Foreword

As an American, I have always associated environmental history with New Zealand. The book that inspired my own doctoral dissertation was Herbert Guthrie-Smith's *Tutira: The Story of a New Zealand Sheep Station*. Guthrie-Smith never imagined that he was writing environmental history—the term did not even exist in the 1920s—he was simply a remarkably astute, observant man with a vernacular sense of botany who was able to connect the changes he saw in the landscape around him with the social changes that he and other immigrants were promoting. It is this connection of environmental change and social change that has been at the heart of environmental history ever since.

The authors of this volume are intellectual descendants of Guthrie-Smith in their ability to connect what appear to be local changes in flora and fauna with broad global changes in the movements of people, goods, and ideas. They, however, explore a far larger span of space and time than Guthrie-Smith's *Tutira* in the late nineteenth and early twentieth centuries. The New Zealand that appears in these pages is a country enmeshed in global changes and reaching into a more distant past as well as to the very present. Its landscape has been profoundly shaped by human actions from the moment the Māori arrived. Guthrie-Smith's generation could embrace the illusion that New Zealand was a wilderness at European settlement, but such illusions are harder to maintain today. New Zealand was a diverse landscape, but not a pristine one.

A volume concerned with the origins, meanings, connections, and consequences of environmental change, and the social, cultural, and economic changes connected to it, takes on matters of considerable controversy. In examining the controversies that embroiled the past, the authors inevitably connect them to present controversies. Such controversies are as much a matter of identity, ideology, and meaning as they are economy and ecology. As these essays detail, the meanings of mountains and grasslands, of gardens and gorse are not purely biophysical; they have become emblems of cultural and national identities.

Taken as a whole, the essays detail a history that cannot be boiled down to any single lesson or set of prescriptions. If they could, this would be a poor and simplistic history hardly worth bothering with. When Thomas Isern quotes the grassland scientist Kevin O'Connor urging New Zealanders to 'try a little harder … to understand better what we, Māori and European, have already done to this land' and to 'create a landscape in which we can all take shelter, a landscape in which no early arrival, no latecomer, plant or animal, is alien', he is indicating a direction rather than suggesting a specific solution. He is combining the social with the ecological, and in that he is true to New Zealand's environmental history. It is timely advice, and this is a timely book. In its sweep, its curiosity, and its ambition, I do not know of an equivalent for any other country in the world.

Richard White
Margaret Byrne Professor of American History
Stanford University

Environmental Histories
of New Zealand

Edited by

Eric Pawson
Tom Brooking

OXFORD
UNIVERSITY PRESS

OXFORD
UNIVERSITY PRESS

253 Normanby Road, South Melbourne, Victoria 3205, Australia

Oxford University Press is a department of the University of Oxford.
It furthers the University's objective of excellence in research, scholarship, and education by publishing worldwide in

Oxford New York

Auckland Bangkok Buenos Aires Cape Town Chennai
Dar es Salaam Delhi Hong Kong Istanbul Karachi Kolkata
Kuala Lumpur Madrid Melbourne Mexico City Mumbai Nairobi
São Paulo Shanghai Taipei Tokyo Toronto

First published 2002

Reprinted 2003

National Library of New Zealand
Cataloguing-in-Publication data:

Environmental Histories of New Zealand/edited by Eric Pawson and Tom Brooking.
Includes index.
ISBN 0 19 558421 X

1. New Zealand—Environmental conditions—History. 2. Human ecology—New Zealand—History. 3. Nature—Effect of human beings on—New Zealand—History. I. Pawson, Eric. II. Brooking, Tom, 1949-

333.70993—dc 21

Typeset by OUPANZS
Printed through Bookpac Production Services, Singapore

The cover photographs are by Charles Wildbore and show the transformation of the bush landscape of the Pohangina Valley of the Manawatu at the turn of the twentieth century. The forest was felled by hand (front cover; photographed c. 1904) before the autumn bush burn. Grass seed was sown in the ashes, and in 1907 Wildbore photographed established houses and farms (back cover). Courtesy of Palmerston North City Library.

Contents

Foreword by Richard White		iii
Figures		vii
Tables		x
Preface		xi
Contributors		xiv
1	Introduction *Eric Pawson and Tom Brooking*	1
PART 1	**ENCOUNTERS**	
2	A fragile plenty: Pre-European Māori and the New Zealand environment *Atholl Anderson*	19
3	Contesting resources: Māori, Pākehā, and a tenurial revolution *Evelyn Stokes*	35
4	Resource frontiers, environment, and settler capitalism: 1769–1860 *Jim McAloon*	52
PART 2	**COLONISING**	
5	Remaking the grasslands of the open country *Peter Holland, Kevin O'Connor, and Alexander Wearing*	69
6	Mining the quarry *Terry Hearn*	84
7	Destruction under the guise of improvement? The forest, 1840–1920 *Graeme Wynn*	100

PART 3 SPECIAL ENVIRONMENTS

8 Children of the burnt bush: New Zealanders and the indigenous remnant, 1880–1930 119
Paul Star and Lynne Lochhead

9 The meanings of mountains 136
Eric Pawson

10 'Swamps which might doubtless Easily be drained': Swamp drainage and its impact on the indigenous 151
Geoff Park

PART 4 MODERNISING

11 The grasslands revolution reconsidered 169
Tom Brooking, Robin Hodge, and Vaughan Wood

12 The state as conservationist, 1920–60: 'Wise use' of forests, lands, and water 183
Michael Roche

13 On the edge: making urban places 200
Eric Pawson

14 Exotic natives and contrived wild gardens: The twentieth-century home garden 214
Helen M. Leach

PART 5 PERSPECTIVES

15 Companions, stowaways, imperialists, invaders: Pests and weeds in New Zealand 233
Thomas D. Isern

16 Bound to the land: Māori retention and assertion of land and identity 246
Danny Keenan

17 A history of New Zealand environmental law 261
Nicola Wheen

18 Losing ground? Environmental problems and prospects at the beginning of the twenty-first century 275
Christine Dann

Glossary 288
Notes 294
Index 333

FIGURES

Figure 1.1	'Man in Forest Avenue, Ninety Mile Bush'	2
Figure 1.2	William Fox, *House in Nelson, 1848*	6
Figure 1.3	Felling of a kauri for the Duke of Gloucester	15
Figure 2.1	Places and districts mentioned in Chapter 2	21
Figure 2.2	The distribution of Rafter Laboratory radiocarbon dates on rat bone	23
Figure 2.3	Windward and leeward provinces in New Zealand, showing pā and moa-hunting sites	26
Figure 2.4	Distribution of forest and open country at approximately AD 1000 and 1800	31
Figure 2.5	A regionally differentiated ecological model of socio-economic change in pre-European New Zealand	33
Figure 3.1	Pākehā encounter before 1840	37
Figure 3.2	Te Hiku o Te Ika: Pākehā land claims and mission stations, 1840	39
Figure 3.3	Te Hiku o Te Ika: Exploitation of resources before 1840	40
Figure 3.4	Te Hiku o Te Ika: Cultural relations, 1840	44
Figure 3.5	The extinguishment of native title	47
Figure 3.6	Alienation of Māori land in the North Island	50
Figure 4.1	New Zealand in the global economy, 1770–1840	55
Figure 4.2	On the edge of the bush: New Plymouth 1850	62
Figure 4.3	Europeans and the south, 1843	65
Figure 5.1	Open-country vegetation: tall tussock, short tussock with matagouri, modified tussock, and severely depleted tussock	70
Figure 5.2	Subdivision of The Point station	73
Figure 5.3	An unusual spell of wet summer months in the Canterbury foothills during the 1870s	75

Figure 5.4	Changing sheep and cattle numbers as indicated by numbers of grazing units	76
Figure 5.5	Open-country sheep and cattle breeds	76
Figure 5.6	Contracts let in 1887 for the purchase of ferrets, and numbers of rabbits shot over a five-year period by members of the Phillips family at The Point	81
Figure 6.1	Goldfields and gold production, 1857–1921	85
Figure 6.2	Damage caused by silting, Waihou River, 1907	89
Figure 6.3	Blue Spur hydraulic sluicing and elevating claim, Gabriels Gully, Otago, 1911	94
Figure 6.4	Coalfields and production, 1883–1920, by decade	96
Figure 7.1	*Primeval Bush*, Julius Geissler, 1919	102
Figure 7.2	The structure of the New Zealand forest	103
Figure 7.3	The forest, c. 1840	104
Figure 7.4	Bullock team and timber workers alongside a kauri tree, 1897, probably Whangarei district	108
Figure 7.5	The North Island forest, c. 1905	109
Figure 7.6	The Ostler farm, showing land clearance, probably in Taranaki, early twentieth century	110
Figure 8.1	Protected areas, 1906–07, showing national parks and scenic reserves and places mentioned in chapter 8	120
Figure 8.2	Kennedys Bush, c. 1920	126
Figure 8.3	Plan of Tongariro National Park, from Leonard Cockayne's report on his botanical survey of the park	129
Figure 8.4	Charles Blomfield, *The Vaulted Aisles of Nature's Cathedral*, 1921	134
Figure 9.1	The mountain and hill areas of New Zealand	137
Figure 9.2	*To the 'Hermitage' Mount Cook*, c. 1925	142
Figure 9.3	Alpine fatalities between 1889 and 1959	147
Figure 10.1	Excavating a drainage canal, Hauraki Plains, 1910	152
Figure 10.2	A plan of swamp drainage, Hauraki Plains, 1908	155
Figure 10.3	Hauraki Plains swamp drainage, 1911–12	157
Figure 10.4	A tidal swamp in its natural state, Hokianga, 1998	161
Figure 11.1	'Fertiliser helped us grow …'	173
Figure 11.2	Cover of the *New Zealand Journal of Agriculture*, July 1946, showing the Four Horsemen of the Apocalypse	175
Figure 11.3	Cover of the *New Zealand Journal of Agriculture*, September 1946. A portrayal of the virtues of rurality and New Zealand's ongoing role as Britain's outlying farm	176
Figure 11.4	Advertisement for Tordon Brushkiller, 1999	178
Figure 12.1	State indigenous and exotic forests, 1930	186
Figure 12.2	The arrival in 1955 of the first trainload of logs at Kawerau, site of the Tasman pulp and paper mill	189
Figure 12.3	'Nature's revenge'	192

Figure 12.4	Aerial topdressing provided a means of stabilising at-risk slopes in higher country	194
Figure 12.5	The SCRCC made use of a range of masculinist images in urging farmers to adopt soil-conservation techniques	196
Figure 13.1	Evoking the modern: Auckland, 1931	204
Figure 13.2	'Civilising' the Waimakariri River since the 1860s	206
Figure 13.3	Auckland suburban development	208
Figure 13.4	Salubrious St Clair	210
Figure 13.5	'Timaru by the Sea'	212
Figure 14.1	*Yates' Garden Guide*, 1934 edition	215
Figure 14.2	At McNab's public garden in Lower Hutt (formerly Alfred Ludlam's)	218
Figure 14.3	The planting of specimen trees on front lawns, especially conifers such as this Chilean monkey puzzle tree, had little regard for their eventual size	219
Figure 14.4	Garden plans from D. Tannock, *Practical Gardening in New Zealand*	221
Figure 14.5	A prize-winning front garden, c. 1960	224
Figure 14.6	This 1945 state house at Naenae possessed a sparsely planted front garden	225
Figure 15.1	'The Only Good Possums'	236
Figure 15.2	Advertisement for rabbit gas, July 1945	238
Figure 15.3	Rabbiting crew at Earnscleugh station, Central Otago, 1996	239
Figure 15.4	Spraying gorse on a hill near Wanganui, 1953	242
Figure 16.1	'Virgin country of great promise'	248
Figure 16.2	New Plymouth, 1856	255
Figure 16.3	Hapū boundaries and seafood resources for Te Āti Awa, North Taranaki	257
Figure 17.1	Location of Lake Manapouri	263
Figure 17.2	'The view stinks but it's worth millions!'	264
Figure 17.3	'Mastering the vast energy potential of the Clutha River'	267
Figure 17.4	The graven image of Aluminium	268
Figure 18.1	Inside a shearing shed, probably in the Chatham Islands, c. 1900	279
Figure 18.2	Cover of *Heritage Destroyed*, 1960	280
Figure 18.3	The thinning of the ozone layer over Antarctica from the 1970s	282

Tables

Table 7.1	New Zealand sawmills: number, distribution, capacity, and output, 1907	107
Table 9.1	Average daily motor traffic on selected alpine roads in the 1930s	143
Table 9.2	High ascents from The Hermitage, 1914–15 to 1938–39	145
Table 9.3	National parks in 1938	148

Preface

To the British author David Arnold, 'Environmental history has been one of the most rapidly growing areas of historical debate and enquiry in recent decades'.[1] This is certainly true of North America, but edited collections have also appeared about Australia and southern Africa. The imprint of imperialism on the lands of the New World has been an important theme in books by Alfred Crosby, Richard Grove, Stephen Pyne, and Thomas Dunlap. The focus is now beginning to broaden to include the impact of contemporary forces of production and consumption. In 2000 John McNeill published a global environmental history of the twentieth century, claiming for it an explanation of how 'the human race, without intending anything of the sort, [has undertaken] a gigantic uncontrolled experiment on the earth' in the last hundred years.[2]

New Zealand has not escaped the attention of overseas environmental historians, as the Introduction to this book demonstrates. This is because, as a small, well-documented land of recent European settlement, it represents a fruitful case study of the political economy, cultural politics, and landscape impacts of McNeill's experiment. A few years ago we decided that it was therefore time to put New Zealand's environmental transformation 'on the map', and to contribute from this country to the growing literature of environmental history as an interdisciplinary enterprise.

The editors and the contributors bring a range of interests to the project. It began in 1998, when Tom Brooking, with a lengthy professional concern with rural history and the politics of land behind him, spent part of a period of study leave touring provincial museums to collect illustrated evidence of people's impacts on the environment. During that winter journey through the North Island, he became more aware of the extent of eroded hillsides in areas deforested years before: processes that had impressed Kenneth Cumberland in the late 1930s and that led to some fine early geographical writing on landscape change in New Zealand.

A growing sense of determination developed during Brooking's 1998 journey. In particular, he felt it necessary to work towards overcoming the amnesia that had enveloped the massive effort by Pākehā and Māori to transform land from bush and scrub into farms, forests, and gardens. He thought that to do this using the extensive provincial archives beyond the confines of the Alexander Turnbull Library in Wellington, whose images have long been the stock-in-trade of scholars, would greatly enrich the story. Reviewing a collection of 'beautiful New Zealand' books revealed to him that there is a pernicious form of 'presentism' abroad in this country: a tendency to portray landscapes as if they 'are' rather than as having histories by which they have come to be. To accept the assumption that this is the harmonious 'clean and green' country of tourism brochures and campaigns is to misread a history of territorial and environmental learning, conquest, and contest, and to miss all that is enlivening about past and present. Scientific writing can be equally bland.

At the end of 1997 another large project was completed, one that did not reproduce these characteristics. It was the *New Zealand Historical Atlas*, perhaps the biggest interdisciplinary exercise ever undertaken in this country.[3] Eric Pawson had been involved for seven years as chair of its advisory committee and as contributing editor. He worked with Malcolm McKinnon, the editor, to ensure that landscape change and the development of places were fully explored in the *Atlas*. One of Pawson's former doctoral students, Russell Kirkpatrick, was its deputy editor, drawing on his considerable cartographic imagination in the representation of the volume's stories. Many of these stories focused on the environment and demonstrated the importance of using historical and geographical insights to situate them in the broader picture.

As editors of this book, we combine the approach of the geographer and the historian, respectively. We were brought together by Linda Cassells, who, as the Oxford University Press editor in Auckland for several years, had built up a widely respected list. Brooking's original hope was that an Oxford environmental history might be modelled on the multi-authored *Oxford History of New Zealand*, to which he had contributed as a young academic. The example of the *Atlas*, as well as his discussions in 1998 with environmental historians in North America, made it apparent that the stories should be multiple, complementary narratives. There is no one history of environmental change; there were too many participants, just as there are many interpreters. Nor is there only one relevant disciplinary perspective, when environmental expertise resides in a wide range of disciplines, including agricultural science, anthropology, archaeology, ecology, geography, history, law, and political studies.

This book is titled *Environmental Histories of New Zealand* in recognition of its plurality as well as its geographical concern with narrating human–environment interactions in the places of Aotearoa/New Zealand. Even so, the title does not do full justice to the range of disciplinary allegiances of the team of contributors assembled in the summer of 1998–99, and described in the List of Contributors. Many gathered at a day-long symposium at the New Zealand Geographical Society Conference held at Massey University in Palmerston North in July 1999. For that opportunity we are grateful to the conference organiser, and contributor of Chapter 12, Michael Roche. In February 2000 many also came to a symposium in the Department of Geography at the University of Canterbury in Christchurch, including the contributor with the greatest distance to cover, Tom Isern from North Dakota. We appreciate the department's covering the on-site costs of this event. Thereafter, the editors worked closely with contributors to ensure that the chapters worked well together and could stand alone.

We hope that the book will go some way towards countering what we referred to above as 'presentism', and enrich New Zealanders' understandings of the role played by the social transformation of environments in the making of their places and pasts. We hope, too, that it contributes internationally to environmental history 'as a rapidly growing [area of] debate and enquiry'. We have intentionally produced a volume that is comprehensive, and not a set of disparate essays. In that we aimed for something akin to the *New Zealand Historical Atlas*, with a strong sense of themes, territory, and chronology, but also embodying a range of perspectives covering topics so often ignored, such as the urban realm and environmental law.

Our thanks go to all our contributors for being willing to share their expertise and for working patiently with us. That the book is so well illustrated is due not only to them, but also to the indulgence of the publisher, the assistance of archivists around New Zealand, and to three cartographers. Max Oulton of the Department of Geography at the University of Waikato drew the figures for Chapter 3, and Bill Mooney of the Department of Geography at the University of Otago drew those for Chapter 5. It is our good fortune to have worked with Tim Nolan, of the Department of Geography at the University of Canterbury (a veteran of the *Historical Atlas*), who took responsibility for the great majority of the book's illustrative work.

The University of Canterbury underwrote editorial costs with a generous research grant. This covered, among other things, reproduction fees of historical photographs from archives around the country. The text and notes for each chapter were moulded into consistent style by Linda Harrison of the Department of Geography at the University of Canterbury, and we are very grateful to her for the skill and experience that she brought to this lengthy task. At Otago a number of colleagues helped with the Glossary, including Jim Williams, Kath Dickinson, and Peter Johnson. Many others, widely spread, have encouraged and assisted us, including Garth Cant, Steve Dovers, Pyrs Gruffudd, Peter Holland, Richard Le Heron, Geoffrey Rice, and the late David McDonald.

The book has benefited from the attention of Richard King, one of New Zealand's finest book editors. We are very grateful to Jill Henry of Oxford University Press for allowing us to work with him. And while we regret that Linda Cassells, after commissioning the book, was unable to see it through to publication, we appreciate the patience and trust that Jill and staff of OUP Australia have invested in our venture.

Eric Pawson
Tom Brooking

Notes

1 D. Arnold, *The Problem of Nature: Environment, Culture and European Expansion*, Blackwell Publishers, Oxford, 1996, p. vii.

2 J. R. McNeill, *Something New Under the Sun: An Environmental History of the Twentieth-Century World*, Norton, New York, 2000, p. 4.

3 Malcolm McKinnon (ed.), *New Zealand Historical Atlas*, David Bateman, Auckland/Department of Internal Affairs, Wellington, 1997.

CONTRIBUTORS

ATHOLL ANDERSON, FAHA, FRSNZ, is Professor of Prehistory in the Research School of Pacific and Asian Studies at the Australian National University and Director of the Centre for Archaeological Research. He has worked on the prehistory of human–environment relationships for thirty years in New Zealand and throughout the Pacific, especially on the exploitation of maritime resources and avifaunal extinctions. He is the author of *Prodigious Birds: Moas and Moahunting in Prehistoric New Zealand* (1989) and *The Welcome of Strangers: An Ethnohistory of Southern Maori, AD 1650–1850* (1998).

TOM BROOKING is Associate Professor of History at the University of Otago. He specialises in New Zealand and comparative rural and environmental history, and has published five books and numerous book chapters, essays, and articles. His most recent major book was *Lands for the People? The Highland Clearances and the Colonisation of New Zealand. A Biography of John McKenzie* (1996). He contributed to the *New Zealand Historical Atlas* (1997) and is currently working on several related projects in environmental history.

CHRISTINE DANN is a Departmental Fellow in the Department of Geography, University of Canterbury, and a researcher in trade and agriculture policy for the Green Party. Her PhD thesis (Lincoln University, 1999) was on the global origins of Green politics, and she contributed a chapter on the environment movement to *New Zealand Government and Politics* (2000) and a plate on the exploration of the South Island to the *New Zealand Historical Atlas* (1997).

TERRY HEARN is a graduate of the University of Otago, his PhD thesis being a study of resource policy and resource-use conflict in nineteenth- and early twentieth-century New Zealand. His publications in environmental history include *Speculators' Dream: Gold Dredging in Southern New Zealand* (1985) (with R. P. Hargreaves), and a contribution to the *New Zealand Historical Atlas*. He is presently the Historian of British Immigration in the History Group of the Ministry for Culture and Heritage, and contributed two essays in Lyndon Fraser (ed.), *A Distant Shore: Irish Migration and Settlement in New Zealand* (2000).

ROBIN HODGE completed her doctoral thesis, 'Nature's Trustee: Pérrine Moncrieff and Nature Conservation in New Zealand 1920–1950', at Massey University in 1999. It was shortlisted in the top three of the 1999 Postgraduate Thesis Award sponsored by the Australia and New Zealand Regional Science Association International. Since then she has been part of the team researching the Indigenous Flora and Fauna claim to the Waitangi Tribunal.

PETER HOLLAND was educated at the University of Canterbury and the Australian National University, and has worked in Canada, Kenya, New Zealand, and South Africa. He has been Professor of Geography at the University of Otago since 1982. Trained as a biogeographer, his current research interests include environmental change during the early colonial period. He also contributed plates for the *New Zealand Historical Atlas* (1997). He has been associate editor of the *Journal of Biogeography* since 1981 and chairs the editorial board of the New Zealand Geographical Society.

THOMAS D. ISERN is Professor of History at North Dakota State University, Fargo, North Dakota, USA. In 1991 he was Senior Fulbright Scholar at the Alexander Turnbull Library, Wellington, and has returned to New Zealand periodically since then to pursue interests in agricultural and pastoral history. He is author or co-author of six books, most recently *Dakota Circle: Excursions on the True Plains* (2000). In 2002 he is working on an intensive study, along the lines of *Tutira*, on the Morven Hills run of Central Otago.

DANNY KEENAN is of Ngāti Te Whiti/Ngāmotu, Te Āti Awa descent. He teaches Māori and New Zealand history at Massey University. His PhD thesis examined the nature of Taranaki tribal and colonial histories and his research interests include Taranaki tribal history, the New Zealand Land Wars, and the post-Land Wars period from 1870 to 1900. In 1998 he was granted a Fulbright Postdoctoral Award to examine aspects of comparative Māori and Native American history. He has contributed to *Fragments: New Zealand Social and Cultural History* (2000) and *A Book in the Hand: Essays on the History of the Book in New Zealand* (2000).

HELEN M. LEACH is Professor in the Department of Anthropology, University of Otago. She completed a doctorate in 1976 on prehistoric horticulture in New Zealand. She wrote *1,000 Years of Gardening in New Zealand* (1984) and *Cultivating Myths: Fiction, Fact and Fashion in Garden History* (2000), and has published many articles on the origins and development of gardening in the Middle East, Britain, Oceania, and New Zealand. She will teach a course on the environmental history of New Zealand with Holland and Brooking from 2003.

LYNNE LOCHHEAD is a freelance environmental historian. She received a PhD from Lincoln University in 1994 for her thesis, 'Preserving the Brownies' Portion: A History of Voluntary Nature Conservation Organisations in New Zealand, 1888–1935'. She lives in Christchurch and is currently researching an ecological history of the Harts Creek–Birdling Brook catchment in central Canterbury.

JIM McALOON is Senior Lecturer in History at Lincoln University. He has research interests on the borders of environmental and economic history, having published widely in the history of nineteenth-century New Zealand and especially the implantation of the capitalist economy in the South Island. His regional history of Nelson appeared in 1997, and a book on rich settlers in Canterbury and Otago will be published in 2002.

KEVIN O'CONNOR is Professor Emeritus in Range Management at Lincoln University, where he maintains contact with the Division of Environmental Management and Design. His interests in the history of pastoral and agricultural land use and its impact on the environment have been nourished since his first post-graduate studies in the Upper Clutha in 1953. He is currently working on an ecological history of New Zealand pastoralism.

GEOFF PARK is a Wellington-based ecologist with a tendency to history, in particular the effects of colonisation on the indigenous Pacific. He is author of *Ngā Uruora: The Groves of Life: Ecology and History in a New Zealand Landscape* (1995). He has contributed to *Edward Gibbon Wakefield and the Colonial Dream* (1997) and to *Quicksands: Foundational Histories in Australia and Aotearoa New Zealand* (1999). He is currently Concept Leader at Papatuanuku at the Museum of New Zealand, Te Papa Tongarewa.

ERIC PAWSON is Professor and Head of the Department of Geography at the University of Canterbury. He chaired the advisory committee of the *New Zealand Historical Atlas* from the project's inception in 1990 to its completion in 1997, and was also its contributing editor. He has a DPhil from Oxford University, and wrote two books on the early Industrial Revolution in Britain. He co-edited the New Zealand Geographical Society's *Changing Places* projects with Richard Le Heron (1992, 1996) and has published on urban environmental history and landscape transformations.

MICHAEL ROCHE is Associate Professor of Geography and Programme Coordinator for Geography in the School of People, Environment and Planning at Massey University. He completed his PhD at the University of Canterbury on forest policy and forest management in New Zealand. He has published two books on the New Zealand timber industry, including *History of Forestry* (1990) as well as *Land and Water: Water and Soil Conservation and Central Government in New Zealand, 1941–1988* (1994). He also writes on landscape transformation in New Zealand, and contributed several plates for the *New Zealand Historical Atlas* (1997).

PAUL STAR has lived in New Zealand since 1972 and has History degrees from Cambridge and Otago Universities. His doctoral thesis examined the changing attitudes of nineteenth-century European settlers to the New Zealand environment, and he has published in the periodical literature on these themes as well as on the debate concerning deforestation. Currently he is researching changing responses to and representations of the Otago landscape between the 1870s and 1900.

EVELYN STOKES, DNZM, holds a Personal Chair in Geography at the University of Waikato, Hamilton. Her research interests include historical geography in New Zealand and North America, Māori land and communities and Treaty of Waitangi issues. She has served on a number of government committees, and since 1989 has been a member of the New Zealand Geographic Board and of the Waitangi Tribunal, contributing to major reports such as that on the Muriwhenua Land Claim (1997). She also authored many of the Māori-focused plates in the *New Zealand Historical Atlas* (1997).

ALEXANDER WEARING is a graduate of the University of Canterbury. His recently completed doctoral research at the University of Otago concerned landscape change in the drylands of Central Otago and the Mackenzie Country over the millennium of human occupation, and his current research and teaching interests lie at the interface of biogeography, environmental history, and landscape management. He is a Senior Teaching Fellow in the Department of Geography at the University of Otago.

NICOLA WHEEN teaches Environmental Law, International Environmental Law, Public Law, and Gender and the Law at the University of Otago. Her research interests and publications focus on conservation and Treaty of Waitangi and New Zealand Bill of Rights Act issues in environmental law. She especially enjoys water law, although her most recent publications concern indigenous forest management. She is currently working on a law and politics book exploring the Waitangi Tribunal's reports.

VAUGHAN WOOD is a doctoral student in History at the University of Otago, where he is drawing on his Honours degree in Chemistry and his Masters degree in History (both from the University of Canterbury) in his thesis on soil-fertility management in nineteenth-century New Zealand. He co-authored a chapter on farming in Canterbury c. 1880–1940 in *Rural Canterbury: Celebrating its History* (2001).

GRAEME WYNN is Professor and Head of the Department of Geography in the University of British Columbia. His longstanding interest in encounters between migrant Europeans and New World environments is reflected in an extensive list of publications focusing on Canada and New Zealand, including plates in the *New Zealand Historical Atlas* (1997). Among his most recent contributions are 'Remaking the Land God Gave to Cain: A Brief Environmental History of Canada', the Canada House (London) Lecture (1999), and a co-authored chapter in *Rural Canterbury: Celebrating its History* (2001).

1
Introduction

Eric Pawson and Tom Brooking

New Zealand holds a special place in environmental history.[1] An isolated land of mountains and forests, it was fished out of the southern ocean by the demi-god Maui, according to the stories of its Polynesian colonists. Their Māori descendants had named and claimed its territories by the time the 'large land, uplifted high' was 'discovered', a few hundred years later, by Europeans. In the stories of these later colonists, named 'Pākehā' by their predecessors, New Zealand is a fragment of the ancient super-continent Gondwana, cast adrift before the advent of mammals. The Australian ecologist Tim Flannery refers to it as 'a completely different experiment in evolution to the rest of the world', showing 'what the world might have looked like if mammals as well as dinosaurs had become extinct 65 million years ago, leaving the birds to inherit the globe'.[2]

The human experiments[3] of making environments for living in these islands are more recent than those conducted elsewhere, probably seven to eight hundred years old at most. The impacts of Māori hunting, fire, and horticulture were extensive. But they were less dramatic than 200 years of Pākehā transformations, part of the European imperial drive to incorporate new territories into the capitalist world economy using the panoply of people, animals, plants, and, less intentionally, pathogens. In turn the consequences of such experiments for human livelihoods have had to be borne. There has been the hazardousness of rapid and sometimes extreme weather changes, and the risk of events such as floods and earthquakes. These result from the country's location astride a tectonic-plate boundary, with its rising mountain ranges intercepting moisture-laden winds from the southern ocean. There have been contests for land between Māori and Pākehā, vigorous throughout the nineteenth century and not forgotten since, and environmental interventions in the form of resource destruction, soil erosion, and the spread of unwanted, and costly, pests and weeds.

Relations between people and environments in New Zealand share many of the characteristics of such interactions elsewhere, particularly in those places that Europeans sought to colonise in recent centuries, but the context for these interactions is unique.

As Joe Powell, the Australian historical geographer, has argued, the complex intersections of local, regional, and international influences produce place-specific outcomes that should not be interpreted in terms of models imported uncritically. In fact 'the best environmental stories ... recognise locational integrities in so far as they have a very definite resonance in [particular] national and regional contexts'. To this we should add cultural contexts, as there is not nor ever has been but one New Zealand. Rather there is a multi-layered complex of Māori and Pākehā territories.[4] It is the purpose of this book to narrate the construction of human–environment interactions in the places of Aotearoa/New Zealand. The Introduction will situate the project in the context of current thinking and practice in environmental history. It will also introduce individual chapters and provide signposts about how further study of New Zealand environmental histories might develop.

Making environments

Consider the photograph in Figure 1.1. This was taken in 1878 by James Bragge, a Wellington photographer, born in County Durham, who, rather than concentrating on portraiture, the lifeblood that sustained his contemporary practitioners, fitted out a horse-drawn cart as a portable darkroom to allow him to capture the development of the new city and its environs. He received an award at the Sydney International

Figure 1.1 'Man in Forest Avenue, Ninety Mile Bush' by James Bragge, 1878.
Collection of the Museum of New Zealand Te Papa Tongarewa, negative number D.0086.

Exhibition in 1879 for a series of views commissioned by the Wellington City Council. This was a year after his second expedition across the Rimutaka Ranges, to the north of the city, where he recorded the extension of the railway, and the farming frontier, into territories previously covered in tussock grass, thick bush, and forest.[5] The photograph is of what Bragge called 'Forest Avenue' in the Ninety Mile Bush in the upper Wairarapa. Outwardly it is a portrayal of the impressiveness of the bush, even, given the small size of the human figure, its oppressiveness.

Bragge's photograph, however, is no more innocent as a record of what he saw than any other of the extensive records that survive from his time as documents of environmental change. Recent scholarship on photography has demonstrated that as a practice it was central to contemporary discourses of colonisation, as were written accounts and maps.[6] Photographers brought to their images, notably in the selection of viewpoints and the manner of framing scenes, an 'imaginative geography' that implicitly betrayed their view of nature and its relation to human endeavour. This photograph highlights not so much the bush but the avenue that draws the invading eye through the trees. And if the smallness of the human figure implies awe of the vegetation, it can equally be suggested that the man is not cowed by it. Rather, he represents the colonial mission to cut or burn the trees, to convert potentially fruitful land to grass for production of goods for profit. The big bush burns of the district were all around Bragge at the time. As the editor of the *Manawatu Times* put it in 1877, 'although the smoke may inconvenience us and the charred avenues offend the eye, we must accept all thankfully as a mark of local progress'.[7] The photograph is a document of culture rather than of nature.

It has thus been suggested that 'the environment[s] we inhabit [are] inseparable from human culture'; in other words, from the ways in which we see and use them.[8] Everything that surrounds us—rural landscapes, cities, seas—is shaped, traversed, and harvested in accordance with cultural imperatives and social needs. Our awareness of these environments, and our representations and interpretations of them, reflect human traditions and expectations. Our awareness is not as objective as we might imagine, but is shaped by deep-seated assumptions about actual or ideal relations between people and nature.[9] It is the role of the environmental historian to dissolve the artificial divisions between nature and culture that characterise Western civilisation (but not, it must be said, that of Māori) and so reveal the deep intertwining of environment and people. The making of environments is a social process.[10]

This last point was recognised by an earlier generation of European commentators. Edward Gibbon Wakefield, the post-Enlightenment dreamer, wrote in his *Art of Colonization* about the necessity of renaming apparently virgin country—including lands occupied by Māori who had not used it in ways recognisable to Europeans—as 'it make[s] part of the moral atmosphere of the country'.[11] To Wakefield, colonisation would produce a new geography, transforming that which had been 'wilderness' into the Eden of the Book of Genesis. Henry Sewell, the Canterbury colonist, proclaimed in the 1850s that 'the first creation was a garden, and the nearer we get back to the garden state, the nearer we approach what may be called the true normal state of Nature'.[12] Karl Marx, one of Wakefield's most severe critics, realised that New Zealand constituted an unusual experiment as British settlers self-consciously set out to make something anew by both transplanting and transforming.

Marx's view was that Wakefield's bold attempt at improving capitalism only reproduced capitalist relations in their universal form;[13] indeed for many years the production of this garden colony was seen as a triumph of progressiveness. It had accomplished in one century, as Kenneth Cumberland put it in the early 1940s, 'what in Europe took twenty centuries, and in North America four'.[14] Cumberland, a geographer newly arrived from Britain, recognised the considerable environmental costs of this transformation. Like Lance McCaskill, working at the same time, he was not open to the later charge of being an impractical or idealistic environmentalist. Both men worked hard to expose the causes of, and remedies for, the extensive soil erosion that had long ravaged large parts of the country.[15] Analysis of resource conservation processes has subsequently engaged several geographers who have been resident in New Zealand, notably Graeme Wynn and Michael Roche.[16] With the exception of these scholars, however, much of the best-known work on New Zealand's environmental histories to date has come from those based elsewhere.

Perhaps the most prominent of these was the Canadian historical geographer Andrew Hill Clark, who was spending a sabbatical break in the Geography Department of the University of Canterbury in the same year that Cumberland published his essay in the American Geographical Society's *Geographical Review*. His sojourn resulted in a book, *The Invasion of New Zealand by People, Plants and Animals*, published in the United States in 1949. Like Cumberland, Clark was impressed by the speed of Pākehā environmental transformation. He essentially downplayed the role of pre-European Māori impacts. His book, he wrote, was 'a report on a revolutionary change in the character of a region, which occurred in a period of less than two centuries'.[17]

The American environmental historian William Cronon has recently reissued, through the University of Washington Press, Herbert Guthrie-Smith's study of environmental change on a Hawke's Bay sheep station, *Tutira*, first published in 1921. Cronon describes it as 'one of the great English-language classics of environmental history' and its re-publication acknowledges a source that more than any other persuaded him to take up environmental history. Richard White, an environmental historian at Stanford University, told Tom Brooking much the same as he drove his visitor around the remnants of the red-wood forest above Silicon Valley in 1998. Both American Scholars heard about the reference originally from Vernon Carstensen, for long an historian of public lands at the University of Wisconsin—Madison, the campus where Clark was a professor of geography.[18]

Other writers have shown great interest in New Zealand. These include the United States-based but New Zealand-trained geographer Alan Grey, whose 1994 historical geography, although terminating in 1935, incorporates insights from generations of geography postgraduate theses up to the early 1980s. Among historians, Thomas Dunlap, following in the footsteps of Keith Thomas, includes New Zealand in his discussion of the impact of the European diaspora on changing understandings of the natural world, whereas Stephen Pyne uses it as a test case for studying the environmental impact of fire. Alfred Crosby, whose book *Ecological Imperialism* incorporates a lengthy New Zealand case study, acknowledges the importance of the archive in the Alexander Turnbull Library in Wellington.[19] Like Cumberland and Clark before him, he regards this land as an ideal laboratory for studying human environmental impacts within an unusually compressed time frame. His research, together with that of John McNeill and Tom Isern, was facilitated by the institutional links between the USA and New Zealand through the Fulbright Foundation.

This overseas enthusiasm has been in marked contrast to the situation in New Zealand itself. Paul Star has noted that 'since Crosby painted the broad brushstrokes in his book, no New Zealand historians have taken a closer look at the paint'.[20] That is not entirely true, there having been some tantalising starts.[21] Nonetheless, European encounters with the New Zealand environment have been largely ignored by historians, with the exception of some recent thesis students, notably at the University of Otago. This reflects in part other preoccupations of a relatively small disciplinary group. The study of history in New Zealand was for long modelled on the British rather than the American profession, hence the absence of environmental themes in Keith Sinclair's standard volume, in both editions of the *Oxford History of New Zealand*, and even in James Belich's *Making Peoples*.[22] There may be a deeper reason. Belich explores at some length the resource dependence of Polynesian colonists in New Zealand, but drops the subject once his attention switches to Anglo-Celtic immigrants. This is in line with the profession's current preoccupation with social history, but is as if culture had without question subsumed nature. That may be the assumption. Given the timing of European colonisation of these islands, and the often-exalted quest of subjecting nature to ever-greater degrees of control, historians seem to take environmental transformation for granted. It has not been seen as of sufficient interest when a belief in the separation of culture from nature renders the former central to enquiry and the latter unproblematic.[23]

New narratives

The narratives in this book incorporate a range of approaches to environmental history, as is characteristic of the field.[24] They reflect the disciplinary allegiances of its authors. They also share, however, a number of conceptual assumptions. The first of these is that discourses of Pākehā colonisation, in written texts, maps, and photographs, embodied a possessive urge to incorporate the so-called 'wastelands' owned by Māori. The urge was often reproduced as a form of panoptical vision, in which the recorder was master of all surveyed (Figure 1.2). This vision, as Giselle Byrnes has pointed out, was both boundless, seeking to draw into its gaze all that lay before it, and bounded, in the sense of desiring to commodify land and resources within Eurocentric delimitations.[25] This is the 'invading eye' that Bragge the photographer draws into his representation of the Wairarapa bush.

The second assumption follows from the first. It is that what we often loosely call the environment is not nearly as 'natural' as it seems. 'Instead it is a profoundly human construction.'[26] The non-human world is neither unreal nor imaginary. Rather, the ways in

Figure 1.2 William Fox, *House in Nelson, 1848*. Fox was an astute observer of colonial life, but his apparently 'topographical' scenes are imbued with contemporary Pākehā conventions. Here he has painted his own house (he was the New Zealand Company agent in Nelson from 1843 to 1850) but with the typical bird's-eye perspective of the coloniser. The garden has been transformed with exotic plants, incorporated as a neat and tidy realm; beyond its boundaries lie apparently empty lands awaiting similar transformation. Reproduced by permission of the Hocken Library, Uare Taoka O Hakena, University of Otago, Dunedin.

which we describe and understand it are so fully a reflection of human ideas and aspirations that it is not possible, for example, to separate landscapes from the people who make them. Hence Māori in Aotearoa/New Zealand have distinctive geographies and environmental constructions, although these have often been obscured, if not erased, by subsequent Pākehā colonisation and its desire for land. As a result, water bodies that long were central to the provision of Māori sustenance have been fouled in ignorance or violation of that role. The changing fortunes of gorse is another illustration of the human construction of nature. Pākehā initially envisioned it as a useful imported hedging plant, before it became a weed so invasive that chemical warfare was waged against it for much of the last half of the last century. Yet more recently it has been reinvented as an ideal nursery plant to encourage regeneration of native species, themselves now often seen as beneficial attributes of landscape after many years of being demonised in the drive to lay down grass.

The third assumption, as expressed by Cronon, is that the 'natural world is far more dynamic, far more changeable, and far more entangled with human history than popular beliefs ... have typically acknowledged'.[27] Indeed, the history of gorse reflects this. The environment was not a neutral stage upon which Pākehā could without encumbrance act out their visions, even though it was often seen that way. Instead, human interventions or lack of awareness could render it hazardous or costly to occupy. Recent consideration of the great Wellington earthquake of 1855, for instance, reveals how poorly prepared many structures were for a shake, despite the experience of one only seven years before in 1848: people had forgotten, and again quickly forgot that which they rationalised as an aberration.[28] Nor was the stage empty of other, Māori, people, as Pākehā representations such as those in Figures 1.1 and 1.2 often implied.

The fourth assumption is that geographical scale matters. In the broadest sense, the political economy of Pākehā colonisation linked the transformation of places and the construction of new landscapes, via a worldwide division of labour and networks of trade and information, with markets, sources of goods and European cultural ideas and legal frameworks. All of these contributed to the capitalist imperative to own and commodify land and resources. In this respect, Rollo Arnold's last two books, with their local focus but broadly drawn contexts, are two of the finest contributions to understanding how New Zealand's environments have been made.[29] Such environments, however, were also immensely variable at the local scale, offering a variety of opportunities but throwing up unexpected responses to human intervention.

The book is divided into five parts. The first, 'Encounters', concerns Māori and Pākehā responses to a new land, and the interaction and contest between them. This is followed by 'Colonising', in which key themes of transformation between the mid nineteenth century and 1920 (grasslands, mining, and the bush) are considered. 'Special Environments', the third part, examines particular initiatives and places, such as nature conservation, wetlands, and mountains, often marginalised by the processes highlighted in Part 2. 'Modernising' takes in the major themes of twentieth-century environmental change: the adoption of science to render economic production and protection of resources more effective, and the making of urban environments. Part 5, 'Perspectives', ranges widely to reflect on contemporary environmental themes.

Encounters

The three chapters in Part 1 explore pre-European Māori environmental impacts, the contest for resources between Māori and Pākehā, and the wider context of settler capitalism within which resources were sought and nature and native subjugated. In Chapter 2, Atholl Anderson discusses the effect of pre-European Māori on what he calls 'A fragile plenty': expanding 'as rapidly as possible using the richest resources with pitiless energetic efficiency'. In so doing, he is placing Māori colonisation firmly within the character, in its early stages, of 'colonisation everywhere and at all times'. His essay re-examines the evidence for the chronology of Polynesian settlement, reaching the conclusion that New Zealand and the outlying islands were not colonised until the twelfth or thirteenth century. Thereafter, however, the environment was culturally and materially appropriated, resulting in widespread vertebrate extinctions and deforestation, before environmental learning brought about the sort of adaptive change that is today often taken—by Māori and non-Māori alike—as somehow inherent to Māori culture.

Anderson thus interprets environmental evidence as a corrective to the mythology of the environmentally benign noble savage that permeates much everyday thinking. His argument is also a counter to those who imagine (as did many European colonists) that pre-European Māori were not capable of environmental change. Chapter 3, by Evelyn Stokes, builds on this view. It is twinned with Chapter 4, by Jim McAloon, with the former assessing European impact from Māori perspectives, while the latter focuses on European colonisation from Pākehā positions.

Chapter 3 recasts the central point that Anderson makes about adaptive change, that a strong sense of territoriality and boundedness developed as Māori became dependent on localised, fine-grained sources of protein and highly productive gardens. Identity became strongly enmeshed in place and ancestry, a world view based on 'a sense of custodial occupation ... that the environment should be maintained in a fit state for generations to come'. Such a sense led to land rights defined in terms of use and occupation, not alienation as was the European way. Stokes stresses the complexity of and scope for misunderstanding in transactions with Pākehā, while emphasising the adaptability of Māori in taking advantage of opportunities to trade in environmental resources. Increasing power and numbers of Pākehā, however, led to appropriation of the resource that both parties valued the most: land. The imposition of British law resulted in alienation to the Crown and private owners of land formerly held under customary title.

Whereas Chapter 3 tends to focus on North Island impacts, Jim McAloon gives Chapter 4 more of a South Island flavour. His emphasis, however, is to place European colonisation in the perspective of the global political economy and cultural politics of the time. From this viewpoint, New Zealand lay 'on the edge of empire', on the edge from a British and American perspective, and also from that of New South Wales. McAloon emphasises how lengthy and involved were the tentacles that enveloped Māori, underlain by what he describes as 'the moral economy of capitalism' and a 'new international division of labour'. These were predicated upon the European concept of land as a tradable commodity, and on organised settlement through establishment of towns. This chapter lays a foundation for Part 2 of the book, 'Colonising'.

Colonising

The next three chapters examine some of the big themes of environmental transformation between the mid nineteenth and early twentieth centuries. These are the reinvention of the grasslands, the impacts of mining and quarrying, and the assault on the forest. The authors of Chapter 5—Peter Holland, Kevin O'Connor, and Alex Wearing—remind us that the grasslands of the open country were already cultural landscapes, altered as Chapter 2 has shown by pre-European human action, but offering complex resource mosaics to Māori despite their deceptively simple appearance to Pākehā. They show how this very assumption led quickly to unsustainable levels of stock use: sheep numbers in much of the high country have never recovered to those of the 1870s. But one of the points of this chapter is to expose how settlers discovered and tried to come to terms with 'boisterous, ramping and uncertain' environmental conditions. Confidence was often knocked by 'people, plants and animals behaving badly', with problems from excessive burning and various introduced species becoming pests. European attempts to come to terms with the open grasslands reveal how much their colonisation relied on experimentation, even if lessons were not always well learned.

In Chapter 6, Terry Hearn focuses on mining, and something that has not had previous systematic investigation: its environmental impacts. Gold was of great importance for nineteenth-century export earnings, but had significance in many other ways, drawing in people and capital from a trans-Pacific circuit of gold rushes, and precipitating conflicts between landholders and miners over the effects of discharge of mine waste in particular. The New Zealand government and its agents were more accommodating of the mining interest than those of either Victoria or California. A detailed case study of the consequences in the North Island's Waihou–Ohinemuri goldfield reveals the extent of conflicts with Pākehā and Māori landholders, through siltation of rivers and flooding. Despite the priority accorded to agricultural land in other resource-allocation debates, gold mining and its impacts were accorded priority, with little overall control until attitudes started to shift about 1900. Coal mining and quarrying were by contrast much more limited in impact. In all, mining law 'imposed few restrictions on the use of resources, while discounting social and environmental costs in the interests of sustained exploitation'.

In Chapter 7, Graeme Wynn describes New Zealand in the nineteenth century as a wooden world. The bush, like the grasslands, might appear of a piece, but varied immensely in composition as well as potential social value. Timber was used for a wide range of purposes, cut from extensive areas to supply towns and cities at the same time as it was burned to clear land for farming. Within the prevailing discourse of progress and improvement, which informs the processes discussed from Chapter 3 onwards, the results, however messy, were seen often as achievements. This chapter also, however, enlarges on a theme introduced in the two that precede it: the growth of disquiet, owing to anxiety about destruction of valuable resources, as well concerns for ecological and aesthetic impacts. The New Zealand Forests Act of 1874, albeit ineffective, was one of the earliest state conservation measures in the British Empire. The arguments for and against 'improvement' and restraint were informed as much by local circumstance as by a wider intellectual climate.

Special environments

The eventual resolution to the timber issue lay with what Wynn calls 'an allocation problem': good land was to be settled, while those areas with little production potential could remain tree covered. In Chapter 8, Paul Star and Lynne Lochhead take up the other side of this allocation, tracing the fate of 'the indigenous remnant'. They identify utilitarian moves to conserve some resources as far back as the 1860s, and show that by 1900, more and more people were drawing a link between the value of the indigenous and identification with New Zealand as home. Nonetheless, it is striking how preservation was usually restricted to small islands, be these literally offshore, or the growing network of tiny onshore scenic reserves. Given the prioritisation of the settlement imperative, this was what was achievable. But Star and Lochhead carefully chart the growth of urban-based conservation bodies, the role of tourism, and scientific arguments that scenic distinctiveness was linked to local flora, in developing a more focused counter to the 'progressive' view. It is apparent that initiatives to conserve flora, fauna, and scenery have far longer and more subtle histories than is often assumed.

Most of the more extensive areas conserved in New Zealand have been mountain landscapes. These have long since been appropriated to do service as the face by which the country is projected to the world. Often, given the prominence of the ranges enclosing the vista from many a suburban street, they have reflected New Zealand back to itself as well. In Chapter 9, Eric Pawson explores some of the meanings of mountains, to Māori and to the Pākehā explorers whom they guided; to nineteenth-century artists representing topography with a 'commodifier's gaze'; and to Victorian and early twentieth-century tourists and day-trippers. Many of these people were attracted by mountain magnificence, but generally not with the intimacy that might have led to the creation of an antipodean equivalent of the American wilderness myth. In fact, numbers of people in the mountains for sport and pleasure were often small before the 1950s, although such activities were less male-dominated than mountain discourse has usually implied. Women were active in high climbing and in the urban-based tramping clubs that developed in the 1920s.

Pākehā colonisation coincided with the softening, worldwide, of European attitudes to mountains, from places of fear to places potentially pleasurable. That the country's conservation estate is so extensive, some 30 per cent of the national land area, reflects the willingness to 'set aside' as national parks areas of value for little else. The estate is therefore quite unrepresentative of other indigenous landscapes, with wetlands in particular being almost wholly absent. In Chapter 10, Geoff Park portrays the demonising of swamps by Pākehā, reflecting the eighteenth- and nineteenth-century European drive to turn these into what he calls 'imperial landscapes', through the desire to convert seeming waste to productive lands. This desire throws into sharp relief some of the distinctions between Pākehā and Māori values in landscape. In the swamp the 'linear logic' of modernity met and beat 'the chaos of nature'. Drained landscapes are therefore sites of 'amnesia and erasure' of alternative geographies. In the swamp, as in the bush, we can read both sides of the process/progress of transformation.

Modernising

The environmental transformations of the twentieth century are those of modernity, although they are portrayed here as deserving of understanding in multi-layered ways. In Chapter 11, Tom Brooking, Robin Hodge, and Vaughan Wood explore 'the grasslands revolution', that marriage of scientific and technical applications with a concerted intensification of land use on which the expansion of primary production, for a world brought ever closer by innovations in transport and trade, was based. The grasslands revolution was seen as permitting what are, on the whole, relatively poor soils to underwrite the country's post-World War II prosperity. This chapter discusses the tensions within this progressivist view, especially between the grassland and the soil scientists, and reveals how agricultural practices have been slowly 'greened'. A minority organic view, connecting with some of the initiatives described in Chapter 8, was long present, but today has achieved greater prominence alongside scientific re-evaluations of what is environmentally and economically sustainable. Nonetheless, the imagery of farming as a 'war' against nature persists.

The state was intimately involved in the development of the grasslands revolution. It was also the central player in another complex twentieth-century environmental initiative: that of the 'wise use' of resources such as forests, soil, and water. To an extent this was a broader fashion among New World lands, although with clear place-specific characteristics. Wise use strategies in New Zealand drew partly on those voices working to temper the excesses of the grasslands revolution; in part they reflected concern for the future of timber supplies. In Chapter 12, Michael Roche makes the point that for much of the twentieth century the state was therefore the most effective proponent of a kind of conservation, which because of its utilitarianism—designed to protect and maintain production values—then became the target of largely urban-based postmodern environmentalists whose interests have lain in fostering amenity and intrinsic values in the landscape. Yet today's focus on this latter type of environmentalism should not obscure the fact that it was state agencies that for many years worked to counter not only resource debasement but also the degradation that unbridled progressivism threatened to wreak.

Above all, however, the twentieth century was an urban century for the majority of New Zealanders. It is in towns and gardens that the majority have experienced the environment, including Māori, who began to shift out of rural areas in growing numbers in the 1950s and 1960s. Eric Pawson, in Chapter 13, argues that despite assumptions to the contrary, towns have always been and remain on the edge of the 'howling wilderness'. Whereas they were founded as bridgeheads of civilisation and assumed many of the attributes of modernity, they have been prone to damage by a suite of environmental hazards such as floods, landslips, and earthquakes. Although experience of such events often constitute markers in the histories of particular places, the threats more apparent to many urban dwellers have been those produced in towns themselves, such as pollution and congestion. Hence the suburb, where most people live, represents a creative compromise between the unruliness of nature on the one hand, and the hazardousness of the town on the other.

The suburb has been intensely consumptive of environmental resources, but it has also been the locus of New Zealanders' most intimate engagements with nature. This is in the garden, the subject of Chapter 14 by Helen Leach. The history of the home garden, perhaps because of the very ordinariness of its subject, is elusive and must be reconstructed from manuals and popular articles. These reveal much about changing fashions and tastes through the twentieth century, but most of all expose the contrived nature of the garden, in this respect reproducing the dynamic of Pākehā environmental encounter elsewhere. Gardens tend to have an accretive history, as assemblages of features and plants popular at different periods and drawn from a wide variety of sources. However, 'Above all the twentieth century New Zealand garden has been a landscape of exclusion', with the desire for shelter, security, and privacy outweighing any attachment to the landscape beyond.

Perspectives

The four chapters in Part 5 range more widely in time than those that precede them, each tackling themes of the present in historical context. They are as informed by evidence and analysis, but are more openly passionate in their advancement of points of view. They underline the fact that all environmental histories are stories, told for a purpose, and from a point of view. Chapters 15 and 16 reflect on the consequences of colonisation and modernity, in terms of ecological disruption and cultural disruption, respectively. Chapters 17 and 18 analyse the dominance of developmental impulses as reflected in environmental law and the industrial modes of land use that have driven colonisation and modernity, and that persist powerfully even in today's more diverse, environmentally aware, postmodern context.

Tom Isern observes in Chapter 15 that 'ambivalence is not the stuff of public discourse on the history and status of pests and weeds in New Zealand'. He explores the patterns and consequences of exotic introductions, but his central message is that our ways of thinking about their 'drastic' impact have never been adequate. The belief of the land-development tradition, that which spurred the 'grasslands revolution', that human manipulation of nature will always win through, has been responsible for the masculinist, bellicose rhetoric[30] of 'control' of 'invaders' that has as often as not failed. Conversely, the popular ecological view, that native ecologies are fragile and will only recover if the adverse hand of humans is withdrawn, has proved equally uninformed in high-country landscapes devastated by rabbits and hawkweeds. Instead, Isern argues that what is done is done, and requires an 'active husbandry', a coming to terms with the complexities of evolving ecologies, seeking solutions 'from the field, from science, and from the record of human experience with the land that is environmental history'.

Writing from the perspective of his home in Taranaki, Danny Keenan reveals in Chapter 16 something of the complexities of the ongoing responses of Māori people to the immense environmental changes wrought by Pākehā colonisation of that region in the nineteenth century. He assesses the range of colonising methods employed at the time, but shows that Pākehā descriptions of their impacts, such as 'erasure', do not reflect the ways in which Māori have sought to control the meaning of change, through the continued assertion of the bonds between land and identity (bonds described, in Chapters 2 and 3). Hence 'iwi everywhere have been more concerned with retaining spiritual and legal links to particular pieces of land, or mana whenua, than with condemning change'. Such links are important in current attempts at redress. Keenan contrasts one of the earliest claims to the Waitangi Tribunal, the Te Āti Awa claim about despoiling of the rich seafood reefs of north Taranaki in the early 1980s, with the generic Indigneous Flora and Fauna claim, which is not rooted in particular tribal landscapes. To him the essential points of reference for Māori remain in the land 'substantially surviving the losses that have occurred'.

The Taranaki story highlights the use of legal instruments to impose Pākehā settlement. Chapter 17 complements this, in exploring the nature and impact of environmental law. Nicola Wheen's thesis is that such law has always facilitated the allocation and protection of property rights and the exploitation of resources. Despite a long history of conservation initiatives, as outlined in Chapters 8 and 12, legislative promotion of resource conservation was for long but a mere ripple 'in the blanket of law enabling resource development'. Has this situation changed with the environmental campaigns in the last third of the twentieth century, with attempts to integrate conservation with development, with the advent of sustainability as the 'golden thread' of resource management? Given the Resource Management Act, no government could now force through a dam-building scheme such as that at Clyde, or get away with the other grand hydro developments of postwar years that proceeded without environmental impact assessments. Yet Wheen sees the Act as being interpreted by the courts in ways consistent with long-held practice; that is, as 'inherently biased towards development'. She considers it 'ecologically derelict', its 'bark ... greener than its bite'.

This analysis is complemented by Christine Dann's wide-ranging final chapter. She reinserts New Zealand's environmental pasts, presents, and futures into the global framework with which the book begins, and which exists, implicitly or explicitly, throughout its pages. She sees three forces as predominant in shaping New Zealand's and the world's environmental realities: colonisation, industrialisation, and modernisation. Today colonisation focuses on the issues of biosecurity as well as genetic engineering; industrialisation has brought about 'the complete commodification of nature'; and modernisation champions development 'as a form of limitless production and consumption'. Such forces take us ever further from any moral commitment to sustainability. Dann, however, sees hope in two alternative pathways. One is growing consumer and producer interest in food produced organically rather than biotechnologically. The other is resistance to 'unfettered global trade' and the more 'mindful consumption of essential goods' that can accompany it, including holding New Zealand producers to account for their claim to be 'clean and green'.

Doing environmental history

What signposts does this collection provide for the ongoing development of environmental history in New Zealand? Practitioners, students, and critics will no doubt decide this matter, but we can suggest three: themes to explore, concepts to develop, and resources to use.

Numerous topics await discovery or more detailed examination. Some that can be mentioned are environmental histories of the coast, of transport development and its consequences, and of tourism. The role of the state as environmental agent, and the history of recent environmental contests (such as those over mining in the Coromandel and forestry on the South Island's West Coast), in which the state has been deeply implicated, deserve attention. So, too, as Stephen Dovers has pointed out, do resource-management institutions, the study of which is one means of ensuring that past insights in the development of environmental knowledge are not lost.[31] In fact relatively little is known about how environmental knowledge evolves through time, or how environmental ideas are transmitted, and when and why they change.[32] How quickly was the hazardousness of different parts of the country understood, for example; what impact did this have on the consciousness of colonists and their successors; and did responses change with experience? There is no equivalent of Donald Meinig's masterly analysis of the response of nineteenth-century South Australian settlers to the peculiarly cyclical nature of droughts,[33] even though similar conditions prevail over much of eastern New Zealand.

The range of methodolgies that can be used in developing environmental histories is a function of its essential interdisciplinarity. This, however, can operate at two levels. In the first, interdisciplinarity involves conscious engagement with other disciplines, driven by a realisation that strict disciplinary allegiance may not allow one's questions to be answered. The implications of statements such as Donald Worster's, that 'wherever the two spheres, the natural and the cultural, confront or interact with one another, environmental history finds its essential themes', are complex.[34] Few disciplines—geography and ecology are exceptions—are used to handling this interaction, which can lead to elementary misconceptions such as the belief that nature has 'agency' in some sort of personalised sense, and that hazards are produced by 'the environment' rather than the interaction of human activity with environmental processes.

The second perspective on interdisciplinarity claims that it is unlikely, given the nature of disciplinary cultures, that a great deal of conceptual and methodological coherence will develop; that pragmatically it may be unwise to pursue such coherence, as many of the insights in books such as this would not emerge without a plural approach.[35] To take one regional example: we know far more about Pākehā environmental histories in central and South Canterbury because of the varied allegiances of its researchers. Peter Holland's work on landscape development, as well as on colonising routines at The Point station, is informed by both an historical consciousness and the ecological awareness of the biogeographer. Michele Dominy, another scholar attracted from North America, has applied her insights as an anthropologist to the development of territoriality among the high-country farming families of the nearby Rakaia Valley. And Karen Beker's masters thesis, on the developing sense of place of the community of Waimate, and rooted in the discipline of history, is a model for postgraduates to emulate. Such work carries on the fine tradition of *Tutira*.[36]

Local studies like these have been described as 'the bedrock of environmental history',[37] although they are always usefully situated within or at the intersection of wider processes. Consider, for example, the photograph in Figure 1.3. It is by the Duke of Gloucester, third son of King George V, who toured New Zealand in 1935. In the Waipoua Forest in Northland, Māori and Pākehā bushmen cut down a six-hundred-year-old kauri tree for his amusement, enabling the Duke to record it using his new hobby of cinematic photography.[38] Here colonial power and the capitalist impulse that drove the exploitation of the kauri forests of the north combine to form a fleeting historical moment in the life of a small place. Ironically, it was by then an area struggling to survive, most of its kauri, the most valued timber tree in the bush, having been previously harvested for export to growing centres of trade such as Auckland and Sydney. Later, however, Waipoua gained a different sort of symbolic status, becoming in the late 1940s the site of the first lowland forest reserve.

Figure 1.3 Felling of a kauri for the visit of the Duke of Gloucester to Waipoua in 1935. Reproduced by permission of the Kauri Museum, Matakohe.

Photographs such as this are part of a rich array of resources for the study of environmental histories, provided they are placed in context and not allowed uncritically to 'speak for themselves'. So, too, are works of art, maps, and advertisements. Films such as those made by the National Film Unit in the 1940s and 1950s about soil erosion and flooding lend insight into how these problems were then conceived.[39] The accessibility of archival materials is better than it has ever been. For instance, the growing number of Waitangi Tribunal hearings and reports since the late 1980s has added immeasurably to the availability of documentation, interpretation, and source materials for pre-European and contact environmental histories. Many repositories have developed improved public access, such as the Auckland War Memorial Museum, the National Museum of New Zealand Te Papa Tongarewa in Wellington, the Canterbury Museum in Christchurch, and the Hocken Library in Dunedin. The online archive of photographs held by the

National Library in the Alexander Turnbull Library is available via any private or public Internet terminal. Debates about topics in environmental history, information, and requests can be found on web sites devoted to the subject.

The interpretation of environmental histories will always be open to change. Some things, however, remain the same. New Zealand is both a vulnerable and a violent land, and it is one that has shown no particular respect for human interests as immigrants have engaged with it over the last few hundred years. Through such engagements, failures as well as successes, people have survived and prospered, although not always equitably or comfortably. There is little point in railing against the past effects of such efforts. Rather, we need better to understand the imaginative worlds that lead people and institutions to behave as they do, to gain a clearer grasp of the consequences of human actions, while appreciating that environmental change, not stability, has always been a factor in the making of places and histories. If the stories of the past show us anything, it is that it is in our own interests to be vigilant, to learn more about the contexts in which we live, and to temper tendencies towards environmental heroics or complacency with an awareness that, slowly or with great drama, the unexpected has always happened.

Part 1
Encounters

2

A FRAGILE PLENTY

PRE-EUROPEAN MĀORI AND THE NEW ZEALAND ENVIRONMENT

Atholl Anderson

The first signs of the considerable pre-European Māori impact on the New Zealand environment came tumbling out of the Taranaki sand at Te Rangatapu in 1847—moa bones dug up with great vigour by local Māori under the bemused gaze of amateur palaeontologist Walter Mantell. He was not entirely sure that the bones were from slaughtered birds, but five years later, in North Otago, his suspicions were confirmed. At the place he named Awamoa, his Māori guides, equipped with tent poles and exhibiting such archaeological enthusiasm 'as would make you shudder', recovered not just numerous remains of moas and other extinct birds, but the butchery knives, oven stones, and charcoal that put the question of a human association beyond doubt. The disappearance of moa, and of other avifauna, became the first and most enduring topic of debate about anthropogenic change in the New Zealand environment.[1]

Debates and perspectives

For more than a century it remained almost the only topic of significance. The other great issue, deforestation, had been foreshadowed by reports from early travellers and surveyors in the eastern South Island of the remains of former forest strewn among the tussock, but the implication of Māori activity in widespread deforestation did not rise to continuing scientific prominence until the mid twentieth century, and then in rebuttal of a contrary hypothesis. Signs of instability in South Island forest structure had been attributed by forester John Holloway, among others, to substantial climatic changes, beginning about the thirteenth century, which ushered in cooler, windier and much drier conditions that affected forest regeneration and set a trajectory towards scrubland and grassland in eastern districts. Burning increased commensurately with desiccation, but climatic change was the forcing agent. In an influential review of this argument, geographer Kenneth Cumberland made out a convincing case for the primacy of cultural firing, a theory that came increasingly to be accepted as palaeoclimatic data failed to confirm dramatic changes in the last millennium and radiocarbon dating documented the coincidence of massive deforestation with initial human colonisation.

Pre-European Māori, it came to be seen, had been involved in the loss of 50 per cent of both the primeval forest area and the late Holocene or postglacial suite of bird species. For some time, the force of this conclusion was blunted by the persistence of an elderly hypothesis that divided the pre-European inhabitants into two populations, early moa-hunters who were then supplanted by Māori immigrants in the fourteenth century. Moa-hunters, it was argued, had been responsible for the massive environmental changes. In comparison, while Māori increased tenfold in population 'nowhere did [they] cause a wholesale transformation of the environment or a disastrous disturbance of the ecosystem'. When it became apparent that neither Māori historical tradition nor archaeological evidence supported the idea of a separate earlier population, the historical reality was clearly exposed: Māori alone were responsible.[2]

Reactions to it have varied. One that commands broad popular appeal is to compress Māori environmental behaviour into an ethnographic present defined by historical snapshots of 'rāhui' and other forms of resource management, to which early faunal extinction and deforestation are distant and minor aberrations. Another, almost the opposite, has proposed that Māori were destructive from the beginning, shattering not only the natural environment but also an earlier population, the 'Nation of Waitaha', a multiracial (including European) community of gentle gardeners steeped in ecological knowledge and reverence. The latter is merely a 'New Age' fantasy that has coopted a genuine tribal name, but it has served to promote a resentful view of pre-European Māori as environmental mismanagers whose descendants are now the undeserving recipients of state largesse in land and resources, delivered upon recommendations of the Waitangi Tribunal.[3]

A third view, which underlies the discussion in this chapter, has developed mainly among archaeologists and ecologists. It originates in evolutionary ecology, notably in the economics of consumer choice, and proposes that within their social rules of resource ownership and use, pre-European Māori operated as optimal foragers, exploiting natural commodities in ways that expended the least effort for the greatest return to promote the comfort and development of individuals and lineages, without consideration for distant communities or the sustainability of any particular resource. Consequently, resources diminished or disappeared in proportion to their desirability and their vulnerability to exploitation.[4] It is axiomatic, in this view of the past, that no substantial, desirable, and easily gathered resource, such as moa or seals, would be left untouched for centuries while less efficient subsistence activities were pursued. However, just that argument has been implied as a means of reconciling evidence of moa-hunting, beginning in the twelfth or early thirteenth century, with speculation about much earlier human settlement. A small, slow-growing, and mainly horticultural population in northern New Zealand, treading environmentally with the delicacy of the mythical Waitaha, is envisaged by some archaeologists as preceding the eventual development of a focus upon big-game hunting and other activities in the south.[5]

Such contrasting scenarios of ecological adaptation underscore three points about the delivery of the pre-European impact to the New Zealand environment. First, much depends upon when the exploitation began. If the loss of forest and megafauna occurred after long occupation had produced conditions of population growth that rapidly accelerated the rate of environmental change, then different processes were at work than if those same changes were the casualties of the first, careless, rapture of overconsumption by newly arrived migrants. Second, the environmental encounter ran in both directions. The growth of Māori society from Polynesian roots owed as much to the constraints and opportunities of the New Zealand environment as the latter was changed by it. Third, considerable environmental variation in New Zealand implies a regionally differential vulnerability of the land and biota to cultural interference. Out of these elements a broad set of ecological

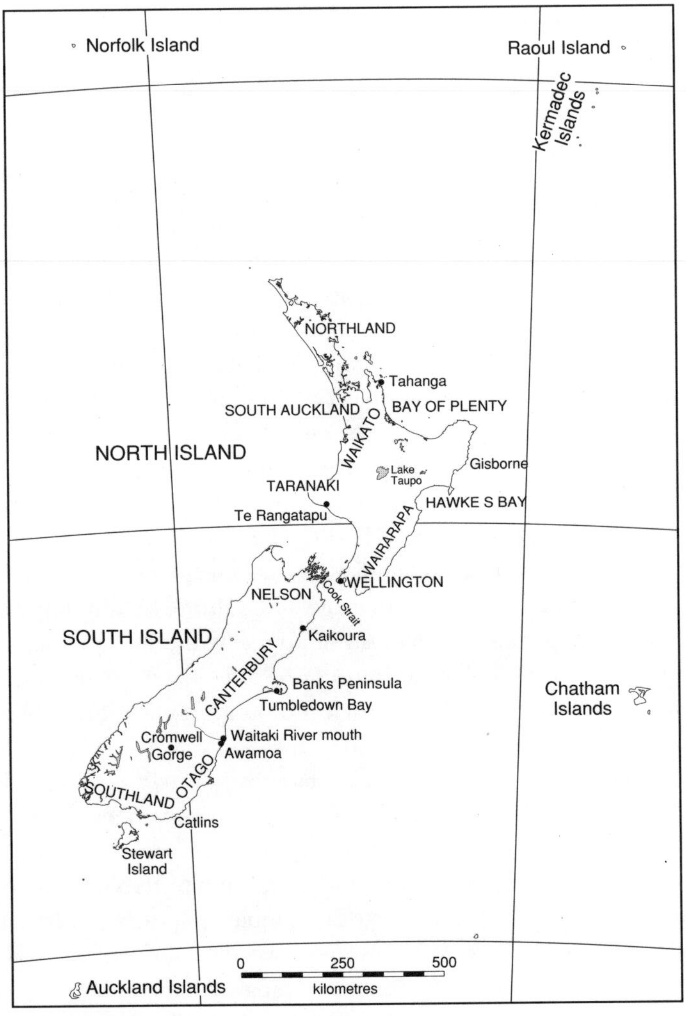

Figure 2.1 Places and districts mentioned in Chapter 2.

relationships is drawn in order to sketch a hypothesis of socio-economic change in pre-European New Zealand (Figure 2.1 shows localities mentioned in the text).

The chronology of colonisation

Three competing hypotheses of initial colonisation in New Zealand have been developed: a long prehistory beginning about 2000 years ago; an orthodox prehistory beginning 1200–1000 years ago; and a short prehistory beginning 600–800 years ago. The idea of a long prehistory goes back more than 150 years, to conjecture by Mantell and, later, the German geologist Julius von Haast, who was the first Director of the Canterbury Museum, but it has been revived recently in arguments that exploit the methodological vulnerability of sedimentary and pollen analyses, and most especially in those that appeal to evidence of early rat colonisation.

In the case of the small Pacific rat, *Rattus exulans*, which was carried, deliberately or stowed away, on large voyaging canoes sailed by the earliest colonists throughout the remote Pacific, it is argued that the people who introduced it either departed more or less immediately or died out, leaving no trace of their settlement. Since rats bred at spectacular rates on islands that previously had no mammalian predators, such as those of New Zealand, they soon became prominent among the prey items of native birds. The earliest radiocarbon dates on the bones of rats from predator-roosting sites should provide, therefore, a reasonable proxy for the age of initial human colonisation. Importantly, the accuracy of the method could be tested by comparing dates on rat bone from the archaeological sites with numerous radiocarbon dates on other materials, such as charcoal, from the same stratigraphic provenances.

Straightforward as the method seems, it ran immediately into controversy. Zoologist Richard Holdaway's early results from predator sites suggested that rats were introduced to the South Island by at least 150 BC, and to the North Island about AD 200. With East Polynesia probably not settled before AD 600, the first people to reach New Zealand would therefore have been West Polynesian or Melanesian, and not directly ancestral to Māori, who have an East Polynesian language and culture. In addition, the existence of rats for three times longer than previously thought in the New Zealand environment must have had a substantial ecological impact on some plants, many invertebrates, and a wide range of smaller vertebrates. With such profound implications at stake, we need to be sure that the results are accurate.

To evaluate them, it is useful to compare radiocarbon dates from predator sites with those from archaeological sites, where rats were probably scavengers on food remains, and occasionally themselves eaten. The largest dataset of radiocarbon dates on rat bone, from the Rafter Laboratory, Lower Hutt, shows that they fall into two groups according to the period in which the laboratory processed the samples (Figure 2.2). In 1995–96, all ten archaeological dates, and twenty of the twenty-two dates from natural sites, were more than 800 years old. In 1997–98, all eleven archaeological dates and fourteen of seventeen dates from natural sites were younger than 800 years old. Furthermore, nearly all of the oldest dates were obtained in the earliest processing, in 1995. Given that the archaeological

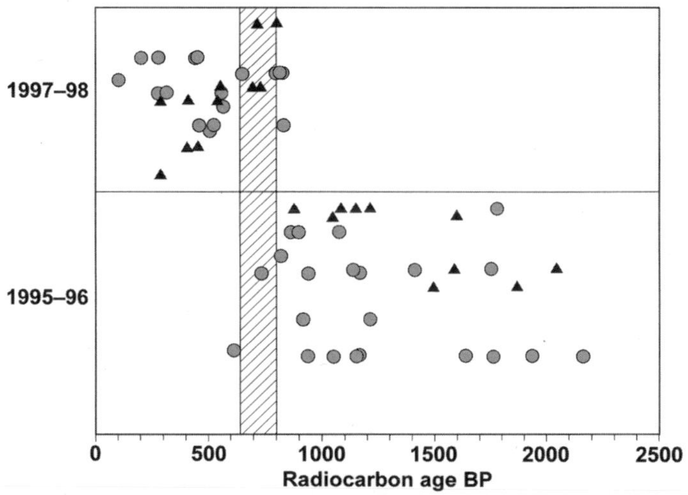

Figure 2.2 The distribution of Rafter Laboratory radiocarbon dates on rat bone. Circles are predator-site samples; triangles are archaeological-site samples. Horizontal axis shows years before present (BP), vertical axis the two periods of sample processing. Vertical shading indicates the expected age of initial rat colonisation.

results are on repeated samples from sites that had been independently dated to no older than 800 years ago, and that the predator-site results mirror the archaeological distribution, it seems that the quality of radiocarbon dating on rat-bone samples improved with experience, eventually to produce results in the expected age range. Opinions are divided as to how this could have happened, but it is widely agreed that there can be no confidence in the early rat-bone radiocarbon dates.[6]

The pre-European history of vegetation change is quite complex and, in some respects, open to debate. Analyses of pollen spectra, and charcoal abundance in sedimentary cores, enable palynologists to argue that certain kinds and scales of change—typically, extensive, unreversed deforestation accompanied by charcoal levels indicative of prolonged burning—were probably anthropogenic in situations where people were present. Reverse that argument, however, and ask how much and what kind of vegetation change could indicate the presence of people, where that is otherwise undocumented, and a difficulty emerges, for clearly almost any kind or scale of change in sedimentary or vegetational conditions *could* be anthropogenic. Given that uncertainty, it has been proposed that brief episodes of charcoal influx or vegetational change extending back several thousand years in New Zealand cases might represent the presence of a human population that remains unnoticed in other kinds of evidence.

Although lacking any archaeological support, this proposition cannot be ruled out entirely, if only on the logical ground that in appealing to a scarcity of evidence it can hardly be tested, but it is improbable at best and the arguments against it are strong. Vegetational and charcoal perturbations of the same kind are evident in sedimentary records extending into the Pleistocene or Ice Ages, long before there were any people in the remote Pacific; even tiny human populations can create a significant impact on the environment by fire; it is improbable that early settlers would ignore the big game, including moa, for more than a thousand years and then fall upon it voraciously, and so on.

Compelling evidence of deforestation associated with fire generally begins after AD 1300 throughout New Zealand. In a few cases, the point of continuous change from forest to scrub, fern, or grass has radiocarbon dates to the first millennium AD, but this seems to reflect difficulties in dating. An important analysis of New Zealand pollen records, by palynologists Matt McGlone and Janet Wilmshurst, shows that whereas radiocarbon dates on the inception of continuous deforestation recorded in peat-bog strata are characteristically late (AD 1300–1400), much earlier dates on the same horizon came from sediments recovered in lakes and swamps that are susceptible to inwashing of old carbon. Dating of offshore pollen cores on samples from marine organisms that lived in deep-sea carbon reservoirs is similarly open to question. Leaving aside such problematic results, the earliest evidence that might be interpreted as anthropogenic is correlated in eleven pollen records from the northern North Island with deposition of the Kaharoa ash, which is dated to about 600 years ago, and similar ages for widespread deforestation occur in South Island pollen cores.[7]

The direct evidence of archaeology offers no support to speculation about early colonisation. Substantial programs of archaeological research have failed to locate evidence of any kind that can be dated to earlier than the twelfth or thirteenth centuries. In particular, large-scale analyses of archaeological radiocarbon ages produced by the Rafter Radiocarbon Laboratory and the Waikato Radiocarbon Laboratory and a wide-ranging study of the calibrated ages have found no evidence of human habitation before 750 years ago.[8]

On rather fewer data, the same story can be read in the records from the outlying islands. The Kermadec Islands were colonised 650 years ago, Norfolk Island perhaps 700 years ago, and the Chatham Islands by at least 450 years ago, although probably somewhat earlier than that, considering the Archaic form of some of the artefacts that have been recovered. Determined voyagers searching in all directions from New Zealand reached even the subantarctic Auckland Islands by 650 years ago, although they did not survive long there.

The rapid discovery of all the outlying islands suggests a substantial early population size, certainly more than the crew of one canoe, and so does the transfer to New Zealand of not just the material supports of a Polynesian existence in plants, animals, and technology, but also a rich cross-section of the social structure, customs, legends, and traditions. Research on Māori mitochondrial DNA sequences has come to a similar conclusion. An original population 800 years ago would have required at least fifty to a hundred women to obtain its genetic diversity, and the retention of rare alleles (the alternative forms of a gene) indicates that the founding population must have been even larger if colonisation occurred earlier than is currently thought.[9]

Therefore, it appears that 'South Polynesia'—New Zealand and the outlying islands—was not reached by people until the twelfth or thirteenth century. A recent review of the various sources of evidence, concluded 'that no human presence in New

Zealand is detectable prior to ca. 1250–1300 A.D... . Our results strongly accord with the late colonisation, or "short" prehistory model.'[10] The founding population was quite large, probably several hundred people at least, implying the arrival of a number of canoes, although not necessarily together. The early archaeological sites, and other contemporary sources of evidence, thus document not a middle phase of the encounter between Māori and the land, reflecting either a deliberate strategic shift in settlement patterns and economic objectives, or simply an expedient extension southwards of big-game hunting and deforestation driven by population pressure. Rather, the evidence illustrates an over-riding will to survive and grow by *initial* migrants in an environment that lay quite beyond their previous experience.

Environmental impact on Māori

The dialectic of human–environmental influence, never a one-way process, opened with the cultural appropriation of the New Zealand environment, marked, we can assume, by the naming of things. This included naming the major topographical features in ways that installed tropical Polynesian claims to ownership. The North Island, for example, became 'Te Ika a Māui', the fish of Māui. It also included imposing the discipline of Polynesian systematics upon the new biota. The northern palm, recalling the coconut, became 'nīkau' (the coconut frond); the Polynesian fibre-plant *Pandanus* or 'fara', was attached to flax as 'harakeke' (strong *Pandanus*); the New Zealand 'pāua' was named for the black-lipped, iridescent-green-eyed giant clam; the tropical snake mackerel bestowed 'mangā' on the barracouta; coral gropers are recalled in 'hāpuku'; while the tiger shark, or 'tanifa', proliferated into a multitude of dangerous water-monsters or 'taniwha'. Parrots remained as 'kākā', owls as 'ruru', rails as 'weka', and long-billed waders added to their name the shore-foraging 'kiwi'.[11]

Much of the tropical Polynesian technology was able to be transferred directly into exploitation of the New Zealand environment. Adze and blade manufacture, developed on oceanic basalts, translated into the crafting of almost identical tools from Tahanga basalt and Nelson-Marlborough metamorphosed argillite. The bait-hook and trolling-lure kit of tropical Polynesia, deprived of *Turbo* and pearl shell, found approximate facsimiles in Cook's turban and mussel shell. Large bone, hardly available in the tropics, was a bonus, and abundant moa bone enabled a proliferation in the shape and size of hooks and many other small artefacts. The tropical fowling spears, lures, and snares worked just as well in New Zealand to take a much wider size range of prey, including moa. Prolonged cooking and soaking to remove the poisons in karaka (*Corynocarpus laevigatus*) and tawa (*Beilschmiedia tawa*) kernels, and to produce sugar from tī (*Cordyline* spp.), were among various ancestral techniques transferred to the processing of New Zealand plant foods.

Yet New Zealand in truth was hardly like anywhere in Polynesia at all. Massive, cloudy, and cold, it stretched to the limit the environmental adaptability of the first settlers. The temperate forest, evolved in the absence of mammals, was poor in large fruits and oil-rich seeds, while the generally humid climate precluded much compensatory development of tubers or starch-rich seeds—dense forest was consequently a significant obstacle to human existence. The bulging 'portmanteau biota' that facilitated an easy accessibility to colonisation in the tropics was in New Zealand stripped, primarily by climate, of most of its more important contents. No coconut, banana, breadfruit, pandanus, pig, or chicken survived, and of the suite of domesticates that did (sweet potato, taro, yam, gourd, tropical *Cordyline*, paper mulberry, dog), only the relatively hardy sweet potato, or kūmara, and the faithful but tasty dog (kurī) became substantial aids to subsistence. Tropical horticulture was adapted to the temperate climate by selection of fast-maturing types, the addition of heat-retaining gravel to soils and winter-storage of tubers in pits, but even the hardiest kūmara needed a minimum of five to six months to mature, which confined its range to lowland regions north of Banks Peninsula, and its economic prominence to the northern two-thirds of the North Island.

A temperate seasonality in climate was sharpened to almost continental severity in many inland areas, and that, coupled with the rapid succession of frontal systems that characterise the New Zealand climate, reduced first-choice human climates to a few

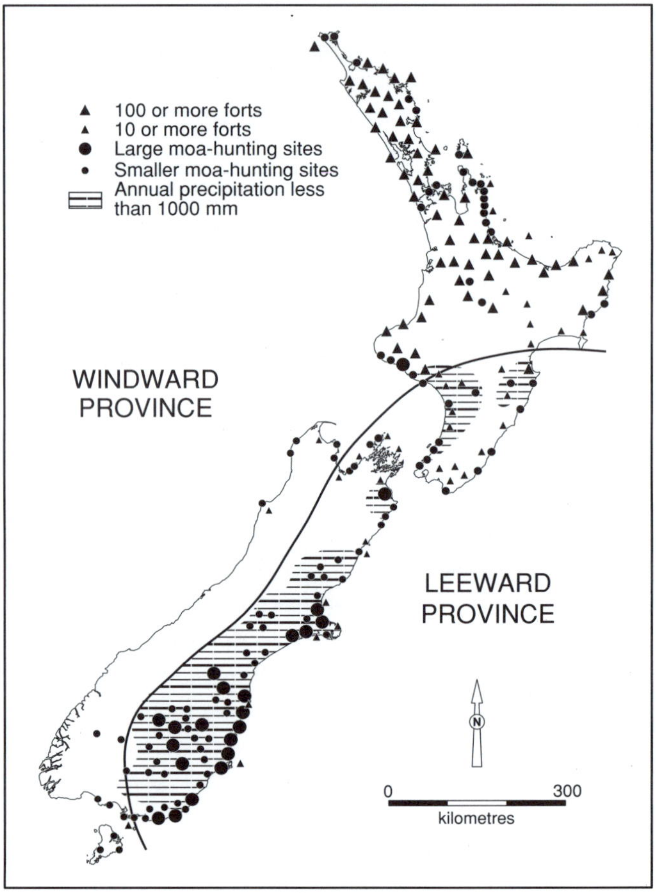

Figure 2.3 Windward and leeward provinces in New Zealand, showing Māori forts (pā) and moa-hunting sites, also the correlation of pā largely with the former, and of moa-hunting sites mainly with the latter.

coastal districts, of which Gisborne and Nelson were the warmest overall. But considerations of comfort had to be balanced by those of survival, so the distribution of native resources also moulded the settlement patterns of Māori from the beginning.[12]

One way of looking at this, and it is one with which Polynesians from high islands were profoundly familiar, is the windward–leeward cline. Like trade winds in the tropics, the dominant westerlies in New Zealand produce contrasting patterns of vegetation and terrestrial life. West to east variations in rainfall (and some rain-shadow reversals) are cross-cut by variations in temperature on islands spread across thirteen degrees of latitude. Consequently, the contours of variation are offset to a northwest–southeast pattern (Figure 2.3). At the time of first settlement of New Zealand the mainly northwest windward province was characterised by heavy, humid forest, much of it, in the north, developed upon soils of volcanic origin. The great trees were rimu, tōtara, tawa, and kauri, and the forest was filled with broad-leaved trees and shrubs. In the mainly southeast leeward province, there was a more open forest dominated by mataī, kahikatea, and tōtara, with beech forest in the mountains and at the eastern edges. In a few districts, such as the Canterbury Plains and inland Otago, there was a low forest of toatoa, kānuka, and kōwhai around open basins covered in light scrub and tussock.

The main biomass of large vertebrates was concentrated in the mosaic vegetation of the leeward province. They comprised, above all, the twelve species of moa (Dinornithiformes)—wingless, browsing birds ranging in weight from 25 to 250 kilograms. In addition, there were large flightless geese and a very large rail-like bird, *Aptornis*, a swan, various species of ducks and parrots, and, among raptors, an immense moa-hunting eagle. The absence of turtles was more than made up for by an abundance of seals, notably the New Zealand fur seal and the sea lion, both most prolific towards the south, although breeding colonies of the former, at least, extended to Northland. Plant foods, also, were probably more accessible initially in the leeward province, because the most useful of them, such as bracken fern root (*Pteridium esculentum*) and the roots and stems of young cabbage trees, or tī, were products of the forest edge and open ground.

The distribution of early archaeological sites is not an infallible guide to the way in which the New Zealand environment influenced initial Māori settlement patterns, because it favours the more visible sites of big-game hunting over those where activities that left less obvious traces, such as plant cultivation or processing, may have been carried out. However, given that early bone and shell middens represent the universal foraging aspect of coastal settlement, it is apparent from their size and distribution that many of the colonists were drawn preferentially to the leeward province. In this region of relatively plentiful resources was first revealed the insular fragility to human intervention of the New Zealand biota.[13]

Vertebrate extinctions

The role of people in faunal extinctions is seldom easily documented. In most cases, unavoidable comparison of data from natural sites where bone accumulated gradually throughout several thousand years or longer with data from archaeological sites representing selective hunting trips over much less than a century raises problems of sampling variation that make it virtually impossible to determine whether a species disappeared only after the arrival of people, let alone whether human activity was the critical factor in extinction.

Expanding on the hypothesis of early rat introductions, and assuming no human survival, Holdaway has proposed that 'many of the extinctions and extirpations occurred when the Pacific rat was the only widespread novel factor in the environment'. For example, he suggests that small petrels such as the diving petrel *Pelecanoides urinatrix* were in decline on the mainland through rat predation before continuous Polynesian settlement began. However, this species is well represented in mainland archaeological sites, considering that small petrels lay outside the preferred size range of Māori fowling. Besides, variations in archaeological recovery of small bones subvert any attempt to define under-representation of species. Only presence or absence across a wide range of sites constitutes reasonably strong evidence. The data there are quite clear. As palaeontologist Trevor Worthy points out, remains of all prehistorically extinct species of late Holocene birds have been found in at least one archaeological site, apart from two tiny wrens and two recently recognised species (the moa *Pachyornis australis* and a petrel *Puffinus spelaeus*), which are expected to be found in re-examination of archaeological collections. In other words, there is no documented extinction of any New Zealand avian species (indeed of any vertebrate) in the millennium prior to demonstrable Polynesian colonisation.[14]

It was the arrival of people, and of rats and dogs, in the thirteenth century or slightly earlier that initiated the great assault upon the New Zealand fauna. Much of this remains poorly documented, and it can be assumed that, were the data available, various invertebrate species would be numbered among the extinct. Evolved in the absence of terrestrial mammals, many of them were comparatively large and flightless, just as in the avifauna, and had become 'invertebrate mice' and other small mammal surrogates. They were immensely vulnerable to the introduction of rats and to forest burning. Much the same is doubtless true of the New Zealand lizards and frogs, several species of which are known to have disappeared in the pre-European era, and others became greatly reduced in range, such as the tuatara, which had been widespread on mainland New Zealand during the late Holocene.

The impact on the avifauna is much better known. The factors of extinction are rather variable, but habitats that were easily accessible to people and often easily burnt, such as light forest, scrubland, or waterside shrubbery, large body size, flightlessness, ground-nesting, diurnal habits, and low breeding rates are common factors. Some species, such as the pelican and swan, were vulnerable to any form of human disturbance, especially at their nesting sites. Small ground-nesting birds generally, such as snipe, snipe-rail, and wrens, were most at risk of direct predation from 'a grey tide' of rapidly expanding rat populations. Larger flightless or poorly flighted geese, *Aptornis*, and various ducks faced rat predation on eggs, competition with rats for some food sources, disturbance by dogs, habitat destruction, and direct human predation, while the moa were largely hunted into extinction and their natural predator, the great New Zealand eagle, lost its means of existence.[15]

There is general agreement that moa extinction occurred rapidly, but perhaps not as quickly as a century or less after human colonisation, as recent zoological modelling suggests. Predator–prey models oversimplify the complexity of cultural systems within which moa-hunting took place. Early colonists, it can be assumed, sought to maintain community integrity, diversity of resources, and external exchange by locating year-round settlements along the coast. These sustained continual predation on local moa populations, but those in less accessible interior districts were probably hunted relatively seldom. Coastal moa populations had probably crashed by the late fourteenth century, especially in the most accessible areas such as the Canterbury Plains, but some archaeological data suggest that they survived rather longer elsewhere. In the Cromwell Gorge (Central Otago), for example, the site at Italian Creek contained large quantities of burnt moa eggshell, from at least two species, concentrated around two hearths. One hearth was radiocarbon-dated to the mid to late fourteenth century, the other to the fifteenth and sixteenth centuries. Similarly, a careful analysis of radiocarbon dates on moa bone by Fiona Petchey, a bone-dating specialist, shows that at least fourteen results spread across two North Island and three South Island sites had ranges extending into the fifteenth century and several into the sixteenth century or later; for instance, at Tumbledown Bay on Banks Peninsula, where a moa bone dated in the range late fifteenth to late seventeenth centuries. None of these data are sufficiently precise to put a date to moa extinction, but they do indicate that while early slaughter was devastating, there were still moa to be found by the mid fifteenth century, if not later, although survival beyond about AD 1500 seems improbable.[16]

Extinction during the pre-European Māori era claimed nearly forty species of birds, a bat, three to five species of frogs, and an unknown number of lizard taxa. This represented a 50 per cent decline in the number of birds breeding on the mainland, most of them predominant in the leeward province. Furthermore, it was the larger species that became extinct, either because they had been especially targeted, as seems to have been the case with moa (which are represented by the bones of thousands of individuals in some sites, such as Waitaki River Mouth) or because a generalised hunting strategy impacted more severely upon species that were conspicuous but relatively scarce.

The loss of moa was especially significant because of the substantial biomass that they represented. This cannot be known precisely, and suggested figures range from one to about thirty medium-sized moa per square kilometre, the latter figure close to modern high-country stocking rates for cattle and sheep. In the best conditions, such as in parts of the eastern South Island, this biomass is not improbable. Even at much lower rates overall, the disappearance of moa significantly lowered the human-carrying capacity of forest and open country, while reduction of fowling opportunity to small birds such as kākā, weka, tūī, and kererū (pigeon) completely removed the early comparative advantage of the leeward province in terrestrial protein productivity.

As moa and other terrestrial vertebrates were heading for extinction, the New Zealand seals were also declining under human predation. The breeding range of the most common species, New Zealand fur seal, marked by pup bone in archaeological sites, retreated southwards from the Northland coast at AD 1300, to Cook Strait by about AD 1600, and to East Otago by AD 1800. The sea lion breeding range contracted similarly.[17]

The Māori encounter with the land- and shore-breeding New Zealand fauna could hardly have turned out otherwise. The large species had conservative life histories, being long-lived and slow-breeding—moa laying only one or two eggs at a time, seals bearing a single pup. This is an efficient long-term strategy for survival in the presence of natural sources of mortality, but it has very little margin for error. The arrival of a super-predator, flanked by dangerous commensals, all with broadly omnivorous habits that released them from the usual swings of predator–prey abundance, that took eggs, chicks, and pups as well as adults, and destroyed vital aspects of the prey ecosystem, could have only one outcome.

Deforestation and its consequences

Having evolved under very low rates of natural ignition, most New Zealand trees and shrubs are killed outright by fire, with only a few species, such as mānuka and tī, able to withstand it. As the majority of tree species are lowland and slow-growing, it takes centuries for full successional recovery. Tussock grassland, however, profits from frequent firing, which may increase growth, flowering, and seed germination. Bracken fern also profits from frequent burning, which eliminates competing species of regenerating shrubs and trees. Consequently, increasing rates of forest firing led to an expansion of fernland and tussock grassland, dotted with tī and fast-growing shrubs.

It is impossible to say whether such effects had been sought by forest firing or were simply the useful by-products of it. It is very unlikely that fires had much to do with moa-hunting, for which snares set on forest or shrubland trails were probably the most effective means. In northern areas, there would have been some deliberate clearance for horticulture, and it is possible that Māori also burnt forest to facilitate cross-country travel. Underlying these possibilities, however, is the important consideration that closed forest was relatively barren of resources, so that its substantial removal, either deliberately or accidentally, did not represent a material disadvantage. The synchronisation of widespread burning throughout much of New Zealand might suggest either that Māori were indifferent to the substantial loss of forest, or perhaps only that they had no control over the impact of an increased incidence of ignition.

Variations within the general trend of fire-induced vegetation change reflect differences in climate, as had earlier changes based upon natural burning and related causes. As the late Holocene climate became cooler and more variable, fire affected some forest in the interior basins of the South Island about 1500–2000 years ago, but devastation in the central North Island wrought by the great Taupo eruption, AD 150, was followed by sustained recovery into a closed forest again after several hundred years.

Māori fires similarly emphasised regional differentiation. Lower rates of widespread conflagration, coupled with relatively rapid regrowth in the humid windward province, slowed and fragmented the advance of deforestation, while fires in the drought-prone leeward province often destroyed large areas of forest, which, being relatively slow to regenerate, were thereafter suppressed by continued burning. It has been estimated from radiocarbon dates on charcoal that fires occurred in some parts of the North Island at about eighty years apart during the pre-European Māori era. In the eastern South Island, by contrast, a fire interval of 200 years in the mid-Holocene had dropped to about fifty years as late Holocene dry conditions took hold, then dropped again to only ten years at about 700 years ago, as human settlement began.

The effect was to virtually eliminate the forests of the eastern South Island in a fairly brief pulse of burning, AD 1300–1450, leaving significant stands only in parts of Southland, the Catlins, Banks Peninsula, and some of the eastern ranges, including the Kaikouras (Figure 2.4). Forest was also burnt out of the lower east coast of the North Island and Hawke's Bay. Throughout the leeward region, tussock grassland was the common result, with fernland prevailing towards the north. At the same time, substantial areas of the windward province (central North Island, inland Waikato, Bay of Plenty, South Auckland, and parts of Northland) were reduced to scrubland and fernland, and although the incidence of major fires was relatively low, the incidence of localised burning must have been much higher, perhaps three to five years, to maintain fernlands. Extensive forest remained in the windward province, and some large stands elsewhere, but 'the forests of New Zealand, lacking resistance to fire, slow-growing and without substantial food resources [for people] were doomed from the moment of first human settlement'.[18]

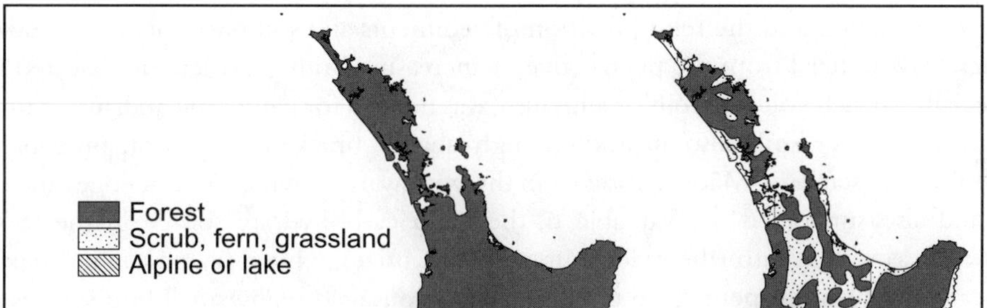

Figure 2.4 Distribution of forest and open country at approximately AD 1000 (left) and 1800 (right). Modified after McGlone, 'The Polynesian Settlement of New Zealand' (See note 2).

A cascade of ecological consequences ensued from deforestation and the loss of the large browsing birds. As zoologist Graeme Caughley has remarked, 'after AD 1400 the major New Zealand grazing systems ceased to exist ... the Polynesians did not just eliminate the moas, they eliminated an ecological and evolutionary process developed over more than 50 million years'. The dispersal of large-fruited seeds, which had relied substantially upon moa and other large birds, declined, while unbrowsed fast-growing shrubs suppressed the growth of podocarp seedlings, perhaps causing a regeneration gap by AD 1400. Such effects, together with the selective loss of the dry lowland forest types, substantially reduced the pre-human forest pattern to its windward and montane types, producing a proportionate increase in beech forest, a relatively barren habitat for birds and people alike.

In the windward province, where fern and scrub colonised the former forest soils, rates of erosion were generally low, although then as now severe episodes of storminess produced substantial slipping in steep hill country. In the leeward province, where tussock grassland was the predominant post-forest cover, rates of soil erosion increased by an order of magnitude. In Canterbury, for example, about three-quarters of radiocarbon dates on charcoal taken from the interface between buried soils and overlying, transported sediments, are in the range 500–1000 years ago.

Deforestation and the remobilisation of sediments and soil nutrients were, however, generally beneficial from the perspective of increasing human settlement. Cleared land, especially on rich volcanic soils or alluvium, was needed for gardening and, just as importantly, the better soils also promoted high-quality bracken fern root, probably the carbohydrate staple of Māori existence in the windward province. Forest edges and open ground also supported the valuable tī, the main carbohydrate source in the leeward province, as well as tutu (the main source of fruit juice), wineberry, pōhuehue, flax, and other useful plants. Opening up closed forest encouraged many small bird species such as weka and quail, while enhanced light and nutrient levels in lakes and waterways increased production of eels and other freshwater fish.[19]

Adaptive change

The broad imperative of environmental change in pre-European New Zealand was to favour a mid-sequence shift in population growth away from the faunally pauperised leeward province towards the plant-favoured windward province, a process that was perhaps reinforced by declining temperatures in the seventeenth century. The historical course of this socio-economic development can be characterised from several perspectives, including those of demographic and societal change, but one that is appropriate here is a simple ecological hypothesis that can be illustrated in archaeological terms by the distribution of moa-hunting versus defensive sites (Figures 2.3).

The nature of the pre-European Māori environmental impact was, in its early stages, almost certainly one that is typical of colonisation everywhere and at all times. Migration into new environments releases a powerful instinct to expand as rapidly as possible, using the richest resources with pitiless energetic efficiency. Evolutionary fitness drives lineage competition in the use of unowned resources towards levels of overexploitation described as the 'tragedy of the commons'. In New Zealand this was played out most visibly between the twelfth and fifteenth centuries in the leeward province, although the loss of moa and seals in the windward province shows that it also occurred there.

Once terrestrial protein resources were substantially reduced to a fine-grained uniformity of small birds, fish, and shellfish, the means of continuing population growth lay in the windward gardens and fernlands (Figure 2.5). These combined high productivity of carbohydrates in an environment where they were otherwise threateningly scarce with strong spatial definition—everybody could see where they were. Around them, and pulling in nearby resource zones of river, lake, coast, and forest, there developed a proprietary sense of boundaries, which became reinforced with population growth into territorial ownership and defence. It is from there but a small step to the systematic regulation of resource use by allocation among related groups and seasonal proscription upon exploitation. How early this began is hard to say, but since construction of pā goes back to the early sixteenth century, it is possible that such regulation was already linked to those developing notions of resource monitoring and conservation that underpin modern Māori perceptions of environmental management.

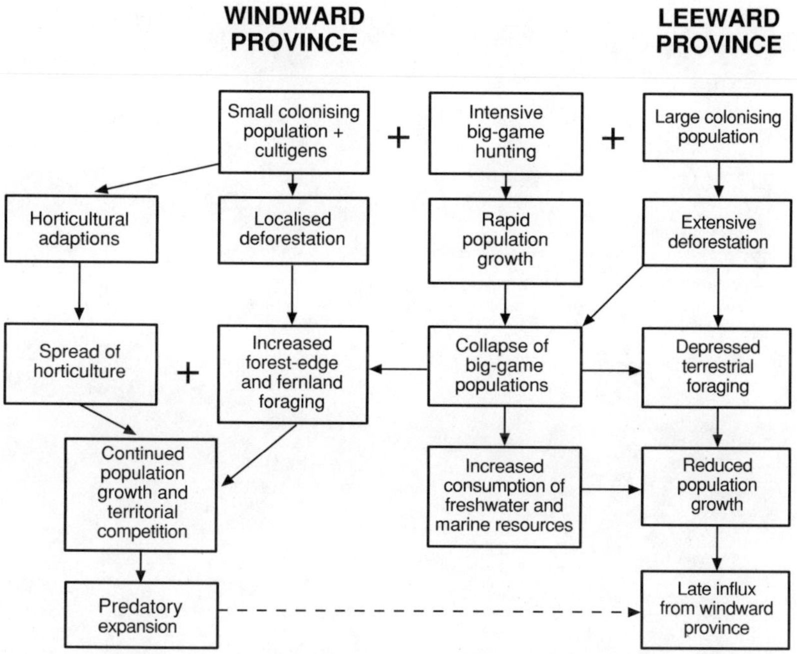

Figure 2.5 A regionally differentiated ecological model of socio-economic change in pre-European New Zealand.

Continuing population growth and territoriality in the windward province initiated, late in the sequence, a movement of some lineages into the relatively underpopulated leeward province, first in Hawke's Bay and Wairarapa, then Wellington and across to the South Island, in a series of migrations that was continuing as Europeans arrived in the late eighteenth century.[20]

Conclusions

New Zealand was the last major landmass in the world to be colonised by people before the modern era, and its record of prehistoric human–environment relationships is correspondingly diverse and well preserved. It describes colonisation about 800 years ago by East Polynesians, who brought the dog and rat plus a suite of domestic plants. Their subsequent environmental encounter focused initially upon the megafauna, most abundant in the relatively dry southeast, and later upon fishing, fern-root collection, and agriculture, especially in the humid northwest region, where resource competition sharpened territoriality and warfare. Sustained predation drove half of the bird species into extinction, and cultural levels of burning devastated the vulnerable forest. Similar changes occurred elsewhere in the Pacific Islands, in Australia, and in the Americas. They are characteristic of the entry of people into previously uninhabited and fragile environments.

3

Contesting Resources

Māori, Pākehā, and a Tenurial Revolution

Evelyn Stokes

In Māori cosmogony the world people live in was shaped by the separation of the original parents, Ranginui, the Sky Father, and Papatūānuku, the Earth Mother. Their children were liberated from Te Pō, the darkness that enveloped them, into Te Ao, the world of light. Some, such as Tāwhirimātea, who was affiliated to atmospheric events, chose to live with Ranginui. Tangaroa chose the sea for his domain. Tāne Mahuta, who was the prime mover in the separation of his parents, was identified with the forests. Rūaumoko, the youngest and still suckling at his mother's breast, remained with Papatūānuku and is associated with earthquakes and volcanoes.

Māori people are the descendants of the union of Tāne with Hine-ahu-one, the woman created out of earth. Therefore Māori saw themselves as part of their environment, at one with it, not dominating it. This relationship was an intensely practical one of using the resources of land and sea for daily sustenance, but was also deeply spiritual, involving recognition and propitiation of ancestor gods. Such ideas do not always sit easily with Pākehā, accustomed to individual property rights and concepts derived from Judaeo-Christian tradition, and the divine command to Adam and Eve, 'Go out and subdue the earth'.

In the *Muriwhenua Land Report* the Waitangi Tribunal noted:

> The fundamental purpose of Maori law was to maintain appropriate relationships of people to their environment, their history and each other ... Maori law described how people should relate to ancestors as the upholders of old values, to the demigods of the environment as providers of life's necessities, to their hapu, which was the primary support system, and to other peoples as necessary for co-existence ... Maori saw themselves as users of the land rather than its owners ... They were born out of it, for the land was Papatuanuku, the mother earth who conceived the ancestors of the Maori people. Similarly, whenua, or land, meant also the placenta, and the people were tangata whenua, which term captured the view that they came from the earth's womb ... That land descends from ancestors is pivotal to understanding the Maori land-tenure system.[1]

A Māori person's identity is thus linked to both place and ancestry. The tenure rights of a Māori community equated with occupation 'from time immemorial', or at least over many generations—ahi kā, keeping the fires burning on the land. Places were identified with deeds of ancestors, frequently recalled in local place names, and detailed knowledge of the landscape and resources of the ancestral estate. There was also imbued in this world-view a sense of custodial occupation, that the environment should be maintained in a fit state for the generations to come.

Māori customary tenure comprised a complex system of overlapping and interlocking usufructuary rights; that is, rights of use and occupation, but with no right of alienation except in very special circumstances sanctioned by the community. Such a situation might be the allocation of rights to some land or resources on the occasion of a strategic marriage to cement a diplomatic alliance, or to redress an imbalance in relationships (utu), or a form of ceremonial gift exchange of valued resources. Conquest did not provide a right unless it was followed by occupation, usually accompanied by strategic marriages with tangata whenua.

Land rights were thus inextricably bound up into the networks of kinship, ancestry, and a political and social structure that acknowledged leadership in senior lines of descent but with the leader unable to make autocratic decisions. Leadership was based on consultation and consensus. The principal social units for day-to-day sustenance were the whānau (extended family) and hapū (group of whānau). In times of threat to life and landholdings a group of whānau may have joined a loose confederation of hapū, sometimes called a tribe, or iwi, but the social structure was flexible, and based on kin networks.

Māori customary tenure was therefore much more complex than any single phrase such as 'ancestral estate' might suggest. A fundamental theme in this chapter is that the nature of the tenure of land and resources is the basis of an understanding the nature of relationships between people and their environment. Before 1840, although there were already some two thousand Pākehā settlers in New Zealand (Figure 3.1), Māori customary law prevailed and Māori retained control of their environment. The history of colonisation after 1840 for Māori is a revolution in tenurial systems, denial of custom law, and incremental loss of control and alienation of land and resources.

Pākehā encounter

In April 1793 two Māori men, Tuki Tahua and Ngahuruhuru, who were sailing off the Cavalli Islands, north of the Bay of Islands, were persuaded to come on board the naval ship *Daedalus*. The commander, Lieutenant James Hanson, had been instructed by Lieutenant-Governor King to bring some Māori back to Norfolk Island to provide expertise in the processing of local flax. The *Daedalus* sailed off with these unwilling passengers, who were taken to Norfolk via Sydney. The young men had limited knowledge of processing flax (it was women's work), but they were treated kindly. King personally escorted them back to their home region in November 1793, and recorded his 'gifts', which consisted of: 'Hand axes; a small assortment of carpenters tools; six spades; some hoes; with a few knives, scissors and razers [sic]; two bushels of maize, one of wheat, two of pease, and a quantity of garden seeds … also ten young sows, and two boars; which Tooke [Tuki] and the Chief promised me should be preserved for breeding'.[2] This was one among many introductions of new plants and animals in the north of New Zealand before the end of the eighteenth century.

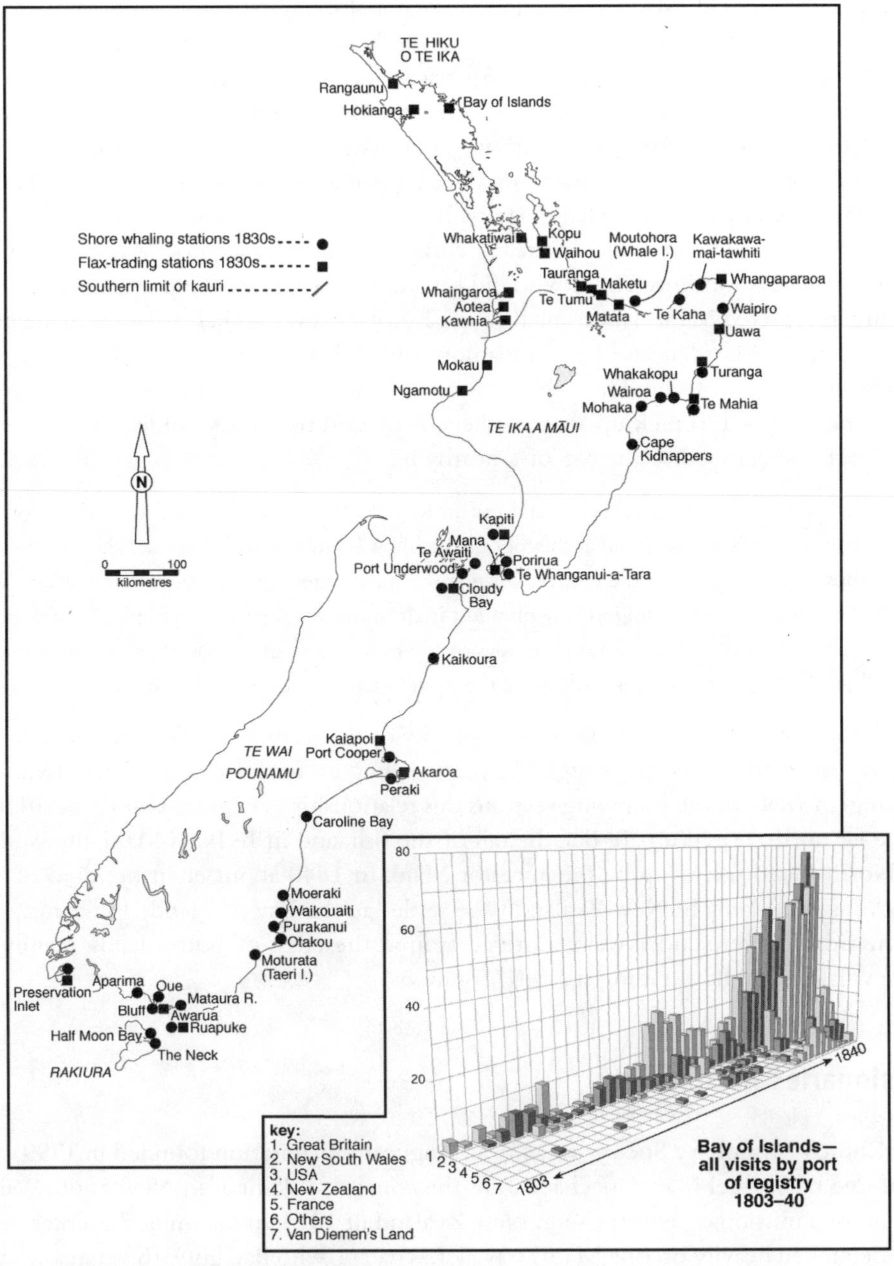

Figure 3.1 Pākehā encounter before 1840.

The introduced pigs fended for themselves and rapidly spread into scrubland and bush, feeding particularly on fern root. Potatoes soon replaced fern root in the Māori diet and were grown as a commercial crop in the Bay of Islands in the early years of Pākehā contact. John Savage, who visited in 1805, commented on the health-giving qualities of potatoes for preventing scurvy among ships' crews, who might be at sea for several months, and was impressed with Māori production of potatoes for trading with visiting ships. By the 1820s, pigs and potatoes had become part of the local economy of most coastal Māori communities, long before Pākehā settlement. American varieties of sweet potato had also been introduced, and from these introductions modern varieties of kūmara have been derived. Fishing, using traditional methods in harbours, along coasts, and often more than thirty kilometres offshore, was also the means to produce a commodity that could be traded. Thus a commercial component was added to established forms of Māori subsistence.[3]

Most European visitors did not really comprehend the nature of Māori society, or iwi and hapū relationships. Those who did record their impressions described what they saw, and interpreted Māori landscape through European eyes. In February 1815, the missionary Samuel Marsden and his companion John Nicholas landed at a village on the coast west of North Cape. Their ship was on its way back to Sydney from the Bay of Islands, but stopped to pick up some baskets of dressed flax. They landed in a canoe in heavy surf and climbed to the top of a nearby hill:

> Below us was a beautiful valley … laid out in neat enclosures, and planted with the coomera [kūmara] and potatoe [sic]; and at the foot of the hill was built a small village … the uncommon neatness and regularity of the cultivated lands; the picturesque form of the valley with its clear and beautiful stream winding its way till it lost itself in the sea; the varied and pleasing foliage of the different coppices scattered on the sides of the hills—these gave altogether such an interesting singularity to this view, as must strike the most tasteless observer with admiration.[4]

This idyllic description masks the complexity of the relationship between Māori and Pākehā that would develop through the years leading up to the signing of the Treaty of Waitangi in 1840. In the following sections this relationship is explored more specifically in the far north, Te Hiku o Te Ika, the tail of the fish, and in Te Ika a Māui, the land of the North Island fished up by the ancestor Māui. In 1840 about eight hundred of the two thousand Pākehā in New Zealand were settled in the Bay of Islands, Hokianga, and northwards. The remainder were scattered around the coast of both islands, mainly in shore whaling and flax-trading stations (Figure 3.1).

Missionaries in the north

The Church Missionary Society (CMS), an Anglican organisation founded in 1799, was persuaded by Samuel Marsden, chaplain to the convict settlement in New South Wales, to sponsor a missionary enterprise in New Zealand in 1814. In planning this enterprise, Marsden relied heavily on one Māori traveller, Ruatara, who had gone to sea in a whaler in 1805. After several voyages he was destitute in London, where Marsden found him, brought him back to his Australian home in Parramatta, and finally in 1812 sent him to the Bay of Islands, equipped with tools and seed-wheat. In March 1814, Marsden sent the brig *Active* (which he had just purchased for the New Zealand trade and mission work) with Thomas Kendall and William Hall on board, and more seed-wheat, a cock, clothing, and other goods destined for Ruatara.

Three Bay of Islands chiefs, Ruatara, Hongi Hika, and Korokoro, sailed on the return voyage to Sydney to help arrange with Marsden for the establishment of a CMS mission station. Judith Binney's analysis indicates the complexity and potential for misunderstanding in this transaction:

> ... the missionaries' purposes and theirs were not the same. Each intended to use the other ... Marsden sought to generate a Maori dependency upon the European missionaries and their ship, and hoped gradually to persuade them to listen to their evangelical message. But on the voyage home Ruatara revealed his ambivalence ... Marsden knew that the survival of the mission depended upon the protection of the chiefs and he assiduously cultivated them.[5]

After Ruatara'a death in 1815, the mission of 'godly mechanics' survived uneasily under the protection of Hongi Hika. However, the CMS presence in the Bay of Islands was probably a significant factor in attracting more whaling ships and traders.

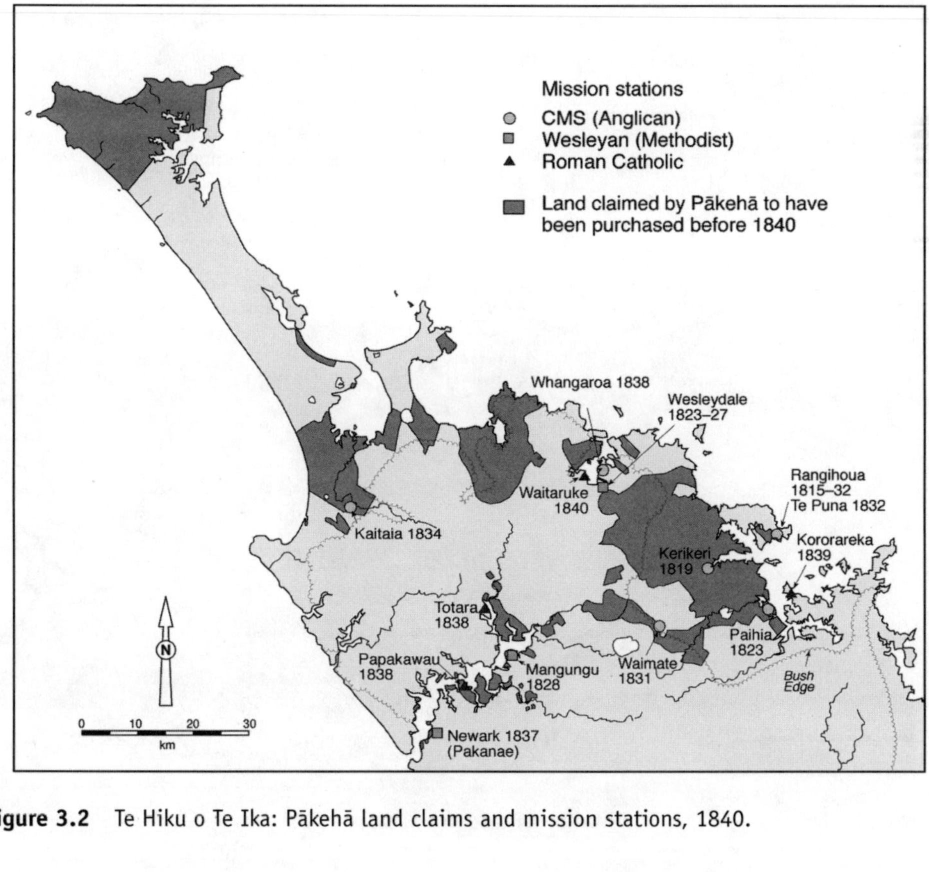

Figure 3.2 Te Hiku o Te Ika: Pākehā land claims and mission stations, 1840.

From an initial base at Rangihoua, further CMS stations were established at Kerikeri (1819), Paihia (1823), Waimate (1831), and Kaitaia (1834) (Figure 3.2). In each of these places there were negotiations with local leaders involving land to be occupied by the missionaries. There was a public signing of a deed that in English appeared to provide some legal right to the land, but it was obvious to the missionaries that their continued occupation depended on the local chiefs. The fate of the Wesleyan mission at Whangaroa provided an example where the station had to be abandoned, when in 1827 the missionaries were caught up in the rivalries between local chiefs of Ngāti Pou and Ngāti Uru, and Hongi Hika's drive to expand his sphere of influence northwards. However, neither the Wesleyans (who were fewer in number) nor the Roman Catholic missionaries (who arrived in the late 1830s) became involved in land transactions in the same way that CMS missionaries did before 1840. The French priests, supported by Irish Catholic traders in the Hokianga, tended to be itinerant. The CMS mission stations developed as settled small communities with a farm to provide subsistence, church, and school, and a settlement of Māori converts close by: an oasis of Anglican civilisation in the Māori wilderness.

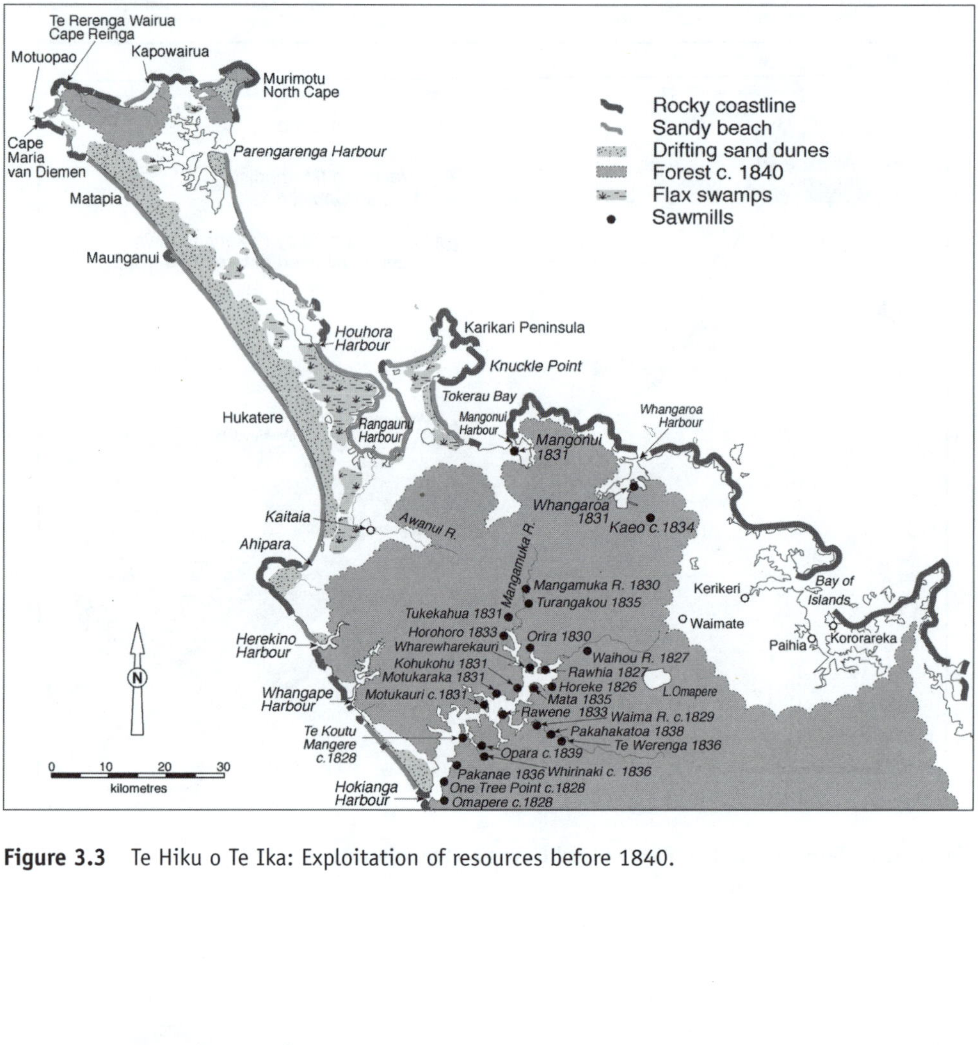

Figure 3.3 Te Hiku o Te Ika: Exploitation of resources before 1840.

Exploiting the resources of the north, 1815–40

During the early 1800s, New Zealand came to be regarded as an integral part of the commercial sphere of Sydney and Hobart merchants. A cosmopolitan population on whaling ships from the Australian colonies, Britain, France, and North America frequented the New Zealand coast by the 1820s. Traders in flax, kauri spars, and timber settled and established trading stations. By the 1830s a number of shore whaling stations had been established (Figure 3.1). The Bay of Islands became the principal provisioning place for ships and the focal point for trade with Māori in the early 1800s. By the mid 1820s the kauri forests of the Hokianga attracted attention sufficient to overcome the difficult entrance to that harbour. Pigs, potatoes, vegetables, dressed flax, and 'curios' were more portable, and were traded by Māori wherever European sailing vessels made anchorage. Apart from the establishment of mission stations, the principal European activities in the north, and contact with Māori, revolved around the provisioning and repair of ships, trade in processed flax, and extraction of kauri spars and sawn timber (Figure 3.3). In all these activities Europeans were totally reliant on Māori cooperation for access to resources, assistance in processing, and transport to and loading of ships. Many Māori also worked as crew on whaling and trading ships, found their way to Sydney, London, and other ports, and brought back a knowledge and experience of the European world that they regaled to kin on their return.

An analysis of 'Shipping Arrivals and Departures' lists compiled for Sydney and other Australian colonies over the period 1803–40 produced a total of 1575 ship visits to the Bay of Islands, including multiple visits by the same ship, although there may have been additional unrecorded visits (Figure 3.1, inset). The number of visits increased through the 1830s to average 118 per year. With an estimated twenty to thirty crew and passengers on each vessel, there would have been some 3000 visitors each year. The sperm-whaling grounds to the north of New Zealand were overfished well before 1840, but the southern right whale in coastal waters between Cook Strait and the Chatham Islands had provided an alternative. However, by 1840 this southern fishery was also grossly depleted. American whalers looked elsewhere, deterred by the prospect of British-imposed port fees, and visits to the Bay of Islands declined in the 1840s.[6]

The flax trade

Of all the strange new plants discovered on Cook's first voyage to New Zealand the flax, harakeke, promised to be the most useful. In a time when sailing ships required ropes and sail canvas, a new source of strong fibre was regarded with considerable interest. It is not surprising, then, that officials and merchants in the colony of New South Wales encouraged the New Zealand flax trade. By 1815 flax was becoming an important item of trade. Between 1815 and 1825 the Church Missionary Society was actively involved in trading flax and timber, and Marsden sold some flax to the Royal Navy. When Henry Williams took over the CMS in New Zealand there was a change in policy, with less emphasis on trade.

There was a continuing problem of satisfactory processing. European flax dressers found their traditional methods of preparing linen flax were not appropriate. Attempts to mechanise processing of New Zealand flax failed. The flax trade therefore relied heavily on Māori willingness to process flax for supply. During the late 1820s there was an increase in Māori production. The organisation of the trade also changed from sporadic collection by trading ships to one of resident agents of Sydney firms and establishment of trading stations. This increased the pressure on Māori producers as only best-quality flax would be accepted, because of the risk of flax cargoes being rejected in London. The major flax-export centres were initially the Bay of Islands and, by the late 1820s, Hokianga. Another important source was the swamps of the Awanui River and around Rangaunu Harbour. By 1830, flax-trading stations were being established further south, into the Thames Valley, Bay of Plenty, and elsewhere (Figure 3.1). Many Māori moved to the swamps to harvest and process flax, which could be traded for European goods, including firearms.

Kauri forest

There are few records of kauri-timber extraction before the 1820s. Whalers used kauri timber for ship repairs and, with Māori assistance, cut tall trees for spars. In 1820 HMS *Dromedary*, having landed convicts in Hobart and Port Jackson, was directed to New Zealand to obtain a load of kauri spars. *Dromedary* was accompanied by 'the Colonial schooner' *Prince Regent*. Negotiations for extracting trees from Whangaroa were entered into with local chiefs, and work commenced on construction of a road from the water's edge to where some suitable kauri trees were growing in a ravine, about two kilometres from a tributary stream that flowed into the harbour.

Removal of the timber took several months. Towards the end of November the job was complete and the crew members working in the forest returned to the ship. Richard Cruise recorded that three local Māori brothers, 'Tippooi, George and Ehoodoo, came on board and received the stipulated payment for the cargo, with which they seemed to be perfectly satisfied'. Cruise also described the difficulties they had encountered in extracting the big logs, which for spar purposes had to be at least 74–84 feet long (22.5–25.6 metres) and 21–23 inches (53–58 centimetres) in diameter and 'perfectly straight' to meet the Royal Navy requirements.[7]

The late 1820s saw the development of a trade in sawn timber destined principally for the growing Australian colonies. Much of this trade was controlled by Sydney merchants, and timber was re-exported to other colonies. Again, few records were kept and it is not possible to give precise quantities. By the early 1830s the Hokianga and Coromandel Peninsula were the principal sources of sawn timber. From the mid 1820s through the 1830s the Hokianga district became the centre of a saw-milling industry that drew many more Māori into trade in ships' provisions and work in the bush felling kauri logs (Figure 3.3).

The missionary James Buller arrived in the Hokianga district by ship and on a sunny April morning in 1836 sailed thirty-six kilometres up the harbour to a point off the

Wesleyan mission station at Mangungu. He noted the 'Native villages perched on the hillsides'. Local people came alongside in canoes to barter fish and potatoes in return for pipes, tobacco, and other goods:

> At nearly every bend, a rude and lonely hut was standing. This was made of slabs, and thatched with grass. A boat, or a canoe, floated in front of it, or was lying on the beach. It was the home of some white man, living in a semi-barbarous style, with a Maori woman, and surrounded by their half-caste progeny. He was perhaps an escaped convict, or a runaway sailor. About two hundred of these classes were living on the shores of the river. They worked as axe-men, sawyers, etc. for the few traders who were located on their respective establishments...[8]

Buller estimated there were between three and four thousand Māori living in and around the Hokianga Harbour. By 1838, of the ninety adult male Europeans listed in British Resident James Busby's census as resident in Hokianga, probably seventy-two were directly involved in the timber trade. It was estimated that between 50 and 60 per cent of all timber exported from New Zealand between 1828 and 1839 came from Hokianga.[9]

Small European settlements associated with production of sawn timber for the Australian market were also established on Whangaroa and Mangonui Harbours. Although high-quality spars had been taken from Whangaroa in the 1820s, the timber trade did not develop here immediately. This was partly because of the reputation of local Māori among European timber men, beginning with the burning of the *Boyd* in 1809 and the sacking of the Wesleyan mission station in 1827. By 1836 Busby recorded twenty-three sawyers and carpenters in residence. The kauri in the Whangaroa district were located well away from the harbour, and Māori labour was needed to get the big logs to a place where they could be cut and loaded.

Exploitation of kauri forests around Mangonui Harbour also began with the spar trade initiated by Sydney merchant Ranulph Dacre. Some of his sawyers—Thomas Ryan, James Berghan, Stephen Wrathall, and others—settled permanently, negotiated land transactions, and married Māori women. By 1839 Busby's census recorded eleven sawyers at Mangonui, and a trade in sawn timber prepared for the Australian market had been built up. It also became a popular spot in the 1830s and 1840s for whaling ships to refit and obtain water and provisions.

The involvement of Yankee whalers in taking kauri logs to supplement their cargo of whale oil was the means of introducing American methods of extraction already developed in New England for white pine.[10] Like white pine, kauri logs cut in the forests inland of Mangonui and Whangaroa Harbours, and in the Coromandel Peninsula, were floated down streams in floods created when purpose-built dams were tripped. Ernst Dieffenbach visited in 1839 and described the impact of logging in the kauri forests between Mangonui and Whangaroa as: 'a melancholy scene of waste and destruction', with the firing of extensive areas of bush 'to make room for the conveyance of logs down to the creek. Noble trees, which had required ages for their perfection, were thus recklessly destroyed in great numbers ...' He commented that this destruction of kauri forests was occurring in many places, and noted that, once cleared, 'kauri-land is so exhausted that scarcely anything will grow on it but fern and manuka'.[11]

Impacts on Māori society

By the end of the 1830s many northern Māori had travelled outside New Zealand. Some had worked as crew on whalers. Others had visited Sydney, including several Bay of Islands chiefs who had been entertained at Government House. Some visited Britain, such as Hongi Hika. Many had learned some English, and some spoke it fluently, although the more usual medium of communication was a jargon language, 'whaler Māori'. Money, often in the form of gold coins, was entering the trading transactions. Elaborate contract arrangements were entered into, with some acting directly for themselves and their hapū, others employing intermediaries, usually Pākehā, or, less frequently, Māori who had acquired some English.[12]

There is little doubt that Māori participated actively in all aspects of the timber and flax trade. Such participation inevitably brought changes in Māori society and economy, not only with the introduction of European goods, but also from the diversion of energy away from customary work patterns into trade. Grudging admiration of Māori proficiency in bartering for goods was shown by many Pākehā commentators. Missionaries also noted the amount of Māori energy expended in trading, and often complained how tiresome Māori demands could be. The writer of an article in the *Sydney Gazette* in 1829

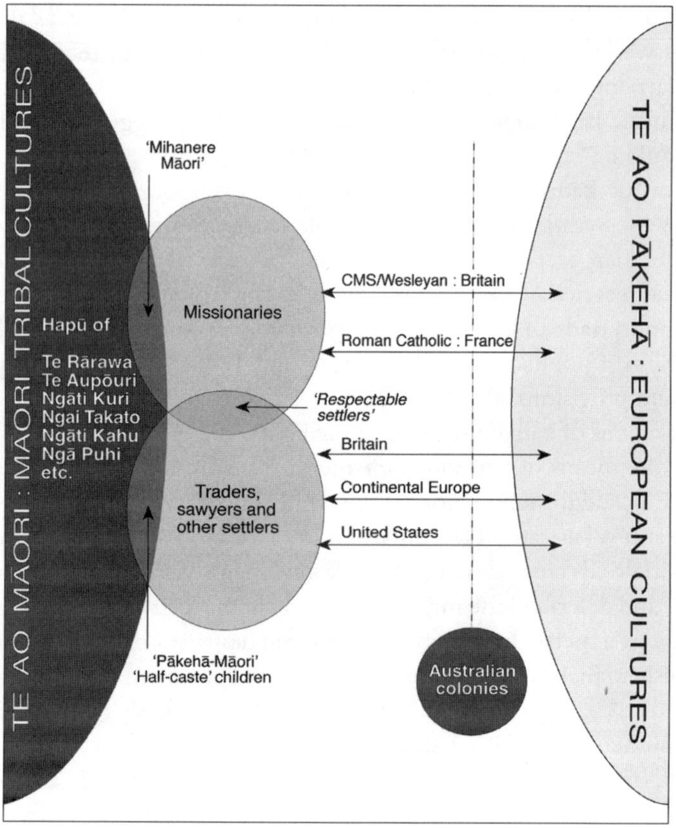

Figure 3.4 Te Hiku o Te Ika: Cultural relations, 1840.

advised that it required 'no common skill to traffic with the New Zealanders, who are extremely shrewd in making bargains'.[13]

Māori encounters with Europeans sometimes ended in violence. Most of the time people from two very different cultures reached out to each other with a great deal of warmth, hospitality, curiosity, and good will. But Pākehā were still in the minority and Māori largely controlled the local economy. Busby's 1839 'census' of the European population for the district from Bay of Islands–Hokianga north recorded 779 people, 377 male and 109 female adults, and 293 children. Many of the women were associated with mission stations. Most of the 197 European children were of mission families, and another ninety-six 'half-caste' children were the offspring of a European man and Māori woman who were 'living as Europeans'. There were probably many more informal relationships. 'Half-caste' children who were brought up in a kāinga (village) were not enumerated.

Edward Markham commented on Europeans settled in the Hokianga in 1834 that '[a]ll the Sawyers live with the Native women',[14] but he observed that such sawyers and traders remained on sufferance of the local Māori chief. Settlement was consolidated by marriage, a traditional Māori way of securing alliances. The pattern of emerging cultural relations is shown in diagrammatic form in Figure 3.4, but Māori and Pākehā still lived in different worlds, barely impinging on each other.

There were also more profound changes in Māori society wrought by the expansion of trade and exploitation of resources, as various local chiefs competed to participate in the new economy. Several hapū in the Bay of Islands consolidated their interests to form the strong Ngā Puhi confederation.[15] With the early acquisition of firearms and other trade goods, Ngā Puhi were in a strong position to settle some old scores with tribes to the south. Through the 1820s Ngā Puhi raids into the Kaipara, Waitemata, Hauraki Gulf, and Bay of Plenty disrupted large areas. Ngāti Whātua and Hauraki tribes retreated into Waikato. There was competition for Pākehā traders in other tribal areas, in order to acquire firearms and other trade goods.

In 1830 Philip Tapsell set up a trading station at Maketu in the Bay of Plenty, acting as agent for a Sydney firm. Te Arawa tribes migrated to the swamps of the Kaituna River nearby, reclaiming lands from which Ngāi Te Rangi had dispossessed them several generations earlier. Inevitably, there was tension, and, in the conflict in 1836, Tapsell's trading station was destroyed. Peace was not made until 1845. In the Waikato the Hauraki tribes had overstayed their welcome, and after a fight in 1830 at Taumatawiwi on the lower slopes of Maungatautari, Hauraki returned to the shores of the Firth of Thames and lower Waihou River, many to scrape flax for one of Tapsell's agents. Other traders also penetrated the Waikato.

The ripple effect continued southwards. In the 1820s and 1830s Waikato tribes had put pressure on Ngāti Toa around Kawhia Harbour, Taranaki tribes, and Ngāti Raukawa of the eastern Waikato. Te Rauparaha and Ngāti Toa were evicted from Waikato and spent some time in North Taranaki before moving to Kapiti Island. Several Taranaki tribes joined a heke (migration) south, displacing tribes in the southern North Island, some moving into the Nelson–Marlborough region. In 1835 Ngāti Tama and Ngāti Mutunga from Taranaki occupied the Chatham Islands. Ngāti Raukawa also migrated to the Horowhenua region. Occasionally, Pākehā settlers were caught up in these conflicts, which represented a massive disruption to Māori tribal and territorial relationships, still fluid in many areas in 1840.

There were other demographic changes. Among the negative impacts of contact with Pākehā must be included the effects of diseases such as measles (with its respiratory complications), influenza, pneumonia, whooping cough, small pox, typhoid, and tuberculosis. Venereal diseases also took their toll and, combined with smoking tobacco, which became a widespread habit, probably contributed to lower fertility rates in women and high infant mortality. There were also changes being wrought by missionary teachings. While the nature of impacts on pre-1840 Māori society and long-term impacts can be debated, it is certain that Pākehā trade and exploitation of resources had profound effects.

The extinguishment of native title

The year 1840 saw the signing of the Treaty of Waitangi and proclamation of a British colony in New Zealand. Article 1 of the Treaty provided for a government to make laws for all—kawanatanga. Article 2 provided a guarantee to Māori of full authority—tino rangatiratanga—over all lands, forests, fisheries, and other property, unless and until Māori willingly chose to sell, and then only to the Crown. Article 3 provided that Māori would share in the rights and privileges of British subjects.

What was not adequately explained to Māori gathered at Waitangi in the Bay of Islands on 5 and 6 February 1840 was that under British law the Crown assumed title to all lands and resources. In this legal fiction the radical title was vested in the Crown, but subject to rights guaranteed in Article 2, and replaced the concept of a communally held Māori ancestral estate. The Crown asserted title to foreshores and seas below high-water mark, to navigable rivers and to other resources, including the royal metals, gold and silver, under Crown prerogative. This was a tenurial revolution that initially was not comprehended by Māori, who continued to live under Māori customary law.

The Crown retained the sole right to negotiate with Māori, protect their interests and to extinguish native title to land. This placed in limbo a large number of pre-1840 transactions between Māori and Pākehā settlers because no title could be recognised in British law unless it derived from the Crown. To resolve this, land claims commissioners were appointed to investigate transactions and determine whether such 'sales' were valid. Limits were placed on grants of land to settlers, but the commissioners accepted in many cases that a valid 'sale' had occurred that extinguished native title. This begs the question whether a private citizen could extinguish a native title when the Crown claimed sole right to this function, and the transaction occurred before a colony and British law were proclaimed.

There is a long history of investigation of these 'old land claims', which has been reviewed recently by the Waitangi Tribunal. The Māori grievance was that when Crown grants were made to settlers who were occupying their lands since before 1840, the 'surplus' reverted not to Māori but to the Crown. The Muriwhenua Tribunal found that these original transactions were not sales because the parties were not of a sufficiently common mind to effect a valid contract. 'Māori contracted with Europeans on the basis of Māori law, which was the only law known to them ... As a consequence, the pre-Treaty transactions were not sales but at best conferred a personal right of occupation conditional upon acceptance of the norms and authority of the local Māori community as represented in the rangatira[chiefs].'[16] Nevertheless, the Crown recognised such titles as the land commissioners recommended for private individuals, or offered 'scrip' to be redeemed in land elsewhere.

New Zealand Company interests were purchased by the Crown. There were also additional Crown purchases around Auckland, the new colonial capital. For a time Governor FitzRoy waived the Crown right of pre-emption, but this was reimposed by Governor Grey in 1846. By then native title had been extinguished in a number of toeholds of Pākehā settlement (Figure 3.5). Māori frustration erupted into armed conflict

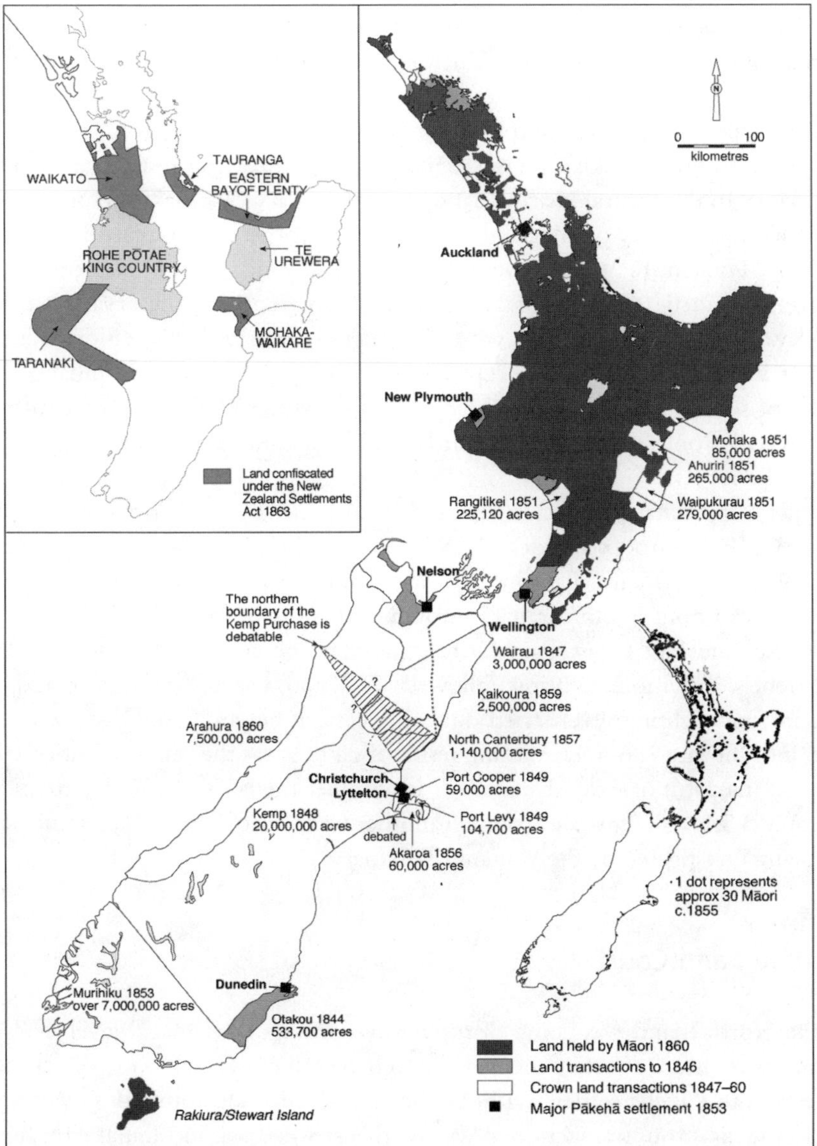

Figure 3.5 The extinguishment of native title.

in the mid 1840s, in the north around the Bay of Islands, in the Hutt Valley near Wellington, and the Wairau Valley in Marlborough. Between 1846 and 1865 the Crown right to extinguish native title was assiduously pursued under pressure to provide land for incoming settlers. The Constitution Act 1852, the British statute that established representative government in New Zealand, provided at section 71 for 'native districts' where 'the laws, customs, and usages' of Māori could 'be maintained for the government of themselves'. But the settler Parliament (which had no Māori representatives until 1867) never invoked this provision, in spite of Māori entreaties, including the petition of King Tawhiao to Queen Victoria in 1884.

The 1850s saw the Crown acquisition of almost the whole of the South Island, with a few small and inadequate reserves left for Māori occupation.[17] In the North Island, where there was a much more numerous Māori population, Crown purchases focused on the Wairarapa, Hawke's Bay, and Manawatu regions, small pockets on the West Coast, and the hinterland of Auckland. The 1850s also saw a growing resistance to land sales among Māori. In the central North Island, from Waikato to Taranaki, a confederation of tribes evolved in a series of meetings, culminating in the ceremonial installation of a Māori king, Potatau Te Wherowhero in 1858. The aims of this confederation, the Kingitanga, included retention of a region in Māori control, preservation of Māori custom law and governance, but with coexistence with Pākehā settlers. The settler Parliament was not prepared to accept any form of Māori self-determination, or the possibility of settlers coming under the control of a Māori king and Māori custom law. There was to be one law for all, British law, and those who did not accept this were deemed to be rebels.

Conflict was inevitable. Fighting began in Taranaki in 1860 and erupted again in 1862. In July 1863, British troops invaded the Waikato, and by early 1864 there were engagements in the Bay of Plenty. Late in 1864 a millennial pacifist movement led by Te Ua Haumene spread from South Taranaki through much of the central North Island to the Bay of Plenty and East Coast. Pai Mārire ('good and peaceful') adherents were labelled fanatical rebels and more fighting followed. Te Kooti was a 'rebel', too, and so was Titokowaru, and fighting was carried on in the eastern ranges, Taupo district and inland Taranaki into the late 1860s. The lasting result of all this was the punishment of rebels by confiscation (raupatu) of extensive areas of land under the New Zealand Settlements Act 1863 (Figure 3.5, inset). Thus was spawned another set of Māori grievances, some of which are still being investigated by the Waitangi Tribunal.[18]

The Native Land Court

While the North Island was being disrupted by fighting, Parliament developed legislation to provide a more effective mechanism to determine ownership of Māori lands and expedite sales to Pākehā settlers without the complexities of competing claims, which had led to the disastrous transaction at Waitara that sparked war in Taranaki. In the Native Lands Act 1862, Crown pre-emption was waived and a Native Land Court established with a purpose as set out in the Preamble: 'And whereas it would greatly promote the peaceful settlement of the Colony and the advancement and civilization of the Natives if their rights to land were ascertained defined and declared and if the ownership of such lands when so ascertained defined and declared were assimilated as nearly as possible to the ownership of land according to British law.'

The machinery for the operation of this Court was set out in the Native Lands Act 1865, which at section 5 defined it as 'a Court of Record for the investigation of the titles of persons to Native land for the determination of the succession of Natives to Native lands'.

Thus was ushered in a new framework for extinguishing customary tenure. The legislation was not specific about how this would be done. Under section 21 an investigation of title began with an application in writing by any Māori. In due course a hearing was notified before a Pākehā judge and a Māori assessor. 'At such sitting of the Court the Court shall ascertain by such evidence as it shall think fit the right title estate or interest of the applicant and of all other claimants to or in the land' (section 23). Similarly, the Court could 'ascertain by such evidence as it may think fit who according to law as nearly as it can be reconciled with Native custom' the succession of Māori interests in land. The Native Land Court was also made the authoritative body in section 41 in the 'determination of the question or fact of or Māori custom or usage' on any matter referred to it by the Supreme Court.

This legislation opened up Māori communities to direct approaches from would-be purchasers of land. Alan Ward described how the operation of the Native Land Court exposed Māori to 'a predatory horde of storekeepers, grog-sellers, surveyors, lawyers, land agents and money-lenders'.[19] The individualisation of title envisaged any owner having an equal right with any other owners in a title to dispose of individual interests in land, thus undermining community political and social structures. Hugh Kawharu has described the Native Land Court as 'a veritable engine of destruction for any tribe's tenure of land, anywhere'.[20]

Two elements of Native Land Court case law significantly differed from Māori custom. One was the '1840 rule', whereby actual occupation of land at the time British law was imposed constituted a right to title. In reality there were areas where occupation was fluid, and was either shared or still being fought over. There is also some evidence that Pākehā judges placed a greater emphasis on conquest, or the 'might is right' argument, in their codification of customary rights. The second element was the acceptance of succession of interests from either male or female line to all descendants, regardless of usual place of residence. This was a denial of customary occupation based on ahi kā, keeping the fires burning on the land, and later led to multiple ownership of blocks of land, with problems of administration on behalf of numerous absentee owners.

The Native Land Court produced a hybrid title that complicated rather than simplified Māori customary land tenure. This also had 'grievous effects on Māori society'. As Ward explained, 'It set up a body of self-proclaimed experts who had to try, and frequently failed, to interpret Māori custom'. The system invited contention and contestation between parties, and the legalistic nature of the court produced a morass in which Māori floundered for decades, frittering away their estates in ruinous expenses and still all too often not getting equitable awards.[21] In a wide-ranging review of the legislation and operation of the Court in the nineteenth century, David Williams remarked on the lack

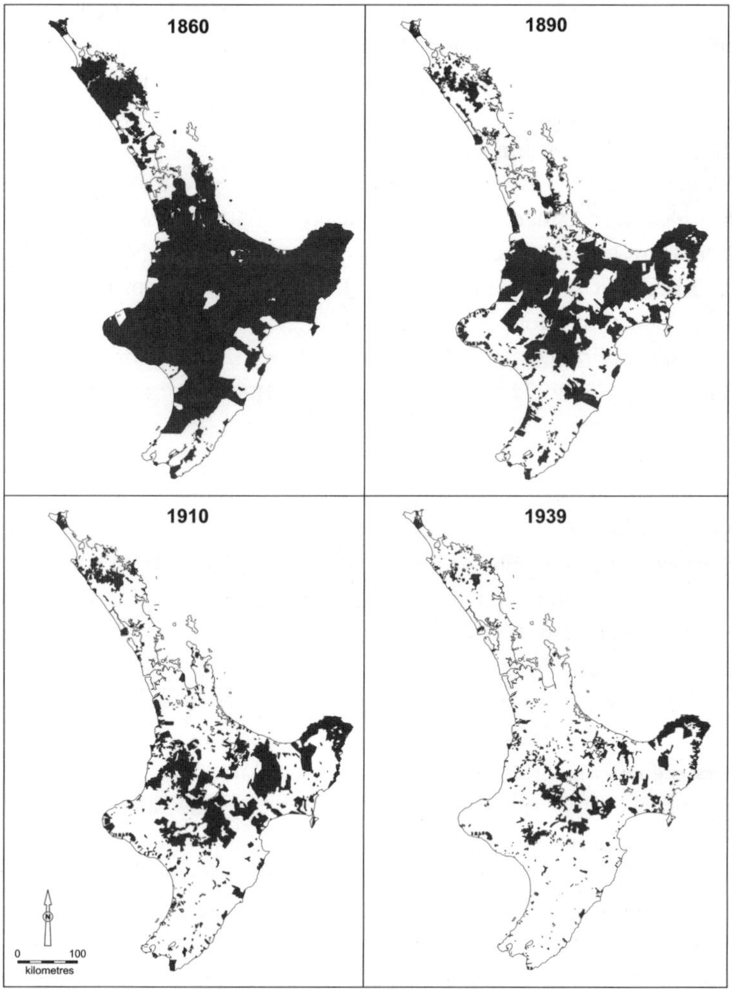

Figure 3.6 Alienation of Māori land in the North Island.

of separation of powers between executive government and the judiciary, and described the Court as 'a willing accomplice in promoting government policy'. He also noted 'a clear pattern' of correlation of Native Land Court operations and alienation to Crown or private purchasers.[22] The pattern of land loss is shown in Figure 3.6.

The machinery of the Native Land Court rolled inexorably across the land. In the Rohe Potae (King Country) legislation was enacted to restore Crown pre-emption and allow the Native Land Court process to operate in the 1880s. The Urewera District Native Reserve, which Tūhoe hoped to retain in tribal title, was subject to an investigation in 1899–1900 by commissioners who divided the land into blocks with lists of owners. By 1907 the Native Land Court jurisdiction was extended there, too. In 1891, T.W. Lewis, the long-serving Under Secretary for Native Affairs, told the Commission on Native Land Laws: 'the whole object of appointing a Court for the ascertainment of Native title was to enable alienation for settlement. Unless this object is attained the Court serves no good purpose, and the Natives would be better without it, as, in my opinion, fairer native occupation would be had under the Maoris' own customs and usages without any intervention whatever from outside.'[23]

The commission in its report strongly criticised the 'pernicious consequences of Native-land legislation' and noted the numerous disputes, litigation, and flood of Māori petitions to Parliament—over a thousand in the decade 1880–90. The legislation was complex and voluminous; in 1888 there were eight separate new statutes, and in 1889 nine more. In reviewing complaints about the operation of the Native Land Court, the commission remarked on 'the confusion both in law and practice', which created 'a state of confusion and anarchy in Native-land titles'. The Waitangi Tribunal in *The Pouakani Report* concluded:

> that Maori paid a disproportionate cost for Pakeha settlement, but little provision was made for Maori participation in the suggested benefits of the introduction of capital and settlers. Indeed, the system of Native Land Court investigation of title and individualisation of interests in land, which could be sold piecemeal, contributed largely to social disruption, dissension over issues of mana and territory, massive debts, costly mistakes in survey boundaries in some cases, and failure to survey in others, and costly litigation ... There is nothing in the Treaty of Waitangi which required the transmuting of traditional Maori forms of tenure into titles cognisable in British law.[24]

Conclusion

The maps in Figures 3.5 and 3.6 illustrate the basis of the piecemeal transformation of the New Zealand environment, a process begun before 1840, as Pākehā settlers acquired land, cut down the trees, drained swamps, developed pasture, and constructed roads and towns. Māori lost control of their ancestral lands and resources, and became marginalised, relegated to small rural pockets of land or remote hill country unsuitable for farming. The legacy of this failure to acknowledge Māori custom law, and the imposition of British law, and a policy of assimilation of Māori under the guise of 'civilisation of the Natives', is the hundreds of Māori claims (see Chapter 16) against the Crown lodged with the Waitangi Tribunal complaining about loss of lands and resources, failure to protect Māori interests, and destruction of environment.

4

Resource Frontiers, Environment, and Settler Capitalism 1769–1860

Jim McAloon

In the middle of 1840 a small schooner, the *Jewess*, sailed from Wellington to Tasman Bay. Part-owned by its master Frederick Moore (the other owners were Wellington and Sydney merchants), the ship had been built in Tahiti. Moore took the opportunity to explore the West Wanganui inlet and quietly examine the northwestern part of the South Island for suitability as a site of European settlement.

This small example highlights some of the connections that placed New Zealand in a Pacific and a world economy. It has been persuasively argued that Australia's frontier at least until the 1830s was not the continental interior but the Pacific. With a range of attractive commodities, New Zealand was part of that frontier, and the colonisation of New Zealand after 1840 relied much on Australia. While the attractions of New Zealand resources have been frequently noted, the literature has usually focused on relations between Māori and the newcomers. The New Zealand environment, the limits it set on human activity, and the varying ways in which it has been perceived have received less attention.[1]

Nor is the economic context emphasised. Particularly, the revolutionary nature of capitalism is underplayed. As Marx and Engels noted in 1848, 'Modern Industry has established the world market … this market has given an immense development to commerce, to navigation, to communication by land'. New industries had been set up 'that no longer work up indigenous raw material, but raw material drawn from the remotest zones; industries whose products are consumed, not only at home, but in every quarter of the globe'. Capitalism, 'by the rapid improvement of all instruments of production, by the immensely facilitated means of communication, draws all, even the most barbarian, nations into civilization'. The global dimension is fundamental to environmental change in New Zealand after 1769, change that amounts to an ecological revolution, a 'major transformation in human relations with nonhuman nature'.[2]

On the edge of empire

European attitudes to nature in the 1760s reflected several themes. On one hand, the study of nature would inspire religious piety and 'veneration towards the Almighty'. Alongside this was the urge to classify and catalogue; Britain led the Western world in systematic natural history by the 1760s. Resources, especially in 'new' lands, became property only through the labour involved in exploiting them and were available to whoever would expend that labour. James Cook proceeded in the service of an expanding commercial empire, and his three voyages to New Zealand anticipated much of the pattern that defined the resource economy. His instructions emphasised exploration as increasing British prestige and trade, and he was alert to potential commodities.[3] Cook also saw New Zealand as ideal for supplying food to ships; he and his French contemporaries introduced plants and animals to this end.

Cook believed that trade facilitated relationships. Tapa cloth was plentiful in the tropics but highly prized in Aotearoa. At East Coast settlements, 'as every one in the Ship were provided with some of this sort of Cloth, I suffer'd every body to purchase what ever they pleased without limitation, for by this means I knew that the natives would not only sell, but get a good price for every thing they brought; this I thought would induce them to bring to market what ever the Country afforded.' Cook regularly traded for fish, even in excess; the critical thing was 'to incourage them [Māori] in this kind of traffick'. From the start Māori were brought into the orbit of British capitalism.

The commercial dimensions of botany were emphasised. Timber and flax stood out; Joseph Banks became an evangelist for 'the most excellent' New Zealand flax, which produced cord and rope 'of a strength so much superior to hemp as scarce to bear a comparison with it'. The mataī was 'tall streight [*sic*] and thick enough to make Masts for vessels of any size', while hard pōhutukawa wood seemed 'well adapted for the Cogs of Mill wheels &c'. Cook repeatedly emphasised the North Island's potential for European settlement. 'It was the opinion of every body on board that all sorts of European grain fruits Plants &c would thrive here. In short was this Country settled by an Industrus people they would very soon be supply'd not only with the necessarys but many of the luxuries of life ...'

Autumn gales and time pressure made for a cursory inspection of Te Wai Pounamu (the South Island), which Cook summarised as 'Ruged and Mountainous', although it was expected to prove rich in minerals and the plains, valleys, and hills in the middle part of the island had 'much the appearance of fertility'.[4]

If the British were overoptimistic, the French dismissal of the country as 'less than mediocre ... unpromising and sterile' may have been excessively pessimistic, and due to their very difficult circumstances, particularly a crew riddled with scurvy. Like Cook, Marion du Fresne in 1772 looked for fertile land, minerals, and 'other products the value of which might induce the state to set up a branch of commerce'. The French crews landed chickens as well as pigs, and wheat, corn, pea seed, and fruit.[5]

Cook used New Zealand as a base in his two later voyages. The *Resolution* spent six weeks in the autumn of 1773 at Tamatea (Dusky Sound). Cook described the timber as among the best in New Zealand. The 114 men had a considerable impact, killed thousands of birds and fish for food, and left other European footprints when they liberated five geese from the Cape of Good Hope. Rats also left the ship. George Forster saw the sojourn as 'demonstrating the superiority of a state of civilization over that of barbarism' by 'the alterations and improvements we had made'—felling trees, taking water, making spruce beer, eating fresh fish. Painting and drawing, 'the polite arts', had appeared, and botany and astronomy marked 'the dawn of science, in a country which had hitherto lain plunged in one long night of ignorance and barbarism'.[6]

Meanwhile the *Resolution*'s sister-ship, the *Adventure*, had arrived at Totaranui (Queen Charlotte Sound), where the two ships were reunited. The *Adventure*'s crew had been busy planting potatoes, turnips, carrots, and parsnips. Cook added wheat, beans, peas, celery, parsley, garlic, onions, and strawberries as well as more roots. Most flourished. As Forster wrote, 'the most precious plant we left here will be the Potatoe, which in length of time will become one of the finest Substitutes for bread, for future Navigators & the Natives'. The Europeans also landed chickens, goats, and pigs, and a ewe and a ram, but these first sheep in New Zealand were also the first to die of tutu poisoning, 'thus all my fine hopes of stocking this Country with a breed of sheep were blasted in a moment'. The pigs were European breeds crossed with Chinese and Indonesian subspecies, and a few Tongan pigs introduced separately. Māori spread the new mammals over both islands, and whalers' liberations and escaped domestic stock reinforced the populations.[7]

Dusky Sound had no permanent Māori settlements, and the European impact, although noticeable, did not provoke conflict. The French experience in the densely populated Far North was different; 400 men required a lot of fish, and Māori were soon reluctant to trade. De Surville was aware of the problem but remained insistent. In 1772 the pressure on resources from 200 extra men was a factor in the bloody end to Marion du Fresne's visit. Similarly, the killing of some of the *Adventure* crew at Totaranui in 1773 was partly due to pressure on resources and relationships.

From 1779 until 1791 no European appears to have visited New Zealand. George Vancouver and the French and Spanish navigators d'Entrecasteaux and Malaspina made brief visits in 1791 and 1793, but the end of isolation swiftly followed the British invasion of the Australian continent in 1788. Australian historians have long debated the motives for the invasion. Some maintain the government was desperate for a penal site; others stress strategic and commercial considerations. Joseph Banks maintained a lifelong interest in New Zealand commodities and in the Australian colony. In 1783 Banks's disciple James Matra, who had sailed on the *Endeavour*, wrote a 'Proposal for Establishing a Settlement in New South Wales', which conveyed Banks's own views, particularly on flax and timber. Banks himself advocated New South Wales to a Parliamentary Committee on Transportation in 1785. The final plan for the penal colony mentioned both commodities.[8]

The resource economy

Whether or not New Zealand resources were a major reason for the convict settlement, they were exploited from the early 1790s. New Zealand was brought into a Pacific economy (Figure 4.1). European interests were specific: timber, flax, seals, whales, and fresh food. Major environmental change resulted, amounting to both plunder and modification. Although Māori society was profoundly transformed, and new diseases wreaked some havoc, the resource economy did not require Māori dispossession; indeed, many Europeans welcomed the integration of Māori into capitalist civilisation.

The Governor of New South Wales, Arthur Phillip, had been instructed to cultivate and prepare flax. The original (1787) plan for William Bligh's ill-fated *Bounty* voyage was for a Sydney-based ship to collect New Zealand flax as well as Tahitian breadfruit. Europeans had no idea how to prepare antipodean flax, hence the proposal of Philip Gidley King, Lieutenant-Governor of Norfolk Island, where flax also grew, that Māori be brought over to demonstrate. This led to the *Daedalus* incident, described in Chapter 3, in which two unwilling Māori were taken on board the ship on its return from picking up a cargo of pigs in Tahiti. Once in Norfolk Island, it was discovered that flax was women's work,[9] and the men were returned home on the *Britannia*, en route from relieving a sealing gang left at Dusky Sound in November 1792. King gave the pair pigs, grain, peas, and potatoes, the makings of 'a local agricultural revolution'; the *Britannia* traded iron for dressed flax, cloaks, and weapons. King justified the modest outlay as 'the means of procuring the goodwill of those who visited us, and the stock, I hope, will prove of publick utility if ever that country should be settled or visited by Europeans'. Firmly convinced of New Zealand's commercial possibilities, King hosted other rangatira (chiefs) in later years.[10]

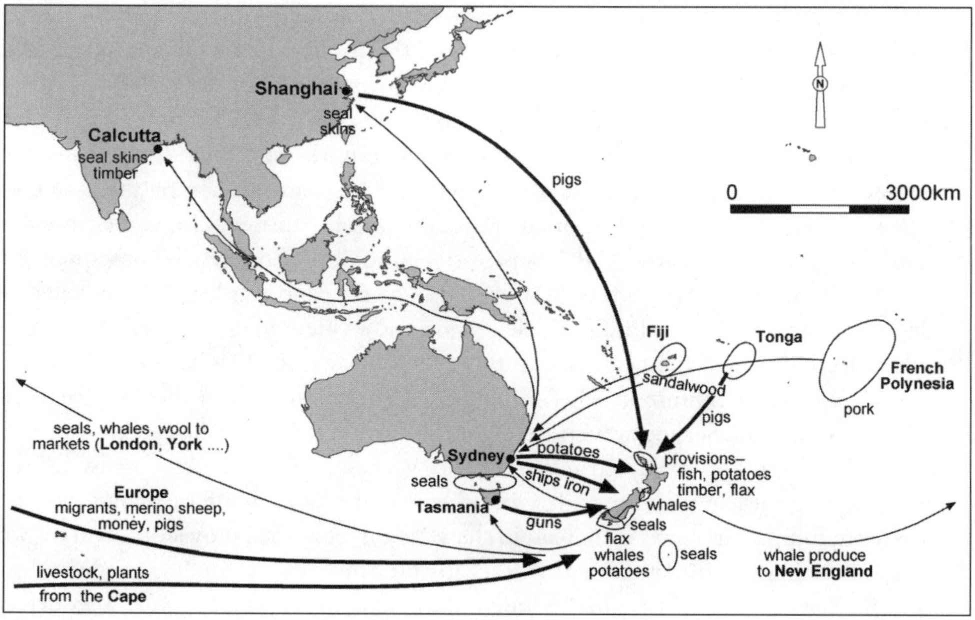

Figure 4.1 New Zealand in the global economy, 1770–1840. This is a schematic representation of the then most important resources and trading links.

The *Britannia* was owned by a London firm and had come out intending to seal, bringing a load of convicts to defray expenses. Before the ship could head for the sealing grounds, in one of the first examples of the New South Wales officer corps moonlighting as merchants, she was chartered to bring cargo from the Cape of Good Hope to Port Jackson. The *Britannia*'s sealers were the first European gang left in New Zealand, and their landing marks the beginning of the globalisation of the New Zealand economy. In ten and a half months the sealers took 4500 skins and built a 40-foot ship. They blamed weather for their low tally, but perhaps spent more time building their ship, a sensible precaution against abandonment. Sealing in Dusky Sound was sporadic throughout the 1790s, but ships took timber for repairs and spars.[11]

In 1801 the *Venus* sailed from Port Jackson to Tahiti, trading for pork. Timber was scarce in Sydney, so the ship stopped at Dusky Sound to collect timber for pork barrels. George Bass commanded this voyage, intending it to be only the first 'speculation'. Successful in pork, Bass was emboldened to propose a government-sponsored fishing expedition. He claimed to 'have every proof, short of actual experiment, that fish may be caught in abundance near the South part of the South Island of New Zealand, or at the neighbouring islands. And that a large quantity might be supplied annually to the Public Stores.' Relying on the fact that Britain asserted a wide jurisdiction, Bass petitioned for a monopoly. As he claimed, 'If I can draw up food from the sea in places which are lying useless to the world, I surely am entitled to make an exclusive property of the fruits of my ingenuity, as much as the man who obtains Letters Patent for a corkscrew or a cake of blacking.'[12] The idea came to nothing, for Bass disappeared on his way home to Britain.

Northern trading voyages were also infrequent and initially concentrated on timber. In April 1793 an East Indiaman, the *Fancy*, visited the Waihou River (Thames) and took two hundred spars back to Sydney for India. In November 1794 she called again, and other vessels visited Thames annually between 1798 and 1801. The timber trade was eclipsed between 1801 and 1808 in favour of Tahitian pork, sandalwood, and sealing on both sides of the Tasman. Interest revived briefly before being shaken by the attack on the *Boyd* at Whangaroa in 1809. Sporadic mutual reprisals continued for some time, and Simeon Lord, who had chartered the *Boyd*, lost a good deal of money in consequence.[13]

Sealing became intensive after 1800, and in New Zealand was largely controlled by Sydney mercantile houses. Philip Gidley King, now Lieutenant-Governor of New South Wales, bemoaned the fact that 'we possess no known staple whatever'. By reducing government expenditure in 1801, King forced entrepreneurs out into the Pacific as well as onto the land. Sealing was an excellent first staple industry. With a cheap process and lucrative commodities, capital accumulation was easy, as Banks had recognised. Small ships could deposit gangs and speculate in other commodities while the gangs worked. Wages were minimal as crews were paid in shares often set against provisions. Seal oil was useful, and China was the traditional market for furs, but new techniques made seal fur sought for hat-making in Britain. Sydney commercial developments were also driven from 1800 by British merchants in India, desperate for return cargoes. Campbell and Co.

were the first and among the most significant Indian firms in Sydney, either buying skins and oil outright, organising sealing themselves, or selling on commission.[14]

The East India Company monopoly, covering most of the Indian and Pacific Oceans, severely restricted trade and shipbuilding. In 1805 the first entirely Australian cargo—of seal oil, skins, and timber, belonging to Robert Campbell—was seized in London. Joseph Banks secured its release and safe landing for two other cargoes. After sustained lobbying, Australian vessels were allowed to trade directly with Britain from 1819, and in 1823 crippling duties on Australian produce were removed. Successive administrations in Sydney and London treated New Zealand produce as Australian for customs purposes; the exploitation of New Zealand resources would otherwise have been much less.[15]

By 1802 the Bass Strait seals had been decimated, and attention shifted across the Tasman. Between 1803 and 1805, ships working for the Sydney partnership Kable & Underwood wrecked the Dusky Sound rookeries; sealers then moved into Foveaux Strait and further south. In October 1809 a Campbell gang was left on Rakiura (Stewart Island) and its overseer became reasonably fluent in southern Māori, trading the first iron tools in Murihiku (Southland) for potatoes. Other gangs experienced much conflict. The most notorious ship was the American *General Gates*, operating right around the Pacific Rim—Canton, Batavia, Manila, Hobart, Tahiti, Sydney, and New Zealand. The *Gates* had little sympathy for Māori sensibilities and its crews were frequently attacked.[16]

During the 1810s, merchants contemplated the virtues of Murihiku flax, but significant trade only began in 1822 with the *Snapper*. Having rescued twelve *Gates* sealers who had been on the run from Ngāi Tahu at Chalky Sound, the *Snapper* party came to an arrangement with the chiefs, mediated by James Caddell, a Sydney lad earlier rescued by a chief's daughter. The ship traded iron and pigs for dressed flax and potatoes. Another ship followed the *Snapper* 'to promote the civilization of the inhabitants of the island by supplying them with British Manufactures in exchange for their flax'. The flax trade combined with sealing. Sealers—Europeans and Māori alike—killed not only mature seals but also pups and pregnant females. By 1827 the average cargo had declined to 2700 skins per ship; a few years previously it was said to have been 80,000. A Hobart newspaper wished 'that some effective steps were taken to protect and cherish this valuable article'.[17]

Capital from sealing allowed Australian entrepreneurs to participate in the London-dominated whaling industry by 1830. Whale oil was used for fuel and for lubricating the machines of the industrialising Atlantic world; whalebone was used in corsets and chairs. Offshore, or bay, whaling was constant by 1807, and ships—British, French, and American—called at the Bay of Islands for fresh food and water. Colonial whalers established shore stations, much cheaper than ocean whaling, along the Foveaux and Otago coasts, at Cloudy Bay and Port Nicholson, and elsewhere. With agreement from Māori, it was easy to lease whaling rights and land for cultivation, and New Zealand's temperate climate meant less oil lost by leakage. The business was speculative and not always profitable, but for some a shore station was the beginning of modest comfort or substantial wealth. In 1840—just before the industry crashed through overhunting—half the southern oil came from New Zealand and reached Britain via New South Wales.[18]

The moral economy of capitalism

Northern harbours were favoured for shelter as much as for resources. In 1805 Governor King reported that the seeds he had given to the unwilling flax dressers from the *Daedalus* had become the basis of a thriving trade in provisions. Looking forward to the continued use of New Zealand as a base, King kept up supplies of livestock, both on his own initiative and in response to requests from visiting northern chiefs. The missionary Samuel Marsden had a major role in the agricultural revolution (see Chapter 3). Critical in this was his close relationship with the Ngā Puhi rangatira Ruatara, who had endured a difficult voyage around the world, worked at Marsden's Sydney farm, and finally returned home in 1813 with seed wheat. Marsden himself crossed the Tasman at the end of 1814. Even this voyage had a commercial as well as an evangelical agenda; Marsden had to report on New Zealand's potential for European settlement. All Marsden's voyages would bring back a full cargo of timber, flax, and salt fish for the Sydney markets.[19]

For both Pākehā and Māori, agriculture and iron implied social as well as economic change. Marsden regarded agriculture as the catalyst of Christianity and civilisation, and tried to persuade Ruatara that agriculture would allow Māori access to European goods; 'all these blessings might be obtained by them by cultivating their land and improving themselves in useful knowledge'. He hosted young Māori for considerable periods at his Parramatta farm. Simeon Lord, proposing to trade in flax and timber, declared that employing Māori would introduce them to 'progressive civilization'. In the 1830s Joel Polack, negotiating for a trading position at Kaipara, made similar appeals to the moral economy of capitalism. If his hosts accepted his proposal, 'they would be enabled to compete with their neighbours ... in possessing articles of clothing to protect them from the wintry blasts, and implements of iron to pursue the labours of agriculture ... [and] ammunition to repel an invader; who, aware of their being in possession of such resources, would themselves ... turn their attention to similar pursuits ... and would war no more.'

Some of the local Māori 'deplored the innovations Europeans would cause, in lieu of their ancient usages'. One old man, Motarou, regretted 'the warrior [being] obliged to give way to women and slaves, whose utmost ability consisted in paddling canoes, pounding fern-root, or scraping flax'. He regarded muskets as inferior to traditional weapons, and regretted the stigmatisation of cannibalism:

> if we want clothing, we have our women to make them ... if food be our object, we have slaves to plant for us; and of them we shall never be deficient, as long as our enemies exist ... No! let the white man go. Who sent for him? He came from beyond the sea to us—he has seen us. What does he further want? Let him go back.

The opposing case was successfully put by another senior chief, Rapu: iron tools saved time and labour, and pork, potatoes, brassicas, corn, onions, and garlic were 'esteemed edibles presented to the country by the white men'.[20]

Botanical change was widespread by the 1820s. Potatoes spread rapidly, reaching Foveaux Strait before 1810. In the south, where the kūmara would not grow, the potato allowed larger permanent settlements. In the north, by the 1830s, many tons of locally grown potatoes supplied visiting ships and Sydney. In 1838 Joseph Montefiore of Sydney imported several thousand bushels of maize from a settler who had married into a Poverty Bay family. Māori traded rather than ate most of the new foods. Fish and potatoes were dietary staples, although younger people were more willing to experiment. A favourite relish combined old and new: tāwhara, peaches, onions, potatoes, kūmara, fuschia berries, pig brains, lard, and tutu juice.[21]

The commodity trade presented threats as well as opportunities and could easily destabilise a society driven by competition for mana. At Maketu the Danish privateer and trader Philip Tapsell, who had spent thirty years in the Pacific, set up as a flax trader on behalf of a Sydney firm, employing 300. Conflict between Ngāi Te Rangi and Te Arawa revived, with considerable bloodshed. Raukawa Moana (Cook Strait) was heavily fought over for its trading opportunities; once there, Te Rauparaha traded flax for guns. For threatened hapū, muskets were equally desirable. Polack had to pay muskets for flax at Kaipara; his hosts were vulnerable to Waikato raiders. If Europeans wanted flax, timber, and a labour force, they would have to arm the locals, whose security from attack was the Europeans' security to trade.[22]

Flax exports soared between 1827 and 1830, in a classic boom and bust, with the material often inadequately prepared and of poor quality; it could end up as mattress stuffing. Even so, flax was often more profitable than timber. Kahikatea—claimed by individual Māori for the birds they attracted—was easily accessible but not durable. Sawmills in the north supplied Sydney with building timber (Chapter 3). Kauri was preferred for spars, but the requirements were precise as to length, diameter, and taper, with one in ten thousand good enough for a mainmast. By 1840 considerable damage had been done to the northern and Port Nicholson forests through indiscriminate logging and, often, much destruction was caused for the sake of a few prize logs.[23]

Initial colonisation

By the 1820s hyperbole featured in European descriptions of New Zealand. Whaling and shipping entrepreneurs began to propose British colonisation. In 1823 a number supported a proposal for a military colony in the north, which stressed the 'delightful climate ... uncommon fertility of the soil, [which gives] ... all the necessaries and most of the luxuries of civilized life ... there is no country on earth more favourably circumstanced for the operations of agriculture than New Zealand'. In 1826 another group petitioned for a colony to secure supplies of timber and provisions, allow naval protection of the Pacific trade, and introduce to Māori the 'peaceful pursuits of industry and the blessings of civilisation and of religious and moral instruction'. With economic advantage cloaked in altruism, it is no surprise that, as well as Samuel Enderby and Son, the signatories included Joseph Somes and L. Marjoribanks and Co.—later luminaries in Wakefield's New Zealand Company.[24]

The colonisation lobby strengthened in the late 1830s. The Wakefield ideals are well known, as is their detachment from reality. On one important issue, however, Edward Gibbon Wakefield anticipated what followed. His prescriptions implied a new international division of labour, with the colonies trading primary produce for metropolitan manufactures. Once in New Zealand, Company agents saw what they wanted to see. William Wakefield described the Hutt Valley 'as of the richest soil, and covered with majestic timber'. Charles Heaphy stressed the climate: summer 'may be said to last for eight months'. Romantic notions of New Zealand were, as a Nelson settler tartly noted, 'written upon the strength of a scramble in the Bay of Islands', and in reality the climate and fertility varied widely.[25]

Systematic colonisation also relied on assumptions about land, particularly that now known as the Waste Lands Doctrine. In 1843 a settler newspaper put the matter baldly:

> Who has the right to most land? He who has cultivated it. This is God's law, and all the chatter about rights of the natives to land, which they have let lie idle and unused for so many centuries, cannot do away with the fact that according to this, God's law, they have established their right to a very small portion of these islands.
>
> Land should no more be considered the property of the uncivilised human beings who find themselves upon it, but cannot use or improve it, than of the wild animals of a lower order who roam over it for food or prey, with as much but scarce more ignorance of its beneficial capabilities, and equal inability to turn them to use.

Grandiose settlement schemes, and the Waste Lands Doctrine, conflicted with Governor FitzRoy's model of European enclaves in a Māori New Zealand. Māori themselves were often influenced in land sales by conflict over trading opportunities. In controlling the Port Nicholson whaling stations, Ngāti Toa had monopolised trade; Te Āti Awa wanted a settlement to secure their own access and to confirm their hold on the district. Sales often over-rode the rights of others living on the ground, and surveying was highly contentious.[26]

Colonisers were also highly optimistic about the prospects for commercial wealth. Ernst Dieffenbach, the German radical and the New Zealand Company's dissident naturalist, sardonically criticised the mania for building towns. 'To found a dozen capitals and commercial ports, and more than two score of villages, before any population is in the island, any produce raised to support a population, or any article of commerce ready to be exported, is subverting the natural order of things, and would have raised a smile on the lips of William Penn, who is often regarded as the father of modern colonization.'

Dieffenbach advocated something like what developed in Nelson: allowing labouring families to squat for fifteen years on ten-acre blocks. That would create a class of peasants; only then would capitalists have a reason for coming. Dispersed settlements, he believed, meant weak centralised government and, conversely, strong and democratic local communities. This yeoman view saw land as the passport to independence and self-respect, and many acknowledged the importance of 'a very large class of peasant Proprietors and small Farmers ... such a class will constitute the surest basis for the durable prosperity of a Colony and the happiness of its Inhabitants'.[27]

Nevertheless, the towns quickly emerged as trading centres. Auckland became a major entrepôt with an aggressive mercantile community. John Logan Campbell, a young Scottish doctor with £1000 from his father, worked his passage as a ship's surgeon to Australia. Plans were indefinite but for the sense that an antipodean fortune was to be made. Campbell and another Scot, William Brown, built a boat and began as 'merchants, commission-agents, pig and potato brokers, anything and everything in both a large and a small way', for Māori were keen to sell their produce and buy clothing, tools, and tobacco. Auckland's merchants relied on Māori supply and demand for most of the 1840s. Campbell was an assiduous promoter of kauri gum, flax, and timber.[28] The trading economy differed only in scale from that of the 1830s.

Agricultural progress was slow. Many settlers preferred fernland to swamp; although the latter was often more fertile, draining proved particularly arduous. Fern was difficult enough. First it was burnt—the fires often spread over miles—then grubbed before ploughing and liming. Settlers often underestimated the amount of work required to bring land into cultivation and few had much capital. At the end of 1843 Nelson counted only eighty-three farmers, not including subsistence squatters. Five hundred and forty acres had been cultivated, with another fifty cleared, and 133 acres in gardens. No farm had more than thirty acres ploughed or in cultivation, and most had less than twenty acres. There were only 1130 sheep, and fewer than 500 grazing cattle. Domestic pigs outnumbered sheep until May 1844, when Edward Stafford brought 1200 sheep from New South Wales.[29]

European exploration of the North Island was also slow. The central North Island was trisected in the 1840s; Dieffenbach travelled from Kawhia to Taupo; Richard Taylor crossed from Wanganui to Taupo in 1845; two years later Colenso reached Taupo from Hawke's Bay. Explorers were avid botanical collectors and forwarded many specimens to the Royal Botanic Gardens at Kew, which received a consignment from somewhere on the globe for every day of the Victorian era and distributed plants and seeds to governments, firms, and individuals throughout Britain and beyond. Pākehā exploration was overwhelmingly driven by utilitarian considerations, but utilitarianism did not imply efficiency.[30]

The towns were beach-heads (Figure 4.2). New Zealand Company surveys were superintended by a surveyor who had never left Britain, a circumstance much in line with the Company's predilection for theorising over practical experience. In Wellington the Company's Principal Agent, William Wakefield, a former convict and mercenary noted for 'capriciousness, ruthlessness ... vindictiveness', autocracy, laziness, and lack of imagination, constantly second-guessed his principal surveyor, William Mein Smith. Nor did the flat and rectangular perfection of the Company's planned towns and farms suit the topography. For a long time Wakefield forbade more practical subdivisions. In addition to Wakefield's meddling, the Company's financial difficulties hampered surveying.[31]

Given the Company's habit of organising colonies in advance of ascertaining suitable land, agricultural and pastoral land was urgently needed. A small number of Wellington settlers established themselves at Wanganui in 1841, farming and selling pork and potatoes to Wellington traders. Fertile soils and plentiful fish and birds made a very pleasant subsistence; one settler enumerated the vast range of cultivated and wild delicacies and concluded, 'Here one can live in ease, without cost or trouble, in one of the most genial and healthy climates in the world, and where it only requires the hand of man to make a Paradise'. The Company's lax purchase filled the role of serpent, and a

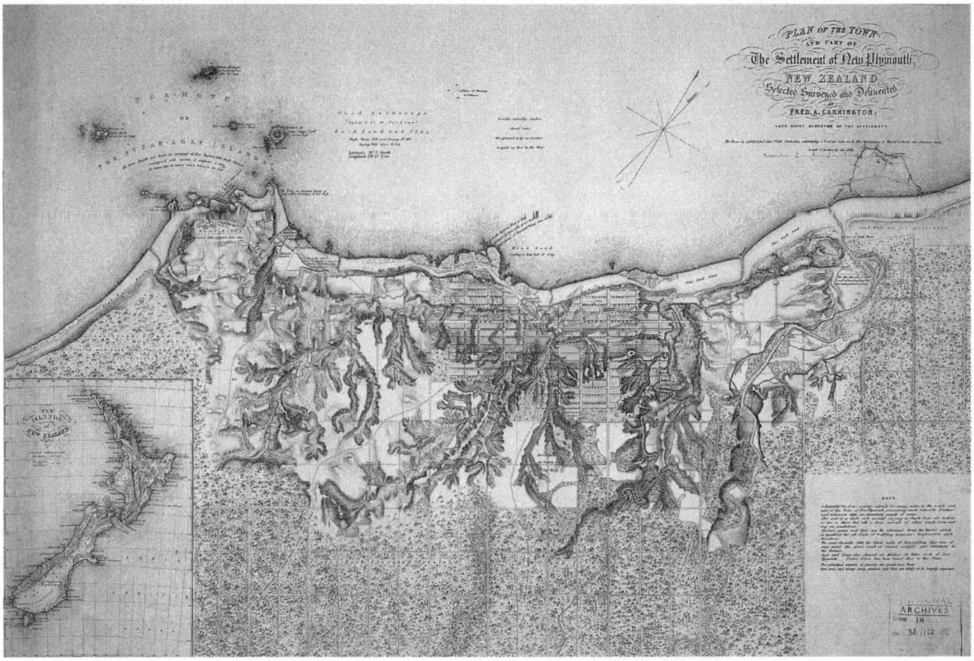

Figure 4.2 'On the edge of the bush: New Plymouth 1850'. Note the manner in which the grid has been superimposed on the landscape. From *Plan of the Town and of Part of The Settlement of New Plymouth, New Zealand. Selected Surveyed and Delineated by Fred. A. Carrington*. Reproduced by permission of Archives New Zealand, IA 36, 122.

Crown purchase was only made in 1848, after prolonged tension and some shooting. The Rangitikei purchase of 2500 acres in 1849, described by Donald McLean as 'superior to any other part of the island for cattle runs', arose from the unsettled circumstances of the 1830s and the desire of some tribes to secure their position against more powerful neighbours. George Grey, Governor of New Zealand from 1845, was under orders to implement the Waste Lands Doctrine and acquire land well ahead of demand.[32] By 1859 a large block from the Turakina to the Manawatu and inland to the Ruahine Ranges had been acquired. Rough surveys accompanied the purchases.

When Company surveyors crossed the Rimutaka Range at the end of 1841 they described level land suitable for Wellington's pastoral hinterland. Other pastoral prospectors, including William Fox and Charles Clifford, followed. In April 1844 the first pastoralists negotiated leases with Māori and established a station at Wharekaka, near Lake Wairarapa. The merino sheep came from Australia, and the station manager from the Scottish Borders. By March 1847 there were 1300 cattle and 13,000 sheep, and the North Island pastoral frontier began to move into Hawke's Bay. Wairarapa flocks stocked much of Marlborough and Canterbury as well, with New South Wales constantly reinforcing the New Zealand gene pool.

The government—contrary to the Waitangi Treaty—forbad Māori from directly leasing land to settlers. This edict proved essential in the purchase of the Wairarapa and

Hawke's Bay, for it threatened Ngāti Kahungunu income and left them with little choice but to sell in order to raise capital, despite the obviously low price. From 1853 Donald McLean secured large blocks, discrediting the missionary William Colenso, whose advocacy of Māori interests was weakened by his marital embarrassments. Pastoralists supported Crown purchase, preferring the familiarity of English tenure. Ngāti Kahungunu had prospered by leasing; an official reported in 1849 that they were 'to a very great extent in the enjoyment of European comforts ... in every village is to be seen the wheat-field, the stack, and mill, and what is still more gratifying, the use of bread is now becoming universal, and is an article of daily consumption'.[33] Inculcating the moral economy of capitalism was now less important than imposing state control, but after Wairarapa and Hawke's Bay, European survey and purchase accounted for little else in the North Island before 1860.

Exploration from Nelson was similarly driven by the desire for grazing land. Golden Bay charmed much but offered little. The Wairau grasslands were disputed, with bloody results at Tuamarina. Misleading or misheard accounts of inland grassy plains prompted various explorations by William Fox, Charles Heaphy, and Thomas Brunner between 1846 and 1849. Heaphy, having travelled as far south as Arahura, reported that 'the Port Cooper country [Canterbury plains] appears to be decidedly the most appropriate locality for the next settlement'. Brunner's epic journey of 1846–48 confirmed that view. A decade later the Nelson government, expecting mineral wealth, commissioned further exploration of the West Coast. Confirmation of the heavy forest did nothing to dent boosters' optimism. Some suggested that axemen could migrate from eastern Canada to clear the land and let 'wilderness become a fruitful field'. Julius von Haast wrote enthusiastically about inland West Coast valleys, particularly the Maruia and the upper Grey, and reported the Grey Valley coalfields 'a vast store of mineral wealth'.[34]

The pastoral south

The South Island east coast, Wairarapa, and Hawke's Bay quickly became the core of the colonial economy, with New Zealand supplying raw materials for the British textile industry. Having learnt from northern embarrassments, the church associations that organised the colonisation of Otago and Canterbury ensured that the land was at least examined before 'purchase'. Frederick Tuckett refused the New Edinburgh (Otago) commission otherwise, and in 1844 the purchasing party travelled extensively. The Canterbury plains had been widely discussed by settlers in Wellington and Nelson. George Duppa enthused in 1841 over 'millions of acres of the richest soil covered with grasses of the most luxuriant growth and dotted with groves of pine trees ... waiting only for the plough and flocks and herds to yield an enormous return'. Isolated cattle runs were established in the bays of Banks Peninsula and on the plains; clearly something more organised would follow, although Tuckett rejected the district on account of the coastal swamps and lack of timber.[35]

Wakefield regarded pastoralism as inherently uncivilised, but the suitability of wool as the principal export staple rapidly became clear. David Monro described the New

Edinburgh expedition for local readers; such accounts were crucial in informing settler efforts. Monro left his readers in no doubt as to the pastoral potential of the east coast, being 'convinced that [wool] can be grown with greater profit there than in any part of Australia'. The sparse Ngāi Tahu population was not expected to present an obstacle.[36] South Island pastoralism spread rapidly from its Marlborough toehold. Clifford and Weld formed the first station in 1846 at Cape Campbell, leasing from Ngāti Toa pretenders to the land and stocking Flaxbourne with 3000 sheep from New South Wales. After the largely fraudulent Wairau purchase in 1847, Nelson capitalists quickly took up the north-eastern valleys. Kemp's massive 1848 'purchase' opened the way for Canterbury and further pastoral expansion (Figure 3.5, Chapter 3).

Pastoralism largely depended on Australia for stock, capital, and expertise. In 1851 William Deans noted the arrival in Canterbury of 'two or three gentlemen Scotchmen who were amongst the earliest settlement of Port Phillip [Victoria, Australia] ... bringing with them some stock ... These gentlemen having colonial experience and capital will make first rate settlers, and in a few years hence we will export large quantities of wool.' Although sheep had been introduced into Australia in 1803, it was not until the early 1830s that wool became the dominant Australian export. For a long time mutton was more lucrative, and British tariff policies hampered colonial wool as much as maritime produce. From the early 1820s power machinery in the Yorkshire woollen industry enabled fine merino wool to supplant coarser fibre, and expert Australian wool growers ran sheep to suit. London and Australian merchants established marketing systems at both ends of the chain, and Australian banks offered capital. From the late 1830s, with wool prices booming and land prices rising, there was a rush to the easy open country of Port Phillip.

In similar fashion Australian pastoralists moved across the Tasman a decade later. Australian pastoralism had reached the end of first expansion, land tenure was becoming complicated, small farmers were assertive, environmental degradation was apparent, and New Zealand was cooler and less dry. A few pastoralists crossed to Canterbury early in 1851; their descriptions attracted a number of others. Australian pastoralists were typically from the rural lower middle classes in Britain. Some worked first as station managers, some profited from the Victorian gold rush; others traded on their skill to form useful connections with richer partners. Some New Zealand pastoral fortunes can be traced back to whaling and shipping, like that of the Rhodes family, who arrived in 1839. Robert Campbell of Otekaieke, although born in England, was related to the Sydney merchant house. George Moore of Glenmark, who may have been the richest man in New Zealand, began as managing partner for his Quayle in-laws and their Kermode kin; both had been Hobart whalers. Such men bridged the resource and settler economies.[37]

Pastoral occupation contributed unevenly to settler geographical knowledge. In Canterbury, except for the determined efforts to find an inland route to Nelson and the Wairau—successful only in 1852—exploration was largely concerned with finding grazing country. John Acland and Charles Tripp explored much of the upper Rangitata and Ashburton, and Samuel Butler the Rakaia, Waimakariri, and other major catchments. The Main Divide passes of Canterbury were all assessed in 1863–64 in terms of their suitability for a road to the West Coast.

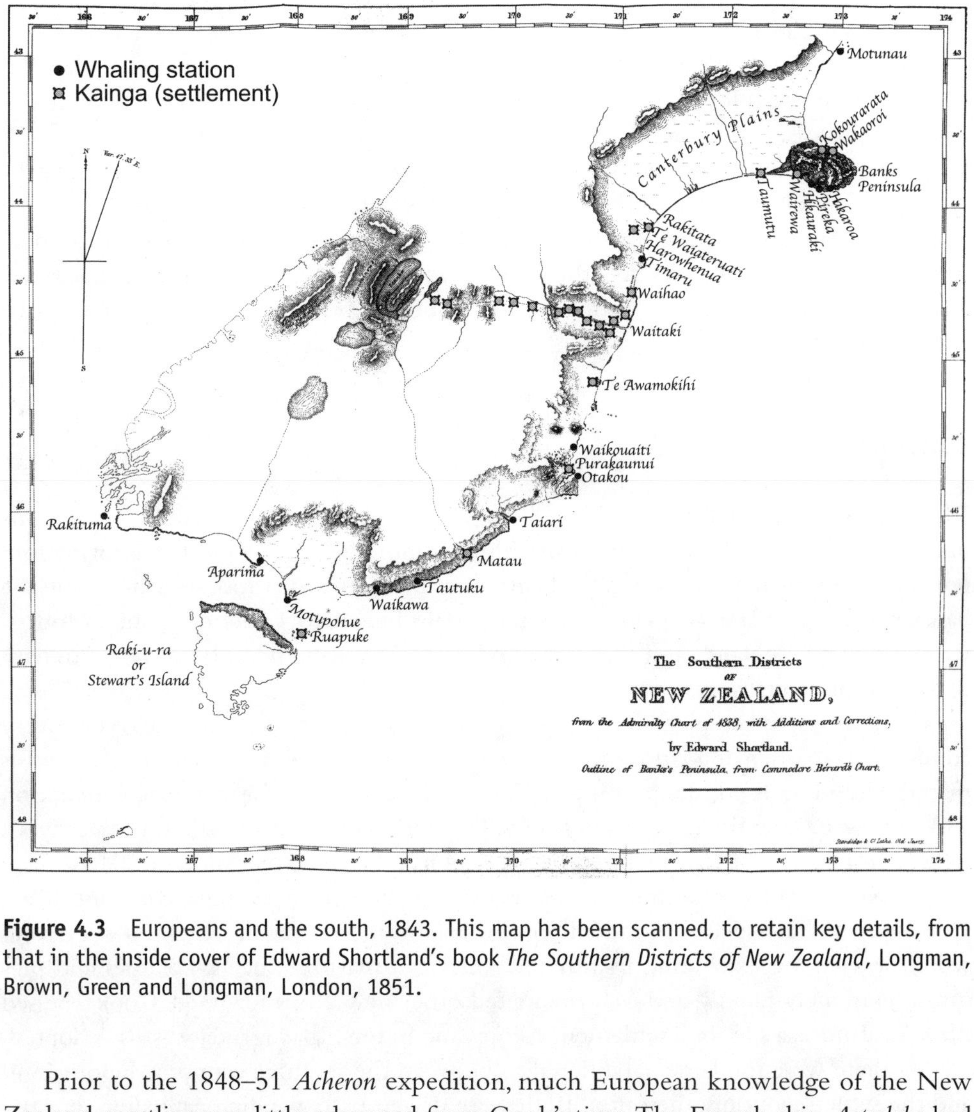

Figure 4.3 Europeans and the south, 1843. This map has been scanned, to retain key details, from that in the inside cover of Edward Shortland's book *The Southern Districts of New Zealand*, Longman, Brown, Green and Longman, London, 1851.

Prior to the 1848–51 *Acheron* expedition, much European knowledge of the New Zealand coastline was little advanced from Cook's time. The French ship *Astrolabe* had charted Cook Strait and the Hauraki Gulf in 1826–27. Edward Shortland's long journey along the South Island east coast in 1843–44 was not published until 1851, and Shortland was more an ethnographer than a cartographer (Figure 4.3). Accurate mapping of the coast was essential for the growing shipping trade and for the infant Otago colony and the imminent Canterbury settlement. *Acheron* parties also explored areas such as the Kaipara Harbour, and (guided variously by Māori and by Pākehā whalers) the Kaikoura Ranges, and the terrain between Foveaux Strait and Dunedin.

The southern interior was filled in for European eyes by John Turnbull Thompson, who walked 2500 kilometres through South Otago in 1857, effecting a reconnaissance survey of a million hectares. Later that year he repeated the exercise in North Otago and inland as far as Wanaka and north to Pukaki. With a clearer map, pastoral occupation proceeded rapidly; 'instead of [the interior] being a dismal wilderness of snowy mountains, as popularly believed, it was found to be one of the finest sheep countries in the world'.[38] Like many other explorers, Thomson had the rough outline of major rivers provided by Māori, in his case Reko of Tuturau.

More detailed surveys swiftly followed in Otago, but in most other provinces the system was much more lax, with very basic surveys only following selection and serious and accumulated error persisting beyond 1870. Surveyors could find themselves arguing with their political masters for the funds necessary to go beyond reconnaissance. The rapidity with which the European footprint was placed on the landscape can be easily overestimated.[39]

Conclusion

The environmental transformation of New Zealand between 1769 and 1860 encompassed European discovery, trade in maritime commodities, biological transformations resulting from the new crops, and the beginnings of organised British settlement and the pastoral economy. Transformation was intimately linked to London, Sydney, Hobart, Calcutta, New England, and Yorkshire, and was a consequence of the revolutionary expansion of capitalism.

Cook's voyages had profoundly utilitarian agendas, despite the romance of discovery admitted by participants and emphasised many times since. Cook and his scientists mapped, listed, assessed, and positioned New Zealand as a base for maritime exploration and commerce over the next seventy years. The penal colony at New South Wales was a direct consequence of British maritime expansion and created the commercial base from which New Zealand maritime resources were exploited, even pillaged, from 1792. Cook's reports and species introductions foreshadowed the way in which New Zealand would service the expanding British and American maritime fleets. Potatoes and pigs spread extremely rapidly, and Māori adopted other new crops for trade. Cook assessed New Zealand as a site for a settlement colony, and in time that agenda was also adopted.

Yet there were fundamental differences between the resource economy before 1840 and the settler economy thereafter. Both were driven by expanding capitalism, but the resource economy could accept tribal autonomy whereas—as it developed—the settler economy could not, and sought systematically to relieve Māori of as much land as possible. Although much attention has focused on the weaknesses and downright failure of the Wakefield schemes, the New Zealand Company shared one critical agenda with yeomen and pastoralists, and the Imperial government from 1846: that of the wholesale implanting of capitalist social relations in New Zealand, beginning with the commodification of land. The commodification of land rather than simply its produce led swiftly to the expropriation of Māori and the beginning of New Zealand's development as Britain's outlying farm.

Part 2
Colonising

5

REMAKING THE GRASSLANDS OF THE OPEN COUNTRY

Peter Holland, Kevin O'Connor, and Alexander Wearing

On the eve of British colonisation of New Zealand, almost anything seemed possible to a nation reaping the benefits of recent developments in science and technology. From afar, the infant colony was perceived to contain broad open spaces suitable for agricultural production, and to offer opportunities for profitable investment. It also lay close to the commercial and administrative centres of southeastern Australia and was viewed by the New Zealand Company as the ideal home for a southern hemisphere yeomanry. Soon after their arrival, however, the first generations of British settlers encountered unforeseen problems. Away from the Canterbury Plains, there was little soil ready for the plough, and in many parts of the colony wetlands, dense forests, fast-flowing rivers, steep hill and mountain country, and unseasonal weather compounded settlers' difficulties.

East of the Main Divide, the 'open country' of New Zealand covered seven million hectares of tussock, fernland, and shrubland extending almost from East Cape to Southland.[1] Pastoralists esteemed grassy areas of the open country (Figure 5.1), especially those lacking dense, coarse tussock. In 1840 John Ward wrote about a small consignment of merino wool reaching the London market, where it surpassed the best from New South Wales for length of staple and fineness of texture.[2] Wool production was economically attractive to colonists, capital and livestock were available, wool could be stored then transported to distant markets, and a pastoral holding operated along Australian lines could be established and run by a handful of energetic people. The early sheep enterprises were in Marlborough, Nelson, and Wairarapa, but the limited area of suitable land there prompted a wider search.[3]

From the earliest days of European settlement, the environmental history of New Zealand's open-country grasslands has been a record of confrontation between image and reality, tension between pastoralism and farming, inappropriate management systems, and ineffective legislation. In this chapter, we highlight the environmental consequences of this colonisation for open-country landscapes and comment on the struggle to sustain extensive pastoralism in the face of the burgeoning demand from farmers for arable land and the

Figure 5.1 Open-country vegetation: (clockwise from top left) tall tussock, short tussock with matagouri, modified tussock, and severely depleted tussock. Photographs by the authors.

progressive deterioration of native ecosystems. In the open country, as elsewhere in New Zealand, lack of sound local knowledge to guide the first two generations of European settlers made major environmental disruption inevitable, and its effects linger to this day.

Open-country landscapes in the 1840s

Present-day studies of remnant vegetation, supplemented by the records of nineteenth century surveyors and travellers, allow an impression of open country landscapes in the 1840s.[4] Open country in the eastern North Island was a mosaic of wetlands, bracken, tall tussock, shrublands, scrub, and forest patches. Apart from their extensive wetlands and remnant forests, the mountains, foothills, downlands, plains, valley floors, and interior basins of the South Island were chiefly covered by tall tussock grassland dominated by species of *Chionochloa*. Red tussock (*Chionochloa rubra*) was common at lower altitudes, with several species of snow tussock predominating on higher ground.[5] The slow-growing, long-lived, tall tussocks produced large amounts of leaf litter that, together with canopy shading, constrained the abundance and growth of smaller grasses and herbs but ensured moisture for plant survival during dry periods.

Most runholders perceived tall tussocks as unpalatable, not nutritious, and generally useless, except during heavy snow or after shoot growth had been stimulated by fire. The maps and field books of John Thomson and Alexander Garvie, who had surveyed parts of Otago and Southland during the 1850s, show pasturage assessed as 'inferior' or even 'very inferior' wherever tall tussocks predominated. The appellations 'good' and 'superior' were reserved for pasturage with abundant fine grasses, such as wheatgrass (*Elymus* spp.), plume grass (*Dichelachne crinita*), a larger form of blue tussock (*Poa colensoi*), and holy grass (*Hierochloe redolens*), as well as the New Zealand anise (*Gingidia montana*). Mostly unpalatable shrubs, such as matagouri (*Discaria toumatou*), mānuka (*Leptospermum scoparium*), and kānuka (*Kunzea ericoides*) were common. Stands of beech (*Nothofagus* spp.) or coniferous forest dominated by members of the Podocarpaceae were widespread in the hill and mountain country. Herbfields above regional treeline often had more fine grasses and other palatable plants than could be found in snow tussock at lower altitudes.[6]

Even in 1840 the open-country landscapes of New Zealand carried the impress of people. A millennium earlier, most of the country below regional treelines was wooded, with grassy, herbaceous, and shrubby vegetation at higher altitudes. Long before human settlement began the forest cover of the South Island interior had been periodically toppled by wind and snow storms, or reduced by fire started by lightning strikes. Induced plant communities dominated by grasses, shrubs, and bracken fern (*Pteridium esculentum*) filled the gaps,[7] yielding slowly to recovering forest communities or persisting as open country in the driest areas. Many centuries of volcanic activity in the North Island had comparable impact. Fire became more frequent during the period of exclusive Polynesian occupation of the land (Chapter 2), and tracts of tussock grassland developed in the absence of grazing mammals. When moa disappeared early in the Polynesian period, native insects became the chief herbivores.

The Canterbury Plains might have struck Archdeacon H. W. Harper in the early 1860s as environmentally simple,[8] but to Māori the lowlands were a mosaic of productive aquatic and dryland habitats for fibre, food plants, and animals. As entries in farm diaries and letter books show, open-country ecosystems were structurally and biologically different from anything a colonist might have known in the British Isles.[9] They were soon to be unravelled and recast.

In 1864 the American natural historian George Perkins Marsh published an influential and widely read book about how human actions affect the environment. He also declared that the late colonisation of Australia and New Zealand would ensure 'the fullest elucidation of some difficult and disputable problems'.[10] W. T. L. Travers, who had corresponded with Marsh, recognised the adverse environmental impact of pastoralism in the northern half of the South Island[11] and attempted to understand the effects of regular burning on forest, grassland and shrubland communities. With respect to the eventual site of Christchurch, Frederick Tuckett concluded that previously extensive stands of podocarp forest had been fragmented and diminished by fire and their soils impoverished.[12] Several years later the naturalist John Buchanan reached a similar conclusion for South Otago.[13] For decades those conclusions were forgotten, and scientists tried to relate grassland distribution to climate conditions. Once carbon dating became readily available, charred logs and fragments of charcoal preserved in the topsoil of native grasslands confirmed earlier views about the impact of fire.[14] In effect, tracts of tussock grassland had been culturally induced, with European settlers continuing and intensifying into the late nineteenth and early twentieth centuries what Polynesian settlers had initiated several centuries before.

Occupying and transforming the land

Pastoralists and farmers on the fertile, better watered lowlands of the open country quickly recognised that exotic or mixed exotic and native pastures were needed if their operations were to thrive. In 1861 there were 158,000 acres of improved pasture.[15] Two decades later the total had reached 3.5 million acres, and by 1925 there were 16.5 million acres of pasture. New Zealand was well on the way to becoming the kingdom of grass as the first two generations of European settlers erased native ecosystems from broad expanses of the open country, replacing them with economically desirable mixes of exotic species.[16]

Until the close of the New Zealand Wars in 1872, difficulty in securing title to agricultural land in the North Island, together with the profitability of raising sheep for wool, gave the edge to the open country of the South Island. Nelson was the first main point of entry, but ports and landing sites along the eastern and southern coasts soon provided beachheads for people, plants, and animals. Large blocks of land were informally occupied and later leased as settlers fanned out from landfalls and drove their sheep and cattle up river valleys, across mountain passes, and into the interior. The principal investment for the pioneer generation of landholders was livestock.

In the spring of 1847, sheep owners in Nelson were anxiously waiting for Governor Grey to purchase the Wairau Plains. The graziers Frederick Weld and Charles Clifford, who had previously run sheep in Wairarapa, occupied Flaxbourne on the Marlborough coast in August 1847, and the occupation of the Wairau Valley by Nelson pastoralists followed. Sheep were driven across easy passes into what is now Marlborough. Imported livestock and natural increase swelled flock numbers, and spare animals were walked from there into Amuri and North Canterbury. Southwards movement was impeded by the large braided rivers, and new landing points were sought.

Absentee investors, business partners, and individuals rushed to join the economically promising new enterprise (Chapter 4). Venture capitalism was the driving force. Most of the lowlands and downs in the South Island open country were occupied by the mid 1850s, with the foothills and inland basins taken up by 1865. As the pace of immigration quickened, so pressure grew to allow subdivision of the fertile lowlands. In 1865, farmers in Hawke's Bay had petitioned government to end the legally dubious occupation by European pastoralists of Māori land because it was frustrating acquisition of fertile lowlands for closer rural settlement.[17] They were not alone. With the exception of landholdings in the inland hill and mountain country, by the 1870s pastoralism was giving way to pastoral farming or mixed crop and livestock farming. Nearer the coast, sowing of introduced grasses and clovers, erection of fences for subdivision, and establishment of fodder crops—or cash crops in mixed farming systems—saw conversion of pastoralist properties to farming by 1880. Individual large holdings were often split into smaller farms and sown with introduced pasture and crop species. Intensive farming practices soon eliminated most native plants from all but roadside areas.

The first generation of pastoralists sought economic benefit from grazing sheep and cattle but their offtake was not sustainable. Stock numbers rose until the late 1870s, wavered for several years, then declined in drier parts of the country. In the hill and mountain country a landholder could respond by resting tracts of grazing land, splitting blocks into fenced paddocks to facilitate pasture management (Figure 5.2), and controlling pest animals and

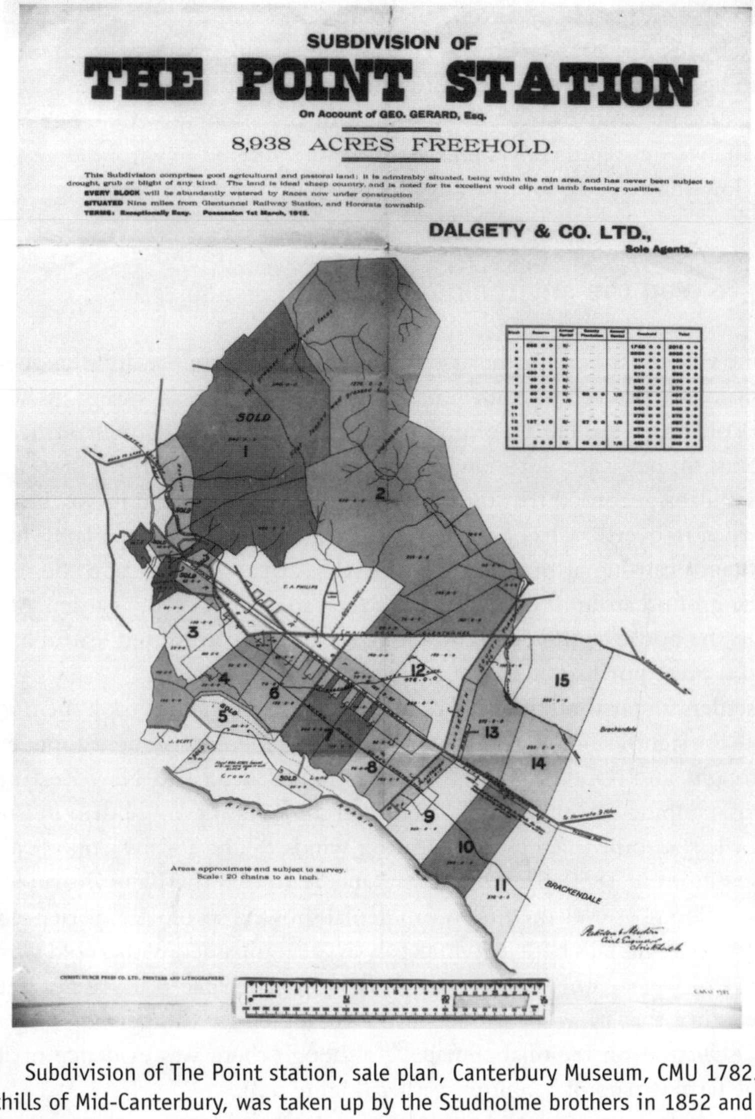

Figure 5.2 Subdivision of The Point station, sale plan, Canterbury Museum, CMU 1782. The Point, in the foothills of Mid-Canterbury, was taken up by the Studholme brothers in 1852 and transferred to the Phillips family in 1862. Freehold was negotiated in 1889, and the run was sold to George Gerard in 1911. By 1912, when the land was subdivided for closer settlement, it had been split into fenced and hedged fields on flat ground and larger fenced paddocks in the hill country.

weeds, but significant environmental improvements were not to come until the 1950s, when aerial topdressing, oversowing, better knowledge of a demanding environment, and money to invest in infrastructure became available.

Throughout the open country, naturalisation of exotic grasses and forbs (non-grassy herbaceous plants such as dandelions) continued. In most upland areas pastoralism remained the dominant land use until the middle of the twentieth century. Limited attempts at sowing grasses and clovers, usually without fertiliser, lack of fencing for grazing management, and ineffective pest control gave rise to environmental problems. Throughout the montane and lower subalpine zones tall tussock grasslands had been transformed by fire and grazing pressure to short grasslands, many of them initially dominated by indigenous species but open to invasion by naturalised grasses and forbs from Australia, California, and Europe. Everywhere in the montane zone, but especially in drier parts, native grassland ecosystems were steadily altered by exotic grasses and forbs tolerant of low soil fertility, sheep and cattle grazing, and rabbit browsing.

Learning to read the environment

Open-country landscapes are areas of environmental uncertainty, and the opportunities for pastoralism were never without limit. Gale-force winds can spring up at any time, unseasonal cold snaps are fairly common occurrences, and snow melt or heavy rain in the mountains flushes water into lowland rivers. On 15 January 1851 a recently arrived farmer, F. S. Pillans, recorded that the 'rain of the last 24 hours did its work well, having caused the river to overflow its banks and inundate a great part of the island [Inch Clutha in South Otago] causing at one time considerable alarm. About noon the water began covering the ground around the house and over a small part of the garden. At 2 o'clock it broke into the house to the depth of about 1 foot and committed fearful havoc in the potato field, a great portion of which I fear is ruined for this year.'[18]

While settlers understood the need to manage economic risk, it took them many years to appreciate the significance of recurrent environmental events brought about by extreme weather, drought, and flood. A book published in 1887 described New Zealand climates as 'boisterous, ramping and uncertain … The sun shines far far more than in England but it is more or less accompanied by high tearing winds.'[19] The Pillans family had recorded similar observations in 1850–51: 'One remarkable feature in the New Zealand weather is that we have seldom or ever the fine warm genial showers so often experienced at home [in Europe]. When rain falls here it is almost always accompanied with a cold wind making a continuance of wet weather in this country far from agreeable.'[20] It was not until the late twentieth century that New Zealanders came to appreciate the periodic impact of the Southern Oscillation on regional climates,[21] although there was evidence of its adverse effects in the farm diaries of a century earlier (Figure 5.3).

Settlers had access to diverse publications that could shape their endeavours in the new land. The Secretary of the New Zealand Company, John Ward, wrote a handbook for intending colonists.[22] Later in the century Charles Hursthouse's book, like

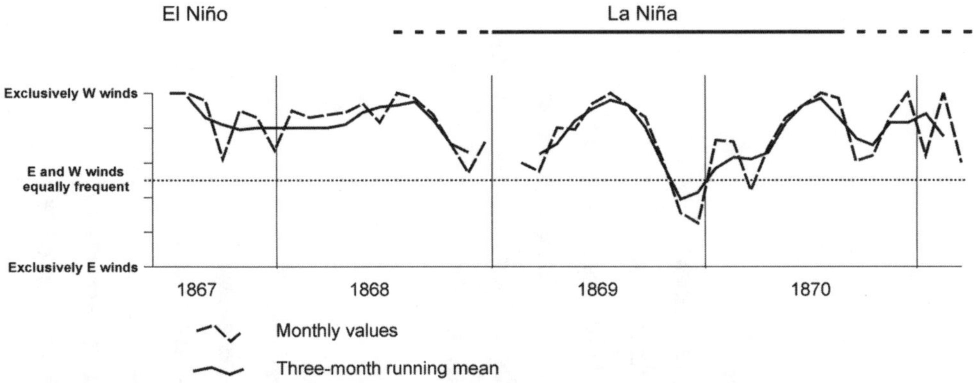

Figure 5.3 An unusual spell of wet summer months shown by the switch from dry northwest to moist winds from the easterly quarter in the Canterbury foothills. Redrawn from Holland & Fitzharris, 'The Wind in the Tussock' (see note 21).

Brett's Colonists' Guide,[23] advised settlers how to become established, while local magazines and the newspapers contained useful hints for a rural family. All provided practical advice about life in a country where cumulative experience could be measured in only a few years.[24]

Making a difference

To colonial society New Zealand lacked the imprint of the human hand. At the time a popular metaphor for the landscape was the garden, with its contrived arrangements of plants and animals, design and control. This justified the comprehensive and rapid environmental transformation of the open country. Settlers used exotic trees, shrubs, herbs, and lawn grasses to make their lives easier and more rewarding in a frequently puzzling, occasionally threatening, environment. Many colonists relished the challenge of ameliorating the environmental conditions of their new home; others could not forget what they had known in rural Britain. To the New Zealand poet Charles Brasch, even a century of European settlement had not been long enough for a consummated marriage between people and the land.[25]

From the outset, settlers brought in plants and animals native to temperate and subtropical regions of the world. Trees and shrubs, herbs and grasses, flowers and vegetables, birds and mammals, game and economic animals, insects, and fish were imported in bulk and widely distributed. After a few years, when native grasses had largely failed to meet pastoralists' expectations, introduced grasses and herbs were either purposefully sown or accidentally introduced as contaminants in the widely used 'station seed mix'. In 1918 the agricultural scientist A. H. Cockayne could state that 'probably no other country uses so many different species in laying down pastures as does the New Zealand farmer'.[26]

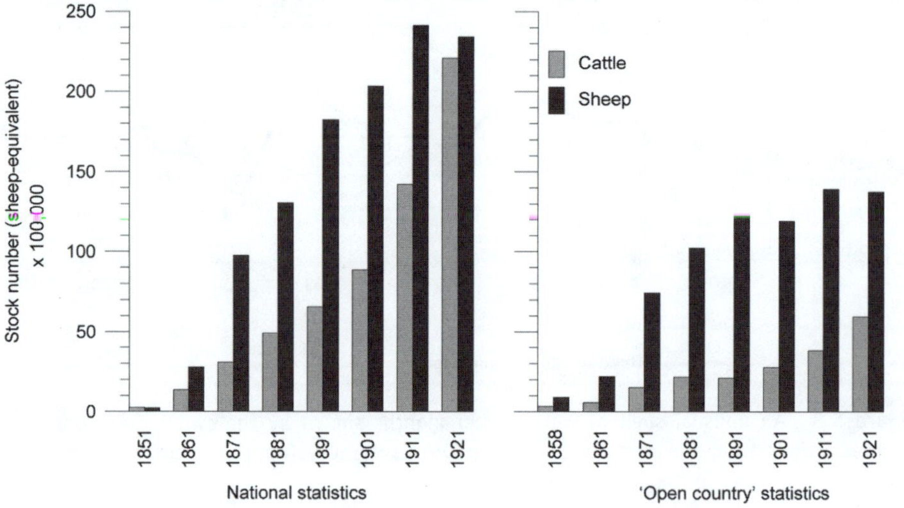

Figure 5.4 Changing sheep and cattle numbers (x 100,000) as indicated by numbers of grazing units (one cattle beast is assumed equivalent to seven sheep). Statistics from G. T. Bloomfield, *New Zealand: A Handbook of Historic Statistics*, G. K. Hall & Co., Boston, 1984.

Many introduced species thrived, several of them doing all too well and becoming pests. As Nugent Wade wrote on 27 June 1876 to W. H. Teschemaker, whose pastoral properties he managed, 'I found sweet briar [*Rosa rubiginosa*] growing very freely as a weed over the flat at Otematata [North Otago], gradually spreading about everywhere … [it] would have assumed great proportions on our soil in a few years, being carried about by rabbits and birds, etc'.[27]

Figure 5.5 Open-country sheep and cattle breeds: (clockwise from top-left) Southdown, Lincoln, Merino, and Hereford. Source: T. W. Leys, *Brett's Colonists' Guide*, Brett, Auckland, 1883.

Early in the 1850s, sheep and cattle were equally important in New Zealand, but sheep quickly commanded the open country (Figure 5.4). By 1860 there were more than 2.5 million of them in New Zealand, and from then until the end of the nineteenth century the national sheep flock steadily multiplied. Merinos (Figure 5.5) from Spain via Germany and South Africa then Australia predominated until the 1860s, when sheep breeds better suited to improved pastures became established. Hursthouse was an early advocate of a national breeding program to increase average body weight and wool yield.[28] Cheviot, Cotswold, English and Border Leicester, Hampshire Down, Lincoln, Romney Marsh, Shropshire Down, and Southdown were the main coarse-wool sheep, and their numbers grew relative to those of merino as the advantage shifted from wool to meat following establishment of the frozen-meat trade in the 1880s. Crosses between merino and English or Border Leicester did especially well, and a New Zealand sheep breed, the Corriedale, was initially developed in North Otago during the 1860s and subsequently refined by James Little of the Hawarden District in North Canterbury before being widely adopted.

A Lincoln averaged twice the wool clip of a merino, thrived on exotic pastures, could be raised in small flocks on farms, was placid, respected fences, willingly grazed with other animals, and produced an abundance of tallow. By the late 1880s, pastoralists were running merinos on areas of rough grazing and in the drier interior uplands, with Southdowns on limestone downlands and improved upland pastures. This matching of sheep breed to environmental conditions was to become a national preoccupation. Cattle breeding, however, was described as neglected or conducted in a slipshod fashion,[29] although there were exceptions such as the Griggs of Longbeach.

What herbivores eat is affected by grazing pressure on the amount of available herbage, and its nutritional value. The relatively small mass of palatable herbs in tussock grassland meant that it could be overgrazed, obliging a sheep to eat less-preferred plants. The outcome was steady depletion of the range lands. Farmers on small properties sought to introduce more palatable plants, and the visit of an eminent Scots agronomist, Professor Wallace, along with establishment of the Department of Agriculture in 1892, encouraged systematic investigations into the dietary preferences of sheep and, to a lesser extent, of cattle.

Dietary preference was a matter of acute concern in the tussock grasslands. In 1919 the plant ecologist Leonard Cockayne reported his systematic observations of a flock grazing a complex sward of a hundred native and introduced grass and broadleaved herb species in modified tussock near Hanmer Springs.[30] Except for its soft young leaves, hard tussock (*Festuca novae-zelandiae*) was seldom touched. Blue tussock (*Poa colensoi*) was found less palatable than most introduced grasses but provided useful winter grazing. Those observations should be seen in the context of earlier and later studies. Although it is not now certain to which fescue he referred, hard tussock had been esteemed as stock feed in the 1870s by John Buchanan, and by Donald Petrie shortly afterwards. In 1911, when hard tussock had become prominent, apparently because of selective grazing of other species, Petrie thought it less valuable for stock but, like Cockayne, he appreciated the shelter it provided for more palatable plants. Recent studies point to its low dietary significance in areas that do not receive regular topdressings of sulphatic fertiliser. After application of fertiliser, however, hard tussock can readily be eliminated by preferential grazing. Then blue tussock may become a valuable component of a sheep's diet because it recovers well from grazing, responds promptly to fertilising, is palatable, and has high nutritive value.

Problems and solutions

Throughout the Western world in the first half of the nineteenth century, the scientific revolution was inspiring confidence among people of their place in nature. Faced with new economic opportunities, and confronted by novel environmental conditions, country people often conducted experiments on their properties. During the 1880s Sir John Hall had advocated the scientific management of soils, productive systems, rural landscapes, even human society.[31] By 1914 there were six experimental stations scattered across the country and an agricultural college at Lincoln near Christchurch. Agricultural topics were taught in primary and secondary schools throughout New Zealand. In one of his many efforts to bring scientific understanding to the management of tussock grasslands, Leonard Cockayne distinguished between 'depletion' (being loss of vegetation cover and associated increase in the area of bare ground) and 'deterioration' (decline in pastoral value through loss of palatable and increase in unpalatable plants).[32] Both are influenced by the grazing preferences of livestock, the adverse effects of which may take decades to work through the system.

Many Victorian certainties shook, and several foundered, when transplanted to the New Zealand open country. European birds had been imported to control the burgeoning insect pests of farm and garden, but things did not always proceed as had been expected, and many introduced species became pests in their own right. Broom (*Cytisus scoparius*) and gorse (*Ulex europaeus*), which had been planted to fence lowland fields, spread to riverbeds and the low hill country. Freed from the biological constraints of their native ecosystems, hundreds of accidentally and purposefully introduced plant and animal species spread and multiplied. The confidently anticipated attainment of Eden in the Antipodes was delayed by people, plants, and animals behaving badly.

Burning issues

In his August 1871 report to the absentee landowner, Nugent Wade wrote that burning of The Levels run in South Canterbury 'has been carried out from the middle of the month and a great deal of rough and useless stuff has been got rid of by these means. I expect to get the whole of the burning for the season finished in about ten days. The country burned from [early] rains to late rains will be greatly benefited thereby.'[33]

The first generation of European settlers learned that, with the exception of new leaves and flowering shoots, tall tussocks provide poor pasturage. Burning to trigger growth of palatable new shoots was therefore deemed imperative, and the firestick became a well-used tool. On 29 September 1859 Frank Mathias, who managed a family holding on the north bank of the Rakaia River, described a grass fire when 'large columns of smoke rose from the country; a most magnificent sight; they look like white trees moving on the top of the hill'.[34] Across the open country, early spring was the preferred season for firing tussock. The plants at their base were then sufficiently moist for a fire to be controlled yet dry enough to burn readily. The wise landholder would start burning early in the morning and ensure flames were extinguished by dusk, but things did not always work out as planned, as this diary entry dated 18 July 1871 for Otaio station in South Canterbury shows: 'Lighted a fire which spread tremendously with a strong N[orth] Wester which sprung up afterwards. Burnt 100 or more [fence] posts out on run; putting out fires till nearly 10 pm.'[35] At times, as when they burned over long fronts or for days on end, grass fires were reported in the newspapers. From 1850 to the end of the century the scale of burning was immense. Fire somewhere on a pastoral property was an annual event during the first two decades of European settlement, less frequent over the next sixty to seventy years, and more rigorously controlled from the 1940s.

Although David Monro and Tuckett in 1844, and Buchanan in 1867 and 1868, had expressed concern over the deleterious effects of burning, they did not deny a role for it in the management of a pastoral property. Buchanan in particular lamented the loss of palatable fine grasses through the repeated burning of pastures in semi-arid districts. It was also clear to pastoralists such as Edward Lee in the Amuri district of North Canterbury in 1852, and to Otago surveyors such as Garvie and Buchanan in 1857, that by turning sheep onto recently burnt tall tussock a pastoralist could induce short grasslands. In the light of current understanding of grazing pressure and the dietary preferences of sheep we can see how, through sustained grazing, stands of tall tussock recovering from fire and made palatable by burning could be transformed from tall to short tussock grassland. If grazing pressure is not sustained, however, tall tussocks recover and gradually become unpalatable, obliging sheep to graze the more palatable inter-tussock plants.

Reduction in the abundance of fine native grasses as tussock grassland recovered from burning was the most serious impact of fire and grazing on pasture quality. That loss was probably less severe once transformation to short grasslands had been effected, but even then the benefits were short-lived, as less palatable plants progressively took over: first speargrass (*Aciphylla* spp.), then sometimes matagouri, Māori onion (*Bulbinella hookeri*), kānuka, cotton plant (*Celmisia spectabilis*), or even silver tussock (*Poa cita*) on fertile country. As the nutritional value and productivity of induced pasturage declined, so the inclination of runholders repeatedly to burn their land became understandable, even though it led to losses in biomass and of plant nutrients[36] through smoke, volatilisation, and blown dust.

There has been persistent public criticism of extensive burning but, given the extent of a pastoral holding and the labour available, it was probably impossible to burn on even a three-year cycle, as Lady Barker's husband had hoped to do at Steventon in the Selwyn Valley.[37] Indeed, apart from incomplete burns, there is little evidence that a block successfully burned one year could be burned again the next, but with the passage of time the careless ambiguity of 'annual burning' has grown. For his part, Leonard Cockayne was rather more tolerant of burning than other observers, but he still argued that it is indefensible where tussock growth is weak, on stony slopes over fragmented rocks liable to slip, where plant cover is damaged, on ground exposed to frost heave and strong winds, anywhere above regional treeline, wherever pest plants might become established, and close to rabbit warrens.[38]

The 'rabbit difficulty'

The first certain record of rabbits in New Zealand was in 1838. From then until the mid 1860s, when their potential as pests was nationally evident, rabbits were imported and liberated by individuals and public bodies.[39] Their environmental impact was soon all too clear.[40] The South Island interior provided safe breeding grounds for rabbits, from which mature animals could later spread into the lowlands. Concerned landholders could only attempt to confine the pest to remote parts of the country until economic and effective means of control had been found. The Rabbit Nuisance Act 1882 was designed to foster just that. Rabbit districts were established, each with its inspector and agents. A select committee was appointed to inquire into the burgeoning rabbit nuisance, and its report was released in 1886.[41]

The committee described the rabbit nuisance as occupying 'a position of importance second to none'. In Otago alone, rabbits had cost the state £32,803 in lost rental income during 1887, when tenants abandoned 414,000 acres of former gazing land.[42] There was also concern that rabbits would infiltrate the area between the headwaters of the Waitaki and Rangitata rivers in South Canterbury. A levy of one penny per sheep was thought sufficient to finance control measures, but it was recognised that delay of a decade would require a three-fold increase in the base rate. Just as sheep scab had been eradicated through rigorous application of control measures, so it was believed the rabbit nuisance would be reduced, if not eradicated, in much the same way.

The control measures involved bran or grain treated with phosphorus and applied throughout the year, plugging burrows and closing water runs, fumigating warrens with carbon disulphide, spreading poisoned carrots, and unleashing dogs, stoats, weasels, ferrets, and cats, all supplemented by shooting and the erection of rabbit-proof fences. The use of mustelids was generally favoured by pastoralists but mostly opposed by farmers.[43] In 1887, contracts were let for the supply of 21,760 ferrets (Figure 5.6). The control measures were costly to implement and required all landholders in a district, including the Crown, to act in concert if they were to be effective. On a large pastoral holding near Tuapeka in South Otago the sum of £3000 was expended on exterminating rabbits in 1885 alone. The projected cost of a rabbit-proof fence from Lake Tennyson in North Canterbury and down the Clarence River, along with another two fences in the Waitaki Valley, was £20,000, enough to absorb the proposed rabbit control levy on grazing land across the entire colony.

In its report to Parliament, the committee endorsed the Rabbit Nuisance Act but advocated harsher penalties and better site inspection. In particular, it identified problems with Crown land reserves and commonages—unoccupied tracts of rough country that offered safe breeding grounds for rabbits—and urged their immediate settlement. It also

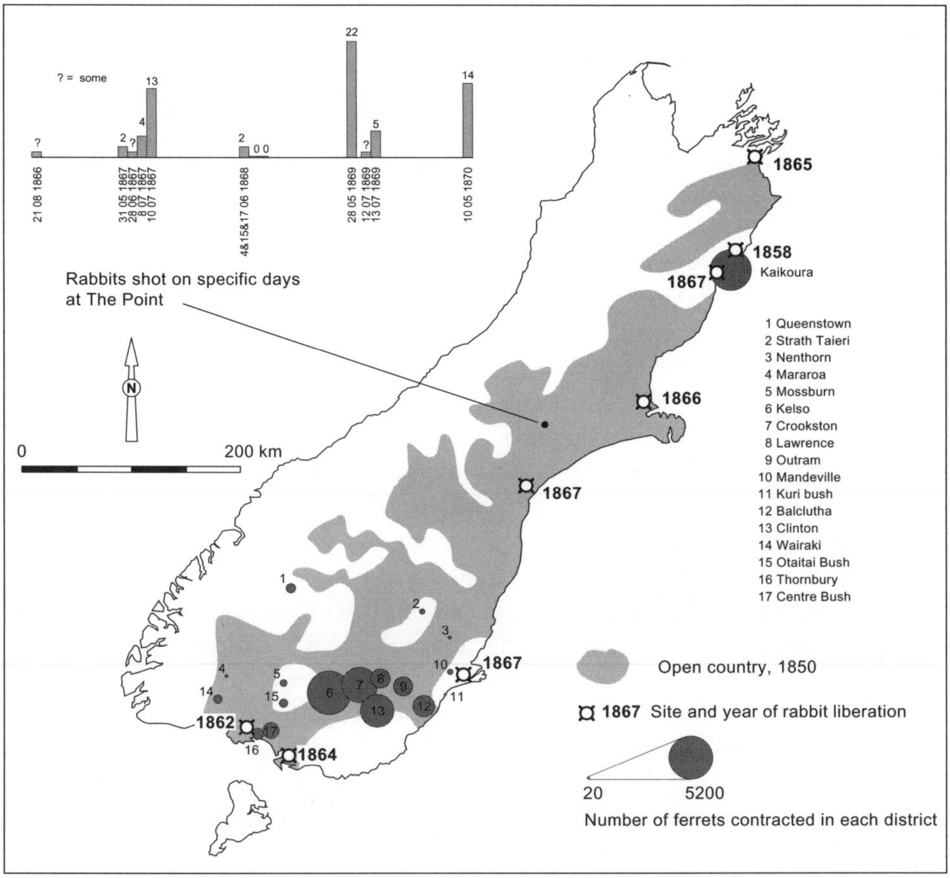

Figure 5.6 Contracts let in 1887 for the purchase of ferrets, and numbers of rabbits shot over a five-year period by members of the Phillips family at The Point in Mid-Canterbury. Source: 'The Supply of Ferrets', *AJHR*, H31, 1888, p. 1; rabbits: see note 9.

recognised that known means of eradication were at best palliatives. The colony's Agent in London was authorised to incur any necessary expenditure to ensure an effective biological means to destroy rabbits without injury to other animal life, and the eminent French microbiologist Louis Pasteur was seen as one who might assist in this task. A major difficulty, and one that touches on many aspects of the wise use of open-country environments, is that, with the prospect of their leases ending, tenants on pastoral properties were alleged to lose interest in pest destruction.[44] The committee therefore urged longer leases and new institutional arrangements that would reward tenants for improvements.

By the end of the nineteenth century only Wairarapa saw rabbits brought under control, through the application of diverse eradication methods and the fortuitous impact of a bladder worm spread by dogs.[45] Rabbit numbers grew to plague proportions in many parts of the high country in the 1890s. The rabbit nuisance then ebbed in most affected places, only to resurge in the early 1920s and late 1940s (see Chapter 15).

Appreciating the need to manage open-country environments

Late in the nineteenth century, landholders and government agencies began to appreciate that open-country environments require diligent management to ensure their continuing productivity. Fire and grazing animals had combined as agents of vegetation depletion and degradation, and stocking rates were plummeting. There were 511,188 sheep in Vincent County, Central Otago, in 1880, but just 315,757 forty years later.[46] On the rabbit-infested lands of Galloway station in Central Otago sheep numbers fell from 75,000 in 1879 to 21,000 in 1904, when land degradation was at its worst. In those parts of the open country that remained as unimproved grassland, carrying capacity began to decline in the 1880s, the area covered by scabweed (*Raoulia* spp.) expanded alarmingly, shingle fans grew, and steeper slopes failed. After the boom year of 1878, falling wool prices and a run of cold winters, culminating in the heavy snows of 1895, coupled with runholders' attempts to maintain sheep numbers in the face of increased numbers of rabbits, led to reduced wool clips from malnourished sheep.

Introduced plants gradually increased in number and abundance, few of them improving the pastoral resource of the high plains and low hill country. In 1917 an agricultural scientist asked why serious efforts had not been made to use native plants for windbreaks, despite the many useful species already known.[47] Thistles (chiefly species of *Cirsium*, *Onopordum*, and *Sonchus*) and sheep's sorrel (*Rumex acetosella*) were among the earliest pest plants, and thistles were subject to provincial ordinances. Inspectors were appointed, but control measures ceased when it was recognised that a landholder's efforts would count for nought if thistles were not eradicated from roadsides, Crown lands, and Māori lands. The same was said of the introduced bird species that raided grain crops. As Nugent Wade wrote to W. H. Teschemaker on 2 October 1861, 'People will not club together to destroy them and it is little sense one doing it and his neighbour not.'[48]

Conclusion

The environmental history of the tussock grasslands in the New Zealand open country is part of the larger story of European contact with the Americas, Australia, and southern Africa, in all of which pastoralism fostered colonial society and supported the developing infrastructure. In the case of New Zealand we may distinguish three significant phases. The first began in the late 1840s with the land rush by squatters to the Wairau Valley, thereby setting the pattern for pastoral land occupation and environmental exploitation for two decades. It was distinguished by investment in livestock rather than land, extraction of forage from standing vegetation, use of fire to improve grazing, and a management system geared to ensuring the greatest fiscal return for the least cost. The second phase began about 1880. While lowland parts of the open country saw accelerated conversion of residual tussock to cropping and livestock production on introduced pastures, high-country areas were the subject of more than thirty years of mostly ineffectual public and parliamentary debate about how best to resolve the economic, social, and environmental problems then plaguing the 'pastoral lands'. The third phase comes at the end of our period, when the Pastoral Lands Commission of 1920 endorsed the continuation of exploitative pastoralism while at the same time urging reductions in the incidence of burning, rabbit numbers, and flock size.

In the 1840s and 1850s, European colonists were occupying landscapes that were adjusting to and recovering from changes initiated several centuries earlier. Since then, agricultural and pastoral systems of land management have favoured early successional plants and animals, and ecological recovery has been suppressed. Colonial society was deeply interested in the New Zealand environment, and some pastoralists, such as Thomas Potts of Mid-Canterbury, W. T. L. Travers of Nelson, and Herbert Guthrie-Smith of Hawke's Bay, had the time, skill, and means to write about their discoveries. The implications of what was learned often proved incompatible with continuing occupation of the open country and exploitation of its resources, yet pastoralism endured only to suffer recurrent upheaval with catastrophic consequences for environmentally unstable areas of hill and low mountain country.

Pastoralism grew too quickly to develop well. Large holdings were occupied before baseline surveys were initiated, let alone completed, and environmental resources were exploited without independent monitoring. Over the eighty years to 1920 the open country was bedevilled by the speed with which introduced species and alien technologies left their mark, by lags in ecosystem recovery, and by inconsistent institutional and management arrangements. All too often, pragmatic solutions were favoured over approaches rooted in objective knowledge, and when times were hard environmental concerns counted for little. Through legislation, official reporting procedures, and the actions of civil servants, central government sought to direct and control landscape transformation while at the same time distancing itself from the consequences of environmental misuse.

Although conversion of dense tall tussock to an open short-tussock grassland better suited to grazing by sheep and cattle was a managed activity, it took decades for its environmental impact to be appreciated. The management systems of pastoral holdings are now and always have been sensitive to macroeconomic conditions. For the first fifty years of European occupation the open country under pastoralism was viewed as a neutral resource, but by the late nineteenth century it had become a loser in the national drive for development. Initially quarried and exploited, only recently sustained and nurtured, the open tussock country is now a beneficiary of the national shift in environmental attitudes. The turnabout is due to better legislation, more sensitive national policies, the work of dedicated scientists, the efforts of concerned citizens, and a new generation of pastoralists drawing upon the growing body of formal and informal environmental learning.[49]

6

Mining the Quarry

Terry Hearn

Mining played a key role in the New Zealand economy through to 1921, encouraging exploration, stimulating immigration and settlement, promoting internal commerce, and fostering technological innovation and industrial development. A wide range of minerals were mined at various times and in various places. These included the metalliferous (especially gold), non-metalliferous (limestone, clays, and aggregates), and fuel minerals (notably coal).[1] For the quinquennium 1861–65, the industry generated 65.2 per cent of New Zealand's export earnings. It still accounted for 15.3 per cent for 1901–05, before declining to 3.2 per cent in 1915–20. It also employed a significant proportion of the European male workforce: 14.5 per cent in 1874, although falling to just 2.0 per cent in 1921, with a pronounced shift during that time from gold mining to coal mining and quarrying. Even so, gold accounted for over 90 per cent by value of mineral exports between 1853 and 1921, and coal just 5.2 per cent.

Mining was, however, recognised as environmentally damaging. In 1890, W. N. Blair attributed the rapidity and scale of landscape change in New Zealand, in part, to 'the washing down of mountains for gold ...'[2] In fact, the environmental impact of mining has not previously been systematically investigated.[3] This essay will therefore explore three major issues involving gold mining—the disposal of mining debris, land settlement, and the preservation of agricultural land—and consider, more briefly, quarrying and coal mining.

The gold rushes

Gold was discovered in New Zealand during the 1850s, but the first large-scale rushes took place to Otago in 1861, followed by Marlborough, Nelson–West Coast, and Hauraki–Thames–Ohinemuri (Figure 6.1). They were part of a nineteenth-century New World series that began in California in 1849 and extended to New South Wales and Victoria in 1851; Colorado and the Fraser, near Vancouver, in 1858; Western Australia

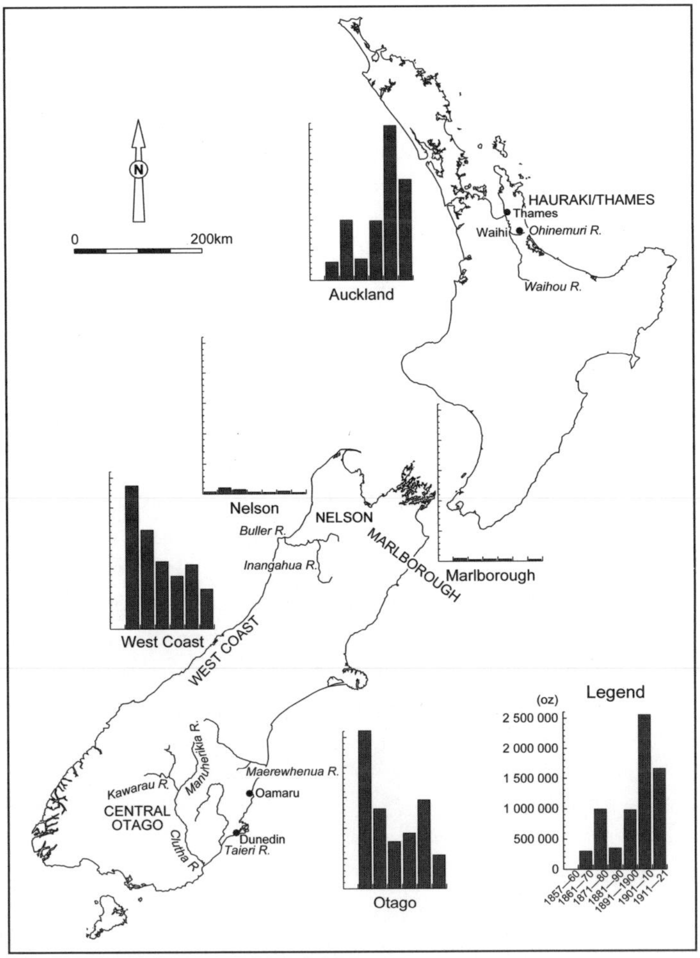

Figure 6.1 Goldfields and gold production, 1857–1921, by decade. Source: *AJHR*, C2, 1916 and 1917–22.

and South Africa in 1886; and the Klondike (Alaska) in 1898. The circulation of capital, participants, and practices linked these discontinuous series of events together, as did experiences of excitement and privation, riches and disappointment. Behind the rushes lay a burgeoning demand for gold to finance the expansion of world trade, to sustain the growth of metropolitan, notably British, industry and commerce, and to stimulate the settlement and development of the colonial periphery. The scale and character of the rushes also reflected the distribution of the gold. Initially at least, this offered ease of entry, required minimal capital outlay, and held out the prospect of sudden wealth.

In order to promote and regulate gold mining, the New Zealand Parliament initially adopted the policy and principles of Victorian mining law. Simultaneously, it laid the basis for conflicts between the private user rights created by that law and the common law rights of private property. As a result, Parliament was compelled to try to reconcile the competing ideals of the freedom of the mines and private property rights. Those efforts offer insights into resource developmental priorities, resource conservation, and environmental protection and management, and into the forces encouraging policy reappraisal and redirection. The policy of gold mining law was clear: to allow the private mining of the public domain with minimal restrictions and at minimum expense, and to accord primacy to miners' requirements. It employed the law of capture to allocate resources among miners, created user rights, and established an institution to apply mining law, resolve disputes, and collect taxes. These private user rights differed sharply from private property rights, the latter including rights of possession, use, management, income, security, capital, transmission, and absence of term.[4]

User rights and private property rights thus constituted two different rights structures. One conferred exclusive enjoyment and freedom of disposition for an unlimited time; the other, occupation and usage for limited periods contingent upon specified performance. The application of these two structures to the same resources of land and water created on- and off-site conflicts between miners and landowners. Miners sought freedom of access to all lands for mining purposes, and the unrestricted right to discharge mining debris into watercourses. Landowners sought security of tenure and protection for investment. Simultaneously, it became apparent that nineteenth-century mining law had been devised for 'pick and shovel' mining, which created relatively minor environmental impacts. It contemplated neither the major changes that took place in mining technology, notably in hydraulic elevating, gold dredging, and hard-rock mining, nor the growing scale of environmental impact.

Discharging mining waste

It was not long before anxiety was being expressed over the discharge of mining debris into rivers, the elevation of their beds, increased susceptibility to flooding, and the dangers posed to farmland. Miners denied both actual responsibility and legal liability, rejecting suggestions that they stack tailings or construct debris dams and settling ponds.[5] Concern that a successful appeal to common law riparianism (that is, the flow of water be undiminished in quality and quantity for the owners of land on both sides of a river) would mean 'the … abandonment of gold mining' induced miners to ask Parliament to enact legislation to confirm the right to dump, and to ask that riparian lands be withheld from sale.[6] Two landowner challenges in Otago in 1875 (*Borton* v. *Howe* and *Glassford* v. *Read*) established three things: riparian rights of freeholders outside the proclaimed goldfields were deemed not to have been affected by mining legislation; the riparian rights of freeholders within the goldfields were deemed to have been affected only in so far as mining law authorised the diversion of water from natural courses; and mining legislation did not authorise miners to pollute streams.[7]

The implications for mining were serious, and hence Parliament enacted measures to extinguish existing and prevent the acquisition of new riparian rights. The Gold

Fields Amendment Act 1875 (No. 1) empowered the Governor to proclaim any watercourse to be a sludge channel open for the dumping of mining debris. Affected riparian proprietors were entitled to compensation, payable by the Crown. The Governor could issue regulations 'prescribing the mode and times at which such tailings mining debris or waste waters may be discharged', and to impose restrictions on the right to discharge. Miners were not satisfied, claiming that mining legislation had created rights that transcended those of common law, and that Parliament could abrogate the latter without paying compensation.

Further, the Act implied that miners were not entitled to discharge into watercourses that had not been proclaimed and for which compensation had not been paid. Continued mining was thus subject to the forbearance of riparian proprietors, or the willingness of the government to utilise the Act's provisions. Its replacement was sought by a measure that would 'afford relief to the miners by securing them in all the rights and privileges which they have fairly and legitimately acquired ...' The Legislative Council declined to approve a repealing measure, and the Act remained the basis for the settlement of riparian rights disputes. It also provided that no person who purchased land after 21 October 1875 (the date the Act came into force) would have 'any right ... to the flow of any watercourse which shall have been at any time proclaimed ... [a sludge channel] running through or upon such land'. Additional provisions limited the acquisition of riparian rights, absolved miners from any responsibility for damage resulting from dumping, and limited compensation claims.[8]

Different approaches to debris dumping

Very different approaches were employed in Victoria and California. In Victoria, miners, claiming a prescriptive right, freely dumped debris. The government appointed a board of inquiry in 1886 when confronted with demands from miners for protection against legal action, and from landowners for the preservation of their lands. Its recommendation—that miners be required to restrain debris—was finally acted upon following the expansion of gold dredging. The Mines Act 1904 defined precise discharge standards and established a Sludge Abatement Board to regulate any form of mining 'by which mineralised or impure water, sludge, or mining debris is discharged into any river stream watercourse lake or reservoir'. The board could inspect, impose, and enforce appropriate orders, including the construction of restraining works, and investigate and prosecute complaints.[9]

In California, prolonged conflict, involving the Hydraulic Miners' Association and the Anti-Debris Association, culminated in *Woodruff* v. *North Bloomfield Gravel Mining Company* (1884). The Supreme Court declared that it had 'never recognised the validity of any custom to mine in such a manner as to destroy or injure the property of others' and issued an injunction that effectively suspended alluvial mining.[10] Claims that the state had indirectly authorised the dumping of debris by according mining a special place in the order of policy priorities were rejected. Various solutions were canvassed. These included that miners pay for the right to discharge debris or purchase affected lands, the construction of river-control works, and legislation to authorise discharge. Neither the Californian legislature nor Congress ever attempted to authorise debris dumping. In 1888 a report ordered by Congress concluded that mining could be resumed if restraining dams were erected in the mountains and wing dams built to constrict rivers on the debris plains. In 1893 an Act created the California Debris Commission and required miners to construct restraining works and fund the commission.

In New Zealand legislative solutions continued to be followed. The expansion of gold dredging after 1895 engendered further conflicts, especially on the Clutha River in Otago. It was claimed that 'The whole of the gold duty obtained would not pay for the compensation that would be claimed if the river were proclaimed', an acknowledgment of the magnitude of the interests involved.[11] Further litigation established that miners had no prescriptive right to foul rivers and that legislation enacted since *Borton* v. *Howe* had authorised neither the discharge of tailings nor the fouling of water. A notice to proclaim the Waipori River produced compensation claims amounting to £18,000. The government declined to act, lest it encouraged riparian proprietors elsewhere to demand proclamation and compensation. The position became increasingly serious from about 1900 with dredges winning some 20 per cent (by value) of the gold produced each year.

This pressure forced the government to appoint a commission to establish the basis for a comprehensive settlement. In fact, the Rivers Commission of 1900–01 simply investigated all watercourses required by miners and recommended proclamation where mining was established or likely to expand, among them the Inangahua River, into which annually 120, 000 tons were being discharged from Reefton's quartz mines.[12] Conversely, it did not recommend proclamation where rivers—including the Clutha, Kawarau, Manuherikia, and Buller—had been long used to carry off mining waste, or where the auriferous character of the ground was uncertain, compensation likely to be substantial, interested parties could reach agreement, or state land-settlement schemes were likely to be adversely affected.

In all, the Rivers Commission considered claims amounting to £150,000. By 31 March 1907, fifty-one watercourses had been proclaimed and over £51,000 paid in compensation.[13] In so doing, the commission discounted the implications of proclamation for river management, public and private property, the protection of agricultural lands, and riverine ecology. It had interpreted its terms of reference as requiring resolution of disputes through the existing mechanism of proclamation, and at the least possible cost to the state. The limitations of that approach became apparent in the major dispute involving the Waihou and Ohinemuri rivers, which drain the North Island's Ohinemuri goldfield.

The Waihou–Ohinemuri dispute

Although the Ohinemuri goldfield was proclaimed in 1875, hard-rock mining awaited the introduction of cyanide extraction in the late 1880s. Then, inflows of English capital, and the amalgamation of small companies into large enterprises, stimulated a major expansion of the industry. Numbers of men employed, stampers installed, tons of ore crushed, bullion recovered, and dividends paid all rose sharply.[14] Mining towns, especially Waihi, boomed. Extensive areas of bush were cleared to satisfy demand for fuel and construction materials. Continuing improvements in ore treatment and recovery rates reduced treatment costs and brought millions of tonnes of low-grade ore within the range of economic working. From 1890 onwards, hundreds of thousands of tonnes of tailings, including cyanide-injected waste, were tipped into the Waihou and Ohinemuri rivers (Figure 6.2).

In 1895 the government, acting in advance of land settlement, declared the two rivers to be sludge channels. Major floods occurred in 1898, 1907, and 1910. In 1901 the Ohinemuri County Council initiated a series of investigations. The council and the Mines and Public Works Departments reached contrasting conclusions concerning the extent of environmental impacts.[15] Miners rejected proposals that they stack tailings clear of watercourses, or construct California-type timber retaining weirs and back-fill stopes as too expensive and unnecessary. The Minister of Mines noted that there had been no objections to proclamation, that miners were legally entitled to dispose of their tailings into the rivers, and settlement had anyway followed proclamation. Any silting, he claimed, was attributable to bush clearance in the watersheds.

Petitions calling for remedial measures were ignored, including that of Ngāti Tamaterā settled along the Ohinemuri. Ngāti Tamaterā acknowledged that in 1875 they had ceded to

Figure 6.2 Damage caused by silting. The top photograph shows a silt bank at Pereniki Bend, Waihou River. 'Settlers used to tie up their boats at willow where figure standing, in about 6 ft. of water.' The bottom photograph shows a view of silt deposit on Barrett's paddock. Both taken in June 1907. Source: *AJHR*, C14, 1910.

the Crown the right to mine over certain lands, but claimed that contamination of the Ohinemuri had rendered the water 'unfit for use by man or beast'. In addition, cultivated land and burial grounds had been covered with tailings, and fish, 'an important part of their sustenance', had been destroyed by cyanide in contravention of the Treaty of Waitangi. under which 'the fisheries of the Natives were specially reserved'. Ngāti Tamaterā insisted that it had never been advised of government's intention to proclaim the two rivers as sludge channels. The iwi petitioned Parliament again in 1907 and presented evidence to the goldfields select committee, the latter being particularly interested in satisfying itself that the iwi had received a monetary benefit arising from the 1875 cession.[16]

Other petitioners claimed that 200,000 acres were 'more or less injured', outlet drains had filled up, navigation was impeded, and the Thames fishing industry had been damaged. They also complained that any scheme for draining the Piako lands would be 'seriously retarded', all to benefit 'wealthy outside companies'. Further investigations by the Mines Department failed to produce a definitive assessment of the actual and potential damage and practical remedies. The flood of 1907 and further petitions led to investigation by the Goldfields and Mines Committee. This committee decided, on the basis that the district's local authorities contribute to any control scheme, to refer the petitions to government for 'favourable consideration'. The short debate in Parliament that followed was remarkable only for the Minister of Mines' insistence that the petitions be rejected, as the area was naturally prone to flooding, and that mined ore was so finely crushed that waste was carried directly out to sea. In any case, the miners would want huge levels of compensation.[17]

Anti-dumping interests formed the Ohinemuri Silting Association, which, familiar with overseas developments, claimed that the miners could stack tailings at minimal cost. Miners called for a commission of inquiry, certain that it would 'explode the contentions of the farmers that the mining tailings are proving a menace, and a source of great danger and loss to them'. The Waihi Gold Mining Company insisted that not more than fifty acres had been affected, and that the Ohinemuri floods were no greater than in the past. The admittedly higher Waihou River floods reflected the 'immense number of artificial drains emptying into the river' and the growth of willows. The company noted that the county had benefited from mining through roads, bridges, and drains, mostly funded by revenue derived from the gold duty. Stacking was not practical and finely ground residues were carried out to sea. Revocation would render government liable to provide both secure storage sites and the means of conveyance.[18]

In 1910 the government appointed a Waihou and Ohinemuri Rivers Commission to investigate these conflicting claims and to propose remedial measures that could be adopted 'without injury to any other persons, corporations, or interests'. This commission found that the annual dumping of 558,000 tons of debris had destroyed 371 acres and affected 'deleteriously' a further 7507 acres of agricultural land.[19] As landowners could not have foreseen the 'wide-reaching and disastrous effect' of proclamation, it recommended that, though not legally entitled to compensation, they should be recompensed. It noted that the adoption of tube mills meant that slimes rather than coarse sands were being discharged into the rivers, and recommended that 'grinding to slimes should be compulsory'. Any restriction to the use of the river as a sludge channel for slimes only would be in the mining companies' interests.

The problems to be remedied related largely to tailings already discharged. While also noting that cyanides were present in the rivers and that fish were no longer found, the commission concluded that farmers had not been affected. Navigation, on the other hand, had been, and 'seriously' so. This it attributed in part to 'the large volume' of light sands discharged into the upper Waihou following settlement. It also predicted future shoaling problems in Thames Harbour, which would require the dredging of both the harbour and the Waihou River. Various schemes for the disposal of tailings were considered. None was felt to be in the state's interests, owing to the likely impact on the cost of gold production, which could well render processing of lower-grade ores uneconomic.

Hence the 1910 commission recommended that the proclamation of the Ohinemuri be amended to allow only the discharge of 'slimes' in the belief that, once the rivers had been straightened and dredged, these would be carried out to sea. Tailings should be stacked or, where that was not possible, discharged under special permit. It recommended revocation of the Waihou River proclamation, although existing mines could continue dumping and 'that if any other mines in its watershed should desire to utilize the river or its tributaries, permission be specially given, after careful investigation and on special conditions, particularly as to fine grinding'. Otherwise the commission proposed extensive river-control works, estimated to cost £150,000, to be raised by loan. It was to be administered by a new river board funded by the miners, rates levied on lands in the river board district, and by the state. The miners' contribution, at the rate of ¾d per tonne of waste, was 'a tax which cannot affect the working of any low-grade ore, and an amount which it is believed the mining industry can well afford ...'

An integral part of this proposal was that Māori riparian lands should be purchased or 'brought into line with lands owned by Europeans in the matters of taxation and contribution towards the construction and upkeep of the new works'. Ngāti Tamaterā interests were accorded no particular recognition, while the proposed membership of the board did not provide explicitly for their representation. The commission's concern was that the large area of land in Ohinemuri County 'held and occupied' by Māori should be rated. No reference was made to the destruction of Māori river fisheries, and it considered that the Thames fishery had not been seriously affected. Were it to become so, 'the industry must give way to the general benefit to the Dominion caused by the continuance of the mines'.

The Waihou and Ohinemuri Rivers Improvement Act 1910 embodied most of the commission's recommendations but did not permit amendments to be made to the 1895 proclamation. That proclamation remained in force, the government not prepared to contemplate action that would have rendered it liable to claims for compensation from miners. The Waihou River was the subject of another inquiry in 1919, but it focused on flood control, while a commission in 1921 investigated the allocation of burgeoning control costs. Miners, insisting that their industry was 'waning and wasting', claimed that they had contributed more than sufficient to remedy any damage from dumping. The Public Works Department claimed that the right to discharge debris 'was a benefit of incalculable value to the gold mining companies', obviating 'enormous' costs in stacking, and that the companies could well afford to pay their share of the remedial works required ...'The commission itself criticised government's refusal to issue amended proclamations, recommending revocation and reissue in a form that would permit dumping 'only on such conditions as will obviate all liability to damage of either the rivers or adjacent agricultural lands, and also on payment of ... charges'.[20]

The fact that in 1921 quartz mining yielded 79.2 per cent (by value) of New Zealand's total gold output, and that 77.1 per cent of that came from the mines of the Thames–Coromandel, ensured that government would respond cautiously. Again the drive for development had triumphed over any impulse to conserve or preserve landscape, ecology, or traditional Māori access to food resources.

The national Rivers Commission 1919–20

The findings of the 1921 Waihou and Ohinemuri Rivers Commission marked a shift earlier apparent in the findings of a national commission appointed in 1919 to investigate river problems. While citing dumping as a major cause, this commission noted, with respect to the Maerewhenua in North Otago, that suspension of mining 'would not mitigate the trouble'. It also judged the value of the gold being won as insufficient 'to justify our recommending any contribution towards the cost of remedial measures being demanded from this source'. On the other hand, the government, having proclaimed the river a sludge channel, 'could not escape liability to contribute a substantial sum towards the costs of the works recommended'. Dumping had damaged Oamaru's water supply, roads, railways, bridges, and 800 hectares of land.[21]

Dumping in the Clutha River—which had never been proclaimed—had resulted in damage of 'a manifold nature', while the costs of protective works was estimated at £165,000. The commission concluded that agricultural and pastoral operations, burrowing by rabbits, and burning of the indigenous plant cover had accelerated the rate of 'natural denudation' as much as had mining, 'and therefore the settlers and miners are equally responsible ...'. Mining operations had displaced some 300 million cubic metres of material, which was then being swept out to sea at an annual rate of 670,000 cubic metres.[22] The similar use of the Taieri River had resulted in damage to some 12,000 hectares and to roads, bridges, and railways.[23]

In each instance, the costs were to be borne by local authorities, the state, and landowners. One important outcome of this investigation was section 48 of the Finance Act 1921–22, which provided that the exercise of the right to discharge mining debris into watercourses or to mine in or on their banks was to 'be subject to such conditions and restrictions as may be set out in the Proclamation'. The state, thereby, assumed more coercive powers to limit damage caused to river systems by mining and dredging.

Mining or land settlement?

The priority accorded mining was apparent in the manner in which the government resolved the conflict between miner and settler over land as well as water. As small-farm settlement was promoted on the goldfields, miners became anxious about the implications for their industry. The goldfields press insisted that 'the miner must not be encroached upon or curtailed in his operations'.[24] In Central Otago the resumption and close subdivision of large areas of pastoral lease land from 1878 onwards aroused alarm. Much of that land, miners claimed, was auriferous with mining being 'capable of almost unlimited extension'. But miners and settlers were in dispute over the priorities to be accorded each group's natural resource requirements, the former stating their concern that litigation as the result of the fouling of watercourses 'would smother the mining industry'.[25]

At the heart of the issue lay the application of the two different rights structures to the same resources of land and water.[26] Resolving the inherent conflict was a complex matter, but the major approach was to establish new forms of land tenure. Between 1860 and 1907, eight tenures were introduced. These were agricultural leases (in 1860), deferred payments licences (1872), perpetual leases (1882), small grazing runs (1885), leases-in-perpetuity (1892), occupation with right of purchase (1892), occupation leases (1894), and renewable leases (1907). All, with the exception of deferred payments, were forms of leasehold. The term varied considerably, but all were renewable, and all eventually offered lessees the right to acquire the freehold, apart from the lease-in-perpetuity.

The desire to promote close settlement was embodied in acreage limitations and mandatory residence and improvement conditions. To meet miner demands, the right of entry to all leasehold lands was reserved, all leases could be terminated if the land were required for mining, and, in the case of four of the tenures, owners or occupiers were not to have any right of action for any damage resulting from the diversion or fouling of watercourses. Thus selected incidents of ownership were modified in the interests of miners, but none of the tenures met their demands for unrestricted and unqualified entry and liability to termination and resumption without compensation. Government also refused to deny would-be settlers right of purchase in gold mining areas.

Freehold lands were not open to miners. Although the Crown retained the ownership of gold or silver found in either Crown or private lands, it had neither the right to enter private lands nor the power to authorise others to enter for mining purposes. An alternative was the sale of all lands, including those sought for mining. Proponents claimed that determining resource-allocation priorities by legislation precluded optimal allocation and use. They alleged that mining was facilitated by the transfer of external costs to the community, while it secured the (largely) untaxed profits. Authorising miners to enter private property meant that Parliament was being asked to pass 'exceptional legislation for the protection of an industry which was not nationally profitable nor nationally desirable to encourage'.[27] Finally, proponents insisted that mining freeholds, by offering greater security of title, would encourage investment and increased production, while land sales generally would effect the rapid settlement of lands closed 'in deference to the wish of goldfields "demagogues"'.[28]

Miners opposed the replacement of the legislatively determined user regime by private property and the competitive market as the allocating mechanism. The sale of mining freeholds would create monopolies and render entry into the industry difficult, while the sale of land for settlement would impede all mining through the multiplication of private property rights. Rejecting claims that their demands amounted to confiscation, miners sought legislation that would allow entry on private lands for mining. The outcome was the Resumption of Land for Mining Purposes Act 1873, by which all lands thereafter alienated were liable to resumption without compensation. Further measures followed, including the Mining Act 1891, which provided that all lands held under lease or licence from the Crown with the right to acquire the freehold were open for prospecting and liable to resumption. But it also established rules to preclude indiscriminate entry and destruction as well as the frustration of legitimate mining enterprise.

Preserving agricultural land

The measures relating to land tenures and to entry to private land applied irrespective of the land's primary-production potential.[29] As early as 1871, Dunedin's *Evening Star* declared that everyone had an interest in the preservation of the soil resource. Parliament should therefore devise some means of restoring the soil in areas once mined.[30] Few listened, until the introduction of hydraulic elevating and gold dredging (Figure 6.3). This allowed the profitable working of low-lying, low-value ground. Vast dredging schemes were proposed. Opponents insisted that the state should preserve 'the staple productive resources of the country' by withdrawing land from the operation of mining law or, in the case of freehold, expropriating it for resale under conditions that prohibited mining.[31] Miners in turn insisted that only rich land would be mined, affecting only a minute proportion of the national land resource. Dredging would anyway improve swampy, cold and sour land, and advance stripping could be employed, although mandatory restoration conditions could render mining unprofitable.

Accordingly, governments up to 1908 dismissed claims over the area being destroyed and insisted that attempts to restrict the sale of land for mining were politically impossible.

Figure 6.3 'Blue Spur hydraulic sluicing and elevating claim, Gabriel's Gully, Otago'. 'At this claim about 50 acres of auriferous fluvio-glacial conglomerate has been removed by sluicing and the remarkable fault-face to the right has been laid bare for a height of about 400 ft.' Source: *AJHR*, C3, 1911.

Landowners believed themselves to be the best judges of the most profitable use of their land.[32] The debate involved the familiar conflict between those who felt that private interest would effect the optimal allocation of resources, and those who wished Parliament to impose controls to ensure resource conservation and sustained yield.

The Australian state of Victoria adopted a different approach. Covenants inserted in mining leases issued after 1906 required advance stripping, redistribution of soil, and sowing of grass seed, while in 1909 the Mines Department was instructed not to issue leases over any land the value of which exceeded £3 per acre. In practice, the covenants were often ignored, an inquiry in 1913 concluding that the sole remedy was to withdraw all agricultural land. In California, the dredging of agricultural land proceeded largely unopposed. Miners claimed that the land involved was largely marginal or had been mined, that overgrazing and soil erosion were more destructive, and that good land could be reclaimed by re-soiling.[33]

In New Zealand the controversy intensified during the 1900s. Arguments were advanced that mining was part of a larger destruction being wrought on indigenous fauna and flora. Land of high agricultural value, it was proposed, should be preserved irrespective of its gold content. The government noted that such land was largely freehold and that owners had 'the perfect right to [do with it] as they wished', rejecting repurchase as a means of ensuring preservation. Objections to the destruction of orchard lands, and a petition seeking to halt mining of agricultural land,[34] finally persuaded Parliament in 1910 to include a clause in the Mining Amendment Act 1910. This allowed wardens to impose conditions on any licence to obviate the destruction of agricultural and pastoral land. It was prospective and discretionary in application, and failed to provide for inspection and enforcement.

In a report to the National Efficiency Board in 1918, the Mines Department conceded that considerable areas of agricultural land had been destroyed, and that little had been done to restore them.[35] The outcome was section 12 of the Mining Amendment Act 1919. This required submission of an application for a dredging claim to the local Commissioner of Crown Lands for assessment of the agricultural value of the land, and the local warden to impose such conditions as were necessary 'to prevent, so far as practicable, the destruction of the surface of the land or the rendering of it unfit for pastoral or agricultural purposes'. The section did not provide for the reservation or other protection of such land. It remained prospective in application and did not apply to freehold land for which a mining licence was not required. Once more use rights triumphed over an attempt at conservation, and control of damage resulting from gold mining remained limited. Given its relative lack of economic importance, compared with farming, gold mining continued to receive preferential treatment.

Mining for coal

Coal was mined in New Zealand from the 1830s, when whalers in Otago exploited sea-beach outcrops. Annual production grew slowly through to 1895, and more rapidly thereafter. The Grey Valley emerged by 1880 as the most important field, although by

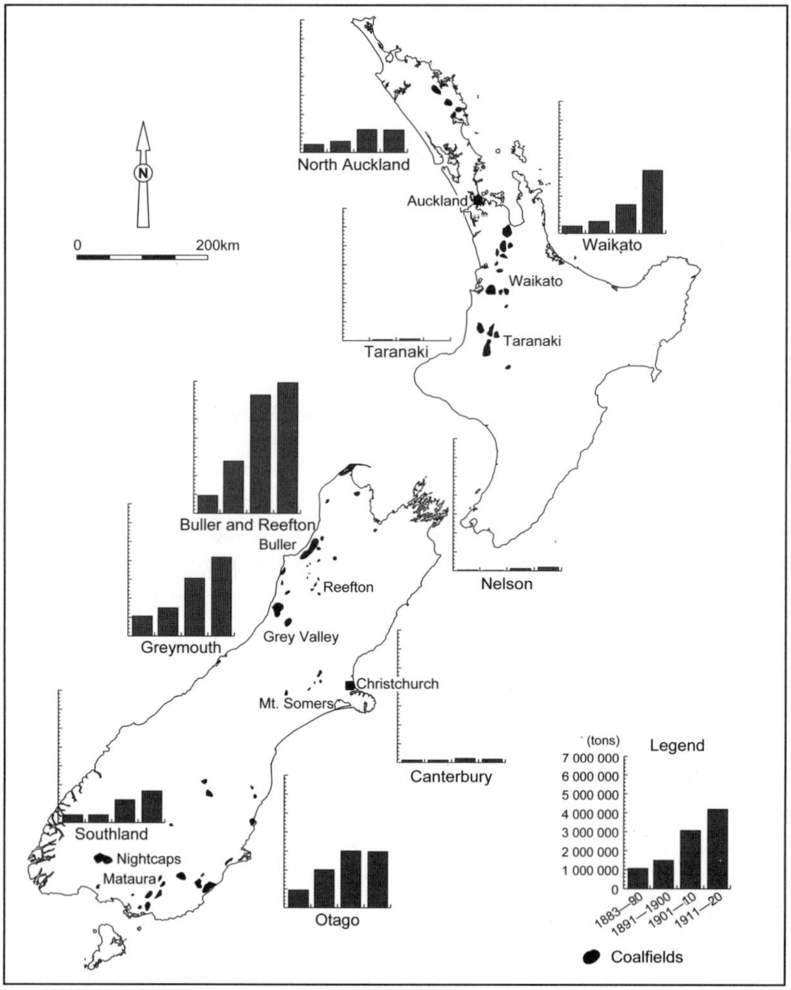

Figure 6.4 Coalfields and production, 1883–1920, by decade. Source: *AJHR*, C2.

1914 the Waikato, responding to the growth of dairy processing and the expansion of Auckland's domestic and industrial markets, produced a quarter of the country's annual output (Figure 6.4).[36] Most of the coal was extracted from underground mines with apparently limited environmental consequences. There were few slagheaps, while land instability and subsidence, accelerated leaching from the surface soil, acid drainage to other areas, soil conservation, site rehabilitation, and grading of spoil dumps were not obvious matters of concern. Investigations into the industry focused on such matters as production and delivery costs; mine management and inspection; health, safety, ventilation, and sanitation; and nationalisation, labour relations, and prices.[37]

While the legislation under which coal mining leases were issued did not require mine owners to assess and make provision for environmental protection, the leases themselves did impose conditions. Those issued over Crown lands, initially under the Land Acts and later under the Coalmine Acts, required lessees to work the mines 'in the most approved manner', and to inflict as little injury as possible to the land surface. Upon the expiry of leases, lessees were required to 'fill up, level, or substantially cover' all pits, shafts, and open works, clear surface slack and stone, and 'restore the surface to its original state, or as near thereto as reasonably may be or be required …'. Such conditions were of a standard rather than site-specific character, and concerned safety and the property's 'tenantable condition' rather than environmental matters.

The same was true of licences issued for the raising of lignite, while the conditions included in leases issued in respect of other minerals matched those relating to coal.[38] Government occasionally imposed other conditions, notably with respect to transport from mine to port.[39] Other concerns related to the clearance of bush around mining towns and the often insanitary state of towns constructed in bush-clad, hilly, and wet areas. However, the isolation of many coal mining townships, especially on the West Coast, the perils of mining, and the fact that many mining families had been drawn from the English coalfields with their traditions of social and political activism and solidarity, helped to create strongly integrated mining communities.

While coal mining legislation reserved the surface, water, watercourses, and trees on all land leased for mining, it also provided that these could be used for mining purposes without further consent having to be obtained. Open-cast mining, with its potentially greater environmental impact, was conducted on a very small scale until 1945 and the introduction of machinery to facilitate the stripping of overburden.[40] Up to 1921 almost all open-casting was confined to the Mount Somers (Canterbury), Mataura and Nightcaps (Southland), and Central Otago fields, with small pits opening and being abandoned as demand fluctuated. Open-cast coal appears not to have exceeded 5 per cent of annual production before 1921.[41]

Quarrying

A widespread form of mining was quarrying—stone for building; aggregates for roading and reclamation; limestone and phosphate for agriculture; and claystone for bricks and tiles. Quarry sites were reserved throughout New Zealand.[42] The few statistics available suggest that between 1911 and 1921 the number of quarries in operation, men employed, and production fluctuated considerably from year to year. In 1921, 257 quarries employed 1561 men and produced 1.19 million tons. Gravel for macadamising and ballast accounted for 56 per cent of this total, stone for harbour works 16.7 per cent, limestone for cement 15.2, limestone for agriculture 10.4, stone for building 1.0, phosphate for agriculture 0.5, and claystone for bricks and tiles 0.2 per cent.[43]

The first Quarries Act, passed in 1910, dealt with the certification of managers, safety, and inspection, making no reference to the discharge of waste and storm water, the control of dust and noise, or site rehabilitation. Moreover, it excluded state quarries, those in which the rock-face was under twenty feet, and those in which explosives were not employed. There seem to have been few problems with rural quarries. The Halswell Quarry, outside Christchurch, which developed into one of New Zealand's largest, did not attract complaints. Nor did the opening of a quarry on Mount Taranaki.[44] Quarries in urban areas, however, did cause some concern.

In 1902 the Heathcote Road Board sought, unsuccessfully, an amendment to the Public Works Act to forbid the operation of quarries within three miles of a city or borough, the object being to preserve property values. Similarly unsuccessful efforts were made to control drainage from quarries alleged to be causing silting in the Heathcote River. Abandoned quarries could also cause anxiety, reflecting the expansion of city suburbs to encompass quarries and industries once located on urban fringes.[45] Of growing concern in Auckland from about 1910 onwards was the quarrying of its volcanic cones. The Reserves and Other Lands Disposal and Public Bodies and Empowering Act 1915 imposed some restrictions and required quarry owners to plant approved trees and shrubs. Not satisfied, the Auckland Town Planning Association campaigned to prevent further despoliation, attracting the support of Māori and tourist interests, while many of Auckland's local authorities accorded preference to scoria obtained from alternative sources.[46]

Conclusion

New Zealand's colonial development involved the conversion of public natural resources into sources of private output and wealth, a process facilitated by legislation and supported by state-funded programs for the construction of roads, railways, and communications. Mining law and land law, in particular, imposed few restrictions on the use of resources, while discounting social and environmental costs in the interests of sustained exploitation. Gold miners interpreted mining law as offering unlimited licence for their enterprise and sought appropriate measures whenever such licence appeared to be under threat. Parliament largely acceded to their demands, proving much less imaginative than its Victorian and Californian counterparts. Controls were only gradually introduced after the costs of unrestrained mining and dumping for water quality and flood control, and the extent of damage to infrastructure and wildlife habitats, became apparent, and only after the community began to realise that it would have to pay for the damage inflicted by companies concerned solely with their own profits. Even then, government attempts at control were intended to resolve conflicts among competing interests rather than to ensure wise resource use.

The first signs of a shift in attitudes and values are apparent from about 1900, in the findings of the rivers commissions as well as inquiries into pastoral and hill lands, forests, and sea fisheries. This shift reflected a growing debate over the social and environmental costs of untrammelled exploitation, technological change that constantly redefined resources and offered an enhanced capacity for environmental change, and the roles of the state and the 'market' in resource assessment and allocation. Further, it reflected concern over the approaching closure of the frontier, the challenge to the notion of 'inexhaustibility', and the shift from 'physical' to chemical wastes.

Although legislative controls were reluctantly enacted, often loosely formulated, and prospectively and sparingly applied, such changes recognised in qualified fashion the principles of 'efficient development', 'wise use', and active management, and did embody new roles for the state beyond those of promoter and facilitator.

7

Destruction under the guise of improvement?

The forest, 1840–1920

Graeme Wynn

Late in life, novelist Frank Sargeson recalled his uncle's farm, high in the King Country beyond Taumarunui. 'Tucked away at the narrow top end of a valley', it was so crowded with 'thick and heavy bush' that its new owner could only imagine its future as a farm when he occupied it in 1913. By 1920, only a few patches of bush remained. On these broken hills, seven years were sufficient to reprise a major theme in the short European history of New Zealand.

A little sawmill, 'not much more than a roof supported on upended logs, with much bigger logs bedded into the ground to take the weight of the machinery', had been built below the farmer's hut. A hauling engine fed the mill, dragging the biggest of the farm's trees roughly across the earth and along a wooden tramline that snaked through the valley. The farmer cut what the millers had left, setting the debris to burn at the end of each summer. Grass was sown, fences were built and sheep introduced. With remarkable speed, it seemed that 'the natural order of things ... had been obliged to yield to intelligent human guidance'. An 'appearance of settled and civilised pastoral order' was imposed on the once-forested landscape.[1]

This 'making over' of the North Island ranked, in the estimation of geographer George Jobberns writing in 1956, as one of 'the outstanding achievements of our people'.[2] The historian G. H. Scholefield measured things rather differently. In *New Zealand in Evolution*, published in 1909, he described the assault on the forest as a 'pitiful war'. The rights given sawmillers were 'simply and solely ... executioner's warrant[s]', allowing greedy, selfish individuals to 'pick out the eyes of the forest, to slay and ruin the rest, and then go elsewhere'. The countryside was being devastated. Hundreds of mills were 'killing, and slaying and burning and wasting'. The prevailing 'doctrine of progress' had unleashed 'unbridled rapine and licence'. The forest was being 'destroyed under the guise of improvements'.[3]

The drama

Achievement or disaster? Why were opinions so different? Such questions lie at the heart of this chapter, and, as always, answers to them will turn upon evidence marshalled and interpreted. But information is collected and preserved for particular purposes; it is often incomplete, inadequate, or inappropriate; all too often it is open to different interpretations. Finding a way through these complexities is a challenge—but it is one that must be joined if the past is to be understood rather than judged anachronistically.

This chapter charts what happened to the forests between 1840 and 1920, striving to understand why those many thousands who played parts in the transformation acted as they did, and to reveal some of the reasons for contemporary and later assessments of these events. The story is complicated because neither forest nor society was of a piece. Between Auckland and Southland, 'the New Zealand forest' varied enormously in species composition, appearance, utility, susceptibility to fire, and so on. Personal and family histories and location differentiated people; their engagements with, and attitudes towards, the indigenous vegetation of the country varied enormously. There was no unanimity of opinion about the processes under way. Important gains as well as distressing losses were recognised.

New Zealanders were, however, late participants in a long-running drama. Like actors in a touring theatre company, they spoke lines adapted to local audiences and comported themselves according to the configurations of the particular stage on which they found themselves, but their performance was shaped by a well-used script. Exploration, encounter, exploitation, adaptation, and transformation were its common acts, and it had been rehearsed for centuries before it reached New Zealand. Those who rendered the South Pacific version of the show felt the burden of this experience.

From the fifteenth century onwards, trade and politics drew European interests outwards. Plants, animals, diseases, and ideas accompanied European voyagers abroad: simultaneously, elements of New World environments became resources for use and commodities for exchange. Place after place was transformed. Progress—from 'wilderness to fruited plain' as one of dozens of works on this theme has it—was widely applauded. But its costs came to be counted as signs that all was not right with the ways in which humans were using the earth.

Incorporated into the New Zealand version of the global drama of colonial settlement, these experiences imparted a distinctive accent to the late local version of the play. It cannot be comprehended without an appreciation of this international context. Conversely, its significance is unlikely to be appreciated unless it is understood that just as the Taumarunui hill slopes served Frank Sargeson as a 'small-scale repetition of … [the] country's history', so the transformation of New Zealand after 1840 epitomises the changes induced in New World lands by the overseas expansion of Europe.[4]

A 'tangled and impervious forest': 1840

Distinctive, impenetrable, and extensive, the forest drew the attention of Europeans in early New Zealand. From Cook and Banks, who noted 'imence woods', 'lofty Trees', and 'the finest timber', through descriptions of views that encompassed 'little else than a succession of steep irregular hills, clothed with dense forests', to claims that these were 'the stateliest forests and the densest underwood in the world', diarists, journal-keepers and

Figure 7.1 *Primeval Bush*, Julius Geissler, 1919, pen. Auckland Art Gallery Toi o Tāmaki, gift of the John Leech Gallery, per Old Colonist's Museum, 1926.

others recorded their impressions of New Zealand's vegetation. Some marvelled at its remarkable trees. Others were fascinated by the luxuriant growth of 'grand broadleaved ferns palmated like the horns of the elk', mistletoes, the clematis that 'spangled' the shade with 'silver stars', 'innumerable parasites and climbing plants, vegetable boa-constrictors in appearance', and a 'carpet of lichens and mosses and fungi'. With the help of several luminous portrayals by early artists (Figure 7.1), this 'forest' is relatively easily imagined—but far from precisely rendered.[5]

Typically, it forms a complex, multi-layered ecosystem, including almost 400 plant species, in five more-or-less distinct strata (Figure 7.2). The giants of the forest are podocarps: rimu, kahikatea, tōtara, mataī, and miro. Below them, hardwoods—taraire, tawa, kāmahi, tōwai, pūriri, black maire—form a dense, diverse canopy. A third layer of tree ferns and small trees—the nīkau palm, māhoe, wineberry—erect a subcanopy. Comprising, in the main, relatively fast-growing pioneer species adapted to colonising open ground, this stratum is most evident in the high-light environments of the forest margins; with time, these trees are overtopped and shaded out by the slower-growing but taller hardwoods and podocarps. Shrubs of the *Coprosma* species, horopito, tutu, rangiora, and the tree nettle comprise a fourth storey; and the ferns, mosses and lichens, the lilies and the grasses that grow on the damp, dark forest floor, a fifth. Vines such as supplejack, bush lawyer, passionflower, clematis, and rātā climb through the forest layers; and epiphytes—orchids, ferns, lilies—form often spectacular hanging gardens high in the trees.

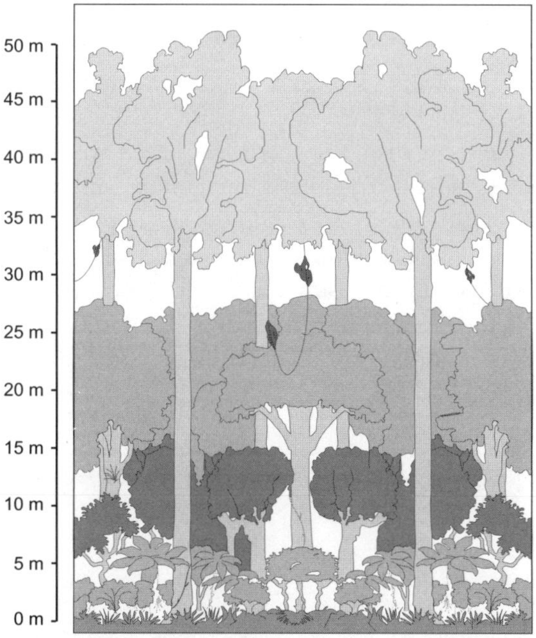

Figure 7.2 The structure of the New Zealand forest.

Variations from this archetype are best understood in biogeoclimatic terms. The forest was richer in species and more luxuriant in appearance in the north than in the south, and on lower rather than higher ground. Differences in humidity and rainfall, soil and drainage conditions, and aspect and exposure altered the vegetation cover. Among the podocarps, tōtara, mataī, and kahikatea favoured fertile soils; tōtara flourished where these were dry, and kahikatea—the 'white pine' of early European parlance—in the swampy ground of tidal estuaries and river banks. In the hardwood canopy, taraire gradually yielded to tawa south of Auckland, and tawa gave way, in turn, to kamahi in the South Island. On coastal sandplains, a great range of forest species grew as low windswept shrubs. On volcanic soils, 'the bush' was generally lighter; on heavier non-volcanic soils, it more closely approached the form that surveyors and settlers came to regard as the quintessential 'dense primeval New Zealand Forest'.[6]

Beyond this, two arbitrary latitudinal boundaries help clarify the form of the forest. North of 38°S (and below the 800-metre contour), that most magnificent—and most commercially valuable—of New Zealand trees, the kauri, rose above all others in the early forest. Typically growing some distance apart, in smaller or larger groups, on slightly elevated sites, the kauri towered over the tōtara, miro, rimu, taraire, tawa, and rewarewa of the mixed podocarp–hardwood forest. South of 42°, many species common in the North Island—nīkau, karaka, tawa, kohekohe, rewarewa, pukatea and tānekaha, rangiora, kanono, and wharangi—disappear. Here, too, subantarctic rainforest, dominated by one or more species of southern beech (*Nothofagus*), becomes more prominent. Although *Nothofagus* grow singly in the podocarp–hardwood forest and are relatively common in lowland Taranaki and the East Cape, as well as in the northern and southwestern parts of the South Island, they occupy the poorer soils and steeper slopes of the cooler south to the virtual exclusion of other trees.[7] In the filtered half-light beneath the close, small-leaved canopy, there are fewer lianes, epiphytes, and tree ferns than elsewhere, and beech seedlings often dominate the understorey, which also includes shrubs such as mingimingi and weeping māpou.[8]

The precise limits of this highly varied forest are impossible to establish. Volcanic eruptions and Māori burning had reduced its area by half well before 1800, and the activities of loggers, reflected in the rising quantities of timber shipped from Hokianga and Whangaroa early in the nineteenth century (discussed in Chapter 3), pushed back its edges on the northern peninsula. Beyond such observations there is only uncertainty, particularly for the interior of the colony. The earliest concerted attempt to estimate

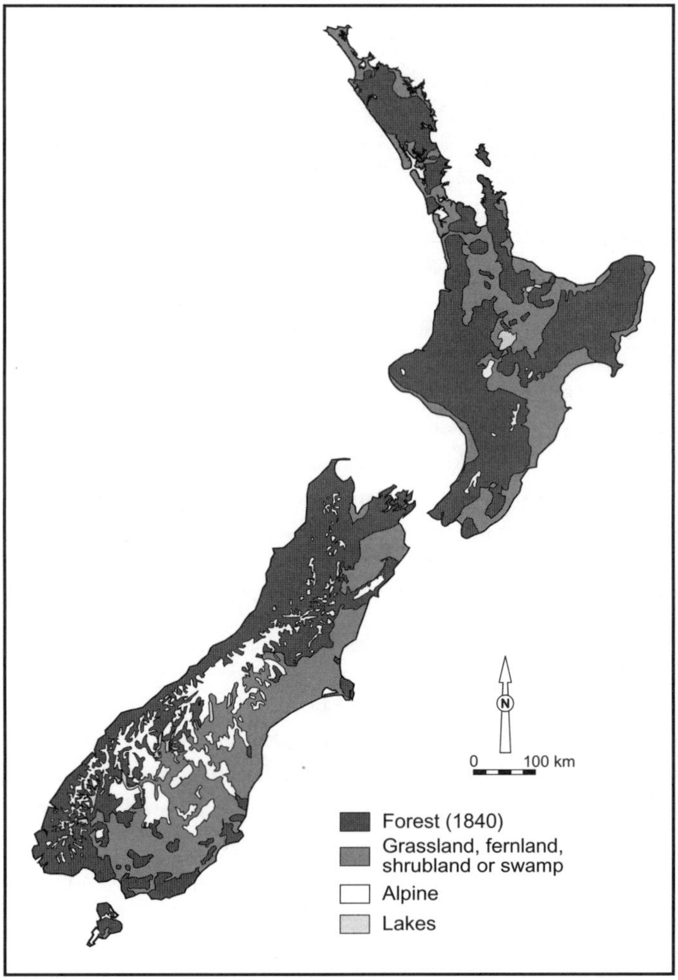

Figure 7.3 The forest, c. 1840. Adapted from *New Zealand Historical Atlas*, plate 12.

New Zealand's forest cover was made by James Hector, Director of the Colonial Museum, in 1874. Based on information collected from provincial superintendents, he stated that 31 per cent of New Zealand was forested in 1830.

Later, more scientific estimates, derived from ecology as well as the historical record, have consistently revised Hector's figures upward. The geographer Kenneth Cumberland suggested about half of the colony was forested in 1840. Others broadly concur. Regional proportions and lines on maps are more difficult to establish. Perhaps the best that can be said is that 'bush' covered some two-thirds of the North Island and rather less (25–30 per cent) of the South (Figure 7.3).

Destruction

Writing to her father and sisters in England, shortly after her arrival in New Plymouth in 1841, Sarah Harris reflected that 'The forest is behind me and the sea in front'. Like countless other nineteenth-century immigrants, she found herself between the bush and the deep blue sea. After their long ocean voyage, most new arrivals had little choice but to confront the interior, into which Sarah initially dared 'not venture … for fear of losing' herself. Enormous effort was spent in this confrontation. Not all of it was directed at the bush, for there were extensive areas of native grassland, and thousands of bracken- and fern-covered acres available to those engaged in realising their 'earthly paradise' in the 'future Britain of the South'. But open country, like the South Island tussock and shrub and fern lands of Hawke's Bay, was quickly occupied—as described in Chapter 5—by runholders and fortunate farmers who found ready markets in the growing towns.

As New Zealand's Pākehā population rose, those who settled the land had to carve farms from the forest. Replacing existing ecosystems by new forms of land use was taken for granted in the march of 'improvement'. The task of 'clearing' was so central that it measured everyday existence. For some it even offered a light to live by. Preaching to his congregation in northern Taranaki in 1844, the Wesleyan Cort Schnackenberg urged them to treat their mortal souls as they did their farms: 'if you find your mind, your heart to be a wilderness, cultivate it in the same manner as you do your fields, cut down the bush, great and small, spare no sin'. Even those who escaped active service in the war on the woods were somehow caught up in the onslaught. Hardly a soul was free from dependence upon the bush and, more pointedly, its exploitation.[9]

Nineteenth-century New Zealand was a wooden world. Its citizens' very existence rested upon the forest's bounty. In 1881, seven of every eight New Zealanders lived in a wooden dwelling; thirty years later, the proportion was even higher. People used wood to warm themselves and to cook and heat water. By the most conservative of estimates, families burned two tons of firewood per person each year; others point to consumption at twice this rate. Wooden barrels and boxes were ubiquitous. Ships that plied the coastal trade, and the carts and carriages that linked farms to markets and ports to hinterlands, were built of New Zealand wood.

Bridges were made of wood, and logs were laid in low-lying areas to form corduroy roads. Wooden sleepers supported the tracks of the expanding railway network. Wooden poles supported telegraph lines the length of the country, and wooden posts carried thousands of miles of fencing wire around the fields of growing numbers of farms. Barns, woolsheds and sheep pens, much furniture, and many implements were made of wood. Countless colonial industries depended upon wood. Without exploitation of the bush, New Zealand could not have developed as it did.

The picture of nineteenth-century forest destruction is a complicated pointillist composition of mini-histories and micro-geographies. Although settlers generally sought to remove bush from their lands, the settings and circumstances of their assault on the forest differed. Wood was produced for different purposes—with kauri, rimu, kahikatea, and mataī favoured for house-building; kahikatea for boxes; tawa for barrels and tubs; tōtara for telegraph poles and railway sleepers—and sent to different markets. Yet the main features of the story are clear. Millers and settlers were the prime movers of change. Their assault on the forest was directed to personal ends—accumulation of profit, establishment of home and family—but it lay squarely within the prevailing discourse of progress and improvement. 'The sawmiller', said one of their number, revealingly, 'cannot be taxed with the destruction of forest, since he merely converts the standing timber into a marketable product.'[10]

For thirty years after 1840, sawmilling was concentrated in coastal districts. Its main centres were the Auckland and Coromandel peninsulas, the northern reaches and west coast of the South Island, Banks Peninsula, and the Catlins River area of Otago, with a smaller concentration in Wellington. Here most of the colony's early mills—six in 1843, twelve in 1847, fifteen in 1855, and ninety-three in 1868—provided timber for growing Pākehā settlements (a population of 32,000 in 1855, and ten times this fifteen years later), as well as trans-Tasman markets. Flotillas of small craft ferried wood from ports near the mills to adjacent settlements—from Catlins River to Dunedin, for example. Slightly larger vessels ran the coast—from Pelorus Sound to Wellington and Lyttelton; from Auckland to ports south. Others carried exports, particularly kauri and kahikatea, overseas.

Generally, the early mills were small, with few capable of producing even one million superficial feet a year. But a combination of wasteful exploitation, and the concentration of production (in 1868 one-third of New Zealand's mills and many of its largest were in Auckland) quickly left its mark on the landscape. Ferdinand von Hochstetter lamented that 'extensive districts ... formerly ... covered with kauri woods are now totally destitute of such'. Meanwhile, James Hector urged millers to practise more careful and selective logging rather than continue their wholesale and rapid destruction of forests.[11]

With population growth and the quickening of economic activity after 1870, the sawmillers' assault on the forest magnified. Railways opened up new areas for exploitation and generated significant demands for wood. In the mid 1880s, timber and firewood accounted for half the freight carried on the Nelson, Picton, and Napier lines, and approximately the same proportion of all goods shipped in the province of Wellington. Railways facilitated sawmilling and settlement in the southern reaches of both islands. Botanist and forester Thomas Kirk, noting the rise of Southland as a supplier of timber to markets 'from

Table 7.1 New Zealand sawmills: number, distribution, capacity and output, 1907. Figures in parentheses indicate percentage of total.

Land district	*No. of mills*	*Horsepower*	*Employment*	*Annual capacity superficial feet*	*Annual output superficial feet*
Auckland	59 (14)	2847 (28)	2367 (33)	256,325,000 (36)	190,543,000 (44)
Hawke's Bay	38 (9)	1059 (11)	721 (10)	70,804,000 (10)	40,868,118 (9)
Taranaki	29 (7)	737 (7)	453 (6)	32,158,000 (4)	16,824,281 (4)
Wellington	83 (20)	1458 (15)	1388 (19)	118,440,000 (16)	70,138,000 (16)
Marlborough	14 (3)	494 (5)	195 (3)	15,770,000 (2)	9,869,000 (2)
Nelson	71 (17)	852 (9)	403 (6)	61,127,000 (9)	16,594,399 (4)
Westland	49 (12)	912 (9)	645 (9)	94,526,000 (13)	44,933,813 (10)
Canterbury	9 (2)	102 (1)	54 (1)	3,000,000 (0.4)	1,164,000 (0.2)
Otago	9 (2)	131 (1)	82 (1)	5,690,000 (0.8)	3,190,000 (0.7)
Southland	50 (12)	1408 (14)	831 (12)	61,100,000 (8)	38,087,000 (9)
TOTAL	411	10,000	7139	718,940,000	432,031,611

Note: Employment total includes sawmill hands only, bush workers not enumerated.

Source: 'The Timber Industry in New Zealand in 1907', *AJHR*, C4, 1907.

Invercargill to Ashburton', Lyttleton, and elsewhere wrote, 'The rapid development of the Southland trade has closed the mills in Catlins River, annihilated the coastal timber export of Westland, and greatly restricted that of Marlborough and Nelson.'

In the hill country of the North Island, mills were established at 'successive railheads' as tracks and settlers pressed into the bush. Although most mills were transitory—several operating for no more than a decade—many underpinned more permanent settlement. By creating markets for supplies as well as timber, and by employing local men as casual labour to build tramways or cut the bush, they helped settlers find their feet in their first years on the land. In many localities, such as Feilding, where eight mills were said to support 1268 men and their dependants, it is fair to say—as H. C. D. Somerset did of 'Littledene' (Oxford in Canterbury)—that 'the mill made the township'.[12]

There were 150 mills in 1876, 204 in 1881, 243 in 1891, and 414 in 1905. Early in the twentieth century, New Zealand's largest mill could produce 18 million feet a year; six others were capable of 10 million, twenty more of 5 million feet plus. Twenty-two of these large mills were in Auckland, and all were in the North Island. Elsewhere, portable mills able to cut no more than 200,000 feet a year, and more permanent structures with capacities of 500,000 to 2–3 million feet consumed their varying shares of bush (Table 7.1). Skid roads, chutes and tramways, dams built to flush logs downstream, the shanties and cookhouses of the workers, marked the landscape. Logging was never a tidy operation. Stumps, sawdust, and vast quantities of debris were left behind; the earth was gouged and disturbed; soils were exposed to rain and wind (Figure 7.4).

Nowhere were the consequences of this onslaught more evident than in the kauri districts. Sawn kauri production peaked early in the twentieth century, at approximately 120 million superficial feet a year, when even the most optimistic contemporary estimates indicated that barely 1112 million feet remained standing, on Crown, Māori, and private lands (Figure 7.5). A forest once among 'the grandest sights to be found in the

Figure 7.4 Bullock team and timber workers alongside a kauri tree, 1897, probably in the Whangarei District. Mrs B. Jones Collection, Alexander Turnbull Library, National Library of New Zealand, Te Puna Matauranga o Aotearoa.

entire range of the vegetable kingdom' had been reduced to the point that trained foresters anticipated its likely extinction. All recognised that the kauri timber used in building 'prosperous provincial cities' (in Australia as well as New Zealand) represented an 'almost fabulous sum of money', but the bonanza had run its course. Despite technological improvements that gave loggers access to formerly uneconomic trees, the annual kauri harvest fell during the 1920s to a tenth of its peak level; thirty years later, output was less than a million feet.[13]

This landscape suffered a double indignity, being further ravaged by a small army of prospectors in search of the gum exuded by kauri trees. From the 1850s through the 1920s and beyond, 'gumdiggers' collected resin from living trees, removing it from cracks in their bark or 'bleeding' them with purposeful incisions. Most, however, simply fossicked for fallen lumps of dried gum deposited on and in the forest floor over thousands of years. Armed with makeshift tools, they searched the swamps and hills north of Auckland for the substance, which was used in making varnish and linoleum. In peak years around the turn of the century, their efforts yielded over 10,000 tons of gum for export. They left behind extensive areas pocked with excavations and tailings, the surface comprising only bare clay of no value for agriculture.

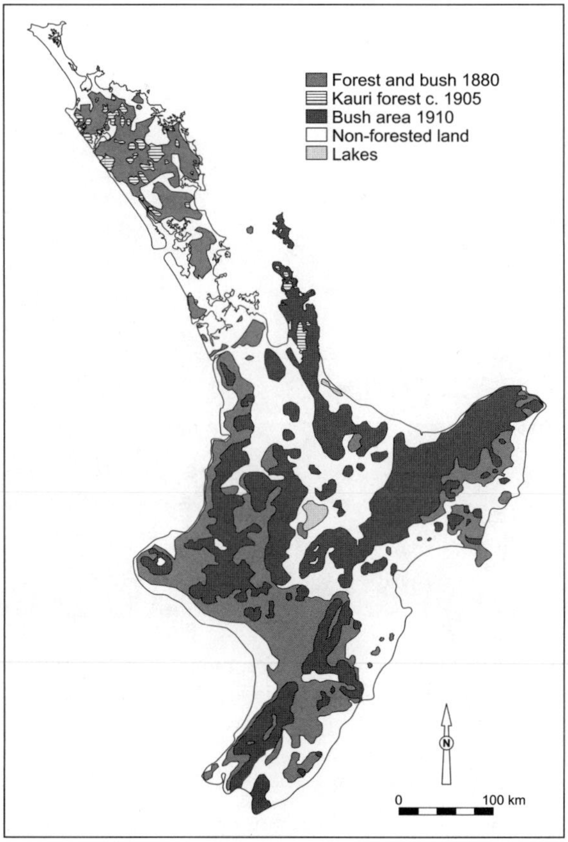

Figure 7.5 The North Island forest, c. 1905. Adapted from *New Zealand Historical Atlas*, plates 47 and 48.

Farmers had their due elsewhere. For forty years or so after 1870, settlers pressed into the bush districts of Taranaki, Manawatu, Hawke's Bay, and, later, the King Country. Each farm created from the bush was a triumph of hard work and resilience in daunting circumstances. Hemmed in by forest, living in a rough hut made of wood slabs or tree ferns, those who pioneered these areas endured a 'Crusoe-like existence'. Their survival rested upon the physically demanding, often dangerous work of bush-felling, as well as upon a thorough late-summer burning of the dried debris.

The surveyor and scholar (and later bureaucrat) Edward Tregear, who watched the process unfold in Taranaki, captured its wider essence. There, he wrote,

> the first settlers ... emulated each other in a struggle of dire economy and stubborn endurance, getting enough perhaps from the grass seed sown on the rich ashes of their first burn to keep life and soul together against another winter of reeking moisture and mud ... The women worked side-by-side with the men from dawn to dark in the work of 'logging

Figure 7.6 The Ostler farm, showing land clearance, probably in Taranaki, early twentieth century. James McAllister Collection, Alexander Turnbull Library, National Library of New Zealand, Te Puna Matauranga o Aotearoa.

> up' the charred and smutty timber and hewing out the massy stumps. Little by little, year by year, their reward became visible; a cow was bought, poultry increased, a better roof was over their heads; schoolhouses began to be built near improved roads ...[14]

These fruits of 'heroic self denial ... [and] patient courage' transformed the interior of the North Island. By 1900 the Seventy Mile Bush, 300,000 acres of forest so intractable that Scandinavian axemen were recruited to lead the charge against it, was no more. Across the drainage divide, sheep and dairy farms covered the Rangitikei–Manawatu area, once among 'the best-timbered districts in the colony' (Figure 7.5). In Waipawa County sown grassland covered an eighth of the land area in 1878; thirty years later it accounted for almost two-thirds. In Manawatu County the proportions rose from less than 5 to more than 50 per cent over the same period. By one account, 1,684,231 acres of land leased or sold by the Crown was cleared between 1895 and 1914. Approximately 60 per cent of this lay in the Wellington and Hawke's Bay districts.[15]

None of this would have been possible without the settler's most essential—and ferocious—tool, the firestick. Burning was the only practicable method of opening up bushland to cultivation. Each new farm was edged by 'blackened prostrate logs', emblems of the 'ever-widening circle' that settlers strove, relentlessly, to expand in the 'seemingly impervious bush' (Figure 7.6). Travelling through the North Island by train in the 1880s, James Inglis noted that clouds of smoke darkened the sun and that the 'deepening gloom' of the evening was broken 'at fitful intervals by the lurid glare of … forest fires'. In the Manawatu, he wrote in *Our New Zealand Cousins*, 'Burning is going on all around. The air is dense with smoke. Our clothes get white with falling ashes, and our eyes smart with the pungent reek.'[16]

But fire is notoriously difficult to control. A rising wind, a shift in the breeze, and away it might go. Sparks from the fireboxes of trains and traction engines, smouldering cigarette butts, scrub fires set by gumdiggers—often disparaged as 'fire raisers in chief'—could also set extensive tracts of forest ablaze. In dry years, with kindling in abundance wherever loggers had worked, 'terrible bush fires … raged throughout the country'. The summer of 1885–86 was especially bad. After months with lower than normal rainfall, it seemed that there was 'scarcely a newspaper in the North Island', that did not 'narrate tales of disaster and peril by reason of the spread of fire'. Losses—of property, of stock, and of prospects—were valued at tens of thousands of pounds by contemporaries.

The magnitude of the impact can only be hinted at by noting occasional references: in forest-scarce Canterbury, the loss of five sawmills and a 'great block of standing bush' at Waimate to fire in the 1870s; in the Puhipuhi kauri forest, almost 12,000 acres (and 130 million feet of timber) burned in the 1880s; at the turn of the century, forester George Perrin's estimate that 'fire has been responsible for more injury to the timber reserves than the sawmillers and all other causes combined'. Perhaps James Inglis made the point as effectively as anyone when he wrote, 'Of the poor forest, if it were sentient, one might say, "The smoke of its torment goeth up for ever" '.[17]

Disquiet

Was this a bad thing? Inglis, a widely travelled, well-educated man, with a dozen years' experience developing and operating an indigo plantation in India, was by no means certain. Although revolted at what he regarded as the destruction of New Zealand's natural endowment, he recognised that 'circumstances alter cases'. Perhaps the profligate haste with which the country was being developed was 'really the cheapest and the best' course. But this was not a question that exercised many nineteenth-century New Zealanders. Caught up in the immediacy of getting on, they saw little reason to equivocate about the future they believed they were bringing into being. The bush was abundant. A yeoman empire was the goal. Reduction of the former was necessary to realise the latter. The 'invariable rule in a new country', observed a prominent member of the New Zealand Parliament in the 1860s, 'was the lavish use of native forest'. The principle seemed self-evident. But Inglis was not alone in his doubts.[18]

Concerned about future supplies of timber for its navy, the British government grew anxious about the destruction of the kauri forests of northern New Zealand as early as the 1840s. A quarter-century later, the sight of Canterbury's Port Hills 'covered, for weeks together, with thick and lurid smoke', led Thomas Potts, an amateur botanist resident on Banks Peninsula, to lament the 'barbarous improvidence' of contemporary attitudes towards the forest. He and a handful of other educated and influential individuals also pointed to the ways in which deforestation worked to disturb the 'equilibrium' arrived at by nature. Removal of the forest was seen to be 'a primary cause of excessive inundations'. Desiccation, too, could result from the 'destructive processes' unleashed in 'attempts to bring new countries under the domain of ... [human] wants'. In the minds of this minority, New Zealanders had a 'duty to preserve' as well as to develop their islands.

A few years later, economic terms were added to the equation of unease. The assault on the forest had proceeded at such pace that some areas were short of wood; in a few more years the progress of the colony might be restricted by a want of timber. Depleting the resource without thought for the future was as foolish a strategy as the decision to consume all of his limited quantity of food in a few weeks would be for a man marooned on an uninhabited island knowing that months must pass before he could replenish his supplies.[19]

Debate about the depletion of New Zealand's forests continued to the end of the century. Still the balance between waste and improvement remained hard to find. Opening a major conference for leading members of the timber industry, convened by the government in 1896, Prime Minister Seddon noted that the timber lands of the colony were 'getting smaller day by day', and lamented that little benefit had fallen to the country or its people from their exploitation. Settlers were encouraged to colonise the backblocks, but by burning bush they destroyed millions of feet of timber 'more valuable than the land' eventually fenced and sown. When interrupted with the question 'Why put them [settlers] there at all?' Seddon was quick to respond, 'If we did not encourage settlers, there would be no sawmills, and there would be very few of you here today'.[20]

The argument was not simply, as forester George Perrin alleged, over 'the destruction annually of thousands of pounds worth of timber—all for the sake of a few sheep'. People, farms, domestic markets—these remained vital to the development of the country and the prosperity of its industries. 'In every new country,' reflected an essayist, 'the first business is to clear the forest, and open up the best land for farming and settlement.' Yet clearing should not go 'too far', because that would make wood scarce, increase its price, and harm the economy.[21]

After almost seventy-five years of sporadic engagement with the issues it framed, this delicate question was resolved into an allocation problem by the Royal Commission on Forestry in 1913. According to the commissioners' recommendations, good land should be settled. This was a fundamental principle. Inaccessible areas, or those with little agricultural potential, should remain forested for watershed protection, scenic benefit, or timber supply. And, given the slow growth rates of New Zealand's indigenous trees, once-forested areas with limited agricultural capability might be afforested with introduced species to meet future timber needs.[22]

Restraint

This resolution was a long time coming. But if the doctrine of 'improvement' defined the fate of the bush for most of eight decades after 1840, it did not do so unchallenged. From the beginnings of European settlement, colonial officials and some settlers sought to regulate and restrain use of the forest. Their efforts were more often intended to control and direct rather than prevent exploitation, and even at that they were more often flawed than effective. But they were not insignificant. They defined an alternative, and sometimes tempered the ethos of exploitation. In their ineffectiveness they revealed much about prevailing attitudes to both the forest and regulation.

Early steps towards forest management in New Zealand came in 1849, with the introduction of licences permitting the cutting of timber on Crown land. Adapted and extended by some provincial governments after 1852, these provisions also saw the establishment of forest reserves, intended to secure timber supplies for the future, in Canterbury and Otago. But inadequate surveillance of reserves and licence-holders allowed 'great waste and destruction' of the bush to continue unabated. Where demand was high and authority weak, it was nigh impossible to deflect sawyers and settlers from exploitation of the forest by fiat alone.[23]

In 1874 the New Zealand Forests Act, introduced by Prime Minister Julius Vogel, allowed for the creation of state forests and gave Parliament authority to regulate access to these, punish trespasses against them, and protect them from fire. Although many of the provisions of this Act were emasculated two years later, the appointment, under its authority, of Inches Campbell Walker as the country's first Conservator of State Forests was important. He introduced cogent arguments against 'mining' the resource, and for the gradual rather than wholesale opening of the public domain for settlement and timber supply.

He also asserted the need for forest reserves on upland slopes beyond the reach of wise settlement. By 1881 half a million acres had been set aside under the 1877 Land Act for the 'growth and preservation of timber' or 'climatic forest conservancy', Little effort, however, was given to managing these or other Crown forest lands. In 1885 the editors of the *New Zealand Times* claimed that regulations governing Crown forests had 'been ill-observed' and that there had been very great 'waste of trees by reckless and extravagant chopping and by fires'. Nonetheless, the creation of reserves was a step back from 'unbridled rapine'.[24]

Further movement in this direction came in 1886, under the provisions of the State Forests Act, passed the year before. The newly appointed Chief Conservator of Forests, Thomas Kirk, insisted that the boundaries of state forests be marked before adjoining land was sold, and imposed penalties for the destruction or damage of the forests by fire, felling, or grazing. New mountain reserves were established to protect rivers, streams, and climate, and several new regulations were imposed on loggers and sawmillers. In the face of widespread sentiment that the wealth of New Zealand nature was for the settlers' benefit, the impact of such measures depended on local officials and the conditions in which they worked.

Kirk was often exasperated by the reports he received. Of one forest ranger charged with responsibility for the kauri district, it was said that 'he resided in Auckland and had only paid two or at most three visits to the Puhi Puhi Forest, although he had spent many days in the Whangerei hotels'. In mid-winter Southland, 'everlastingly overhung' with cloud, physical circumstances made the work of even the most dedicated ranger difficult. Every step in the often 'scrubby tangled broken' bush seemed to bring down 'a drenching shower'. Sleeping on bare boards, or in a bed and clothes that were rarely dry, Thomas Hickson captured the harshness of this life when he wrote, 'One would require the constitution, hide and coat of a seal or polar bear to stand it.'[25]

In 1887, with another change of government, Thomas Kirk's role was terminated and the State Forests Department, which he had set up, was abolished. Most of the rangers were discharged. In the 1890s (through to 1919) large areas of land were withdrawn from state forests to promote settlement. In 1897 alone, over 20,000 acres of bush was cleared from former state forest land. However, some influential people still clung to the principles Campbell Walker had introduced in the 1870s. Thus attempts to open bush in Southland to settlement brought a reminder that 'the preservation of a reasonable share of the forest lands of the colony was a matter of great importance'. In the Lands Department, where settlement was always a priority, officials acknowledged the importance of forest cover for watershed protection, and some grew concerned about the ecological consequences of turning marginal land into farms.[26]

Early in the twentieth century, as timber production climbed towards a peak of 432 million superficial feet in 1907, growing anxiety about future timber supplies also tempered spendthrift attitudes towards the forest. There was no reliable inventory of the resource—of one estimate, made in 1909, it was said 'no-one can say whether the amount is too much or too little'. But the notion of an impending timber famine was powerfully underwritten by the sharp fall in estimates of how long timber supplies would last, from seventy years in 1905 to thirty years in 1913. Coupled with a growing sense that the battle to settle the land had been won, and rising interest in the conservation of New Zealand's indigenous flora and fauna, this was enough to initiate an important shift in the terms on which New Zealanders treated the bush. In this respect the Surveyor General's turn-of-the-century recommendations that forests be conserved to maintain water supplies and climatic equilibrium, to prevent degradation of the high country and deposition in the lowlands, and to protect flora, fauna, and natural beauty, were a prescient blend of the utilitarian and aesthetic concerns that would shape the future.[27]

Reflection

Speaking in the parliamentary debate on the Forests Bill of 1874, Mr Hunter of Wellington City questioned the very foundations of Julius Vogel's arguments in support of the proposed legislation. Vogel, known as an impassioned advocate of economic expansion who considered colonisation the 'heroic' work of New Zealanders, had come to his understanding of the forest question by combining local knowledge with book learning. A journey through the South Island alerted him to the rapidity with which domestic demands were reducing forests and altering the landscape. From American and European literature dealing with human impacts on nature he gained broader insight into the environmental consequences of forest destruction.

Vogel imagined a future blighted by climatic changes induced by deforestation—by the drying-up of streams, the erosion of soils, the desertification that had overtaken once-forested North Africa and Asia Minor. It was time, he insisted, to curb the heedless and irresponsible destruction of New Zealand's forests. But Hunter would have none of this. In his view, the Prime Minister's examples from Mediterranean Europe and the United States were irrelevant. They were 'a mere history of the past' of little consequence to people 'in a young country and in a new land'.[28]

There were other arguments against the Bill, but Hunter's intervention went to the heart of the matter. Few of those who opposed the Bill were prepared to accept the collective, ecological, and long-term viewpoints upon which it rested. The forest question, said Vogel, was 'something for New Zealand to cling to for generations', it was about preserving the 'intrinsic value' of the country. Most who spoke against the Bill expressed immediate concerns and specific anxieties. Individualism, self-interest, and material progress were the bedrocks of their understanding. They preferred 'the gospel of trade' to official regulation; they railed against the government's 'desire to become paternal' and argued that settlers should be 'left alone' to conduct their lives.

Knowledge derived from everyday local experience—common sense—was valued above expert opinion from overseas. Formal efforts to conserve forests before real shortages emerged were alarmist, and probably completely unnecessary: 'Nature', after all, had been an effective 'conserver of forests ages before the science of forestry was known'. Nelson was a 'sleepy hollow' compared with those 'hives of industry' Christchurch and Dunedin, precisely because it stood amid 'almost interminable forest', while the other cities were surrounded by 'grass-covered plains'; clear the forest, make waste lands fit for settlement, and Nelson, too, would enjoy prosperity. All the people of his province wanted, said Mr Bunny of Wellington, was to 'disforest' their land, foster development, and produce a large profit.

These arguments echoed the central principles of mid-nineteenth-century liberalism—*laissez-faire*, localism, economy, and progress—but they owed at least as much to colonial circumstances as they did to the intellectual climate of Victorian Britain. New Zealand *was* a 'young country'. Having abandoned the places of their pasts in anticipation of better futures, its Pākehā settlers faced the daunting task of establishing homes in a new territory. Social capital, in the form of houses, barns, fences, roads, bridges, farms, and cities, had to be developed, and exploitation of the colony's natural capital offered the most direct means to this end. From this perspective, the onslaught on New Zealand forests after 1840 was a constructive rather than a destructive process, yielding valuable export revenues, providing essential commodities, and bringing 'unproductive' bush into 'higher use'.

Only slowly were most of those caught up in the work of colonisation able to look differently at the world they were making, to consider the wider consequences of their actions upon the environment and future generations. In this context, expressions of disquiet at, and efforts to restrain, the onslaught on the forest were more remarkable than the assault on the bush itself. But they, too, are attributable to the particular circumstances of colonisation. Such developments owed much to the timing of European settlement in New Zealand and the composition of the colony's migrant stream. Without the insights derived from the hillsides of Vermont and the fringes of the Mediterranean by George Perkins Marsh, without the voyage of the *Beagle* and all that Darwin meant to understanding of the natural world after 1859, without the experience of European-trained foresters and the work of the Forest Conservancy in India, and without the presence in New Zealand of a group of settlers spared, by their wealth, from the general struggle to gain a sufficiency from the land, the assault on the bush might have been more unfettered and protracted than it was.[29]

Conclusion

New Zealanders, said Captain Campbell Walker, with reference to the prospects for New Zealand's forests in 1877, 'can not be wise too soon'. But it would be a mistake to offer a blanket indictment of the attitudes and actions of late-nineteenth-century New Zealanders. Even as they watched, as Sargeson's uncle did in the 1920s, the creeks through their new-cleared land rising quickly after rain and running discoloured where once they had been clear, as they saw landslides scar once-forested slopes and pondered the invasion of briefly lush pastures by biddy-bid and bracken, there were reasons, in the sheep, taut fencelines, orchards, and dwellings that had replaced the bush, to take pride from the transformation of the landscape. Setbacks, such as declining soil fertility, could be addressed, it seemed, by clearing more land or, later, by using chemical fertilisers.[30]

The ambivalence James Inglis felt about the course of New Zealand development was, however, not unwarranted. Consider the heartfelt cry offered by Herbert Guthrie-Smith near the end of his remarkable life as a Hawke's Bay runholder, natural historian, and author. No one in New Zealand between 1880 and 1940 had a closer knowledge of or love for the land. Yet for years he had followed the common 'stream of tendency' in his development of Tutira station, valuing it for its 'ability to grow meat and wool' and failing, he said, to afford his acres the respect that the long view demanded. In search of pastoral perfection, the hills had been remade, and left largely 'bare of trees, of woodland, of sedge'. He harboured some misgivings about this along the way, but not until 1939, looking back on a lifetime's work, did he come to ask, 'Have I for sixty years desecrated God's earth and dubbed it improvement?'[31]

Part 3

Special Environments

8

Children of the Burnt Bush

New Zealanders and the Indigenous Remnant, 1880–1930

Paul Star and Lynne Lochhead

Naked, denuded,
Forestless, fernless,
Mute, now, and songless,
Sharp on sheer sky gape the lips of the gully;
Burden'd with black is the grass of its pasture;
On whose long slopes
The sheep in their browsing
Must leap o'er a million,
Strewn, helter-skelter, headlong and helpless
Burnt bones of the Bush …[1]

The scene described by Blanche Baughan was familiar to New Zealanders at the dawning of the twentieth century. They lived as people still very much engaged in the rapid transformation of the environment. Baughan was one of a growing number in that generation who questioned the direction of settler society, who challenged the assumptions on which the rate and extent of the transformation were based, and who considered it vital to preserve an indigenous remnant.

The forest area of New Zealand, in 1886 still 22 million acres or about a third of the total land surface, had been reduced to 17 million by 1909 (Figure 7.5). Correspondingly, the total area 'under occupation' increased from 35 million acres in 1901 to 40 million in 1910. This reflected the Liberal government's settlement policy and its accelerated purchase of remaining Māori bushland after 1892.[2] But, at the same time, efforts were made to reserve some of the pre-European natural heritage. By 1909, over 2 million acres had been set aside under the State Forests Act of 1885, but timber on this land was intended for eventual milling. More significantly, the Land Act 1892 was the first to cater for scenic reservation, and by 1907 nearly 3 million acres had some such classification, much of it as national park (Figure 8.1). Our purpose in this chapter is to describe and analyse the movement to protect a part of the native environment during the decades of its greatest destruction.

The rapidity of change has led to the assumption that the settlers feared and hated the bush, but the reality was rather more complex.[3] The grandeur and luxuriance of the forest were widely appreciated, and though it was often described as 'gloomy', this needs to be understood within the context of nineteenth-century canons of taste. Whereas it may suggest negativity to us, any literate Victorian would recognise this as a conventional expression of the sublimity of nature.[4] But actual experience of travel on foot was apt to change appreciation into a feeling that the forest was interminable, and experience of the difficulties in removing it could lead to a negative assessment.

Victorians were as ready as we are to suppress aesthetic feelings in the name of utility. They were helped by a belief that the progress of civilisation depended on their efforts to 'subdue and replenish' nature. Whether or not they appreciated its beauty, the

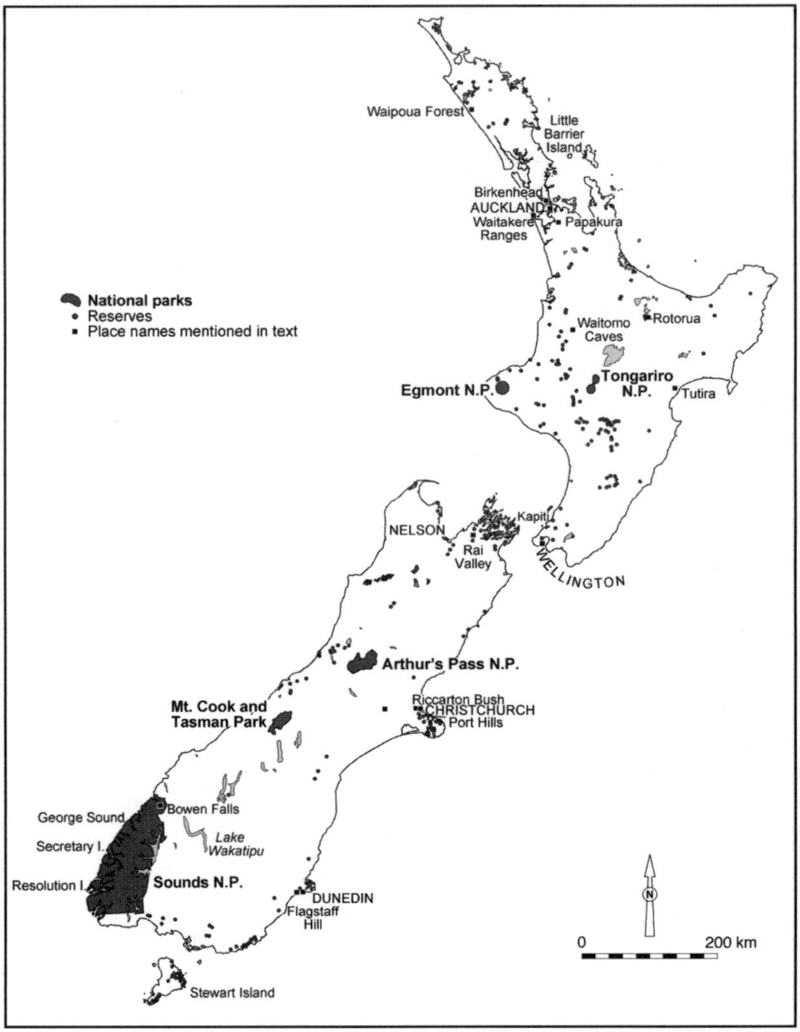

Figure 8.1 Protected areas, 1906–07, showing national parks and scenic reserves and places mentioned in Chapter 8. Source: *AJHR*, C6, 1907.

majority felt morally bound to turn uncultivated nature ('wilderness', 'barren' or 'waste' land) to domesticated, civilised use.[5] Any regret felt for the passing of indigenous flora and fauna diminished with the conviction that they merely hastened a natural process. Until the 1880s the inevitable displacement of weak southern hemisphere species by more vigorous northern hemisphere species that had evolved with greater competition was perceived as a universal law by most scientists and laymen alike.

Economic motives for conservation

Given this frame of mind, it is not surprising that the earliest conservation measures were utilitarian in motive. Government designed the Forests Act 1874 and its successors to ensure future supply in the interests of long-term development of the colony, prompted by growing recognition that timber was a limited resource. The legislation also reflected anxiety that loss of forests contributed to droughts and increased downstream flooding, both of which imposed economic costs on settlement.

There was concern, too, about the depletion of marine resources. In 1870 the Otago Institute investigated coastal whaling stations and the resulting slaughter of young whales. A closed season was introduced for oysters (1866) and seals (1872), and the Fish Protection Act 1877 allowed for protection of fish through closed seasons and control of the mesh size of nets. Fears that a burgeoning flounder export trade might be 'nipped in the bud' through flouting of the law led to a strengthened Fisheries Conservation Act 1884, with provision for the protection of breeding areas. It also contained a first anti-pollution measure, against the dumping of sawmill waste into streams.[6]

From the 1860s to the 1880s, economic arguments at times carried the day over the protests of many who believed nothing should stand in the way of settlement. But, for a few, concern went beyond the purely utilitarian. In 1874 Premier Julius Vogel contended that forests also affected the 'beauty, healthfulness, and pleasure-bestowing qualities' of the nation and, even more significantly, 'its character and intrinsic value'. Discussion of 'forest influences' signalled some realignment in thinking about the human relationship with nature. Science had been linked to the goal of dominating the environment since the seventeenth century, but just when the rapid advance of technology and the spread of 'civilised and civilising' Europeans throughout the globe seemed to bring that dream close to fulfilment, some scientists began to sound warnings. An American, George Perkins Marsh, wrote of limits to the control that could be exercised over nature. No one yet spoke of sustainability, but the recognition of limits was an essential step towards acceptance of this concept.[7]

Island reserves and native bird protection

The need for preservation remained a minority viewpoint throughout the nineteenth century, but the pace quickened in its final decade. The year 1891 proved a landmark for fauna preservation, with the establishment of Resolution Island in Fiordland as a sanctuary in response to a recommendation from the Australasian Association for the Advancement of Science. Others followed—Secretary Island (1893), Little Barrier Island (1894–97), and Kapiti (1897). The specific idea of *island* reserves was probably a 'world first' for New Zealand, a nation of islands. An appreciation of the frequent incompatibility of indigenous fauna and European settlement had led T. H. Potts, a Canterbury runholder and keen ornithologist, to suggest in 1872 that Resolution Island 'might be placed under tapu from molestation of dog and gun' as a refuge for 'wingless species'. The Auckland-based botanist Thomas Kirk envisaged a similar future for Little Barrier Island.[8] (see Figure 8.1 for locations).

Implementation of this idea seemed increasingly urgent after 1884 when, in a misguided attempt to reduce the vast population of rabbits, which ravaged pasture intended for sheep, the government introduced stoats and weasels. While these creatures were the 'natural enemy' of rabbits in England, in New Zealand the flightless birds made easier prey. Native bird populations decreased rapidly at the same time as interest in them increased, and stoats became the scapegoats for a decline that probably resulted more from destruction of habitat.

In Europe, zoological gardens and private collectors paid good money for unusual antipodean specimens. Lord Rothschild of Tring amassed nearly two hundred kiwi skins and skeletons. As its scientific name (*Apteryx*, or 'no-wing') indicated, the bird challenged European taxonomists as profoundly as had Australia's duck-billed platypus. International fascination with such evolutionary oddities as the kiwi, the takahe, and the lizard-like tuatara helped the government to appreciate that, in these species, New Zealand had something worthy of protection. Reserving one or two island refuges where at-risk species might be spared from extinction was quite easily done. It proved much harder to gain government support for action on the mainland, where protection of stoats and weasels, even in areas without rabbits, remained until 1903.

The declining numbers of many species of native birds proved unquantifiable, but it was a fact no one doubted. It went with the removal of native vegetation and the introduction of exotic species of flora and fauna, and was recorded in broad outline by many early settlers.[9] While the best accounts of the process of ecological transformation did not appear until the 1920s, these were written by two men—Herbert Guthrie-Smith and G. M. Thomson[10]—who had themselves participated in the revolution for half a century and had published earlier, less extensive commentaries. First efforts to protect native birds therefore occurred against a background of quite widespread awareness of cause and effect.

But these early measures were half-hearted at best, occurring on an ad hoc basis under the Animals Protection Acts. Based on British game laws, they were primarily concerned with protecting acclimatised species. An 1864 provision for a closed season for native ducks and pigeons—species that settlers recognised as worth shooting for sport—was clearly utilitarian. The list of game species expanded over the years, including kākā and morepork in 1887, but since the law was not strictly enforced it afforded little protection.

Protection of tūī proceeded from a different motive. Canterbury's Superintendent William Rolleston advocated legislation to counter the destruction of native birds 'characteristic of the country'. He observed that one saw 'bundles of tuis hanging up for sale in shops and heard of people dining off kiwis', which he considered 'gross abuse of the present privilege to kill'.[11] Sale of tūī was prohibited in 1872, but kiwi, which would become a synonym for New Zealanders from around 1916, were not protected. An 1873 amendment added tūī to the schedule of native game, effectively giving them permanent protection, as an open season was never declared. Crested grebe and white heron were similarly treated from 1888, huia in 1892, tuatara in 1895, and finally kiwi, kōkako, kākāpō, saddleback, stitchbird, and bellbird, in 1897.

While this gradual addition of native species was in part a colonial response to Britain's Wild Bird Protection Bill 1872 and its subsequent legislation, there was a growing locally inspired feeling for native and especially endemic species. According to the Minister of Internal Affairs, by the 1900s 'most of our older settlers [had] practically disassociated themselves from the bird-life of the older countries'. The occasional one even acknowledged that 'we are sadly inferior to the old Native chiefs in this matter', describing rāhui (Māori protection orders), which prevented unseasonal slaughter of tūī, kiwi and muttonbirds. The Christchurch politician Harry Ell sensed within Parliament in 1900 a 'unanimity of opinion that every effort should be made to save our native birds from destruction', but only during debate in 1910 does this appear a genuine concern for most MPs. The result was a significant amendment to legislation that, rather than listing favoured species, protected them *all* unless, like the predatory harrier and kea, they were specifically exempted.[12] Comparable recognition of the special value of native plants—simply by the fact of indigenousness—did not follow until the Native Plants Protection Act of 1934. Despite gradual legislative improvement, protection of native fauna remained haphazard until the formation of the Wildlife Service in 1945.

Early scenery preservation and tourism

In 1874 ex-Premier William Fox introduced the national park idea to New Zealand in a letter urging public acquisition of the Rotorua thermal region to ensure its controlled development for the public benefit. He cited as a precedent the recent protection of Yellowstone's volcanic wonders within a public park. But the resulting Thermal-Springs Districts Act 1881 did not emulate the Yellowstone model. Rather, it was designed to promote settlement to take advantage of the revenue-producing potential of sanatoria. However, with the example of Yellowstone in mind, the 1885 Land Act made provision for designating mineral springs and 'natural curiosities' as reserves. This was amended in 1892 specifically to include scenery, but the provision was seldom used before 1900. Nevertheless, there was a growing realisation that New Zealand's finest scenery could attract tourists and that by failing to protect it, one risked killing the goose that would lay the golden egg.

The Union Steam Ship Company began cruises to Fiordland in 1877, though the area did not gain protection until 1905. Following a private initiative that established the Hermitage in response to growing international interest in mountaineering, the Department of Lands designated Hooker Valley near Mount Cook a recreation reserve in 1885.

The Tasman Valley was added in 1887. That same year the government also finally turned to the national park idea after Te Heuheu Tukino IV, the leader of Ngāti Tūwharetoa, gifted the three volcanic peaks of the central North Island to the nation.[13] The Tongariro National Park Act 1894 formally constituted New Zealand's first national park. General acceptance of the park owed much to the fact that the land was 'almost useless as far as grazing was concerned', and that as a tourist attraction it was likely to be 'worth ten times more to the country than if it was agricultural or pastoral land'.[14] In contrast, a debate on scenery preservation in 1891, prompted by Clutha Member of the House of Representatives Thomas Mackenzie's call to improve tourist access, revealed a widely held view that roads should not be opened solely for tourism at the expense of the needs of settlers. For many in the community, tourism was only acceptable provided it did not hinder the dominant goal of settlement. Despite this perception, the government remained committed to tourism, as signalled by the creation of the Department of Tourist and Health Resorts in 1901. The department's annual reports regularly stressed the importance of protecting scenery.

The growing support for scenery preservation throughout the 1890s was also manifested in the formation of scenery preservation societies. The Dunedin and Suburban Reserves Conservation Society was established in 1888 to improve and preserve the natural attractions of that city. Other societies followed between 1891 and 1899 in Taranaki, Nelson, Wellington, Christchurch, Auckland, and Birkenhead. Most chose to use the name Scenery Preservation Society, and, though independent, they felt they were part of a nationwide movement. They were not slow to recognise the tourist potential of scenery. The Taranaki society published a guide to Mount Egmont in 1892, setting out routes and accommodation and describing the flora and fauna. Participants in these groups felt a genuine love of nature but recognised 'that the faculty of comprehending, reverencing and loving natural beauty grows up slowly and gradually'. Promoting utilitarian benefits offered the best hope of achieving protection until others shared their sense of reverence. Members knew their contemporaries well enough to recognise that they would be regarded as 'fanatics not untouched with lunacy' if they stressed preservation for its own sake.[15]

Participants were mainly middle-class males—lawyers, politicians at national and local level, newspapermen, and businessmen—while the most active members of the groups were typically scientists or men with surveying experience. Historian Ross Galbreath has said in explanation of the movement, which was predominantly urban-based, that distance from the bush lent enchantment to the view, but supporters were conscious that continued indifference on the part of most settlers was the more likely result.[16] They stressed the need to encourage contact with nature. This was one reason behind publication of the guidebook. It also led to an emphasis on protection of accessible areas. Although designation of Egmont National Park (1900), including the valuable lowland forest of the Kaitake Range, and the Otira/Arthur's Pass Reserves (1901), which formed the nucleus of the later Arthur's Pass National Park (1929), were important results of this activity, protection of forest remnants in or near the city, as at Riccarton Bush, Birkenhead, Papakura, and the Waitakere Ranges, or in the town belts of Dunedin and Wellington, was more characteristic (Figure 8.1).

Portrayal of an early conservation movement preoccupied with offshore islands, remote mountains, or 'ferny glades, waterfalls and forest clearings for bush picnics' does not present a rounded view.[17] Certainly, ferny glades and other favoured picnic sites were protected, which was consistent with the goal of encouraging contact with nature. But far from focusing on offshore island reserves, the preservation groups advocated reserves where birds were actually breeding, as with the 1893 campaign by the Taranaki Scenery Preservation Society to protect coastal bush at White Cliffs.

There were boundaries, however, beyond which indigenous protection could not at first extend, as clearly signalled by the attempt to preserve the Ronga and Opouri Valleys, near Rai Valley on the Nelson–Blenheim road. The area was rich in millable forest but also provided a major lowland breeding and feeding ground for species such as pigeon and kākā. Local millers sought revocation of its existing forest reserve status in 1897. The Nelson Scenery Preservation Society responded in 1898 with a counter-petition for a national park of some 20,000 acres, claiming that birds should be preserved in a mainland sanctuary where they were thriving, rather than removed to places where they might perish. In addition, they argued, the area contained some of the densest, grandest, most diversified forest in New Zealand, and had the advantage of low fire risk and ready accessibility. Reversing the usual settler equation of undeveloped land with wilderness, a key supporter of the park claimed that if the valleys were 'subjected to the usual ravages of milling and fire, nothing but a howling wilderness would be the result'.[18]

Never before had conservationists sought to preserve in perpetuity such a large area of demonstrably high-value timber on land suitable for settlement. Its very suitability for those purposes meant that it was an increasingly scarce example of the finest forestland, some of which, supporters argued, should be preserved for posterity. They reasoned that, if future generations were to experience not just the trees but also a forest teeming with life, small blocks would not suffice because they were 'absolutely useless for birds'. Opponents, arguing that a national park would mean 'complete stagnation' for the district, pointed out that other parts were far more picturesque. But having dismissed its scenic value, they had to concede that the 'one unique peculiarity' about the Rai was that 'you can see grand forestry'. In fact, Charles Adams of the Land Board admitted he had 'never seen better forest ... anywhere in New Zealand'.[19] The campaign highlighted a difficulty with the term 'scenery preservation', soon to be enshrined in legislation. In the popular mind it was associated with particular types of scenery and did not sit comfortably with the ecological approach towards which some campaign participants were already feeling their way.

The Waste Lands Committee recommended that the government carefully consider how best to conserve the forests of the Rai, but milling rights were granted in 1906, and in 1914 it was opened for settlement. This conclusively answered the question raised during the conflict, whether 'in this young country, the fringe of which is not yet tilled, land is in such demand that 20,000 acres cannot be spared for a National Park'. They could not if they contained good timber or were suitable for settlement. New Zealand did not prove ready to save a major commercially valuable lowland forest until Waipoua was set aside in 1952 (see Chapter 12).[20]

The significance of the scenery preservation societies went beyond campaigns to reserve land. They sought effective management of reserves at a time when there was scarcely any political awareness of the need. They drew attention to damage caused by vandalism, browsing animals, weed invasion, and fire. The Taranaki society undertook fencing of reserves, and a campaign launched by it in 1898 resulted in the Noxious Weeds Act 1901. This group also successfully lobbied for a Board of Conservators for Egmont Reserve. Appointed in 1892, it set a precedent for Tongariro and later national parks, while curators were also appointed for the island sanctuaries. Approval was given for the first of these, Richard Henry of Resolution Island, in 1893, but for the majority of reserves there was no improvement, and there was no official inspector of scenic reserves before the appointment of E. Phillips Turner in 1907.

Arguably the greatest achievement of the early groups was the Scenery Preservation Act 1903, which in turn provided the groundwork for the current system of parks and reserves. Scenic preservation in the 1890s had been the responsibility of the Ministry of Lands and could only apply to Crown land. The new Act paved the way for compulsory purchase of private or Māori land if their features were of sufficient note. Between 1904 and 1906 a commission, reporting to the Tourism Department, identified 380 scenic and historic places throughout New Zealand worthy of preservation. The first reserve made under the Act was Waitomo Caves, on Māori land, and Flagstaff Hill behind Dunedin was repossessed from its European owners soon after, but most reserves

Figure 8.2 Kennedys Bush, c. 1920. Reproduced with permission of the Aotearoa New Zealand Centre, Christchurch City Libraries. Kennedys Bush was the first of the scenic reserves gazetted (in 1906) in association with Harry Ell's Summit Road.

were on Crown land, involving the government in no additional expense. About 214,000 acres had been preserved under the Act by 1914, in 363 different locations (Figure 8.1). Scenic reserves covered a smaller total area than national parks, but they resulted from a more continuous effort.[21]

Harry Ell, who ardently campaigned for it in Parliament, is usually given credit for the Scenery Preservation Act, but Parliament's willingness to listen resulted from a decade of lobbying on a range of preservation issues by the scenery preservation societies. Paradoxically, the Act then seems to have contributed to their demise. Having achieved government action, some societies lapsed, others turned increasingly to the provision of amenities, while in Christchurch the nature protection role was taken over by Ell's Summit Road Association, formed in 1909 to promote his far-sighted schemes for the Port Hills.[22] (Figure 8.2). A few groups modelled on these early societies continued to form after 1903, but there was a temporary loss of vigour prior to the emergence of nationally based groups in the second decade of the century.

An eye to the tourist dollar continued to motivate scenery preservation at the official level. Particular emphasis was given to major travel routes such as the Main Trunk line between Auckland and Wellington. Thomas Donne, the Superintendent of Tourism, believed that 'magnificent areas of forest ... preserved in its primeval beauty contiguous to the railway, will afford a great attraction to travellers ... whereas miles of burnt and blackened logs would prove a weariness to the spirit'. As long as there was no interference with settlement, Donne considered it a 'national obligation' to preserve such patches of bush, which would 'not only agreeably adorn the routes of travel, but also serve as a last home for the rarer New Zealand birds'. Consistent with this attitude, the government's Scenery Preservation Board bent over backwards not to alienate settlement interests, stressing that they never withdrew farmland for 'aesthetic purposes'.[23]

A sense of scarcity

Before protection could extend beyond the parameters so vividly shown in the case of the Rai Valley, new factors had to emerge. Undoubtedly, the increasing scarcity of some native bird species and of certain kinds of native forest was a stimulus towards their preservation. In 1907, when the Department of Lands expressed concern that the quantity of millable native timber had fallen from 43,000 million to 36,000 million superficial feet in just two years, one of the most striking facts was that less than 650 million superficial feet of kauri, the most sought-after timber, remained. There was general acceptance that kauri would soon be milled out, and this focused attention on the need to preserve at least one representative sample of original kauri forest. The decline in overall area of bush was harder to appreciate, and for many the impression remained that there was ample left.

Nor did calls for preservation necessarily follow with increasing scarcity. Many argued, rather, that acclimatisation of introduced species, such as insectivorous birds and exotic timbers, was all the more important as native species grew rarer. The 1913 Royal Commission on Forestry (which included botanist Leonard Cockayne) was frequently urged to recommend planting of indigenous trees to help prepare for a forthcoming 'timber famine' (see Chapter 12), but concluded that no native timber, save perhaps beech, would grow or regenerate quickly enough.[24] The solution lay with the continued one-off utilisation of native forest until sufficient exotic timber became available. While a regard for native species was increasing, few of the requirements of settler society seemed likely to be met by them. Basic need favoured the exotic, which did not improve the case for preservation of native forests.

On the other hand, the rejection of a crude displacement theory, which had been used in support of suppression of the pre-European environment, increased respect for the indigenous remnant. Already in the 1880s New Zealand-based botanists and some other colonists, trusting more to their own eyes than to the generalisations of overseas theorists, questioned the notion.[25] By the 1920s, Cockayne had published evidence that native plants could hold their own unless humans (directly or through the grazing of their beasts) continued to modify the environment in favour of exotics. Displacement theory was disproved—which meant that preservation was not, intrinsically, a lost cause—and, in its place, ecology gained credence.

Leonard Cockayne and ecological motives for preservation

Much as, in the 1860s and 1870s, Marsh's *Man and Nature* had crystallised the forest conservation ideas of Potts and Vogel, so the ecological studies of the Dane Eugene Warming provided a focus in the 1890s for the botanical conservation work of Cockayne. His 'oecological' survey of the Chatham Islands (1901) described a vegetation destined for extinction through the combined influence of exotic plants, introduced animals, and fire—all initiated by human action. Cockayne's government-financed surveys of Kapiti, Tongariro, Waipoua and Stewart Island (1907–09) then familiarised him with a series of remarkable environments that appeared capable of protection. He seized this opportunity to develop the arguments for protection of the indigenous remnant, and his persuasive introductions to the resulting botanical reports provided an influential rationale for conservation in New Zealand over the ensuing decades.

Cockayne adduced all the usual arguments for preservation based on tourism and protection of lowland farms from erosion and flooding. His particular insight was to link the distinctiveness of New Zealand's scenery with its flora, an argument expressed most cogently in his recommendations for extensions to Tongariro National Park (eventually achieved in 1922). Progressing beyond the standard argument that Tongariro was a scenic wonder, he reasoned that similar geological features could be found elsewhere.

> ... the special features of any landscape depend upon the combinations of plants which form its garment, otherwise a monotonous uniformity would mark the whole earth. Therefore the more special the vegetation, the more distinctive the scenery. And nowhere does this dictum carry more weight than in New Zealand, where the vegetation is unique ... Nor is it merely the individual species which are interesting, but equally important and of greater moment to the scenery is the manner in which they are associated together.[26]

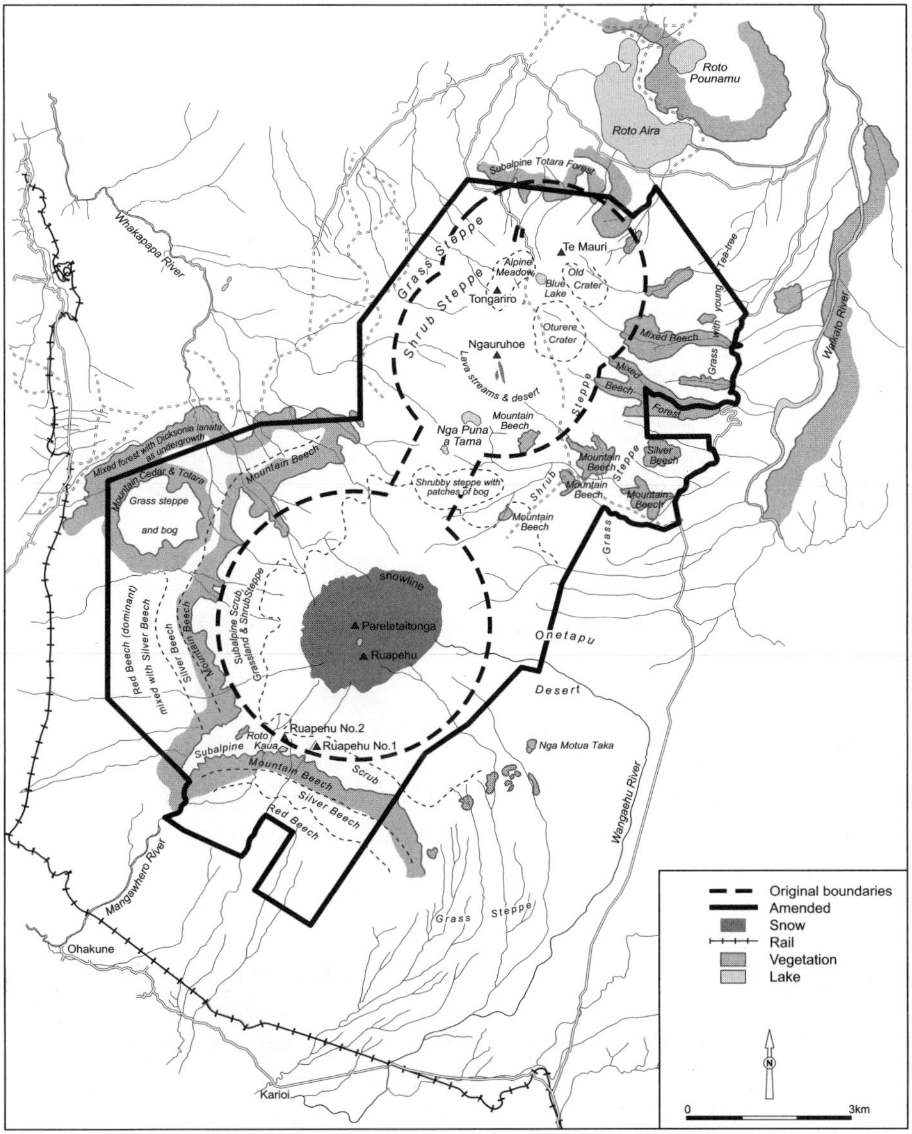

Figure 8.3 Plan of Tongariro National Park, from Leonard Cockayne's report on his botanical survey of the park. Source: *AJHR*, C11, 1908.

Extensions to the park should not be into the forest alone, since 'no area gives an accurate picture of the district ... if it does not contain typical examples of all those combinations of species called scientifically "plant associations"'. Here was a specifically ecological argument for the preservation of the *range* of habitats, one that could be assimilated into the popular and legislative emphasis on scenery. It opened the way for protection of areas that were not conventionally scenic, such as tussock, low shrub, and bog associations of the Volcanic Plateau (Figure 8.3).

The corollary of Cockayne's emphasis on plant associations was stress on the importance of reserves as natural museums. Individual species could be preserved in botanic gardens, but plant communities could not. Once destroyed, they were lost forever. If necessary, conservation should take priority over access, as on Kapiti, which was not for the 'merely curious' and 'no place on which to picnic'. Cockayne believed that Kapiti and the kauri forests of Waipoua were examples of 'actual primitive formations'. Since nothing comparable remained in the Old World, they were 'of extreme botanical interest to foreign scientists'. He further remarked that preservation of forests such as Waipoua, by facilitating the study of ecological succession, not only advanced science but also had a 'distinct economic bearing'.[27]

Cockayne claimed that his recommendations for the extension of Tongariro included 'no land which could finally become of economic value'. He consistently endeavoured to accommodate the needs of settlement as well as preservation, a position that aided his public employment as a botanist and commissioner, and prevented his dismissal as a crank. It also facilitated a gradual acceptance of his ecological approach to conservation. Yet he was surely aware that, at a time when even Campbell Island and the Auckland Islands were leased for grazing, few areas were considered devoid of economic value. When unique remnants such as Riccarton Bush, Waipoua, the subantarctic islands or the environs of Tongariro itself were threatened, Cockayne pushed for preservation ahead of economic gain.

Nature conservation and management after 1914

European botanists held Cockayne in the highest esteem for his work in plant ecology, but his significance to us lies more in his readiness to utilise his science in the cause of preservation. He became a commanding presence in the New Zealand Institute (later the Royal Society), which under his influence (and that of like minds such as G. M. Thomson and Thomas Kirk) became increasingly active in this respect. Cockayne also participated in the popular preservation movement, both through the Christchurch Beautifying Association and the short-lived New Zealand Forest and Bird Protection Society (1914 to about 1918), the first conservation organisation with a national constituency—not to be confused with the still-extant Royal Forest and Bird Protection Society, which began as the Native Bird Protection Society in 1923.

This latter group, together with its companion, the New Zealand Forestry League (1916), marked a new departure. Nationally based, it developed a network of active branches and regional representatives. It also formed working relationships with locally based conservation groups, such as the Nelson Bush and Bird Society founded by Pérrine Moncrieff in 1928, and the tramping clubs that emerged in the 1920s with the growth of outdoor recreation. Building on the work of the earlier groups, Forest and Bird brought a new depth of purpose to the cause.[28]

Administering agencies were exposed to a high degree of scrutiny and public criticism. They could not afford to ignore relentless pressure through the press, direct political lobbying, and the groups' own publications. This ensured that existing laws were adequately implemented and improved. Particular emphasis was placed on the need for active management. With the support of the Royal Society, the groups helped to shape policy on the control of browsing animals and of erosion and flooding. They also influenced the creation of an administrative structure for protection of native flora and fauna.

In 1919 the Forestry League secured the establishment of an independent Forestry Branch, which, initially at least, seemed to offer better hope of protection than Lands or Internal Affairs. But challenging the dominance of agriculture was no easy task, and little came of the movement's proposals for an expert 'demarcation' of remaining forest land into areas best suited for forestry or farming. Conflict increased as the State Forest Service gradually abandoned its initial commitment to sustained-yield management of indigenous forests (see Chapter 12). It was only with the establishment of a Department of Conservation (1987) that the 'unity of control' the groups had long advocated was fully achieved.

Most importantly, the preservation movement continued to shape the definition of parks and reserves, which had begun with no concept of indigenous integrity. Thomas Donne believed that, though New Zealand was extraordinarily beautiful, wealthy tourists would only visit if there were things to shoot as well as to see. Through the Tourist Department he had promoted both scenery preservation and deer acclimatisation, even though attention was already being drawn to the harm that browsing animals caused. In 1904, while supporting a successful move by Thomas Mackenzie to make much of Fiordland a national park, Donne 'enhanced' the area by releasing wapiti at George Sound and white-tailed deer at Lake Wakatipu.

The close link between scenery and preservation had also created ambiguities. For instance, in an 1897 report on the conservation of New Zealand forests, George Perrin, Tasmanian Conservator of State Forests, suggested that mānuka scrub should be replaced with 'more ornamental and useful trees' to render thermal areas attractive.[29] Cockayne's identification of the relationship between vegetation and the uniqueness of scenery helped to alter perceptions. By 1905, for Riccarton Bush, and again in 1907 for Kapiti, he argued that no exotic species, even those that were apparently harmless, had a place in such reserves.

The rapid spread of heather, introduced at Tongariro National Park from 1914, helped to crystallise views on the need to keep reserves 'inviolate'. As a result, by the mid 1920s the Forestry League, the Bird Society, and the Royal Society all adopted the principle that national parks and reserves should be preserved in a natural state. In 1925 the Native Bird Protection Society, influenced by the entomologist J. G. Myers, went further and argued that reserves must also be kept free of indigenous species that had not formerly been present in the area. This lay behind a successful campaign in 1927 to prevent transfer of South Island robins to Kapiti, where it was feared they would have hybridised with the northern species.

Preservation and nationhood

Increasingly, native flora, fauna, and scenery were not merely appreciated, but also fulfilled a psychological need. Native birds, scenic wonders, and mountains first appeared on New

Zealand postage stamps in 1898. Four years later, Harry Ell wanted schools provided with pictures that would make the new generation 'more familiar with our beautiful flowers, and the more interesting specimens of the New Zealand native birds, instead of having only as an object lesson the cards of English birds'. Indigenous nature became linked to both individual and national identity.[30]

Scientists supportive of conservation tapped into a gathering sense of nationhood. Dunedin scientist G. M. Thomson, in 1901, regretted that in towns 'the native flora had been more or less displaced by introduced species, so that there was nothing in the vegetation to tell a visitor he was in New Zealand'. To counteract this trend, he suggested plantings by the Natives' Association, which comprised a growing number of New Zealand-born Europeans who felt pride in the country of their birth. The following year Cockayne called for 'a national garden in the centre of the colony' (Wellington) to protect native plants. Such remarks fell short of any direct statement linking native flora with national identity, but they demonstrate the interplay of developing ideas. Protection of scenery, flora, and fauna was justified on the grounds of their New Zealandness, while, in parallel, landscape and biota helped to define the values a New Zealander would hold.[31]

By the early 1920s the link with national identity was being made explicit. In 1924 J. G. Myers associated exotic-free reserves with patriotism. He argued against the 'abominable practice' of introducing foreign species, considering it a 'sin against posterity' to allow them in parks and reserves. He was scathing of those in authority 'whose patriotism, scorning those natural glories which embody the very spirit of our country, rises no higher than a desire to create in New Zealand a paltry replica of other lands'. In 1925 James Cowan, opposing proposals to generate power and manufacture fertiliser at Bowen Falls in Fiordland, argued that 'landscape beauty is bound up with the soul of a country'. National parks should be treasured not so much for tourists as for New Zealanders, since 'they make a definite impress on our spirit of nationhood'. In a slightly different vein, another well-known writer, Johannes Andersen, argued that the sparsity of New Zealand's human history, compared with European countries, was more than compensated for 'by the rich offering from the hands of Mother Nature'.[32]

Both to the natural scientist and the nationalist, the indigenous remnant was greater in value the less it had been subject to external influences. For contemporaries with ethnological interests such as Andersen and Cowan, evidence of the indigenous human impact had tremendous value in the creation of a national identity, but for a botanist such as Cockayne it was an external factor interfering with the pristine environment preceding *any* human occupation. In common with most of his contemporaries, Cockayne underestimated Māori impact on the indigenous environment, but this did not negate his insight that the endemic quality of vegetation (and indeed birds) mattered most. Of all the plants that hold a place in our affections, he believed 'none can ever rank quite as high as those which slowly took their shape on New Zealand soil in the far-distant past'. For naturalists, personal identity was particularly likely to find expression through the indigenous biota; but, increasingly, all Europeans who settled became 'Kiwis'.[33]

Preservation and appropriation

Ross Galbreath, in 1989, analysed the development of a protective attitude towards the indigenous remnant within the wider context of a society engaged in its destruction. He found that 'as British colonists became settled New Zealanders they began to develop a sentimental attachment to native bush scenery and birds, and to elevate images of them into symbols of their new country and their new identity'. More recent studies have supported this analysis, but whereas Galbreath made no suggestion that the process he described was anything other than wholesome, some writers have viewed it as what might be called '*environmental* appropriation'. For historian Paul Hamer, 'the active incorporation of nature into the realm of settlement—to create a national *park*, for example, was to lessen nature's threat and make it seem accessible to settlers'.[34]

In 1995 another young scholar, the Canadian James Muir, described settlement as a process of 'ecological colonialism', the final stage characterised by 'the beginning of a celebration of the new world's environment'. Reservation of Little Barrier Island, an example of the final stage, involved the eviction of Māori —an 'anti-Māori position'. Similarly the Animal Protection Act 1907, by protecting over twenty native bird species, effectively outlawed traditional Māori bird-hunting. Most recently, ecologist Geoff Park has argued that the park and reserve system starts from 'the Western, imperialist principle that people and nature are irreconcilably opposed, and that the victory of one necessarily entailed the vanquishing of the other'. Thus, for him, 'today's conservationists are the obvious descendants of the pioneers' in that both deny the impact or relevance of indigenous people on a land deemed 'original' prior to the advent of the European.[35]

The reservation of Little Barrier Island was important, but the reservation of Resolution Island was equally significant. Here there was *no* conflict with Māori land claims, only an interest in the preservation of native species. Further, the Animals Protection Act 1907, listed for protection some species rarely hunted by Māori, and others, such as the huia, that had already been the subject of rāhui. Arguably, it was as much an extension of Māori concerns as a denial of them. Conflict occurred, but there was also cooperation. In Taranaki, the scenery preservation society worked with Māori to preserve pā sites. And when Te Heuheu gave Tongariro and adjacent peaks to the nation, he was in effect utilising European concepts of sanctity and conservation to ensure that his tribal land remained sacrosanct.

As contemporary newspapers make clear, the New Zealand situation was most similar to, and most influenced by, parallel situations in Australia and North America, where alongside the assertions of nationhood by settler populations, indigenous rights were also being eroded.[36] But a variety of motivations and influences lay behind conservation in this period, including a shift in Western thought *away from* the idea of opposition between people and nature. By 1900 this was strengthening the protection movement not only in colonies and ex-colonies, but also in long-settled European countries, where subjugation of a native race was clearly not a major factor.

Is protection of the indigenous remnant best viewed as part of an evolving process whereby European New Zealanders embraced and dominated a land and its people, or did preservation genuinely challenge the vision held by most of settler society around 1900? Our analysis favours the latter approach. There might have been a degree of cynicism and calculation in the extent to which Parliament and society as a whole yielded to the preservationist lobby, but for many the concern was sincere, at times even noble.

Conclusion

The society that reduced so much of the country's landscape to the 'burnt bush' of Blanche Baughan's poem did so consciously, but, for many individuals, this was accompanied by an increasing sense of sadness. Charles Blomfield thought it impossible to exaggerate 'the exquisite beauty' of the bush that he had known from the 1860s and celebrated in his

Figure 8.4 Charles Blomfield, *The Vaulted Aisles of Nature's Cathedral*, 1921. Oil on canvas, Auckland War Memorial Museum.

paintings. For him, it was 'a crime to destroy so much'.[37] Like Baughan in her poetry, he developed a reverential attitude towards 'the vaulted aisles of Nature's cathedral', powerfully evident in his 1921 painting with that title (Figure 8.4).

Baughan and Blomfield were exceptional individuals whose art gave heightened expression to the stirrings felt by many around 1900. The increasing sense of both response and responsibility towards the indigenous remnant cannot readily be quantified, but that sense was there, and the attempts towards environmental preservation that we have analysed were its clear manifestation.

9

THE MEANINGS OF MOUNTAINS

Eric Pawson

The first set of 'pictorial' New Zealand postage stamps was issued in 1898. There were thirteen stamps in this set, the earliest to depict anything other than one-colour portraits of Queen Victoria. Three featured native birds, and two, thermal terraces at Rotorua. But no fewer than seven displayed mountain scenes. Mount Cook framed the set, being on both the lowest and highest denominations—the halfpenny and the five-shilling stamps. Milford Sound (twice), Lake Wakatipu and Mount Earnslaw, Lake Taupo and Tongariro, and Otira Gorge with an inset of Ruapehu, also appeared.[1]

If Taranaki/Mount Egmont were to be added, this list would be a good illustration of those mountain landscapes then best known, within and beyond New Zealand. That a set of pictorial stamps with a strong alpine theme should be issued at all at the end of the nineteenth century is indicative of early Pākehā pride in such landscapes. Mountains have always been an inescapable part of New Zealand's topography, to Pākehā and Māori alike, in a land where a considerable portion of the surface area lies above 600 metres, with the ranges being visible from many towns (Figure 9.1). The backbone of the South Island is the extensive chain of the Southern Alps, whose highest peak, Aoraki/Mount Cook (3754 metres), is surrounded by permanent icefields and glaciers. If the North Island is less alpine in nature, it is still characterised by rugged hills, and by the volcanic peaks of Tongariro and Egmont National Parks. The ways in which these mountains and ranges assumed social significance is the focus of this chapter. Four themes are examined in turn.

The first outlines the meanings of mountains both to Pākehā and to Māori, and the extent to which the former relied on the knowledge of the latter in their explorations of hill and mountain country. This is followed by discussion of the relationship between the mountains, their discovery and use by tourists, and an emerging sense of Pākehā national identity. Third, the growing popularity of mountain-based sports, such as mountaineering, tramping, and skiing, is traced, between the founding of the first New Zealand Alpine Club (NZAC) in 1891 and the 1950s. The fourth theme explores the relationship between mountains and the creation of national parks over a similar time frame. Whether or not the landscapes of national parks naturalised a particular idea of New Zealand, in the process 'silencing' other environmental meanings, is questioned in the chapter's conclusion.

Cultural meanings

Mountains have not always had an unequivocally positive hold on the European imagination. When John Ruskin wrote *Modern Painters* in the 1860s, he felt obliged to distinguish between 'mountain gloom' and 'mountain glory' as Western responses to alpine regions. He was very much a proponent of the latter, but dread or death had been associated for hundreds of years with mountains in Europe. Anxiety of the unknown, about the apparent wildness of unfamiliar environments, and often about their animal

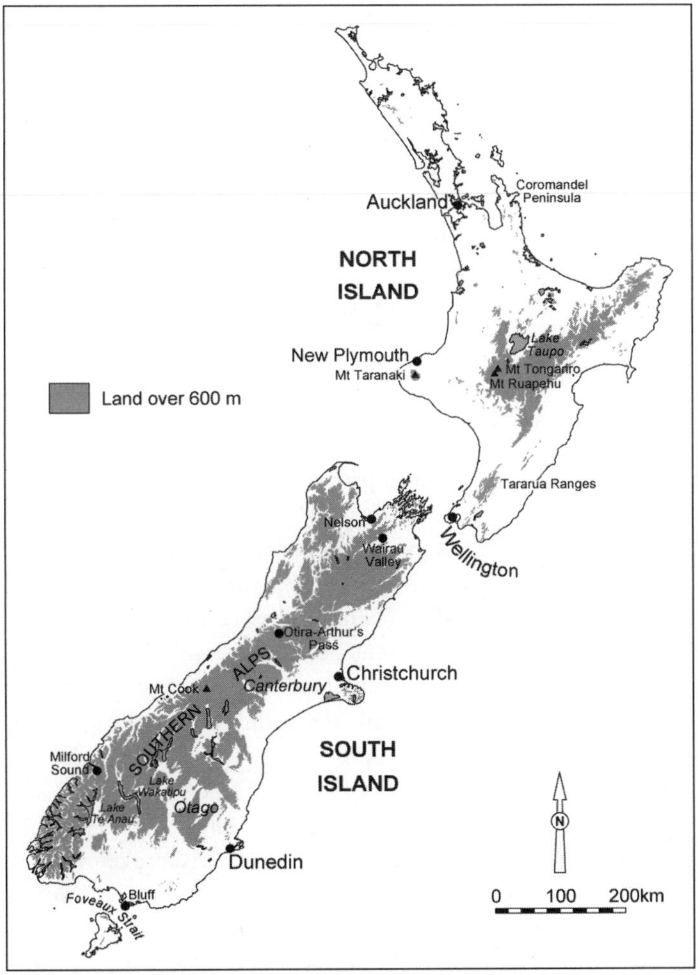

Figure 9.1 The mountain and hill areas of New Zealand, showing also the proximity to them of main towns.

and human inhabitants as well, heightened fears of the realm that Simon Schama has characterised as the meeting point of the terrestrial and the celestial. Mountains were then, as now, places of the imagination, lying beyond the borders of social control.[2]

Some accounts from early colonial New Zealand share this alienation from what was frequently termed the 'wilderness'. 'The summits of the mountain-chain are ... barren and rude, where jetting precipices ... are disjoined ... by deep gorges and ravines ... and deeper chasms that, Erebus-like, appear awfully fearful.' Other observers, however, experienced awe and exhilaration in the face of 'sublime' vistas. Julius von Haast's accounts of his explorations in the Southern Alps are riddled with superlatives. Many painters embellished their portrayals of mountains; Charles Heaphy, for instance, exaggerating the prominence of peaks such as Taranaki. But other colonists were dismayed by the apparent uselessness of the uplands, at a time when, employing the Eurocentric convention of the pastoral, godliness was seen as synonymous with transformed landscapes of tidy productiveness. 'A dismal looking country ... fearfully mountainous, some of them almost perpendicular' was the verdict of a prospective Nelson settler in 1859.[3]

The Māori understanding of mountains has long been rather different. Certainly they are not useless, and the formation of ranges, peaks, and lakes was written into the stories of the ancestors. Tribal territoriality was often linked to one mountain in particular. What Hong-key Yoon has called 'motto maxims' were, and are, used by speakers to identify themselves before an audience, in so doing reciting their whakapapa, or genealogy, in relation to mountain, river, and locality. In this way, prominent features of the land anchor people to place (see Chapter 16). The peaks were the homes of atua, or spiritual beings, and often also the burial places of high chiefs. They were simultaneously places of attachment and apprehension. The explorer and scientist Ernst Dieffenbach made two attempts to climb Mount Taranaki in 1839, on both occasions with Māori guides. The second attempt succeeded, although the guides refused to go further than the snowline because, he recorded, of their superstitions and the cold affecting their uncovered feet. In the Tararua Ranges, such guides interpreted poor weather as indicative of the displeasure of the atua.[4]

Nonetheless, it should not be assumed that Māori were unfamiliar with hill or mountain terrain. Far from it. Archaeological finds suggest they explored the Tararuas early, and travelled along the tops. Ten years after Dieffenbach's climb, Lieutentant-Governor Eyre ascended Tapuae o Uenuku, the prominent peak in the Inland Kaikoura Range in the South Island. He took with him four Māori guides, one of whom, William Hoeta, slipped and was killed. There was a network of trails across the Southern Alps, connecting population centres in the east with sites of greenstone in the west, and with inland food sources. The naturalist Walter Mantell observed how his guide Te Wharekorari could recite a long list of important sites, such as wetlands, up the Waitaki Valley. The surveyor John Barnicoat recorded that the Māori of Foveaux Strait 'sometimes make excursions to the Snowy mountains and catch 300 woodhens per night'. Ngāi Tuahuriri went birding and trapping native rats in the ranges behind Kaiapoi, especially from April to July when prey had overfed on the tawai fruit. The rat was the most prized food, with rat runs being strictly controlled by family groups against poaching.[5]

Consequently, the Waitangi Tribunal has recorded how 'European names [in the hills and mountains] ... celebrate the deeds of the nineteenth-century explorers ... These later adventurers were not the first, neither were the paths they took untrodden. Māori guides often accompanied such men, using trails with landmarks long familiar to them and places named after their ancestors'. When Heaphy and Thomas Brunner undertook their epic journey from Nelson down the South Island's West Coast in 1846, they were accompanied by Kehu, and as they progressed southwards, they 'recognised mountains, hills, rivers, streams, headlands and other natural features from [his] prior description'. Europeans first found a route over the Main Divide when Leonard Harper and a Mr Loch, guided by four unnamed Ngāi Tahu from Kaiapoi, 'discovered' the Harper Pass from Canterbury to the West Coast. But when John Henry Whitcombe, the Canterbury Provincial Surveyor, attempted the apparently shorter pass that also bears his name with a Swiss companion alone, he ended up drowning in the Taramakau River, trying to save himself from starvation after a badly miscalculated journey over treacherous terrain.[6]

These early European travellers in the mountains were not out to experience scenery. Their motives were utilitarian: the search for routeways, resources, or land (Chapter 4). From this perspective, mountains were obstacles. The Tararua and Rimutaka Ranges were formidable barriers between the infant settlement of Wellington and the pastoral lands of the Wairarapa, which the New Zealand Company's surveyor had painted as 'a vast English park'.[7] Heaphy and Brunner were looking for places into which the sheepmen of the hemmed-in colony of Nelson could expand. On another journey south, earlier in 1846, they had been accompanied by William Fox, New Zealand Company Agent in Nelson, who subsequently became a prominent politician and four times prime minister. Fox was also a prolific painter, who used a Claudian style of perspective in his views of valleys and lakes that they encountered. European eyes appropriated the land for European use, renaming it as well: Lake Rotoroa became 'Lake Howick'. It has been said of Fox that he recorded 'not so much unspoiled primeval nature, but potential productivity'.[8]

Mountains, tourism, and nationalism

Colonial artists often applied the 'commodifier's gaze' to mountain landscapes. Fox, after all, enclosed copies of his watercolours with the written dispatches he sent to the New Zealand Company in London. He ruminated on Lake Howick as a site for a spa, with hotel and pleasure boats. In 1858, the surveyor and painter J. J. Thomson wrote a glowing description of the country of inland Otago and the 'magnificent spectacle' of Mount Aspiring, concluding that, within a lifetime, one might yet 'see these beautiful lakes frequented as summer retreats for a change of air and recreation from business'. In 1865–66, the well-known Australian-based artist Nicholas Chevalier visited the South Island, and was supported to the tune of £200 apiece by both the Otago and Canterbury Provincial Councils. Their interest in his trip was that he would produce a series of his spacious, atmospheric paintings that would, by being shown overseas, encourage immigration and tourism. Chevalier obliged, exhibiting in Melbourne on his return, in Paris in 1867, and at the Crystal Palace in 1871.[9]

The best-known late-Victorian artist resident in New Zealand was John Gully, who—like Fox—worked for some time out of Nelson, where from 1863 he was a draughtsman in the Provincial Surveyor's office. Etchings of his drawings appeared regularly in publications such as the *Illustrated New Zealand Herald*, a monthly newspaper 'for Home readers', published in Dunedin 'in good time for transmission home by the San Francisco mail'. In 1874 this paper used several of Gully's drawings of the mountains in the upper Wairau and Aorere Valleys. When it printed a picture of his of the Remarkables above Queenstown in 1878 (the year after he resigned to paint full time), the *Herald* claimed that 'the chief characteristics of New Zealand scenery have become by this time familiar to the Australian public, and that they have done so is to a large extent due to the pictures of Mr Gully'.[10]

Gully produced some famous paintings of the Fiordland Sounds, which by this time was one of the better known alpine districts. Initially, the only way to see the Sounds was on a summer excursion by steamer from Melbourne, such as aboard the *Alhambra*, which visited in 1874, although there appear to have been Australian tourist ship visits before this. Soon the intercolonial steamers between Melbourne and New Zealand were calling at one or other of the Sounds, usually Milford, in the summer months. In 1877 the Union Steam Ship Company started its 'alpine excursion by steamer' from Port Chalmers, near Dunedin. A traveller on one of these, in 1883, noted that the vessel carried 250 passengers and crew to the Sounds, but that another fifty hopefuls had been turned away. By 1884 there were two such excursions each January.[11]

Other visitors went overland. There were two popular alpine tourist routes in the South Island. The first was from Bluff, north to the Otago lakes, often called the 'Lake District' at the turn of the twentieth century, and back to Dunedin. The second was the road from Christchurch, over Arthur's Pass, to the West Coast. Overseas visitors on both routes were prone to all sorts of comparisons as they struggled to fit the scenery into a European frame of reference. Anthony Trollope, here in 1872, found a steamer at Kingston, at the lower end of the lake from Queenstown, even at that early date. 'I do not know that lake scenery can be finer than that of the upper ten miles of Wakatip,' he wrote, but then added, confusingly: 'In New Zealand everything is English ... The shape of the hills, are altogether un-Australian, and very like to that with which we are familiar in the west of Ireland and the highlands of Scotland.' A decade later, the Reverend W. S. Green was more effusive: 'Wakatipu is amazingly beautiful; the only lake in Europe which can surpass it is Lucerne.'[12]

The Fiordland Sounds, however, were more likely to be compared with Norway, whereas the Otira road was described by a visitor writing in *The English Illustrated Magazine* as 'one of the sights of the world ... compared with which in dizzy boldness of engineering and road-making, those of which I have had experience—whether in the Alps, the Carpathians, the Balkans, or the Himalayas, are tame and prosaic'. This was quoted with approval in *Maoriland*, the Union Steamship Company's guide to New Zealand.[13] One description that has stuck through time was that added as the headline by the editor of the London *Spectator* to an article by Blanche Baughan on the Milford Track: 'The finest walk in the world'. The track had been opened in the late 1880s, with government encouragement, as a means of reaching Milford Sound overland. 'Everything is Titanic in scale,' said the Department of Tourist and Health Resorts in *Overland to Milford Sound*, published in 1903, including it seemed, the cost. This was nearly £15, covering first-class rail travel from Dunedin to Lumsden, coach to Te Anau, then boat to the start of the track.[14]

Despite the hyperbole, the actual numbers of people making such journeys were therefore small. Only 287 people walked the track in the 1905–06 season, although this had risen to 484 three seasons later, of whom 137 were women. In 1905–06, there were 185 guests at The Hermitage at Mount Cook, which had been opened in 1885 before being taken over by the government eleven years later. The next year numbers rose to 304, with the replacement of the coach by a motor service, which reduced travel time from two days to one from the rail head at Fairlie; but there were still only 539 guests in 1913–14. The most accessible mountains at this time were in the North Island. Mount Taranaki was close to the town of New Plymouth, which had been connected by rail to the capital, Wellington, by 1885. In the 'record season' of 1902–03, the combined number of visitors to the three houses on the mountain, at North Egmont, East Egmont, and Dawson Falls, was about 2500. In 1910, over a thousand people climbed Mount Holdsworth in the Tararuas, accessible from Wellington.[15]

In 1919 the *Timaru Herald* called for more accommodation at Mount Cook, asserting that 'if railway facilities were available this would surely be the most popular resort in the country'. But it noted that 'in the absence of the railway ... the car road is, with exceptions, surprisingly good—better on the average than some country main roads near the coast'.[16] After the Mount Cook Company took over the hotel in 1922, it was promoted vigorously. The £6 return fare by company car from Timaru was reduced to £3 10 shillings in 1926, and to £2 in 1935. A frequent byline for the resort was that it was 'Thousands of Feet Above Worry Level', and its advertising regularly contrasted the virtues of alpine freedoms with the confining nature of office work (Figure 9.2). There were some clever plays on New Zealanders' underlying fears (see Chapter 13) of the polluted nature of towns:

> The air is so dry, pure and invigorating —
> As to make the winter climate at the Hermitage —
> The most delightful, cheering and healthful in the Dominion —
> GET AWAY FROM THE FOGGY, STUFFY TOWNS ...

The extension of the railway system certainly popularised a few alpine districts, such as Arthur's Pass (the Otira tunnel was opened in 1923), and the peaks of Tongariro National Park (the Main Trunk railway was completed near Ohakune in 1908). The Railways Department was soon running day excursions to 'the alpine wonderland' of Arthur's Pass from Christchurch. With a 10-shilling second-class return fare, about 10,000 people a year were making this trip in the 1930s. It was claimed that nine-tenths of them accompanied a 'well-informed railway officer' on the 'World-Famed Otira Walk', a ten-mile trek from Arthur's Pass station 'across the ridge of the Alps into Westland'.[17]

Such initiatives were consistent with the views of the Minister of Works in the first Labour government, who was 'firmly of the opinion that the natural beauties of our country shall be within easy reach of all our citizens and not merely those who visit us from overseas'.[18] To this end, the state invested increasingly in highway development. The

Figure 9.2 *To the 'Hermitage' Mount Cook,* c. 1925. Pamphlet collection, the Hocken Library, Uare Taoka O Hakena, University of Otago.

Lewis Pass road was opened across the Alps from North Canterbury in 1937. People were put on public works projects in South Westland, in the Haast Pass, and on the road to Milford Sound (although the Homer tunnel was not completed until 1953). The summer-only road (today's State Highway 1) from Waiouru to Taupo, on the eastern flank of the central North Island volcanoes, was upgraded, across what a contemporary motorists' guide referred to as 'the Gobi Desert'.[19] Access to Whakapapa on the western flank had improved sufficiently for a hotel, the Chateau Tongariro, to be opened in 1929,

Table 9.1 Average daily motor traffic on selected alpine roads in the 1930s.

Route	*1934–35*	*1937–38*
Taumarunui–National Park	NA	552
National Park–Taupo	144	227
Waiouru–Ohakune	NA	97
North of Otira–Otira	31	61
Harihari–Whataroa	NA	74
Pukaki–Hermitage	3	12
Pukaki–Tekapo	17	25
Pukaki–Omarama	13	18
North of Te Anau–Te Anau	84	37

The traffic census was taken for a complete week during the months of August 1937 and January 1938, to compare with a similar census in 1934–35.

Source: Selected data in the Public Works Statement, *AJHR*, D1, 1938.

in an area becoming popular for skiing. But despite high levels of car ownership in New Zealand by international standards, a traffic census in 1937–38 revealed that daily use by motor vehicles of mountain routes was low (Table 9.1).

Given the praise, the pictures, but the apparently small number of visitors to all but a few alpine districts, to what extent were the mountains important in an emerging national consciousness? In the United States, Alfred Runte has claimed that wilderness has been an integral aspect of American nationalism, in a country with spectacular scenery but lacking the 'great art, literary attainments and time honoured traditions' of Europe. He dates its significance from the popularity of the Hudson River school of painters in the 1820s–1830s, with its flowering in the writings of Whitman, Thoreau, Muir, and Leopold. New Zealand, however, with a European history that is far shorter, lacked an equivalent wilderness culture. It has even been claimed that 'as a people we are afraid of the "wilderness myth" '.[20]

At the time of the New Zealand Centennial in 1940, M. H. Holcroft wrote of the absence of the physical environment, of itself, in the imagination of Pākehā: 'The general crowd of New Zealanders likes to read the laudatory remarks of tourists ... If there is a sentimental interest in the country for its own sake, it remains more or less inarticulate.' In an uncanny echo of today's careless enthusiasm for 'clean and green', he observed that 'the nearest approach to it, perhaps, is a kind of complacency, as if the beauty of the land were something for which we were somehow responsible'.[21] Holcroft's view was not inconsistent with much of the literary writing of the 1930s. But there had been earlier writers who urged enjoyment of scenery for its own sake, such as Blanche Baughan. Another was Leonard Cockayne, at a time when he was campaigning for national park status for the Arthur's Pass and Otira landscapes. 'Mountains are the noblest recreation ground,' he wrote, 'the finest school for physical and moral training, a source of perfect health for those that visit them, and the place of all places for enlarging our minds by the study of nature in Nature's greatest laboratory.'[22] His words appeared in 1900, as part of a publication marking Canterbury's fiftieth jubilee. Nonetheless, every other essay in this volume celebrated the virtues not of nature but of culture.

Mountains and sport

In the late nineteenth century small numbers of overseas and local climbers had started to discover the potential of New Zealand peaks for mountaineering. The NZAC was founded in 1891, by a group of Canterbury and Otago enthusiasts, who consciously modelled it on the Alpine Club of London. On Christmas Day 1894, Tom Fyfe, George Graham, and Jack Clarke climbed Mount Cook to the summit for the first time, described a century later as 'a symbolic event not to be underestimated in its contribution to the self-respect of a [country], painfully emerging from 19th century colonialism'.[23] This statement is well worth examination.

The first attempt on Mount Cook had been by the Reverend W. S. Green in 1882. An Irishman, he had climbed in the European Alps since the late 1860s, and had seen some photographs of the peak, taken 'by a lady recently returned from New Zealand', at a British Association meeting in York in 1881. 'They showed me enough to convince me that Mount Cook was a splendid peak, and the conquest well worth the trouble of the long journey.'[24] If the wilderness could not be transformed, it could still be humanised by individual skill and effort. However, in reaching the summit, the three New Zealanders deliberately forestalled an attempt by a visiting Englishman, Edward FitzGerald, and his Swiss guide.

Fyfe, Graham and Clarke were not monied and leisured as were the foreign climbers who came to the Southern Alps, nor were they middle class like those who had founded the NZAC. They were young labouring men from the small South Canterbury towns of Timaru, Waimate, and Temuka. They had come to The Hermitage, combining paid guiding—usually of tourists onto the glaciers—with self-motivated climbing. This was not the European model, where guides served clients alone, but then New Zealand climbers—both middle and working class—usually had to be more self-reliant. Compared with Switzerland—which A. P. Harper, a New Zealander who had climbed in both countries, thought full of 'feather bedded mountaineers'—high-altitude guides were initially scarce, porters hard to get, tracks and accommodation rudimentary: all of which gave colonial mountaineering a more expeditionary feel.[25]

But if the mountaineers saw themselves partly in terms of colonial pride, and if their early feats have entered New Zealand mountain lore, their achievements seem not to have had wider meaning at the time. The Mount Cook climb was not widely reported in the press. The *Otago Witness* was enthusiastic, but the *Otago Daily Times*, the *Oamaru Herald* and Auckland's *New Zealand Herald* ignored it. The Christchurch *Press* was curmudgeonly: why hadn't the New Zealand climbers 'played the game' and waited to take FitzGerald with them? A recent historian considers that 'the ascent led to no outpouring of patriotic pride'.[26] In fact, the NZAC went into recess not long after, and did not re-emerge until after World War I. The weather at Mount Cook in the summer of 1895–96 was poor. Then five of the leading lights of the club moved away, to the North Island or overseas. Instead, the quarter-century from 1910 became the heyday of guided climbing at The Hermitage (Table 9.2).

An important development was the establishment of the Tararua Tramping Club (TTC) in 1919. It was convened by W. H. Field, Member of Parliament for Otaki, who

Table 9.2 High ascents from The Hermitage, 1914/15 to 1938/39.

Season	*High ascents*	*All-male parties*	*Mixed parties*	*All-female parties**	*Guideless parties*†
1914–15	42	24	5	13 (10)	1 M, 1 M/F, 1 F
1915–16	48	23	4	21 (19)	–
1916–17	32	11	8	13 (3)	2 M, 1 M/F
1917–18	42	15	17	10 (5)	5 M, 3 M/F
1918–19	17	6	5	6 (5)	1 M
1919–20	33	7	15	11 (11)	–
1920–21	26	16	9	1 (1)	–
1921–22	6	1	3	2 (2)	–
1922–23	7	3	4		
1923–24	5	2	3		
	12	10	1	1 (1)	2 M
1924–25	35	21	3	11 (11)	8 M
1925–26	10	5	2	3 (3)	1 M
1926–27	31	17	9	5 (1)	11 M, 5 M/F
1927–28	28	19	7	2	4 M
1928–29	37	20	7	10 (9)	7 M, 1 M/F
1929–30	24	17	6	1 (1)	1 M/F
1930–31	41	26	2	12 (12)	5 M
1931–32	20	12	1	7 (6)	3 M
1932–33	45	30	2	13 (13)	15 M
1933–34	22	11	2	9	9 M, 2 F/M, 3 F
1934–35	no list				
1935–36	50	42	1	7 (6)	26 M
1936–37	20	11	1	8 (5)	–
1937–38	no list				
1938–39	5	2		3 (3)	1 M

* Parties consisting of women climbers only, usually with male guides. Figures in brackets indicate number of parties comprising a single woman (with guide).

† M= all male parties, M/F = mixed parties, F = all women parties. Numbers represent number of parties.

Source: Annual Reports of the Department of Tourist and Health Resorts, *AJHR*, H2.

had been active for many years in scenery preservation and track development in the area, and F. Vosseler, a Wellington businessman. The generational tensions between the club leaders—many of whom were city professional people and believers in a 'safety first' policy in the hills—and their younger members echoed those of class between the alpine climbers in the 1890s. Field and Vosseler saw the TTC's mission as introducing more people to the Tararuas 'so they could visit them and enjoy the great beauty and healthy recreation of these areas without risk'. Guy Mannering of the NZAC had similarly written in 1892 that '... the very presence of danger draws out of a man all the caution he possesses, and brings his most admirable qualities into play'.[27]

Another characteristic of New Zealand mountain recreation, however, was that it was by no means a male preserve. A woman had climbed Mount Taranaki as early as 1855, and the first woman to walk the Milford Track did so in 1890—the same summer that three women together climbed Tapuae o Uenuku. In the summer of 1912–13, her fifth season in the Southern Alps, Freda Du Faur of Sydney made five guided ascents from The Hermitage, causing 'quite a sensation amongst those interested in alpine work' with the first traverse of the three peaks of Mount Cook, and the first traverse of Mount Sefton. She had earlier become the first woman to climb Mount Cook. In fact, as Table 9.2 shows, quite a high proportion of high climbs at The Hermitage involved mixed or women-only parties. However, social convention decreed that female participation was no simple matter, both dress and company being problematic. Miss Du Faur records how older women at The Hermitage, fearing for her reputation, implored her not to climb alone with a male guide.[28] The TTC resolved this issue by the using female chaperones. Dress remained a problem, for both sexes.

The TTC's initial tramps were not difficult, and it was January 1922 before it arranged one across the Tararuas from Otaki to the Wairarapa (the 'Southern Crossing', which Field had completed in 1912). Yet on this first strenuous outing, one member died of exposure; so did another tramper five months later, one of two travelling the same route independently. These incidents brought home the need for well-located huts for shelter, and better clothing. The first waterproof garments did not begin to appear until the mid 1920s. Despite this, tramping flourished in the Tararuas. The TTC had over 300 members by 1923, but the attitude of its leaders remained that of safety first. One interpretation of this was to travel in large parties: John Pascoe, the famous alpine writer and climber, who moved to Wellington from Canterbury in 1937, referred to the TTC's 'alarming caravanserai'.[29]

Students preferring a less organised attitude created the Victoria College Tramping Club in 1921. Manual workers in the Hutt Valley—inviting Vosseler to speak at a meeting to discuss formation of another group—founded the Hutt Valley Tramping Club in 1923. It was more accepting of women as equals from the start. In the same year, having written to the TTC for advice, the Otago Tramping and Mountaineering Club was formed, with university students prominent among a membership, after twelve months, of 157.[30] Two years later the Christchurch Tramping Club, soon to be renamed the Canterbury Mountaineering Club, came into being. It was an alpine specialists' group; like the Wellington and Otago clubs, it put a lot of effort into building huts in the back-country. Until the late 1970s it also excluded women. In 1931, twenty clubs around the country, including the NZAC, joined forces to establish Federated Mountain Clubs (FMC). Of the twenty, eight were tramping clubs, five were skiing clubs, and one was a climbing club, while six promoted a combination of activities.

The first president of the FMC had been a founding member of the TTC, so safety issues were to the fore. In 1932, a subcommittee was set up to investigate mountain accidents to see what could be learned. Older club members expressed concern about the adventurousness of younger colleagues. Table 9.2 shows the growth in the number of unguided high climbs from The Hermitage. Climbers were also breaking away from the ridges and snow slopes, and targeting harder rock climbs, ridges, and peak traverses. Partly this reflected the more widespread use of crampons. Anxieties within the NZAC were echoed at the time within the American Alpine Club. Training camps were organised, an idea borrowed from the Alpine Club of Canada. The FMC published *Safety in the*

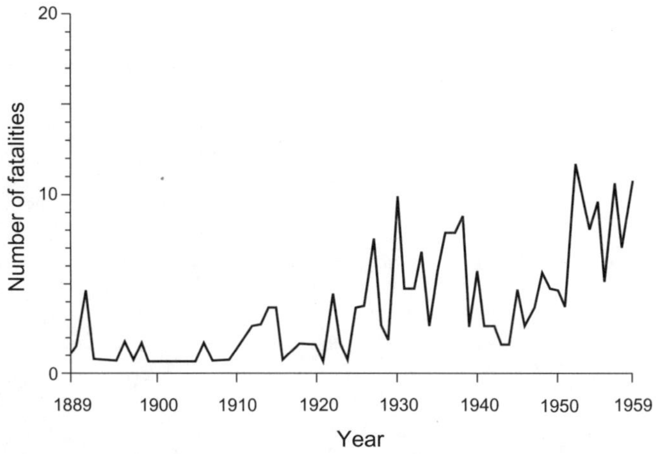

Figure 9.3 Alpine fatalities between 1889 and 1959. Redrawn from M. Johnston, 'Peak Experiences: Challenge and Danger in Mountain Recreation in New Zealand', PhD thesis, University of Canterbury, 1989, p. 56.

Mountains in the mid 1930s, and facilitated a national search and rescue system, under the aegis of the police, based on one developed by the TTC.[31]

The growing popularity of mountain recreation, and these changing attitudes towards challenge and danger, were reflected in the growing fatality record in the hills (Figure 9.3). Social attitudes, however, were moving towards those expressed—ahead of his time—by Leonard Cockayne in 1900. The Labour government's Minister of Internal Affairs, promoting state support for outdoor recreation, asserted that '... good physical and mental health should be the foundation of a good life, besides making the individual profitable to the nation'. The hills provided opportunities for individuals to test themselves in the wilderness in a way the frontier, now closed, had once done. And in 1953, the year of the successful ascent of Everest by a New Zealander, an MP urged that nothing should be done 'to discourage young people from going into the mountains. [They] are one of the best training-grounds ... some of our best soldiers overseas ... have done mountaineering.'[32] Most of these training grounds were national parks.

Mountains and national parks

The pattern of establishment of national parks in New Zealand was a function of the relationship between mountains and the frontier of settlement, as well as of the popularity of particular places with tourists and recreationists. It is often said that the early motivation for national parks was utilitarian, and this certainly helps to explain the sort of roles that those parks were seen as playing. Wilderness had to have a use and purpose, rather than being there for its own sake, as the American wilderness ethic implied. 'Utility' needs to be unpacked, however, in order to understand why certain places were designated as parks, and others were not.

Table 9.3 National parks in 1938.

Name	*Approximate size (acres)*	*Legislative authority*
Tongariro*	150,000	Tongariro National Park Act 1922
Egmont*	79,000	Egmont National Park Act 1924
Arthur's Pass•	117,000	Part III, Public Reserves, Domains and National Parks Act 1928
National Park in Minchin, Bealey, Davie and Hawdon Survey Districts•	94,060	Reserved under Land Act 1892
Sounds (Fiordland)•	2,407,000	Reserved under Land Act and special legislation
In addition, the following areas were commonly regarded as national parks:		
Peel Forest Park*	1305	Peel Forest Act 1926
Hooker Glacier†	28,000	Reserved for recreation purposes under Land Act 1885
Tasman Park†	97,800	Reserved for recreation purposes under Land Act 1885, 1908
Godley Glacier†	18,900	Reserved for recreation purposes under Land Act 1924

* administered by special boards appointed under their Acts and Part III of the 1928 Act

† administered under Tourist and Health Resorts Control Act 1908.

• administered under Part I of 1928 Act.

Source: Annual Report on Public Domains and National Parks, Department of Lands and Survey, *AJHR*, C10, 1938, pp. 4–5.

The introduction of the national park concept into New Zealand, at Tongariro, was discussed in the preceding chapter. This concept remained rather flexible: not until 1952 was there coordinating legislation to deal with each park in the same way. Table 9.3 illustrates the confusing situation in 1938. The underlying rationale, however, was clear. The Department of Lands had asserted that 'the vast and magnificent national parks of Mount Egmont, Mount Cook, Tongariro and Ruapehu, and the West Coast Sounds, embrace country that can never be suitable for close settlement, but is of world-wide fame as the home of scenery'. Consistent with this, it stated that '... it has never been the practice of the Department to unduly withhold from settlement areas of rich soil and well adapted to pastoral or agricultural pursuits merely because they are also suited for scenery preservation. The needs of settlement are imperative ...'[33]

Mountainous national parks were therefore the bits left over, those that could not be made to fit into the pastoral vision of Britain's southern farm. Both Tongariro and Egmont parks, however, had their origins in fear of the impact of the frontier on particular values of the wild: in the former case, sacred peaks that Ngāti Tuwharetoa did not want violated by farms and mills; in the latter, to preserve forests for purposes of catchment control, so guarding against the risks of flooding new farmlands. Egmont and the other parks were in the areas in which alpine tourism was most significant at the turn of the century: Fiordland and the lakes, Mount Cook, and Arthur's Pass. A Canterbury MP, urging action, with pressure from Cockayne and the newly formed Christchurch Beautifying Association, claimed that a national park incorporating the Otira Gorge 'would prove ... a gold-mine in the future in the way of inducing tourists to visit that part of the colony'.[34]

Less accessible or less spectacular mountain areas, lacking attention from tourists or recreationists, were unlikely to become national parks. A good example is the glacier district of South Westland. South of Fox Glacier in 1906, Miss Moreland had found herself 'in a world untouched by man'. The famous Fox Glacier Hotel did not open until 1928, and only in the 1930s was bridging and roading put in place. The *New Zealand Motorists' Road Guide* of 1938 referred to Fox Glacier as 'the centre of the proposed National Park', but this status was not attained until 1960. On the other hand, a request from the MP for Timaru that a national park be created in the accessible Rangitata Valley of South Canterbury, owing to its scenery and potential for ice skating, came to nothing.[35]

There were other mountain areas that did attract plenty of human use but nonetheless also failed to become national parks. The Tararua Ranges, north of Wellington, are the best example. In 1936 a proposal emerged from within the TTC to have the Tararuas set aside as a national park. The idea was to construct a network of new huts and tracks, with enhanced roading access, as Wellington's centennial memorial, marking the hundred years since the signing of the Treaty of Waitangi. Younger members were opposed, but eventually it gained sufficient support for official consideration. It was turned down as being too expensive and lacking wide enough appeal. Representations to the Minister of Internal Affairs were also unsuccessful; he may have reasoned that national park status would be incompatible with the potential for hydro power development on several Tararua rivers.[36]

The Waitakere Ranges are another interesting case. To the mountaineer Pascoe, they 'looked like a hedge on part of Auckland's low horizon', pleasant enough for 'hedge-hopping'. The Auckland City Council had begun buying land there for water-catchment purposes in 1899, as well as for scenic reserves. In 1924 the Auckland Blue Mountains Society called for creation of a park. The following year the Waitakere Association was founded to attain national park status for the area. In the late 1930s 'the Waitakere National Park' was the goal of those who wished it to become the chief centennial memorial for Auckland, as 'a perpetual source of health and enjoyment'. An Act of Parliament in 1941 created the 'Centennial Memorial Park', but as the country's first regional, rather than as a national, park.[37]

Accessibility was therefore not a sufficient condition for the creation of national parks, although perhaps a necessary one. Nonetheless, parks needed to be beyond the frontier, lacking development potential for farming, forestry, or power generation. Equally important was that the landscapes involved conform to the ideals of spectacular scenery that the nineteenth-century artists and, increasingly, photographers had created as representing 'New Zealand'. On this score, neither the low-level Waitakeres nor the rugged Tararuas passed muster. A degree of exclusivity was required, although the in-club opposition to the Tararua proposal revealed the tension between this and access: the challenge of the hills being lost for some if they became too 'easy'. When parts of existing parks became very popular in the 1950s, this tension was partially resolved by the creation of a small number of wilderness areas within them, using the provisions of the 1952 National Parks Act. These were remote places without huts and tracks, the first designated being Otehake in the Arthur's Pass National Park.

Conclusion

To a considerable extent the mountains of New Zealand have become known through the icons of the national park system, just as New Zealand itself is often known through its national parks. Gully's representations of alpine peaks may have been the picture that 'Home' readers of illustrated newspapers got of the colony in the 1870s, but posters and photographs played the same role for New Zealanders in the 1920s and 1930s. And just as mountains had been prominent in the 1898 stamp issue, so too did they feature in the next pictorial set, in 1935, with Mount Cook and Mount Taranaki gracing, respectively, the cheapest and most expensive denominations. When the 'Peace' stamps were issued in 1946, the halfpenny showed the Southern Alps reflected in the still waters of Westland's Lake Matheson, while the ninepenny—one of the most popular of New Zealand's stamps—portrayed the Franz Josef Glacier through the chancel window of the local chapel.

These examples underline a point that has been central to this chapter, namely that mountains are not neutral landscapes but features of the environment employed to various social ends. They are, in other words, charged with meanings, even if to Pākehā these meanings have tended to be more detached than for Māori. In colonial times, mountains were often viewed as wastelands, unless commodified for purposes of tourism or used for character-building recreational pursuits. As in North America, significant alpine areas were then reserved as national parks, providing they were good for nothing else. After the passage of the 1952 Act, which brought into being for the first time a body, the National Parks Authority, charged with extending that system, a creditably large proportion of the national land area became part of the national conservation estate. Yet attempts to use this as indicative of a national respect for environment conveniently overlooked the fact that 'less than 0.5% of New Zealand's area has been designated National Park or Reserve in preference to a use foregone'.[38]

This statement was made in 1980, since when it has become a little less true, with national park extensions and new designations made in areas of lowland native forest and downland, such as the river landscapes of the Whanganui, the karstlands of Paparoa, or the Kahurangi wilds of northwest Nelson. It remains the case, however, that the national park system is overwhelmingly mountainous in nature, and lacks representativeness of other pre-European landscape types, such as tussock grasslands or wetlands, which, as Chapters 5 and 10 show, had all the attributes for conversion into 'productive' areas. Yet paradoxically, as order was wrought across the land, leaving the hills and mountains aside because they alone were invulnerable to conversion, it was the wild areas that assumed the role of representing New Zealand not only to itself but on an international stage. This is despite a history in which relatively few New Zealanders have gained much personal knowledge of the mountains.

Nonetheless, we have needed them. For some people, with the peaks being visible on urban horizons, it has been the mountains that have kept alive dreams of challenge and a pioneering spirit. For others, they have represented the appeal of peace and contemplation, a welcome counterpoint to the drudgery of suburban routine. For most of us, however, they have long been landscapes of renown, taken-for-granted national 'possessions' that do service as New Zealand's face to the world: rendering distinct, and distinguished, a homeland otherwise too often marked by little but its ordinariness.[39]

10

'Swamps which might doubtless Easily be drained'

Swamp drainage and its impact on the indigenous

Geoff Park

> ... Swamps which might doubtless Easily be drained, and sufficiently evinced the richness of their soils by the great size of the plants that grew upon them ... indeed in every respect the properest place we have yet seen for establishing a Colony. —Joseph Banks, 1769[1]
>
> The cultivation of a new country materially improves its climate. Damp and dripping forests, exhaling pestilent vapours from rank and rotten vegetation, fall before the axe; and light and air get in, and sunshine ripening goodly plants. Fen and march and swamp, the bittern's dank domain, fertile only in miasma, are drained; and the plough converts them into wholesome plains of fruit, and grain, and grass. —Charles Hursthouse, 1857[2]

One of the truly great landscape changes in modern times, according to the eminent historical geographer Clarence Glacken, has been marsh, bog, and swamp drainage.[3] If the magnitude of the change from swamp to farm is any gauge, the flat lowlands of New Zealand must be among the world's most modern landscapes. Drainage has reduced the 670,000 hectares or more of freshwater wetlands that existed at the commencement of European settlement to some 100,000 hectares. Twenty per cent of New Zealand's indigenous birds use wetland environments as their primary habitat.[4] In evolutionary terms, New Zealand's swamps contain some of its most ancient lifeforms. But lowland New Zealand today is dramatically altered from the swampy country in which its unique, indigenous ecosystems evolved—and in which the Treaty of Waitangi was signed.

The 85 per cent decline in New Zealand's wetlands since European settlement is one of the most dramatic known anywhere in the world; far higher than the countries in which modern agriculture began large-scale draining of swamps and marshes. The Netherlands and Britain are believed to have lost around 60 per cent of their original wetland areas; France only 10 per cent. The New Zealand figure is also considerably greater than in most countries that received what Alfred Crosby has termed 'the biological expansion of Europe'.[5] In the continental United States, for example, about 53 per cent of the original area of wetlands has been lost.[6] In many parts of lowland New Zealand, such as the Bay of Plenty, where less than 1 per cent of the natural wetland area remains, the change has been so comprehensive that the full extent of swamp and other wetland environments prior to European settlement can only be inferred from soil evidence.[7]

Imperial landscapes

The vanishing of New Zealand's swamps was a consequence of what has been called 'ecological imperialism'.[8] Their cardinal environments—the lowland plains where the country's most productive lands lie, where the prime export produce is grown, and a great many of us live—are like our laws of justice. They appear and function as they do to us today because of England's eighteenth- to twentieth-century extension into New Zealand; a cultural spreading that carried with it a deep antipathy to leaving country to the grip of the swamp.

Joseph Banks, the explorer–natural scientist, and Charles Hursthouse, colonist–farmer, believed certain things would have to be done to New Zealand were it truly to become the country that, to Hursthouse, deserved to be called 'South Britain'. No haunts of ancient peace to them, its swamps would have to go. Depicting swamps as 'wilderness' and 'waste' and forcing their native fluidity into the straight, criss-crossing channels of man-made drains was fundamental to the Western cultural construction of nature of which Banks and Hursthouse were prime agents and advocates (Figure 10.1).

Banks and Hursthouse were Englishmen. Lincolnshire lads both, native to the low, watery Fenland country of marsh and fens; a vast, damp flatness broken only by the

Figure 10.1 Excavating a drainage canal, Hauraki Plains, 1910. Source: *AJHR*, C8, 1910.

Gothic spires of its market towns' cathedrals. Inheritor of some two hundred farms by the time he visited New Zealand with Cook on the *Endeavour*, Banks was one of those men of Empire, of inordinate power, who shaped the world as it came to be for the people of Australia, New Zealand, and the South Pacific. No less than his enthusiastic discernment of the Pacific as 'an arcadia of which we were going to be kings',[9] and his influence on British colonisation, trade, and imperial science, was his passion for creating pasture and cropland from nature's swamps. In an 1813 portrait, Banks, at the height of his power as President of the Royal Society, holds not an explorer's chart or botanical specimen, but the map of a fen drainage scheme.[10]

That drainage of the Lincolnshire Fens was concluding when Hursthouse, who emigrated to Taranaki with a New Zealand Company scheme, was a child. 'A few years since,' he recollected, 'the ague was the scourge of my native swamps in Lincolnshire; and fen infants, like myself, were only preserved by copious cups of bark and wine. But now, reed and rush and snake and buzzard, rat and eel have vanished before the plough; the "reek o' the rotten fen" is gone, and the ague is a tradition of the past.' Settlement and cultivation in New Zealand, he said, with more than a hint of Sanitary Movement speak,[11] would produce the same effects.[12]

The only great swamp that the *Endeavour* people encountered at close quarters was what is today the Hauraki Plains. But Joseph Banks knew what he had seen there, and what could now happen. To someone with such an eye for colonising opportunity, New Zealand's swamps had three values: their watery acres of tall trees were so vast he could 'see no bounds' to them; their rich soil would make 'ample returns of any European Vegetables sown in it';[13] and, other than those in the raised swamp village or fishing camp who welcomed the *Endeavour* party ashore 'in the most friendly manner imagineable',[14] they appeared surprisingly devoid of people.

The marshes of Banks's Lincolnshire estate had been busy with people since before Saxon settlement in about AD 700. Through medieval times, former tidal marshes around the Lincolnshire fen edges had been reclaimed piecemeal, divided by drainage ditches and surrounded by sea banks, behind which farmers became wealthy from the valuable new pastures.[15] Nonetheless, until the 1760s most of the fens still lay in their natural state. Their diversity of oak and alder woodlands, sedge, rush and reed swamps, open water and tide-swept salt marsh sustained a way of life that was luxurious compared with that of similar people elsewhere. The poorest people had common rights access to fish, wildfowl, timber, peat, thatch reeds, and hay. But they faced ruin when the fens and marshes were enclosed and drained by estate owners such as Joseph Banks.[16]

One of the reasons that the Pākehā settler culture has never held swamps in esteem as picturesque—compared with the wooded edges of rivers and lakes, for example—is that the confines of closed, wooded wetlands posed a problem for an aesthetics of sight accustomed to more open space and invulnerability in watery environments. When Englishmen raised in and habituated to the flat openness of the Fens confronted the densely wooded swamps and wetlands of their far antipodean discoveries they were in for a culture shock of the most profound magnitude—and with durable after-effects.[17] To such a sense of swamp country, the towering, vine-tangled kahikatea swamp forests that the

Endeavour shore party encountered in the Hauraki must have been dizzying. We know from the traditions of Hauraki people that, unknown to the Englishmen, their boats were shadowed across the swamp country.[18] But their invisibility and the way that, beyond the fishing settlement, such palpably fertile a plain was 'completely cloathed' with heavily timbered forest would have given Joseph Banks a whole new quickened sense of what wilderness meant.

Twentieth-century archaeology would reveal otherwise. The ecological diversity of the Hauraki swamp made it about as rich in food resources and raw materials as anything in Aotearoa. Furthermore, the pattern of Māori settlement it sustained, reflected it. There were many more villages than Cook and Banks saw. Archaeologists estimate that swamp drainage and flood-control works have destroyed 70 per cent of the sites of dozens of kāinga up the labyrinth of myriad hidden waterways that English eyes were unable to discern.[19] But the seed that drove Edward Gibbon Wakefield's colonisation schemes of the 1840s—the impression, as Charles Hursthouse would recount, of 'immense districts of teeming fertility, literally without an inhabitant, [that] did not produce a mouthful of food for a single human being'[20]—was sown.

The history of swamp drainage is substantially the linear logic of modern book law meeting and beating the chaos of nature. As the draining of swamps produces the flat and relatively dry surface of the earth on which the straight, equilateral lines of the settlers' towns and cities—and the agricultural space to sustain them—can be laid out, it purposefully obliterates nature's organic flow lines (Figure 10.2). Nothing that meets the eye on a New Zealand coastal plain that has been the subject of a swamp-drainage scheme is yet a century old. No plant or animal it sees, other than the odd raupō plant and cabbage tree, or eel in a farm drain, is indigenous. Yet the recognisable combination of trees, pasture, and human structures makes it seem as if perhaps that they are all that was ever there. In countries such as New Zealand and Australia, what is termed 'spatial history'[21] tends to interpret such a landscape as one of imperialism.

A landscape of swamp drainage such as today's Hauraki Plains is undoubtedly an imperial landscape, a place of amnesia and erasure in whose shaping political passions have been mobilised; 'a potent, ideological representation that serves to naturalise power relations and erase history and legibility'.[22] But ridding country of its low-lying, wet, fecund places is an imperialism not confined to the former European colonies. Nor is it restricted to the colonisation phase from the second half of the nineteenth century, or its European antecedent, the agricultural revolution from the late seventeenth century in England's Fens and the polders across the Channel. Some would give swamp drainage and wetland reclamation an even wider cultural framework than a millennium or more in the countries around the North Sea:

> Postglacial Europe, even the periglacial Mediterranean shores, was a swampy place. The most fertile soils were often those, from an agricultural and medical point of view, most in need of drainage. The reclamation of wetlands played an enormous role in the civilized history of the continent and an equal role, I believe, in the psychohistory of those for whom the symbols of a new duality were being shaped ... the fearful potential of organic fructification and the muckiness of wet decay, as opposed to the order of the farm or the city itself.[23]

Figure 10.2 A plan of swamp drainage, Hauraki Plains, 1908. Source: *AJHR*, C1, 1908.

Despite the postmodern trend of wetland restoration, the same dualism is everywhere today, as indeed swamp drainage and wetland reclamation continue to be wherever nature's wet, uncultivated places are in close proximity to culture.

Taming the wet wild

The significance to New Zealand historiography of fen drainage in eastern England between the 1760s and 1840s, and the agricultural revolution therein, is in part to do with the timing of the colonial project here; led as it was from that particular corner of the world. Its greater significance perhaps has been its demonstration of the massive scale and almost military-style organisation and control of the landscape (both water and land) that was necessary, which in New Zealand only the Crown could undertake—as settlers attracted to the great Rangitaiki Swamp in the Bay of Plenty were to discover.

In 1890 a commercial traveller proposed draining the Rangitaiki Swamp and converting it to farmland. The government surveyed the swamp into 500-acre sections, and the first settlers arrived to take up their land in 1891. Their piecemeal approach of each draining their own section failed because of the lack of adequate outfalls. So in the early 1900s the settlers formed a drainage board, it having become obvious by then that drainage of the swamp would have to be under a comprehensive scheme to be successful. The scale of the operation proved well beyond the board's resources. It lacked what the historian of Rangitaiki Plains Drainage Scheme called 'a vital prerequisite for the successful prosecution of any drainage proposals—control over Crown Lands and Native Land'.[24] Thus, by way of the Rangitaiki Land Drainage Act 1910, the government took over.

The following year work began on the long drains and cutting a direct outlet to the sea for the Rangitaiki River. By 1924 both the Rangitaiki and Tarawera rivers had been diverted out to sea, their floodplains drained, and their courses straightened and stopbanked. By 1925 the drainage of the Rangitaiki Swamp was substantially complete, except for a major drain outfall to the sea near Whakatane, for which Māori kāinga land was taken under the Public Works Act. Like other drainage schemes, it was dependent on Māori swampland, which, if Māori did not want to sell, they were forced to part with compulsorily. Of the land affected by the time of the scheme's completion, only 8 per cent was freehold land, 35 per cent was Māori land, 42 per cent was land leased from the Crown, and 11 per cent unoccupied Crown land.[25]

The consequence a little north in the landscape of the Hauraki Plains Act 1908 was little different (Figure 10.3). That same year the government commissioned a survey of what the local county's centennial historian would describe as 'a desolate wasteland of swamp and alluvial flats'.[26] The following year government-facilitated works began clearing much of the Piako and Waitoa rivers and constructing stopbanks along the foreshore and the rivers to prevent tidal and flood overflow. Behind them they began criss-crossing the plain with miles of canals and drains. The Hauraki Plains Act also gave the Crown the power to take Māori swampland compulsorily. In the three years following its passage, almost 2000 acres of Māori land were acquired to facilitate what the Act termed 'the more effective carrying out of drainage works'. By 1911, 5200 acres of the plain were drained and burnt ready for balloting to eager waiting settlers. By 1918, newspaper columnists were describing the 'splendid results' of making 'a wilderness carry a prosperous population and produce ever increasing wealth, of changing 'useless swamp into rich farm land'. Not too different at all from the conclusion Arthur Young

Figure 10.3 Hauraki Plains swamp drainage, 1911–12. Source: *AJHR*, C8, 1911; C8, 1912.

had come to in England in 1799: 'fens of water, mud, wild fowl, frogs and agues, have been converted to rich pasture and arable'.[27]

One of Britain's most regarded historical geographers, H. C. Darby, has described the drainage of England's fens as giving 'man and his conquest of nature' its 'full meaning'. In a context such as the colonisation of New Zealand, with the imperative (in a promoted-as-flat but actually very unflat land) to obtain for agriculture any fertile, level ground, a large swamp like the Hauraki, Rangitaiki or Manawatu was readily constructed as an easily vanquished foe.[28] The Australian cultural theorist who described swamp drainage as 'a colonial device for subduing an ostensibly recalcitrant, even rebellious, indigenous population and wetland environment'[29] had Vietnam's Mekong Delta and Plain of Reeds more in mind than the Rangitaiki or Hauraki swamps in New Zealand. But his portrayal of drainage as a threat and obstacle to progress that the colonial project would have to subdue is not an inaccurate appellation of the New Zealand situation.

New Zealand was settled on the promise of soil; of 'level ground … space so ample … soil so fertile',[30] a North Island 'full two-thirds rich alluvial'[31]. Inland from the coast, but believed to be low and level, James Cook's River Thames (the Waihou) was thought to flow navigable all the way from Hauraki to the strait named after him. It was also settled on the premise that the native landscape of that low sprawling country would be of no use as it was, and that large-scale conversion of it to agricultural production would be vital to the colony's success. It is this, the British settler perception of what Māori considered among their most productive resource environments (and thus refrained from clearing and cultivating) as land still in 'the primeval dress of nature'—'wilderness' and 'waste', in other words—that is the root cause of swamp drainage having so comprehensively eliminated the indigenous.

The swamp became an obstacle to progress from the moment the first settlement scheme's colonists walked up the beach to discover that New Zealand's plains were far from the grassy, alder and oak woodland version. There was relief, in Charles Heaphy's description, that the Petone shore of the New Zealand Company's intent at least had *something* of level ground, but shock at its being 'covered with high forest to within a mile and a half of the beach, when swamps full of flax ... intervened'.[32] The next New Zealand Company shipload to Port Nicholson, the surveyors, discovered that where they were meant to lay out Britannia, 'a great many of the streets would run through swamps and marshes, in some places six and ten feet deep'.[33]

After a day in the swamp with his chief surveyor, the Company's Principal Agent, William Wakefield, acknowledged that while 'perfectly level, and of considerable extent ... the marshy nature of the soil, and its liability to inundation' made the Hutt Valley 'at present unfit for the settler'. It would nevertheless 'with draining become valuable'.[34] Within weeks the whole place did inundate. The settlers, waiting in tents and makeshift huts, protested at the choice of site, but Wakefield declared 'the swamps would be thrown out'.[35] Days later, however, he was persuaded to move the colony across the harbour to the present-day site of Wellington.

As the Company's draughtsman, Charles Heaphy was required to prepare drawings of the chosen site for the colony for advertisements back in England. However he actually depicted the swampy kahikatea and flax country behind Petone Beach, it appeared in the Company's promotional lithographs as sprawling, well-drained, well-wooded open plains country. To have presented thickly timbered swamps as thickly timbered swamps would not have attracted the ships of settlers that were needed. Ruth France's poem of the colonising moment may have urged: 'There is no need to remember swamp-grass/Or how the first women (let the rain pass, They had prayed) wept ...'.[36] But although excised and omitted so as not to unsettle potential settlers, the obstacle to progress at Petone would not be forgotten.

Modernity takes all

> If you bid me of the features most remarkable to speak,
> I should say a spur, a gully, then a swamp, then a creek,
> A little distance further on there will recur
> First a swamp, and then a gully, then a creek, and then a spur.
> —William Pember Reeves, 1889.[37]

Swamps abounded in lowland New Zealand in the early phase of European settlement. Prior to the discovery of refrigerated shipping spurring settler demand for flat land, they were a common part of the landscape. We today need to be very careful about reconstructing how lowland New Zealand looked and how it functioned ecologically when it had its swamps. The documents of colonisation on which environmental historians draw are not exactly cluttered with descriptions of swamp country. To the patriarchal cultural tradition that brought the demands of Western modernity to New Zealand, swamps were places of disease and decay, melancholy and horror, absolutely inimical to modern ways.[38] They were places to dredge, drain, or fill in, but rarely places to write about. Few nineteenth-century writers thought well of swamps, though William Pember Reeves saw a native quality in the landscape to be admired in its vanishing:

> Small streams ran out of the swamp ... and disappeared in the shingle of the beach. When not disturbed with draining work, their water was sweet and clear. The swamps had been covered with tall flax, toetoe, rushes and small bushes, green and beautiful in the sunlight, but as the drains did their work, the peat sank, cracked and dried, the surface was systematically burnt and became stretches of black, hideous ashes and mud, poached up by the hoofs of cattle.[39]

Swamp *drainage*, on the other hand, was described because it was settlement history. It had Acts of Parliament in its name and purpose. The swamps themselves, however, were merely empty wilderness to the eyes of the literate; waiting for their place in history.

Swamp drainage as history is, to an ecologist, a process by which a thriving, powerful expansionist culture learns how to wring wealth from a certain kind of country by cleverness and industry; comes, inevitably, to need more of it to swell its success; goes searching for it; finds it lying, seemingly vacant and unused, in another culture's land; and, declaring it 'wilderness' and 'waste', claims it and transforms it into wealth.[40] In New Zealand the declaring and transforming was effected by laws—laws of the Crown.

A powerful principle of English land law that, prior to its arrival in New Zealand had facilitated the landscape revolution of the enclosures in the Lincolnshire Fens, was the dictum enunciated by the seventeenth-century philosopher John Locke. Land 'left wholly to Nature, that hath no improvement of Pasturage, Tillage, or Planting,' wrote Locke in his *Two Treatises of Government*, 'is called, as indeed it is, *waste*'.[41] To the eyes of colonists from civilised England, the swampy flats lying inland of so many a New Zealand beach were 'waste' at its most profound. To those who believed their civilising and 'reclaiming' of land from the wilderness to be 'God's work',[42] the only possible purpose of swamp country, unpeopled and uncultivated as it seemed, was what they believed it was waiting for: providing the productivity that would sustain the cities they could imagine their culture building here. That is why Cook called the river that took his *Endeavour* party into their New Zealand swamp the Thames.

But as the New Zealand Company settler William Swainson would later write of Māori and their whenua, 'Land, apparently waste is highly valued by them'.[43] The great swamp of Hauraki, the vast wetland systems of the Piako and the Waihou rivers, had a human-sustaining productivity of a very different kind to that desired by James Cook's culture. In 1840 George Clarke, Protector of Aborigines in New Zealand, visited what his Instructions termed 'by far the largest block of land in New Zealand that is, in its whole extent, fit for cultivation'—'to treat with the natives for such portions of their land as they may be disposed to part with and can conveniently spare'.[44]

It was early summer, but Hauraki Māori told him how 'every winter the swamps from the entrance of Piako to the interior for about thirty miles is an inland sea in which nothing but water and the tops of a few kahikatea trees are to be seen with canoes sailing in all directions over the expanse of water. The only place secure from these inundations ... in winter season becomes an island.'[45] One 'island' was Oruarangi; the oldest permanently inhabited settlement site known in New Zealand,[46] and the site of the 'Indian village' that Cook and Banks visited when they came inland from the *Endeavour* in 1769. Another 'island', well up into the kahikatea forests beyond where they ventured, was Kakaramea; a major swamp pā from which Ngāti Maru traded timber in the 1790s, but merely a rise on a dairy farm today, indistinguishable from the stopbanks.

Clarke was in no doubt about the fertility of the Hauraki flat country. But its wetness overwhelmed him. He could see 'no probability of redeeming a country lying so low and receiving such an immense body of water from the interior'.[47] Water was not the only drawback: the plain was only 'part clean'. Much of it was kahikatea forest. As such, the Hauraki swamp was one of the biological pump-houses of the New Zealand ecosystem; where both biodiversity and nutrient turnover reached peak levels; where birds of forest, scrubland, and water and fish of fresh water and sea bred and fed. Just a few miles away, over a few low, wooded hills, was another even greater example: the Waikato swamplands, where the river that had once formed the alluvial plain of the Hauraki swamp had flowed since the Taupo eruption in the second century AD. By the time the century was out, the 'redeeming' of both the Hauraki and the Waikato was being effected by what the government officially called 'land improvement' schemes.

From prodigious ecology to geometric settlement

But in a landscape that actual European settlement had revealed to contain only too few Haurakis and Waikatos, the premium on any level acres was substantial. In the Crown colony New Zealand was, swamps and swamp drainage became the subjects of legislation.

Central to English land laws are the distinctions between waterways and dry land. Swamps, rivers, and lakes are interconnected ecologically; that is the key to their biological productivity and resource value. Many cultures make neither distinction nor division between them. Rather, the ecological processes that link them, such as fish-spawning and eels running to sea, are what matters. As traditional Māori fishers knew, river and lake fisheries are productive in relation to the areas of swampland they water.[48] But for a culture accustomed to its rulers using legal boundary lines as means of asserting governance, swamp environments provided a real problem. Where does a swamp become river or lake? What are the delineating features? Is a swamp merely a shallow lake with plants growing through the water? Or is it is dry land only temporarily or ephemerally wet? To such a perspective, like English law, that needs classificatory order and that is predicated on a hard and fast distinction between land and water, swamps were anomalous

Figure 10.4 A tidal swamp in its natural state, Hokianga, 1998. Photograph by the author.

(Figure 10.4). Untamed places where all was yet to be done, their indeterminate nature, in space and time both, does not readily lend them to such absolute linear logic.

Māori settlement in 1840 had a particular pattern to it. It was concentrated along the floodplains and mouths of rivers and at estuaries and lagoons—the environments in which the indigenous flora and fauna tended to be most diverse and rich.[49] While the presence of European crops for fifty years prior had expanded Māori agriculture, the primary resources of the Māori economy continued to be the indigenous forests and fisheries referred to in the Treaty of Waitangi. Some of the richest and most productive resources of all were the coastal swamps in which those forests and fisheries co-occurred in the same immediate environment.

The high regard for lowland swamps in the traditional Māori landscape derived from the often vast areas of country that they watered and gave access to, from the birds that were attracted to them for food and breeding sites, and from the native fish that came to spawn.[50] Dominating the swamps were rushes, reeds, flax, and the kahikatea, or white pine. Mature fruiting kahikatea were a seasonal mecca for birds and people. Waikākā (spring eels, mudfish), a traditional delicacy for presentation at feasts, hibernated during summer drought beneath kahikatea roots. Myriad indigenous fish species such as inanga, kōaro, waikākā, and the kōkopu species, migrated through the estuaries and lagoons that would be taken by Crown law for swamp drainage scheme spillways, through into the pools enclosed by flax and raupō in the gaps in the kahikatea swamp forests. It was these conditions that made tidal swamp-plain rivers such as the Waihou, Waikato, and Manawatu great fisheries prior to British agricultural settlement.[51]

Ecologically, these were landscapes of interconnection and interaction, the antithesis of the boundary lines and the subdivision of the country into legally separated units desired by English land laws. It is in this sense that the American ecologist Daniel Janzen has commented how 'what escapes the eye is the most insidious kind of extinction—the extinction of interactions'.[52] Using the body-as-system analogy, the ecological effect of swamp drainage in New Zealand was as if a major organ such as the heart had been ruptured and removed. When the native birds no longer had the premium breeding and feeding zones that the lowland swamps provided, the hill forests, too, went silent.

The small-scale geographic diversity of New Zealand meant that, in most districts, the birds of interior forest country were never far from the relatively food-rich swamps of the coastal lowlands. Birds such as kererū, the New Zealand pigeon, would flock across country in huge numbers when a swamp food species such as kōwhai was in season. That, no less than the colonial evisceration of forest habitat, is why native bird numbers began plummeting dramatically, when swamp drainage facilitated by government schemes really got going comprehensively in the 1900s.

The cumulative impact of that period's agricultural settlement on the customary Māori swamp resource was reported to the Waitangi Tribunal by the South Island tribe Ngāi Tahu: 'European settlement inevitably began to impinge on Ngai Tahu mahinga kai resources ... By the late nineteenth century, most sources of mahinga kai in the Otakou Block had been destroyed or enclosed by settler occupation ... Streams, drains and lagoons were much more important to us than the main rivers. These smaller water bodies are the first to disappear when farmers or catchment boards start land drainage or river management works.'[53]

The advent of refrigerated shipping in the 1880s opened up huge European markets for dairy produce and made great demands for land on which to grow it. The concomitant draining of swamps and alteration of lakes and rivers to bring any level land into agricultural production was deemed in the 'national interest'. As the Waitangi Tribunal historian Ben White has observed, the country's future lay in sheep and cattle, not eels and kōura.[54] Swamps and the people who valued them as key mahinga kai were caught between the settler–colonist imperative to drain and reclaim any low-lying land that could become fertile pastures and the Crown imperative to control waterways. Customary Māori rights to swamps and waterways, those with which Article the Second of the Treaty of Waitangi terms 'taonga'— 'fisheries', 'forests', and 'properties'—are concerned, were primarily about use rights, from which ownership derives. Under English law the reverse applied; the right to use and manage a resource flowed from ownership of it. The way Māori were forced to reconceptualise their customary resource rights and laws in order that they be cognisable under English common law is one of the key issues of the colonial encounter in New Zealand (see Chapter 16).[55]

As White has said, while many colonists regarded the notion that Māori had rights in waterways as far-fetched, they considered idiotic any contention that Māori had rights in swamps. They believed tacitly that any rights to swamps on the land to which they held title were exclusively theirs. No less perhaps than Māori who sold lands containing swamps believed, from *their* customary standpoint, that they would continue to enjoy usufructuary rights in them. Little did they realise that not only would settler title to their swamps preclude their future access them, but also that drainage would transform their mahinga kai—by removing them.[56]

A succession of Crown laws effected swamp drainage, with increasingly deleterious repercussions for an economy with any reliance on freshwater resources. The earliest legislation pertaining to swamps vested power to drain land in provincial councils and other local authorities. With the 1876 Public Works Act the Crown formally empowered itself to control waterways. Any natural watercourse in which fluvial action occurred—thus any swamp—could be declared 'a public drain'. Councils could be empowered to undertake large-scale drainage operations, and could take any land required for drainage purposes. Ratepayer boards, which enabled farmers with a vested interest in drainage and the prevention of flooding to dominate decision-making and override other community interests, were set up by the 1884 Rivers Board Act and in 1893, the Land Drainage Act. White has recounted how such boards acted to the detriment of Māori, of whom only the trustees of landowner trusts could claim ratepayer status.[57]

By 1913 it was recommended to the government to eliminate swamps from the national landscape altogether. If there is a single tree species that characterises New Zealand's swamp environments, it is kahikatea, or white pine as settlers knew it. While Europe inched towards war, the Royal Commission on Forestry was deciding the future of land 'still under standing forest'. The government's policy of 'close settlement' and the 'pressing demand' for New Zealand's 'limited area of first class land' meant one kind of indigenous forest had to go: 'As is well known the soil of the white-pine swamps, when drained and the trees removed, forms one of the richest of agricultural land, which when grassed, is extremely useful for dairy farms ... Since no land is more suitable for occupation than that of the white-pine swamps, when drained ... their value in this regard is a strong plea in favour of the removal of the trees forthwith.'[58]

The Swamp Drainage Act 1915, extending government powers to undertake large-scale drainage operations, was enacted with a view to making more agricultural land available for settlement. Māori settlement land could be taken under the Act if, as in the case of the outfalls of the Rangitaiki Drainage Scheme in the Bay of Plenty, the Crown considered it essential for the completion of a drainage operation.

Wetlands rediscovered

'Wetlands,' said a recent Asian and Pacific UN Environment Programme, 'are vital life-support systems for many communities throughout the world. The traditional [i.e. Western] world view of wetlands as wastelands is being overturned and there has been a rise in awareness of their importance.'[59] From the beginning of the twentieth century most elements of New Zealand's indigenous life that British colonists had considered 'wasteland' became protected in some way; as ecosystems as well as species (Chapter 8). But not swamps. As early as the 1930s, ornithologists had tied the national decline in indigenous birds to agriculture's transformation of lowland swamps. In the 1950s the impact of lowland swamp clearance on indigenous fauna became a conservation issue as, in district after district, once-common wetland birds such as matuku (bittern) became rare. But it was not until the end of the 1960s that there was any acknowledgment by the state that swamps had intrinsic, indigenous values, over and above their potential productivity as farmland.

The recognition was initiated by the Wildlife Service undertaking a series of wetland surveys in the Bay of Plenty.[60] Such surveys led to the Service, by opposing local drainage schemes and proposing protection, becoming a counter-force to the Crown's traditional policy role of draining and developing wetlands. But it was not until the 1980s that New Zealand government sufficiently accepted the principle to state, as policy, that swamps have not been adequately represented in the reserve system; that 'if samples of the whole range of natural wetlands are to be retained as part of the landscape, many existing wetlands must be reserved'.[61] Just as wetland drainage quintessentially characterises modernity, wetland restoration, perhaps, characterises postmodernity.

Conclusion

It is no coincidence that the Crown's firm tightening of its animal protection laws as the nineteenth century ended and through the first decade of the twentieth, prohibiting hunting of native birds such as kererū, straddles the same passage of time in which the Crown undertook its great swamp-drainage schemes. They were years of change and crisis in the Māori landscape, as the Native Land Court worked its way through tribes' estates, and as the natural life-support systems that had traditionally sustained them vanished (Chapter 16).

The Crown's concern was with what 'would be appreciated by many settlers.'[62] In turn-of-the century parliamentary debate, swamps were seen as country whose settlers faced particular difficulties in helping the colony realise prosperity. William Massey described the situation in 1903 that led to the Crown becoming the key agent in swamp drainage:

> A settler goes onto swamp land. The first thing he has to do is to get in his drains—not only his main drains but also his side drains. Then, if the swamp has too much water thereon, after the settler has got his drains in and got the water off he has to allow the scrub to grow upon it before he can get a burn. That may take two or three years. After the scrub has grown sufficiently he has to wait for a dry summer. Then, when he gets it burnt off, he has to wait another year before he gets the grass to grow, and probably two to three years after that before it is sufficiently consolidated to carry heavy stock. That is the situation of many of the swamps in the North Island.[63]

Ecological landscape change takes time even when a colonising culture is in landscape transformation mode. Yet by the late 1890s, anyone who had anything to do with the land and nature was aware of the dramatic decline in bird numbers occurring. But the MP for Northern Māori, Hone Heke Rankin, objected in Parliament to 'any legislation that tends to take away any of the native rights to shoot or kill birds' as the closed-season clauses in the Animals Protection Act 1895 were doing.[64] It would, he said, have massive impact on his Tai Tokerau people. Heke repeated an argument that Māori had made consistently since the 1879 Māori Parliament—that the government should not be able to dictate bird protection or game management on Māori land.[65] His opposition was on the basis of rights. Castigating the new legislation for doing nothing to halt the loss of forest habitat that European settlement was causing, and for putting the burden of impact on Māori who had kept their forests, he called for flexibility in the timing of closed seasons to allow for phased fruiting of the birds' berry trees.[66] 'The birds suffered,' he said, 'because settlers cut down the bush, not because of hunting.'

Te Tai Tokerau was one of New Zealand's swampiest regions, wet climatically and with countless low-lying valley flats winding inland from its many harbours. Much of the bush that settlers were downing was swamp forest, in order to get to the rich soil of the flats—then to drain, burn, fence, grass, and stock it. As a factor that collapsed the indigenous resource of Hone Heke Rankin's concern, the succession of changes to Te Tai Tokerau's swamps would have paralleled in magnitude the massive settler clearance of hill forests that was occurring.

It was in Te Tai Tokerau, too, that a coastal swamp resource had first initiated Māori into the Western trade economy (Chapters 3 and 4). The exchange of flax fibre for muskets began the massive readjustment of tribal power that preceded the Treaty of Waitangi. And in the concomitant change in Māori lifestyle and settlement pattern it produced lay the root cause, some colonists believed, of Māori becoming the vulnerable, vanishing race they appeared to be when swamp drainage was in full swing. Consumption, 'the chief disease that kills the Maoris', according to Alfred Newman in 1881, was widely considered the consequence of the shift from the 'old hill-forts' of their 'former wild' habitat to 'live at the edge of a bush or a swamp, almost always on low-lying, damp, ill-drained spots'.[67]

Swamps and Māori alike had little place in Newman's New Zealand. Both had threatened, but none of the country would be allowed to remain as Charles Hursthouse's 'bittern's dark domain, fertile only in miasma'. No New Zealand environment has seen greater loss of its indigenous life than its swamps. None has so little future prospect for native flora and fauna as the 'portion of the wilderness' for which Hursthouse foresaw the plough converting into his 'wholesome plains of fruit, and grain and grass'. 'The sanatorium of a large body of ... wealthy invalid-emigrants', he called it: 'cultivating a few acres for amusement near the towns and profiting by the fine scenery and the really good society of the young Land'.[68]

Part 4

Modernising

11
THE GRASSLANDS REVOLUTION RECONSIDERED

Tom Brooking, Robin Hodge, and Vaughan Wood

P. W. Smallfield, retired Director-General of Agriculture, published *The Grasslands Revolution in New Zealand* in 1970. In his account of the substantial improvement of New Zealand pasture lands since the 1890s he recalled the words of A. H. Cockayne, famous agricultural scientist and later Director-General of Agriculture. In the 1920s Cockayne had likened New Zealand's farming land to 'a magic hat which, while still retaining its original size, allowed the conjurer to draw a seemingly never ending stream of objects from its interior'. It appeared to Smallfield that spectacular production increases on an essentially static land area between 1920 and 1966, and especially between 1949 and the 1960s, 'more than vindicated Cockayne's simile'. Smallfield attributed the three-fold increase in production from the 1920s to the 1960s not to 'the conjurer's magic wand', as Charles Darwin earlier had on seeing the English-style farm established by the Anglican missionaries at Waimate, but to 'the combined and sustained efforts of farmers, research and advisory services, marketing boards, merchants and successive governments'.[1]

This chapter outlines the 'revolution' as described by its major architects and promoters, discerns variations among them, and analyses New Zealanders' obsession with the development of grasslands at the expense of other land-development strategies. It explores briefly the alternative organic approach to farming, which did not have much influence outside the suburban garden until the 1990s. It concludes by examining the slow 'greening' of mainstream agriculture, as the grasslands revolution was questioned for its less desirable environmental impacts, and draws together the mainstream and alternative paths.

What was 'the grasslands revolution'?

Smallfield, along with Sir Bruce Levy (Director of the Grasslands Division of the Department of Scientific and Industrial Research (DSIR)), the geographer Kenneth Cumberland, and soil conservators Lance McCaskill and Douglas Campbell, coined the term 'grasslands revolution' to celebrate the huge increase in farming output that occurred after the acquisition of phosphate-rich Nauru Island in 1919, and especially after the introduction of aerial topdressing in 1949. The application of superphosphate and an increasing amount of variants (particularly serpentine) peaked at over 3 million tonnes in 1985, or about 2 per cent of the world's total. Sheep numbers had stagnated at around 20 million in the early 1900s, but then increased between the wars to around 30 million before rocketing from 32 million in 1949 to a peak of 70 million in 1982. This occurred with only a small increase in the area of cultivated land. Tonnages of fertiliser and sheep numbers fell dramatically from 1985, when the fourth Labour government removed subsidies and recast traditional agriculture as a 'sunset' industry.[2] Until then New Zealand had prospered as a direct result of the revolution maintaining a standard of living from the 1920s to the 1970s that ranked between the fifth and third highest in the world.[3] Little wonder, therefore, that agricultural historian B. L. Evans and historian of New Zealand science F. R. Callaghan confirmed the notion of a revolution in grasslands farming by treating the men who directed it as heroic champions of the application of science to agriculture.[4]

The story told by both historians and agricultural scientists praised nineteenth-century farmers for converting bush to pasture because New Zealand's temperate and moist climate supposedly made it the country most suited in the British Empire, and even the world, to growing grass and carrying stock year-round. Rarely was this simple environmental determinism tempered by acknowledgment of the country's relative paucity of fertile soils. Instead, such modernist authors argued that a combination of planting exotic pastures and application of artificial fertilisers easily compensated for any such natural deficit. They therefore praised enlightened pioneer farmers who had used fertilisers from the 1890s, especially blood and bone from the burgeoning number of freezing works.

But, with the advantage of hindsight, the modernists also condemned the ignorance of the pioneers and hill-country farmers for pushing New Zealand farming past its ecological limits by 1920. Difficult economic times compounded such apparently intractable problems as regenerating bush and erosion when, according to Cumberland, nature exacted its revenge from the early 1920s.[5] The huge effort in laying down some 14 million acres of English pastures by 1911 seemed wasted as productivity declined dramatically once the initial virgin fertility had been worked out.[6] Failure forced many soldier–settlers to leave the land. Production, which climbed in the early 1920s in response to increasing mechanisation and the application of superphosphate made at fertiliser plants by mixing sulphuric acid with phosphate from Nauru, fell back. Failure heaped up when commodity prices collapsed during the 1930s Depression. The 'Bridge to Nowhere' became a potent symbol of the chronic underperformance of New Zealand agriculture. War compounded the situation by interrupting supplies of phosphate and discouraging farmers from adopting more innovative approaches. Unbeknown to pessimists, however, war also held the key to recovery through developing greatly improved aircraft. The Royal New Zealand Air Force and Douglas Campbell worked together to adapt military planes for the difficult task of dropping superphosphate from the air.[7]

Improvements in the understanding of soil nutrients (particularly the role of such crucial trace elements as cobalt and molybdenum), and advances in pasture ecology in the 1930s, also enabled farmers to develop the old gum lands of the Far North and the pumice lands of the North Island's Volcanic Plateau after World War II. The development of more vigorous strains of exotic pastures, especially clovers and rye grasses, along with Bruce Levy's notion of heavy stocking to create 'urine and dung showers', led to spectacular increases in production from 1949 onwards. Bulldozers apparently minced secondary growth into submission while applied science and increased aerial topdressing raised soil fertility and increased carrying capacity of formerly marginal land. Research and development and government assistance propelled New Zealand to the world leadership of grassland farming and enabled it to maximise supposed 'natural advantages'.

The end result was the conversion of 51 per cent of New Zealand's surface area to grasslands by the 1970s. This far exceeded the world average of 37 per cent.[8] Overseas scientists marvelled at New Zealand's super-efficient grassland farming. Little wonder that agricultural scientists celebrated this conversion from a giant rainforest to smiling pastures apparently free from 'Old World' soil exhaustion and the curse of regenerating bush.

This glorification of agricultural science, downplaying any negative impacts, survived largely unchallenged from within mainstream agricultural science until the 1980s, despite queries raised by some microbiologists and ecologists. Cumberland's 1981 television series and book *Landmarks* then popularised the notion that agricultural science had saved New Zealand from economic and environmental disaster.

Variants of the revolution

Agricultural scientists (especially agrostologists—grassland scientists), however, were generally more enthusiastic than soil scientists. Levy, in particular, became less critical as the years passed. As a young instructor to the Department of Agriculture, he had acknowledged that the forest had a key role to play in New Zealand's future and had adopted an ecological perspective that placed him in the vanguard of contemporary scientific thought in the first edition of *The Grasslands of New Zealand* (1923). By 1951, as Director of the Grasslands Division, he had become obsessed with grass and his sense of ecology did not extend beyond the paddock fence. In his final 1973 version the retired scientist and international eminence wanted every possible hectare of New Zealand covered in high-producing pasture so that it could carry 111 million sheep.

Few authors could see beauty or worth in scrub or gorse, but Levy differed from others in not lauding the fact that the actual increases had occurred without much expansion of the farming area. On the contrary, he seemed annoyed by the reluctance of government and farmers to undertake such expansion. In contrast, Kenneth Cumberland, like P. W. Smallfield, expressed pride in so much more being produced from a virtually static area of land. Cumberland muttered darkly that the threatened removal of the herbicide 2,4,5-T (finally banned in 1988) would give gorse the 'half chance' it needed to flourish. Smallfield expressed hopes of a massive increase in sheep numbers and thanked science for making available to farmers some 243 chemical fertilisers and herbicides rather than the 'handful' present in the 1920s.[9]

Lance McCaskill was always more guarded because he realised that Levy's beloved 'dense sward' could not hold the land by itself. Even so, like Campbell, he praised aerial topdressing as a useful ally in the fight against soil erosion. McCaskill also portrayed the restoration of Molesworth station in Marlborough as a miracle of agricultural science, the lesson of which was that production could be maintained by resting pasture from grazing and by greater use of cattle as opposed to sheep.[10] Although like Levy and other agricultural scientists McCaskill and Campbell had considerable state support, they struggled to change farmer attitudes towards erosion control compared with the success of grassland scientists in persuading them to utilise aerial topdressing.

Levy, whose heavy stocking and high fertiliser inputs approach is still shared by farmers in some parts of Southland, Canterbury, Taranaki, and Waikato, acted as a radical revolutionary with his 'unbridled pasture' system. McCaskill held a more conservative position. Some mainstream grassland scientists such as Kevin O'Connor, successor to McCaskill at the Tussock Grasslands and Mountain Lands Institute at Lincoln, shared the soil conservators' reaction against Levy's excess, but still accepted that applied science had achieved much and would continue to do so for the foreseeable future. Another group, represented by P. D. Sears (Director of the Grasslands Division of the DSIR, 1956–63) and J. K. Syers (Professor of Soil Science at Massey University, 1972–85), positioned themselves somewhere between the uncompromising Levy and the more cautious McCaskill. Sears, for example, advocated more extensive sowing of white clover in country suited to sheep farming, but also recommended that pasture be retired in steep areas and turned over to trees.

All the 'grasslands revolutionaries' remained oblivious to the extraordinary environmental damage to Nauru, and rarely questioned the energy costs involved in shipping phosphate to New Zealand and then distributing it by fuel-guzzling aeroplanes. When they did investigate this issue, a consensus soon emerged that New Zealand's grassland farmers remained far more efficient users of energy than the cropping farmers of North America and Europe.[11] They believed that solutions to farming problems would always involve the use of artificial fertilisers, herbicides, and pesticides. Like the New Zealand Institute of Agricultural Science (founded in 1953 by Campbell), they agreed that, while mistakes had been made, repair had succeeded and would continue to succeed; to them the gains far outweighed any problems and losses. In this respect the mainstream differed from the much smaller group discussed in the second section of this chapter who reacted totally against the enthusiasm for applied science and artificial fertilisers and differentiated themselves with the label of 'organic farmers'.[12]

Most discussions of the 'grasslands revolution', however, tend to hide the fact that the changes occurred in stages rather than in one long, uninterrupted progression, and that the 'revolution' occurred at very different rates in the North and South Islands. Initially, superphosphate brought most benefit to the dairy farmers of the North Island, who wanted to end time-consuming and costly reliance upon supplementary crops. Growing a single crop of grass proved much more attractive. South Island farmers, in contrast, other than the grain growers of Canterbury and Southland dependent on such fodder crops as turnips, did not use superphosphate on any scale until the advent of aerial topdressing. Consequently 2.1 million of the 2.4 million acres topdressed with artificial fertilisers in 1934 were in the North Island. Southern farmers preferred to retain short rotations of pasture and crops, and failed to increase production much between 1900 and 1950.

South Island sheep numbers fell behind those of the North Island from 1899 and increased by only 38 per cent from 11.3 million in 1910 to 14.8 million in 1950. In contrast North Island sheep numbers increased by 47 per cent over the same period from 12.9 million to 19 million. Indeed, the initial concern of A. H. Cockayne with grasslands related to the South Island's relative underperformance. From the establishment of the Department of Agriculture's Grasslands Research Station at Palmerston North in 1926 (transferred to the DSIR in 1936), attention shifted to bringing pumice land, gum land, and land that had reverted to secondary growth into production, and with repairing the damage caused by erosion on the east coast of the North Island. McCaskill was left to cure the South Island's ills. The drier areas of the South Island also required irrigation before farming could push past nineteenth-century production levels. In combination, irrigation and aerial topdressing closed the gap somewhat between 1950 and 1980 (from 14.8 million to 32.8 million sheep as against the North Island's 19 million to 36.9 million).[13]

Figure 11.1 'Fertiliser helped us grow ...' A romantic portrayal of the technology that delivered the 'grasslands revolution'. Advertisement from the *New Zealand Journal of Agriculture*, June 1977.

The upsurge in fertiliser usage of the 1950s gathered momentum through the 1960s, supported by both subsidies and the advocacy of the Department of Agriculture and the Grasslands Division. It only began to slow from the mid 1970s when the rising costs of superphosphate and aviation fuel forced farmers to reconsider the rate of application (Figure 11.1). The amount of superphosphate and additives dropped over the green fields of New Zealand peaked at over 3 million tonnes in 1985. This then fell dramatically when, rather than phasing out subsidies, the fourth Labour government ended them abruptly.

Changes in infrastructure, advances in related technological areas, and shifts in government policy are always necessary before a technology can surge ahead. The remarkable feature of the grasslands revolution is that it advanced as rapidly as it did, despite checks imposed by bureaucracy, inadequate means of transport, unreliable markets, the natural scepticism of farmers, and the environment itself.

Why did the grasslands revolution occur in such extreme form?

Why did the agricultural establishment become quite so obsessed with establishing grasslands as a kind of monoculture? The obvious answer is economics, because fat-lambing, wool growing, and dairying won New Zealand a considerable degree of prosperity. Only worsening terms of trade, exacerbated by Britain's manoeuvring to join the European Economic Community from the 1960s, and the oils shocks of the 1970s, threatened the continuance of that prosperity and forced a major rethink on how the country earned its living.

Concern to reduce escalating labour costs was influential in persuading agricultural scientists to advocate greater use of artificial fertilisers and chemicals. Smallfield admitted that cropping could improve feed but lamented that it 'needed too much labour for production and feeding out'. He praised chemical weedkillers for promoting 'a revolution in weed control from the days when we used to bend hour after hour'. A more organic approach seemed laborious, slow, and expensive in comparison.[14] The topdressing plane, especially once the specialist Fletcher had been developed from 1957, also liberated hill-country farmers from drudgery.

Yet much more than economic imperatives and fascination with high-tech innovation was involved in explaining the pursuit of a grasslands paradise. Scientific conceptualisation and practice is never innocent and objective. It is rather a product of its time, especially of the climate of opinion, intellectual fashions, and changing cultural norms. During the period from the 1920s to the 1960s, faith ran high in the limitless possibilities of science and technology to resolve humanity's problems. Cynicism concerning the claims of mainstream science lay well in the future. Two world wars raised serious doubts about humanity's moral capacity but reinforced this blind faith by accelerating technological and medical advances. Gains in areas such as aviation were so spectacular that this optimism became 'scientism', or a kind of substitute religion.[15] Agricultural scientists, who held considerable power and influence in New Zealand over this period, shared this optimistic faith in 'man's' capacity to tame and improve upon nature.

Figure 11.2 Cover of the *New Zealand Journal of Agriculture*, July 1946, showing the Four Horsemen of the Apocalypse. The message is New Zealand's role as a bread basket feeding a hungry world.

Noble intentions also played a vital role in driving the grasslands revolution, especially the determination to ensure the success of rehabilitation. Levy, Smallfield, Cumberland, and McCaskill all shared the first Labour government's determination to avoid the disasters of the 1920s and to build a stronger economy and a better society.[16] So too did the report of the Sheep Industry Commission in 1949 and editorials in the *Journal of Agriculture*.[17] The high wool prices induced by the Korean War seemed to confirm this confident prognosis. The commissioners also talked incessantly about feeding a hungry world, as did Federated Farmers, which metamorphosed out of the older Farmers' Union between 1944 and 1946. New Zealand's future as a food producer seemed guaranteed by the global population explosion. Until postwar idealism waned in the 1960s, numerous conferences also echoed this optimistic reading[18] (Figure 11.2). It also reflected a much older and deeper belief in 'ruralism'—the notion that the country way of life is morally superior and socially preferable to city living. Levy and Cumberland, along with the *Journal of Agriculture* and *Straight Furrow*, portrayed the city as an unproductive and vice-ridden problem[19] (Figure 11.3).

Figure 11.3 Cover of the *New Zealand Journal of Agriculture*, September 1946. A portrayal of the virtues of rurality and New Zealand's ongoing role as Britain's outlying farm, with St Paul's, London, representing the temple of Empire.

Some other factors also influenced the narrow concentration on improving grassland farming. One was the direct impetus coming out of English agronomy from the 1920s as it attempted to catch up on the gains made at the Svalof Plant Breeding Station in Sweden. Reginald George Stapledon, champion of pasture improvement at the Royal Agricultural College at Cirencester (and later the Welsh Plant Breeding Station at Aberystwyth and the Grassland Improvement Station at Drayton), visited Levy in 1926 and encouraged New Zealand experimentation. No one seemed to note the irony involved in the rejection by New Zealand 'agrostologists' of Stapledon's suggestion that evolution equips indigenous grasses best to cope with environmental particuliarities. Instead they went ahead with improving imported English grasses. Levy later worked with one of Stapledon's star students, William Davies, to develop even more vigorous strains of rye grass and clovers. Stapledon also moved agrostology away from a broader ecological perspective and contradicted his arguments in favour of indigenous adaptation by fixating on improving a narrow range of easily controlled grasses that he hoped would expand production within the Empire as well as within Britain. Lord Bledisloe, New Zealand's Governor-General at this time and a successful and enthusiastic farmer himself, articulated a similar agenda.

Lingering imperialist ties and ongoing commitment to the project of colonisation underpinned such influences. Cumberland and Levy responded to the imperial rallying cry by suggesting that Māori land currently covered in weeds and gorse needed 'vigorous occupancy' if it was to be converted into the best pasture. Men of Levy's generation continued to envisage New Zealand as Britain's farm and could not tolerate the idea of places within it that did not operate at the highest levels of productivity. They ignored the irony that their revolution could never have been implemented without the land removed from Māori ownership by dubious purchase and confiscation.

Certainly the agrostologists' obsessions mesh with the argument of Libby Robin, Australian environmental historian, that ecology became 'a science of Empire'. She points out that ecology grew out of the earlier 'Systematics', which had been developed to help administrators better understand the new lands of their ever-expanding domains. Ecology gained official recognition in 1913 with the establishment of the British Ecological Society. This development lagged behind the United States, where land-grant colleges had linked the 'science of development' with agriculture in the 1890s. New Zealand followed over a generation later with the establishment of Massey Agricultural College and the Department of Scientific and Industrial Research (DSIR) in 1926, and the modernisation of Lincoln (established in 1878) to provide the South Island with an up-to-date, American-style agricultural college. Developments in Australia also followed the American model but paralleled New Zealand chronologically. The key agency, the Commonwealth Scientific and Industrial Research Organisation, was also set up in 1926. Like New Zealand's DSIR, it represented a local institutional response to the urgings of politicians and administrators to increase the productivity and wealth of the Empire.

As in New Zealand, most Australian 'applied science' soon focused on agriculture rather than manufacturing, reflecting the colonial division of labour and reinforcing dependence of the Australasian periphery on the British core (Figure 11.3). Australian agricultural scientists turned their attention to pasture improvement and pest control. Severe soil-erosion problems, however, forced ecologists and other agricultural scientists to carry out much more research beyond the farm and paddock. Yet even today Robin argues that the essential 'Western nature' of ecological science means that its practitioners still concentrate their labours on improving economically valuable 'imported' floras and faunas. Much the same could be said of New Zealand before the late 1980s. Bledisloe's 1934 address to the Grasslands' Association Conference underscored this point when he praised grassland scientists as 'progressive far sighted patriots' and argued that grasslands constituted 'the true wealth' of New Zealand.[20]

Things might also have been different if another year like 1938, with its disastrous floods and soil erosion on the North Island's east coast, had occurred before Cyclone Bola in 1988. New Zealanders, therefore, had only to accept the flood control initiatives of catchment board engineers (see Chapter 12), rather than rethinking how bush clearance and overgrazing damaged the land. Many farmers consequently ignored the warnings of soil conservators regarding flooding. Indeed, the Sheep Industry Commission set up during World War II to discover how this key engine of the economy could operate more efficiently, when it finally reported in 1949, argued that farming had nothing to do with erosion. This view remained largely unchallenged within orthodox farming circles until Bola.[21]

From the 1960s the shift to town became relentless as sons gave up the rigours of farming for more lucrative careers in the urban professions and joined the cohort of deserting daughters. Worse, political power, held for so long in the strong hands of farmers, slipped away faster than an East Cape hillside. The old order increasingly appeared to constitute a golden age as suburb, rather than farm or small town, became the abode of most New Zealanders.[22] Increasing productivity through the application of fertilisers, herbicides, and pesticides via aerial topdressing represented a tangible way of retaining prosperity, power, and lifestyle. It also maintained the pugnacious, masculinist attitudes of landholders against nature, a perspective that persists among some to the present day (Figure 11.4).[23]

Figure 11.4 Advertisement for Tordon Brushkiller, 1999. The imagery of war against nature continues down to the present.

Greening the green sward: the 'organic' alternative

Despite the almost complete dominance of mainstream grasslands agriculture there was nonetheless a persistent, if low-profile, interest in organic farming in New Zealand. Artificial fertilisers became more popular with grassland and arable farmers from the early 1900s as their cost fell.[24] In contrast, market gardeners, especially those of Chinese extraction, and orchardists continued to use whatever natural fertilisers they could to reduce costs as these specialisations developed from the 1870s. An alternative approach, developed in Europe and Britain, began to have a much bigger influence from the 1920s, especially on suburban gardeners.

Organics, as a self-conscious movement in New Zealand, began with the formation of the Food Reform Society in 1922 to improve the nutrition of New Zealanders. It followed the teachings of Albert Howard, who had developed greater use of compost at the Indian research centre of Indore; another example of ecology as 'science of Empire'. The society promoted Howard's composting methods before forming the first Humic Compost Club in Auckland in 1941. Prominent supporters included the poet A. R. D. Fairburn and the advocate of Abel Tasman National Park, Pérrine Moncrieff.[25] By 1956, fifteen branches were established throughout New Zealand with 4000 members, although membership declined thereafter. A report in 1984 noted 'there were no more than 70' organic farmers, as opposed to home gardeners.

'Biodynamics', the organic method advocated by the philosopher Rudolf Steiner, also began in New Zealand in the late 1920s when George Winkfield, having learnt the techniques at Steiner's research institute, the Goetheanum, in Switzerland, began to make and distribute biodynamic preparations. Numbers of adherents grew slowly, particularly in clusters of orchardists around Kerikeri and Te Aroha, until in 1939 they formed an association that was registered in 1945 as the Biodynamic Association of New Zealand. By 1985 they had 500 members, including farmers, orchardists, and viticulturists, but again precise numbers of each cannot be established.

Members of these New Zealand groups, as in Britain, Germany, and elsewhere, held the older world-view of Earth as a living organism, whose plants, animals, and human beings are interconnected by a life force or vital spirit. One reason for the reappearance of this world-view was in reaction to the substantial increase in the use of artificial chemical fertilisers and, later, pesticides. Organic farmers and gardeners saw themselves, unlike champions of orthodox farming, as working with nature rather 'than constantly fighting it'.

Yet despite endless pamphlet writing and public-speaking campaigns neither Soil and Health (the name adopted when the Food Reform Society and the Humic Compost Club joined forces in 1943) nor the Biodynamic Association had much impact outside the suburbs. In the countryside, only orchardists showed much interest, apart from a few notable eccentrics. The wealthy owner of a rubber plantation in Malaya, Alma Baker, for example, invested considerable money during the 1930s in attempts at organic farming on his Limestone Downs property near Raglan. His trustees worked with Massey University after his death to moderate his apparently 'impractical' ideas, based on Steiner's teachings, into a more workable 'low-input' agriculture. The methods used for thirty years by one organic farmer in North Otago, J. W. Nicolls, are detailed in his 1964 book *It's a*

Pleasure. Observing one of his cows selecting goose grass from a roadside pasture, Nicolls remembered thinking, 'Strewth, [Bruce] Levy's spent his life on the wrong grass'. He farmed on what he called a long cycle of more than four years, alternating stock and cropping on his paddocks, never ploughing wet ground, and applying as much organic compost to his farm as possible. The latter task became much easier when his neighbour, organic farmer Harry Leaman, began a business to compost the borough wastes of Oamaru, one of several towns and cities to establish such a scheme. Dannevirke operated the first from 1946 under its borough engineer, Harold A. Truman. It ceased operations in 1967 when the borough council declared it financially unviable.

The Auckland City Council also operated a municipal compost scheme from 1950, but it closed in the 1960s, possibly because of contamination by inorganic materials. The New Zealand branch of the British Medical Association and the Inter-Departmental Committee on Utilization of Organic Wastes gave support to these schemes. Official recognition came from the Department of Agriculture and from the Royal Commission on the Sheep-Farming Industry, while Ben Roberts, Minister of Agriculture, pledged his support to the Biodynamic Association conference in 1945. But large-scale composting ventures ended in the 1960s and were not revived until the 1990s.[26]

The slow greening of mainstream grassland farming

Despite the limited impact of organic farming, a few more orthodox farmers, including the noted botanist and sheep farmer Herbert Guthrie-Smith, had doubted the efficacy of so-called scientific farming since the troubled 1930s. The massive floods and land slips of 1938 confirmed his worst fears. The preface to Guthrie-Smith's third edition of *Tutira*, for example, reveals considerable anxiety about orthodox farming and the wholesale replacement of trees by pasture. His essay published in 1940 in the illustrated school series *The Making of New Zealand* lamented that the soil had deteriorated so badly that grasses that 'used to flourish with enthusiasm grow now with philosophic calm, almost with the senility of age'. He concluded gloomily that grass could not hold the land, and that erosion had become an 'inevitable, uncontrollable process' without a massive attempt at reforestation. Yet such voices were very few in number. The great majority of farmers believed in the heroic version of the grasslands revolution.[27]

Reference to Rachel Carson's disturbing critique *Silent Spring* (1962) appeared in the *Journal of Agriculture* from 1965, but sustained questioning of chemical farming did not occur until the 1980s, and topdressing planes dropped DDT in a mix with superphosphate from the 1950s to 1970s. Carson had also condemned the overconfidence and carelessness associated with 'scientism', but few seemed to notice in rural New Zealand. Dichlorophenoxyacetic acid, or 2,4-D, which Carson highlighted as particularly toxic, remained our most common herbicide until 1997, when it began to be phased out and replaced with a less volatile ester formulation.[28] The *Journal of Agriculture*, Federated Farmers, and most agricultural scientists lamented the demise of the insecticide DDT when United States authorities banned its use in 1979 but welcomed the arrival of the powerful new herbicide 2,4,5-T. Farmers and the *Journal* initially sided with 2,4,5-T manufacturer Ivon Watkins Dow against criticism of 'Agent Orange'. Many also argued that DDT residues did not constitute a long-term problem, even though some soils in Southland and Canterbury still require careful treatment because of excessive use of this insecticide.[29] The *Journal* condemned the failure to clean up thousands of toxic dumps often associated with dipping from 1975, and blamed the problem on an 'out of sight, out of mind' approach. In 1989, farmers and government finally drew up an Agrichemical Users' Code of Practice and established a New Zealand Agricultural Chemical Education Trust to promote wise use of agricultural chemicals.[30]

Women seemed to be concerned earlier than men, with the Women's Division of Federated Farmers calling for greater attention to environmental matters from the 1970s.[31] The realisation that agriculture rather than manufacturing was the greatest national polluter did not dawn upon the broader rural community until the late 1970s, when scientists calculated that New Zealand sheep and cattle produced as much organic waste as 150 million people. Concern about effluents appeared from the late 1960s, as microbiologists confirmed that dumping of dairy waste into creeks and streams, along with fertiliser runoff, could enrich, or eutrophy, waters to such an extent that most animals and plants within the affected streams or lakes died. Alternatively, weed growth stimulated by the excess of nitrogen and phosphorus strangled all other forms of life and gave off noxious odours.

The *Journal* responded by suggesting several alternative ways of disposing of this waste. The 1967 Water and Soil Conservation Act tried to regulate such practices and established a National Water and Soil Conservation Authority to monitor this work, with mixed results. *Straight Furrow*, the official organ of Federated Farmers, began to advocate lower stocking rates from the early 1980s. Tree planting was endorsed by the 1949 Royal Commission on the Sheep Industry, and the *Journal* chipped in with lots of advice on how and what to plant from the 1950s. The Farm Forestry Association, founded in 1959, enthusiastically promoted planting of 'useful' species. Government meanwhile established the Queen Elizabeth II National Trust in 1977 to protect open spaces, including wetlands, by voluntary covenant. Such moves towards more cautious husbandry won the support of much of the mainstream farming community by the 1990s. Federated Farmers, working with Landcare Research, also revitalised the older farmer-support groups of catchment board days in the form of landcare groups in the South Island high country from the late 1980s. These groups spread into the erosion-ravaged east coast of the North Island in the 1990s.[32]

Such questioning of the old orthodoxy had practical spin-offs as New Zealand Federated Farmers and the Ministry of Agriculture and Fisheries began serious investigations of organics. Two MAF surveys resulted, in 1983 and 1987, the second of which gave guarded approval to organic farming. When, in 1983, Dr Bert Quin argued that New Zealand's pastoral farming had always been essentially organic because the great majority of farmers raised stock rather than crops, did not inject stock with hormones and kept chemical, herbicide, and pesticide use to a minimum, Bob Crowder, lecturer in horticulture at Lincoln, and practising bio-dynamic farmers such as Ian Stephenson disputed this comforting interpretation. Some agricultural scientists, such as R. J. Haynes of the Agricultural Research Division at Lincoln and R. S. Swift, head of Soil Science at Lincoln, initially ridiculed such protestations as bad science.[33] Within a year, however, editor, journalists, and readers accepted Crowder's enthusiastic review of Miguel A. Altieri's *Agroecology: The Scientific Basis of an Alternative Agriculture* without adverse comment. Mainstream farmers implemented integrated pest-management schemes employing a whole range of controls instead of relying upon highly toxic pesticides. Leading grassland scientists such as O'Connor joined the growing chorus of opinion in favour of making farming 'sustainable' from the mid 1980s.[34] Research by social anthropologist Hugh Campbell also suggests that 'new' horticulturists and viticulturists, largely from urban backgrounds, are much more amenable to following organic alternatives than are traditional grassland farmers.

Conclusion

Unsurprisingly, recent studies of high-country farming cited in the 1997 report on *The State of the Environment* suggest that struggling farmers in difficult environments are still responding more to cost signals than concern for sustainability. Thus the greening of New Zealand farming still has a long way to go before the more negative impacts of the grasslands revolution can be ameliorated.[35] Nevertheless, we are slowly coming to realise that the old paradigm of relentless scientific and technological progress does not provide an adequate understanding of the complex and special environment in which we live. One solid proof of this shift is *Pastures: Their Ecology and Management* (a completely new edition of the 1972 *Pastures and Pasture Plants*), edited by R. H. M. Langer, Emeritus Professor of Plant Science at Lincoln, and published in 1990. Unlike Bruce Levy's original work, this volume acknowledges the problem of environmental degradation and the worth of indigenous grasses, admits the limits of intensive farming based on high technological inputs, and calls for the preservation of indigenous landscapes. Even that old demon gorse is reassessed, because its nitrogen-fixing ability enables it to act as nursery for regenerating bush.[36]

By the later 1980s, organic challengers were no longer marginalised, but nor were they in the mainstream. Between 1920 and 1960 they had some success in having organic compost accepted by home and market gardeners, but because of cost, the perceived necessity for high yields, and philosophies of progress, they had little impact on New Zealand farmers or agricultural science. By the early 1990s, however, assisted by international reappraisal of the environmental impacts of chemical farming, they had helped 'green' New Zealand agriculture to the extent that their methods were seriously researched and considered suitable for export niches. More importantly, 'organic farming' suddenly became profitable as a large market for such products developed in Europe and Japan. Heinz Wattie, for example, has recently directed some suppliers to adopt 'organic' methods in search of market niches. In the new millennium an organic dairy farmer even serves as vice-president of Federated Farmers. Keith Holyoake's optimistic retelling of the old English adage to 'Live as though you were going to die tomorrow, but farm as if you were going to live forever', delivered at the Takaka Agricultural and Pastoral Show of 1938,[37] takes on a new relevance as greater environmental awareness develops and as alternative economic opportunities beckon.

12

THE STATE AS CONSERVATIONIST, 1920–60

'WISE USE' OF FORESTS, LANDS, AND WATER

Michael Roche

By 1920 New Zealand's biophysical environment had undergone widespread, rapid, and often irreversible change as a consequence of colonisation. The role of the state in bringing this about as an agent of land development, while also ameliorating natural resource exploitation in the interests of conservation, tends to be overlooked. The designation of large portions of New Zealand as Crown land conferred a number of possibilities for state-led conservation, particularly through the activities of government departments responsible for lands and forests. These included the creation of national parks, reserves, and state forests.

This chapter examines state-led conservation initiatives from the 1920s to about 1960, when a belief in superabundant resources gave way to concerns about rates of exploitation and the possibility of resource exhaustion. It is a period that has been comparatively neglected by environmental historians. The nineteenth century has been more fully explored in a search for conservation origins, and the 1970s have attracted attention for the emergence of environmentalism. Yet in New Zealand, as elsewhere, there were significant conservation episodes between the 1920s and the 1950s.

The 1920s were marked by the development of state conservation initiatives overseen by a small number of technical experts within the bureaucracy. Tensions existed, however, between such experts, dedicated to what they saw as 'wise use' of resources, and public preservationist groups, with both sides labelling themselves as 'conservationists'. The state also focused its attention on Crown land rather than regulating use of private land. Tentative steps in the latter direction awaited passage of the Soil Conservation and Rivers Control Act 1941. Until then forestry was the state's major concern. Difficulties with sustained-yield indigenous forestry in part contributed to establishment of an exotic coniferous plantation estate in the 1920s that was large by world standards. Disputes over indigenous forest management in the 1950s foreshadowed the emergence of contemporary environmentalism in New Zealand.

State conservation

The New Zealand experience both mirrors and contrasts with contemporary environmental histories in other lands of recent European settlement. Donald Worster has stressed the importance of understanding how capitalist production has shaped the US environment.[1] This viewpoint is significant in that it reconnects environmental history with wider social processes, but his analysis has tended to underplay the role of the state, even in the USA. Michael Williams observes that from the 1900s to the 1950s in the USA, 'The focus was on limits, availability, and ownership of some of the earth's key renewable resources, particularly, land, timber, soil and water, which led to the quest for conservation'.[2]

Conservation as the wise use of natural resources can arguably be traced back to medieval forest game reserves in Europe. Wise use developed as a utilitarian approach to regulating natural resource use so that future needs were considered. It was also an anthropocentric notion: the resources were being reserved for future human use, not because of any intrinsic qualities that they might have. As it developed in the USA from the 1890s, wise-use conservation became the realm of the technical expert, particularly as management increasingly involved active intervention; for example, to manipulate forest age-class distributions. Samuel Hays depicted conservation in the USA immediately and after World War II as mostly concerned with forests, soil erosion, and game management. Forest conservation was associated with 'scientific forestry', particularly sustained-yield management. Conflict occurred between those wishing to preserve forest environments as amenities, and others who saw them as commodities. Soil conservation was allied with 'efficiency in resource production'.[3] This view of wise-use management as technical also tended to imply that natural resource management problems could be resolved by expert managers rather than by overtly political processes.

Australian geographer Joe Powell remains wary of uncritically importing American models of environmental history. Instead, he emphasises the connections between local, regional, national, and international scales of analysis. Some of the themes he suggests for study in Australia, such as the 'interpretation, management, mismanagement of soils' and 'the appearance of an array of entirely commercial and environmentally vulnerable monocultures',[4] can be translated usefully to the New Zealand context.

The New Zealand experience, however, is also distinctive. Its colonial past provided an opportunity for state management of Crown lands. In a unitary state, there was scope for innovation on the part of creative individuals who could institute effective national policies; for example, aerial topdressing. On private land, the engagement of the state was more tentative, with soil conservation being pursued by emphasising its economic advantages to farmers. Many of New Zealand's endemic species were not, however, amenable to existing Anglo-American management strategies, and specific forms of forestry management had to be developed.

The particular role played by the state in conservation in New Zealand is explored next in terms of forest-conservation and soil-conservation activities. The proposition is that the New Zealand experience can inform the wider writing of environmental history in settler societies where North American models have, not surprisingly, prevailed.

Nineteenth-century conservation legacies

During the nineteenth century British colonial officials throughout the Empire set aside land as reserves for various 'wise use' as well as preservation purposes. By 1903, in New Zealand, these included forest reserves for the growth and preservation of timber; flora and fauna reserves; and initiatives for national parks and scenery preservation. Such efforts palled beside the 1.5 million acres of forest cleared off Crown land opened for settlement from 1896 to 1914. Much of the expanded Crown estate was purchased by the Liberal government from Māori, a point obscured by the contemporary rhetoric of breaking up the great estates.

By 1919, however, there were 512 scenic reserves totalling 306,888 acres, national parks of 1,654,234 acres, and state forests amounting to 1,654,214 acres. The relatively pragmatic expansion of state functions meant that different branches of a single department such as Lands and Survey could be engaged simultaneously in both land settlement and forest conservation, albeit with the emphasis in favour of the former. The 'best use' of land was for agriculture, but it was recognised that some land was uneconomic for farming and that it was better to set this aside as forest reserves for soil and water protection, for the timber industry, or for scenery preservation purposes. The boundaries between such uses were, however, contested into the 1960s and beyond.

Forest conservation

Deforestation provides one of the major traces of environmental change in New Zealand. In 1900 forest covered approximately 25 per cent of the country, a reduction from about half in 1840, and perhaps 80 per cent when Polynesians first arrived. The main agents of ongoing deforestation were small farmers occupying land on deferred payment from the Crown. In Northland and Westland the timber industry itself was a major cause. In areas such as the upper Rangitikei and Dannevirke, a symbiotic relationship existed between sawmillers and settlers. Forest cut over by the millers was easier to convert to pasture, and sale of cutting rights to them provided welcome cash for settlers. New Zealand's close economic links to the United Kingdom as a supplier of frozen meat and dairy products helped drive continued expansion of the settlement frontier into the 1920s as sawmillers followed the forest margins into the King Country and Westland. Between 1905 and 1913, official estimates of the exhaustion of merchantable forests were reduced from seventy to thirty years.[5]

The state's reaction to fears of a future timber famine was twofold. One response was to seek efficient utilisation of remaining resources by imposing more restrictive regulations for harvesting forests on Crown land (although the industry cutting off freehold land remained comparatively unregulated). This eking out of forest resources culminated in a series of export controls imposed from 1918 to 1922 to prevent the sale of kahikatea, kauri, rimu, mataī, and tōtara. The slogan 'New Zealand timber for the New Zealanders' defined these efforts, which also sought to protect the local timber industry from North American timber imports.

The second response was to support exotic afforestation. Some commentators placed their faith in exotic timber species. A. H. Cockayne in 1914 boldly predicted that *Pinus radiata* would become the timber tree of the future in New Zealand.[6] Private plantation forestry experiments, which revealed rapid growth rates, dated back to the 1860s, the decade in which *Pinus radiata* was introduced from its native California. A Forestry Branch of Lands and Survey had been established in 1897. The efforts of the branch were concentrated on afforestation at Waiotapu on the Volcanic Plateau. By 1921 it had created 38,461 acres in thirteen plantations in both islands. Already Whakarewarewa,

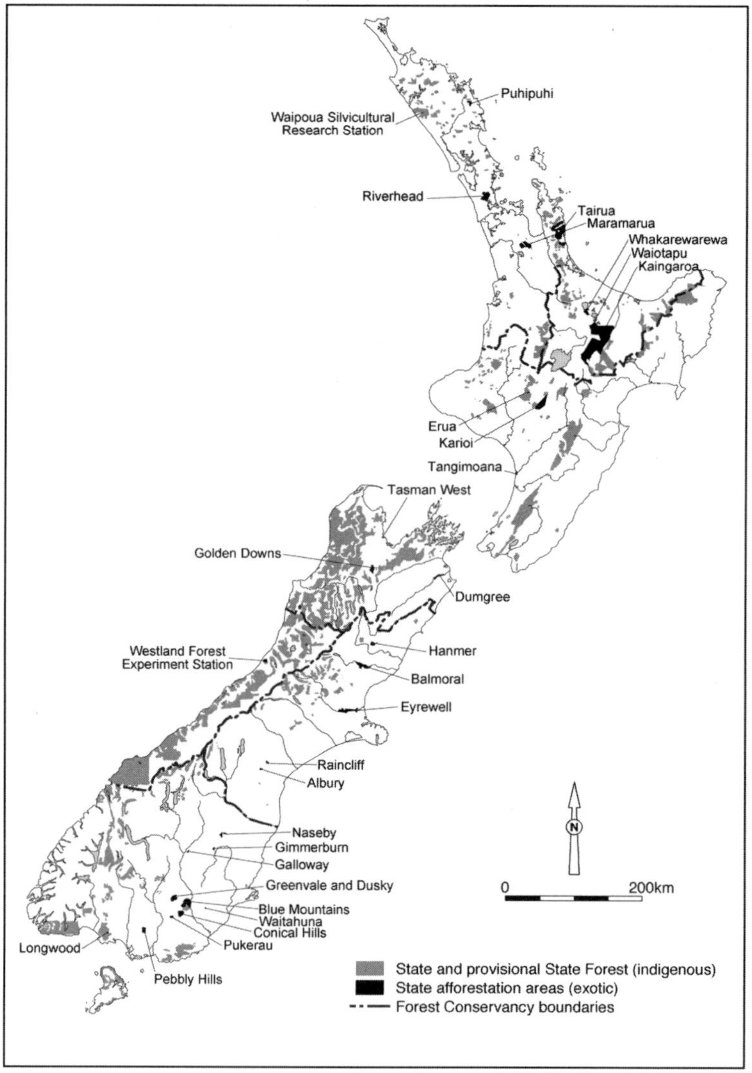

Figure 12.1 State indigenous and exotic forests, 1930. Source: *AJHR*, C3, 1930.

Waitotapu, and Kaingaroa plantations amounted to nearly 25,000 acres, or 64 per cent of the total area of state plantings (Figure 12.1).

In 1915 the colonial forestry expert David Hutchins, then visiting Australia with the British Association, was invited to report on the New Zealand's forests. The government intended that Hutchins should consider mainly afforestation for the provision of a long-term timber supply. But Hutchins himself, in line with the canons of scientific forestry at the time, successfully redefined forestry to officials as management of natural forests in perpetuity. He was, however, slow in completing his reports, and Prime Minister Massey was unenthusiastic. Real progress on the forestry question was delayed until the separation of the Forestry Branch from the Department of Lands and Survey in 1919. This led to the appointment in 1920 of Canadian-trained forester Leon McIntosh Ellis as Director of Forests and the creation in 1921 of the State Forest Service (SFS).

Ellis was only thirty-three on his appointment: energetic, totally committed to forestry, and frequently at odds with other officials. On arrival he reported on forest conditions and made recommendations, which were incorporated into the Forests Act 1921–22. This Act charged the SFS with six main functions: the control and management of forest policy; control and management of permanent and provisional state forests; the planting and maintenance of nurseries; enforcement of leases, licences, and permits; the collection of rents, fees, and royalties; and administration of the Forests Act.

Ellis quickly set about regulating the timber industry, which was by now largely dependent on Crown forests, putting in place a set of forest-management strategies as well as developing a research and education programme. The first step was to concentrate responsibility for all forests on Crown land in the SFS; this involved regaining some control from Lands and Survey and the mining wardens. Once under SFS jurisdiction, the onus was on the other departments to justify removing these areas from its control. In this respect Ellis was in the mould of natural resource managers who saw themselves acting as technical experts in the public interest. In 1926 he replaced the wasteful royalty payments on sawn output with a new system of tendering for standing-block sales. This, he argued, would produce more efficient felling and sawing, as well as preventing monopolising of cutting rights.

Another priority was the National Forest Inventory, conducted from 1921 to 1923. This yielded information on the quantity and quality of forest growth, the extent of fire damage, the effects of grazing, and regional distributions of forest types. Despite its limitations, it was superior to the earlier estimates of forest area. The 'rational control of forest exploitation to secure constant renewal and perpetuation of the resources' was a cornerstone of Ellis's forest policy.[7] Following orthodox European and American forestry principles, he sought to understand indigenous-forest regeneration and growth rates in order to implement sustained-yield forestry.

Research suggested the possibility of managing beech forest on an 80–120-year rotation, with 135–150 years for kauri. However, slow podocarp growth rates and poor regeneration, along with projections that local demand would exceed timber supplies by 1965, prompted Ellis to make an unexpected and imaginative change of direction.

Afforestation embraced

In 1925 Ellis announced an unprecedented planting target of 300,000 acres to be achieved over ten years. After he had worked so hard to convince politicians and public that forestry was about the management of natural forests, this was a dramatic about-face. But the plan was consistent with Ellis's view of himself as a man of action, and with emerging evidence about the potential of afforestation. Improved nursery techniques and less arbitrary planting practices had reduced the cost of planting from over £26 per acre to less than £2 by 1925, and the speed of tree growth helped in overcoming orthodox forestry objections to large-scale afforestation. The programme was acceptable politically because it coincided with the long-standing popular view that tree planting was the solution to a timber famine, and because there were sizeable areas of Crown lands unwanted for pastoral agriculture and available for afforestation: particularly the 'bush-sick' districts of the Volcanic Plateau.

Ellis's embrace of the possibilities offered by afforestation went as far as instigating some technological investigations for converting *Pinus radiata* into wood pulp. When he unexpectedly resigned in 1928, the afforestation momentum was sustained and the SFS and private afforestation companies continued to plant until their efforts came to a rather abrupt end in 1934. By then the SFS had planted 406,179 acres—the bulk at Kaingaroa in the central North Island—and private companies 272,326 acres (Figure 12.1). Much of this planting pre-dated the years of the Depression, despite popular mythology that it was a response to that event.[8]

In 1939 Alex Entrican, who was in time to become a more dominant figure than Ellis, became Director of Forests. A university-trained engineer, he had joined the SFS in 1921. His appointment was significant because a technical expert was again in charge. Entrican was emphatic that forestry was 'one of the few activities which is recognised as essential a function of government as the maintenance of law and order'.[9] Under his directorship a full inventory of indigenous forest resources was undertaken (1946–55) that provided vital information about indigenous forests on lands of all tenures. It revealed that many of those remaining were on Māori lands. Responsibility for protection forestry, in a move symptomatic of head office tensions, was passed to the deputy director, A. L. Poole.

Entrican's major contribution came not in the area of forest management but in forest utilisation and industrial processing. He had gathered information on pulp and paper making for Ellis in the 1920s. Entrican's vision was for a large, integrated forest industry, with the state as tree grower as well as wood processor. Originally, he envisaged a large-scale state-led industrial development in the form of a fully integrated sawmill and pulp-mill plant that would also process trees from private company plantations. The companies distanced themselves from the proposal, but by 1946 the Labour government was committed to proceeding.

An incoming National government in 1949 was more sympathetic to business but, with planning already well advanced, could only rework the scheme to give more scope for private enterprise. The tender for the forests from Kaingaroa was let to Tasman Pulp and Paper Ltd, a public–private consortium that included Fletcher Holdings, a New Zealand construction firm (Figure 12.2). Entrican served as a director and was dismayed

Figure 12.2 The arrival in 1955 of the first trainload of logs at Kawerau, site of the Tasman pulp and paper mill. The Director of Forests, Alex Entrican, is shown on the right. He was a strong believer in integrated state forestry, from indigenous management to afforestation through to industrial processing. AAQA 6395 M1159, National Archives Head Office, Wellington.

when James Fletcher, the chairperson, wrested control away from government representatives on the board.[10]

Kaingaroa and Tasman Pulp and Paper Ltd are illustrative of the extent to which the state in New Zealand by the 1950s was involved in the forest economy as both a regulatory agent and a participant. Kaingaroa Forest grew to be one of the largest contiguous plantations in the world and is a local expression of Joe Powell's observations about the appearance of environmentally vulnerable monocultures. Not only have there been disease threats to New Zealand forest monocultures, such as that posed by the wood wasp (*Sirex noctilio*) epidemic in the 1940s, but also monoculture vulnerability was a vehicle for contentious debate between forestry professionals, who generally downplayed the risks, and environmentalists, who tended to accentuate them.

Entrican, who always maintained a critical eye over private sector forestry, also questioned the ability of the afforestation companies to adequately protect their forest monocultures against the threat of disease. And in the late 1950s he became convinced that even the existing exotic-forest estate would not meet future wood demands. He also saw an opportunity for forest products to help diversify New Zealand's narrow range of agricultural and pastoral exports. He set a new target of 1.2 million acres by 2000. This had already been exceeded by the time new planting ceased in the mid 1980s.

Indigenous forest management revisited

It proved much harder for foresters in New Zealand to understand regeneration processes in indigenous forests than they had imagined. After World War II the SFS, renamed the New Zealand Forest Service (NZFS) in 1949, renewed its efforts at wise-use indigenous forestry. The intention was to reduce harvest levels to a point matched by rates of indigenous regeneration. Ecological investigation of podocarp and beech forests suggested, however, that regeneration processes were more complex than previously realised, and that management would be difficult. A selection logging system rather than clear-felling was proposed, but anxieties remained. This is encapsulated in the NZFS annual report for 1956, which commented that 'Above all there must be faith in the final outcome to visualise the seedling Rimu full grown' three and four generations hence.[11] Forestry science was now a matter of faith, at least as far as indigenous forests were concerned.

The NZFS faced other pressures in the 1950s with the demands of postwar housing policy, which ensured that government wanted to keep harvest levels high and timber prices controlled. This was not the ideal political climate for advancing indigenous sustained-yield management. Further attempts were made to understand regeneration processes in order to implement rotational management of indigenous forests, particularly in Westland. Kauri and the less valuable beech species seemed to offer the best prospects. By the late 1950s Entrican's frustration was evident when he observed that 'sustained yield silviculture of kahikatea would promise better than with another indigenous soft wood species, were it not for the prior claims of agriculture to the rich lowland soils'.[12] Similar comments were made for other timber species such as tōtara and mataī.

Entrican's parting rebuke to the politicians was that 'the pioneering instinct that trees are a liability and not an asset has survived for over a century ... as a result forestry has had to accept mostly submarginal or marginal land'.[13] This also signals the limits of state conservation; efforts were largely confined to Crown lands and there was a reluctance to regulate land use on private lands or pursue forestry on lands where agricultural development was possible.

Classical sustained-yield forest management balanced harvests against annual growth increments and was underpinned by a number of social and economic assumptions, including scarcity of timber products, stability of wood-flow requirements, certainty in planning for timber consumption, and a closed economy. None of these translated easily to New Zealand circumstances. Forest land was more sought after for pastoral agriculture, and demand for timber fluctuated, with occasional flooding of the local market with imports. Public and private afforestation apparently offered alternatives to indigenous forest management. Furthermore, as the remaining indigenous forest was reduced in area there were calls for its preservation from the scientific élite and popular preservationist groups, from some politicians, and from the Lands and Survey Department.

The first major challenge to SFS management proposals occurred over plans to initiate sustained-yield management of Waipoua kauri forest in Northland. Originally purchased by the Crown for land settlement in 1876, and gazetted as a state forest of 22,650 acres in 1906, the forest had been surveyed two years later by botanist Leonard Cockayne, who unsuccessfully suggested its scientific and scenic values were such that it ought to become a national park. Descendants of the original Māori owners of Waipoua maintained into the 1930s that the sale to the Crown included a condition that the forest now had a rāhui, a traditional concept embodying physical and spiritual preservation, placed on it and that it should be protected in perpetuity.

In 1921 Ellis funded William McGregor from Auckland University College to investigate kauri regeneration. An initial research programme was completed, but McGregor's working relationship with the SFS quickly disintegrated. The combative researcher then emerged as one of the protagonists behind the Auckland Institute and Museum's moves in 1932 to have the whole of Waipoua preserved. That same year a committee was established to seek the 'absolute and permanent protection' of the kauri at Waipoua. The Depression and war delayed any resolution of this preservation versus wise-use controversy.

In 1946 a Waipoua Forest Preservation Committee was re-formed and renewed its efforts, calling for a reserve of at least 10,000 acres. With support from prominent zoologist Professor Valentine Chapman and McGregor, a 'Preserve Waipoua' campaign gathered momentum, even though professional foresters derided its 'irrational and unyielding depth of conviction'.[14] In what was to be a decisive move, a petition was launched in 1947 by the Whangarei Progressive Society and the Whangarei branch of the Forest and Bird Protection Society calling for the preservation of the entire forest as a national park. The society presented 50,000 signatures to Parliament after it had circulated nationally through its branches.

Recognising that it was losing this political contest, the SFS devised its own proposal for a 7200-acre kauri preserve. Entrican, meanwhile, lambasted the petitioners as wanting to create a 'tree cemetery'. The hosting of the Pacific Science Congress in Auckland in 1949 provided additional scientific support for the proposed national park. Slowly the balance tipped in favour of preservation until, in 1952, Parliament gazetted the whole of Waipoua forest as a sanctuary under the Forests Act 1949, which left it under NZFS jurisdiction but set aside for preservation. Waipoua was a bitter defeat for wise-use forest management, particularly as few lowland sites were available for the sustained-yield management of indigenous forests. This was an occasion when other scientists and members of the public challenged the foresters' judgment. In so doing, the Waipoua Forest Preservation Committee implicitly rejected the notion of the apolitical expert natural resource manager and appealed directly to the public and politicians for a policy change. The campaign is also noteworthy in that the tactics used foreshadowed those of the environmental movement in its challenges to the NZFS in the 1970s and 1980s.

Figure 12.3 'Nature's revenge'. The Forest and Bird Protection Society, in articles and cartoons, regularly identified an erosion problem in the 1930s. Its message was that forest clearance for farming on steeplands would lead to flooding and accelerated erosion. The sketch of the half-buried hut at the bottom is taken from a photograph of the aftermath of heavy rain at Pukatea, Admiralty Bay, near French Pass in 1938. *Forest & Bird*, No. 51, 1939.

Soil and water conservation

Auckland University College's Professor Joseph Grossman, in a polemic entitled *The Evils of Deforestation*, pointed to strong connections between deforestation and erosion, as well as flooding, in New Zealand as early as 1909.[15] Land settlement in the nineteenth century involved forest clearance of increasingly hilly country and, in the South Island, was accompanied by annual burning of tussock grasslands. The environmental consequences were clearly recognisable by the turn of the twentieth century.

The most evocative contemporary statement about land degradation was Herbert Guthrie-Smith's *Tutira: The Story of a New Zealand Sheep Station*, first published in 1921.[16] By then soil erosion was in evidence throughout the East Cape and Hawke's Bay, and land deterioration and reversion to scrub was occurring in the interior Whanganui and King Country (Figure 12.3). A series of severe floods on the east coast of the North Island awakened political interest initially in flood-control engineering, and subsequently to the wide problems of soil erosion.

In the South Island, concern about land condition was expressed to various commissions examining land tenure. The Southern Pastoral Lands Committee of 1920, for instance, investigated the extent and causes of land depletion and deterioration. At issue was the use of fire, which runholders asserted was a necessary management tool. Official discussion of water conservation dated back even further but was unrelated to land degradation, being primarily concerned with ensuring water availability for the gold mining industry in Otago (see Chapter 6).

The Department of Agriculture by the 1920s was committed to improving farming productivity by ushering in an era of more intensive agriculture. The limits of settlement for extensive pastoralism had, under prevailing technology, been reached and, with prices for New Zealand commodities in the United Kingdom falling, sizeable increases in production were necessary to maintain export income. The department sought to improve production levels by matching farm practices with soil fertility and land capability.

The Department of Scientific and Industrial Research (DSIR), established in 1926, was also involved in identifying the severity and extent of soil erosion in the 1930s. This work included Soil Bureau surveys in Mid-Canterbury and Taranaki as well as land-utilisation mapping, notably in Hawke's Bay. Particularly important was work undertaken by Norman Taylor that revealed that accelerated soil erosion was widespread across the North Island. He tactfully called into question the efficacy of continuing to farm some of the more remote and erosion-prone lands. Equivalent but less controversial work was also published on the South Island tussock lands.[17]

The Department of Agriculture only reluctantly agreed with these assessments, but a turning point came in 1939 when R. P. Connell acknowledged that land deterioration, including soil erosion, was now a serious threat to the national economy. For Connell, at least, the problem was serious enough to warrant state action on the grounds that individuals could not effectively counter the problem.[18] There was not, however, complete unanimity among government scientists as to what constituted effective action. The eminent grasslands scientist Bruce Levy, for example, tended to argue that a good sward of pasture alone was sufficient to counter soil erosion problems (see Chapter 11).

The Esk Valley flood of 1938 hastened political action. Ernest Marsden, Secretary of the DSIR, was able to orchestrate a motion from the Royal Society of New Zealand, calling for a royal commission to investigate vegetation preservation and soil erosion. Norman Taylor was asked to chair the resultant committee of inquiry in 1939, which recommended statutory measures to institute a soil conservation programme.[19] There was some initial opposition from farmer groups wary of outside 'experts' restricting their land use options.

Meanwhile, the efforts of Lincoln College's Lance McCaskill and geographer Kenneth Cumberland of Canterbury University College were also important in keeping soil-erosion problems in front of the politicians and public alike. McCaskill had benefited from a Carnegie Grant to tour the United States, where he observed soil erosion and soil conservation programmes. His lantern slide show for parliamentarians was decisive in expanding the scope of a new rivers control bill to encompass a more broad-based approach, combining river engineering for flood control with soil conservation in a single Act. The Esk Valley event gave moment to the claims of soil-erosion campaigners and provided a dramatic example of their concerns, one that was too significant in terms of size and damage to be ignored.

The Soil Conservation and Rivers Control Act 1941 ushered in a new era of land management in New Zealand. It signalled a change of approach from that of Frederick Furkert, the head of the Public Works Department, who believed that the 'abandonment of flooded country' implied 'a retreat of civilisation before the forces of nature'.[20] It established the Soil Conservation and Rivers Control Council (SCRCC), composed of representatives of a number of government departments, local authorities, and agricultural and pastoral interests. This body first met in 1942 and was chaired by a senior government engineer, signalling that it would adopt a path of evolutionary and incremental, rather than revolutionary, change from earlier engineering solutions to flooding.

Figure 12.4 Aerial topdressing provided a means of stabilising at-risk slopes in higher country. Doug Campbell of the Soil Conservation and Rivers Control Council was instrumental in organising the original trials and promoting topdressing as a means of soil conservation. He wrote two SCRCC bulletins on the subject (this one in 1955) and spoke at many meetings in New Zealand and overseas.

Simultaneously, new regional authorities termed catchment boards could be voluntarily established. The most severely affected areas quickly set up such boards, including most of the South Island between 1943 and 1948, and the southern portion of the North Island and East Cape from 1943 to 1944. The voluntary arrangement was deliberate: the SCRCC emphasised education, promotion, and demonstration of soil conservation techniques rather than more direct regulation of land use. Even so there was some farmer concern about the SCRCC and its activities. This was apparent in evidence given to the Royal Commission on the Sheep Farming Industry in 1947 and 1948, which led to a recommendation in its final report that catchment boards be abolished. Even National Party MPs spoke out against this, but the episode did point to farmer concern about external restrictions on land use represented by the presence on catchment boards of elected urban members who were regarded as antagonistic to farming.

The SCRCC was able to make more rapid progress after the war. It focused on demonstrating the utility of soil conservation techniques, working to an implicit assumption that soil conservation was in the national interest. Publicity efforts included a series of bulletins (with poignant titles such as *Down to the Sea in Slips*) and films shown widely throughout the country. New techniques were showcased on demonstration farms, and a research programme was initiated that, by 1963, included seventeen soil conservation reserves, each with specific regional erosion problems. These were used for hydrological research and land-capability surveys, with a view to devising farm-level soil conservation plans.

Aerial topdressing was perhaps its most innovative area of investigation. This was to prove a real boon for soil conservation in New Zealand (Figure 12.4). It facilitated the effective stabilisation of at-risk slopes in the hill and high country, and was particularly associated with Doug Campbell, the Senior Soil Conservator who orchestrated the original trials in 1948. Campbell had been interested in soil conservation issues since the 1930s, and his efforts in publicising the benefits of aerial topdressing extended even beyond New Zealand. The salient feature of the aerial topdressing programme was that not only did it allow successively grander soil conservation targets to be set, but also that it enabled farmers to continue farming without having to sacrifice overall production levels. By the time he retired in 1967, Campbell perhaps sensed that it would not be possible for these two goals of soil conservation and increasing production to coexist indefinitely.

Soil conservation was able to be promoted in the 1950s, however, as not only in the public interest and unquestionably something that the state ought to be engaged in, but also as leading to a rational system of land utilisation that would enable the farm sector overall to lift production levels. Soil conservation was promoted very much in utilitarian terms, which was perhaps a necessity in that education and financial incentives were the favoured implementation mechanisms. The scale of bureaucracy and regulatory power available to soil conservators in New Zealand was comparatively less than that associated with such famous American programmes as the Tennessee Valley Authority.

During the 1950s there was also an energy- and morale-sapping contest, behind the scenes, between the Department of Agriculture and the Ministry of Works as to where the soil conservators should be based. Initially part of Works, they were separated from the river engineers and transferred to the Department of Agriculture in 1956 after a five-year

Figure 12.5 The SCRCC made use of a range of masculinist images in urging farmers to adopt soil conservation techniques. This example is from the *New Zealand Farmer*, 17 August, 1961.

bureaucratic struggle. Here they remained until they were returned to Works in 1967. Having the staff supporting the SCRCC divided between two departments was a hindrance to achieving soil conservation targets in the 1950s. This separation arose from the competing views of the Department of Agriculture—that soil conservation was a legitimate part of its farm extension activities—and of the Ministry of Works—that soil conservation was part of its flood-control programme.

Education campaigns and demonstrations aside, what gave real impetus to soil conservation and rivers control in the 1950s and 1960s was the availability of government subsidies to undertake on-farm works and regional flood-control schemes. From 1943 to 1962, a total of £14.5 million was spent on a range of river works and soil-erosion subsidies and grants.[21] Expenditure varied regionally across the country, reflecting the mix of soil-erosion and flooding problems; for example, river-channel clearance work predominated in Canterbury, while tree planting was a particular feature of the Wairarapa, Hawke's Bay, and East Cape regions.

Soil erosion never generated the same sort of popular concern as deforestation in New Zealand, although the use of films to publicise its impact heightened public awareness in the 1940s and 1950s. Even so, soil conservation tended to be regarded by the public as a problem for the expert. The caveat was that on-farm soil erosion was a significant problem in some regions, and the onus was on remedial action at the farm level. To this end, soil conservators helped farmers to develop land utilisation plans (Figure 12.5). Unlike foresters, soil conservators had to persuade farmers to adopt soil conservation techniques. They were aided by the availability of subsidies through catchment boards for on-farm works.

However, river engineering remained an important part of the SCRCC's work. Engineers shared some characteristics with the foresters as natural-resource managers of the technical expert type. They also tended to capture the bulk of the funding; flood-control engineering works by their very nature being expensive. Less obviously, but equally significant for the organisation, the engineers tended to dominate senior staff positions. There was special recognition of their professional training within the public service salary structures, which did not extend to the soil conservators. The legacy of the soil conservation programme and the major river engineering schemes in the landscape was significant but perhaps skewed in favour of the latter.

There was a loss of momentum in soil conservation in the late 1960s. The benefits of aerial topdressing were becoming problematic, and there were new and complex water-quality and allocation issues facing the state and the community. This gave rise to new legislation in the form of the Water and Soil Conservation Act 1967, and saw the emergence of a number of linked organisations to manage water and soil conservation under the umbrella of the National Water and Soil Conservation Authority. Water, rather than soil, provided the most difficult issues in the 1970s and 1980s, including challenges to attempts to establish water classifications, granting of water rights for the Clutha Dam, and protests about hydro development threatening wild and scenic rivers (see Chapter 17). In the early 1980s, Māori increasingly challenged the monocultural nature of the legislation, notably in three claims to the Waitangi Tribunal to do with the waste outfall at Motunui, piping of Rotoura's sewage into the Kaituna River, and pollution of the Manukau Harbour.[22]

Conclusion

The scope of state-led conservation activity in New Zealand from the 1900s to the 1950s was similar to that found in Australia and the USA. There were differences of emphasis, game management being less significant in New Zealand than in the United States, and deforestation and forest management being comparatively more important than in Australia. State conservation in New Zealand was informed by an amalgam of views of élite public perspectives and technical experts, with the former gradually giving way to the latter. Conservation interpreted by technical managers was largely a matter of the 'wise use' of natural resources, although it was extended in New Zealand as elsewhere to include aesthetic and ecological ends (in the form of limited preservation of flora and fauna).

Forestry provides a fascinating example of conflicting currents of thought, as popular notions of 'timber famine' and the inevitable decline of indigenous forests pointed to exotic afforestation as a long-term solution. The first trained foresters advising the government reinstated sustained-yield management of indigenous forests, but in turn expanded their efforts into large-scale exotic afforestation, initially to win time to enable the mechanisms of indigenous forest regeneration to be understood, and later because of the possibilities conferred by industrial forestry and a local pulp-and-paper industry for broadening the export basis of the economy.

'Wise use' was something of a foil to the developmentalist push within government and from within the agricultural sector. It secured the protection of some areas of Crown land, but ultimately it unravelled as a concept. This was due to internal contradictions, particularly the long-standing tension between 'wise use' as utilitarian conservation and the counter-position of conservation as inviolable preservation, especially when the former was espoused by state officials, and the latter was increasingly advocated by members of the public and took on a more environmentalist character.

Soil conservation was taken up by the state only in the 1940s, and there was a reluctance to prescribe land use on privately owned land, with education and subsidised works being favoured strategies. Aerial topdressing as a new technology was critical to the success of soil conservation efforts on the steeper lands, but underpinning the whole soil conservation initiative was the explicit assumption, unchallenged until the neo-liberal experiment of the 1980s, that such work was in the national interest.

By 1955, harvests of exotic plantation sawlogs (1.65 million cubic metres) had exceeded those from indigenous forests (1.5 million cubic metres). A *Pinus radiata*-based pulp-and-paper industry had been established. It was proving technically and politically difficult to institute a sustained-yield management regime for indigenous forests. Furthermore, from the late 1950s there were renewed moves by public preservationists to protect scenery (including forests), lakes, and waters from development. The dominance of the technical expert model of natural resource management was under threat.

Some important contests over vegetation remnants continued into the 1980s. Resolution appeared to have been reached in 1986, when the West Coast Forest Accord was signed by government, local body, industry, and conservation groups. Perhaps the last round of the 'wise use' versus preservationist contest was fought in late 1999, when the incoming Labour government required state-owned enterprise Timberlands West Coast to abandon its plans—consistent with that accord—for sustainable beech forest management.

Donald Worster's popular model of environmental history does not adequately conceptualise much of a role for the state, yet in New Zealand from the 1920s to the 1970s the state, nationally and locally, not only played an important role in terms of natural resource development and its regulation, but also in key aspects of environmental conservation. There is perhaps a tendency among scholars to seek shortcomings in the achievements of the state. These are apparent in the conservation arena from the 1920s to the 1960s, particularly in the failure to implement a sustained-yield indigenous forest management, in the reluctance to regulate agricultural land uses to the full extent provided for by the legislation, and in the limitations of aerial topdressing as a long-term solution. The dominance of the expert resource manager well into the 1960s, before public participation and environmental perspectives were recognised officially, has to some extent perpetuated the frequently antagonistic debates over indigenous forests.

Looking back at the efforts of twentieth-century forest management, it might even be observed that 'wise use' of forests did not advance much beyond the eking out of resources, more efficient felling and milling, and recovery of higher royalties. The objectives of professional foresters have been repeatedly thwarted, first by indigenous forest ecology, then diverted by exotic afforestation, and most recently countered by a preservationist approach to conservation very similar to that articulated in New Zealand as long ago as the 1890s.

What such a perspective overlooks is that the state was active in pursuing natural-resource conservation from the 1920s, guided by some notion of 'the national interest' through the efforts of a few professionals. They had limited resources available to them, were typically running counter to the mainstream development ethos in government, and were often in advance of public opinion. On occasions, however, they developed bold and imaginative solutions to real environmental problems, as in the cases of afforestation and aerial topdressing.

13

ON THE EDGE

MAKING URBAN PLACES

Eric Pawson

New Zealand since European settlement has arguably always been an urban land. Not withstanding the emphasis on primary production for the last 150 years, European colonisation has been urban-focused, the towns acting as 'beach-heads' (Chapter 4). Wakefieldian ideals decreed that it should be so, to promote economic advancement, cultural stability, and political control. New Zealand was therefore systematically settled from planted towns, its important trades have always been coordinated through towns, and since the early twentieth century a majority of its people have lived in towns. In 1931 *Auckland City and Province* was claiming that in terms of population, output, and imports, it already accounted for one-third of the country's total. The everyday experience of most people for most of the twentieth century was therefore urban. In her poem 'Living Here', Cilla McQueen imagines that 'this place is just one big city' with its 'suburbs strung out in a long line' from north to south, between ocean horizon and mountain ranges.[1]

There is, however, relatively little in domestic or international literature that assists in the development of a New Zealand focus for urban environmental history. In those countries where it has been relatively strong, environmental history has not emphasised urban themes. William Cronon has noted, in respect of North America, that 'cities in particular deserve much more work than they have received'. Stephen Dovers has recently written of 'the glaring need for a consolidation of the environmental history of Australian urban areas'. Jock Phillips implies that in New Zealand there may be a historical reason for this lack. In *A Man's Country?* he suggests that in the construction of male mythology, 'because it was the most distinctive aspect of Pakeha society, the frontier experience was universalised and the urban world was ignored'. 'On the edge' is therefore a metaphor for marginalisation, a statement to the effect that the writing of environmental history has been heavily ruralised. As an academic enterprise, it has been built upon wilderness and farm perspectives, and, more broadly, from a long tradition among historical geographers of analysis of landscape construction and environmental change.[2]

More recently, environmental historians, in North America at least, have become mildly critical of their own rural preoccupations, as well as of their lack of conceptual clarity when considering urban topics.[3] In this respect 'on the edge' assumes some analytical value. It is employed in this chapter as a working metaphor to construct a framework for urban environmental history. This framework consists of three themes that explore the roles that towns and 'the urban' have occupied relative to both 'the natural' and 'the rural' in New Zealand between about 1900 and the 1960s. The chapter concludes with the application of these themes in a case study of a resort town.

A framework

The town was long promoted, and understood, as a vanguard of colonisation in 'new' lands. In this view, the making of urban places encapsulated and symbolised the taming of the 'howling wilderness', a biblical phrase in wide use in nineteenth-century Otago.[4] Colonial towns stood on the edge of 'civilisation', providing the agencies by which modernisation proceeded: capital, military and cultural power, information, infrastructure, and onward connection to a wider world. As a functional perspective on urban history, this has been less readily recognised in New Zealand than in North America, where geographers such as Vance and Gottmann (the latter with his idea of the Seaboard hinge of settlements) long since conceptualised it, although it was picked up here twenty years ago by Neil Quigley. Such work is based on the thesis that it is the town that made the country, as Cronon has more recently argued in his work on Chicago.[5]

The environmental discourse underlying this first theme was progressivist: that culture was destined to triumph over nature. Indeed, wilderness was often represented as an empty stage, benignly awaiting the imprint of the European. As the French visitor André Siegfried said of the Canterbury Plains, 'No Maori came to trouble the peace of these new settlers, and the large and beautiful plain open before them needed nothing but cultivation.'[6] But the blitheness of this viewpoint belies a second sense in which the urban has been 'on the edge': the vulnerability of these new towns to the unpredictability of the 'howling wilderness'. A way of thinking that imposed false expectations upon the environment was particularly open to hazards, be these native peoples contesting colonisation, or physical processes that were, and to an extent remain, little understood.

In many of the neo-Europes, the threat posed by indigenous competitors was accommodated, although often not without more prolonged and effective resistance than standard sources reveal. The inhabitants of towns such as New Plymouth and Wanganui in the mid nineteenth century attested as much.[7] However, it was the openness of new urban settlements to physical threats that became so important in the history of these places, the more so because urban growth greatly accentuated, rather than lessened, human exposure to natural variability. This is a matter of wider significance than the combating of air and water pollution in degraded cities that fills those accounts of urban environmental history that do exist. Rather, it involves the extent to which multiplying assets, and numbers of lives, were put at risk from flood, fire, storm, and earthquake, owing to the assumption that nature could be tamed. In fact it was rendered more dangerous to people by towns placed in harm's way.

The third sense in which the urban is 'on the edge' was of particular significance in the making of twentieth-century urban places. In New Zealand the bulk of people live and work on the fringes of cities and towns, rather than at the centre of them. It is a pattern prominent in other affluent countries, too, with which 'the broad economic, technological, and political forces associated with major [urban] environmental transformations—industrialization, automobility, suburbanization, and dependence on [government] initiatives' are shared.[8] At a cultural level, however, the meaning of suburbs has lain deeper. They can be represented as places that were believed to embody high levels of environmental amenity, or, put another way, as a realm in which resolution was sought of the dangers of nature untamed and of the city degraded.

These three themes—of the progressive town built boldly on the edge of wilderness; of the vulnerable town placed unwittingly on the edge of unpredictable nature; and of suburbs in search of environmental amenity on the edge of town—form the basis for a more extended analysis of New Zealand's urban environmental histories.

The progressive town

A recurring theme in urban boosterism, as well as in local histories written in the first six or seven decades of the twentieth century, was the role of the town as a centre of progress. This was celebrated by means of comparisons with other towns and other countries; by civic achievements in terms of cultural icons and the healthiness of the population; and by constant reference, implicitly or explicitly, to nature conquered. Writing of Auckland in 1917, James Cowan described it as '... one of the wealthiest and most sightly of young colonial cities ... Though many parts of the province, forest covered and imperfectly roaded, are still in their rough pioneering days, Auckland City is well past that stage ... and the citizens have sufficient time and taste to cultivate the City Beautiful, and to add vastly to the graces of their nature favoured home.' For at least the first thirty years of the century, the motto of Auckland Corporation was 'Advance'.[9]

In 1931 a guide to the city, *The Gateway to New Zealand*, told 'intending settlers and those wishing to invest their wealth', that they could 'know that sure, certain and safe progress is inevitable'. 'To have achieved [so much] in so short a space of time ... reflects the magnificent future which assuredly must lie in front.'[10] The markers of this assurance were evident in the townscape. Art Deco architecture and design for instance signified the technological optimism of the modern world, a universal style adopted from Europe and North America. Today it is recognised as typifying the new Napier, rising phoenix-like from the devastating earthquake of 1931, but it was widely adopted in urban New Zealand and Australia in the 1930s. It helped that its lightly decorated concrete box structures were cheap and could be built quickly.[11] Two decades later another Auckland guide proclaimed that 'Where once there were silent hills and valleys, to-day there stand tall spires and towers of stately churches; institutes of culture and of learning; business houses, modern apartments and fine homes of the people ...'[12]

Such publications portrayed these points boldly on their covers and in their illustrations. In those about Auckland, the Grafton Bridge was prominent: 'the World's largest single span concrete bridge', said the 1931 guide, along with pictures of the geometrically neat Albert Park, 'adorned with statuary, lawns, trees, and walks', the epitome of nature ordered and contained for human pleasure. However, the most striking photograph in this particular guide, entitled 'The Picture of Health', is that of the smiling boys of Auckland Grammar School informally posed in front of its Spanish Mission buildings (a style closely related to Art Deco). That they are boys, or that this is a select educational establishment, is not remarked upon. The subtitle reads, 'Auckland's good Anglo-Saxon stock, her marvellous climate, garden homes, recreational facilities, and happy democratic atmosphere, build sturdy citizens'. The environment both facilitated and was transformed in the pursuit of progress.

The development of urban New Zealand was celebrated, as elsewhere, with major exhibitions. One of the largest was the Christchurch International Exhibition of 1906–07, which attracted nearly two million visits that summer. Subsequently, Cowan wrote about it, averring that 'in the essentials of modern progress the four cities are well advanced', going on to praise Christchurch as 'architecturally ... a very sightly city', to which for him its wide streets contributed.[13] Most towns, large and small, had been built on a generously proportioned grid, with much ink later expended in trying to explain the ubiquity of this device.[14] The desire for order was part of it, but more commonly explanations have focused on its simplicity for the surveyor, and that it was evidence of mastery over nature, or at least the need for it.

This can perhaps explain why grids were persisted with in unlikely situations, such as New Plymouth (Figure 4.2), Wellington, and Dunedin, and underlines the symbolic role of towns on the edge of the frontier. There is a more essential reason, however, although it reinforces this point. The grid was one of the 'civilising' influences of capitalist colonisation. It was the most straightforward way of delineating private property rights in land, of commodifying nature for those asserting a stake in it. It was the most efficient means of accommodating capital in space, providing a stage from which that capital could be used in the conversion of nature into resources. This after all was the driving force of modernisation.

The cover of the 1931 Auckland guide is particularly evocative of the modern (Figure 13.1). There are multi-storeyed office buildings, surrounded by all the signs of growing traffic: motor vehicles and trains; a large ship, docks, and cranes as symbols of trade; and, across the harbour, generously spaced suburbs. The whole picture is liberally dotted with benign vegetation and bathed in sunshine. The sun was often used as a metonym for progress, hence the sunburst symbol of Art Deco. So, too, was the garden, which was seen as the antithesis of idle wilderness. Taranaki, for instance, called itself 'the Garden of New Zealand', with New Plymouth being promoted for 'Health, Sunshine, Happiness'. In the 1940s Gisborne ('a magnificently appointed modern town ... on which Nature, in her bounty, has seen fit to bestow her richest gifts') saw itself as both 'Gisborne the Golden' as well as 'The California of New Zealand'. This encapsulated, at one level, its orchards and vineyards, and 'Miles of splendid beaches'; and at a deeper level was meant to evoke, by association, prosperity and glamour.[15]

Figure 13.1 Evoking the modern. In 1934 George Bernard Shaw found Auckland 'bright, clean, sunny and happy' (quoted in David Eggleton, 'Introduction', *Here on Earth: The Landscape in New Zealand Literature*, Craig Potton Publishing, Nelson, 1999, p. 21). The illustration is the cover of the 1931 guide to the city, reproduced with permission of Aotearoa New Zealand Centre, Christchurch City Libraries.

Many towns at this time had progress leagues, which went under various names. In Gisborne and Napier the '30,000 Clubs' were dedicated to raising their town's populations to that level. The goals of the 'New Plymouth Tourist and Expansion League' were self-evident; in Christchurch the Canterbury Progress League aimed to complete the city's rail links to the West Coast and to Picton. When Rotorua attained city status in 1962, it claimed to be the 'HAPPY, FRIENDLY, PROGRESSIVE CITY'. Synonymous with this, at a time—during the post-World War II long boom—when there was unanimity over the extensive role of the state in society, was substantial government investment in urban fabrics. This took the form of new offices for its agencies, roading schemes, and state housing. Wellington, as the centre of government, was a particular beneficiary, displaying many of the early high-rise buildings in New Zealand. It was said of the capital in 1960 that 'in the last ten years the erection of many handsome buildings have [*sic*] changed the skyline of the city, giving it, with the ever-increasing motor traffic, an atmosphere comparable with the great cities of Europe and America'.[16]

This was the period when, internationally, the city was being lauded as the crucible of modernism. Hence the desire of New Zealand's main centres to be seen as equal to, or in advance of—to use the language of the time—those elsewhere. Commenting on the growing focus on the city for artists, Frank Whitford writes that 'Nature now seemed finally to have been mastered. The city, in which nature was most obviously tamed, confined in parks, tubs, and pots, seemed to be the symbol of that mastery.'[17] There is a sense, however, in which this statement is inaccurate, at least for New Zealand towns. They remained very much on the edge of nature in their vulnerability to hazards. In fact, as urban growth proceeded, the extent of this exposure escalated.

The vulnerable town

One of the revelations of recent hazard research in New Zealand is that the more that has been spent on control measures, the greater the loss of assets because of events such as flood, fire, and quake. The resolution of this paradox lies in the realisation that people often interpret technical interventions in the environment as returning it to a 'safe' state, one that is again convenient for human endeavours. Damaging natural events are considered to have been banished, owing to the underlying progressivist assumption of nature tamed. Urban growth has therefore proceeded apace in risky places. The most devastating critique of this position is Mike Davis's exposé of the growing vulnerability of twentieth-century Los Angeles to environmental hazard, based upon what he calls 'disaster amnesia' and decisions to base development on short runs of optimistically interpreted data about natural variability.[18]

In New Zealand these characteristics apply equally, with much of the country at risk from seismic events, land instability, and floods. For example, the vulnerability of central Wellington to earthquakes, revealed in the events of 1848 and 1855[19] (the latter resulting in the emergence from the harbour of much of what is now the downtown area, as well as of the lip of land that carries the rail and road lines north to the Hutt Valley), seems to have been quickly forgotten. Perhaps this was because the alternative location for the city, at the Hutt River mouth in Petone where the grid was initially laid out, was fortuitously flooded—as described in Chapter 10—not long after European settlers landed. Had it not been, then no doubt, as was the case with countless other New Zealand towns, a flood-prone site would have been chosen on the basis of not even a short run of environmental data. Hence the nineteenth-century epithets for places such as Blenheim ('Beavertown') and Westport ('the Venice of the South').

Between 1920 and 1953, 64 per cent of the 136 places with more than 1000 people listed in the 1956 census experienced one or more floods. 'The most frequent flooding occurred in the metropolitan areas of Auckland (33), Hutt (36), Wellington (29), and Christchurch (26), as well as the small West Coast towns of Greymouth (33) and Hokitika (29).'[20] The Christchurch problem—because of its location at the seaward edge of the Waimakariri River fan—was grasped by some in the early days of settlement. James Balfour, a Dunedin-based engineer, reported to the Canterbury Provincial Council in 1866 after Waimakariri floodwaters had several times poured down the Avon through the town. 'It must be remembered,' he wrote, 'that if the Government once commit themselves to the policy of confining the river absolutely to its present channel, they undertake a work which must be never ending and which must grow in magnitude from year to year'.[21] Politically and publicly, however, the message was barely understood.

Flood-control measures were taken to ensure that the Waimakariri remained, as best as could be managed, in its existing channel rather than switching—as is natural—to any number of other outlets. A report in 1928 put this propensity down to 'the continued rise of the bed of the lower course', as indeed is to be expected at the edge of a gravel fan. The report drew another conclusion: 'It shews that the inability of the river to get rid of its shingle is due to a deficiency of nature which must be made good by the art of man.' Hence the philosophy of 'training of the river ... [so as to make it] flow in an orderly manner'.[33] On this basis the Waimakariri was artificially canalised along the northern fringe of the fan, both to encourage it to carry more of its load into the sea, as well as to constrain its flow away from Christchurch and its suburbs (Figure 13.2). So far the scheme, modified over the years but essentially as conceived in the 1920s, has protected the city. But this has been at the price that Balfour foresaw—of ever-increasing investment in stopbanks, revetments, and

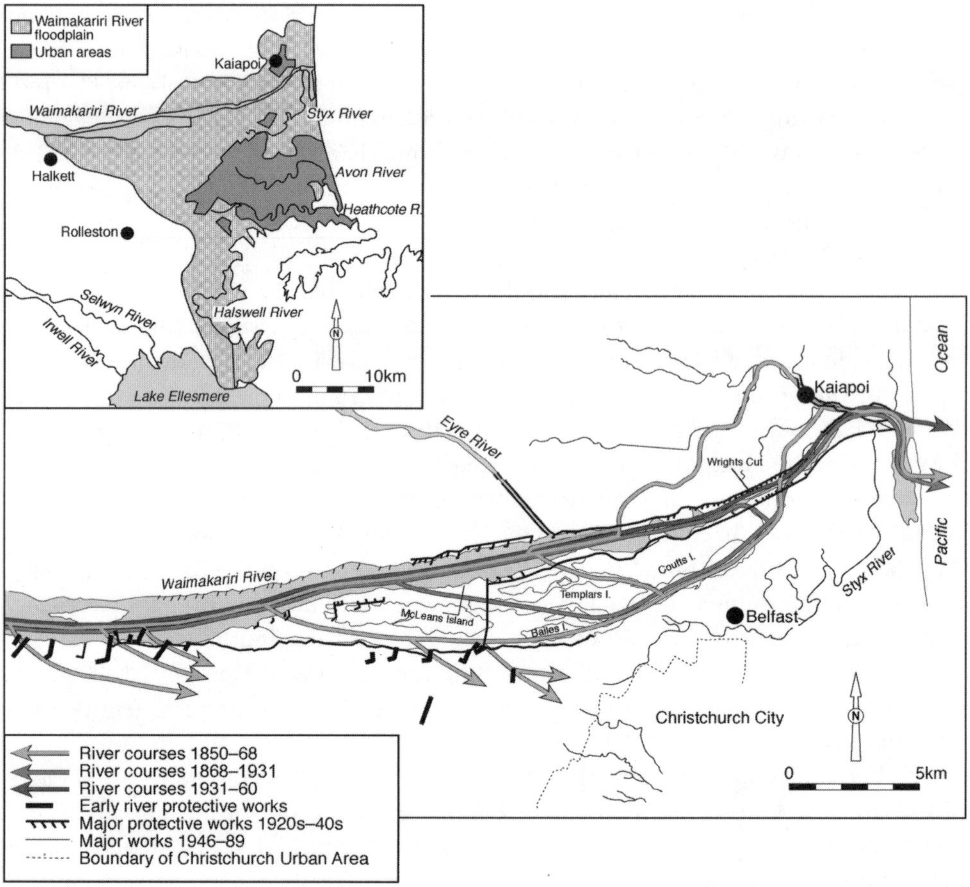

Figure 13.2 'Civilising' the Waimakariri River since the 1860s: its changing courses and flood-control works. The inset shows the relationship of Christchurch to the river's flood plain. Adapted from *Draft Waimakariri River Floodplain Management Plan*, Report R91 (9), Canterbury Regional Council, Christchurch, 1991.

plantings—and with the effect of ever-greater urban expansion over the flood plain. The flood hazard now posed by the Waimakariri is the largest in the country.

Canalisation of streams and rivers was undertaken in many urban areas of New Zealand in the first half of the twentieth century. It was as if they were being demonised in the same way as swamps (Chapter 10). In reality, control over nature was sought in order to develop flood plains rather than to allow them to remain sodden. Extensive works were put in hand on the Water of Leith in Dunedin, which, because of its steep, small catchment, is very responsive to intense rainfall on the hills behind the city. The Otago Harbour Board concreted the walls of its lower course and provided a lined outlet to the sea—the Leith Canal—across reclaimed land just before World War I. The scheme had to be expensively revised in the 1930s after it was shown to be too constricting during extensive floods in 1923 and 1929, the latter washing away several bridges and inundating 500 houses.[23]

Hazards such as flood and earthquake were the result of urban development carried out in the face of natural variability. Other hazards were the result of urban concentration. Early on, a dent to the image of towns as centres of progress was the prevalence of disease caused by pollution of water supplies. Wells and river waters were all too easily contaminated by crude disposal of wastes. The advent of sewerage systems and reticulation of water supplies in the late nineteenth century usually resolved these problems at the local scale, displacing that of sewage discharge out of sight, for some years at least. Air pollution, however, remained very much in view, although observers could interpret it in a positive light. For instance, one, standing on top of Christchurch's cathedral tower in 1900, rejoiced in the 'intense activity that prevails' in the smoke-covered city.[24]

It seems not to have been until the early 1950s that the term 'smog' came into general use in Christchurch, although it had been introduced by the city's Sunshine League during its campaigns against the 'smoke nuisance' in the 1930s. Even when Mabel Howard, as MP for the industrial constituency of Christchurch South, raised the matter in Parliament, the government view was that air pollution was essentially a South Auckland issue.[25] This was due to long-standing stenches from disposal of industrial and animal wastes into the Manukau Harbour, and from air-borne pollutants from local factories (Figure 13.3). The district around Mangere Inlet was colloquially known as 'Lavender Flat'. Such was the problem that the government set up an official 'Fumes Inquiry' in 1955. Action thereafter was piecemeal: the Auckland City Council opened a new sewage-treatment works in the area in 1961, but industrial pollution of the Manukau was still in evidence when the Waitangi Tribunal investigated this problem in the mid 1980s.[26]

Meanwhile in Christchurch, Miss Howard's intervention drew attention to the role of domestic as well as industrial sources in the generation of smog, a factor that was still being disputed by some people fifty years later. She also highlighted the unequal way in which the costs of such pollution fell on the community, with poorer people being closest to smoke from factory chimneys and steam trains. However, the accentuation of the flood hazard, owing to residential development alongside flood-escape routes from the Waimakariri main channel, potentially placed better-off residents at greater risk.[27]

The effects of hazards such as water and air pollution on the health of urban populations, as well as the alleged incidence of disorder and drunkenness, were factors used by

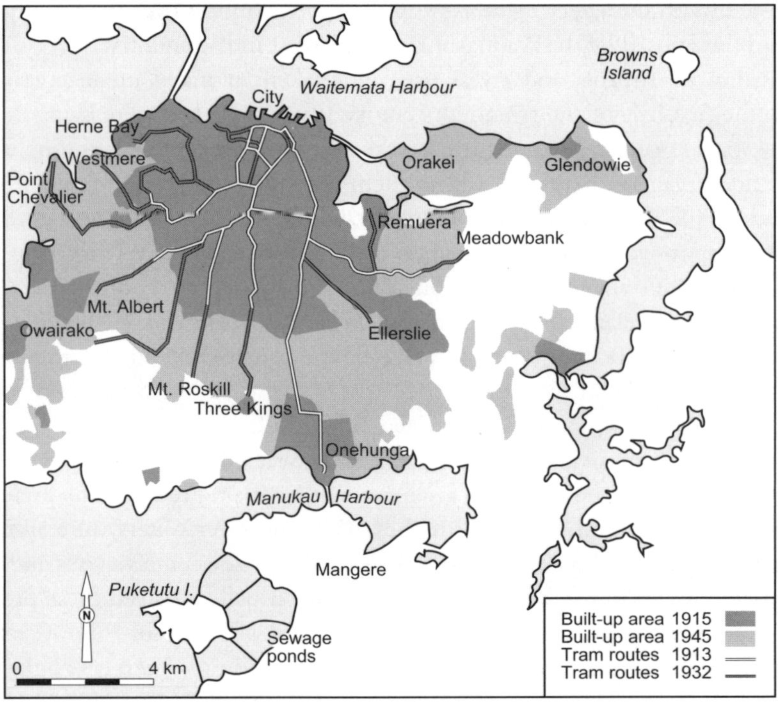

Figure 13.3 Auckland suburban development. Adapted from K. Cumberland, *Landmarks*, Reader's Digest, Surry Hills, 1981, p. 247.

rural interests from the late nineteenth century onwards to fuel animosity between town and country. This grew as New Zealand became more obviously urban. Miles Fairburn has argued that this animosity was based on an underlying desire for arcadia, a safe orderly haven, that farming areas could no longer accommodate as population grew, and that towns had demonstrated they were unfit to meet. Hence an underlying ambivalence about the town, in a land dependent on primary exports and sustained by frontier mythologies, was resolved in the twentieth century by the mass development of suburbs.[28] Urban history moved to its own edges.

The suburban town

The growth of suburbs, however, was well under way by the early 1900s. André Siegfried commented of his visit to Auckland in 1899 that:

> The town, with its suburbs, contains 67,000 inhabitants … But, a common phenomenon at the Antipodes, the suburbs, to the number of a dozen, are almost as important as the city itself, having nearly 33,000 inhabitants … The suburbs of Auckland are renowned for their beauty. The town is confined into a narrow space; but on the hillsides the villas stretch at their ease, surrounded by luxuriant vegetation, and looking down on the magnificent roadstead …

To Cowan this beauty seemed to be entirely imposed: he wrote of the city that 'What she lacks in the seven lamps of architecture she more than makes up in the charms of public gardens … of streets which are leafy avenues, cool and fresh with their rows of spreading oaks and ash and elms and tall colonnades of whispering poplars'. Beatrice Webb, visiting from Britain in 1898, saw it differently, as have many later writers: 'unlovely bungalows … small and uninteresting'.[29]

Home-ownership reached high levels early, exceeding 50 per cent of households by 1916. Sales advertisements for suburb and section development are useful representations of the 'meaning system' underlying this drive for property. Such advertisements were selling a 'good', in both senses of the word, and designed to enable consumers to envisage a suburban future.[30] Certain themes recur. First there are those relating to arcadian environmental dreams, identifying characteristics less readily available in the town. Sections in suburban Christchurch were frequently labelled in the 1920s and 1930s as receiving 'All the Sun that Shines!', as well as being well drained and possessing good gardening soil. In Dunedin promotion of new suburban subdivisions often focused overtly on health and the excellence of the view. Andersons Bay in 1910 was the 'Sunshine Township', and Calton Hill was promised in 1923 to be 'SUNNY! CHEERFUL!! HEALTHY!!!' Sun, of course, symbolised optimism as well.

A second group of themes emphasised access to urban infrastructures: on the edge but never isolated. Tramline extensions were a common selling point, as well as sewer, gas, and electricity connections. In Dunedin proximity to schools and churches was highlighted. Suburban expansion was therefore promoted by drawing attention to the ways in which it shared the advantages of both country and town. A third group of themes, usually interwoven with the others, centred on the benefits of investment. So just as it was claimed in 1913 that 'THOUSANDS OF LIVES made HAPPY and HEALTHFUL through residence in such a district as SALUBRIOUS ST CLAIR!', so prospective owners were assured: 'THOUSANDS OF POUNDS have been made by … far-seeing investors in ST CLAIR PROPERTY!' (Figure 13.4). Similarly, Mosgiel in 1927, given its '… Nearness to the City, is bound to grow, and is a delightful place in which to live. WATCH IT GROW!! REAP YOUR PROFITS!!'

The belief in the right to acquire and own property was institutionalised early in New Zealand. State lending support for home purchase extends back to 1894, and was greatly augmented in the 1930s. In debates in Parliament, the role of property and good housing in integrating people into the social structure, promoting citizenship, and diminishing threats of disorder featured frequently. The orderly suburbs in which family life would be underwritten were removed from the social as well as environmental dangers of both frontier and town. The first Labour government's state-housing scheme opened similar opportunities to those unable otherwise to afford them, so 'democratis[ing] the middle class suburban life-style'.[31]

The lifestyle being sought (in the 'typical residential street' of an Auckland guidebook: 'garden-surrounded houses, tidy hedges, shady trees, broad footpaths, and well kept roads') was based on what the American environmental historian Samuel Hays has described as 'beauty, health and permanence', or enjoyment of amenity, freedom from pollution, security, and social stability.[32] Houses were built with balconies and sunrooms, with sections

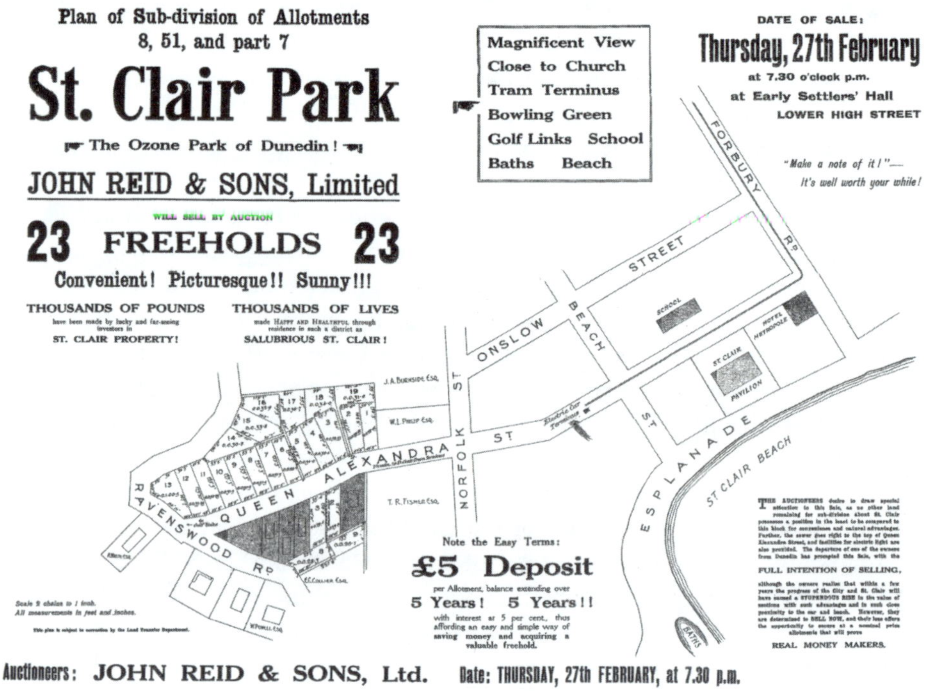

Figure 13.4 'Salubrious St Clair'. Auction notice for suburban sections in 1913. Reproduced with the permission of the Hocken Library, Uare Taoka O Hakena, University of Otago.

spacious enough for vegetables and play space as well as shrubs and flowers (Chapter 14). The 1920s saw rapid suburban growth, being the heyday, for instance, of the Californian bungalow in Auckland (Figure 13.3). That city, it was said, 'is capable of almost unlimited expansion, as both unoccupied and partially developed lands are awaiting the necessary population and capital to bring them into full production'. Penrose interests claimed in 1946 that 'in 25 years, this rural wilderness has been transformed into an intensely developed manufacturing area …' by 'young and lusty industries'.[33]

An American firm of consultants planned Auckland's pattern of motorways in the early 1950s, a further sign of the international style of urban modernism being adopted in New Zealand. It was largely in place by the mid 1960s, a state investment furthering suburban growth that was also fuelled by large-scale state housing development in Mangere and Otara. What was occurring in South Auckland was also happening around other cities and towns. In part, state-housing areas were used to accommodate Māori people who were moving from the countryside in great numbers in the 1950s and 1960s. For example, many Māori from rural East Cape and Hawke's Bay moved to the new forestry towns of the North Island interior, and to Rotorua, as well as to Wellington and Christchurch.

It was the expansion of suburban Wellington into the Hutt Valley, where in the 1940s the Naenae state-housing scheme caused controversy because of the loss of market gardens (relocated in the event to Otaki), that raised another matter: the environmental price of suburban development *per se*. In the early 1970s New Zealand's report to the first international environmental conference of government representatives in Stockholm described the national loss of good farming land to urbanisation as being 'most acute around Auckland',[34] turning round the progressive interpretation of suburban expansion of forty years before. Such anxieties had already led in the 1950s to the implementation of town and country planning legislation, designed to encourage more efficient use of existing urban space, and to give some protection to agricultural lands.

The regulatory role of the state, at national and local levels, thus became increasingly important in moulding urban development, although often its lack of investment in environmental-care schemes left the contemporary suburban city with a range of problems. These included traffic congestion, in the Auckland metropolitan area in particular (no longer the marker of the modern that it was in 1960s Wellington); sewage disposal (the favoured long-term solution to Auckland's post-World War II water-supply problems being a pipeline from the Waikato River, into which towns such as Taupo and Hamilton still discharged their barely treated sewage); and growing exposure to hazards such as flooding. Analysis of two urban floods, at Invercargill and Paeroa in the early 1980s, showed that they were so expensive in damage terms because so much development had been permitted to occur in flood-prone areas by the respective local authorities since the 1950s.[35]

On the beach

Using the metaphor 'on the edge', this chapter has set out to construct a framework for analysis of New Zealand's urban environmental histories. Towns were created on the edge of wilderness, centres of civilisation for the reclamation of nature. Functionally and symbolically, they came to represent progress expressed as the conquest of nature. But nature has not been tamed, and towns remain on its edge, subject to environmental hazards of their own making. These hazards have contributed to New Zealanders' ambivalence towards the urban, which has in part been resolved by creating a landscape on the edge that is neither urban nor rural, but suburban. In conclusion, these three themes are drawn together in a short case study that focuses on a coastal town.

The town of Timaru was created in the late 1850s to open up the district of South Canterbury. Its port exported wool from a landscape where previously (according to the progressive narrative of a 1926 guide) 'the ti-tree, tussock and flax clump rustled in the breeze, unheeded and unmolested'.[36] By the early years of the twentieth century the prosperity of the town was expressed in its public and commercial Edwardian architecture. Trade had been encouraged by construction of a breakwater, begun in 1878 to shelter shipping and much extended thereafter. Simultaneously, however, this breakwater interrupted the northward drift of sediment along the coast. The result has been the creation of both a hazard—as beach barriers to the north have been starved of gravel, thereby threatening low-lying coastal land—and a resource, as fine sand settled in the calm waters in the lee of the harbour to build a golden beach. Much of Timaru's twentieth-century history focused on this fortuitously produced beach in Caroline Bay.

Figure 13.5 'Timaru by the Sea.' Promotional image from the 1930s. Reproduced with the permission of South Canterbury Museum.

Elsewhere 'the beach' has been described as a liminal zone, a place on the edge in yet a further sense, where behavioural norms of what is (and with whom it is) legitimate can be relaxed to provide pleasures for people otherwise bound by convention.[37] Yet this was not the image constructed for Caroline Bay. It was promoted as modern (for example, having in the 1920s 'the longest chain of [electric] lights on any waterfront in the Southern Hemisphere'),[38] as family-oriented, and as 'sunny and safe' (Figure 13.5). It was the destination for regular and large train outings from Christchurch and Dunedin. Far from being risqué, its name was synonymous with that deemed healthy and non-threatening. Caroline Bay was dedicated to the reproduction, rather than the contest, of suburban values. And it was something of which to be immensely proud:

> New York has Coney Island and Timaru has Caroline Bay. He who will admit to the comparison is not a good citizen; for Timaru's Caroline Bay means just as much to Timaru as does

> Coney Island to New York ... In very few towns in New Zealand are there such safe bathing places. Caroline Bay is safer than Takapuna at Auckland, than Island Bay at Wellington, than Brighton, than Sumner, than St Clair, than Lyall Bay, than Milford Beach.[39]

Continued accumulation of sand in front of the breakwater, however, has built the beach outwards to such an extent that the seaside facilities of the bay are now isolated a kilometre or more from the water's edge. Combined with changing holiday fashions, which have taken people away to adventure destinations as well as overseas, the town has been undermined both economically and physically. In a further irony, a replacement source of prosperity for Timaru, its industrial area of Washdyke to the north of the bay, is at risk of inundation as the barrier beach that protects it continues to shrink because of the loss of gravel trapped behind the breakwater. Timaru's environmental history has therefore been 'on the edge' in all three senses—progressive, suburban, and vulnerable—that this chapter has employed to interpret the topic in New Zealand between the 1900s and the 1960s.[40]

14

EXOTIC NATIVES AND CONTRIVED WILD GARDENS

THE TWENTIETH-CENTURY HOME GARDEN

Helen M. Leach

Two paradoxes are evident in late twentieth-century New Zealand gardening. The first, and most obvious to visitors, is that the native plants that gardeners proudly display do not really look like the native species to be seen in wild habitats, being generally much more highly coloured. The second is that gardeners who claim to be imitating nature or creating a transition zone between nature and culture usually practise their art behind walls, fences, hedges, or other forms of barrier that exclude the external environment. How these paradoxes developed in the context of changing popular tastes, and how gardeners create one landscape while excluding another, will be the subject of this chapter. After justifying the emphasis on the history of the home garden, and the significance of popular manuals in moulding garden practice, the chapter will describe the features commonly seen in home gardens during the course of the twentieth century, before proposing an explanation of the paradoxes in the final discussion.

New Zealand garden histories

Just as gardens come in many forms, serving various purposes, there are potentially as many garden histories. Since the early nineteenth century, New Zealanders have made gardens around their homes and, from the establishment of the first towns, have regarded public gardens as important civic amenities. Because of the need to document decisions and account for the expenditure of public funds, archival records exist of many municipal gardens, which have been used in the histories so far completed, such as that of the Wellington Botanic Garden. Several preliminary studies have been made of the nurserymen who, from the 1850s, supplied ornamental and plantation trees in their hundreds of thousands for farms and parks, fruit trees for orchards, and shrubs, roses, and climbers to home gardeners. These have revealed how significant were nurserymen such as David Hay of Auckland, William Hale of Nelson, William Wilson of Christchurch, and William

Martin of Dunedin in propagating the imported plant materials used in the rapid transformation of the nineteenth-century New Zealand landscape.[1]

The history of the New Zealand home garden is more elusive. A small number of garden 'diaries' have been published, in the same literary tradition as the writings of Mrs Earle and Vita Sackville-West in England, but these describe exceptional gardens.[2] The 'average' suburban or rural home garden is accessible not through such eloquent accounts but in instructional manuals and articles that span the century, influencing and simultaneously reflecting popular practice.

The manuals were usually authored by professional gardeners and in some cases were published by companies selling garden products, such as the Auckland firm established by Arthur Yates in 1883. The most long-running examples are *Brett's Gardening Guide* (1920–) and *Yates' Garden Guide* (1895–), which since its twentieth edition (1934) has been 'printed in New Zealand for New Zealand conditions' (Figure 14.1).[3] Commercial pressures have led to frequent revisions of these manuals, and they can thus be used to track the changing popularity of plants and garden features. National and provincial publishers (especially Whitcombe & Tombs and later A. H. & A. W. Reed) have also produced practical gardening manuals that have had multiple editions.[4] Gardening notes have been published in numerous newspapers and magazines. From these sources it is possible to derive a description of the types of private garden considered achievable in both rural and suburban settings.

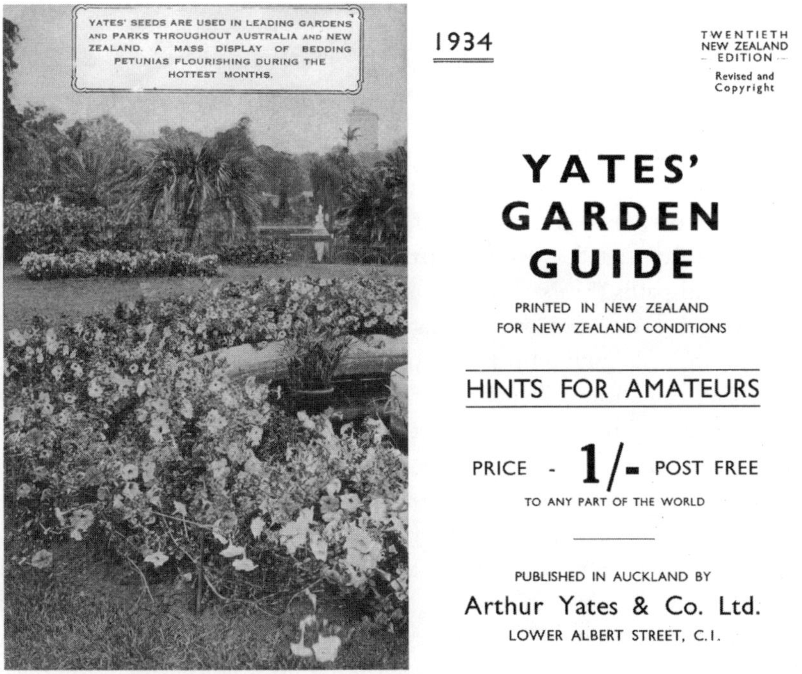

Figure 14.1 It was not until 1934 that *Yates' Garden Guide* appeared in an edition specially prepared for New Zealand gardening conditions.

What distinguishes these from the great international gardens on which garden historians write at length is the lack of unifying design. Rather than being planned as a whole, according to a shared ideal of beauty, they consist of elements, both botanical and structural, that are added and removed through time. Research on public gardens has shown that they, too, are assemblages of features, in this instance the elements perceived as important by ratepayers and the professional horticulturists put in charge. Thus many have been furnished with heated glasshouses for winter floral displays, with duck-ponds, bandstands, rose gardens, rockeries, woodland dells, arboreta (tree collections), herbaceous borders, expansive lawns cut by flowerbeds, mazes, sunken gardens, Japanese gardens, pergolas, and playing grounds. In many cases new features have been added alongside the old, to the point where municipal public gardens are effectively living museums of garden history without an integrated design.

The same accretive history is evident in the homestead gardens of many large rural properties, with few having been designed professionally, let alone maintained to the designer's specifications.[5] The suburban home gardener is even less likely to employ a professional landscape architect, instead laying out the section around the house to satisfy multiple, often conflicting, social needs, such as for privacy and display, domestic requirements such as drying clothes, and individual tastes. The quarter- or eighth-acre section common in most cities and towns is therefore also an assemblage of disparate features, despite its small size. Because the suburban home garden was numerically dominant throughout the twentieth century, it will be the focus of this chapter. However, the sharing of popular features between town and country gardens, as well as private and public gardens, means that the conclusions are broadly applicable to most twentieth-century New Zealand gardens.

The early twentieth-century home garden

At the beginning of the twentieth century the basic ornamental garden, or 'pleasure ground' as it was often called, consisted of the formal flower garden proper, lawn, informal shrubbery, and paths ('walks'). It lay to the front and sides of the house, while the kitchen garden and service areas were situated out of sight at the rear. Optional extras in the pleasure ground, depending on its extent, were a rockery, pond and bog garden, wild garden, rose beds, greenhouse, fernery, and lawn tennis court. Rural homestead gardens had space for more ornamental features, but in other respects they differed little from the large suburban garden.

The origins of all these features can be traced to Britain. Some came as the conceptual baggage of the first settlers in the 1840–60 period. Others arrived later in the nineteenth century as established settlers returned from visits 'Home' and the flow of British horticultural publications increased. In his 1907 manual Michael Murphy explicitly acknowledged his experience of gardening in 'the Old Country' and his English textual sources, while David Tannock reported on the latest trends to be seen at the 'great flower shows in London'.[6]

As was still current practice in Britain, geometrical flowerbeds provided a formal element in the Edwardian flower garden. New Zealand gardeners had adopted each of the 'bedding-out' styles of the nineteenth century, from massed planting of primary colours, to ribbon borders, spring bedding, subtropical, and carpet bedding, to sculptural bedding using wire frames, and several of these styles were described in the twentieth-century New Zealand manuals.[7]

The fernery was popular as a 'romantic retreat' from 'the dazzling beauty of the flower garden'. Elaborate roofed ferneries were built at ground level or as partly subterranean structures. Less formal were the ferneries made by heaping up earth and rocks on either side of an excavated pathway. Constructed ferneries were clearly inspired by British examples designed since the 1850s for growing ferns in a harsher climate. Their social significance as fashion features gave them a role in New Zealand gardens until the 1940s, despite the relative ease of growing ferns under shrubs and trees in a fully outdoor setting through most of New Zealand.[8]

House verandahs were covered with climbing and trailing plants 'to blend and soothe the work of man into harmony with nature', although the wooden fabric of most New Zealand homes was more likely to be damaged than the brick or plaster used in Britain. The arrival of the fashionable pillar and rambler roses from Europe and North America also led to the proliferation of pergolas, arches, and poles in rose gardens. In smaller gardens, however, roses 'invaded the flower garden', competing for attention with the beds of annuals.[9] The separate rose garden, or rosary, had been a high-status element of British gardens since the early 1800s when Humphry Repton incorporated them into many country estates.

Rustic finishes had been fashionable for timber structures supporting roses since the late eighteenth century, as for garden bridges, arbours, and summerhouses; mānuka was found to be the best native timber 'for rustic work'. The summerhouse was usually situated in the informal section of the pleasure ground, an area in which serpentine paths wound through shrubberies, as they had in English gardens since the late eighteenth century. The shrubbery was a common location for clumps of subtropical plants and, in some larger gardens, merged into the wild garden advocated by the influential British garden writer William Robinson, and itself the romantic descendant of the sixteenth- and seventeenth-century formal garden wilderness.[10]

The rockery emerged as a fashionable feature in Britain by the 1850s, but poor design and construction had led to criticism. However, under the direction of plantsmen such as Reginald Farrer it became 'the height of fashion in horticulture' from the Edwardian era. Tannock advocated it as a way of dealing with a bank or of screening an undesirable feature, and saw it as the miniaturisation of a natural landscape, advising that 'before commencing operations it is well to study a mountain range'. But few New Zealand alpine plants were to be found in these rockeries, especially in warm North Island localities, and Murphy reported that there was still 'a feeling amongst many that these denizens of our forests and mountains are difficult to cultivate'. For Tannock, a rock garden 'devoted to the cultivation of natives is most interesting and very bright, particularly at celmisia [mountain daisy] time', but he conceded that though the celmisias might reproduce themselves from seed, 'others have to be renewed from time to time from their native haunts'. Not surprisingly, therefore, New Zealand rock gardens featured mostly northern hemisphere plants.[11]

Figure 14.2 At McNab's public garden in Lower Hutt (formerly Alfred Ludlam's), native nīkau palms substituted for exotic species in a box-edged avenue (c. 1890s). Reproduced with the permission of the Hocken Library, Uare Taoka O Hakena, University of Otago.

It was not always a case of colonial imitation of the 'motherland', however. Adaptability was often necessary, and Murphy's (1907) fourth edition included chapters on 'trees and shrubs suitable for small gardens', reflecting the growth of suburbs in New Zealand cities. Also added to manuals and almanacs reflecting South Island experience were more details on managing the ornamental greenhouse, vinery, and orchard, a sign of greater ability to invest in capital improvements than had been possible in the pioneering era. Victorian fascination with subtropical vegetation, evident since the 1860s, was also exported to New Zealand, manifest in signature plants such as agaves, yuccas and aloes, pampas, bamboos, and palms. Several New Zealand native plants were adopted for their subtropical effect, especially the toetoe, *Phormium* flax, and cabbage tree[12] (Figure 14.2).

Unlike British gardens in long-established suburban and rural settings, most New Zealand gardens required substantial windbreaks. By the time that Murphy was writing, early misjudgment of ultimate tree dimensions was evident:

> A very common mistake which prevailed in the early days of settlement throughout the colony, but nowhere more prevalent than in Christchurch, was the planting of such trees as Wellingtonias, Pinus insignis, Oaks, Elms, Blue Gums etc., in quarter, and eighth of an acre sections. The idea was to get shelter, as soon as possible. This was an obvious mistake, as they soon outgrew everything else and had to be cut down, leaving ugly blanks.[13]

The macrocarpa was found too large for suburban hedging, while experiments with certain natives such as the matipo showed them intolerant of frequent clipping. It was not merely the use of tall-growing trees for suburban shelter that was a mistake, but also their planting as specimen trees in front lawns, a practice going back to the eighteenth-century English landscape garden. The highest-status trees in the nineteenth century included exotic evergreens such as the Chilean monkey puzzle, Californian redwood, and Atlantic and Himalayan cedars, all of which grew faster and taller in New Zealand. Even the Douglas fir and Monterey pine (*Pinus radiata* syn. *insignis*), which subsequently became New Zealand's main timber tree, were initially esteemed as lawn specimens. In 1914 the Dunedin horticulturist David Tannock complained that these conifers were being cut down as having grown too big 'just as many are becoming beautiful' (Figure 14.3).[14]

In country districts, high shelter belts were frequently planted right around homesteads. While W. C. Hyde recommended to readers of the *Journal of Agriculture* that they

Figure 14.3 The planting of specimen trees on front lawns, especially conifers such as this Chilean monkey puzzle tree, had little regard for their eventual size. Subtropical-looking flax bushes flank the front steps. Reproduced with the permission of the Bathgate Collection, the Hocken Library, Uare Taoka O Hakena, University of Otago.

have just a fence on the north side to allow the house and its grounds a vista of the surrounding countryside, J. A. Campbell argued against any form of blending:

> With regard to work on a large scale, probably the two main points to observe in designing the work are: when the surrounding country is rough and rugged the ground should be treated as artificially as possible—neat level lawns, walks, flower-beds, borders, etc., should be aimed at in order to form a contrast; on the other hand, should the surroundings be made up of neatly laid-out and well-kept green fields, etc., more natural ruggedness may be introduced.[15]

Thus the principle of exclusion, applied to British gardens primarily for social reasons, was reinterpreted in New Zealand as an environmental or aesthetic necessity. Other justifications for exclusion were also offered: as early as 1914 David Tannock was aware of the common practice in the United States of leaving the fronts of gardens 'open to the street and unfenced', and regretted that it could not be carried out in New Zealand, 'owing to our out-of-date ideas of maintaining swarms of stray dogs in our towns'. But considering his advice that the front door be screened by a rustic fence, arch, or shrubbery from the sight of someone passing the front gate, it seems that the unstated social imperative for privacy also prevailed.[16]

The home garden between the wars

In the 1920s garden writers commented on the growing trend towards informality in the New Zealand flower garden. Although some people preferred 'a stiff formal garden, with neat clipped hedges and shrubs, and the flowerbeds planted out in regular designs, such as carpet bedding, ribbon borders, etc.', a 'much freer and more individualistic treatment' had begun to prevail, with less emphasis on mass effects and more on standard roses and fuchsias. This did not mean that formal design elements were abandoned—the symmetrical rose garden was still evident in large gardens (both public and private), and can be seen in many municipal gardens today. By 1934 Tannock was convinced that for the small suburban garden, 'a more or less formal design' was preferable. This included the sunken garden with its geometrical lily pond and crazy paving, made fashionable by English designers such as Gertrude Jekyll and Edwin Lutyens in the Edwardian period (Figure 14.4). The hallmark of their collaboration was formal hard landscaping softened by luxuriant planting, and it was informality in both plant varieties and their positioning that became apparent in New Zealand. Specimen trees and shrubs were planted in mixed borders rather than on the lawn itself. While this trend re-established the lawn as a formal design feature, the borders that it 'set off' were increasingly informal. To a large extent this was the result of an ever-increasing choice of flowering or coloured-leaved shrubs.[17]

The bush-house, of probable Australian origin, became a popular alternative to the conservatory or greenhouse in warmer parts of New Zealand. With a roof of mānuka brushwood, its purpose was to reduce the intensity of sunlight, protect the contents from drying winds, and increase humidity around plants such as gloxinias and begonias that in cooler climates would be grown under glass. The bush-house was also the only part of

Higher End

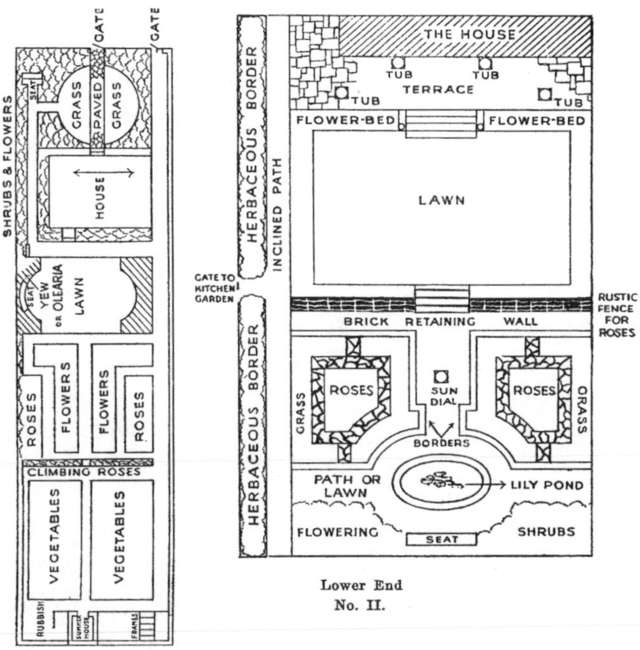

Lower End
No. II.

No. I.

No. I.—This plan would be suitable for a long town section, and provides for both flowers and vegetables with suitable lawns. The path through the front lawn could be omitted. Climbing roses on a rustic fence could separate the vegetables from the flowers. A sweet pea fence or espalier fruit trees could be substituted for the roses. A hedge of Escallonia or Olearia Fosteri could form the boundary on one side.

No. II.—This plan would be suitable for a sloping site, the house occupying the higher position. A low rustic fence would separate the lawn with its surrounding flower borders from the rose garden, and on it climbing or rambler roses could be grown. The rose beds are surrounded by paved paths and there is really no need to have grass at all, if more roses are desired. The long path would be a suitable place for a pergola, which would provide a vista the whole length of the garden. This plan provides a good view of the garden from the house as well as a good view of the house from the garden.

Figure 14.4 The suburban garden designs provided in David Tannock's *Practical Gardening in New Zealand* (1934) were strongly influenced by the formal, symmetrical style then popular in Britain. The olearia suggested as an alternative to yew hedging was the only distinctive New Zealand element.

the warm-climate garden where the fashionable English wall garden might succeed. This was a roughly built stone wall covered with ferns, mosses, or mat-forming alpine plants. Such 'artificial rock works' were seen as contributing to the charm of the bush-house, just as they had in late Victorian conservatories in England. This is an interesting example of colonial adaptation by substitution.[18]

Rock work became even more popular in the form of the outdoor rockery, which Yates presented as an important form of home improvement capable of changing 'an unattractive or unsightly corner or wall' into 'quite a beauty spot'. But it had to look 'natural' and 'never obtrude on to a formal garden'. An ideal position was a rocky bank backed by the raised foundations of the house, or the back of a terrace cut into a hillside. As the rockery's popularity returned, it was not surprising that gardening manuals added new sections on pools and fish-ponds, for it was believed that a background of rocks made a water feature immediately 'impressive'. There were now several variants of rock garden, including the moraine or scree garden popularised by Tannock as the answer to growing the most difficult alpines, the dry streambed, and the alpine lawn. With the spread of bungalows, some gardeners dispensed with hedges and adopted the Californian system of marking the front boundary with rough rock kerbing backed by a wire fence, 'leaving the garden practically open to the view of the street'. This practice was later criticised by Douglas Elliott for making such gardens look 'like public parks'.[19]

Woodland gardens flourished in damper areas, such as New Plymouth, Wellington, and Dunedin, where there was space for canopy trees, often deciduous, under which bulbs, rhododendrons, hydrangeas, tree ferns, and woodland perennials such as primroses would thrive. Although there was little discussion of these in the practical handbooks, they also became a hallmark of the rural gardens attached to wealthy homesteads, especially in the foothills of Canterbury. Several were subsequently opened for public viewing. They were undoubtedly influenced by Gertrude Jekyll's woodland variety of wild gardening, extensively practised in Surrey and West Sussex.[20]

Vegetable gardens were an important component of the inter-war home garden. More appropriate windbreaks had now been devised, including 'the use of a framework of wires, interlaced with ti-tree [tea-tree, mānuka]' and covered with 'useful and profitable' plants such as roses, runner beans, and chokos. By this time the choko (*Sechium edule*) was a distinctive Australasian vegetable, though not of high status. In layout the vegetable garden still followed basic nineteenth-century English practice in its division by permanent paths into at least four large beds. The means of restoring soil nutrients were undergoing major change, however, and the manuals document the declining use of stable manure, considered 'practically unobtainable' by the 1930s. Artificial fertilisers were promoted as science's answer, along with the commercially profitable concept of 'the proper fertilizer for the particular crop'.[21]

Suburban sections that were too small for a home orchard benefited from the spread, in the 1930s, of new fruits from the Pacific rim, such as Chinese gooseberries (renamed kiwifruit in 1973), cranberries, feijoas and guavas, and small citrus varieties, which took up less space or could be grown over fences. By 1945 *Brett's Gardening Guide* had dropped its section on the orchard, incorporating instead new paragraphs on small back and front gardens, as well as the proliferating types of rock garden.

In 1934 Tannock could claim that native plants had 'received such increased attention during recent years that a native section is now an accepted as well as an interesting feature of most large gardens'. Eleven years earlier the botanist and pioneer ecologist Leonard Cockayne had published a practical manual on the cultivation of New Zealand plants (1923). It is difficult to estimate the role this book played in their acceptance by the public. Innate patriotism as a motivation, as argued by Cockayne, may not have been as significant as the popular desire for novelty. Throughout the 1920s nurserymen were actively promoting purple-leaved cabbage trees and native fuchsias, variegated pittosporums, coloured *Phormium* flaxes, the bronze-leaved rangiora, and crimson and double mānuka, to the point where Tannock believed that the increased popularity of natives was 'to some extent due to the introduction of the new brightly coloured varieties of the manuka'.[22]

Tannock's descriptions of individual native plants often invoked comparisons beyond New Zealand. For example, when allowed to grow in isolation, 'shapely round-headed specimens of totaras, knightias, and beech' give 'that park-like effect to the landscape which is so characteristic of the English countryside', while the native *Libocedrus doniana* (now *L. plumosa*) was described as of 'upright pyramidal growth not unlike the Italian cypress in appearance'. Particular emphasis was given to the qualities of native species as potential lawn specimens in large gardens or for providing a tropical effect. Even after World War II the native plants singled out as of particular merit in the new magazine the *New Zealand Gardener*, were the coloured mānuka, hebes, red-flowered kākā beak, golden tainui, purple rangiora, and bronze akeake, all of which were unusually bright in flower or leaf colour compared with wild species. It might be concluded from this that native plants were valued by the gardening public only to the extent that they looked 'exotic'.[23]

From the 1950s to the 1980s

World War II stopped the flow of seeds and new plant varieties from overseas until 1946, though nurserymen were able to bulk up new bulb varieties obtained from South Africa just before the war, ready for the postwar boom in ornamental gardening. Wartime disruption had also affected phosphate imports from Nauru, strengthening interest in compost making and soil health (Chapter 11). This was reflected in a page inserted in the 1943 *Yates' Garden Guide* claiming that the early success of 'the celebrated world-beating All Black football team' had been based on reserves of humus and minerals built up in the country's 'virgin lands' but now largely consumed with the complicity of 'chemical acid-forming water-soluble stimulating manures such as Sulphate of Ammonia and Superphosphate'. By 1950, however, this organic message had been removed and a revised edition was promoting numerous artificial fertiliser mixes, hormone weedkillers such as 2-4-D, and grass-grub treatments containing DDT and arsenate of lead—all available from Yates and their retailers. By 1957 superphosphate and sulphate of ammonia replaced animal waste products as the compost activators recommended by Yates, and a newspaper extract headed 'Starvation Diet in the Home Garden' was reprinted in their guide, accusing home gardeners of starving their crops by using insufficient quantities of compound artificial fertiliser. This extract appeared in each edition up to the late 1970s, doubtless influencing the countless home gardeners whose only gardening book was *Yates'*.[24]

The flower garden retained many pre-war features over the 1950–70 period, such as the rose arch and pergola, various types of rock work, pools and fish-ponds, and the use of standard roses (Figure 14.5). The manuals gave increasing emphasis to the lawn, no doubt influenced by the growth of the multi-million-dollar lawncare industry in the United States, the source of many of the chemical products advertised in New Zealand. Flowerbeds cut into lawns were openly criticised, while ornamental shrubs competed with flowers for space in the borders. A second attempt was made to introduce the American-style open front yard, this time to postwar state-housing developments. In these new suburbs front and dividing fences were eliminated from the area between the house and the street. Cedric Firth argued that though some loss of privacy would occur, the system would give 'a more unified street

Figure 14.5 Despite its size, this prize-winning front garden (c. 1960) displayed a modern-style pergola, a pond and fountain set into a small front lawn, and standard roses underplanted with annuals. Reproduced with the permission of the Hocken Library, Uare Taoka O Hakena, University of Otago.

picture' and contribute to the sense of being 'part of a large community garden'[25] (Figure 14.6). Many became extended street playgrounds rather than gardens, and when the state-owned properties were later sold to private owners, fences and walls were erected in keeping with the widespread desire for a garden that excludes the external environment.

The home vegetable garden became smaller and received less attention in the manuals from the 1950s until organic gardening and the ornamental potager style made it fashionable again in the 1990s. The decline began as early as 1947 when Douglas Elliott's articles on landscape design in the *New Zealand Gardener* pointed out that if a garden feature had to be dispensed with for lack of space, it was better to be the vegetable plot: 'The value of a flower garden is something that cannot be priced, and you can never buy its equivalent from a florist's shop as you can buy vegetables from the greengrocer.' By 1957 *Yates'* recommended that the vegetable garden 'be confined to the end of the garden' instead of merely separated from the flower garden. At the same time its coverage of the home 'nursery', with its paraphernalia for raising seedlings and cuttings, was dropped. Gardeners were now expected to purchase their plants from professionals, who were portrayed as knowledgeable in the science of seed testing, selection, and breeding. A special section on herb growing was added to the 1961 edition, but it was not until 1987 that a chapter on organic gardening was included. Against the previous trend, *Yates'*

Figure 14.6 Mr Ian Holmes and his family outside their home in Naenae Road, Lower Hutt. Their 1945 state house had a sparsely planted front garden with a post-and-chain fence marking its street boundary. John Pascoe Collection, Alexander Turnbull Library, National Library of New Zealand, Te Puna Matauranga o Aotearoa.

recognised that the majority of urban New Zealanders still buying seed and growing vegetables did so as a lifestyle choice, not out of necessity. The vegetable garden was now treated as an optional feature, comparable to a rock garden or 'theme' garden.[26]

The most significant changes over the period took place close to the house, and often involved considerable expenditure on hard landscaping. The Californian concept of the outdoor room promoted by designers such as Thomas Church between the wars was quickly adopted in the 1950s. Features associated with the new outdoor room competed for space with older ones like the traditional formal rose garden. The new 'sun patio' was portrayed as a 'feature for gracious living', which required shade and privacy, supplied by vine-covered trellising, as well as outdoor furniture. Decorated with potted shrubs and wall gardens, it often featured a barbecue fireplace, an American development whose construction was described in imported lifestyle magazines such as *Sunset*. Another modern feature was the children's playground containing a sandpit and swing. It was promoted as 'an added inducement for young children to keep away from the garden beds', but it also reflected parental desire to have children under closer supervision, in private rather than public places. In the 1980s the swimming pool began to dominate the outdoor living area in affluent suburbs of northern New Zealand cities, restricting both the play area available for small children and the planting space for keen gardeners, but increasing entertainment opportunities for young adults. In cooler zones the attached conservatory was revived, but more as a living area for people than plants.[27]

More attention was given to integrating house and garden. Not only was the patio linked by 'ranchsliders' to the living area inside, but the new fashion for picture windows required that 'displays of showy annuals and perennials should be so arranged as to create a vista of colour when seen from the inside of the house'. Significantly there was no comparable discussion of vistas linking the home garden with the external landscape. Advice given by books on landscaping was to enhance views 'of any desirable scenery, while screening out unwanted features ... Shelter planting, fences and screens will define the extent to which you allow the outer environment to be included.' Such was the need for privacy as New Zealand suburban housing densities increased that screening became a higher priority than viewing.[28]

As section size decreased, shrubs and ornamental trees were selected for suitably restrained growth habit and attractive flowers, berries, or foliage. The aim was to provide 'colour in the garden for the greater part of the year', an indication that colour was still judged more important than texture or form. With low-maintenance shrub borders becoming more numerous, the quest for 'permanent' weed suppression gained momentum in the 1960s. To those unwilling to apply weedkillers, a polythene barrier seemed ideal, provided it could be concealed. The pebble-over-polythene garden emerged in the early 1970s, presented as a derivative of a Japanese style. Pebbles were later replaced by bark and woodchip mulches, a cheaper by-product of the expanding timber industry.[29]

Attitudes to native plants were highly variable during this period, ranging from tokenism to deep commitment. In the early 1950s *Yates' Garden Guide* had urged gardeners not to 'overlook our New Zealand native shrubs and small trees, many of which are most ornamental'; however, only ten native genera were included in their tree and shrub lists. In 1958 a photo of native bush was captioned 'It is a fortunate gardener indeed who has remaining or who has recreated, a small piece of "New Zealand as it was"', but it was not until 1987 that *Yates'* devoted a major section to native plants. In contrast, *Brett's Gardening Guide* had listed six pages of native species by 1963. Most gardening manuals included the few popular native plants in their general lists of ornamental shrubs or trees. The true successors to Cockayne's (1923) work were two specialist books published in the 1970s by Muriel Fisher, E. Satchell, and Janet M. Watkins, and by Lawrie Metcalf. This time the message that the decline of native species in the wild should be matched by their increased cultivation in gardens fell on the receptive ears of the growing numbers of New Zealanders sympathetic to the conservation movement.[30]

The home garden at the end of the twentieth century

By the end of the twentieth century the old binary division of the home garden into pleasure ground and kitchen garden/orchard (1900–20), followed by flower garden and vegetable garden (1920–90), was being replaced by an array of styles from which one or more could be selected, or purchased like a commodity, according to personal taste. The new suburban home-owner of the 1990s might no longer start with a front and back garden, but with a house and its outdoor living area. Plants were decorative additions to this zone but no longer essential. Where there was additional space beyond the deck, paved area, and pool, a choice could be made as to what type of garden should be created. The manuals, television garden programmes, and horticultural shows suggested a number of styles, including Japanese, alpine, riverbed, subtropical, old English or cottage, native, Mediterranean, tropical Polynesian, potager, organic, Californian, beach-front, and desert—all with overseas precedents or parallels, and all offered as a self-contained microcosm with no apparent connection to the external landscape. In centres such as Auckland these could be professionally installed in a few hours, as a 'garden make-over'. Although popular media have presented the smorgasbord approach to horticulture as a *fait accompli*, many New Zealand gardens are maintained in more traditional styles consistent with their age and architecture. But equally these exist with little reference to their external environment.

Discussion

The New Zealand garden assembled features and styles from external sources throughout the twentieth century. Britain contributed most, but there were significant inputs from the United States, especially California, and Australia. A diversity of features was valued ahead of any unity of design, as can be seen in responses to the diminishing size of town gardens where miniaturisation of elements was preferred to abandonment. The styles were more or less modified to suit New Zealand's social and natural settings. For example, the low front boundary wall was adopted with the Californian bungalow, but there was resistance to the idea of the unfenced front lawn. Most modifications can be classified as adaptation by substitution. Native ferns were assimilated into Jekyll-style woodland gardens, replacing English ferns, and grown beside exotics such as rhododendrons and camellias. Rock gardens were made in imitation of mountains and ravines, but usually planted with alpine species from the northern hemisphere. The subtropical style of British summer bedding displays was enhanced with native plants selected for their 'tropical' appearance. Shrubberies and shrub borders accommodated native species if they satisfied popular taste for colour in flowers or foliage. Since most native shrubs in the wild have small pale flowers, and foliage in subtle shades of green and grey, the paradox of the atypically bright native cultivar can be interpreted as a response to the imported subtropical style. Only the functional vegetable garden exemplifies adaptation by innovation, in this case by the adoption of new fruits and vegetables from the Pacific Rim; however, this distinctiveness has recently been undermined by the spread of the fashionable potager from Britain.

Above all, the twentieth-century New Zealand garden was a landscape of exclusion.[31] Its preoccupation with boundaries, whether shelter belts or hedges against strong winds, dog- or child-proof fences, trellises for privacy, or walls for security, suggests that the gardening tradition brought to New Zealand was inherently inward-looking and has remained so to the present. The readiness of contemporary gardeners to re-create Mediterranean courtyards or Japanese moss gardens in the suburbs of Auckland or Christchurch is further evidence of their perception of the garden as a self-contained environment. This paradoxical focus on a miniaturised artificial environment, when attractive backdrops of hills, oceans or harbours surround many New Zealand gardens, suggests that the desire for social exclusion outweighs our attachment to the natural landscape.

For most of the century the external environment beyond the garden has been primarily a source of materials. Mānuka, for example, has provided long-lasting poles for arches and rustic arbours. It has also supplied brushwood to cover newly sown lawns, for the roofs and walls of ferneries and bush-houses, and windbreak fences for vegetable gardens. Early in the twentieth century its inherent beauty as a plant was briefly acknowledged, but its commonness disqualified it from the garden until the rare pink and red forms were discovered. By the 1940s many New Zealanders considered the white-flowered mānuka simply a pest.[32] The external environment supplied weathered rocks for rock gardens and slabs for paving. Coarse sand was extracted for horticultural use, and a commercial peat industry was in place by the 1960s. Alpine herbfields were visited by collectors stocking and restocking their rock and scree gardens. Forests supplied rotted kiekie foliage for potting mixes, as well as tree ferns and seedling podocarps.[33] At first, plant collecting was seen as a source of pure pleasure and healthy recreation, although Cockayne and McPherson deplored the loss of ferns and alpines in gardens through failure to understand their needs. When the postwar building boom led to the felling of tree ferns to build retaining walls, their cheapness and effectiveness was tempered by a growing awareness that it was an inappropriate use. Douglas Elliott wrote, 'Another objection I have—mere sentiment: I don't like to think of all those beautiful ferns being squandered in this way.'[34]

Two beliefs that have affected interpretations of garden history in New Zealand need further clarification. The first is that the English settlers attempted to make another England in their new land; the second is that they saw the garden as an interface between wild nature and human culture. Thus the formal parts of the garden lay close to the house, while the informal parts, being closer to nature, merged with the landscape on the fringe of the garden.[35]

The first contention is relevant to the negative attitudes to New Zealand's native plants evident through much of the twentieth century. Victorian gardeners in England did not value English native trees or shrubs, believing them to be common, and aggressive in growth habits—indeed, the influential John Claudius Loudon accepted English trees only if they had a different habit from those growing naturally in woods and forests. It was not until the appearance of William Robinson's (1870) book on the wild garden that English gardeners showed more interest in native wildflowers. In fact Robinson's book was chiefly concerned with the naturalisation of hardy exotic plants on the fringes of country gardens. This attitude to native species explains the preoccupation of Victorian gardeners in both Britain and New Zealand with trees from North and South America, the Mediterranean, East Asia, and the Himalayas. The English landscape to be re-created in New Zealand was already full of exotic species and was the product of a value system, duly exported to the colonies, that placed the rare and exotic above the native.[36]

The second belief appears to be supported by statements from the garden writers themselves. For example, the ultimate aim in making a rock garden was 'to imitate Nature as closely as possible', to make it a 'mountainside in miniature', which ideally looked 'as if it were part of the landscape'. Similarly, the artificial fernery 'should imitate nature' to the extent of banning concrete arches within it and selecting mossy stones 'to give it a more natural appearance'. Home-owners seeking low-maintenance gardens in the 1960s were advised to have 'a more or less natural and informal garden', and 'to follow nature by having as few straight lines as possible'.[37] Intellectually the European gardening tradition has, since the Italian Renaissance, situated the garden between art (culture) and nature. In keeping with this, garden writers in the twentieth century positioned the different garden types that lie between the house and the wilderness along a continuum from 'outdoor room' to 'wild garden'. However, this model has been questioned by Geoffrey Dutton, by Michael Pollan, and by Helen Leach, who have argued that most 'wild' or 'natural' gardens are no less artificial than formal gardens—they are landscapes cleverly contrived to conceal their cultural origins.[38] From this perspective, the New Zealand garden proves to be as 'constructed' as the house, and the two characteristics of the twentieth-century garden that we started with cease to be paradoxical. The persistent use of barriers to exclude the 'wilderness' and other variants of the external environment is comparable to putting walls on a house, and a preference for certain native plants, which look more like domesticated garden cultivars than wild species, is akin to the keeping of pets.

Part 5
Perspectives

15

COMPANIONS, STOWAWAYS, IMPERIALISTS, INVADERS

PESTS AND WEEDS IN NEW ZEALAND

Thomas D. Isern

In 1991 the proprietor of a venerable sheep station in the Mackenzie Country of inland Canterbury looked about from rim to rim of the basin and explained how the property had been degraded by rabbits and hawkweeds. He gestured down at the ground on which he stood—though the ground was not soil at all, but a five-centimetre-thick mat of rabbit excrement. The only green peeking through was a few tawny spears of hawkweed. The station had been destocked, there had been no sheep on this land for five years—but nature was not healing itself; rather the pests and weeds were multiplying.[1] This is a compelling image given the mythic standing of the Mackenzie in the New Zealand identity.

A shocking situation indeed, but by no means a singular one in the environmental history of New Zealand. Ninety-nine years earlier, the first English sparrows nested on Tutira, the Hawke's Bay station made famous in the environmental classic penned by its owner, Herbert Guthrie-Smith. The birds, which habitually nested in and around buildings, offered chirping comfort in colonial lands; they were released by the Auckland Acclimatisation Society in 1867 and subsequently by colonists elsewhere. At first settlers greeted the birds with 'interest and incredulity', which in but a few years shifted to 'considerable alarm'—the birds 'appearing as if by magic', descending on fields of small grains.[2]

To say that the history of introduced animals and plants in the environments of New Zealand has been chequered would be unduly kind, according to scholars of the subject, who portray it as folly or aggression. George M. Thomson, in his pioneering study of 1922, *The Naturalisation of Animals and Plants in New Zealand*, while carefully cataloguing the specific introduction of each species, observes more generally that acclimatisation 'has hitherto been carried on in the most haphazard and irresponsible manner'.[3] A generation later, Andrew Hill Clark, in *The Invasion of New Zealand by People, Plants and Animals*, held to that rhetorically provocative term 'invasion' to label the introduction of foreign species and systems and the resulting disruption of native species and formations. Clark codified common conceptions of the problem—a land of poor soils clothed tenderly in bush and grass, formations evolved without the presence of significant grazing, browsing, or predator animals, hammered by invading species. He advanced understanding by placing pests, weeds, livestock, crops, and the entire transformation of the landscape into one complex, rather than simply dwelling on the rogues' gallery of recognised problem species.[4] Global context is provided by Alfred W. Crosby's more recent and sweeping *Ecological Imperialism*, a book wherein the lowly dandelion is freighted with empire, Crosby's general thesis being, 'Perhaps the success of European imperialism has a biological, an ecological, component'. New Zealand is his case study for the 'runaway propagation and spread' of the 'portmanteau biota' of 'Europeans and all the organisms they brought with them'.[5]

It is valuable to broaden perspectives, as Clark and Crosby have done, by considering systems, not only species, and by doing so globally, not just locally. Yet as Guthrie-Smith showed in *Tutira*, it can be useful, too, to focus on conception and scale. The focus in this essay is on pests and weeds in New Zealand—that is, on those plants and animals that New Zealanders commonly have identified as problems in their fields, paddocks, and forests. The public and private efforts of New Zealanders to deal with pests and weeds are instructive; the lessons are discouraging, hopeful and, most of all, challenging. The impact of pests and weeds in New Zealand is so drastic, and of such peculiar nature, that it cannot be explained in traditional terms of ecology or environmental history. It requires rather a reconsideration of the place of humankind in nature, the abandonment of passive environmentalism, and the pursuit of active husbandry.

Animal pests: disorder mammalia

The 'small bird problem' that agitated Guthrie-Smith and generated hot discussion in the 1880s, like the Canada goose problem at mid twentieth century, was transitory. Mammal pests posed the great and intractable problems to farmers, pastoralists, foresters, and citizens of New Zealand. Pigs were the pioneer pest, but in this case the distinction between pest and resource was often fuzzy. Wild pigs were a serious problem only in a thinly populated land, although deer cullers in the twentieth century still took pigs for bounty. Cullers were dispatched by the Wildlife Service (established in 1945) to reduce the burgeoning and destructive population of red deer—the irony being that the animal that most embodied the aristocratic sporting impulse should be reduced to the status of a pest to be extirpated by the unemployed poor of the Great Depression. Well-to-do colonists organised into acclimatisation societies had landed deer at multiple points on both islands during the mid nineteenth century. Proliferation and spread of these imports was uneven, some prospering. Introductions continued until the beginning of World War I, including government initiatives to establish herds in the Southern Alps for the enjoyment of tourists.[6]

Even before introductions had ceased, warnings had been voiced about the take-off of deer populations. The browsing habits of deer made them a threat to native bush in the most direct fashion—the consumption of young growth, creating forests that were superficially charming in their open character, but barren. The animals were regarded as problems in the North and South Island alike, but their persecutors and their defenders were more agitated on the latter, where, despite the relative paucity of forests, hope persisted for an economically and recreationally beneficial deer population. An official of the State Forest Service estimated with alarm that there were 300,000 deer in 1922, by which time organised culling already had begun in Otago. Two years later the Native Bird Protection Society (see Chapter 8) made red deer the poster pest of a bulletin exhorting, 'New Zealanders, are you content with New Zealand as nature has made her, or shall introductions continue until not a vestige of the real New Zealand exists outside the pages of history!'[7] Sentiment had turned against deer by 1930 when, at the Deer Menace Conference in Christchurch, ecologist Leonard Cockayne denounced their ravages. During the 1920s all legal protection of deer was lifted, national park officials were authorised to destroy them as they saw fit, and government assisted with marketing of deerskins. During the 1930s men welcomed gainful government employment as cullers, supervised for the Department of Internal Affairs by the legendary G. F. ('Skipper') Yerex. Its employees killed more than 100,000 deer between 1930 and 1934; estimates for 1938–41 ran to some 90,000, with perhaps as many killed for their skins by private shooters. Deer culling then lapsed on account of wartime exigencies.

The rise of deerstalking organisations of sportsmen in the 1940s failed to turn official policy in favour of deer preservation. Rather, deer culling was renewed with vigour after the war and through the following two decades (a development shaped by author Barry Crump into a classic of Kiwi popular culture, the humorous coming-of-age memoir *A Good Keen Man*).[8] The tone of Crump's work aside, deer culling became serious business. Returning veterans armed with military .303 rifles and paid by the tail proved effective killers of the unwanted browsers. Buoyed with postwar confidence, the government declared a policy of deer eradication in 1950. In 1956 the Department of Internal Affairs turned over deer control to the Forest Service, and 63,000 deer were shot in 1957 alone. As early as 1963, and especially following the Vietnam war, the deer campaign was escalated by employment of helicopters and shooters with automatic weapons. By this time private shooters harvesting skins and venison for export were doing most of the eradication. Such concentration of resources drastically reduced the herds, so that by the late 1960s and early 1970s some citizens were anticipating the day when feral deer would be rare and domestic deer might have value. Some deer were captured for domestication by homely methods, such as luring them into camouflaged pens with feed. Others were taken by use of helicopters. The first daredevil to 'bulldog' a deer from a helicopter did so in the Kaweka Ranges of Hawke's Bay in 1966. This was the beginning of the commercial deer industry and the end of deer as a pest. The deer campaigns had proved that concentrated, relentless efforts could effectively eliminate a mammal pest.[9]

That lesson was not necessarily transferable; other pests, such as the Australian possum, might not go so quietly. The origins of the possum in New Zealand, introduced in hopes of establishing a fur resource, go back nearly as far as those of red deer, for small numbers were brought over at least by 1858. The people of New Zealand were much slower in awakening to the menace of the furry tree-dweller, however. Its nocturnal habits made it an invisible pest. It fed heavily on native bush, but a modest return from fur production offset the loss of bush. Indeed, the legislation codified in 1921 limited the taking of possums to set trapping seasons and required permits. Not until the 1940s did

Figure 15.1 This photograph, labelled 'The Only Good Possums', appeared in a report of the Northland Regional Council describing its pest campaign in the 1990s. Northland Regional Council.

any significant public discussion of a possum problem emerge. In 1947 all legal protections were removed, and from 1951 to 1961 the government paid a bounty for possum scalps (Figure 15.1). During the 1960s and 1970s local pest destruction boards and Forest Service personnel waged targeted campaigns using the pesticide sodium monofluorocatate, commonly known as 1080, but these were scaled back on account of cost. It was hoped then that local control efforts, coupled with the fur market, would keep the possum pest in check.[10]

Three factors converged in succeeding decades to stimulate public alarm about possums and dissipate public sympathy for them. First, possums were found to carry bovine tuberculosis. The disastrous potential of such infection stirred livestock interests. Second, environmental interests in New Zealand became more active, particularly the Forest and Bird Society. It was bad enough that alien possums were destroying plant life, worse still that research in the 1980s and 1990s disclosed the adverse effects of possums on native birds, both indirectly through competition and directly through predation on eggs. In a contest for public affection the alien possum, however cuddly, had no chance against the native pigeon (kererū) and, most tellingly, the kiwi. 'Kiwi are silently disappearing from our forest,' cried a spokesperson for the Forest and Bird Society in 1998, 'and their nightly call has been replaced by the screech of possums.'[11] The third adverse factor converging on the possum was that as urban New Zealand sprawled into what had been bush, suburbanites found their gardens ravaged by nocturnal feeders; pest control permeated cocktail party conversation. Common estimates gave the number of possums in the land as 70 million. In 1994 the Parliamentary Commissioner for the Environment issued a major report, *Possum Management in New Zealand*. Without fear of contradiction the commissioner intoned, 'The possum problem is very serious'. Possums had no friends left.[12]

A key reason for the 1994 report was that although the public was aroused against possums, there were serious concerns about heavy aerial application of 1080 for control. Such practice continued, and control costs continued to rise from the $30 million spent in 1993–94. In an update of 1998, the commissioner admitted, 'Despite real progress since 1994, possums are still a very significant risk to New Zealand.'[13] Moreover, public concerns about use of 1080 in the bush persisted, ranging from complaints of poisoning of family dogs to Māori concerns over spiritual implications.

Documentation from the Northland Regional Council provides a case study of the continuing possum problem. The council's 1996 plan for pest control named possums as 'known carriers of bovine tuberculosis' and 'a serious threat to Northland's farming industry', and cited damages to 'forests, farmland and native bush'. It resolved 'to treat the whole of Northland for possums by the year 2000, and to maintain possum numbers at low levels across the whole region'. Professional pest contractors would be sent into localities to do the 'initial knockdown' once landholders pledged to conduct follow-up work (Figure 15.1).[14]

As illustrated by possums, and in contrast to deer, smaller and more prolific mammal pests can be much more troublesome in the long term. The outstanding example is the European gray rabbit. In New Zealand today an attitude of uneasy calm prevails in regard to the long-debated issue of rabbit control. On conclusion in 1995 of the five-year Rabbit and Land Management Programme, high-country pastoralists, now responsible for their own rabbit control, were assisted by unusually abundant rainfall, which encouraged recovery of grass and discouraged propagation of rabbits. Demands for introduction of the rabbit disease myxomatosis stilled as attention shifted to the rabbit calicivirus, which, accidentally released in South Australia, had proven devastating to rabbit populations. Pastoralists and public officials alike regarded it as inevitable that the disease would be released in New Zealand; if public officials demurred, private citizens would bring it in illegally. That was exactly what happened, as in 1997 'a person or persons' unknown, in what the Parliamentary Commissioner for the Environment called 'a major breach of New Zealand's biosecurity', introduced the calicivirus.[15] Its deadly effect in the rabbit-infested regions was immediate and apparent; its long-term efficacy remained to be tested.

It is possible to outline the rabbit history of New Zealand in chronological periods (see Chapter 5), which generally correlate with other developments. For instance, the time of introduction of the rabbit corresponds to what has been termed the 'eruptive' phase of pastoral expansion. No single individual or organisation bears credit or blame for introducing the rabbit to New Zealand; there were numerous instances of introduction by private parties from the late 1830s to the 1860s. From swelling rabbit population concentrations in Marlborough and especially Southland, the rabbits followed pastoralism inland, so that by the 1870s substantial tracts of pastoral land were rendered unproductive.[16]

Public alarm resulted in a period of mobilisation against the menace: a series of Rabbit Nuisance Acts and amendments were implemented, and this legislation became more and more coercive and sought to stimulate local action through the formation of rabbit districts and the appointment of rabbit inspectors. During this time, counsel was divided and contention constant. Some commentators considered rabbit killing useless and said only closer settlement by agriculturists would solve the problem, thus implicitly laying blame for rabbits on large pastoralists. Others thought the rabbit should be embraced as a cash crop by harvesting skins, which prompted outcries from rabbit inspectors and their allies against neighbours who were 'farming the rabbits'. This also was the period of the great rabbit fences erected as public works, including one 120 kilometres long across South Canterbury—all proved futile. In 1887, 164,000 rabbits were killed on one pastoral run in Central Otago. The period of mobilisation and turmoil ended during the demoralising depression of the early 1890s. The semi-arid interior, mainly Central Otago, was given over to rabbits. The skin harvest and a burgeoning meat market made rabbit revenue a consolation prize for the destruction of pastoralism. Elsewhere in pastoral country, rabbit control became an accepted cost of production.

This was the situation until new and disruptive circumstances—the Great Depression and World War II—upset the balance. During the Depression private landholders and local government lacked the means to maintain conscientious control. During the war they lacked the manpower. The result was a serious outbreak of rabbits, rabbits rampant, and a substantial extension of the area of infestation (Figure 15.2). Following the war this destruction could no longer be suffered. The Rabbit Nuisance Act of 1947 established a

Figure 15.2 Advertisement for rabbit gas in the *New Zealand Journal of Agriculture*, July 1945. Alexander Turnbull Library, National Library of New Zealand, Te Puna Matauranga o Aotearoa.

Figure 15.3 Rabbiting crew at Earnscleugh station, Central Otago, 1996. Photograph by the author.

national Rabbit Destruction Board charged with implementation of what became known as the 'killer policy', its ultimate goal the eradication of the European gray rabbit from the land. Government employees, professional rabbit killers, took the field against the pest and used the most modern methods. These included poisoning with 1080, dropping of poisoned carrots from aircraft, and night shooting with shotguns from Jeeps and Land Rovers. The cost of bringing rabbits back under control through these methods was high.

Despite the massive kills, total eradication was a mirage, and by the late 1960s public officials were prepared to return responsibility to local bodies. By 1971 the killer policy had given way to containment, which then failed during the mid 1980s. As part of a general rethinking of agricultural policy, funding for rabbit control was sharply reduced. Pastoralists and local governments lost the capacity to control rabbits. The resulting plague resembled that of forty years earlier and produced the desertification of the Mackenzie Country described at the outset of this chapter. Meanwhile a series of task forces and policy studies eventuated in the legislative creation of the Rabbit and Land Management Programme, which operated from 1991 to 1995. Government support to regional councils and individuals fighting rabbits was renewed, but tied to land use planning and conservation measures, the rabbit work being rationalised as merely a transition on the way to more sustainable patterns. However envisioned, the programme was expensive: the plan for Earnscleugh in Central Otago, the most notoriously rabbit-infested sheep station, called for spending $2.1 million on rabbit-proof fencing, shooting, gassing, and trapping the pests (Figure 15.3).[17]

Arguably it was an improved agricultural economy and kinder weather that produced the lull in rabbit infestation just prior to importation of the calicivirus. Popular expectation is that the history of the rabbit nuisance is over, but a disease introduced as a biological control may produce merely a respite rather than a long-term solution. It seems premature to pronounce the rabbit history of New Zealand at an end.

Like other episodes in the history of pest control, this one yields lessons and principles that can be catalogued and compared. One lesson is that matters of pest control, which at first glance may seem to be technical issues, are in fact social issues. The proliferation of pests pits neighbour against neighbour, creating class cleavages. Blame is exchanged. Another lesson is that pest control in a sparsely populated pastoral grassland, as in remote bush, is difficult. Likewise, it makes a difference, particularly in public rhetoric, whether the pest of the day is a native animal or an exotic invader; militaristic rhetoric against rabbits was acceptable to the public because they were invading animals. Perhaps most salient is the lesson that pest control hereafter must take into account the desires of distant consumers as well as those of urban Greens close by. One reason advanced for the curtailment of rabbit killing in the 1980s and 1990s, or at least for requiring land use reform along with it, was that foreign buyers of wool and lamb were repulsed by the carnage. Meanwhile, environmentalist groups at home made legal introduction of the calicivirus politically unacceptable.[18]

It is possible to induce more basic insights from this country's rabbit history. New Zealand has been home to two intellectual traditions having to do with agriculture and nature. The first is that of English high farming, which evolved into the positivist enthusiasm for land development articulated by P. W. Smallfield (see Chapter 11). The high-farming, land-development tradition was enthusiastic—all too enthusiastic—for human manipulation of nature. This view conflicted with that of grasslands ecology, which had its New Zealand origins in the writings of Leonard Cockayne. Grasslands ecology said that ecological systems in semiarid lands were fragile and must not be abused; human intervention in nature should be minimised. Much popular comment in recent years is to the effect that pastoralists have abused the land through unwise development, and that if only they were expelled, the land would heal itself. The history of the rabbit nuisance shows that this is a mistaken notion. Certainly pastoralism—the application of sheep and fences and fertiliser to the land—changed the natural order, but its removal did not solve the problem; rather, the problem was exacerbated. In the presence of an aggressive exotic animal such as the rabbit, the withdrawal of human agency brought not healing but ecological chaos. Land development was discredited by its excesses; popular ecology vainly hoped that nature would heal itself; and there was between the two poles no tradition of moderate, responsible human engagement with nature.[19]

Weeds: plants out of place

The destructive agency of rabbits in pastoral country was exacerbated in the late years of the twentieth century by the spread of an invasive weed, *Hieracium pilosella*, or mouse-ear hawkweed. The origins of this Eurasian weed in New Zealand are unknown, but it came into public notice during the 1980s, some pastoralists saying that *Hieracium* was a greater threat than the rabbits. This grey, yellow-flowering, low-growing matweed, first introduced by seed, spread by vegetative reproduction through the vulnerable inter-tussock seams of tussock grassland. Many pastoralists observed that it was an invasive weed displacing native and desired exotic species alike, possibly with the advantage of allelopathy, or the production of chemicals harmful to other plants. More traditional ecologists doubted this and insisted that the weed could not have penetrated a healthy plant formation; the system must have been weakened by grazing and burning. There were no known biological controls, and direct applications against a weed spread across extensive pastoral lands were not feasible. The only way of checking the weed was, ironically, to be more aggressive in land development, applying seed and fertiliser so that desirable exotics could hold the ground against the hawkweed.[20]

This hawkweed, which appeared to defy all traditional assumptions of ecology, brought the conflicting perceptions of pastoralists and scientists into clear relief. Strong difference of opinion about noxious exotic weeds has prevailed from the time of the first broadly noticed noxious weed, *Cirsium arvense*, known in New Zealand as Californian thistle. This persistent perennial weed in croplands spreads vegetatively, but more alarming is the capacity of its purple flowers to produce prodigious amounts of seed that is carried down on the wind. Even repetitive tillage is of little use against the weed once established. Californian thistle first received public notice as a problem in the most intensively farmed province, Canterbury, in the 1880s. 'From every district comes news of the appearance or identification of this pest,' wrote a Canterbury correspondent in 1888, 'and it is evidently so thoroughly established in the country that the strongest measures for its extermination are called for.' By 1912 A. H. Cockayne of the Department of Agriculture would term Californian thistle 'the most wide-spread and most injurious' of weeds in the land.[21]

The Californian thistle was the main concern prompting the government to bring forward a noxious weeds bill in 1893. The pervasiveness of the weed, and thus farmers' fears that they would be compelled to undertake costly eradication, was the reason the bill initially failed. After passage of the Noxious Weeds Act in 1900, contention over thistles continued. Agriculturists prescribed smother crops, ritual fallowing (in what was called the 'Canterbury system'), religious tillage and, in extreme cases, salting to rid cultivated land of infestations, and farmers largely complied. The problem lay in rough grazing lands, low-value lands where graziers were loath to make high investments. Local weed inspectors appointed under the Act were subjected to abuse by landholders, who also complained to their members of parliament. Farmers of improved lands pleaded for enforcement, but holders of hilly lands decried the tyranny of weed inspectors. A. H. Cockayne analysed a nationwide weed survey of farmers in 1917 and observed that although weeds might be a question of 'national character'—one affecting national productivity and thus deserving of government attention—it had to be 'governed by local conditions and requirements'. He argued that compulsion had damaged the culture of husbandry, so that landholders did the least amount of weed control required of them, grudgingly. The thistle issue thus faded from broad public scrutiny, becoming a matter of local good judgment. Coercive weed control was discredited.[22]

Weed policy was even more complicated when public opinion about a plant was diverse and ambivalent—as in the case of gorse, which as a living fence assumed a prominent place in the settlement landscape. Like many other plant and animal introductions, however, gorse refused merely to serve its intended purposes. It escaped cultivation and earned a reputation first as a pesky weed and then as an invasive species dominating large tracts of countryside. Gorse flowers yellow and profusely for most of the year. Its pods burst in warm weather, scattering seeds, and the plant also spreads from the roots. Gorse came to New Zealand with missionaries prior to organised colonisation, for Darwin noted gorse hedges at Waimate North in 1835. It went everywhere organised settlement went at mid century and was particularly favoured on the plains of Canterbury. The gorse plant responded well, perhaps too well, to the New Zealand environment. As early as 1859 Taranaki and Nelson provinces prohibited the planting of additional gorse. Canterbury in 1861 prohibited planting it in town but not in the country, and gorse hedges would be a hallmark of the progress of closer settlement in the wake of the break-up of great estates into the twentieth century.[23]

The folk culture of gorse was recorded in the nineteenth-century agricultural press. The best description of the construction of the classic ditch-and-bank hedge fence was by the correspondent 'Komata' in the *New Zealand Farmer* in 1888.[24] He prescribed a ditch 2 feet 6 inches deep and 3 feet 6 inches wide alongside a sod bank of comparable dimensions. Gorse was planted on the ditch-side face of the bank. Gorse barriers required serious maintenance. Cropping was commonly done by hand using traditional long-handled knives. Availability of tractors with power take-off, as well as the shortage of labour during World War II, brought mechanised contractors to the fore. Among the few still carrying on the hedge-trimming business in 1991 were brothers Alister and Warwick Wooding, of Geraldine.[25]

Figure 15.4 Spraying gorse on a hill near Wanganui, 1953. Reproduced by permission of Archives New Zealand, DA 34, 550.

The nineteenth-century agricultural press held up the standard of 'well-cropped gorse hedges with seedlings annually grubbed'; gorse allowed to spread was the sign of a farmer 'on a low scale in an agricultural point of view'.[26] Gorse thus was the subject of considerable discussion in the years leading up to passage of the Noxious Weeds Act of 1900. The consensus of farmers and legislators was that gorse could and should be controlled in arable lands, roads, or anywhere there was concentrated attention to it, but coercion should not be extended where there was no good reason for it.

There, exactly, lay the problem as defined in the next generation. Gorse escaped to hillsides and other lands neither ploughed for crops nor intensively developed for grazing. Following World War II, as New Zealand entered a period of enthusiasm for land development aimed at increasing exports, the campaign against gorse became more intensive and employed heavier weaponry, particularly in North Island hill country. Land developers brought in crawler tractors to knock down gorse. Effective (or at least supplementary) chemical control of gorse became possible in the 1950s with the general availability of 2,4,5-T products (Figure 15.4). Still, reminded a senior scientific officer of the Department of Agriculture, 'A dense, vigorous pasture is the best and cheapest insurance against reinfestation'.[27]

Interest in biological controls on gorse, tried but found unsatisfactory in the 1930s, resurged during the 1980s. Over the next decade such controls accomplished no major reduction of gorse. In the first place, opinion against the plant was by no means unanimous. Impact studies disclosed that beekeepers valued the shrub as a basis for honey production. A more peculiar argument came from advocates for native forests. Whereas they might have been expected to cheer on any campaign against an exotic shrub, they instead insisted that gorse was useful as a nurse crop for regrowth of native bush. This argument, however, may have been a stalking horse for a more general and rising conviction among New Zealand Greens—a determination that the introduction of any additional exotic species, even an insect imported to fight an introduced weed, was wrong and dangerous. In the reconsideration of biological controls little thought was given to gorse hedges. From the 1960s on there was steady removal of gorse hedges. Farmers determined that they could achieve better shelter benefits for livestock by planting more substantial shelter belts of *Pinus radiata* or *Cupressus macrocarpa*—other exotics—than by retaining gorse hedges.[28]

Perils of biodiversity

The story of gorse is one of ambivalence. Ambivalence is not the stuff of public discourse on the history and status of pests and weeds in New Zealand, however. In 1998 a spokesperson for the Forest and Bird Society declared, 'New Zealand's history is littered with well meaning but disastrous introductions'—and the tone was cautionary.[29] New Zealanders were to heed the lessons of environmental history. In 1869 W. T. L. Travers addressed the New Zealand Institute 'On the Changes Effected in the Natural Features of a New Country by the Introduction of Civilized Races'. Citing Darwin on the 'struggle for existence' among all creatures 'both animal and vegetable' in 'any particular Zoological or Botanical province', he concluded that the 'new and rival organisms' introduced to Newest England had rendered 'the indigenous flora and fauna ... unable to cope with the intruders'.[30] More than a century apart, these two commentators were on the same page in their assumptions: alien species are potent and will prevail. That the earlier writer was pleased with this, and the latter alarmed, does not gainsay their common paradigm.

If there are lessons in the history of pests and weeds in New Zealand, they have to do with the perils of all such paradigms. As Rob Hengeveld has outlined in *Dynamics of Biological Invasions*, there have been two paradigms dominant in the conception of species migration or relocation. The first is that of biogeography, which assigns to every species or complex of species a home. The distillation of this line of thought, as described by animal ecologist Charles S. Elton, was the delineation by Alfred Russel Wallace of Wallace's Realms. Kiwi commentators from Travers on had to deal with the disruption of this neat view of the world, and the writings of Elton were some comfort. Elton subsumed the alien animals into a balance-of-nature style of ecology, theorising that outbreaks of pests were mere interludes, and that a new balance would emerge.[31]

The problem with ecology in New Zealand was that the pests and weeds did not read Elton. Other exotic species might find a comfortable niche, but these did not; that was how they became pests and weeds. Instead of relapsing into a proper place in a new, synthetic order, they continued to wreak havoc until somebody stopped them. The theory that emerged to explain this and to assign blame was that humankind had so disrupted the natural order of things—the realms of nature—that the natives had no fair chance. Christopher Lever has summarised this idea as the artificial creation of 'vacant niches' that alien species are better fitted to occupy than natives. Other commentators, frustrated by persistent pest problems, ceased explaining and commenced blaming. A good example was the Parliamentary Commissioner for the Environment's 1991 report on sustainable land use in the South Island tussock grasslands. The assumptions underlying this document, reflecting an anachronistic sense of grassland ecology, were that any problems on the land were due to exploitation and abuse by humankind. All that was necessary to solve environmental problems was to remove the human pressure on the land and the balance of nature would reassert itself. This attitude, which might be termed a passive-green approach to environmentalism, failed to reckon with the patterns of pest and weed history in New Zealand.[32]

At the turn of the millennium the Department of Conservation and the Ministry for the Environment have proposed to recast the principles of environmental policy to emphasise 'biodiversity'—defined as the defence of native species, 'New Zealand's Living Treasures', against 'burgeoning pests and weeds and the destruction of habitat'. The new cast is appealing in that it is not passive-green but active-green, calling on citizens to nurture biodiversity not only in 'remote nature reserves' but also in 'our backyards and neighbourhoods', and also in its appeal for '"number 8 wire" Kiwi ingenuity to tackle conservation problems'. It is disappointing in its adoption of a jingoistic rhetoric—references to 'predatory rats, mice and other mammals', to 'hordes of animal pests', and to all manner of hostile and potent threats are contrasted with 'our vulnerable species' that are 'uniquely imperilled'. By defining introduced species as an unmitigated evil, as 'invasive pests' that do nothing but 'demolish our native species', the new policy statement encourages an unrealistic seal-the-border mentality.[33]

A bellicose, national-security rhetoric that pits virtuous natives in moral contest against an evil empire of alien invaders may be useful as a stimulus, but it also raises impossible expectations. It disregards the sensible and synthetic traditions of New Zealanders in their paddocks, forests, and gardens, the best work of recent ecological science, and the history of pests and weeds. This history offers no hope of resolution, only continued struggle calling, as Crosby has said, for 'unprecedented ecological and diplomatic sophistication'.[34] It might be wise to look back, as Lincoln University grassland scientist Kevin O'Connor has done, to the founder of ecology in New Zealand, Leonard Cockayne, who in his late years adjusted his formal conceptions of nature to account for the presence of humankind and other immigrant species in the land. Taking his cue from Cockayne, O'Connor urges us to 'try a little harder ... to understand better what we, Māori and European, have already done to this land', to be willing to abjure models and slogans and embrace complexity. 'Then,' he hopes, 'we may better create a landscape in which we can all take shelter, a landscape in which no early arrival, no latecomer, plant or animal, is alien.'[35]

This is a hard teaching. When architects of the killer policy promised extermination of the last rabbit, it was appealing, because although they called for battle, they promised that there would be an end to it; after the last rabbit was killed, the country would rest easy. Likewise, when the next generation of policy-makers determined that land use reforms would stop the spread of rabbits and hawkweed, they promised a resolution to the situation. Simply restrain or remove the pastoralists and things would be all right. More recently, public officials have oversimplified biodiversity by reducing it to the neat categories of native versus alien. Sometimes, as the history of pests and weeds affirms, a simple approach will do. Deer could be controlled by direct action. The small-bird pest, left alone, went away with changing land use, as did the problem with the California thistle. What of gorse, however? Historically it was a useful plant, then a pernicious weed, and finally, though itself alien, an ally in restoration of native bush. No simple solutions or categories applied. Possums, too, are a conundrum. Everyone hates possums, but other than those misguided souls in the distant past who introduced them, there is no one to blame for them. Protection of native species requires large and continual human intrusions into nature so as to knock back possums; when kiwi are threatened, ardent environmentalists no longer trust the balance of nature to make things right.

Where simplicity, passivity, and categorical programs fail, the only responsible course is active husbandry. Active husbandry requires the acceptance of corporate responsibility, rather than the laying of blame on factions. It requires the relinquishment of hope for permanent solutions and the long-term commitment of thought and effort. It recognises human agency in nature. Most of all, in a practical spirit, active husbandry seeks its solutions where they may be found—from the field, from science, and from the record of human experience with the land that is environmental history. The history of pests and weeds in New Zealand, however chequered, is no unmitigated disaster if it at least compels consideration of such lessons of husbandry.[36]

16

Bound to the Land

Māori retention and assertion of land and identity

Danny Keenan

> Ko ngā Honotanga, a iwi a hapū a whānau, e whakapumautia
> ana te hononga o ngā mātua tūpuna me o ratou uri whakatipu.
> Those things that bind Māori people together must remain unbroken, as are those things that bind our ancestors passed away to descendants yet unborn.

Turbulent change, substantially arising from colonisation, affected Māori at every level of society in the nineteenth century. Underpinning this was the transformation of the land into which Māori society and culture had long been firmly anchored. Māori people responded to this change in many ways, but perhaps most markedly by reaching back into ancient knowledge in order emphatically to locate a presence and legitimacy on the land. This chapter seeks to describe and explain these responses to changes over which Māori people often felt they had little control, especially as the land was slipping from their grasp. It focuses particularly on Taranaki and explores the persistence of such responses to the present day.

Māori expressed their responses to vanishing landscapes in many different forums, some of which were reasonably well reported. For example, there is the evidence available through the Native Land Court after 1865, especially the investigation of title hearings. There is also Compensation Court testimony of Māori people from those areas caught up by the land confiscations after 1863, in particular Taranaki, Tauranga, and the Waikato. The Compensation Court offered Māori an opportunity to argue a case for the return of land taken by the Crown, even though the process was seriously flawed, with Māori people seldom allowed to present testimony in a form consistent with Māori convention.

Paradoxically, however, it is possible to find within this court testimony indicators of how Māori sought to retain and assert connections between land and identity on the basis of ideas that were current then, and which largely remain intact today. For example, much of the court evidence has a certain narrative value about what was really happening to people, kinship groups, boundaries, wāhi tapu (sacred areas), and ancient landscapes. One needs to be aware, however, of how the conventions of the marae were brought to bear upon such evidence, in order to obtain some sense of what was actually being said. Māori would have prioritised evidence in a certain way, mediating knowledge of the past through testimony with particular political considerations in mind. In so doing, Māori were trying to make some sense of what was happening to the land and to themselves.

Substantial native land legislation enacted throughout the nineteenth century (see Chapter 3) impacted heavily upon Māori customary tenure, landholdings, and livelihoods. The Native Land Court was established for the express purpose of extinguishing native title. Hence Hugh Kawharu's description of it as the 'engine of destruction' or David Williams' more recent, softer preference—'Te Kooti Tango Whenua—The Land-Taking Court'.[1] Testimony in this court shows how Māori people responded to the court's impacts on their livelihoods, security of land ownership, settlements, cultivations, fishing grounds, and resource trails. Debates over who owned what, and who had primary access to which resources and which use rights, under customary law, are evident in great detail. There are even notes scrawled across the survey maps, as judges sought to disentangle competing claims. Much of this detail is today still recalled to a significant degree on the marae, from the paepae (the place where orators stand). It has also been brought to light by the Waitangi Tribunal, today's process for hearing claims of breaches of the Treaty of Waitangi.

Taranaki narratives

This chapter focuses on Taranaki because it is the tribal district from which I descend, and I am following the convention that operates among Māori historians that 'one writes about one's own area'. This conforms to the general marae imperative that operates among all Māori—that one speaks from his or her own paepae. In Taranaki, tribunal hearings were always major occasions and important histories were heard. Most accountings of the past, however, were of a fairly recent origin, essentially addressing the land grievances of the nineteenth century. These were matters of considerable importance to the tribes of Taranaki. In 1991 I had an opportunity to contribute when I presented evidence on behalf of my hapū, Ngāti Te Whiti. We drew the tribunal's attention to a number of land issues arising from the early Wakefield settlement of New Plymouth after 1840.

When the first settlers arrived from England they generally saw the land as vast and hostile. Incessant rain seemed to exacerbate a difficult terrain. Many Europeans recorded their impressions of this 'wilderness', seeing it as primordial and intimidatory. The places over which Māori exercised mana whenua (absolute authority over the land) seemed instead to be untamed, awaiting purchase and intensive economic utilisation. Māori communities were often a physical constraint to such ambitions. Opportunities to negotiate accommodations with local Māori were overtaken by increasingly severe land disputes and ultimately war (Figure 16.1).

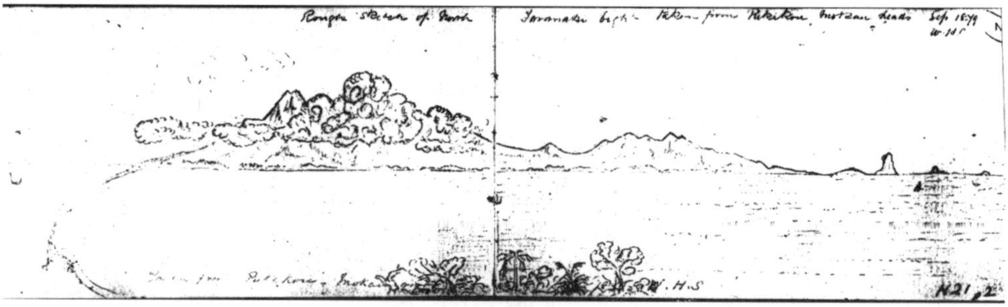

Figure 16.1 'Virgin country of great promise.' The North Taranaki coastline, 1879, looking south from Mokau towards Mount Taranaki (left) and the Ngamotu Islands, site of present-day New Plymouth (right). Sketch by W. H. Skinner, surveyor, ethnologist, and later founder of the Taranaki Museum. Fieldbook N21, p. 2, Department of Survey and Land Information, New Plymouth.

Before the tribunal we discussed how Ngāti Te Whiti responded to these circumstances, and we canvassed some alternative approaches to the researching and constructing of our hapū and tribal histories. I concluded that the material generated by the tribunal process, while significant when emphasising loss, was nonetheless interesting if utilised differently. Perhaps the stories of contact and interaction, of conflict and material loss, might be moved to the outer edges of the colonial contact narrative. If that were the case, then the question arose—what, or whose, story was one left trying to tell? If one is to get closer to how nineteenth-century Māori people themselves perceived the totality of environmental change and sought to relate to it in a positive way—since identity and mana are positive things—then one should be looking beyond the stories of contact, conflict, and deprivation.

But how could these histories of intense land conversion and dispossession be retold? An important clue lay in the Māori notion that constructions of the past should provide validation for the present. As Joe Pere of Rongowhakaata has argued, Māori histories and traditions should not be mere histories of convenience—they should enhance the importance of tribal ancestry, whakapapa (genealogy), karakia (prayer), waiata (song), poetry, and other cultural institutions as of right. They should, says Pere, 'give me the basis of my identity and my mana'.[2]

When recalling the past, it is customary for Māori to mediate history through certain traditions, always with a strong sense of identity, legitimacy, and mana to the fore. These mediated histories were always firmly located in specific historic landscapes, though these landscapes may have undergone marked and permanent change, and may even have slipped from the ownership of the people. In a sense, such assertions of identity and mana were as important as the history of how that land was changed and even lost. This type of approach gives a better sense of how Māori people responded to change. It even suggests how Māori sought to control the meanings of that change—or perhaps even to assert that no real change had occurred, but that continuities with pre-contact tradition had been preserved, as the whakatauki, or proverb, cited at the beginning of this chapter proposes.

The landscape was changed significantly, almost beyond recognition, for most Māori in the nineteenth century. Important customary and cultural markers on the land were removed as communities were destabilised. In response, Māori people represented themselves and their pasts as a validation of their descent, their historic occupation of the land, and their ongoing political activity. Much of the evidence used for this approach, which comes from a number of Taranaki kaumātua, lies primarily in its reconceptualising nature, not in its historical content. Often the processes of constructing a past are more interesting than the literal narratives we produce. Waitangi Tribunal material presented in Taranaki has therefore been extremely useful as it serves as an essential focus and conduit for observations about the nature of the Māori past as envisaged or as re-envisioned in Taranaki today.

The evidence produced by the claims process has revealed four major features of the response of Taranaki in particular, and Māori in general, to the rapid transformation of environment and landscape discussed in this book. First, iwi everywhere have been more concerned with retaining spiritual and legal links to particular pieces of land, or mana whenua, than with condemning change. Certainly there is disappointment and anger at the loss of traditional food sources, fouling of clean water, and blatant disregard of tapu sites and historically important places. But maintaining mana whenua has been paramount. Second, disruption began well before formal colonisation, because the musket wars of the 1820s and 1830s brought the mana whenua of Taranaki iwi under great pressure. Third, hapū, or family groups rather than iwi, increasingly bore the brunt of defending and maintaining mana whenua as disruption quickened with formal colonisation from 1840 and accelerated because of the confiscation policy and the operations of the Native Land Court from 1864. Claims consequently became more individualised, often down to whānau (family) level, and more localised. Fourth, the complexities caused by confiscation and subsequent compensation distorted history because of the clumsy attempts of government to define hapū as either rebellious or loyal.

Mana whakapapa: binding people to the land

Assertions of mana whenua by Māori over ancestral lands after 1841 were activated through the authority of tribal whakapapa connections. These connections underpinned tribal and hapū activity as colonial pressures on land increased and new concepts of land tenure were enacted. The assertion of mana whenua often compelled tribes, hapū, and other kinship units to redefine their functional kinship bases in both customary and deliberate ways to sustain tribal claims to land in the wake of intense contest with the Crown. It was an activity validated over time by the tribe's mana and its history. It also reflected a certain expedient fluidity of Māori kinship structures, though these were nonetheless always fixed within the broadest context of conventional whakapapa relationships. These relationships were always held to be constant.

A feature of Taranaki history after 1830 was the intense competition for land. New settlers in Taranaki complained that they did not have sufficient pasturage for their flocks and were 'dissatisfied with the Government and ill pleased with the Maories, who ... possess large tracts of land which they cannot occupy'.[3] But the basis of the tribal hold on land remained constant. Assertions of mana whenua over customary lands constituted a sense of attachment that was described by Chief Judge Eddie Durie of the Waitangi Tribunal as inherent in the 'vastly complex spiritual world through which Maori sought to maintain balance and harmony in his modification of the environment'.[4]

To Māori, the land was paramount. It was the foundation of social and economic life, and it also provided the cultural stability essential to survival. Every aspect of life for Māori could be anchored into the land, as mana whenua was exercised within a long-standing continuum of generations that, together, attached specific tribes, hapū, and other kinship units to specific localities. The exercise of such mana whenua was ongoing, particularly in situations of duress and conflict. This was especially so after 1841, when sporadic hostilities between new European settlers and tribes commenced. According to Wiremu Te Kupenga Kaha of Te Āti Awa, speaking in 1925, 'the tribes joined because of the obvious injustice of the Government. Wherefore they said these words, "Let the land be first and land afterwards" '.[5]

In the normal course of events, recognised subordinate kinship groups within a tribe might be numerous. Each hapū or whānau possessed a mana whakapapa of its own that connected it with others and located it into a well-known portion of the landscape. Such areas were well sustained within tribal histories and traditions. However, hapū and whānau in Taranaki generally recognised the tribe's superior mana whakapapa and rights. Such recognition implied a certain reciprocal relationship, empowering hapū and whānau to act in defence of tribal mana in certain circumstances, at the same time as it acknowledged the mana and rights of each entity. It operated more strongly in the north of Taranaki than in the south, where, among the 'Tokomaru confederation'[6] a clear basis for concerted activity functioned among the Te Āti Awa whānui tribes.[7] All tribes in Taranaki, however, recognised subordinate kinship groups, which 'acknowledged themselves bound to join the other sections in defending all or any part of the tribal estate from encroachment by strangers'.[8]

Whakapapa remained a key device of 'intellectual management' with increased utility where appropriate as a vehicle of a tribe's history.[9] Such devices attracted intense, if misdirected, colonial attention. As Durie has written, the courts 'did not appreciate the idiom, the customary predilections for synecdoche, where ancestors are used as symbolic of their descendants and posited as living at a later period, retrospectively'.[10] Notions of the past as reflected in whakapapa and the more expressive whaikorero (speech-making) therefore continued to 'reach back to bring (them) forward ... everything a Maori ever knew was memory ... it was all coming from behind, bringing it forward'.[11]

Such realities of the 'past in the present' were evident to the ethnographer, and advisor on Māori Affairs, I. L. G. Sutherland, following a visit to Māori settlements in Taranaki in the late 1940s. He observed that 'the past is still very real (here) ... the past is always nearer to Maoris than it is to Europeans'. He further observed that Māori districts where there was 'no heritage of war' were making great progress and were, in comparison with Taranaki, 'almost a half century ahead'.[12]

Complications of earlier incursions

Less complex but equally current in tribal recall were the earlier catastrophic wars visited upon Taranaki from the hostile north. Incursions of Ngā Puhi, Ngāti Toa, and especially Waikato wreaked havoc throughout Taranaki for at least a generation, bearing heavily on land and people. Ferocious battles would end with the complete destruction of villages, people, and property. Exacting destruction on real or imagined enemies of the past through conquest seems to have been the primary motivation for conducting these fierce and arduous campaigns.

The taking of new land was not, therefore, necessarily a motive for the waging of war. Consequently, the Waikato tribes did not remain in occupation of conquered Taranaki lands long enough to constitute new title, or to extinguish the mana whenua of Taranaki whānui. The Church Missionary Society missionary and champion of Māori land rights Octavius Hadfield thought as much, declaring that Waikato had not held possession of Waitara. As a consequence, they had not acquired rights to it.[13] Nonetheless, incursions from the north impacted on coastal and inland papa kāinga almost as heavily as would the later European conversion of the ancient tribal landscape. At the time of the earliest Ngā Puhi and Ngāti Toa raids some local tribes also waged war on each other, continuing to fight out their own long-standing internecine conflicts. According to Ngāti Mutunga kaumātua Lou MacDonald, such wars and the ensuing migrations south—to the Otaki–Waikanae area—seemingly left behind a deserted and disfigured landscape as tribes and hapū 'became nomads'.[14]

The material havoc wrought on Taranaki communities left, according to Governor Gore Browne, 'a conquered, broken and scattered tribe … the fairest and most fertile country in New Zealand, their ancient inheritance, was a deserted wilderness at the time of the European colonisation'.[15] Settlements and villages were devastated, sacred places desecrated, and populations annihilated or forced to move away. Such disruption severely destabilised the long-established structures in Taranaki of mana whenua, and mana history itself, but did not destroy them. Waikato could not transform the essential apparatus of cognitive thinking and activity, the Taranaki 'Māori philosophy', to use Moana Jackson's term. Only its material and external manifestations were affected. Many artefacts were preserved in flight, especially carvings, which were frequently buried, so confining them to the protection of Hine-i-te-huhi, the Maiden of the Swamps, for subsequent rediscovery and restoration.

Much of the history of the Taranaki tribes, hapū, and communities after 1835 sought to reimpose their mana whenua and their mana histories upon the landscape where 'the blood of kinsmen' lay in profusion. The advent of colonisation rendered this process increasingly complex. Before colonisation, for most Māori, the intellectual management of knowledge was considered to be sequential. Despite physical devastation, the underlying means of establishing and asserting mana whenua, linked to long-standing mana whakapapa that anchored tribes into localities, were not transfigured. The local Taranaki tribal processes of mana history remained intact, though the land over which these processes acquired their essence and significance might be stripped of occupation.

British colonisation and the fragmentation and individualisation of land

After 1800, hapū emerged as the most important basis of activity. In Taranaki, hapū are held by the tribes to have evolved out of the larger tribal kinship base that expanded over time, giving rise to small groups breaking away to form smaller entities. Angela Ballara has proposed a different model for Ngāti Kahungunu of Hawke's Bay, that of small and disparate hapū clusters ultimately coming together, propelled by a growing iwi consciousness.[16]

In Taranaki, such hapū and whānau mounted their defence of land from within the continuum of descent that rooted that unit into the known landscape. The tribes and hapū defended mana whenua throughout the Waikato wars as best they could, and continued this defence across the period of colonisation. Contests for land with the Crown usually involved tribes and hapū that were readily identified with assertions of distinct identity. Tribal declarations, such as that made by Tunga Paekawa in 1925, were clearly stated. In a petition seeking redress from the Crown for the 'injustice inflicted upon us by the confiscations of the lands of our fathers', Paekawa cited ancestors connected to known landscapes and people—those of the 'tribes of Ngati-Uenuku and Kai-tangata'.[17] Other contests after 1830, however, involved smaller kinship units, with varying and primarily individual motivations born of the debilitating conflicts with new settlers and legislation, as diminishing amounts of land remained in collective possession.[18]

After 1830, then, the defence of mana whenua in Taranaki compelled some changes to kinship-group arrangements within tribes. These reconstituted 'families' acted independently to defend smallholdings but continued to acknowledge the superior status of the tribe. This strategy was long-standing and remained central to ongoing demonstrations of tribal mana whenua. By 1870 the incidence of dispossession in Taranaki had sharply increased as lands were moved from effective hapū control. Hapū identities tended to consolidate as determined ongoing assertions of mana whenua evolved from assertions of actual occupation to those of customary, yet dispossessed, occupation.

The Compensation Court, after 1865, was a principal arena in which to assert mana whenua, in rhetoric as well as reality. Later Commissions of Inquiry also provided important forums, as did the Native Land Court. However, given that in the court tribes and hapū contested with each other, Māori pitted against Māori often at the expense of collective identity, direct assertions of mana whenua became less common once early investigation of title hearings were completed. Hence the Native Land Court represented, in Taranaki as elsewhere, a steady diminution of Māori customary title.

Throughout the nineteenth century certain common narratives of the past, and a common geography centred on Taranaki, the mountain, continued to provide the basis for a sense of unity among the tribes of the region. But notions of unity were for a time ambivalent because, as land fragmentation increased, not all the tribes, hapū, and communities subscribed to the expansive 'Taranaki whānui'. Nonetheless, such common narratives of the past found frequent expression before later Commissions of Inquiry. Such ancient knowledge therefore remained central to the Taranaki sense of tribal history.

This was seen in 1880 when Māori laid claim to lands 'all the way from the Tukeho Stream to Taitairamaka'. Landmarks were described as 'the fixed boundaries of the Taranaki people. [They] include Mount Egmont. These are the original boundaries and we claim within these ... our ancestor was called Rua Taranaki and the tribe is called Taranaki.'[19] This citing of Rua Taranaki constituted an ancient mana whakapapa reference, one recalled to validate the mana whenua of Ngāti Tu, Te Kaingati and Ngāti Haumea over lands within the coastal Taranaki rohe (tribal region). This represented a claim to specific title, lands over which individual families had long been settled.[20]

Later land sales especially rendered such assertions more complex in Taranaki as elsewhere. The Rarangi Ingoa O Te Karapapa (Piri Pono) me ona uri papers in 1927, for example, describe 'Ngāti Awa' as being 'landless or practically landless'.[21] Even so, the mana whenua recall of the tribes in Taranaki had not diminished, remaining manifest in the ancient landscape. But the incursions did impact to the extent that tribes thereafter reconstituted whakapapa based on new realities as tribal structures broke down. Some mana whenua attachments as a result became indistinct and weakened,[22] and there were frequent declarations of 'individuated' whakapapa from a seeming fragmenting of hapū identities. Many Māori then became protective of their whakapapa, which, according to Lou MacDonald, came to be considered 'a dangerous thing, especially in Māori company, [because] there was always someone who would pick you out'.[23]

Important references to celestial or mana wairua descent largely gave way, for pragmatic purposes, to the utility of recent mana tūpuna, people known to have lived and whose deeds were well remembered. The reasons for this may have been due to missionary monotheistic influences, the advent of colonial ethnographical research, or the Native Land Court's disregard of celestial lineage. Under Chief Judge Francis Fenton the court certainly placed greater emphasis on recent occupation, as recent as 1840, as the basis for land claims. The preferred citing of mana tūpuna descent lines therefore comprised recently distinguished ancestors who were specifically recalled as 'You bring a whakapapa down so far, to an ancestor, then he'll say, he'll relate himself to that ancestor, and go no further'.[24]

Therefore, recent ancestors who were carefully recalled linked certain individuals directly to lines of descent and attendant lands. Such individuating of whakapapa for pragmatic purposes did not necessarily bear directly on the recognised whakapapa kinship bases of hapū and whānau. For their part, whānau groups operated at a different social level and were often quite unique and broad in composition. The seeming profusion of hapū and whānau was evident to officials such as Police Inspector Donald McLean, who conducted an extensive survey of Māori in North Taranaki in the late 1840s, soon after the tribes began to reoccupy ancestral estates in large numbers.

Mana whakapapa therefore remained important to Māori as a basis of organising and asserting mortal descent traditions and histories across the nineteenth century, histories that were anchored in locality, at the hapū and tribal level. There is much evidence to suggest that these assertions were ongoing. The post-confiscation land claims in particular provided a context for them to continue. Some claims involved hapū, as that of Tapa Te Waero, who in 1876 declared, 'You have got the land, I and my hapū will merely wander about the earth ... the land is mine because it descended to me from my ancestors.'[25] Most, however, seemed to involve smaller kinship groupings best able to locate themselves with specific lands, lying within the customary hapū or whānau estate. The reverence for land did not diminish, as Wiremu Kingi's later waiata illustrated:

> Grieved am I for my seaward land
> Pekapeka looms in the distance
> My beloved home
> Kaiwaka appears vividly, my seaward land
> Kohia stands prominent, my seaward land
> O tribe, cease from war
> I have finished.[26]

Equally, reverence for wāhi tapu, burial, and other historic sites was maintained. Vigorous collective defences of these wāhi tapu were mounted by hapū and whānau in the wake of confiscations, as defences to the Native Land Confiscation Commission of 1927 illustrate.[27]

However, the customary basis of mana whenua did also fragment under the pressure of land sales and confiscations. The issue of precise hapū boundaries within North Taranaki was thereafter frequently rendered uncertain. This was exacerbated by legislation that required tribes and hapū to establish boundaries commensurate with, for example, section 2 of the Native Territorial Rights Act of 1858, which stated that 'no such Certificate shall be issued until a Survey of the lands … shall have been made … and the boundaries thereof distinctly marked out'.

Confiscation, the Native Land Court, and reforming of hapū

Later consolidated hapū groupings in North Taranaki were therefore largely reconstituted hapū, having adopted a collective identity superseding a possible multitude of previous divisions. In 1927, when extensive lists were presented of the Taranaki district with the tribes or hapū as then known and the approximate areas of land occupied by them, it was clear that earlier and complex tribal–hapū configurations had become smaller and more consolidated in nature.[28] After 1841, then, tribes, hapū and communities had constructed and reconstituted their mana wairua, mana tūpuna, and mana whenua to reflect the new realities. Thereafter, such mana histories and traditions became the collective focus as tribes and hapū faced the processes of Crown inquiry.

The messy process of confiscation and subsequent redress complicated matters considerably by trying to define hapū and whānau as 'kūpapa' (loyal to the Queen), or 'rebel'. The origins of the Compensation Court process in Taranaki lay in the impacts on tribal lands of the New Zealand Settlements Act 1863. This Act was the primary instrument of the land confiscations, although the word 'confiscation' does not appear in it. The Governor was authorised to place tribal districts under the Act, thereby forcibly setting apart sites for colonisation and settlement. Monies raised from sales of land were to be used to

Figure 16.2 New Plymouth, 1856, with Mount Taranaki and the Marsland Hill Barracks, which housed a British Army contingent after 1855. The landscape shows signs of new settler influence—cottages, small fenced plots and extensive ground clearance, with secondary undergrowth appearing. Reproduced by permission of the Museum of New Zealand Te Papa Tongarewa.

defray the 'expenses of suppressing insurrection', and to meet the costs of surveying new settlements, primarily for military settlers. These settlers were moved into confiscated areas, in the Waikato as well as Taranaki, to create a buffer zone between Pākehā and Māori still thought to be potentially hostile.[29] The first reference to confiscations in Taranaki appeared in a proclamation of 17 December 1864. Although primarily focusing on impending confiscations in the Waikato, it also advised that the Governor would take possession of and retain in the country between Wanganui and New Plymouth such land as belonging to the rebels 'as he may think fit' (Figure 16.2).

Māori deemed to have 'adhered to the Queen' would retain their land, as would those previously in rebellion 'who shall submit to the Queen's authority'. Those tribes deemed to have been guilty of violence would be 'punished as had the Waikato tribes been punished'. Later that year the Governor was empowered to award compensation for continuing losses of land,[30] with a subsequent stipulation that confiscations were to cease by 3 December 1867.[31] On 16 June 1866, regulations were gazetted establishing Compensation Courts for the purposes of awarding or increasing compensation as stipulated under the various Settlements Acts.

The key personnel of the Compensation Courts came from the Native Land Court, which was also the source of precedents and experience. The Compensation Court subsequently convened in New Plymouth from 1 June 1866 until late September of that year. 'Rebels' were deemed to have forfeited their land, but in reality Māori claimants were so numerous as to render such distinctions difficult to confirm prior to the hearings. Some considerable effort was devoted by the courts to identifying rebel individuals and those hapū members thought to have joined the fighting.[32]

Thereafter, separating 'loyalist' from 'rebel' was never a straightforward process. At any time during the period of hostilities, individuals or disparate groups of Māori throughout Taranaki were as likely as hapū and tribes to have been involved, or not involved, in conflict with or in support of the Crown, or in conflict against each other. The situation in Taranaki was altogether more complex than that suggested by Keith Sinclair, who wrote that about half of the Māori people were neutral, or kūpapa.[33]

The term 'kūpapa' has limited value in Taranaki, as it has for Māori in other parts of New Zealand. 'Kūpapa' first referred to those Māori who were not involved in conflict, who 'remained seated on the ground when others rose to the debate or departed for war'.[34] However, such neutral Māori were later described by colonists as friendly to the Crown since they were not actually fighting against it.[35] However, it was soon found to be impracticable to ascribe this status to specific hapū or tribes. Some tribes argued that they were loyal, while others such as Ngāti Mutunga said they had specifically demonstrated loyalty. Substantiating loyalty to the Crown was an important factor bearing on the successful filing of claims for lost lands. Hemi Matenga's right to petition in 1878 for the return of Waitara South lands was examined on the grounds of rebellion or loyalty. To the question, 'Were any members of [your] tribe in rebellion against her Majesty', Matenga replied, 'No, none of the Ngatihinetutu.'[36]

Issues of loyalty were rendered more complex by later claims that lands returned as Crown grants went to Māori people without rightful claim to the land in question. This was evident in 1927 when Kaho Heremia was asked, 'Do you say that the land where these weirs are situated ... was not returned to the natives after the war?' Kaho Heremia replied, 'It was returned to the loyalists ... that land was confiscated, and that was part of the land which caused the fight. It was afterwards that some of the loyalists were put onto the list of title.'[37] By implication, these were names not previously linked to the land in question.

The haphazard process of land reallocation also contributed to land claim difficulties, as with Taurua and his Pakakohe people, who were placed on to reserves 'somewhat promiscuously ... the boundaries of which had never been definitely fixed or surveyed'.[38] Subsequently, the later grievance of Ngāti Maru was one experienced by many of the tribes in Taranaki, that some of those persons were not genuine Ngāti Maru people at all but that some belonged to Ngā Puhi, some to Te Āti Awa and some to Whanganui. On the other hand, many genuine Ngāti Maru who were and are landless were left out of the said grants of land altogether.[39]

As late as 1940, Māori in Taranaki were still being required to state their loyalty to the Crown. Māori petitioners addressing 'claims and grievances remaining outstanding of the Aboriginal Natives of New Zealand' were still compelled to include references to past loyalty to the Crown to demonstrate 'that your Petitioners and their ancestors ...

always have been since the signing of the Treaty of Waitangi, loyal British subjects, and have not in any way been concerned in hostility against the Crown'.[40]

Continuities with today's claims process

Māori people have continued to file claims for material loss before judicial bodies such as the Waitangi Tribunal. Established in 1975 to consider argument from Māori alleging breaches of the Treaty of Waitangi, the tribunal has conducted a large number of complex historical inquiries dealing with Māori material and cultural loss, tied to specific histories and landscapes. The tribunal has also considered a range of generic issues that are not, on the face of it, connected to land. Māori language retention is one example. Although the Māori language has local nuance and dialect, it might be argued that the fate of Te Reo Māori is an issue that transcends whakapapa-based arguments that emphasise specificity of land, history, and protocol. Before a forum of discerning Māori, such argument might even

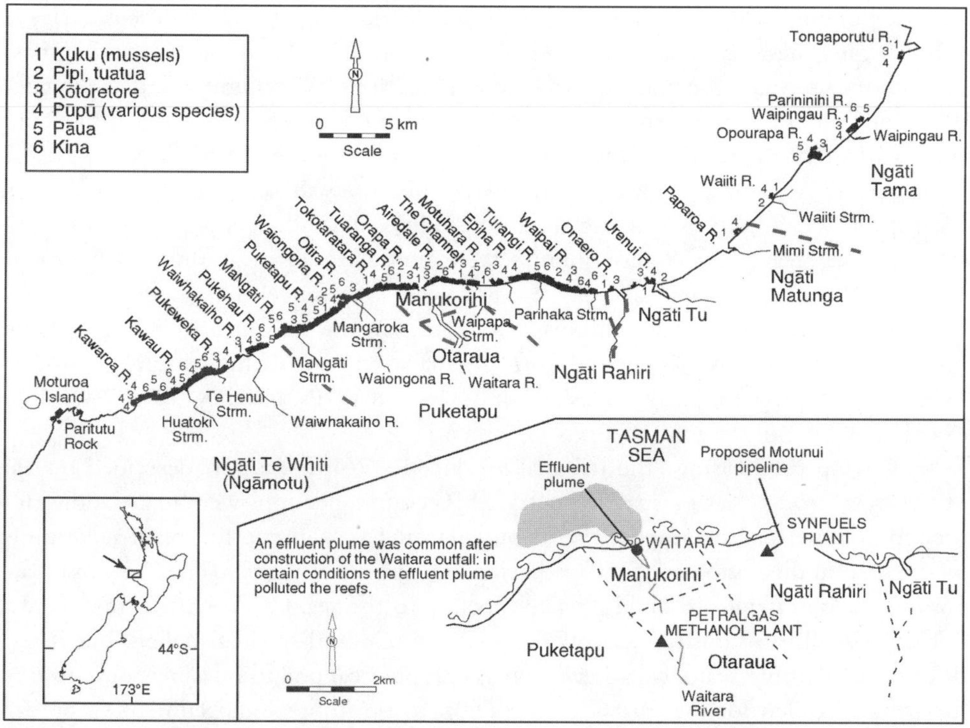

Figure 16.3 Hapū boundaries and seafood resources for the Te Āti Awa tribe, North Taranaki. As presented to the Waitangi Tribunal by Te Āti Awa in 1981. This traditional food-gathering area faced extensive pollution from the Motunui waste outfall. In defence of this coastline, Te Āti Awa established clear whakapapa connections between these resource areas, and tūpuna (ancestors) who had long exercised kaitiakitanga (guardianship) over the reefs. Aila Taylor and members of Te Āti Awa (Wai 6, 4 June 1981), courtesy of Northern Taranaki Iwi Crown Progression Team, New Plymouth.

succeed, if only for pragmatic purposes. However, where the losses argued by Māori relate more directly to land and resources, generic arguments that do not connect those directly to particular histories and landscapes have less chance of succeeding.

One early tribunal case, where historically specific evidence grounded in whakapapa proved to be persuasive, was the Te Āti Awa Motunui claim of the early 1980s. This turned on the fouling of seafood-rich reefs by waste outfalls (Figure 16.3), and it resembled claims brought before other like forums during the nineteenth century by Māori who were aggrieved at the despoiling or outright loss of their resource areas. Critical to such claims in Taranaki was the capacity of Māori, from the paepae, to locate themselves—their tribes and hapū—in the lands and resources under inquiry. This was achieved through whakapapa; and at such hearings, in the past as in the present, much whakapapa was heard, binding people and places together, clearly demonstrating the mana whenua of claimants.

The Te Āti Awa Motunui claim originated in the late 1970s when a small but dedicated group of Te Āti Awa, led by kaumatua Aila Taylor, 'fought judicial snubs; prejudiced attitudes; antagonistic bureaucrats … and stalling officials … to pursue a long, legal path that led to the Treaty of Waitangi Tribunal'.[41] Throughout the hearings Te Āti Awa laid emphasis upon their perceptions of the natural world as connected to their stories of tribal origin. These connections provided, among other things, the long-standing basis for resource use, management, and protection. Thus, the atua traditions (deities) provided the mauri (life force) that, when planted into a specific resource area, acted as the kaitiaki (guardian) of the resource area—specifically, in this case, the much valued reefs north of Waitara. Te Āti Awa, as tangata whenua of the area, drew these connections from their whakapapa, which imposed additional responsibilities upon the people to care for these taonga (resources). These responsibilities were met through institutions such as tapu (sacredness), noa (non-tapu), ihi (power), and wehi (reverence). The guiding principle that recognised Te Āti Awa authority to care for this resource was kaitiakitanga (guardianship), and this was derived from the mana whenua of the people. Te Āti Awa followed this process of recall and assertion in the mid 1970s, and they would have done exactly the same in the mid 1870s.

Following the hearings, the tribunal produced a 76-page report described by one observer as 'strong clear persuasive poetry'.[42] Recommendations were made addressing the central issue, that the proposed waste outfall from the synthetic-fuel plant at Motunui would despoil the customary food-gathering areas north of Waitara. The Motunui plant possessed a water right to build a waste pipeline to the sea. However, said Te Āti Awa, not only would its construction offend their cultural and spiritual beliefs, but it also threatened an entire seafood-gathering area with physical pollution. In response to this, the tribunal called for the outfall construction to be stopped and effluent to be discharged through the existing Waitara outfall. It also recommended that a new regional outfall be constructed to handle all the projected North Taranaki 'Think Big' projects. Perhaps inevitably, these recommendations ran foul of local and national political interests, though the initial negative stance taken by the National government was moderated with further mediation. The Waitangi Tribunal also recommended a change to the regulations restricting Māori access to pāua and sought the easing of special licences to allow for the harvesting of kaimoana (seafood) for occasions such as tangi. It further called for a study to clearly define the customary fishing grounds in North Taranaki, as well as to measure the impact of pollution within those grounds.

Much of the testimony laid before the tribunal by Te Āti Awa was structured and presented in a form consistent with normal marae convention and protocol. As with nineteenth-century testimony, weight was placed on utilising processes of historical recall that emphasised clear whakapapa connections between people and places, tied to known historic landscapes over which claimants exercised mana whenua. Throughout the later Taranaki whānui claim that commenced hearings in 1992, this approach was also followed,[43] as it has been by other tribal or hapū claims elsewhere in New Zealand. And, as with all tribunal cases since Motunui, this was hardly surprising, since, unlike in the nineteenth century, hearings were now located on the marae.

We might contrast this approach with another claim currently before the Waitangi Tribunal, the Indigenous Flora and Fauna claim, sometimes known by the shorthand 'Wai 262', the number by which it was registered. This claim was filed in 1991 by Haana Murray of Ngāti Kuri and Del Wihongi of Te Rārawa, along with a number of other Māori. Since then at least two amended claims have also been filed alongside the primary claim.[44] Few could argue with the central point, which deals with the material and spiritual loss to Māori of indigenous flora, fauna, and resources. The claim argues that Māori have been 'prejudicially affected by the actions and omissions of the Crown … in denying the tino rangatiratanga o te iwi Māori'. It therefore proceeds on the basis that the Treaty of Waitangi ought never to have subordinated Māori people.

As a consequence of the Crown assuming all authority to itself, the claim argues, Māori people were consistently denied the right to conserve their indigenous knowledge and resources, to develop that knowledge, and to control its use. The claim cites numerous Acts of Parliament and specifically identifies a large range of affected native plants, trees, birds, and animals. Through this claim, Māori people are said to be asserting a prior right to breed and propagate a range of select species for the purposes of research or commercial sale. The claimants conclude by seeking the Crown's acceptance of these arguments, the payment of compensation for losses, and a return to Māori of the sovereign right of control over such flora and fauna.

The Wai 262 claim represents a huge undertaking by its primary claimants, and it has acquired a high level of interest from both Māori and Pākehā, since its potential to influence control of key resources in New Zealand is enormous. It is a very broad-brush claim. However, its ability to achieve redress and restitution for Māori is seriously weakened by its generic nature, by its lack of geographic and historic specificity, and because the cited losses are not sourced within particular tribal landscapes. For all of its scope and detail, and the merit of its arguments, this is not a claim where local resources, flora, fauna, and land are referred to within a mana whakapapa context that emphasises places and people possessing those resources, and over which the claimants exercise and assert mana whenua.

Thus the atua of the named flora and fauna, and the mauri, are difficult to discern, as are the connections with the appropriate kaitiaki. Of course, this is not possible because one needs to know the tangata whenua first, allowing them to speak from their paepae of their lands where their species can be located, and whakapapa connections made: as, for example, the reefs north of Waitara. There kaumātua of Te Āti Awa named and pointed to specific mauri. The kaitiakitanga of all such taonga is derived from the mana whenua of the people.

This was the approach used by Māori during the nineteenth century when faced with the highest stakes imaginable: the fate of the land itself; and it is the approach preserved by the paepae today. The paepae continues to serve as the place where Maori define themselves and their histories, and determine how, among other things, tribal or hapū resource issues will be addressed, as occurred with Te Āti Awa over the Motunui outfall.

Conclusion

This chapter has reflected on the nature of Māori processes of historical recall and how these have functioned within the claims process. It has proposed an interpretation that suggests how, on what basis, and for what purposes the tribes and hapū in Taranaki have utilised such processes. The primary structuring device for this kind of approach was undoubtedly whakapapa, as asserted from the paepae. The function of whakapapa was to anchor claimants into known landscapes, and to establish the ongoing basis from which tribal and hapū mana, identity, and activity in the present could be validated by the past.

Central to this process is loss of land, or forced and permanent change to the names, the burial places, the wāhi tapu, the cultivations, the entire physical cover. Yet, for Māori, all of these have remained as the essential material points of reference for interpreting the landscape, substantially surviving the losses that have occurred. Great pains have been taken by Māori to assert their rights to retain and control land and resources. The Crown has frequently been challenged as to the circumstances and iniquities of their losses. Yet the mana of the people has continued to be maintained from the paepae, with the old people and sacred places remembered in whakapapa. Now, as then, what matters most to Māori in the context of marked change and loss is the mana whakapapa assertion of continuing mana whenua. Despite everything, Māori remain forever bound to the land.

17

A HISTORY OF NEW ZEALAND ENVIRONMENTAL LAW

Nicola Wheen

New Zealand environmental law has long facilitated resource development to promote social and economic growth.[1] Despite significant changes since the 1960s, the law remains very accommodating in this respect. Only in the conservation estate are environment and conservation interests legally paramount, appearing in the general body of environmental law in terms and contexts that allow them to be compromised and avoided. High, well-meaning principles such as sustainability are set out, especially in more recent legislation, but then defined so loosely that they lose impact. In particular, the Resource Management Act 1991, which aims to promote the sustainable management of natural and physical resources including land, air, and water, fails to provide any real checks against development and resource exploitation.

By the time English common law was introduced in the nineteenth century, Māori environmental management had assumed a strong underlying conservation ethic. Concepts such as whānaungatanga, arohatanga, mānakitanga, mauri, and utu directed human interactions with the environment. Straddling both the physical and metaphysical, this indigenous law was enforced by quasi-religious/quasi-legal mechanisms such as tapu, mana, and rāhui. The courts' misguided view that '[o]n the foundation of this colony, the Aborigines were found without ... any settled system of law',[2] allowed English common law to take over. Environmental law became one branch of the law of property and focused on defining entitlements to resources according to land ownership.

The legislative take-over

Fuelled by the pace of European settlement, legal change in the form of statutory encroachments into the common law came quickly. Initially these were fragmented and overlapping, reflecting local government patterns of the time, and the prevailing 'tinkering, and engineering approach to "resource" management'.[3] With time, many have been integrated into fewer, more comprehensive pieces of legislation. The aim of such encroachments was seldom to conserve, but rather to establish 'a legal and administrative order within which property rights could be allocated, transferred, and protected, [and] resources could be exploited'.[4]

Legislation enabled access to resources such as gold and other minerals (see Chapter 6), geothermal energy, fossil fuels, and water. Usually it did so by assuming Crown ownership or control of resources, and then authorising allocations of new rights to private users. Further, public bodies were empowered to use resources to attend to the needs of settlements for supply of water, provision of roads and bridges, sewage disposal, electricity, and so on. Agricultural interests were protected by legislation authorising the construction of works to control floods and erosion, and restricting or preventing the introduction of plant and animal pests.

When provision was made to protect the quality of natural resources, this was only where human health, safety, or economic interests were at stake. For example, the early Marine Boards, Marine, and Harbours Acts controlled and prohibited discharges of ballast into harbours (until 1950, expressly to prevent damage to shipping); the Thermal Springs legislation probably offered a little protection to such features, although its true purpose was to facilitate European settlement; and, in 1953, steps were taken to protect ground water for domestic, farming, and industrial uses. Clearly the primary object of these provisions was not nature conservation.

Where access to resources was already open under the common law, legislative intervention took the form of restrictions and controls to prevent over-exploitation. For example, restrictions on the time, place, and means of fishing, or on the size or weight of the fish, could be imposed to protect parts of the sea-fisheries resource. Little was done, however, to protect forests. Even when in 1949 the notion of 'balanced use' was introduced to direct state forest management, this was expressed as one principle among many, with the emphasis on production, water and soil conservation, scientific objectives, and recreation and amenity values.

Some steps towards resource conservation were taken in early legislation, but these were mere ripples in the blanket of law enabling resource development (see Chapter 8). What is more, the emphasis was undeniably on recreational and scenic (that is, human-centred) values. Late nineteenth-century moves to set aside reserves, domains, or national parks, so as to provide scenic, historic, nature, and recreation areas for public benefit and enjoyment, were fragmented. They involved a series of Acts empowering various public authorities. Sometimes the law provided that the reserve, domain, or park should be managed so as to protect the animals and plants living there, or the quality of water in rivers, streams, or lakes flowing through or on the land.

Plants, animals, and water were also protected, piecemeal, in other limited Acts. The Oil in Territorial Waters, and Oil in Navigable Waters Acts (of 1926 and 1965 respectively) purported specifically to control oil pollution in waters within New Zealand's territorial limits. The Waters Pollution Act 1953 had more general application but was practically ineffective. The animals and birds at first protected by legislation were the game species, but since 1953 a presumption of protection for all wildlife has applied.[5] The Native Plants

Protection Act 1934 made it an offence to take, without authorisation, protected native plants from public reserves, Crown land, roads, or private land. Most native plants are protected, but the Act has never been vigorously enforced and its penalties are derisory.

Both the main development-oriented body of environmental law and the more fragmented collection of conservation legislation have been subject to significant change in the last forty years or so. The law's provision for environment and conservation has expanded, at first on an ad hoc basis in response to particular problems, but later in more comprehensive and integrated ways. This reflects the growing politicisation of the environment, which was kick-started by the Manapouri controversy.

The Manapouri controversy

Arguably the most beautiful of New Zealand's southern lakes, Manapouri, and its neighbour, the South Island's largest lake, Te Anau, were first earmarked for hydroelectric development in 1903. After World War II, with state development priorities shifting towards industrialisation, the need for cheap power became more insistent.[6] In September 1959 a proposal to develop the lakes' hydroelectric potential for aluminium production was announced. To that end the National government entered into an agreement with an

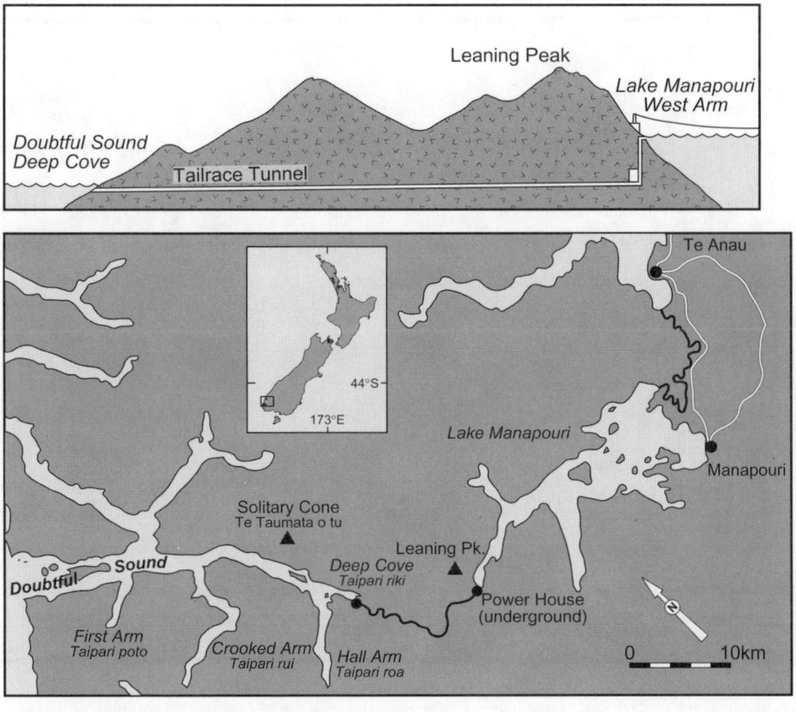

Figure 17.1 The location of Lake Manapouri, with a schematic representation of the power scheme and tailrace tunnel.

Australian company, Consolidated Zinc Proprietary. Within a year, however, the company had cried too poor to build the power scheme.

Undeterred, the government secured the enactment of the Manapouri–Te Anau Development Act 1963; the water rights reverted to the Crown, enabling it to develop the hydro resource itself. An underground power station of a scale unprecedented in the southern hemisphere was constructed. Water from the lakes was diverted from its natural course into the Waiau River, down vertical penstocks onto turbines and then out through a tailrace tunnel to a new outfall at Deep Cove on the Fiordland coast (Figure 17.1). Power output would be maximised by raising lake levels, and a rise of eight to ten metres was proposed.

Manapouri's turbines first turned in 1969—and only then was the need for some kind of environmental-impact assessment realised. The issues focused on the likely effects of raising lake levels on wildlife habitats, on the Waiau River, and, especially, on the lake's shoreline (Figure 17.2). Public feeling was mobilised in the country's first large-scale environmental campaign, that to 'Save Manapouri'.[7] The campaign peaked when the government changed in 1972 and the new Minister of Energy instructed the Electricity Department to keep the lakes within their natural levels. The new Labour Prime Minister, Norman Kirk, then approved terms of reference for the appointment of Guardians for the Lakes, who were to devise and supervise the implementation of guidelines for lake management.

Figure 17.2 'The view stinks but it's worth millions!' Sid Scales, *Otago Daily Times*, originally published 22 October 1959; republished 26 February 1970. Reproduced with the permission of the Hocken Library, Uare Taoka O Hakena, University of Otago.

Six leading members of the Save Manapouri campaign were appointed as the first Guardians, beginning a new relationship between conservation and development interests that endures today. These steps were formalised with the amendment of the Manapouri–Te Anau Development Act in 1981. The provisions providing for raising of the lake levels were repealed and a new provision for guidelines to protect ecological stability and recreational values of the shorelines (at the same time as optimising energy production) was inserted. Guidelines were devised and officially published in the *New Zealand Gazette* on 3 December 1981. One of the guardians, botanist and conservationist Alan Mark, argues that the campaign was a 'milestone in the transition from the pioneering era of resource exploitation to one aimed at integrating conservation with development, and associated with the sustainable management of our natural resources'.[8]

The road from Manapouri: environmental gains

The impact of Manapouri should not be underestimated but must be placed in context. The 1960s was a period of rapid growth in levels of public concern for environment and conservation throughout the Western world. The Manapouri campaign was a product, as much as anything, of its time. With the 1981 amendment, it clearly had a direct impact on New Zealand environmental law. The government also responded to post-Manapouri public expectations by creating new environmental institutions, chief among which were the Nature Conservation Council, the Environmental Council, and the Commission for the Environment. One role of the commission was to implement the Environmental Protection and Enhancement Procedures adopted in 1973. Under these procedures, environmental-impact assessments were required for all government works likely to have significant environmental effects. The politicisation of the environment also had flow-on effects for the wider body of New Zealand environmental law.

In 1967 water management was completely overhauled. The Water and Soil Conservation Act put in place a single licensing system to control water use for industry, town supply, fisheries, wildlife habitats, and recreation. The Act took a catchment-wide approach and so helped to focus local government by advancing regionalism. To be authorised, proposed uses of water had to prove beneficial when weighed against anticipated losses. But the environmental flaws inherent in this balancing approach were vividly illustrated by the 1978 decision approving the hydro development of the Rangitaiki and Wheao rivers. This was despite the anticipated loss of an outstanding trout fishery and the destruction of the habitat of two endangered duck species.[9] One critic, lawyer Tony Black, argued that the decision showed the law had 'a decided bias towards resource development as opposed to environmental conservation ... For in the process of balancing tangible economic benefits and tangible social benefits against intangible and generally misunderstood environmental benefits the tangible wins out every time.'[10]

Environmentalists urged that some way of conserving rivers and lakes of national significance was needed. In 1981 Parliament introduced a water conservation scheme to preserve the natural, wild, scenic, recreational, wildlife, or scientific features of water bodies, and the Motu became the first river for which a water conservation order was issued. Public pressure by conservationists in the post-Manapouri period also brought improvements to the law relating to the marine environment and forests. 'New Zealand's past is steeped in the blood of whales and seals';[11] indeed, the last whaling station did not cease operations until 1964. Then one of the most widely supported of all environmental campaigns—'Save the Whales'—forced a turnaround in government policy and the law. The Marine Reserves Act 1971 (under which reserves can be established to protect scenic areas, natural features, or marine life in the national interest and for scientific study), and the Marine Mammals Protection Act 1978 (which protects these animals in their natural habitat) were the legislative results.

The 1971 publication of a government proposal for large-scale harvest of South Island beech forest, much of which is adjacent to alpine national parks, generated another significant environmental campaign. Two new and powerful lobby groups—the Native Forests Action Council and the Friends of the Earth—were formed. In response to mounting public concern, the emphasis on natural, intrinsic, and scientific values was increased in the reserves and national parks legislation when this was consolidated in 1977 and 1980. In 1976 'balanced use' became the foremost management goal for the Crown's own production forests, making water and soil management, land conservation, indigenous flora and fauna, recreation, education, and historic, cultural, scenic, aesthetic, amenity, and scientific values all relevant concerns, along with production.

Finally, the 'growing concern for the protection of the environment' in the post-Manapouri period was behind changes to town and country planning legislation.[12] These recognised the need to preserve the natural character of the coast and of river and lake margins, and to conserve the physical environment. More specifically for urban environmental quality, the Clean Air Act 1972 made a small inroad into air pollution. Its general duty to adopt the best practicable means to minimise air pollution was only enforceable against industry, and although it authorised the creation of zones where domestic pollution could be controlled, only one limited zone—Christchurch City—was ever created. Despite all these improvements, however, the main body of environmental law continued to enable and facilitate resource exploitation.

The road from Manapouri: developmentalism resurgent

Manapouri and Te Anau were only two of the lakes targeted for hydroelectric development. Others, including Waikaremoana, Monowai, and Hawea, were also affected, along with the Waikato, Tongariro, Waitaki, and Clutha rivers. The controversy caused by the damming of the Clutha River, which drains around one-twelfth of the country's land surface and flows through some of its most dramatic scenery, constitutes the next thread in this history (Figure 17.3).

Serious investigations into the Clutha River's hydro potential began in 1962. In 1965 the investigations were officially announced and rumours—later to prove justified—that the historic township of Cromwell would be flooded and that the levels of Lake Wanaka

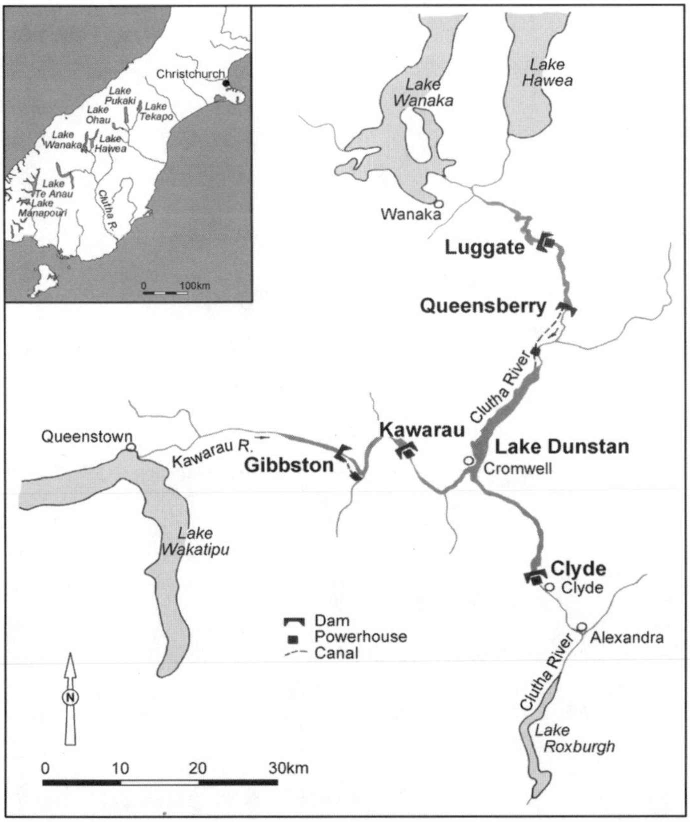

Figure 17.3 'Mastering the vast energy potential of the Clutha River.' The map shows Scheme F, approved in 1976. By 1983 the two dams on the Kawarau had been abandoned because of geological problems. The two dams on the upper Clutha towards Wanaka were later abandoned by the fourth Labour government. Adapted from *Clutha Power*, Ministry of Works and Development, revised December 1983.

would be raised began to circulate. The 1972 general election, which brought the Kirk-led Labour government to power, also saved Lake Wanaka. The Manapouri example was followed with the passage of the Lake Wanaka Preservation Act 1973, and guardians were appointed to protect its natural values.

However, also in 1972 an official report put forward six alternative schemes for the hydro development of the Clutha. The option finally selected, by a National government in 1976, was the second-most destructive, involving construction of a 195-metre-high dam at Clyde. Old Cromwell town and several of the pip-fruit orchards in the Clutha Valley would be flooded. Public opposition mounted as it became apparent that part of the government's goal was to generate cheap power for a new aluminium smelter.[13] The smelter proposal was itself highly contentious, the intended site being at Aramoana, directly across Otago Harbour from Tairoa Head, the only mainland royal albatross colony in the world. Both the dam and smelter disputes moved into the courts (Figure17.4).

Figure 17.4 Government ministers kneel before the graven image of Aluminium, as the Minister of Energy offers a jug of Clutha water into the sacrificial sink. Sid Scales, *Otago Daily Times*, originally published 13 December 1980. Reproduced with the permission of the Hocken Library, Uare Taoka O Hakena, University of Otago.

The government's application for the water rights to dam the Clutha was initially approved, despite a recommendation from the local catchment board that it be declined in favour of a smaller scheme. Some protesters appealed, but their appeal was dismissed. When the Aramoana smelter proposal finally lapsed, because of the withdrawal of likely corporate investors, another appeal was taken to the High Court. In it the objectors claimed that the proposed end use of the power to be generated by damming the Clutha had not been taken into account in the original decision, and that this was contrary to law. The decision in *Gilmore* v. *National Water and Soil Conservation Authority* (1982), that the end use of the power was relevant, was the final straw. Irked by the protesters' success, the government decided to take legislative action. It secured the necessary support of two minor-party members of Parliament just as the court decided that, once the end use of the power was considered as required by *Gilmore*, the objectors' appeals must succeed.

The Clutha Development (Clyde Dam Empowering) Act 1982 conferred the water rights to dam the river on the Minister of Energy. In so doing, it effectively reversed the court's decision to the government's advantage. This gives the Act a constitutional notoriety unmatched in New Zealand's legal history. It breached an important constitutional convention and underscored the government's willingness and ability to manage and control parliamentary processes to its own ends. It illustrated a determination to see the dam built no matter what, and a derisory attitude towards the objectors and the courts.[14]

In 1979 the National government had also been responsible for enacting the National Development Act. This was the legislation under which the Aramoana aluminium smelter was initially considered. It provided a fast-track procedure to assess and authorise proposed works deemed to be of national importance, with final decisions resting with government ministers. The Act was an integral part of National's 'Think Big' policy, which promoted large-scale industry exploiting New Zealand's natural resources. Both the policy and the Act were very controversial. Ministerial decisions were vigorously challenged in the courts,[15] but schemes such as petrochemical developments in Taranaki using the country's limited supplies of natural gas proceeded.

The fourth Labour government and environmental reform

There is little doubt that 'the perceived indifference, if not open hostility' of the National government towards environmental interests was exploited by the Labour Party in the run-up to the 1984 election.[16] Ostensibly, Labour offered a significant shift in environmental policy, along with institutional reform to provide a more effective voice for conservation.

Policy generation within the fourth Labour government (1984–90) was, however, dominated by Treasury and a core group of half a dozen 'free market' ministers. Their perspective on government was that in order to reinvigorate economic development, the extent of state activity and regulation had to be 'rolled back'.[17] Environmentalists were not, in principle, opposed to this approach: 'for many ... the State had been the main culprit of environmental degradation'.[18] In hindsight, it is not at all clear that the ensuing reforms have benefited environmental and conservation interests, but the fact that they were initially supported by advocates of both areas most affected—economy and environment—made them easier to implement. The extent of the program was such that it was, in several respects, unfinished by the end of Labour's second term in office in 1990.

Labour began by disestablishing the existing 'mixed mandate' environmental agencies. These included the Ministry of Works and Development (which had been responsible for hydroelectric schemes, as well as for oversight of water conservation orders) and the Department of Lands and Survey (which was both a land development agency as well as having a role in administration of the conservation estate). Commercial functions were transferred to new state-owned enterprises, which were instructed to operate as successful businesses. Conservation functions were allocated to a new Department of Conservation. A new Ministry for the Environment, with a policy role, and the new office of Parliamentary Commissioner for the Environment, with audit functions, were established.

The functions of the Ministry for the Environment are directed by a range of matters, including the intrinsic value of ecosystems, resource sustainability and the needs of future generations, aesthetic, cultural, recreational, scenic, and scientific values, and the principles of the Treaty of Waitangi. One of the architects of the Office of the Parliamentary Commissioner for the Environment, Phillip Woollaston, Minister of Conservation and Local Government, and Associate Minister for the Environment in the fourth Labour government, points out that when it was established, and for nearly a decade following, the office 'was unique in the Westminster ... system [in that it held] the power to examine critically the policy decisions of the executive government ... [This] was undoubtedly the outcome sought by the policy's authors ... [who were responding] to "Think Big", the Clyde Dam legislation and the kneecapping of the Commission for the Environment ... by the [previous National Government].'[19] The wide range of the commissioner's powers is, however, compromised by their relative weakness and the office's limited resources.

The Department of Conservation is a 'hands-on' agency that administers most conservation legislation and manages the conservation estate. The Conservation Act 1987 requires it to preserve and protect resources, maintain intrinsic values, provide for appreciation and enjoyment, safeguard future options, and give effect to the Treaty of Waitangi. The Act's central virtue is that it enables a level of cohesion and integration in planning for, and management of, the conservation estate that was previously virtually absent.

Another plank in Labour's program of reform was the reorganisation of local government. The environmental functions of almost all residual specialised agencies (such as catchment boards) were devolved on to general-purpose territorial authorities and regional councils. This nationwide tier of regional administration, based to a considerable extent on catchment boundaries, and introduced in 1989, was to provide the framework within which newly formulated resource management law could be administered.

The resource management law-reform process proper began in January 1988, when the review was announced, and ended in October 1991, when most of the Resource Management Act came into force. Additional reforms made since then are, however, also part and parcel of the process. The reforms as a whole were motivated primarily by the increasing prominence and widening appeal of environment and conservation issues. An apparent commitment to sustainability characterises the resulting legislation, which has also significantly integrated and cohered New Zealand's environmental law.

The Resource Management Act 1991 replaced nearly sixty existing Acts, including the Town and Country Planning Act 1977 and the Water and Soil Conservation Act 1967. Created after unprecedented consultation, it covers the use, development, and protection of air, land, and water. It puts in place a three-tiered (national, regional, and local) management system and a scheme for allocating rights to use land, air, and water. When the Resource Management Bill was introduced into Parliament in December 1989, Ministry for the Environment staff enthused:

> a new era in environmental management has begun. Our existing ... laws ... have evolved in a piecemeal fashion, resulting in a set of complex, overlapping, and sometimes conflicting rules. As a result, the outcomes for the environment are often inadequate ... The ... Bill proposes to change all this. In a world where concern for the environment grows stronger every day, New Zealand has recognised that the clean-up must begin at home.[20]

The Act seeks to facilitate sounder environmental decision-making by prescribing guiding principles and objectives. Before any proposed use of land, air, or water is authorised, the actual and potential effects on the environment must be assessed and a whole raft of interests, including development, amenity and intrinsic values, and the principles of the Treaty of Waitangi, must be considered. Most importantly, decisions made under the Act must promote sustainable management. By adopting sustainability as its core purpose, the Act broke new ground. Sustainability has since become the 'golden thread' of resource management in New Zealand, finding its way into other legislation, including the Forests and Fisheries Acts.

Commercial fisheries are managed under the Fisheries Act 1996, which aims to provide for the conservation, use, enhancement, and development of fisheries resources while ensuring sustainability. This is the first piece of New Zealand legislation expressly to adopt the precautionary principle. The fisheries are managed using a quota management system (QMS), which was introduced in 1986. A total allowable catch (TAC), designed to maintain, or move fisheries stock towards, the maximum sustainable yield (MSY), is set for each nominated fishery. Within the TAC, a total allowable commercial catch (TACC) is determined. Individual tradable quotas, representing a proportion of the TACC, are allocated to fishers. This market-based system was introduced to promote industry efficiency and conserve the fishery.

The introduction of the QMS was the single most radical change ever made to commercial fisheries management. It forced government to settle outstanding Treaty of Waitangi commercial fisheries grievance's by propelling the claims into court, and undertake negotiations that eventually generated the Treaty of Waitangi (Fisheries Claims Settlement) Act 1992. The system's ability to conserve the fishery remains contentious: everything hinges on the level at which the minister sets the TAC. In 1995 Greenpeace challenged the TAC set for orange roughy in 1993–94, claiming there was no chance of the fishery being restored to its MSY. Controversially, the court held that it was lawful for the minister to set the TACC at a level allowing the attainment of the MSY over a ten-year (or other 'reasonable') period.[21]

Sustainability was introduced to privately owned indigenous production forests by the Forests Amendment Act 1993. Labour's institutional reform had split state-forest management between the commercial and conservation estates, and put the bulk of the Crown's indigenous forests into the latter. Cutting rights to most exotic and indigenous production forests were corporatised and, in some cases, subsequently privatised, though the Crown retained large tracts of indigenous production forest on the South Island's West Coast. Until 1993 the only attempts to control logging in indigenous production forests were the accords negotiated between conservation interests, the Crown, and the timber industry in 1986, 1989, and 1991. The exact status and weight of these agreements was always unclear.

Under the 1993 Act, indigenous timber cannot be milled and indigenous timber product cannot be exported unless the timber has been harvested sustainably. 'Sustainable forest management' is defined as management that 'maintains the ability of the forest growing on that land to continue to produce a full range of products and amenities in perpetuity while retaining the forest's natural values'. Controversially, the Crown's own West Coast forests were expressly exempted from the Act, on the grounds that they were covered by the West Coast Accord. Recent government policy has, however, put an end to logging in the Crown's West Coast forests, thus undermining the accord. This policy has been formally implemented in legislation.

Sustainability therefore now stands as the management focus of commercial fisheries, indigenous production forests, and land, air, and water. The interests of future generations are to be considered in environment and conservation policy, and in the administration of the conservation estate. This does not mean, however, that there has been a complete shift in environmental outcomes. Sustainability is a very general concept, and the breadth of the statutory definitions has caused problems. More resources are always needed, and seldom forthcoming. Furthermore, there has been a failure to deal with some of the more challenging (and controversial) environmental issues such as agricultural pollution of waterways and greenhouse gas emissions. The latter is of particular note in the context of international obligations.

New Zealand is a signatory to the Framework Convention on Climate Change that was agreed to at the Rio Earth Summit in 1992. Unfortunately, its approach as a signatory has been merely to make well-meaning but empty policy statements. On the one occasion the law offered the Minister for the Environment a specific opportunity to do something to reduce carbon dioxide emissions, little was done. In *Decision of the Minister for the Environment on Air Discharge Permit: Taranaki Combined Cycle Power Station* (1995) the minister was asked to approve a proposal to construct a new thermal power station. This he did, but imposed a special condition requiring the consent holder to take 'such steps as are necessary and effective to avoid, remedy, or mitigate the effects of the additional amount of CO_2 being discharged as a result of the exercise'.

Although the new power station should therefore not add to CO_2 emissions, our international obligation is actually to *reduce* emissions to 1990 levels. In the Taranaki case, the minister also affirmed New Zealand's net approach to greenhouse emissions and our emphasis on using carbon sinks to absorb emissions rather than reducing emissions at their source. Both of these have been challenged as flawed and inadequate responses to climate change.[22] In 1999 New Zealand was awarded the Climate Action Network's fossil award for actually increasing greenhouse gas emissions by 30 per cent since Rio.

The Energy Efficiency and Conservation Act 2000, however, offers some cause for optimism. It enables development of national energy efficiency and conservation strategies, and the making of regulations prescribing performance standards for energy-using products and services, including vehicles. If it is to make a practical difference, action will have to be taken. Recent government practice has been to shy away from opportunities to provide national guidance or control, because of a continued commitment to non-interventionist economic policies. The Resource Management Act provides government with significant opportunities to develop policy statements and technical standards. So far it has refused to get involved, despite many calls for guidance.

High (but indeterminate) principles

Of all the principles adopted by international environmental law and policy worldwide, sustainability is both the most important and 'the most wonderfully wide'.[23] In New Zealand, it has been incorporated into the Environment Act 1986, the Conservation Act 1987, the Resource Management Act 1991, the Fisheries Act 1996, the Hazardous Substances and New Organisms Act 1996, and the Energy Efficiency and Conservation Act 2000.

For the purposes of the 1991 Act 'sustainable management' is defined in section 5, in what can best be described as 'open' language, as:

> Managing the use, development, and protection of natural and physical resources in a way, or at a rate, which enables people and communities to provide for their social, economic, and cultural wellbeing and for their health and safety while—
> (a) Sustaining the potential of natural and physical resources (excluding minerals) to meet the reasonably foreseeable needs of future generations; and
> (b) Safeguarding the life-supporting capacity of air, water, soil, and ecosystems; and
> (c) Avoiding, remedying, or mitigating any adverse effects of activities on the environment.

According to the courts, section 5 'should [not] be subjected to strict rules and principles of statutory construction which aim to extract a precise and unique meaning from the words', but instead must be read so as to 'allow the application of policy in a general and broad way'.[24] A very broad 'overall judgement' approach that 'allows for comparison of conflicting considerations and the scale or degree of them, and their relative significance or proportion in the final outcome' has been adopted.[25]

This dashes hopes—including those of Geoffrey Palmer, Minister for the Environment in the fourth Labour government, and architect of the Act—that section 5 would 'overturn the whole philosophy of the decision-making process' in place under the previous legislation.[26] By reading section 5 as creating what is essentially a balancing test, the courts have opened it up to the same central criticism as was made of earlier legislation. Balancing tests are inherently biased towards development, 'for in the process of balancing tangible economic ... and ... social benefits against intangible ... environmental benefits the tangible wins out every time'.[27]

The balancing approach is ecologically derelict in its failure to provide uncompromising environmental standards. *Even if* a balancing test had not been adopted for section 5, its very wording is so wide that it can support almost any decision on a given set of facts. This is illustrated by *Canterbury Regional Council* v. *Selwyn District Council*. Counsel argued that allowing residential development on land with food production potential would 'not safeguard the life supporting capacity of soils but destroy their capacity and further ... [would] not sustain the resource represented by the soil for the reasonably foreseeable needs of future generations'. The Planning Tribunal (now the Environment Court) replied that 'an equally valid argument could be advanced' that 'to blindly protect soils of high value does not sustain the resource represented by the community ... for its foreseeable future needs if it deprives future generations of the ability to live in an expanded community.'[28]

The fact that there is no preference for conservation over development means there is no preference for the existing state. In 1995, local residents sought to stop (or at least slow down) fast ferries operating a service between the North and South Islands. They alleged that the ferries' wakes had caused physical and ecological changes to the coastline. The Planning Tribunal refused to intervene, taking 'the view that [the changes that had] happened [had] reach[ed] equilibrium'. While the ferries' activities 'may [have] result[ed] in a modified natural environment', stopping them would result in a reversal of that new equilibrium.[29]

Bruce Pardy, a legal academic specialising in environmental law, explains the ecological flaw in this approach:

> The ecosystem of the Sounds prior to the fast ferries could not be described as virgin ... Why then should the equilibrium prior to the fast ferries be preferred to the equilibrium after? The objective of environmental protection is the preservation of the existing state because it is closer to the natural or pristine state than the one that follows the new impact. The existing state is the best case scenario remaining (in the absence of remedial measures to repair the effects of previous impact).[30]

Because sustainability is defined similarly in other legislation—especially the Fisheries Act 1996—similar problems will permeate decision-making in those areas.

New Zealand Law Commissioner D. F. Dugdale postulates that some of the 'voluntary ambiguity' of recent legislation may be 'attributable to ... politic uncertainty, a desire for an appearance of agreement despite the existence of nettles left ungrasped'.[31] But by using high principles such as sustainability in environmental law, and not defining and prioritising them tightly enough, Parliament has created a situation where the law's bark is far greener than its bite.

Conclusion

For the last century or so New Zealand environmental law has comprised an increasingly comprehensive body of legislation designed to manage (and promote) resource development. Ripples have been made in this body of law by statutes that aim to conserve the natural environment. Otherwise, conservation and environment have been, and still are, relegated to the periphery. Today this relegation occurs mainly because of the vague standards and definitions used to guide environmental decision-making. Of these, the foremost is sustainability. This is a fine principle, to be sure, but 'the existence of a principle in itself never saved a tree or cost a logging company any money. Where the benefit and the pain come from are the laws implementing that policy, and the administrative decisions derived from it.'[32]

The implementation of sustainability has been hampered by a legislative preference in New Zealand for widely framed and flexible definitions. The aim is to be embracing and to leave plenty of discretion to decision-makers so that they can tailor outcomes to the facts of each case. The problem with discretion is that it leaves (too much) room for compromise, and allows pre-existing values to prevail. Compromise tends to result in developments proceeding, so long as the environmental impacts are somehow reduced. As Bruce Pardy argues, 'significant long-term environmental changes can be caused by the accumulation of small impacts. Compromise allows environmental death from a thousand inconsequential cuts.'[33] The underlying value preference in New Zealand favours development and the management of environmental impact. Without either very clear and uncompromising ecological bottom lines, or a transition to a greener value paradigm, this bias will continue to manifest itself in environmental decision-making.[34]

18

Losing ground?

Environmental problems and prospects at the beginning of the twenty-first century

Christine Dann

A southerly storm in Koukourarata/Port Levy, Banks Peninsula. The creeks run high and brown, and flash streams course straight down steep, bare hillsides, taking with them the yellow loess soils that the roots of tōtara used to bind to the slope. On the hill opposite the old cook's quarters, the dead and dying kānuka trees thrash in the wind. Helicopter spraying killed them along with some gorse. The kōwhai on our side of the creek also copped the spray. They are still alive but won't flower this spring. The creek rampages by, carrying dead trees and dead sheep. The head of the harbour is already smothered in fine silt as deep as my thighs, and I see the spreading brown stain from the hills stretch out to the open sea, carrying still more mud to settle. The depleted cockle beds in the harbour are currently protected from plundering by a special five-year rāhui, but what shellfish can withstand this slow death by suffocation as hills keep sliding into the sea?

Horomaka/Banks Peninsula is where the Ngāti Irakehu hapū of Ngāi Tahu maintains four marae. This is all that is left from earlier, denser patterns of settlement. Dozens of British and French farmers settled here around the time that the Treaty of Waitangi was signed, and a few of their descendants still remain. Hardly anything remains of the original 56,600 hectares of virgin forest they encountered when they arrived—by the late twentieth century only 61 hectares were left.[1] Living here, one is surrounded by stories of settlement, which are still being inscribed in the land and drawn on the sea.

An environmental history of New Zealand is primarily the story of the environmental impacts of human settlement. In concluding this volume I look at the forces that have driven, and continue to drive, three centuries of environmental intervention. In doing so, I am mindful of the critique of colonialist ways of conceptualising the past provided by the authors in *Quicksands: Foundational Histories in Australia and Aotearoa New Zealand*.[2] Stephen Turner discusses why and how Pākehā culture exhibits a 'will to forget' the realities of colonial settlement that has detrimental cultural and political effects in the present day. Other contributors contrast the 'clean break' and 'progressive conquest' narratives of Australian history provided by white settlers and their descendants (which invariably emphasise discontinuities) with the Aboriginal emphasis on the continuity grounded in contiguity of past and present experience.

The emphasis on disjunction and discontinuity is particularly evident and probably functional in Western political histories—the stories of finite governments, rulers, political movements, and empires. It is less obviously useful when dealing with social and economic history, where underlying structures and patterns of long duration are as significant as abrupt shifts. An environmental history necessarily deals with long-term 'events'. For example, the reduction of New Zealand's native forest cover is an 'event' that took place over centuries, and it is still happening. Uncovering why this is still happening or, in other words, what drove the environmental behaviour of past settlers that is still influencing the behaviour of their descendants, is the subject of this chapter.

The storm at Koukourarata writes on the land the forces that have shaped and continue to shape the environmental history of New Zealand. At the beginning of the twenty-first century we can expect to see, in the words of Colin McCahon's painting, that 'Tomorrow will be the same but not as this is'. What are these shaping forces? They are not unique to New Zealand. Three core processes that have been making history across the world are also at work here. They are colonisation, industrialisation, and modernisation. Corresponding roughly to the political, the economic, and cultural realms, they are nevertheless inextricably linked, and each contains elements of the other. They need to be teased out separately to understand what each contributes to environmental change.

In focusing on these three forces I do not mean to imply that they are the only ones worthy of consideration, but I do believe that they hold the key to understanding what drives the environmental problems and concerns, past, present, and future, that are documented below. Nor do I seek to reify them as monolithic and inexorable forces. Of course there are discontinuities, contradictions, and resistances, and these are also considered.

Colonisation

Colonisation is such a given for New Zealand that it is usually accorded little or no consideration in histories dealing with anything other than the period of first occupation by British rulers and settlers. It is assumed to have happened in the past and to be over. Hence we speak of 'postcolonial' politics and literatures. Yet a closer examination of how settler stories are told and 'postcolonialism' is constructed provides evidence that the colonisation process is not over. Julian Thomas examines the writing of histories of 'great moments' in Australian history, uncovering the ways in which indigenous people and native species are relegated to the margins and are literally put out of consideration.[3] Stephen Turner argues that until New Zealanders come to terms with the fact of settlement as an ongoing political and social process, attempts to form a new polity that is independent of the British Crown, founded on a constitution arrived at by consensus, are doomed to failure.[4]

Turning to the environment, there is further evidence that the colonial approach to the land and its indigenous species is far from dead, and continues to generate seemingly intractable problems. The imposition of alien agricultures and exotic biota on indigenous ecosystems causes problems in time and space that have spread far beyond the point of initial introduction. Alfred Crosby has documented the nature and extent of this 'ecological imperialism' for the Pacific region[5], while Tim Flannery provides further evidence of utterly inappropriate and disastrous approaches in the colonial management of natural resources in Australasia.[6]

But have we learned from our mistakes? For Māori, the process of environmental colonisation is still being contested. In 1991 six iwi lodged the Indigenous Flora and Fauna and Māori Intellectual and Cultural Property Claim (Wai 262) with the Waitangi Tribunal (see Chapter 16). This claim seeks to establish Māori rights to 'intellectual property' in the indigenous flora and fauna of New Zealand. This would in turn create a legal and commercial framework within which to resist attempts at bio-piracy and to profit from selective breeding.

This property rights approach to nature has been criticised by non-Māori environmentalists, who distinguish between private rights and public goods, and place most natural resources and processes in the latter category. Many Māori may share this view, but they are between a rock and a hard place. The property rights approach has already been enshrined in laws that they must obey; their only choice is between letting others profit from this system or establishing their own rights to profit. Land is not the only thing that can be colonised—and lost.

For the British settlers, colonisation was based on rights to ownership of the land and also on the taken-for-granted right to do what one liked with that land. Hence the introduction of exotic species on an individual, local, and national scale. Colonisation in this sense was a replacement of 'old and feeble' indigenous species with 'new and vigorous' stock. Colonists may have regretted the passing of the old,[7] but that did not stop them from setting up new social mechanisms (such as acclimatisation societies) to deliberately replace old species with new ones. New species were introduced not just for their economic and productive value, but also for recreation or purely sentimental reasons.

Bio-colonisation can hardly be said to be over when, every year, hundreds of millions of taxpayers' dollars are spent on dealing with the adverse environmental effects of the policy of species replacement.[8] Although by the late twentieth century the policy had changed from helping them in to keeping them out, and a new term to describe this policy—biosecurity—was coined, during the same period conditions for effective border protection deteriorated markedly. World trade increased twelve-fold after World War II, and the volume of New Zealand's exports and imports rose considerably. Mass foreign travel for First Worlders, including New Zealanders, also became common. By 1991 over two million people were leaving or entering New Zealand annually.[9] Announcing the formation of the new Biosecurity Authority in July 1999, the Minister of Biosecurity stated that by that year the numbers had reached 3.16 million. The number of sea containers arriving in New Zealand increased from 200,000 to 316,000 between 1994 and 1999, and the number of used motor vehicles imported during the same period rose from 50,000 to 120,000. These are major sources of deliberate or accidental introduction of alien species, and place New Zealand in environmental jeopardy. The situation was described as a state of siege by the Parliamentary Commissioner for the Environment in his December 2000 report on the management of biosecurity risks. This report highlighted major weaknesses in management of the risks.[10]

In the last five years of the twentieth century, new pests such as the gypsy moth, the white-spotted tussock moth, the painted apple moth, and the varroa bee mite entered the country. They all require extensive and expensive control measures.[11] History may show that the recognition of the need for biosecurity measures for New Zealand was 'too little, too late', coming as it did in the face of acceleration in the globalised capacity for contamination.

While government spent millions on measures for preventing further bio-colonisation, at other levels of society assisted species colonisation was still going on. In 1997 farmers in the South Island illegally imported and spread the RHD (rabbit haemorrhagic disease) virus. By 2000 they had not been identified or prosecuted and the law had been changed retrospectively to legalise possession of RHD virus.[12] This case is well documented, but generally it is impossible to know what other species may be being brought in deliberately and illegally.

Yet there is a final irony to the story of biosecurity in New Zealand. At the same time that the government was spending millions on keeping potentially troublesome non-native species out, it was also spending millions on creating new and potentially troublesome organisms within New Zealand. In 2000 more than one-third of the money provided for public science research in New Zealand was spent on genetic engineering projects.[13] This was despite the fact that, by 1999, scientific studies showed that genetic engineering had created and had further potential to create superweeds (plants resistant to herbicides) and superpests (resistant insects) and to damage beneficial and harmless species.[14] In addition to their existing concerns about the environmental impacts of pesticides and herbicides used as agricultural tools, genetic engineering in itself became a primary concern for New Zealand environmental advocates at the turn of the century.

Genetic engineering as currently practised represents both a particularly insidious form of colonisation (expropriation of ownership of the building blocks of life), and the late twentieth-century pinnacle of the second major force shaping the environmental history of New Zealand, namely industrialisation.

Industrialisation

New Zealand was colonised by Britain during the Industrial Revolution. In both agriculture and manufacturing, great increases in productivity, and hence in profit, were made possible by the substitution of machinery powered by fossil fuels for the human labour energy source. Also essential was a reorganisation of land and labour, with both becoming market commodities to be bought, sold, and used as efficiently as possible. This 'great transformation' is explained in detail by Karl Polanyi.[15]

This was the social, political, and economic context within which New Zealand was settled by British farm owners and workers in the nineteenth century. The history of New Zealand primary production—then and now the dominant form of economic

Figure 18.1 Inside a shearing shed, possibly in the Chatham Islands, c. 1900. W. B. Burt Collection, Alexander Turnbull Library, National Library of New Zealand, Te Puna Matauranga o Aotearoa.

production, accounting for around 60 per cent of export commodities in 2000—is one of intensified application of industrial methods.[16]

The industrialisation of New Zealand agriculture relied first on the 'Taylorisation' of labour (the division of work into repetitive, specialised tasks—epitomised by the early twentieth-century Ford car-assembly line but actually practised in New Zealand shearing sheds long before then (Figure 18.1) and on primitive coal- and water-powered machinery.[17] Then came imported machines powered by imported energy—petrol-driven tractors, harvesters, etc. After World War II the regular application of imported and synthetic fertilisers and agricultural chemicals became widespread (Chapter 11).

This agro-industrial revolution was a worldwide phenomenon and produced similar environmental and social effects wherever it occurred.[18] It could be seen, literally, in the radically changed rural landscapes of New Zealand, with their geometric patterns of monocultures, devoid of indigenous species.[19] Further evidence of treating the land like a factory without understanding its ecological capacities was the extensive erosion apparent from the early twentieth century, and the associated silting up and eutrophication of lakes and harbours (see Chapter 12).[20] Another striking feature, and one of major concern to conservationist John Salmon when he published *Heritage Destroyed* in 1960 (Figure 18.2), was the dominance of the artefacts of hydro-industrialisation—dams and power pylons (see Chapter 17).[21]

But most of the environmental damage from industrial agriculture is invisible. Extensive water pollution from concentrated animal waste, artificial fertilisers, and pesticides, for example, is a significant problem.[22] Nevertheless, intensive animal farming is

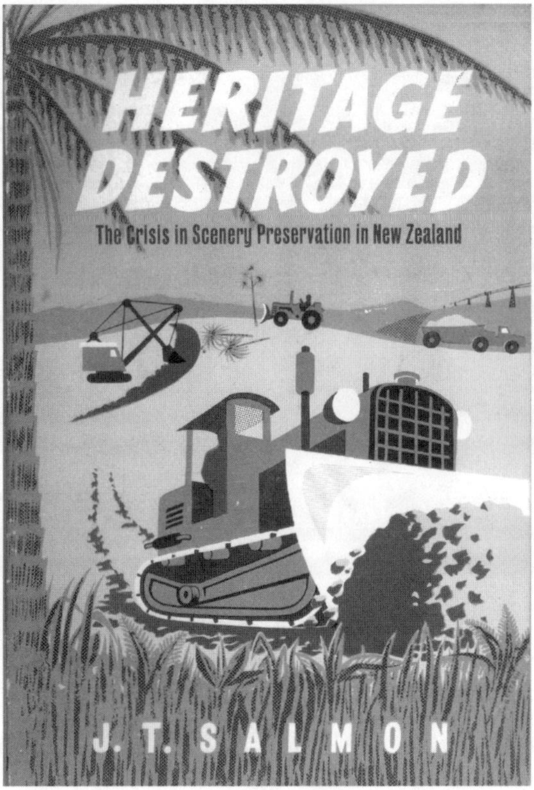

Figure 18.2 Cover of *Heritage Destroyed*, 1960, John Salmon's seminal text in the development of environmental consciousness in New Zealand.

still permitted and there are few restrictions on the application of fertilisers and pesticides. Soil remains tainted by organochlorine pesticides that were phased out in the 1960s.[23] The current generation of organophosphate pesticides are less likely to contaminate soil, but little is known about their residue levels in New Zealand soils.[24]

Another area of invisible damage from industrial farming is one where there is literally nothing left to see. Drainage and irrigation schemes, which both use and permit intensive industrial methods of farming, are responsible for the loss of around 85 per cent of New Zealand's wetlands in the past 150 years (Chapter 10). Many of those that remain are degraded by pollution and introduced species.[25]

Out of sight was out of mind as far as policy-makers in the late twentieth century were concerned. New Zealand lagged far behind Europe in calculating and redressing the environmental and economic costs of industrial agriculture. Acting on studies such as that of Pretty et al.,[26] which put the cost of the 'externalities' of industrial agriculture (loss of biodiversity, cleaning up pesticide and nitrate contaminated water, flood control, etc.) at £208 per hectare, the British government began offering farmers £450 per hectare over a five-year period to convert to organic production.[27]

Goodman, Sorj and Wilkinson, in *From Farming to Biotechnology: A Theory of Agro-industrial Development*,[28] document how agriculture moved through its mechanical and chemical industrial intensification phases from the late nineteenth to the mid twentieth century. In the late twentieth century it entered its biological industrialisation phase. The net effect of this three-pronged industrialisation of agriculture has been the compression and, in some cases, the virtual elimination of the basic stuff of farming—land to grow crops and animals plus time in which to grow them. Industrial practices such as factory farming, mechanisation, and artificial fertilisation have all speeded up the time and reduced the space it takes to produce food and fibre. The agricultural biotechnologies of the late twentieth and early twenty-first centuries remain meshed in this industrial approach, with land, plants, and animals regarded as malleable and substitutable inputs and outputs. This has reached the extreme of biofeedstocks, which are based on the mass production of one basic agricultural commodity, such as maize, which is then transformed by chemical and biological technologies not just into the basis for processed human food products, such as flour and syrup, but also into the essential ingredient for other industrial and industrially processed commodities such as glue, paint, starch, and ink.

The industrial approach to agricultural production and consumption has increased both enormously. It has also resulted in the complete commodification of nature, with disastrous consequences for human health and for the health and sustainability of other species. Genetic engineering is both the effect of industrialising agriculture and a cause of further industrialisation. It is based on a modernist scientific paradigm that is deeply implicated in the late twentieth-century environmental and human tragedies of Chernobyl and the BSE/vCJD epidemic. Modernisation is the third global historical force shaping the environmental history of New Zealand.

Modernisation

The salient features of the current phase of world-historical development known as modernity include the two already discussed—colonisation and industrialisation on a global scale. Also significant are representative democracy within nation-states, self-regulating national markets, secure national currencies, and the establishment of science and technology in place of religion as dominant ways of knowing and intervening in the world. Originating with economic and social élites, the spread of these features to mass publics has been important to the self-definition of individuals and of nations. Even where things appear to have changed—for example, with decolonisation and de-industrialisation—old patterns of economic and political dependency persist in former colonies, and the personal service work available to displaced manufacturing workers is organised into 'industries' of tourism, childcare, and so on.

The discourse of development, in both the First and Third Worlds, has been one of becoming modern. Traditional societies produce and consume small amounts locally; modern societies produce and consume large amounts on a global scale. The difference in the impact on the environment was characterised by Raymond Dasmann as the difference between ecosystem people and biosphere people. Ecosystem people know the ecological characteristics and limits of their region, and generally manage to stay within them, whereas biosphere people draw their support not from the resources of any one ecosystem but from the entire biosphere. Any large modern city is the focus of a network of transportation and communication that reaches throughout the globe—drawing perhaps beef from Argentina, lamb from New Zealand, wheat from Canada, tea from Sri Lanka, herring from the North Atlantic, and so on. Local catastrophes that would wipe out people dependent on a single ecosystem may create only minor perturbations among the biosphere people, since they can simply draw more heavily on a different ecosystem. Consequently, biosphere people can exert incredible pressure upon an ecosystem they wish to exploit—something that would be impossible or unthinkable for people who were dependent upon that particular ecosystem. The impact of biosphere people upon ecosystem people has usually been destructive. Even if the intentions of the biosphere invaders are the best, and they seldom are, their effect is to break down the local constraints, the

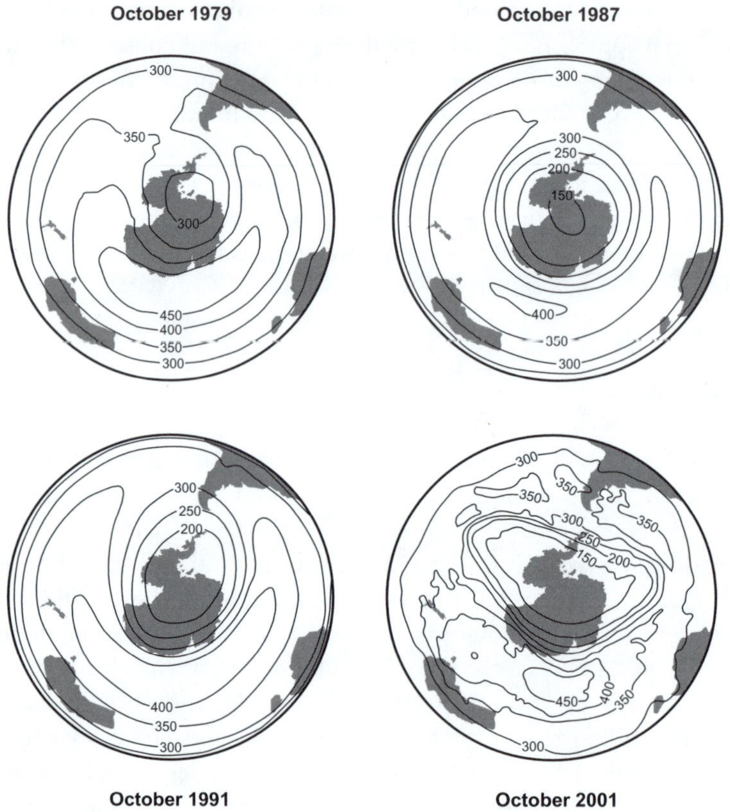

Figure 18.3 Distribution of mean monthly stratispheric ozone concentrations, centred over the Antarctic. The contours are in Dobson units. Adapted from A. Sturman and N. Tapper, *The Climates of Australia and New Zealand*, Oxford University Press, Melbourne, 1996, p. 397, and updated with data from NASA.

traditional practices that have held the delicate balance between humanity and nature, and thus allow ecosystem destruction to take place.[29]

By 2000 the economic and industrial activities of biosphere people had led to a marked thinning of the ozone layer over Antarctica (Figure 18.3), despite progress being made on the banning of ozone-destroying CFCs under the 1987 Montreal Protocol.[30] It clearly takes a long time to repair the global atmosphere. Yet at the end of 2000 the sixth international conference of the parties to the UN Kyoto protocol on climate change in The Hague could not agree on how best to begin reducing global carbon emissions. New Zealand was part of the 'Umbrella Group', headed by the USA, at that conference. With other members of the group, New Zealand was given a 'Fossil of the Day' award by environmental NGOs for supporting the move to remove references to existing environment agreements (such as the Conventions on Biodiversity, Wetlands, Forests, and Agenda 21) from eligibility rules for land use, landuse change, and forestry.[31]

New Zealanders operate nationally and internationally as biosphere people, acting out the modernist definition of 'development' as a form of limitless production and consumption without rational consideration of genuine physical limits to such behaviour or moral concerns about its negative social and environmental impacts. This definition of development, as well as its environmental impacts, has been heavily critiqued by First and by Third World authors.[32] John McNeill argues that the rate of environmental change in the twentieth century was unique and unprecedented, both in scale and intensity. The motor-force for change was economic growth. The world economy at the end of the twentieth century was fourteen times larger than it was at the beginning,[33] and this growth was powered by cheap, non-renewable energy sources. The carbon and other emissions from these sources led to the climate effects that the international community was struggling to address and reverse via the climate-change protocol.

Regardless of the ostensible economic creed of a twentieth-century state—capitalism, communism, nationalism—'economic growth became the indispensable ideology of the state almost everywhere'.[34] This belief in and pursuit of endless economic growth could only be based on a 'science' of economics that was reduced to abstract rationalist calculations that denied the reality and relevance of the natural world. In this reductionist 'science', behaviour was atomised and simplified, and real-life observation was considered of less interest and importance than thought experiments. The 'science' was based on the fundamental, albeit disputable, assumptions that maximising profit for the individual and economic growth for the state and should be the means and ends of life, and will also maximise individual and social functionality and utility.

The parallels with contemporary biological science are striking and not accidental.[35] Genetic engineering is based on similarly simplistic and amoral assumptions and approaches. It has been analysed and criticised on both grounds by biological scientists who are also environmentalists.[36] Peter Wills' submission to the Royal Commission of Inquiry into Genetic Modification provides a reality check when he considers the socio-political and economic context within which genetic engineering currently takes place. He concludes his summary:

> The ambition of the biotechnological governmental-industrial-academic complex to bring the processes of genetic change under global human control is driven and supported by the misrepresentation of scientists themselves as a morally neutral egalitarian community of scholars who work for the common good. Scant consideration has been given by the broader scientific community to the overall effects of the enterprise of genetic engineering and its capability of transforming biological reality beyond historical recognition.[37]

It is small wonder, then, that the eco-political resistance to the environmental impacts of colonisation, industrialisation, and modernisation has moved on from the nature preservation and conservation lobbying approaches dominant in New Zealand and elsewhere from the late nineteenth to the late twentieth centuries.[38] Radical action to protect the environment is now based on a critique of the physical and economic 'scientific' premises that have led to environmental destruction and degradation on a local and global scale.

Alternative pathways

At the end of the twentieth century new forms of resistance to industrial modernisation on a global scale appeared. The two that seem to me to have most relevance to whether the future is ecologically sustainable or not are the two that directly address the causes of unsustainability: industrialised primary production, and the economic growth fetish.

The move away from industrial agriculture based on the reductionist and amoral modernist scientific paradigm is a move towards environmentally sustainable primary production based on a holistic and ethical 'postmodern' scientific paradigm. The first steps on this road were taken in 1941 with the foundation of the Compost Society (now known as the Soil and Health Association).[39] For around forty years 'organic' gardening and farming remained the province of a minority of committed amateurs, doing it for love not a living (Chapter 11). There was little interest in it from the state, the scientific community, or business. In the 1980s that situation began to change. Alternatives to the environmental damage done by industrial agriculture were sought, and a movement of consumers seeking safe, healthy food produced by ethical and sustainable means began to grow in size and influence, and to create a market for organically produced food. By the end of the century this was the fastest-growing food market in New Zealand and worldwide.[40] Even global food processors were seeking to capitalise on the 'clean, green' image of New Zealand and its products.[41]

The state continued to direct most of its scientific research funding towards old-paradigm agricultural research: $130–135 million went to genetic engineering, versus $2.6 million for organics, in 2000.[42] However, the first organic farmer MP was elected to the New Zealand Parliament with six other Greens in 1999. The Greens were then able to institute the first select committee inquiry into organics, and obtain some budget funding for increased state support for them. A Sustainable Farming Fund of $5 million set up by the Minister of Agriculture in 2000 received 350 applications chasing five times the amount offered.[43] Thirty-seven per cent of New Zealand farmers surveyed in 2000 expressed an interest in going organic.[44]

The jury is still out on whether this seemingly dramatic re-orientation from industrial to sustainable primary production is more apparent than real, and whether and how quickly ambitious conversion targets can be met. The biotechnology industry has billions of dollars invested in genetic engineering and related research, development, marketing, and sales—and in lobbying and other public relations work to maintain its market position.[45] But consumers traumatised by contaminated food scares and associated deaths and injuries have become suspicious of industrially produced food, and have collapsed the market for genetically engineered food while boosting that for organic food.[46]

Consumer choice expressed via markets became the 'democracy of default' in the late twentieth century for citizens concerned about the environmental behaviour of their nation-states and big business. A major achievement of twentieth-century modernity was the social democratic form of the state, in which citizens supported the role of government in regulating, and in some cases managing (via state-owned industries and companies), economic production and consumption. This was in addition to the role of the state in ensuring fair distribution of the fruits of economic activity.

The major environmental conflicts in New Zealand in the twentieth century focused on how the state managed its economic resources, where these were also natural resources such as indigenous forests (potential timber) and rivers (potential hydroelectric power). By the end of the twentieth century, the economic nationalists of classic social democracy had mutated into the economic rationalist defenders and promoters of global economic growth and 'development'.[47]

National economic management was left to 'the market', which operated within a relatively low set of consumer and financial regulatory standards and guidelines determined or set by default by non-democratic international institutions such as the World Trade Organisation.[48] Citizen participation was possible via submissions to regulatory agencies such as the Environmental Risk Management Authority (ERMA) and the Australia New Zealand Food Authority (ANZFA), but as both authorities allow(ed) active industry participation, after their first three years of operation neither authority had proven responsive to citizen submissions overwhelmingly in favour of stopping genetic engineering experiments and fully labelling all foods containing engineered ingredients or produced by engineering processes.

ERMA and ANZFA are local examples of the trend towards global regulatory bodies that base their decisions on old-paradigm scientific advice and privilege economic considerations over environmental and ethical concerns.[49] They were at the service of a new phase in the pursuit of economic growth—export-led growth. With a small domestic market, this growth path was particularly appealing to New Zealand, although it has thus far been singularly unsuccessful.[50] By 1999, however, environmentalists worldwide had made the connections between increasing trade on a global scale and damage to local and global environments, particularly that which export-led agro-industrialisation was doing to humans and other species in the Third World.[51]

Hence the World Trade Organisation's attempt to begin a Millennium Round of global trade talks in Seattle at the end of 1999 was stymied by an eruption of street protest on a scale not seen in the USA for almost thirty years. This time environmentalists from the First and Third Worlds joined with labour and farmer activists and Greens of all hues in actions aimed at understanding and preventing the seemingly inexorable trend towards expanding production, consumption and trade on a global scale, regardless of negative social and environmental impacts. According to the protestors, this trend is exacerbating, not relieving, human poverty and misery worldwide, while destroying non-human species and complex ecosystems at an unprecedented rate.[52]

Some New Zealand environmentalists had already reached this conclusion. It was most forcefully expressed by the Green Party as part of its economic policy for the 1999 election, *Thinking Beyond Tomorrow*.[53] This critique of and opposition to the expansion of unfettered global trade, which is in essence an opposition to economic growth at any cost, is the second significant environmental resistance movement to come out of the late twentieth century.

Unlike the dominant conservation and environmental lobby and pressure groups of that century, this movement aims to contest the assumptions of colonisation, industrialisation and modernisation directly, and to develop alternatives of local, fair, and environmentally sustainable economic activity. It also differs from its predecessors in that it focuses as much on causes as effects, and hence on prevention as much as or more than amelioration. Another major difference is that this environmental resistance movement is moving beyond the colonialist and modernist assumptions inherent in the twentieth-century emphasis on 'wilderness' preservation and 'scientific' resource management, and has a greater respect for traditional and indigenous knowledge. It also has more interest in reconciling the needs of human beings to make a decent living with the needs of other species to exist in their own right, via informed and ethical coexistence, rather than strict separation of species and activities into 'natural' and 'non-natural' zones and categories. This shift in thinking between twentieth- and twenty-first-century environmentalism is well expressed in 'Resisting Green Globalism'.[54]

The new resistance is surely a sign of new times, yet whether it will be any more successful at making New Zealand truly the 'clean, green' paradise that marketing hype makes it out to be remains to be seen. Paradoxically, certain unsustainable features of New Zealand's current phase of economic development may have more influence on environmental outcomes than green attempts to convert governments and corporations to new-paradigm science and technology, let alone ecological ethics.

The preferences of consumers across the world for 'clean, green' foods and fibres, which, ironically, are delivered to them by means that are neither clean nor green, has already been raised. Similarly, when the dark age of cheap fossil fuels ends somewhere in the mid twenty-first century, it will take unsustainable long-distance mass tourism with it. But meanwhile those tourists who come to New Zealand to have a 'natural' experience are interested in seeing for themselves how the 'clean, green' products are produced. New Zealand's first-ever Wine and Food Tourism Conference was held in November 2000, and, as this movement grows, it has potential to act as a counterweight to corporate, industrialised production.[55] Mindless consumerism is a major part of the problem—but moves towards mindful consumption of essential goods produced sustainably and ethically may well be part of the solution.[56]

The problems New Zealand faces in reaching environmental sustainability within the context of the relentless global drive for more economic growth were highlighted in

November 2000 when the international climate-change talks collapsed. Major exporting, mining, and manufacturing states such as Japan, the USA, and Australia were not prepared to consider direct ways of reducing fossil-fuel emissions, fearing to jeopardise their economic growth and expanding trade opportunities. New Zealand identified with this group of nations, not with its Pacific Island neighbours, although these are likely to be among the first victims of climate change, with rising sea levels and an increase in extreme climate events such as hurricanes.

In the 1980s, when nuclear war seemed the most pressing global environmental problem, research was done into the environmental, economic, and social effects that a 'nuclear winter' caused by a northern hemisphere nuclear war would have on New Zealand and Australia.[57] New Zealand enhanced its clean, green image—or reality—by creating a nuclear-free zone. This may well have helped reduce the nuclear-winter possibility. By 2000 a 'carbon summer' was a very real and increasing threat, yet New Zealand was not taking similarly bold steps, nationally or internationally, to counter the threat and to give a lead to other small states. It had gone from being a country that refused to shelter under the American nuclear umbrella to one that, fifteen years later, was huddling under the American carbon umbrella.

Glossary

MĀORI NAMES AND TERMS

Ahi kā literally 'keeping the fires burning on the land'; a Māori system of claiming rights to land through regular reoccupation.

Arohatanga 'aroha' means love or compassion, and 'arohatanga' suggests relationships based upon love and empathy.

Hapū group of extended families or clan.

Harakeke or New Zealand flax (*Phormium tenax*).

Hine-ahu-one first woman created out of the earth.

Iwi tribe.

Kahikatea (*Dacrycarpus dacrydioides*) tall, soft-wooded native tree of the podocarp family that dominated the wetlands but was heavily milled to make butter boxes, among other things.

Kāinga village, often of a single hapū.

Karaka (*Corynocarpus laevigatus*) native tree with broad green leaves and edible fruit.

Karakia prayer or incantation.

Kawanatanga governance.

Kauri (*Agathis australis*) a native conifer tree, among the largest in the world, that produces excellent timber suitable for both house and boat building and resin that can be used in industrial processes such as varnish manufacture.

Kererū (*Hemiphaga novaeseelandiae*) native pigeon.

Kingitanga Māori King Movement.

Kōwhai (*Sophora* spp.) native tree famous for its yellow flower.

Kūmara (*Ipomoea batatas*) sweet potato brought to New Zealand from Polynesia.

Māhoe (*Melicytus ramiflorus*) small native tree.

Mahinga kai traditional resource-gathering area.

Mana prestige and status reflected in genealogy, attachment to place and achievement.

Manākitanga generosity, care-giving, or compassion.

Mana whenua right of an iwi, hapū, or whānau to claim land through genealogy, occupation and use, or conquest.

Mangā (**makā** in the southern dialect) barracouta (*Thyrsites atun*).

Mānuka (*Leptospermum scoparium*) shrub with small leaves and usually white flowers though coloured forms are widely cultivated.

Māpou or **matipou** (*Myrsine australis*) small native tree sometimes cultivated for its reddish stems and foliage.

Mataī (black pine) (*Prumnopitys taxifolia*) a native tree of the podocarp family.

Matuku (*Botaurus stellaris or Botaurus poiciloptilus*) bittern, a swamp bird.

Mauri life force or vital essence of an individual, species, or place.

Miro (*Prumnopitys ferruginea*) a native tree of the podocarp family.

Moa (*Dinornithiformes* spp.) extinct native ratites (flightless birds) ranging from small to even larger than modern-day ostrich and emu.

Moriori separate tribe of Māori who lived on the Chatham Islands from the fifteenth century rather than an earlier non-Polynesian stratum of people in New Zealand as imagined by the early twentieth century ethnographers Percy Smith and Elsdon Best.

Muriwhenua northern area of North Auckland with which the Te Rārawa, Te Aupōuri, Ngāti Kahu, Ngāti Kuri, and Ngāti Takoto iwi are associated.

Ngāti Toa iwi from the Kawhia area who migrated south to Kapiti Island and Otaki in the 1820s under the leadership of the chief Te Rauparaha. They also ventured into the top of the South Island in the early 1830s and clashed with the major South Island tribe of Ngāi Tahu.

Nīkau (*Rhopalostylis sapida*) New Zealand palm tree.

Paepae horizontal beam on the marae from which speeches are made.

Pai mārire 'good and peaceful religion' founded in the early 1860s by Te Ua Haumene in Taranaki and revived by Princess Te Puea of Tainui and the Kingitanga in the 1920s.

Papatūānuku Earth Mother

Pāua (*Haliotis* spp.) black-lipped, iridescent-green, univalve shellfish.

Rāhui prohibition on harvesting of food supplies, normally enforced in the interests of resource management and conservation.

Rangatiratanga full, chiefly authority.

Ranginui Sky Father.

Rimu (red pine) (*Dacrydium cupressinum*) native podocarp tree that produces top-quality timber ideally suited to furniture making.

Rohe territorial area claimed by an iwi, hapū, or whānau, including all resource rights.

Rūaumoko god of earthquakes and volcanoes.

Tāne mahuta god of the forest.

Tangaroa god of the sea.

Tangata whenua people of the land; i.e. all Māori rather than the iwi or hapū occupying a rohe, who are known as 'manwhenua'.

Taniwha water monster; often a guardian.

Tapu under restriction (sacred). Once a food resource such as an eel weir or a tree housing nesting birds was declared tapu it could not be touched other than by specially designated persons. More commonly declared under a rāhui.

Taro (*Colocasia* spp.) edible root plant brought from Polynesia and grown in the northern parts of the North Island.

Tawa (*Beilschmiedia tawa*) native tree.

Tāwhirimatea god of wind and atmospheric events.

Te Ao the world of light.

Te Hiku o Te Ika the tail of the fish of Māui; North Auckland.

Te Ika a Māui the fish of the demi-god Māui; North Island.

Te Pō primeval darkness before creation.

Tī (*Cordyline australis*) native cabbage tree. An imported variant (*Cordyline terminalis*) was cultivated along with *Cordyline australis*.

Toatoa (*Phyllocladus glaucus*) native tree.

Toetoe (*Cortaderia* spp.) robust New Zealand tussock grass, closely related to the pampas grasses of South America.

Tōtara (*Podocarpus totara and P. hallii*) tall native podocarp trees having resistant wood, prized for carving, and once used for fence posts.

Tuatara (*Sphenodon punctatus*) ancient and long-lived native lizard.

Tūī (*Prosthemadera novaeseelandiae*) native bird.

Tūpuna or **tīpuna** ancestors.

Utu redressing an imbalance in relationships to maintain harmony, rather than simple 'revenge' as claimed by some Pākehā.

Waitaha early South Island tribe.

Weka (*Gallirallus* spp.) small flightless native bird.

Whakapapa genealogy.

Whānau extended family.

Whanaungatanga the primacy of kinship bonds in determining action and in settling rights and status.

SCIENTIFIC NAMES AND TECHNICAL TERMS

2, 4, 5-T powerful organochloride herbicide banned from use in New Zealand in 1989 because it produces dioxins that are dangerous to both animal and human life.

Acanthisittidae wren (most species extinct).

***Aciphylla* spp.** speargrass.

Agrostologist grasslands scientist interested in pastoral farming, as opposed to an agronomist, who concentrates more on agricultural farming and cropping.

Allelopathy capacity of some plants to produce chemicals harmful to other plants.

***Anguilla* spp.** eels.

Anthropogenic induced by human agency.

***Apteryx* spp.** kiwi.

***Aptornis* spp.** large, poor flying goose, now extinct.

Arctocephalus forsteri fur seal.

Aristotelia serrata wineberry.

Avifauna birdlife.

Beilschmiedia tawa tawa tree.

Biodynamic method of growing foods that minimises the use of artificial fertilisers and chemicals.

Biomass the sum of organic mass per unit area represented in one or a group of species.

Broussonetia papyrifera paper mulberry.

Bulbinella hookeri Māori onion.

Bush Australian term referring to scrubby savannah lands remote from settlement, also applied to New Zealand's heavy rainforest from the early nineteenth century.

Capellirallus karamu snipe-rail (extinct).

Celmisia spectabilis tikumu, or mountain daisy.

Chionochloa genus of mainly stout grasses, mostly tussock-forming, and the common dominants of New Zealand upland and alpine grasslands.

Chionochloa rubra red tussock.

Cirsium, Onopordum and ***Sonchus*** varieties of thistles. *Sonchus* is a genus of soft plants with the common name sow thistle, distinct from the prickly genera of real thistles.

***Cnemiornis* spp.** goose (extinct).

***Coenocorypha* spp.** New Zealand snipe.

Commensal animal living in, or on, another but not at the expense of the other, hence different from a parasite.

Cookia sulcata Cook's turban shell.

***Cordyline* spp.** cabbage tree.

Coriaria arborea tutu.

Corynocarpus laevigatus karaka tree.

Coturnix novaeseelandiae New Zealand quail, now extinct.

Cupressus macrocarpa macrocarpa tree, or Monterey cypress; originally from California, widely cultivated in New Zealand.

Cytisus scoparius broom.

DDT (Dichloro-diphenyl-trichloroethane) long-lived organochlorine insecticide much used during and after World War II, restricted use from 1970 and finally banned from any use in New Zealand in 1989.

Desiccation increasing dryness of climate.

Dichelachne crinita plume grass.

Dichlorophenoxyacetic acid common herbicide also known as 2, 4-D, finally banned in 1997.

Dinornithiformes australis species of moa, now extinct.

***Dioscorea* spp.** yam.

Discaria toumatou tumatakuru, or matagouri; a prickly high-country shrub inedible to soft-mouthed herbivores but relished by native insects.

DSIR Department of Scientific and Industrial Research; established 1926, disestablished in 1992.

Ecosystem a functioning complex of living organisms and their environment.

***Elymus* spp.** Blue wheat grasses.

Evolutionary fitness a measure of the relative breeding success of a lineage.

Festuca novae-zelandiae New Zealand fescue grass, hard tussock.

Gingidia montana New Zealand anise.

Harpagornis moorei Haast's eagle (extinct).

Hieracium (especially ***H. pilosella***) hawkweeds; a genus of low-growing weedy daisies that has infested much of the South Island high country, especially in the Mackenzie Basin, Central Otago and inland Marlborough.

Hierochloe redolens holy grass, so named for its scent.

Holocene the most recent geological period, from 10,000 years ago to the present,

Kunzea ericoides (previously ***Leptospermum ericoides***) kānuka; second-growth shrubby native tree similar to mānuka.

Lagenaria siceraria bottle gourd.

Libocedrus doniana (now ***L. plumosa***) kawaka, or New Zealand cypress tree.

Lignite low-quality brown coal common in many parts of New Zealand.

Lolium perenne perennial ryegrass.

Megafauna animals that were conspicuously large within their class, such as moas among flightless birds.

Miasma pre-Pasteur (germ theory) notion that disease was spread by bad odours/vapours/effluvias from swamps, sewers, etc. rather than spread by germs (viruses and bacteria).

Nestor meridionalis kaka, a native green parrot.

***Nothofagus* spp.** southern beech; *N. menziesii* silver beech; *N. fusca* red beech; *N. truncata* hard beech; *N. solandri* var. *solandri* black beech; *N. solandri* var. *cliffortioides* mountain beech.

Palaeontology the study of fossil remains of plants and animals.

Palynology the study of pollen grains, especially those surviving in sediments, from the analysis of which former patterns of vegetation can be deduced.

***Pandanus* spp.** Tropical plants, often small trees, with fibrous leaves used for weaving and cordage.

Pelecanoides urinatrix diving petrel.

Phocarctos hookeri sea lion.

Pinus radiata radiata or Monterey pine, now the basis of New Zealand's artificial and commercial forests.

Pleistocene the last episode of Ice Ages, which occurred in the approximate period 10,000 to 1,000,000 or more years ago.

Poa cita silver tussock.

Poa colensoi blue tussock.

Podocarp member of the Podocarpaceae, a mainly southern hemisphere family of conifers.

Polyprion oxygeneios hāpuku, a native fish.

Portmanteau biota the suite of plants and animals carried from one island to another by human colonists.

Pteridium esculentum aruhe, or bracken fern.

Puffinus spealus petrel.

Radiocarbon dating a technique that estimates the time elapsed since the death of a plant or animal by measuring the level of decay in the unstable radioactive carbon isotope ^{14}C, relative to its stable isotopic forms, in surviving organic remains such as charcoal or bone.

Raoulia australis scabweed.

Rattus exulans kiore, or Pacific rat.

Revetment rock facing to protect a stopbank or river bank from erosion.

Riparian rights rights pertaining to land on either side of a body of water.

Rumex acetosella sheep's sorrel.

Sechium edule choko, the fruit of a rampant vine, eaten as a vegetable in Australasia. Common in northern parts of New Zealand.

Sirex noctilio wood wasp that threatened *Pinus radiata* plantations from the 1940s and was subsequently subjected to biological control.

Stope a step-like excavation in mining.

Trifolium repens white clover.

Trifolium subterraneum subterranean clover.

Ulex europaeus gorse.

Notes

1 Introduction

1 Paul Star, 'New Zealand's Changing Natural History. Evidence from Dunedin, 1868-1875', *New Zealand Journal of History*, vol. 32, no. 1, 1998, pp. 59–69; Kenneth B. Cumberland, 'A Century's Change: Natural to Cultural Vegetation in New Zealand', *Geographical Review*, vol. 31, no. 4, 1941, pp. 529–54.

2 Tim Flannery, *The Future Eaters: An Ecological History of the Australasian Lands and People*, Reed Books Australia, Chatswood, NSW, 1994, p. 55, quoted in Star, 'New Zealand's Changing Natural History'. The 'large land, uplifted high', is from the journal of Abel Janszoon Tasman, commander of the first known European voyage to sight New Zealand's shores. It refers to the mountains of the northwest of the South Island: M. F. Vigeveno (trans), 'Tasman's Journal or Description', in *Abel Janszoon Tasman and the Discovery of New Zealand*, Department of Internal Affairs, Wellington, 1942, p. 45.

3 Peter Holland, 'Cultural Landscapes as Biogeographical Experiments: a New Zealand Perspective', *Journal of Biogeography*, vol. 27, no. 2000, pp. 39–43; Eric Pawson & Peter Holland, 'The New Zealand Environmental Experiment', *Proceedings of the Joint Conference of the New Zealand Geographical Society and the Institute of Australian Geographers, Dunedin, 2001*, New Zealand Geographical Society, Hamilton, pp. 96–100.

4 J. M. Powell, 'Historical Geography and Environmental History: An Australian Interface', *Journal of Historical Geography*, vol. 22. no. 3, 1996, p. 293; 'Historical Geographies of the Environment', in Brian Graham & Catherine Nash (eds), *Modern Historical Geographies*, Pearson Education, Harlow, 2000, pp. 186–7; Eric Pawson, 'Senses of Place', in Richard Le Heron & Eric Pawson (eds), *Changing Places: New Zealand in the Nineties*, Longman Paul, Auckland, pp. 345–84.

5 William Main, *Bragge's Wellington and the Wairarapa: Images of a City and its Provinces from the 1860s to the 1890s as Recorded by Photographer James Bragge 1833–1908*, Millwood Press, Wellington, 1974; 'James Bragge, 1833?–1908, Photographer', *Dictionary of New Zealand Biography*, vol. 2, Bridget Williams Books/Department of Internal Affairs, Wellington, 1993, pp. 54–5. In the 1870s Wellington interests were working hard to extend the city's hinterland: David Hamer, 'Wellington on the Urban Frontier', in David Hamer & Roberta Nicholls (eds), *The Making of Wellington, 1800–1914*, Victoria University Press, Wellington, 1990, pp. 227–54.

6 James R. Ryan, *Picturing Empire: Photography and the Visualization of the British Empire*, The University of Chicago Press, Chicago, 1997; 'Photos and Frames: Towards an Historical Geography of Photography', *Journal of Historical Geography*, vol. 26, no. 1, 2000, pp. 119–24; J. M. Schwartz, 'The Geography Lesson: Photographs and the Construction of Imaginative Geographies', *Journal of Historical Geography*, vol. 22, no. 1, 1996, pp. 16–45; J. B. Harley, 'Maps, Knowledge and Power', in D. Cosgrove & S. Daniels (eds),

The Iconography of Landscape. Essays on the Symbolic Representation, Design, and Use of Past Environments, Cambridge University Press, Cambridge, 1988, pp. 277–312.

7 Quoted in I. R. Matheson (ed.), 'The Birth of Palmerston North', supplement to the *Evening Standard*, 13 March 1871, p. 53.

8 H. Morphy & K. Flint, 'Introduction', in Kate Flint & Howard Morphy (eds), *Culture, Landscape and the Environment. The Linacre Lectures 1997*, Oxford University Press, Oxford, p. 1.

9 P. Slack, 'Introduction', in P. Slack (ed.), *Environments and Historical Change. The Linacre Lectures 1998*, Oxford University Press, Oxford, 1999, pp. 1–9.

10 Eric Pawson & Tom Brooking, 'Landscape Change and Environmental Histories', *New Zealand Geographer*, vol. 56, no. 2, 2000, pp. 52–6; for a political ecology perspective, see Erik Swyngedouw, 'Modernity and Hybridity: Nature, Regeneracionismo, and the Production of the Spanish Waterscape, 1890–1930', *Annals of the Association of American Geographers*, vol. 89, no. 3, 1999, pp. 443–65.

11 Edward Gibbon Wakefield, *View of the Art of Colonization with Present Reference to the British Empire: in Letters Between a Statesman and a Colonist*, Parker, London, 1849, p. 118.

12 Sewell quoted in Eric Pawson, 'Confronting Nature', in John Cookson & Graeme Dunstall (eds), *Southern Capital: Christchurch, Towards a City Biography, 1850–2000*, Canterbury University Press, Christchurch, 2000, p. 63.

13 Karl Marx, *Capital. A Critique of Political Economy*, vol. 1, with an introduction by Ernest Mandel, Penguin, London, 1990, pp. 931–42.

14 Cumberland, 'A Century's Change', p. 529.

15 Kenneth B. Cumberland, *Soil Erosion in New Zealand: A Geographic Reconnaissance*, Soil Conservation and Rivers Control Council, Wellington, 1944; L. W. McCaskill, *Hold This Land: A History of Soil Conservation in New Zealand*, A. H. & A. W. Reed, Wellington, 1973.

16 Graeme Wynn, 'Conservation and Society in Late Nineteenth-century New Zealand', *New Zealand Journal of History*, vol. 11, no. 3, 1977, pp. 124–36; 'Pioneers, Politicians and the Conservation of Forests in Early New Zealand', *Journal of Historical Geography*, vol. 5, no. 2, 1979, pp. 171–88; M. M. Roche, *Forest Policy in New Zealand: An Historical Geography 1840–1919*, The Dunmore Press, Palmerston North, 1987; *Land and Water. Water and Soil Conservation and Central Government in New Zealand, 1941–1988*, Historical Branch, Department of Internal Affairs, Wellington, 1994.

17 A. H. Clark, *The Invasion of New Zealand by People, Plants and Animals: The South Island*, Rutgers University Press, New Brunswick, 1949, p. v.

18 H. Guthrie-Smith, *Tutira: The Story of a New Zealand Sheep Station*, Random House, Auckland/University of Washington Press, Seattle, 1999 (first published 1921). Foreword by William Cronon, p. xi; Richard White, pers. comm.

19 Alan Grey, *Aotearoa and New Zealand: A Historical Geography*, Canterbury University Press, Christchurch, 1994; Thomas Dunlap, *Nature and the English Diaspora: Environment and History in the United States, Canada, Australia and New Zealand*, Cambridge University Press, New York, 1999; S. Pyne, *Vestal Fire: An Environmental History, Told through Fire, of Europe and Europe's Encounter with the World*, University of Washington Press, Seattle, 1997; A. W. Crosby, *Ecological Imperialism: The Biological Expansion of Europe, 900–1900*, Cambridge University Press, Cambridge, 1986.

20 Star, 'New Zealand's Changing Natural History', p. 60.

21 Rollo Arnold, *New Zealand's Burning: The Settlers' World in the Mid-1880s*, Victoria University Press, Wellington, 1994; Geoff Park, *The Groves of Life: Ngā Uruora: Ecology and History in a New Zealand Landscape*, Victoria University Press, Wellington, 1995; Giselle Byrnes, 'Surveying Space: Constructing the Colonial Landscape', in Bronwyn Dalley & Bronwyn Labrum (eds), *Fragments: New Zealand Social and Cultural History*, Auckland University Press, Auckland, 2000, pp. 54–70.

22 Keith Sinclair, *A History of New Zealand*, rev. edn, Penguin Books, Auckland, 2000; W. H. Oliver (ed.), *The Oxford History of New Zealand*, The Clarendon Press, Oxford, Oxford University Press, Wellington, 1981; G. W. Rice (ed.), *The Oxford History of New Zealand*, 2nd edn, Oxford University Press, Auckland, 1992; James Belich, *Making Peoples: A History of The New Zealanders from Polynesian Settlement to the End of the Nineteenth Century*, Penguin Books, Auckland, 1996.

23 It is symptomatic of this lack of understanding of environmental history that our first article on the subject was promoted on the cover of the journal that commissioned it as 'A Green History of New Zealand', when it is nothing of the sort: Tom Brooking & Eric Pawson, 'Writing New Zealand's Environmental Histories', *History Now*, vol. 5, no. 2, 1999, pp. 28–32.

24 W. Cronon, 'A Place for Stories: Nature, History and Narratives', *Journal of American History*, vol. 78, no. 4, 1992, pp. 1349–76; Pawson & Brooking, 'Landscape Change and Environmental Histories'.

25 Giselle Byrnes, 'Surveying Space'; Julie King, 'Facing up to Fox: The Colonial Watercolours of William Fox', *Art New Zealand*, no. 95, 2000, pp. 84–87; also Mary Louise Pratt, *Imperial Eyes. Travel Writing and Transculturation*, Routledge, London, 1992.

26 William Cronon, 'Introduction: in Search of Nature', in William Cronon (ed.), *Uncommon Ground: Toward Reinventing Nature*, W. W. Norton & Co., New York, 1995, p. 25.

27 Cronon, 'Introduction', p. 24.

28 Rodney Grapes, *Magnitude Eight Plus: New Zealand's Biggest Earthquake*, Victoria University Press, Wellington, 2000.

29 Arnold, *New Zealand's Burning: Settler Kaponga 1881–1914: A Fragment of the Western World*, Victoria University Press, Wellington, 1997.

30 Michael Roche, '"The Land We Have We Must Hold": Soil Erosion and Soil Conservation in Late Nineteenth- and Twentieth-Century New Zealand', *Journal of Historical Geography*, vol. 23, no. 4, 1997, pp. 447–58.

31 Stephen Dovers, 'Still Settling Australia: Environment, History, and Policy', in Stephen Dovers (ed.), *Environmental History and Policy: Still Settling Australia*, Oxford University Press, South Melbourne, 2000, pp. 2–23.

32 Paul Shepherd's early monograph deserves mention in respect of environmental ideas: *English Reaction to the New Zealand Landscape before 1850*, Pacific Viewpoint Monograph no. 4, Department of Geography, Victoria University of Wellington, 1969.

33 D. W. Meinig, *On the Margins of the Good Earth: The South Australian Wheat Frontier, 1869–1884*, Rand McNally, Chicago, 1962.

34 Erica Schoenberger, 'Interdisciplinarity and Social Power', *Progress in Human Geography*, vol. 25, no. 3, 2001, pp. 365–82; Donald Worster, 'Transformations of the Earth: Towards an Agroecological Perspective in History', *Journal of American History*, vol. 76, no. 3, 1990, p. 1095.

35 Stephen Dovers, 'Commonalities and Contrasts, Pasts and Presents: an Australian View', in Stephen Dovers, Ruth Edgecombe, & Bill Guest (eds), *Perspectives on South African Environmental History*, David Philip Publishing, Cape Town, in press.

36 Peter Holland, 'Plants and Lowland South Canterbury Landscapes', *New Zealand Geographer*, vol. 44, no. 2, 1988, pp. 50–60; P. G. Holland & R. P. Hargreaves, 'The Trivial Round, the Common Task: Work and Leisure on a Canterbury Hill-Country Run in the 1860s and 1870s', *New Zealand Geographer*, vol. 47, no. 1, 1991, pp. 19–25; Michele Dominy, *Calling the Station Home: Place and Identity in New Zealand's High Country*, Rowman & Littlefield Publishers, Lanham, 2001; Karen Beker, Encountering Te Waimatamate: An Historical Investigation of Engagement with a Local Landscape, MA thesis, Massey University, 2000; Graeme Wynn, 'Remapping Tutira: Contours in the Environmental History of New Zealand', *Journal of Historical Geography*, vol. 23, no. 4, 1997, pp. 418–46.

37 Dovers, 'Commonalities and Contrasts'.

38 *New Zealand Herald*, 25, 26 January 1935. See also A. H. Reed, *The Kauri*, A. H. & A. W. Reed, Wellington, 1953, pp. 36–7; and *Trounson Park*, Department of Lands and Survey, Wellington, 1971.

39 New Zealand National Film Library, *16 mm Film Catalogue 1978*, Government Printer, Wellington. See, for example, *Ruin by Rabbits*, 1949 (catching up on rabbit 'extermination' after World War II in Hawke's Bay); *Grass-New Zealand*, 1950 (its importance to the economy, and pasture management and conservation); *To Save a Valley*, 1957 (catchment-board work to contain flooding in the Waipoa Valley, Gisborne); *Giving Wings to Conservation*, 1957 (hill-country conservation practices, including aerial topdressing).

2 A fragile plenty: pre-European Māori and the New Zealand environment

1 Richard Taylor had visited Te Rangatapu in 1843 and was similarly equivocal about whether the moa bones represented hunted birds: A. J. Anderson, *Prodigious Birds: Moas and Moa-hunting in Prehistoric New Zealand*, Cambridge University Press, Cambridge, 1989, p. 99. Except in relation to Figure 2.1, all dates mentioned in this chapter are calendrical ages.

2 J. T. Holloway, 'Forest and Climates in the South Island of New Zealand', *Transactions of the Royal Society of New Zealand*, vol. 82, no. 2, 1954, pp. 329–410; K. B. Cumberland, 'Man's Role in Modifying Island Environments in the Southwest Pacific, with Special Reference to New Zealand', in F. R. Fosberg (ed.), *Man's Place in the Island Ecosystem: A Symposium*, Bishop Museum Press, Honolulu, 1963, pp. 187–206, quote p. 193. The role of climatic change remains debated, e.g. P. J. Grant, 'Effects on New Zealand Vegetation of Late Holocene Erosion and Alluvial Sedimentation', *New Zealand Journal of Ecology*, vol. 12 (supplement), 1989, pp. 131–44; and opposing views in M. S. McGlone, 'The Polynesian Settlement of New Zealand in Relation to Environmental and Biotic Changes', *New Zealand Journal of Ecology*, vol. 12 (supplement), 1989, pp. 115–29; J. M. Wilmshurst, 'The Impact of Human Settlement on Vegetation and Soil Stability in Hawke's Bay, New Zealand', *New Zealand Journal of Botany*, vol. 35, no. 1, 1997, pp. 97–111. The supposed pre-Māori population was often called 'Maruiwi' or 'Moriori', the latter term being, in fact, the correct name for the original population of the Chatham Islands.

3 B. Brailsford, *Song of Waitaha: The Histories of a Nation*, Ngatapuwae Trust, Christchurch, 1994.

4 A. J. Anderson, 'Prehistoric Polynesian Impact on the New Zealand Environment: Te Whenua Hou', in P. V. Kirch & T. L. Hunt (eds), *Historical Ecology in the Pacific Islands*, Yale University Press, New Haven, 1997, pp. 271–83.

5 D. G. Sutton, 'A Paradigmatic Shift in Polynesian Prehistory: Implications for New Zealand', *New Zealand Journal of Archaeology*, vol. 9, 1987, pp. 135–55; P. V. Kirch, 'Review of Geoffrey Irwin, *The Prehistoric Exploration and Colonisation of the Pacific*', *Pacific Studies*, vol. 20, no. 2, 1997, pp. 119–29.

6 A. J. Anderson, 'Research Report: Was *Rattus exulans* in New Zealand 2000 Years Ago? AMS Radiocarbon Ages from Shag River Mouth', *Archaeology in Oceania*, vol. 31, no. 3, 1996, pp. 178–84; R. N. Holdaway, 'The Arrival of Rats in New Zealand', *Nature*, vol. 384, 1996, pp. 225–6; R. N. Holdaway, 'A Spatio-Temporal Model for the Invasion of the New Zealand Archipelago by the Pacific Rat *Rattus exulans*', *Journal of the Royal Society of New Zealand*, vol. 29, no. 2, 1999, pp. 91–105; A. J. Anderson, 'Differential Reliability of ^{14}C AMS Ages of *Rattus exulans* Bone Gelatin in South Pacific Prehistory', *Journal of the Royal Society of New Zealand*, vol. 30, no. 3, 2000, pp. 243–61. Also, radiocarbon dating of land snails exhibiting rat-gnawing from various localities in Northland, found none dated earlier than about AD 1200.

7 M. S. McGlone, 'The Polynesian Settlement'; Sutton, 'A Paradigmatic Shift'; M. S. McGlone & J. M. Wilmshurst, 'Dating Initial Māori Environmental Impact in New Zealand', *Quaternary International*, vol. 59, no. 1, 1999, pp. 5–16; R. M. Newnham, D. J. Lowe, M. S. McGlone, J. M. Wilmshurst & T. G. F. Higham, 'The Kaharoa Tephra as a Critical Datum for Earliest Human Impact in Northern New Zealand', *Journal of Archaeological Science*, vol. 25, no. 6, 1998, pp. 533–44.

8 A. J. Anderson, 'The Chronology of Colonization in New Zealand', *Antiquity*, vol. 65, no. 249, 1991, pp. 767–95; T. G. F. Higham & A. G. Hogg, 'Evidence for Late Polynesian Colonisation of New Zealand: University of Waikato Radiocarbon Measurements', *Radiocarbon*, vol. 39, 1997, pp. 149–92; B. G. McFadgen, F. B. Knox & T. R. L. Cole, 'Radiocarbon Calibration Curve Variations and their Implications for the Interpretation of New Zealand Prehistory', *Radiocarbon*, vol. 36, 1994, pp. 229–32.

9 R. P. Murray-McIntosh, B. J. Scrimshaw, P. J. Hatfield & D. Penny, 'Testing Migration Patterns and Estimating Founding Population Size in Polynesia by using Human mtDNA sequences', *Proceedings of the National Academy of Sciences*, vol. 95, 1998, pp. 9047–52.

10 Quote from D. J. Lowe, R. M. Newnham, T. G. F. Higham, J. M. Wilmshurst, M. S. McGlone & A. G. Hogg, 'Dating Earliest Human Impact and Settlement in New Zealand', in D. G. Sutton (ed.) *The Origins of the First New Zealanders*, 2nd edn, Auckland University Press, in press.

11 A. K. Pawley & M. D. Ross, *Austronesian Terminologies: Continuity and Change*, Pacific Linguistics, Series C-127, Australian National University, Canberra, 1994.

12 A. J. Anderson & M. S. McGlone, 'Living on the Edge—Prehistoric Land and People in New Zealand', in J. Dodson (ed.), *The Naïve Lands*, Longman Cheshire, Melbourne, 1992, pp. 199–241; H. M. Leach, *1000 Years of Gardening in New Zealand*, Reed, Wellington, 1984; S. E. Tuller, 'Summer and Winter Patterns of Human Climate in New Zealand', *New Zealand Geographer*, vol. 33, no. 1, 1977, pp. 4–14.

13 Anderson, 'Prehistoric Polynesian Impact', on the windward–leeward model.

14 R. N. Holdaway, 'Introduced Predators and Avifaunal Extinction in New Zealand', in R. D. E. MacPhee (ed.), *Extinctions in Near Time*, Kluwer Academic/Plenum, New York, 1999, pp. 189–238, quote p. 216; T. H. Worthy, 'What Was on the Menu? Avian Extinction in New Zealand', *New Zealand Journal of Archaeology*, vol. 19, 1997, pp. 125–60.

15 R. N. Holdaway, 'New Zealand's Pre-human Avifauna and its Vulnerability', *New Zealand Journal of Ecology*, vol. 12 (supplement), 1989, pp. 11–26, quote p. 15.

16 R. N. Holdaway & C. Jacomb, 'Rapid Extinction of the Moas (Aves: Dinornithiformes): Model, Test and Implications', *Science*, vol. 287, pp. 2250–4; Anderson & McGlone, 'Living on the Edge'; Anderson, 'Prehistoric Polynesian Impact'; Worthy, 'What was on the Menu?'; N. A. Ritchie, 'The Prehistoric Role of the Cromwell Gorge', *New Zealand Journal of Archaeology*, vol. 4, 1982, pp. 21–43; F. J. Petchey, 'New Zealand Bone Dating Revisited: A Radiocarbon Discard Protocol for Bone', *New Zealand Journal of Archaeology*, vol. 19, 1997, pp. 81–124.

17 C. L. Batcheler, 'Moa Browsing and Vegetation Formations, with Particular Reference to Deciduous and Poisonous Plants', *New Zealand Journal of Ecology*, vol. 12 (supplement), 1989, pp. 57–66; G. Caughley, 'New Zealand Plant-Herbivore Ecosystems Past and Present', *New Zealand Journal of Ecology*, vol. 12 (supplement), 1989, pp. 3–10; I. W. G. Smith, 'Maori Impact on the Marine Megafauna: Pre-European Distributions of New Zealand Sea Mammals', in D. G. Sutton (ed.), *Saying So Doesn't Make it So*, New Zealand Archaeological Association Monograph 17, Dunedin, 1989, pp. 76–108.

18 Anderson & McGlone, 'Living on the Edge'; J. Ogden, L. Basher & M. McGlone, 'Fire, Forest Regeneration and Links with Early Human Habitation: Evidence from New Zealand', *Annals of Botany*, vol. 81, 1998, pp. 687–96; M. S. McGlone, 'Polynesian Deforestation of New Zealand: A Preliminary Synthesis', *Archaeology in Oceania*, vol. 18, no. 1, 1983, pp. 11–25, quote p. 23.

19 Caughley, 'New Zealand Plant-Herbivore Ecosystems', p. 7; M. N. Clout & J. R. Hay, 'The Importance of Birds as Browsers, Pollinators and Seed Dispersers in New Zealand Forests', *New Zealand Journal of Ecology*, vol. 12 (supplement), 1989, pp. 27–34; M. J. McSaveney & I. E. Whitehouse, 'Anthropic Erosion of Mountain Land in Canterbury', *New Zealand Journal of Ecology*, vol. 12 (supplement), 1989, pp. 151–64; M. S. McGlone, A. J. Anderson & R. Holdaway, 'An Ecological Approach to the Polynesian Settlement of New Zealand', in D. G. Sutton (ed.), *The Origins of the First New Zealanders*, 1st edn, Auckland University Press, 1994, pp. 136–63.

20 Anderson, 'Prehistoric Polynesian Impact'; A. J. Anderson, *The Welcome of Strangers*, University of Otago Press, Dunedin, 1998.

3 Contesting resources: Māori, Pākehā, and a tenurial revolution

1 Waitangi Tribunal, *Muriwhenua Land Report*, GP Publications, Wellington, 1997, pp. 21–4.

2 R. McNab, *Historical Records of New Zealand*, Government Printer, Wellington, 1914, vol. 2, p. 550.

3 J. Savage, *Some Account of New Zealand, Particularly the Bay of Islands and Surrounding Country*, John Murray, London, 1807; Waitangi Tribunal, *Muriwhenua Fishing Report*, Government Printer, Wellington, 1988.

4 J. L. Nicholas, *Narrative of a Voyage to New Zealand*, James Black, London, 1817, vol. 2, pp. 209–10.

5 J. Binney, 'Tuki's Universe', in K. Sinclair (ed.), *Tasman Relations: New Zealand and Australia*, Auckland University Press, 1988, p. 19.

6 R. Richards & J. Chisholm, *Bay of Islands Shipping Arrivals and Departures 1803–1840*, Paremata Press, Wellington, 1992; H. Morton, *The Whale's Wake*, John McIndoe, Dunedin, 1982.

7 R. A. Cruise, *Journal of a Ten Months' Residence in New Zealand*, Longman, London, 1824, p. 157.

8 J. Buller, *Forty Years in New Zealand*, Hodder & Stoughton, London, 1878, pp. 27–8.

9 R. P. Wigglesworth, The New Zealand Timber and Flax Trade 1769–1840, PhD thesis, Massey University, 1981, pp. 135–6.

10 E. Stokes, 'Kauri and White Pine: A Comparison of New Zealand and American Lumbering', *Annals of the Association of American Geographers*, vol. 56, no. 3, 1966, p. 446.

11 E. Dieffenbach, *Travels in New Zealand*, John Murray, London, 1843, vol. 1, pp. 227–8.

12 Binney, 'Tuki's Universe', p. 24; see also Morton, *Whale's Wake*, pp. 166–9, 216.

13 Quoted by Wigglesworth, New Zealand Timber and Flax Trade, p. 193.

14 E. Markham, *New Zealand or Recollections of it*, Government Printer, Wellington, 1963. p. 40; see also Wigglesworth, New Zealand Timber and Flax Trade.

15 J. Sissons, W. Wi Hongi & P. Hohepa, *The Puriri Trees are Laughing: A Political History of Nga Puhi in the Inland Bay of Islands*, Polynesian Society, Auckland, 1987.

16 *Muriwhenua Land Report*, p. 392; see also E. Stokes, *A Review of the Evidence in the Muriwhenua Land Claims*, Waitangi Tribunal Review Series No. 1, Wellington, 1997.

17 See Waitangi Tribunal, *The Ngai Tahu Report*, Brooker & Friend, Wellington, 1991.

18 See Waitangi Tribunal, *The Taranaki Report: Kaupapa Tuatahi*, GP Publications, Wellington, 1996, and *The Ngati Awa Raupatu Report*, Legislation Direct, Wellington, 1999.

19 A. Ward, *A Show of Justice*, Auckland, Auckland University Press, 1973, p. 185.

20 I. H. Kawharu, *Māori Land Tenure*, Clarendon Press, Oxford, 1977, p. 17.

21 Ward, *A Show of Justice*, pp. 185–6.

22 D. V. Williams, *Te Kooti Tango Whenua: The Native Land Court 1864–1909*, Huia Publishers, Wellington, 1999, pp. 44–6.

23 *Appendices to the Journals of the House of Representatives*, Session II, G1, 1891, p. 145.

24 Waitangi Tribunal, *The Pouakani Report*, Brooker & Friend, Wellington, 1993, p. 307.

4 Resource frontiers, environment, and settler capitalism, 1769–1860

1 On the Pacific frontier, see J. M. R. Young, 'Australia's Pacific Frontier', *Historical Studies, Australia and New Zealand*, vol. 12, no. 47, 1966, pp. 373–88; D. R. Hainsworth, 'Exploiting the Pacific Frontier: The New South Wales Sealing Industry 1800–1921', *Journal of Pacific History*, vol. 2, no. 1, 1967, pp. 59–75. See also Geoffrey Blainey, *The Tyranny of Distance*, Pan Macmillan, Sydney, 1983, esp. p. 115ff. Of other works dealing with this period, Anne Salmond's *Two Worlds: First Meetings Between Maori and Europeans, 1642–1772*, Viking, Auckland, 1991, and *Between Worlds: Early Exchanges Between Maori and Europeans, 1773–1815*, Viking, Auckland, 1997, are the most recent detailed studies to 1820, although more concerned with culture than environment. Alan Gray, *Aotearoa and New Zealand: A Historical Geography*, University of Canterbury Press, Christchurch, 1994, addresses many themes of the present chapter. There is little recent detailed work on the period between 1840 and 1850, and most of it treats New Zealand in isolation and deals with the well-established themes of Wakefieldian schemes and colonial reality, without emphasising environmental or imperial themes.

2 The observations on revolutionary capitalism are from Karl Marx & Friedrich Engels, *The Communist Manifesto*, Penguin, Harmondsworth, 1967, pp. 81–4. Ecological revolution is defined by Carolyn Merchant, *Ecological Revolutions: Nature, Gender and Science in New England*, University of North Carolina Press, Chapel Hill, 1989, pp. 2–3.

3 See, generally, Keith Thomas, *Man and the Natural World: Changing Attitudes in England 1500–1800*, Allen Lane, London, esp. pp. 281–85; a classic formulation of the doctrine of property is Chapter 5 of John Locke, 'Second Treatise', in *Two Treatises of Government*, Cambridge University Press, Cambridge, 1988: 'whatsoever then he removeth out of the State that Nature hath provided, and left it in, he hath mixed his *Labour* with, and joyned to it something that is his own, and thereby makes it his *Property*'. Cook's instructions are quoted in Salmond, *Two Worlds*, p. 99.

4 Cook on trade is in J. C. Beaglehole (ed.), *The Journals of Captain James Cook,* Cambridge University Press, Cambridge, 1968, vol. 1, pp. 186, 194–5. Flax and timber are described by Beaglehole (ed.), *The Endeavour Journal of Joseph Banks: 1768–1771,* Angus & Robertson, Sydney, 1962, vol. 2, p. 10. Other observations are Beaglehole, *Cook Journals*, vol. 1, pp. 176, 269–70, 277–8; Beaglehole, *Banks Journals*, vol. 2, p. 4.

5 Isabel Ollivier & Cheryl Hingley, trs., *Extracts from Journals Relating to the Visit to New Zealand of the French Ship St Jean Baptiste ...* , Alexander Turnbull Library Endowment Trust, Wellington, 1987, pp. 136–8; Salmond, *Two Worlds*, pp. 331–8, 383, 406.

6 Beaglehole, *Cook Journals*, vol. 2, pp. 126, 133–5; Salmond, *Between Worlds*, p. 52. Forster is quoted in Salmond, *Between Worlds*, p. 63.

7 Beaglehole, *Cook Journals*, vol. 2, pp. 167–9, vol. 3, pt 1, p. 63; Michael E. Hoare (ed.), *The Resolution Journal of Johann Reinhold Forster, 1772–1775*, Hakluyt Society, London, 1982, vol. 2, pp. 287–98, who gives a longer list of vegetables than Cook; C. M. H. Clarke & R. M. Dzieciolowski, 'Feral Pigs in the Northern South Island, New Zealand: I. Origin, Distribution, and Density', *Journal of the Royal Society of New Zealand*, vol. 21, no. 3, 1991, pp. 237–47; Harry Morton, *The Whale's Wake*, Otago University Press, Dunedin, 1982, p. 164.

8 Generally, Ged Martin (ed.), *The Founding of Australia*, Hale & Iremonger, Sydney, 1978; Margaret Steven, *Trade, Tactics and Territory: Britain in the Pacific, 1783–1823,* Melbourne University Press, Melbourne, 1983, chapters 1–2; Harold B. Carter, *Sir Joseph Banks*, British Museum, London, 1988, pp. 213–14; Robert McNab (ed.), *Historical Records of New Zealand*, Government Printer, Wellington, 1908, vol. 1, pp. 36–7.

9 The affair is discussed in Salmond, *Between Worlds*, chapter 9. For detail, see Carter, *Banks*, p. 218, and Lieutenant-Governor King to Nepean, April 1791, McNab, *Historical Records*, vol. 1, p. 126.

10 Salmond, *Between Worlds*, p. 232 and chapter 15; for detail, King to Nepean, 19 November 1793, in McNab, *Historical Records*, vol. 1, p. 180; King to Dundas, 19 November 1793, in McNab, *Historical Records*, vol. 1, pp. 171–5; King to Dundas, 10 March 1794, in McNab, *Historical Records*, vol. 1, p. 192.

11 Much of the detail on the *Britannia* is in Robert McNab, *Murihiku and the Southern Islands*, William Smith, Invercargill, 1907, chapters 4–6; Salmond, *Between Worlds*, pp. 285–94; D. R. Hainsworth, 'Trade within the Colony', in G. J. Abbott & N. B. Nairn (eds), *Economic Growth of Australia 1788–1821,* Melbourne University Press, Carlton, 1969, p. 268; Steven, *Trade, Tactics, Territory*, p. 87.

12 George Bass to Capt. Waterhouse, 30 January 1802, in McNab, *Historical Records*, vol. 1, p. 225; George Bass to Capt. Waterhouse, 5 January 1803, 2 February 1803, in McNab, *Historical Records*, vol. 1, pp. 240–2, 245; Bass to King, 30 January 1803, in McNab, *Historical Records*, vol. 1, pp. 242–4.

13 McNab, *Murihiku*, pp. 57–8; Salmond, *Between Worlds*, chapters 11, 16; R. P. Wigglesworth, The New Zealand Timber and Flax Trade 1769–1840, PhD thesis, Massey University, 1981, pp. 14, 259–61.

14 M. J. E Steven, 'Exports other than Wool', in Abbott & Nairn, *Economic Growth of Australia,* p. 289; R. B. Joyce, 'Government Policy', ibid., p. 70; Abbott, 'Economic Growth', ibid., pp. 147–8; see also Steven, *Merchant Campbell, 1769–1846: A Study of Colonial Trade*, Oxford University Press, Melbourne, 1965, and Hainsworth, 'Exploiting the Pacific Frontier'; details in 'Some Remarks on the Present State of the Colony of Sidney 4 June 1806', in McNab, *Historical Records,* vol. 1, pp. 271–4; Morton, *Whale's Wake*, p. 113. For a general account of Australian trading and strategic considerations, see Blainey, *Tyranny of Distance*, chapters 4 and 5.

15 Morton, *Whale's Wake*, pp. 90–4, 106, 121, 134, 144; Carter, *Banks*, pp. 433–4.

16 McNab, *Murihiku*, chapters 8–10 and 16, esp. pp. 113–14, 182.

17 McNab, *Murihiku*, chapters 12, 18, 23; esp. pp. 230, 261.

18 Morton, *Whale's Wake*, chapter 15 and esp. pp. 51–3, 121–5, 131–3, 140–7. On whaling rights see Edward Shortland, *The Southern Districts of New Zealand*, Capper Press, Christchurch, 1974, pp. 83–91.

19 Salmond, *Between Worlds*, chapters 17 and 18 and p. 339; Morton, *Whale's Wake*, p. 126; 'Rev. S. Marsden's Account of his First Visit to New Zealand', in McNab, *Historical Records*, vol. 1, pp. 343–8; Young, 'Australia's Pacific Frontier', p. 379; 'Governor King to Earl Camden 30 April 1805', in McNab, *Historical Records*, vol. 1, p. 255; Morton, *Whale's Wake*, p. 126; Salmond, *Between Worlds*, p. 339; 'King Papers, 2 January 1806' in McNab, *Historical Records*, vol. 1, pp. 263–6.

20 On Marsden, see 'Rev. S. Marsden's Account of his First Visit to New Zealand', McNab, *Historical Records*, vol. 1, p. 358; and 'Letter from Marsden 20 September 1815', McNab, *Historical Records*, vol. 1, p. 403; Salmond, *Between Worlds*, p. 445. For Polack's dealings, see Joel Polack, *New Zealand,* Capper Press, Christchurch, 1974, vol. 1, pp. 172–82.

21 'Report on New Zealand Flax', by R. Williams, in McNab, *Historical Records*, vol. 1, pp. 463–4; Morton, *Whale's Wake*, p. 183; Polack, *New Zealand*, p. 251; Richard A. Cruise, *Journal of a Ten Months' Residence in New Zealand*, Capper Press, Christchurch, 1974, pp. 38, 48; William Yate, *An Account of New Zealand,* Reed, Wellington, 1970, pp. 107–11; for the 1838 committee, see *Irish University Press Series of British Parliamentary Papers. Colonies: New Zealand*, Irish University Press, Shannon, 1968, vol. 1, pp. 60, 64, 68.

22 Evelyn Stokes, *A History of Tauranga County*, Dunmore Press, Palmerston North, 1980, p. 55; Polack, *New Zealand*, p. 120.

23 Generally, Wigglesworth, The New Zealand Timber and Flax Trade, pp. 71–110. For detail, 'Robert Torrens to Under-Secretary Horton', 14 June 1827, in McNab, *Historical Records*, vol. 1, pp. 676–8; Augustus Earle, *A Narrative of a Nine Month's Residence in New Zealand in 1827,* Whitcombe & Tombs, Christchurch, 1909, pp. 66, 68, 82; Salmond, *Between Worlds*, p. 250; Cruise, *Journal*, p. 21; Ernst Dieffenbach, *Travels in New Zealand,* Capper Press, Christchurch, 1974, vol. 1, pp. 201–53; E. J. Wakefield, *Adventure in New Zealand,* John Murray, London, 1845, vol. 1, p. 412. The spar specifications are in Wigglesworth, The New Zealand Timber and Flax Trade, pp. 108–9.

24 For example, 'Robert Sugden to Earl Bathurst, 18 January 1821', in McNab, *Historical Records*, vol. 1, p. 516; 'Lt-Col Nicholls (Royal Marines) to Earl Bathurst 8 November 1823', McNab, *Historical Records,* vol. 1, pp. 599–603; 'Memorial to ... Earl Bathurst, 24 April 1826', McNab, *Historical Records,* vol. 1, pp. 663–5.

25 The point about a new international division of labour is made by Erik Olssen, 'Wakefield and the Scottish Enlightenment', in Friends of the Turnbull Library (eds), *Edward Gibbon Wakefield and the Colonial Dream: A Reconsideration*, Government Printer, Wellington, 1997, p. 58. Descriptions are from Wakefield, *Adventure in New Zealand*, pp. 77, 92; Charles Heaphy, *Narrative of a Residence in Various Parts of New Zealand*, Capper Press, Christchurch, 1972, pp. 3, 22–3; David Monro, 'Notes of a Journey Through a Part of the Middle Island of New Zealand', Appendix C, in T. M. Hocken, *Contributions to the Early History of New Zealand*, Sampson Low, London, 1898, p. 231.

26 Newspaper quotes: *Nelson Examiner*, 10 June 1843, p. 262; 8 March 1845, p. 2. On FitzRoy, see Dean Cowie, 'To Do All the Good I Can': Robert FitzRoy, Governor of New Zealand 1843–45, MA thesis, University of Auckland, 1994; on complexities of purchase, see Robyn Anderson & Keith Pickens, *Waitangi Tribunal Rangahaua Whanui Series: District 12—Wellington District*, Waitangi Tribunal, Wellington, 1996.

27 Dieffenbach, *Travels in New Zealand*, vol. 1, pp. 15–19; *Journal of the Canterbury Provincial Council*, no. 11, 13 April 1855.

28 R. C. J. Stone, *Young Logan Campbell*, Auckland University Press, Auckland, 1982, quote at p. 86; generally, chapter 8.

29 Fox to William Wakefield, 1 December 1843, *Fourteenth Report of the New Zealand Company*, London, The Company, 1884, Appendix 17; *Nelson Examiner*, 8 June 1844, p. 54; Ruth M. Allan, *Nelson: A History of Early Settlement*, Reed, Wellington, 1965, pp. 237–8; *Nelson Examiner*, 16 December 1843, p. 370; Edmund Bohan, *Edward Stafford,* Hazard Press, Christchurch, 1994, p. 23.

30 Donal P. McCracken, *Gardens of Empire: Botanical Institutions of the Victorian British Empire*, Leicester University Press, London, 1997 p. 85; utilitarian exploration is modelled by John Overton, 'A Theory of Exploration', *Journal of Historical Geography*, vol. 7, no. 1, 1981, pp. 53–70.

31 Brad Patterson, 'A Queer Cantankerous Lot', in David Hamer & Roberta Nicholls (eds), *The Making of Wellington, 1800–1914,* Victoria University Press, Wellington, 1990, esp. p. 65.

32 L. J. B. Chapple & H. C. Veitch, *Wanganui*, Wanganui Historical Committee, Hawera, 1939, esp. p. 49. Donald McLean is quoted by Robyn Anderson in *Rangahaua Whanui Wellington*, p. 63. On Grey and land, see Ann Parsonson, 'The Challenge to Mana Māori', in G. W. Rice (ed.), *The Oxford History of New Zealand*, 2nd edn, Oxford University Press, Auckland, 1992, pp. 167–98; and Harry C. Evison, *Te Wai Pounamu/The*

Greenstone Island: A History of the Southern Maori During the European Colonization of New Zealand, Aoraki Press, Wellington, 1993.

33 See generally A. G. Bagnall, *Wairarapa*, Masterton Trust Lands Trust, Masterton, 1976, chapters 2–4. James Kemp on prosperity quoted in Paul Goldsmith, *Waitangi Tribunal Rangahaua Whanui District 11A: Wairarapa*, Waitangi Tribunal, Wellington, 1996, p. 26. See also John C. Weaver, 'Frontiers into Assets: The Social Construction of Property in New Zealand 1840–1865', *Journal of Imperial and Commonwealth History*, vol. 27, no. 3, 1999, pp. 17–54.

34 Heaphy quoted in N. M. Taylor (ed.), *Early Travellers in New Zealand*, Clarendon Press, Oxford, 1959, p. 248; *Nelson Examiner*, 2 June 1860, p. 3; Julius Haast, *Report of a Topographical and Geological Exploration of the Western Districts of the Nelson Province*, Nelson Provincial Government, Nelson, 1861, pp. 43, 130–2.

35 Tuckett's Diary, in Hocken, *Contributions*, Appendix A, p. 207.

36 Monro in Hocken, *Contributions*, p. 258–60.

37 Canterbury Museum Archives, Deans Family Papers, William Deans to John Deans snr and James Deans, 4 June 1851, folder 4. On Australia, see Sylvia Morrissey, 'The Pastoral Economy, 1821–1850', in James Griffen (ed.), *Essays in Economic History of Australia*, Jacaranda, Milton, 1967, pp. 51–112; Jill Ker, 'The Wool Industry in New South Wales 1803–30', *Business Archives and History*, vol. 2, no. 1, 1962, pp. 18–54; E. A. Beever, 'The Origin of the Wool Industry in New South Wales', *Business Archives and History*, vol. 5, no. 2, 1965, pp. 91–106; S. H. Roberts, *The Squatting Age in Australia*, Melbourne University Press, Carlton, 1970; Lynette Peel, *Rural Industry in the Port Phillip Region*, Melbourne University Press, Carlton, 1974; Tony Dingle, *The Victorians: Volume 2—Settling*, Fairfax, Syme & Weldon Associates, McMahons Point, 1984.

38 On the *Acheron*, see R. J. B. Knight, 'John Lort Stokes and the New Zealand Survey, 1848–1851', in Alan Frost & Jane Samson (eds), *Pacific Empires: Essays in Honour of Glyndwr Williams*, Melbourne University Press, Melbourne, 1999, pp. 87–99; Sheila Natusch, *The Cruise of the Acheron*, Whitcoulls, Christchurch, 1978; on Thomson, see John Hall-Jones, *John Turnbull Thomson*, John McIndoe, Dunedin, 1992, esp. p. 83.

39 On the practice of surveying, see Giselle Byrnes, 'Surveying Space: Constructing the Colonial Landscape', in Bronwyn Dalley & Bronwyn Labrum (eds), *Fragments: New Zealand Social and Cultural History*, Auckland University Press, Auckland, 2000, pp. 54–75.

5 Remaking the grasslands of the open country

1 The terminology follows I. A. E. Atkinson, 'Derivation of Vegetation Mapping Units for an Ecological Survey of Tongariro National Park, North Island, New Zealand', *New Zealand Journal of Botany*, vol. 23, no. 3, 1985, pp. 361–78. 'Forest' is woody vegetation with trees and shrubs covering at least 80 per cent of the ground. 'Scrub' is dominated by smaller trees with bole diameter at breast height less than 10 centimetres and covering at least 80 per cent of the ground. 'Shrubland' has shrubs as the dominant lifeform and a discontinuous canopy. 'Grassland', while dominated by grasses, may contain shrubs or low trees.

2 J. Ward, *Information Relative to New Zealand, Compiled for the Use of Colonists*, 2nd edn, John W. Parker, London, 1840.

3 B. E. King, 'Farming in New Zealand: the Pastoral Age', *New Zealand Journal of Agriculture* (hereafter *NZJA*), vol. 74, no. 3, 1947, pp. 243–7, 249–55.

4 H. E. Connor, 'A Tall-Tussock Grassland Community in New Zealand', *New Zealand Journal of Science*, vol. 4, no. 4, 1961, pp. 825–35; H. E. Connor, 'Tussock Grassland Communities in the Mackenzie Country, South Canterbury, New Zealand', *New Zealand Journal of Botany*, vol. 2, no. 4, 1964, pp. 325–51; E. Dieffenbach, *Travels in New Zealand with Contributions to the Geography, Geology, Botany and Natural History of that Country*, John Murray, London, 1843; A. Garvie, 'Report on the Reconnaissance Surveys of the South-Eastern Districts of the Province of Otago', *Otago Provincial Government Gazette*, vol. 3, 1859, pp. 276–82; F. W. Hilgendorf, 'The Grasslands of the South Island of New Zealand: an Ecological Survey', *New Zealand Department of Scientific and Industrial Research*, Bulletin 47, 1935; A. Mark,

'Indigenous Grasslands of New Zealand', in R. T. Coupland (ed.), *Ecosystems of the World 8B. Natural Grasslands: Eastern Hemisphere and Résumé*, Elsevier, Amsterdam, 1993, pp. 361–410; J. McKerrow, 'Reconnaissance Survey of the Wanaka and Hawea Lake Districts', *Otago Provincial Government Gazette*, vol. 6, 1862, pp. 11–18.

5 Common names for plants (with formal names in brackets on first reference) are used throughout this chapter. The terminology follows E. R. Nichol (compiler), *Common Names of Plants in New Zealand*, Manaaki Whenua Press, Lincoln, 1997.

6 J. Buchanan, 'Sketch of the Botany of Otago', *Transactions of the New Zealand Institute* (hereafter *TNZI*), vol. 1, 1868, reissued 1875, pp. 181–212.

7 M. S. McGlone & J. M. Wilmshurst, 'Dating Initial Maori Environmental Impact in New Zealand', *Quaternary International*, vol. 59, no. 1, 1999, pp. 5–16.

8 H. W. Harper, *Letters from New Zealand, 1857–1911*, Hugh Rees, London, 1914.

9 We have drawn on the following farm diaries and letterbooks for examples: Phillips family diaries for The Point in Mid Canterbury: copy held by Canterbury Museum, Christchurch; Pillans family diaries for their farm on Inch Clutha in South Otago: copy held by Hocken Library, Dunedin; Teschemaker diaries for Otaio station in South Canterbury: originals held by South Canterbury Museum, Timaru; and Wade's letterbooks for Kauru Hill in North Otago: originals held by South Canterbury Museum, Timaru.

10 G. P. Marsh (ed. D. Lowenthal), *Man and Nature*, Harvard University Press, Cambridge, 1965. See also D. Lowenthal, 'Nature and Morality from George Perkins Marsh to the Millennium', *Journal of Historical Geography*, vol. 26, no. 1, 2000, pp. 3–27.

11 W. T. L. Travers, 'Remarks on a Comparison of the General Features of the Flora of the Provinces of Nelson and Marlborough with that of Canterbury', *TNZI*, vol. 1, 1868, reissued 1875, pp. 174–9.

12 F. Tuckett, *Do not Emigrate Until You Possess that Portion of the Land which Should be Yours: Being a Few Remarks on the Sufferings of Emigrants in Ships and Colonies Addressed to the People*, Charles Gilpin, London, 1844.

13 Buchanan, 'Sketch of the Botany of Otago'.

14 B. P. J. Molloy, C. J. Burrows, J. E. Cox, J. A. Johnston & P. Wardle, 'Distribution of Sub-Fossil Forest Remains, Eastern South Island, New Zealand', *New Zealand Journal of Botany*, vol. 1, no. 1, 1963, pp. 68–77.

15 English measure is retained where used in the source: one pound is 0.45 kilograms; one mile is 1.61 kilometres; one acre is 0.40 hectares.

16 K. F. O'Connor, 'The Use of Mountains: A Review of New Zealand Experience', in A. G. Anderson (ed.), *The Land Our Future: Essays on Land Use and Conservation in New Zealand in Honour of Kenneth Cumberland*, Longman Paul/New Zealand Geographical Society, Auckland, 1980, pp. 193–222; K. F. O'Connor, 'The Implications of Past Exploitation and Current Developments to the Conservation of South Island Tussock Grasslands', *New Zealand Journal of Ecology*, vol. 5, 1982, pp. 97–107.

17 'Petition of the Settlers in the Province of Hawke's Bay', *Appendices to the Journals of the House of Representatives* (hereafter *AJHR*), G2, 1865.

18 Source given in note 9.

19 *'Hopeful', 'Taken In': Being, a Sketch of New Zealand Life*, W. H. Allen, London, 1887.

20 Source given in note 9.

21 P. G. Holland & B. B. Fitzharris, 'The Wind in the Tussock: the Weather in the Foothills of Mid Canterbury During 1866–71', in G. Kearsley & B. Fitzharris (eds), *Southern Landscapes: Essays in Honour of Bill Brockie and Ray Hargreaves*, Department of Geography, University of Otago, Dunedin, 1990, pp. 39–53.

22 Ward, *Information Relative to New Zealand*.

23 C. Hursthouse, *New Zealand the 'Britain of the South'*, 2nd edn, Edward Stanford, London, 1861; T. W. Leys (ed.), *Brett's Colonists' Guide and Cyclopaedia of Useful Knowledge*, Brett, Auckland, 1st edn, 1883; 2nd edn, 1897; 3rd edn, 1902.

24 P. McConnell, 'British, American and New Zealand Agriculture: a Comparison', *NZJA*, vol. 9, no. 6, 1914, pp. 430–7.

25 C. Brasch, 'New Zealand, Man and Nature', *Geographical Magazine*, vol. 12, no. 5, 1941, pp. 332–43.

26 Reported in B. L. Evans, 'Grassland Research in New Zealand', *New Zealand Official Yearbook, 1960*, pp. 1243–64.

27 Source given in note 9.

28 Hursthouse, *New Zealand the 'Britain of the South'*.

29 See note 23.

30 L. Cockayne, 'An Economic Investigation of the Montane Tussock-Grassland of New Zealand: Relative Palatability for Sheep of the Various Pasture-Plants', *NZJA*, vol. 18, no. 6, 1919, pp. 321–31.

31 S. H. Olson & P. G. Holland, 'Maintaining the Rural Landscape: Expectations and Costs of Hedging', *New Zealand Geographer*, vol. 51, no. 1, 1995, pp. 16–24.

32 R. T. Sadd et al., 'Report on the Pastoral Lands of Otago, Southland and Marlborough', *AJHR*, C15, 1920, pp. 4–24; see also K. F. O'Connor, 'The Influence of Science on the Use of Tussock Grasslands', *Review, Journal of the Tussock Grasslands and Mountain Lands Institute*, no. 43, 1986, pp. 15–78.

33 Source given in note 9.

34 Source given in note 9.

35 Source given in note 9.

36 K. F. O'Connor, A. H. Nordmeyer & K. Svavarsdottir, 'Changes in Biomass and Soil Nutrient Pools of Tall Tussock Grasslands in New Zealand', no. 200, *Rala Report*, Reykjavik, 2000, pp. 125–45.

37 M. A. Barker, *Station Life in New Zealand*, Macmillan, London, 1870.

38 See note 32.

39 K. A. Wodzicki, *Introduced Mammals of New Zealand: An Ecological and Economic Survey*, New Zealand Department of Scientific and Industrial Research, Wellington, Bulletin 98, 1950.

40 D. Petrie, 'Some Effects of the Rabbit Pest', *New Zealand Journal of Science*, vol. 1, 1883, pp. 412–14.

41 'Report of the Joint Committee on Rabbit and Sheep Acts', *AJHR*, I5, 1886.

42 'Lands Thrown-Up in Rabbit-Infested Districts in Otago and Southland', *AJHR*, C17, 1887.

43 'The Supply of Ferrets', *AJHR*, H31, 1888.

44 G. A. Dunbar & J. G. Hughes, 'Effect of Land Development on the Environment', *New Zealand Agricultural Science*, vol. 8, no. 3, 1974, pp. 110–19.

45 'Report of the Australasian Stock Conference', *AJHR*, H2, 1893, pp. 1–56.

46 Sadd et al., 'Report on the Pastoral Lands of Otago, Southland and Marlborough'.

47 J. A. Simmonds, 'Wind-breaks for Fruit-farms', *NZJA*, vol. 15, no. 5, 1917, pp. 253–62.

48 Source given in note 9.

49 In preparing this chapter we acknowledge the suggestions of Garth Cant, Ray Hargreaves, Helen Leach, and Jim Williams. Andrea Howard provided research assistance, Bill Mooney drafted the diagrams, and the late David McDonald of the Hocken Library pointed us towards useful sources of information.

6 Mining the quarry

1 For brief surveys of mining in New Zealand, see the *New Zealand Official Yearbooks*. G. J. Williams, *Economic Geology of New Zealand,* Office of the Congress and of the Australasian Institute of Mining and Metallurgy, Melbourne, 1965, includes a brief survey of the history of mining in New Zealand. The history of mining for minerals other than gold and coal remains largely untold, although M. Johnston, in *High Hopes: The History of the Nelson Mineral Belt and New Zealand's First Railway,* Nikau Press, Nelson, 1987, offers an account of Nelson's mineral belt of Dun Mountain–Red Hills.

2 W. N. Blair, 'Artificial Earth Sculpture', *Zealandia*, vol. 1, no. 8, 1890, pp. 474–81. Reprinted, and with an introduction by R. P. Hargreaves, in *Earth Science Journal*, vol. 2, no. 2, 1968, pp. 175–81.

3 The same is largely true for Australia. See, for example, J. M. Powell, *Environmental Management in Australia, 1788–1914. Guardians, Improvers and Profit: An Introductory Survey*, Oxford University Press, Melbourne, 1976; W. Lines, *Taming the Great South Land: A History of the Conquest of Nature in Australia,*

Allen & Unwin, North Sydney, 1991, p. 91; N. Barr & J. Cary, *Greening a Brown Land: The Australian Search for Sustainable Land Use*, Macmillan, South Melbourne, 1992, pp. 54–5; S. Dovers, 'The History of Natural Resource Use in Rural Australia: Practicalities and Ideologies', in G. Lawrence, F. Vanclay & B. Furze (eds), *Agriculture, Environment and Society: Contemporary Issues for Australia*, Macmillan, South Melbourne, 1992, pp. 1–18.

4 A. M. Honoré, 'Ownership', in A. G. Guest (ed.), *Oxford Essays in Jurisprudence,* Oxford University Press, London, 1961, pp. 107–47.

5 See, for example, Votes & Proceedings, Otago Provincial Council, Session 27, 1870, Appendix, p. 94; *Mount Ida Chronicle*, 7 February 1873; *Dunstan Times,* 21 February 1873.

6 *Appendices to the Journal of the House of Representatives* (hereafter *AJHR*) G18, 1871, p. 4; G4, 1872, p. x.

7 *Borton* v. *Howe* and *Glassford* v. *Read*. See *New Zealand Jurist* 2, 1874–75, pp. 97–100; *New Zealand Court of Appeal* 3, 1875–1877, pp. 17–18.

8 See Land Act 1877; Land Amendment Act 1882; Mining Act 1886; Mining Amendment Act 1887 (No. 2); Mining Amendment Act 1888; Mining Act 1891; Mining Amendment Act 1892; Mining Act 1898.

9 Victorian Parliamentary Papers, *Report of the Board Appointed to Inquire into the Sludge Question 1887*, pp. xv–xvi. See also R. Southern, 'Mining Wastes, Bucket Dredging, and Public Policy: The Sludge Abatement Board in Victoria', unpub. paper; R. Southern, 'John Montgomery Coane (1848–1923), Surveyor and Consulting Engineer', *Victorian Historical Journal*, vol. 49, no. 2, May 1978, pp. 119–28.

10 See C. W. McCurdy, 'Stephen J. Field and Public Land Law Development in California 1850–1866: A Case Study of Judicial Resource Allocation in Nineteenth Century America', *Law and Society Review*, vol. 10, 1976, pp. 235–66. See also R. L. Kelley, *Gold vs Grain: The Hydraulic Mining Controversy in California's Sacramento Valley*, A. H. Clark Co., Glendale, California, 1959; C. C. Spence, 'The Golden Age of Dredging: The Development of an Industry and its Environmental Impact', *Western Historical Quarterly*, vol. 11, October, 1980, pp. 401–14.

11 See *New Zealand Parliamentary Debates* (hereafter *NZPD*), vol. 134, 1905, p. 240; *NZPD*, vol. 135, 1905, p. 315; *AJHR*, I4, 1905, p. 4; *Bruce Herald,* 23 October 1905.

12 *AJHR*, H21, 1901, p. 12.

13 *AJHR*, C14 and C14A, 1907.

14 For a brief history of the field, see J. H. M. Salmon, *A History of Gold Mining in New Zealand*, Government Printer, Wellington, 1963; J. B. McAra, *Gold Mining at Waihi, 1878–1950*, Waihi Historical Society, Waihi, 1978; L. Barber, *No Easy Riches: A History of Ohinemuri County, Paeroa and Waihi: 1885–1985*, Ray Richards Publisher, Auckland; Ohinemuri County Council, Paeroa, 1985. A more recent essay, dealing largely with post-1970 mining, is J. Dixon, 'Coromandel Gold: Conquest and Conservation', in J. Connell & R. Howitt (eds), *Mining and Indigenous Peoples in Australasia*, Sydney University Press, Sydney, 1991, pp. 169–82. See also G. Watton, *Taming the Waihou: The Story of the Waihou Valley Catchment Flood Protection and Erosion Control Scheme*, Waikato Regional Council, Hamilton, 1995.

15 National Archives, Mines Department file, MD 1910/402.

16 See *AJHR*, I4, 1903, p. 3; I4, 1904, p. 5; I4, SII, 1906, pp. 1–3; I4A, 1907, pp. 16–18; MD 1910/402.

17 *NZPD*, vol. 142, 1907, pp. 813–18.

18 *Waihi Daily Telegraph*, 1 July 1907; *New Zealand Herald*, 24 April 1909.

19 The following sections are based on *AJHR*, C14, 1910.

20 See *AJHR*, D6F, Session 2, 1921–22.

21 *AJHR*, D6, 1920, pp. 1–2.

22 *AJHR*, D6B, 1920, pp. 5, 7, 15.

23 *AJHR*, D6D, 1920, p. 13.

24 *Mount Ida Chronicle*, 17 June 1870. Concern that that principle was not being observed led the Alexandra Miners' Association to urge the classification of all lands within the goldfields and the strict reservation of all potentially auriferous land from settlement, a demand endorsed by the Otago Mining Conferences in 1873 and 1874. See National Archives, Legislative Department file, Le 1, 1873, p. 5; *AJHR*, C6, S2, 1873, pp. 3–4; A8, 1874, p. 3.

25 *Dunstan Times*, 8 July 1881.

26 T. J. Hearn, 'After the Gold Rush: Economic Change and Resource Use Conflict in Central Otago', in G. W. Kearsley & B. B. Fitzharris (eds), *Southern Landscapes: Essays in Honour of Bill Brockie and Ray Hargreaves*, Department of Geography, University of Otago, Dunedin, 1990, pp. 55–76.

27 See, for example, *NZPD*, vol. 43, 1882, pp. 690–1.

28 *New Zealand Times*, 28 March 1876.

29 See T. J. Hearn, 'Mining and Land: A Conflict Over Use 1858–1953', *New Zealand Law Journal*, August 1983, pp. 235–8.

30 *Evening Star*, 30 April 1871. The issue was raised in the Otago Provincial Council in 1874, but no action ensued. See Votes & Proceedings, Otago Provincial Council, Session 33, 1874, p. 4.

31 *Otago Witness*, 17 June 1903; *Evening Star*, 17 April 1903; *NZPD*, vol. 133, 1905, p. 58.

32 *Otago Witness*, 17 June 1903. See also *NZPD*, vol. 134, 1905, pp. 615–16.

33 Victorian Parliamentary Papers, *Report of the Dredging and Sluicing Inquiry Board*, 1914, p. 18; Spence, *The Golden Age of Dredging*, 1980.

34 *Dunstan Times*, 28 April 1903; *Otago Witness*, 17 June, 1 July 1903; *Evening Star*, 17 April 1903; *Tuapeka Times*, 29 September 1906; National Archives, Mines Department file, MD N12/123.

35 MD N12/123.

36 L. Richardson, *Coal, Class and Community: The United Mineworkers of New Zealand 1880–1960*, Auckland University Press, Auckland, 1995, pp. 24, 92.

37 *AJHR*, Session II, C3, 1891; C4, 1901; *AJHR*, Session I, C4, 1912; H44A, 1919.

38 Clyde Warden's Court, Leases for coal mining purposes, 1873–1904; Cromwell Warden's Court, Coal mining leases, 1881–1942; Cromwell Warden's Court, Lignite licences, Cromwell, 1899–1920; Queenstown Warden's Court, Mineral licences, Queenstown.

39 When the Nelson Provincial Council, in 1865, granted a lease for the first mine on the Brunner field, the company concerned was required to build a railway to Greymouth. In fact, it merely constructed a horse track along the northern bank of the Grey River, with coal barges being towed upstream. A report in 1891 indicated that 'enormous damage' followed on the destruction of the banks and the widening of the river channel to 'a great shingle-bed, and thus supplying the shingle-bars that are continually on the move downstream, and add to the cost of the [Greymouth] harbour-works'. Failure to meet that condition resulted in the cancellation of the lease. See *AJHR*, Session II, C3, 1891, p. 25.

40 On the Nightcaps–Ohai field, overburden was removed by hand shovels, skips, horses and drays, traction engines, and hydro-sluicing, local streams being used as sludge channels. See J. S. Thomson, *Pasture, Coal Seam, and Settlement: A Centennial History of Nightcaps and District 1880–1980*, Nightcaps and District Centennial Committee, Nightcaps, 1979, p. 225; also D. C. W. Muir, *Mataura: City of the Falls*, Mataura Historical Society, Gore, 1991.

41 See *AJHR*, C3B, 1892, pp. 18–24; C3B, 1896, pp. 20–6; C4, 1901, pp. 28–33; C3A, 1906, pp. 32–44; C3A, 1911, pp. 31–9; C2, 1916, pp. 75–6; C2, 1922, pp. 46–50.

42 In the former Ashburton County, for example, two-hectare gravel reserves sited some three kilometres apart were set aside from 1868, while extensive quantities of gravel were also removed from local riverbeds. See R. Britten, *Between the Wind and the Water: Ashburton County Council, 1876–1989*, Ashburton District Council, Ashburton, 1991, p. 50.

43 See *AJHR*, C2, each year from 1912.

44 I. McBride, *The Paparua County: A Concise History*, Canterbury Public Library, Christchurch, 1990, p. 38; G. C. Smith, *Divine Rock: The Quarrymen's Gift*, Christchurch City Council, Christchurch, 1993; I. Church, *The Stratford Inheritance: A History of Stratford and Whangamomona Counties*, Heritage Press, Waikanae, 1990, pp. 160–71.

45 J. Watson, *Along the Hills: A History of the Heathcote Road Board and the Heathcote County Council 1864–1989*, Heathcote County Council, Christchurch, 1989, pp. 73–4.

46 See Auckland Planning Association, *Auckland's Unique Heritage: 63 Wonderful Volcanic Cones and Craters*, Auckland, 1925. The association insisted that 'Our heritage in these hills must be guarded', their scenic value, geological interest, and 'their close association with and evidence of the work of the Maori people', necessitating measures to prohibit further quarrying. See also G. M. Fowlds, 'The Volcanic Cones of Auckland', *Journal of the Auckland Historical Society*, vol. 1, no. 2, October 1963, pp. 25–8.

7 Destruction under the guise of improvement? The forest, 1840–1920

1 Frank Sargeson, *Sargeson*, Penguin Books, Auckland, 1981, pp. 53–6.

2 George Jobberns, 'Life and Landscape: 50 years in Retrospect', in *New Zealand: Inventory and Prospect*, New Zealand Geographical Society, Wellington, 1956, p. 3. See also K. B. Cumberland, 'A Century's Change: Natural to Cultural Vegetation in New Zealand', *Geographical Review*, vol. 31, no. 4, 1941, pp. 529–54.

3 G. H. Scholefield, *New Zealand in Evolution*, T. Fisher Unwin, London, 1909, pp. 45–59.

4 There is an enormous international literature in environmental history and historical geography: R. Grove, *Green Imperialism: Colonial Expansion, Tropical Island Edens and the Origins of Environmentalism. 1600–1860*, Cambridge University Press, Cambridge, 1995; A. W. Crosby, *Ecological Imperialism: The Biologcal Expansion of Europe, 900–1900*, Cambridge University Press, Cambridge, 1986; G. G. Whitney, *From Coastal Wilderness to Fruited Plain: A History of Environmental Change in Temperate North America from 1500 to the Present*, Cambridge University Press, Cambridge, 1994; W. Cronon, *Changes in the Land: Indians, Colonists and the Ecology of New England*, Hill & Wang, New York, 1983.

5 Cook and Banks quoted by G. Park, *Ngā Uruora: The Groves of Life*, Victoria University Press, Wellington, 1995, pp. 30, 34; 'Steep and Irregular Hills', from G. F. Angas, *Savage Life and Scenes in New Zealand and Australia*, Elder, London, 1847, vol. I, p. 233.

6 G. C. Petersen, 'Pioneering the North Island Bush', in R. F. Watters (ed.), *Land and Society in New Zealand*, A. H & A. W. Reed, Wellington, 1965, pp. 66–79.

7 This picture is simplified. The range of southern beech forests extends from the Coromandel Ranges to Southland; in more northern areas they are generally confined to the most barren slopes, with mixed conifer–broad-leaved forest occupying the flats and valleys.

8 This discussion draws from Park, *Ngā Uruora*; N. Bishop, *Natural History of New Zealand*, Hodder & Stoughton, Auckland, 1992, pp. 43–72; L. Cockayne, *New Zealand Plants and Their Story*, 4th edn, Government Printer, Wellington, 1967; R. G. Robbins, 'The Podocarp–Broadleaf Forests of New Zealand', *Transactions of the Royal Society of New Zealand*, vol. 1, no. 5, 1962, pp. 34–75; P. Wardle, 'Facets of the Distribution of Forest Vegetation in New Zealand', *New Zealand Journal of Botany*, vol. 2, no. 4, 1964, pp. 352–66.

9 Sarah Harris quoted in R. Dalziel, 'Popular Protest in Early New Plymouth: Why Did it Occur?', *New Zealand Journal of History*, vol. 20, no. 1, 1986, p. 12; Schnackenberg quoted in Park, *Ngā Uruora*, pp. 134–5; F. W. Strum, 'Timber and Firewood', *Transactions to the New Zealand Institute* (hereafter *TNZI*), vol. 11, 1878, pp. 568–70.

10 W. J. Butler of Kokiri Mills, Greymouth, quoted in T. E. Simpson, *Kauri to Radiata: Origin and Expansion of the Timber Industry of New Zealand*, Hodder & Stoughton, Auckland, 1973, p. 249.

11 F. von Hochstetter, *New Zealand: Its Physical Geography, Geology, and Natural History*, Cotta, Stuttgart, 1867, p. 141; Hector, Journal of the House of Representatives, 1870, both cited by Simpson, *Kauri to Radiata*, pp. 224, 226.

12 T. Kirk, *Appendices, Journals of the House of Representatives* (hereafter *AJHR*), C3, 1886, p. 5; R. Arnold, 'The Virgin Forest Harvest and the Development of Colonial New Zealand', *New Zealand Geographer*, vol. 32, no. 2, 1976, pp. 105–26; M. M. Roche, 'From Forest to Pasture', plate 47 in M. McKinnon (ed.), *New Zealand Historical Atlas*, David Bateman, Auckland, with Department of Internal Affairs, Wellington, 1997; H. C. D. Somerset, *Littledene: A New Zealand Rural Community*, New Zealand Council for Educational Research, Auckland, 1938, Auckland. I am indebted to J. Belich, *Making Peoples: A History of the New Zealanders from Polynesian Settlement to the End of the Nineteenth Century*, Penguin Books, Auckland, 1996, p. 372, for this point.

13 Timber merchant W. Leyland of Auckland, 1896, cited in Simpson, *Kauri to Radiata*, p. 252; G. S. Perrin, Report upon the Conservation of New Zealand Forests, *AJHR*, C8, 1897; E. Stokes, 'Kauri and White Pine: A Comparison of New Zealand and American Lumbering', *Annals of the Association of American Geographers*, vol. 56, no. 3, 1966, pp. 440–50.

14 Tregear cited from the Wellington *Evening Post*, 14 January 1886, by R. Arnold, *New Zealand's Burning: The Settlers' World in the Mid 1880s*, Victoria University Press, Wellington, 1994, p. 158; Petersen, 'Pioneering', pp. 66–79.

15 Tregear, 14 January 1886; Petersen, 'Pioneering'; "rough bush" in a letter from immigrant settler John King, 27 October, 1875, cited in R. Arnold, *The Farthest Promised Land*, Victoria University Press, Wellington, 1981, p. 300; Roche, 'Forest to Pasture'.

16 J. Inglis, *Our New Zealand Cousins*, Sampson, Lowe Marston, Searle & Rivington, London, 1887, pp. 103, 108.

17 Simpson, *Kauri to Radiata*, p. 264; D. E. Hutchins, *Forestry in New Zealand. Part 1: Kauri Forests and Forests of the North and Forest Management*, Government Printer, Wellington, 1919; Arnold, *New Zealand's Burning*, p. 84; Inglis, *Cousins*, p. 104; S. J. Pyne, *Vestal Fire: An Environmental History, Told Through Fire, of Europe and Europe's Encounter with the World*, University of Washington Press, Seattle, 1997.

18 J. Vogel, *New Zealand Parliamentary Debates* (hereafter *NZPD*), vol. 4, 1868, p. 190.

19 G. Wynn, 'Conservation and Society in Late Nineteenth-Century New Zealand', *New Zealand Journal of History*, vol. 11, no. 2, 1977, pp. 124–36; G. Wynn, 'Pioneers, Politician and the Conservation of Forests in early New Zealand', *Journal of Historical Geography*, vol. 5, no. 2, 1979, pp. 171–88; M. M. Roche, *Forest Policy in New Zealand: An Historical Geography 1840–1919*, Dunmore Press, Palmerston North, 1987.

20 Simpson, *Kauri to Radiata*, pp. 245–6; *AJHR*, H24, 1896.

21 *AJHR*, C8, 1897; Anon, 'Forestry and Land Settlement—A New Zealand View', *The Australian Forestry Journal*, vol. 2, 1919, p. 58.

22 *AJHR*, C12, 1913.

23 Roche, *Forest Policy*.

24 I. Campbell Walker, 'State Forestry: Its Aim and Object', *TNZI*, vol. 9, 1876, pp. 187–203; I. Campbell Walker, 'The Climatic and Financial Aspects of Forest Conservancy as Applicable to New Zealand', *TNZI*, vol. 9, 1876, pp. xxvii–xlix; L. Brown & A.D. McKinnon, *Captain Inches Campbell Walker, New Zealand's First Conservator of Forests*, NZFS Information Series, No. 54, 1966; Roche, *Forest Policy*, pp. 76–92; *New Zealand Times*, 15 December 1885.

25 L. Brown, *The Forestry Era of Professor Thomas Kirk, FLS*, NZFS Information Series, No. 56, 1968; T. Kirk to Commissioner of State Forests, 1 May 1886, National Archives, LS 53/15, p. 113; T. W. Hickson to T. Kirk, 1 November 1886, National Archives, LS 53/4 F & A 87-59; T. Hickson to Chief Conservator of State Forests, 4 July 1887, National Archives, LS 53/6 F&A 87-339.

26 Roche, *Forest Policy*; T. Brooking, *Lands for the People: The Highland Clearances and the Colonisation of New Zealand*, University of Otago Press, Dunedin, 1996.

27 Simpson, *Kauri to Radiata*, pp. 272–3; W. H. Guthrie-Smith, *Mutton Birds and Other Birds*, Whitcombe & Tombs, Christchurch, 1914, and his retrospective *Sorrows and Joys of a New Zealand Naturalist*, A. H. & A. W. Reed, Dunedin, 1936; E. Phillips Turner, 'A Retrospect of Forestry in New Zealand, 1894–1931', *Empire Forestry Journal*, vol. 11, no. 1, 1932, pp. 198–212.

28 The debate on the Forests Bill is in *NZPD*, vol. 16, 1874, pp. 79–94, 350–81, 399–426. For discussion, see Wynn, 'Conservation', and 'Pioneers', Roche, *Forest Policy*, pp. 76–93.

29 G. P. Marsh, *Man and Nature*, Scribners, New York, 1864.

30 *AJHR*, C3, 1877; J. P. Grossman, *The Evils of Deforestation*, Brett & Co., Auckland, 1909; Sargeson, *Sargeson*, pp. 55–7.

31 H. Guthrie-Smith, *Tutira: The Story of a New Zealand Sheep Station*, 4th edn, Godwit, Auckland/University of Washington Press, Seattle, 1999, p. xxiii.

8 Children of the burnt bush: New Zealanders and the indigenous remnant, 1880–1930

1 'Burnt Bush', in Blanche Baughan, *Shingle-Short and Other Verses*, Whitcombe & Tombs, Christchurch, 1908, pp. 63–7.

2 Michael Roche, *Forest Policy in New Zealand: An Historical Geography, 1840–1919*, Dunmore Press, Palmerston North, 1987, pp. 96–9; Tom Brooking, *Lands for the People? The Highland Clearances and the Colonisation of New Zealand*, University of Otago Press, Dunedin, 1996, pp. 131–56.

3 Judith Johnston, 'The New Zealand Bush: Early Assessments of Vegetation', *New Zealand Geographer*, vol. 37, no. 1, 1981, pp. 19–24; Paul Star, From Acclimatisation to Preservation: Colonists and the Natural World in Southern New Zealand, 1860–1894, PhD thesis, University of Otago, 1997.

4 Francis Pound, *Frames on the Land: Early Landscape Painting in New Zealand*, Collins, Auckland, 1983.

5 Lynne Lochhead, Preserving the Brownie's Portion: A History of Voluntary Nature Conservation Organisations in New Zealand, 1888–1935, PhD thesis, Lincoln University, 1994, pp. 10–46; Paul Star, 'Plants, Birds and Displacement Theory in New Zealand, 1840–1900', *British Review of New Zealand Studies*, no. 10, 1997, pp. 5–21.

6 Otago Institute Minutes, Hocken Library, 11 January 1870; *New Zealand Parliamentary Debates* (hereafter *NZPD*), vol. 48, 1884, p. 340.

7 *NZPD*, vol. 16, 1874, p. 93; Graeme Wynn, 'Conservation and Society in Late Nineteenth-Century New Zealand', *New Zealand Journal of History*, vol. 11, no. 2, 1977, pp. 124–36; Graeme Wynn, 'Pioneers, Politicians and the Conservation of Forests in Early New Zealand', *Journal of Historical Geography*, vol. 5, no. 2, 1979, pp. 179–85; George Perkins Marsh, *Man and Nature*, 1864, ed. David Lowenthal, Harvard University Press, Cambridge, Mass., 1965.

8 Susanne and John Hill, *Richard Henry of Resolution Island*, John McIndoe, Dunedin, 1987; Ross Galbreath, *Walter Buller: The Reluctant Conservationist*, GP Books, Wellington, 1989; Chris Maclean, *Kapiti*, Whitcombe Press, Wellington, 1999; T. H. Potts, 'Help Us Save Our Birds', *Nature*, 2 May 1872, p. 6.

9 W. T. L. Travers, 'On the Changes Effected in the Natural Features of a New Country by the Introduction of Civilized Races', *Transactions of the New Zealand Institute* (hereafter *TNZI*), vol. 2, 1869, pp. 299–313, 313–30; vol. 3, 1870, pp. 326–36; W. W. Smith, 'On the Birds of the Lake Brunner District'; *TNZI*, vol. 20, 1887, pp. 205–24; T. H. Potts, 'Stock in the Chathams', *New Zealand Country Journal*, vol. 12, 1888, pp. 370–5.

10 W. H. Guthrie-Smith, *Tutira: The Story of a New Zealand Sheep Station*, Reed, Dunedin, 1921; G. M. Thomson, *The Naturalisation of Animals and Plants in New Zealand*, Cambridge University Press, Cambridge, 1922.

11 *NZPD*, vol. 13, 1872, p. 204.

12 *NZPD*, vol. 152, 1910, p. 326; vol. 113, 1900, pp. 25–6, 34.

13 W. W. Harris, Three Parks: An Analysis of the Origins and Evolution of the New Zealand National Park Movement, MA thesis, University of Canterbury, 1974; David Thom, *Heritage: The Parks of the People*, Lansdowne Press, Auckland, 1987.

14 *NZPD*, vol. 86, 1894, p. 678; *NZPD*, vol. 57, 1887, p. 401.

15 Lochhead, Preserving the Brownie's Portion, pp. 82–180; *Taranaki Herald*, 5 May 1891.

16 Ross Galbreath, *Working for Wildlife: A History of the New Zealand Wildlife Service*, Bridget Williams Books/Historical Branch, Department of Internal Affairs, Wellington, 1993.

17 Geoff Park, *Ngā Uruora: The Groves of Life: Ecology and History in a New Zealand Landscape*, Victoria University Press, Wellington, 1995, p. 318.

18 *Nelson Evening Mail*, 23 February 1898; Lochhead, *Preserving the Brownie's Portion*, pp. 160–80.

19 *Appendices to the Journals of the House of Representatives* (hereafter *AJHR*), I5B, 1898, pp. 27, 6, 16.

20 *Evening Post*, 10 August 1898; Michael Roche, *History of New Zealand Forestry*, GP Books, Wellington, 1990, pp. 405–14.

21 Michael Roche, The Origins and Evolution of Scenic Reserves in New Zealand, MA thesis, University of Canterbury, 1979.

22 Paul Dingwall, 'Harry Ell's Vision in Nature Conservation', *Landscape*, vol. 10, 1981, pp. 23–7; Lochhead, Preserving the Brownie's Portion, pp. 181–91.

23 *AJHR*, H2, 1902, p. 21, H2, 1903, pp. iii–iv, C6, 1909, p. 2.

24 *AJHR*, C12, 1913, pp. xlv, xxii.

25 T. F. Cheeseman, 'The Naturalized Plants of the Auckland Provincial District', *TNZI*, vol. 15, 1882, pp. 268–74, *Otago Witness*, 30 June 1883, p. 17.

26 *AJHR*, C11, 1908, pp. 2–3.

27 *AJHR*, C8, 1907, pp. 15, 4; C11, 1908, p. 31.

28 Lochhead, Preserving the Brownie's Portion, pp. 192–295; Chris Maclean, *Tararua: The Story of a Mountain Range*, Whitcombe Press, Wellington, 1994.

29 *AJHR*, C8, 1897, p. 43.

30 *NZPD*, vol. 122, 1902, p. 26; Keith Sinclair, *A Destiny Apart: New Zealand's Search for National Identity*, Allen & Unwin/Port Nicholson Press, Wellington, 1986; Ross Galbreath, Colonisation, Science, and Conservation: The Development of Colonial Attitudes toward the Native Life of New Zealand, PhD thesis, University of Waikato, 1989; Peter Gibbons, 'Going Native': A Case Study of Cultural Appropriation in a Settler Society, PhD thesis, University of Waikato, 1992; Claudia Bell, *Inventing New Zealand: Everyday Myths of Pakeha Identity*, Penguin, Auckland, 1996.

31 *Otago Daily Times*, 29 June 1900, 28 June 1901, 2 October 1902.

32 *Birds*, No. 6, c. 1924; *New Zealand Life*, vol. 1, 1925, p. 3; vol. 5, 1925, p. 7.

33 *AJHR*, C12, 1913, p. 16; Leonard Cockayne, *The Cultivation of New Zealand Plants*, Whitcombe & Tombs, Christchurch, 1923, p. 8.

34 Galbreath, Colonisation, Science, and Conservation, p. 350; Paul Hamer, Nature and Natives: Transforming and Saving the Indigenous in New Zealand, MA thesis, Victoria University of Wellington, 1992, pp. 11, 105–7.

35 James Muir, Changing the Forest: Ecological Colonialism, Statute Law and the New Zealand Bush, 1840–1940, MPhil thesis, University of Waikato, 1995, pp. ii, 172, 174; Geoff Park, 'Going Between Goddesses', in Klaus Neumann et al. (eds), *Quicksands: Foundational Histories in Australia and Aotearoa New Zealand*, UNSW Press, Sydney, 1999, pp. 177, 189–90.

36 Thomas R. Dunlap, *Nature and the English Diaspora: Environment and History in the United States, Canada, Australia, and New Zealand*, Cambridge University Press, Cambridge, 1999, pp. 71–163; Ian Tyrrell, *True Gardens of the Gods: Californian-Australian Environmental Reform, 1860–1930*, University of California Press, Berkeley, 1999, p. 15.

37 Muriel Williams, *Charles Blomfield: His Life and Times*, Hodder & Stoughton, Auckland, 1979, pp. 35, 168.

9 The meanings of mountains

1 L. Franks, *All the Stamps of New Zealand*, A. H. & A. W. Reed, Wellington, 1977, pp. 26–8. Mountain scenes also feature prominently on early banknotes, particularly those of the Bank of New Zealand.

2 John Ruskin, *Modern Painters*, Smith, Elder, London, new edn, 1873; Marjorie Hope Nicolson, *Mountain Gloom and Mountain Glory: The Development of the Aesthetics of the Infinite*, Cornell University Press, New York, 1959; Simon Schama, *Landscape and Memory*, HarperCollins, London, 1995.

3 Paul Shepard, *English Reaction to the New Zealand Landscape before 1850*, Pacific Viewpoint Monograph no. 4, Wellington, 1969, p. 42; A. Fell, *A Colonist's Voyage to New Zealand under Sail in the 'Early Forties'*, J. Townsend & Sons, Exeter, 1927, p. 107.

4 Hong-key Yoon, *Maori Mind, Maori Land*, Peter Lang, Berne, 1986; Ernst Dieffenbach, *Travels in New Zealand*, John Murray, London, vol. 1, 1843; Chris Maclean, *Tararua: The Story of a Mountain Range*, Whitcombe Press, Wellington, 1994.

5 Maclean, *Tararua*; John Pascoe, *Land Uplifted High*, Whitcombe & Tombs, Christchurch, 1952; Waitangi Tribunal, *The Ngai Tahu Report 1991* (Wai 27), Brooker & Friend Ltd, Wellington, 1991, pp. 186–98.

6 *The Ngai Tahu Report*, pp. 186–8; *Lyttelton Times*, 20 January 1858; G. M. Mitchell, *Maori Place Names in Buller County*, A.H. & A.W. Reed, Wellington, 1948, p. 19; John Pascoe (ed.), *Over the Whitcombe Pass: The Narrative of Jakob Lauper. Reprinted from the Canterbury Gazette, July 1863*, Whitcombe & Tombs, Christchurch, 1960.

7 Maclean, *Tararua*, pp. 80–1.

8 Cheryll Sotheran, 'The Later Paintings of William Fox', *Art New Zealand*, no. 11, 1978, p. 45. See also Julie King, 'Facing up to Fox: The Colonial Watercolours of William Fox', *Art New Zealand*, no. 95, 2000, pp. 84–7, 99.

9 Jill Trevelyan, *Picturing Paradise. The Colonial Watercolours of William Fox*, National Library of New Zealand, Wellington, 2000; John H. Angus, *Aspiring Settlers: European Settlement in the Hawea and Wanaka Region to 1914*, John McIndoe, Dunedin, 1981, p. 52; Melvin D. Day, *Nicholas Chevalier Artist: His Life and Work with Special Reference to His Career in New Zealand and Australia*, Millwood Press, Wellington, 1981; N. Roberts, *Nicholas Chevalier: An Artist's Journey through Canterbury in 1866*, Robert McDougall Art Gallery, Christchurch, 1992.

10 *Illustrated New Zealand Herald*, 21 September 1878.

11 *Illustrated New Zealand Herald*, 12 March 1874; *Otago Witness*, 28 March 1874; J. Hingston, 'The New Zealand Sounds', *The Victorian Review*, 1 September 1883, pp. 622–36; *Maoriland: An Illustrated Handbook of New Zealand*, issued by the Union Steamship Company of New Zealand, George Roberston & Co., Melbourne, 1884, pp. 136–7.

12 Anthony Trollope, *New Zealand*, Chapman & Hall, London, 1874, pp. 43, 50; W. S. Green, *The High Alps of New Zealand*, Macmillan & Co., London, 1883, p. 303.

13 *Maoriland*, p. 116.

14 B. E. Baughan, *The Finest Walk in the World*, Whitcombe & Tombs, Christchurch, 1917; *Overland to Milford Sound*, Department of Tourist and Health Resorts, 1903, pp. 25, 46.

15 Annual Report of the Tourist and Health Resorts Department, *Appendices to the Journals of the House of Representatives* (hereafter *AJHR*), H2, 1906, pp. 10–11; 1909, p. 15; 1914, p. 4; Annual Report of Department of Lands and Survey, *AJHR*, C1, 1903, p. 153; Maclean, *Tararua*, p. 112.

16 *Timaru Herald*, 29 March 1919.

17 Pamphlet collection, Hocken Library, Dunedin; verse from an advertisement for the 'Great Alpine Carnival, Mount Cook' in *The Press*, 15 July 1923.

18 *AJHR*, D1, 1936, p. xi.

19 *The New Zealand Motorists' Road Guide (North Island)*, Andrews, Baty & Co., Christchurch, 1935, p. 244.

20 A. Runte, 'The West: Wealth, Wonderland and Wilderness', in J. W. Watson & T. O'Riordan (eds), *The American Environment: Perceptions and Policies*, John Wiley & Sons, London, 1976, pp. 47–62; L. Molloy, 'Wilderness Recreation—the New Zealand Experience', in L. Molloy (ed.), *Wilderness Recreation in New Zealand*, Federated Mountain Clubs of New Zealand, Wellington, 1983, p. 6.

21 M. H. Holcroft, *Discovered Isles: A Trilogy*, The Caxton Press, Christchurch, 1950, pp. 22–3.

22 L. Cockayne, 'A Glimpse into the Alps of Canterbury', in *Canterbury Old and New 1850–1900*, New Zealand Natives' Association, Christchurch, p. 215.

23 Molloy, 'Wilderness Recreation', p. 7.

24 Green, *The High Alps*, p. 4.

25 A. P. Harper, 'Climbing in the Alps of Switzerland and New Zealand', *New Zealand Alpine Journal*, vol. 1, no. 3, 1893, pp. 134–42.

26 G. Langton, A History of Mountain Climbing in New Zealand to 1953, PhD thesis, University of Canterbury, 1996, p. 116.

27 Maclean, *Tararua*, from which much of the material on the TTC is drawn; W. H. Field & F. W. Vosseler, 'Message for the Founders', in B. D. A. Greig (ed.), *Tararua Story: Jubilee of a Mountain Club*, Tararua Tramping Club, Wellington, 1946, p. 4; G. E. Mannering, 'The Ascent of Mount Rolleston', *New Zealand Alpine Journal*, vol. 1, no. 2, pp. 98–112.

28 Annual Report of the Tourist and Health Resorts Department, *AJHR*, H2, 1913, p. 5; Freda du Faur, *The Conquest of Mount Cook and Other Climbs*, George Allen & Unwin, London, 1915. In 1914 Miss Du Faur had moved to England. 'She never climbed again … she was entirely deterred by the fact that women were not allowed to join the English Alpine Club' (Bee Dawson, *Lady Travellers: The Tourists of Early New Zealand*, Penguin Books, Auckland, 2001, p. 194).

29 Pascoe, *Land Uplifted High*, p. 217.

30 Maclean, *Tararua*; R. J. Keen (ed.), *Outdoors: the Official Journal of the Otago Tramping and Mountaineering Club*, Fiftieth Anniversary Issue, 1973.

31 M. Johnston, Peak Experiences: Challenge and Danger in Mountain Recreation in New Zealand, PhD thesis, University of Canterbury, 1989.

32 *New Zealand Parliamentary Debates* (hereafter *NZPD*), vol. 249, 1937, p. 415; vol. 299, 1953, p. 189.

33 Annual Report, Department of Lands, *AJHR*, C6, 1907, pp. 2–3.

34 *NZPD*, vol. 100, 1897, pp. 155–6.

35 A. M. Moreland, *Through South Westland*, Whitcombe & Tombs, Christchurch, 1911, p. 56; Public Works Statement, *AJHR*, D1, 1937; *The New Zealand Motorists' Road Guide (South Island)*, 1938, p. 259; *NZPD*, vol. 271, 1945, p. 233.

36 Maclean, *Tararua*, who mentions the hydro potential. In fact the Public Works Statement of 1912 refers to investigations for this purpose on the Hutt River and the Waiohine and Tauherenikau, both major eastern Tararua rivers: *AJHR*, D1, 1912, p. 85.

37 Pascoe, *Land Uplifted High*, pp. 32–3; *Centennial Memorial Park Golden Jubilee Edition 1940–90: Conserving the Waitakere Ranges*, Auckland Regional Council Parks Department, Auckland, 1990; E. E. Vaile, *Waitakere National Park, With A Short History of the Ranges*, Waitakere National Centennial Park Citizens' Association, Auckland, 1939, p. 4.

38 'Landscape and Nature Conservation', in L. F. Molloy (comp.), *Land Alone Endures: Land Use and the Role of Research*, Discussion Paper 3, Department of Scientific and Industrial Research, Wellington, 1980, p. 67.

39 I am grateful to Julie King and Paul Star for references and discussion on the themes of this chapter.

10 'Swamps which might doubtless Easily be drained': Swamp drainage and its impact on the indigenous

1 J. C. Beaglehole (ed.), *The 'Endeavour' Journal of Joseph Banks, 1768–1771*, 2 vols, 2nd edn, Public Library of New South Wales/Angus & Robertson, Sydney, 1962.

2 Charles Hursthouse, *New Zealand or Zealandia, the Britain of the South*, Edward Stanford, London, 1857, p. 69.

3 Clarence J. Glacken, *Traces on the Rhodian Shore: Nature and Culture in Western Thought from Ancient Times to the End of the Eighteenth Century*, University of California Press, Berkeley, 1967, p. 348.

4 Figures from Ministry for the Environment, *The State of New Zealand's Environment*, Wellington, 1997, 7: pp. 24, 62.

5 Alfred W. Crosby, *Ecological Imperialism: The Biological Expansion of Europe, 900–1900*, Cambridge University Press, Cambridge, 1986.

6 Figures from E. B. Barbier, J. C. Burgess & C. Folke, *Paradise Lost? The Ecological Economics of Biodiversity*, Earthscan, London, 1994.

7 Analysis by Landcare Research commissioned for Ministry for the Environment, *The State of New Zealand's Environment*.

8 Crosby, *Ecological Imperialism*.

9 Beaglehole, *The 'Endeavour' Journal*, September 1769, p. 252.

10 Patricia Fara, 'Presidential Portraits: Joseph Banks in the National Library', *National Library of Australia News*, December 1998.

11 The nineteenth-century Sanitary Movement began in Britain and spread to its colonies. It was based on the utopian and educative impulse that good drainage meant good morals. See Rod Giblett, *Postmodern Wetlands. Culture, History, Ecology*, Edinburgh University Press, Edinburgh, 1996, pp. 120–5.

12 Hursthouse, *New Zealand or Zealandia*, p. 69.

13 Beaglehole, *The 'Endeavour' Journal*.

14 J. C. Beaglehole (ed.), *The Journals of James Cook, Vol. 1: The Voyage of the Endeavour*, Cambridge University Press for the Haklyut Society, Cambridge, 1955, p. 207.

15 Robert Silvester, 'Medieval Reclamation of Marsh and Fen', in Hadrian Cook & Tom Williamson (eds), *Water Management in the English Landscape: Field, Marsh and Meadow*, Cambridge University Press, Cambridge, 1998, p. 127.

16 Christopher Taylor, 'Post-medieval Drainage of Marsh and Fen', in Cook & Williamson (eds), *Water Management*, pp. 142, 149.

17 Giblett, *Postmodern Wetlands*, pp. 11, 116.

18 Geoff Park, *Ngā Uruora;The Groves of Life. Ecology and History in a New Zealand Landscape*,Victoria University Press, Wellington, 1995, p. 38.

19 Simon Best, 'Oruarangi Pa: Past and Present Investigations', *New Zealand Journal of Archaeology*, vol. 2, 1980, pp. 56–71: cited in Park, *Ngā Uruora*, p. 49. Wendy Pond, *The Land with All Woods and Waters*, Waitangi Tribunal Rangahaua Whanui Series, Wellington, 1997.

20 Hursthouse, *New Zealand or Zealandia*, p. 33.

21 For example, Paul Carter, *The Road to Botany Bay: An Essay in Spatial History*, Faber, London, 1987.

22 W. T. L. Mitchell, 'Holy Landscape: Israel, Palestine, and the American Wilderness', *Critical Inquiry*, vol. 26, no. 2, 2000, p. 194.

23 Paul Shepard, *Nature and Madness*, University of Georgia Press, Athens & London, 1998, p. 83.

24 George J. Murray, *The Story of the Rangitaiki*, Presbyterian Bookroom, Christchurch, 1968.

25 Chairman (Assistant Director General of Lands) to the Director General of Lands, National Archives, Auckland, ABWN 6095 W5021/421 15/11 p.1–S.A.L.D.–Rangitaiki Drainage.

26 Rufus Tye, *Hauraki Plains Story*, Thames Valley News, Paeroa, 1974.

27 Arthur Young, 1799, quoted in Giblett, *Postmodern Wetlands*, p. 111.

28 Giblett *Postmodern Wetlands*, pp. 114–15.

29 Ibid., p. 219.

30 Edward Gibbon Wakefield, *The British Colonization of New Zealand*, John W. Parker, London, 1840, p. 25.

31 The New Zealand Colonisation Company to be Incorporated by Charter, or Act of Parliament, New Zealand Company Papers, Alexander Turnbull Library, Wellington, q.325.931.77099

32 Charles Heaphy, 'Notes on Port Nicholson and the Natives in 1839', *Transactions of the New Zealand Institute* (hereafter *TNZI*), vol. 12, 1879, pp. 32–9.

33 Charles McGurk, *Aurora* letter, in 'Extracts from Colonists' Letters', *New Zealand Journal*, vol. 1, 1840.

34 William Wakefield, Journal, No. 2, 1839–1842, Typescript, New Zealand Company Papers 131/9, Alexander Turnbull Library, Wellington.

35 Wakefield, Journal.

36 Ruth France, 'Return Journey', in Allen Curnow (ed.), *The Penguin Book of New Zealand Verse*, Blackwood & Janet Paul, Auckland, 1966.

37 William Pember Reeves, *An Old Chum on New Zealand Scenery*, in G. P. Williams & W. P. Reeves, *Colonial Couplets: Being Poems in Partnership*, Simpson & Williams, Christchurch, 1889.

38 Giblett, *Postmodern Wetlands*.

39 George Phipps Williams ans W. P. Reeves, 'An Old Chum on New Zealand Scenery', in *Colonial Couplets: Being Poems in Partnership*, Simpson and Williams, Christchurch, 1889, p. 2.

40 Modified, considerably, from Paul Colinvaux, *The Fates of Nations: A Biological Theory of History*, Simon & Schuster, New York, 1980.

41 John Locke, *Two Treatises of Government*, 12th edn, C. J. Rissington and Partners, London, 1824, p. 362.

42 'Is it not the will of God that the earth should be replenished and subdued, that the desert should give rise to the fruitful field, the frantic war-cry to the hymn of praise, and the frightful depository of the unburied dead to the country steeple and the village school?' said 'MA of Trinity College Cambridge', 'Exceptional Laws in Favour of the Natives of New Zealand', Appendix A in E. G. Wakefield, *The British Colonization of New Zealand*, John Parker/New Zealand Association, London, 1837, p. 417.

43 William Swainson, *New Zealand and its Colonization,* Smith Elder & Co, London, 1859.

44 Geo Gipps, 7 March 1841 (letter incl. Clarke's Instructions), Governor's Despatches, vol. 35, A 1224, Mitchell Library, Sydney, CY POS p. 657.

45 George Clarke, Report on the River Thames in New Zealand, from Extracts from the Final Report of the Chief Protector of Aborigines in New Zealand, Mitchell Library, Sydney, CY POS, pp. 679–92.

46 Best, 'Oruarangi Pa'.

47 Clarke, Report.

48 Pond, *The Land with All Woods and Waters*, p. 129.
49 Park, *Ngā Uruora*, p. 54.
50 Pond, *The Land with All Woods and Waters.*
51 Pond, citing R. M. McDowall, *Gamekeepers of the Nation: The Story of New Zealand's Acclimatisation Societies, 1861–1990*, Canterbury University Press, Christchurch, 1994.
52 The US ecologist Daniel Janzen quoted in Gary Paul Nabhan, *Cultures of Habitat: On Nature, Culture and Story*, Counterpoint Press, Washington, DC, 1997, p. 259.
53 *Ngai Tahu Report*, vol. 1, Waitangi Tribunal, Wellington, p. 158.
54 Ben White, *Inland Waterways: Lakes*, Waitangi Tribunal Rangahaua Whanui Series, Wellington, 1998, p. 1.
55 White, *Inland Waterways.*
56 ibid.
57 ibid., notably chapter 2, Wairarapa Lakes.
58 Recommendations, Report of the Royal Commission on Forestry, *Appendices to the Journals of the House of Representatives*, C12, 1913.
59 United Nations Environmental Programme and Wetlands International—Asia Pacific, *Wetlands and Integrated River Basin Management: Experiences in Asia and the Pacific*, Kuala Lumpur, 1997, p. 15.
60 *A Wetlands Guideline*, National Water and Soil Conservation Organisation, Wellington, 1982.
61 Geoff Park, *Effective Exclusion? An Exploratory Overview of Crown Actions and Māori Responses Concerning the Indigenous Flora and Fauna, 1912–1983*, Waitangi Tribunal, Wellington, 2001.
62 William Massey in parliamentary debate the on Bush and Swamp Crown Land Bill, *New Zealand Parliamentary Debates* (hereafter *NZPD*), vol. 124, 1903, p. 491.
63 ibid.
64 Hone Heke Rankin, quoted in Evaan Aramakutu, Colonist and Colonials: Animals Protection Legislation in New Zealand 1861–1910, MA thesis, Massey University, 1997; see also Geoff Park, 'Going between Goddesses', in Klaus Neumann, Nicholas Thomas & Hilary Ericksen (eds), *Quicksands: Foundational Histories in Australia and Aotearoa New Zealand*, UNSW Press, Sydney, 1999, pp. 176–97.
65 Hone Heke Rankin, *NZPD*, vol. 113, 1900, pp. 32–3.
66 ibid.
67 Alfred K. Newman, 'A study of the causes leading to the extinction of the Maori', *TNZI*, vol. 14, 1881, pp. 459–77.
68 Hursthouse, *New Zealand or Zealandia*, p. 71.

11 The grasslands revolution reconsidered

1 P. W. Smallfield, *The Grasslands Revolution in New Zealand*, Hodder & Stoughton, Auckland, 1970, p. 97. On Darwin's metaphor, see John Stenhouse, The Battle between Science and Religion over Evolution in Nineteenth Century New Zealand, PhD thesis, Massey University, 1985, p. 11.
2 See R. J. Bremer, 'Federated Farmers and the State', in Brian Roper & Chris Rudd (eds), *State and Economy in New Zealand*, Oxford University Press, Auckland, 1993, p. 121. Figures on economic production and fertiliser use are from *New Zealand Official Yearbooks* (hereafter *NZOYB*), 1920–90. International figures come from John McNeill, *Something New Under the Sun: An Environmental History of the Twentieth-Century World*, W. W. Norton, New York, 2000, p. 25.
3 On this and economic history, see Tom Brooking, 'Economic Transformation', and Gary Hawke, 'Economic Trends and Economic Policy', in G. W. Rice (ed.), *Oxford History of New Zealand*, 2nd edn, Oxford University Press, Auckland, 1992, pp. 230–53, 414–21; John Gould, *The Rake's Progress*, Hodder & Stoughton, Auckland, 1982; C. B. Schedvin, 'Staples and Regions of Pax Britannica', *Economic History Review*, vol. 43, no. 4, 1990, pp. 533–59; Brian Easton, *In Stormy Seas: The Post War New Zealand Economy*, University of Otago Press, Dunedin, 1997.
4 B. L. Evans, *A History of Agricultural Production and Marketing in New Zealand*, Keeling & Mundy, Palmerston North, 1969, and 'Grasslands Research' in *NZOYB*, 1960, pp. 1248–64; F. R. Callaghan, 'Science and Agriculture', in F. R. Callaghan (ed.), *Science in New Zealand*, Reed, Wellington, 1957, pp. 137–53.

5 This summary of the writing up of the 'grasslands revolution' by both participants and observers is based on: A. H. Cockayne, 'Grasslands of New Zealand: A Grasslands Philosophy', *Proceedings of the Seventh International Grasslands Conference*, 1956, pp. 585–95; K. Cumberland, *Landmarks*, Reader's Digest, Surry Hills, 1981, pp. 152–207, and *Soil Erosion in New Zealand: A Geographic Reconnaissance*, Soil Conservation and Rivers Control Council, Wellington, 1944; Ross Galbreath, 'A Grassland Utopia? Pastoral Farming and Grassland Research in New Zealand', in *DSIR: Making Science Work for New Zealand, 1926–1992*, Victoria University Press/Historical Branch, Wellington, 1998, pp. 58–79; E. Bruce Levy, *The Grasslands of New Zealand*, three editions, 1923, 1951 and 1973, Government Printer, Wellington; Lance McCaskill, *Hold This Land: A History of Soil Conservation in New Zealand*, Reed, Wellington, 1973; K. J. O'Connor, 'The Improvement and Utilization of Tussock Grasslands: A Scientist's Viewpoint', *Proceedings of the New Zealand Grasslands Association*, vol. 28, 1966, pp. 59––78; Smallfield, *The Grasslands Revolution*; essays in *New Zealand Agricultural Science*, vol. 8, no. 3, 1974, especially J. K. Syers, 'Effect of Phosphate Fertilizers on Agriculture and the Environment', pp. 149–64.

6 See J. D. Gould, *The Grass Roots of New Zealand History: Pasture Formation and Improvement, 1871–1911*, Massey University Occasional Publications, Palmerston North, 1974.

7 D. A. Campbell, 'Developments in Aerial Top-dressing During 1949', *New Zealand Journal of Science and Technology*, vol. 33A, no. 3, 1951, pp. 1–12.

8 Ministry for the Environment, *The State of New Zealand's Environment 1997*, Wellington, 1997, chapter 8, p. 9.

9 Levy, *Grasslands*, 2nd edn, pp. 285–304; 3rd edn, pp. 238–70. On the loss of agricultural land to sprawling Auckland and Christchurch, see *New Zealand Agricultural Science*, vol. 8, no. 4, 1974; on agricultural chemicals, see Cumberland, *Landmarks*, pp. 191, 295; Smallfield, *Grasslands Revolution*, p. 130.

10 L. McCaskill, *Molesworth*, A. H. & A. W. Reed, Wellington, 1969, pp. 257–70.

11 W. Maslyn & Barrie Macdonald, *The Phosphateers: A History of the British Phosphate Commissioners and the Christmas Island Phosphate Commissioners*, Melbourne University Press, Carlton, Victoria, 1985; T. W. Walker, 'Superphosphate and Biological Nitrogen Fixation', in B. E. Williamson & Dennis Hogen (eds), *New Zealand is Different: Chemical Milestones in New Zealand History*, New Zealand Institute of Chemistry, Christchurch, 1999, pp. 37–39.

12 P. D. Sears, 'The Potential of New Zealand Grassland Farming', *Proceedings of the Third New Zealand Geography Conference*, Palmerston North, 1961, p. 66.

13 The 'Southern Pastoral Lands Commission', *Appendices to the Journals of the House of Representatives* (hereafter *AJHR*), C15, 1920; L. McCaskill, Fertilisers in New Zealand, 1867–1929, MAg. thesis, University of Otago, 1929; 'Royal Commission To Inquire Into And Report Upon The Sheep Farming Industry', *AJHR*, H46A, 1949; H. Belshaw et al., *Agricultural Organisation in New Zealand*, Melbourne University Press/OUP, Melbourne, 1936, pp. 386–7; A. N. Tait, 'The Growth of Fertiliser Use in New Zealand', *New Zealand Journal of Agriculture* (hereafter *NZJA*), vol. 95, no. 2, 1957, pp. 186–97; *NZOYB*, 1920–90. See W. J. Gardner, *The Amuri: A County History*, 2nd edn, Amuri County Council, Culverden, 1983, pp. 448–58, on irrigation.

14 Smallfield, *Grasslands Revolution*, pp. 49, 99, 87.

15 See Helge Kragh, *An Introduction to the Historiography of Science*, Cambridge University Press, Cambridge, 1989, p. 180.

16 For example, Labour's Minister of Agriculture, Ben Roberts, stressed New Zealand's role in 'winning the peace', *NZJA*, vol. 73, no. 6, 1946, pp. 345–7. National's Minister of Agriculture, K. J. Holyoake, talked of New Zealand's role in feeding a hungry world, vol. 80, no. 1, 1950, p. 3.

17 On disasters resulting from noble intentions, see Nancy Langstone, *Forest Dreams Forest Nightmares: The Paradox of Old Growth in the Inland West*, University of Washington Press, Seattle, 1995. Cumberland claimed 'the lessons of the failures after 1918 had been thoroughly learned', *Landmarks*, p. 166. 'Sheep Industry Commission', *AJHR*, H46A, 1949, p. 88, warns of 'the tragedy of abandoned lands'.

18 Edward Cullen, Labour Minister of Agriculture, urged farmers to increase food production to head off totalitarianism, *NZJA*, vol. 78, no. 3 (March 1949), p. 227. Similarly, Cumberland wrote in *Landmarks*: 'Food and Agricultural Organisation researchers predict substantially increased world demand for New Zealand's main export foodstuffs', p. 295.

19 On 'ruralism', see T. Brooking, 'Use it or Lose it: Unravelling the Land Debate in Late Nineteenth-Century New Zealand', *New Zealand Journal of History*, vol. 30, no. 2, 1996, pp. 145–7; Miles Fairburn, *The Ideal Society and its Enemies: The Origins of Modern New Zealand Society*, Auckland University Press, 1988, pp. 19–73; Rodney B. Lyon, The Principles of New Zealand Liberal Thinking in the Late Nineteenth Century, PhD thesis, University of Auckland, 1982, p. 355; on the 'rural problem', see David B. Danbom, *Born in the Country: A History of Rural America*, The Johns Hopkins University Press, Baltimore, 1995, pp. 185–232.

20 B. L. Evans, 'Grasslands Research', in *NZOYB*, 1960, pp. 1254–5; Sir E. John Russell, *A History of Agricultural Science in Great Britain*, Allen & Unwin, London, 1966, pp. 380–409; Libby Robin, 'Ecology: A Science of Empire?', in T. Griffiths & L. Robin (eds), *Ecology and Empire: Environmental History of Settler Societies*, Melbourne University Press, Melbourne, 1997, pp. 63–75; T. Brooking, *Massey: Its Early Years: A History of Massey Agricultural College to 1943*, Massey Alumni Association, Palmerston North, 1977, pp. 13–52; I. D. Blair, *The Seed they Sowed: Centennial Story of Lincoln College*, Lincoln College, Lincoln, 1978; Lord Bledisloe, *Grasslands: The Main Source of the Nation's True Wealth*, Third Conference of the New Zealand Grasslands Association, Wellington, 1934, pp. 20–5, 35; Galbreath, *DSIR*.

21 *AJHR*, H46A, 1949. The 'Problems' section, p. 42, blamed erosion on the nature of New Zealand soils, low fertility, rivers, and rabbits, and concluded, 'The hue and cry on erosion is, therefore, misleading.' Similarly, in 1985 economist Dr Alistair McArthur in *NZJA*, vol. 150, no. 5, p. 14, argued that there was no proof of the link between soil conservation and flooding.

22 On urbanisation and the dwindling political power of farmers, see Graeme Dunstall, 'The Social Pattern', in Rice (ed.), *The Oxford History of New Zealand*, pp. 455–8; R. J. Bremer, in Roper & Rudd (eds), *State and Economy in New Zealand*, p. 116.

23 M. Roche, '"The Land We Have We Must Hold": Soil Erosion and Conservation in the Late Nineteenth- and Twentieth-Century New Zealand', *Journal of Historical Geography*, vol. 23, no. 4, 1997, pp. 447–58.

24 Vaughan Wood, 'Soil Fertility Management in Nineteenth Century New Zealand', PhD in progress, University of Otago.

25 Robin Hodge, Nature's Trustee: Pérrine Moncrieff and Nature Conservation in New Zealand 1920–1950, PhD thesis, Massey University, 1999, chapter 8.

26 On organic farming, see Jack Meechin (ed.), *Healthy Soil Healthy Food Healthy People*, Soil and Health Association of New Zealand Inc, Auckland, 1993, pp. 3–5, 19; *Compost Club Magazine*, 1943–51, p. 24; Rudolf Steiner, *Spiritual Foundations for the Renewal of Agriculture*, Bio-Dynamic Farming and Gardening Association, Kimberton, 1993; Anna Bramwell, *Ecology in the Twentieth Century: A History*, Yale University Press, New Haven, 1989, p. 200; Bio-Dynamic Association Minute Book, 1945–69; J. W. Nicolls', *It's a Pleasure*, Awa Moa, Oamaru, 1964, pp. 41, 1–3; New Zealand Inter-Departmental Committee, *The Utilization of Organic Wastes in New Zealand: An Interim Report*, Wellington, 1948, 1951, 1955, 1965; Barrie MacDonald, *Imperial Patriot: Charles Alma Baker and the History of Limestone Downs*, Bridget Williams Books, Wellington, 1993.

27 Herbert Guthrie-Smith, *Tutira: The Story of a New Zealand Sheep Station*, Godwit, Auckland/University of Washington Press, Seattle, reprint, 1999; 'The Changing Land', in *Making New Zealand*, II, No. 30, Department of Internal Affairs, Wellington, 1940, pp. 12, 19–20.

28 McCaskill, *Hold This Land*, p. 260; Margaret Ritchie & Hugh Campbell, 'Historical Development of the Organic Agriculture Movement in New Zealand', in Hugh Campbell (ed.), *Recent Developments in Organic Food Production in New Zealand*, Department of Anthropology, University of Otago, Dunedin, 1996, pp. 10–18; Anthony Haystead, 'Organic Farming Survey', *Soil and Health*, Spring 1987, pp. 8–12; Frank Bradshaw, 'Disposing of Farm Wastes', *NZJA*, vol. 132, no. 3, 1975, p. 25; Rachel Carson, *Silent Spring*; Houghton, Mifflin Co., Boston, 1962, pp. 75–78, 204, 213; *State of New Zealand's Environment*, chapter 6, p. 17.

29 Carson: *NZJA*, vol. 110, no.1, 1965, p. 9; 2,4,5-T: vol. 140, no. 4, 1980, pp. 28–34; vol. 146, no. 1, 1983, p. 29; DDT: vol. 140, no. 2, 1980, p. 5; *State of New Zealand's Environment*, chapter 8, pp. 66–7.

30 QEII Trust: *State of New Zealand's Environment*, chapter 9, p.139; Agrichemicals: *State of New Zealand's Environment*, chapter 8, p. 36.

31 Jenny Philips, editor of *Women's World*, championed legislation to protect the environment and recycling, *Straight Furrow*, 12 December 1974, p. 18.

32 'Effluent disposal': *NZJA*, vol. 120, no. 3, March 1970, pp. 25–37; 'Dairy Effluent Disposal': vol. 130, no. 2, 1975, p. 14; 'Farm Forestry': vol. 100, no. 4, 1960; vol. 110, no. 6, 1965, pp. 34–7 advocated the planting of 'radiata'. Planting of native trees was not advocated until vol. 153, no. 1, 1988, p. 50. *Straight Furrow* advocated harmonious landscape and planting more trees, including natives, from 5 February 1982, p. 13. Two months later, however, it expressed concern at good farming country being lost to forest planting. May 1982, p. 4; landcare: *Landlink*, Summer 1994–95; stocking rates: *Straight Furrow*, 14 May 1982, p. 19.

33 Quin: *NZJA*, vol. 146, no. 3, 1983, pp. 4–6; Stephenson: vol. 148, no. 2, 1984, pp. 7–8; Haynes & Swift: vol. 148, no. 2, 1984, pp. 9–11.

34 Crowder, *NZJA*, vol. 147, no. 4, 1983, pp. 6–7; K. F. O'Connor, 'The Sustainability of Pastoralism', *Proceedings of the 1987 Hill and High Country Seminar*, 1987, Tussock Grasslands and Mountain Lands Institute Special Publication No. 30, pp. 161–88.

35 *State of New Zealand's Environment*, chapter 8, p. 33.

36 R. H. M. Langer (ed.), *Pastures: Their Ecology and Management*, Oxford University Press, Auckland, 1990: especially W. Harris, 'Pasture as Ecosystem', pp. 75–131; K. F. O'Connor, 'Pasture and Soil Fertility', pp. 157–96; R. J. Field & G. T. Daly, 'Weed Biology and Management', pp. 409–47.

37 Takaka A&P Show 1938, 'Sir Keith Holyoake Collection', MS 1814, Box 2, Alexander Turnbull Library, Wellington.

12 The state as conservationist, 1920–60: 'Wise use' of forests, lands, and water

1 Donald Worster, 'Transformations of the Earth: Towards an Agroecological Perspective in History', *Journal of American History*, vol. 76, no. 3, 1990, pp. 1087–110.

2 Michael Williams, 'The End of Modern History', *The Geographical Review*, vol. 88, no. 2, 1998, p. 276.

3 Samuel Hays, *Beauty, Health and Permanence. Environmental Politics in the United States 1955–1985*, Cambridge University Press, Cambridge, 1987, p. 18.

4 Joseph Powell, 'Historical Geography and Environmental History: An Australian Interface', *Journal of Historical Geography*, vol. 22, no. 3, 1996, p. 258.

5 These early estimates were of merchantable timber remaining. In 1905 this was put at 43 million superficial feet, or seventy years' duration. The Royal Commission on Forestry of 1913 put forward a figure of thirty years, corresponding to exhaustion by 1943, *Appendices to the Journals of the House of Representatives* (hereafter *AJHR*), C4, 1905; C12, 1913.

6 Alfred Cockayne, 'The Monterey Pine, The Great Timber-Tree of the Future', *New Zealand Journal of Agriculture* (hereafter *NZJA*), vol. 8, no. 1, 1914, pp. 1–26.

7 *AJHR*, C3, 1921, p. 7.

8 *New Zealand Official Year Book*, Government Printer, Wellington, 1936, pp. 375, 378. The State Forest Service took on over a thousand men during the winter planting season in 1929. Others were employed under the Unemployment Board's Scheme No. 5, and during the winters from 1932 to 1935 over a thousand were employed on tree planting, but the decision to expand the exotic forest estate had been taken much earlier, in 1925.

9 Alexander Entrican & V. Rapson, 'The Establishment of a Local Pulp and Paper Industry in New Zealand' PR 347 1943 [Permanent Record Collection], Forest Research Institute, Rotorua. Entrican in many ways typified the expert natural-resource manager: 'The State and The Development of Natural Resources', *New Zealand Journal of Public Administration*, vol. 3, no. 4, 1958, pp. 29–36; 'Additional Reflections on the Expert in Administration', Address to the Wellington Branch of the New Zealand Institute of Public Administration, 1959 (typescript).

10 The early years of Fletcher's is discussed in Neil Robinson, *James Fletcher: Builder*, Hodder & Stoughton, Auckland, 1970, while the involvement in Tasman is described from a company perspective in Selwyn Parker, *Made in New Zealand: The Story of Jim Fletcher*, Hodder & Stoughton, Auckland, 1994.

11 *AJHR*, C3,1956, p. 28.

12 Alexander Entrican, Hugo Hinds, & J. Stanley Reid, *Forest Trees and Timbers of New Zealand*, New Zealand Forest Service Bulletin No. 12, Government Printer, Wellington, 1957.

13 *AJHR*, C3, 1961, p. 15.

14 'Editorial Notes', *New Zealand Journal of Forestry*, vol. 5, no. 3, 1946, p. 175.

15 Joseph Grossman, *The Evils of Deforestation*, Brett, Auckland, 1909. This was reprinted in *AJHR*, C4, 1909, pp. 93–6.

16 Graeme Wynn, 'Remapping Tutira. Contours of the Environmental History of New Zealand', *Journal of Historical Geography*, vol. 23, no. 4, 1997, pp. 418–46.

17 Norman Taylor, 'Land Deterioration in the Heavier Rainfall districts of New Zealand', *New Zealand Journal of Science and Technology*, vol. 19, no. 11, 1989, pp. 657–81; Vladimir Zotov, 'Survey of the Tussock Grasslands of the South Island, New Zealand', *New Zealand Journal of Science and Technology*, vol. 20, no. 4, 1938, pp. 212A–244A.

18 R. P. Connell, 'Land Deterioration as a Grave Phase of Our National Economy', *NZJA*, vol. 59, no. 1, 1939, pp. 4–12.

19 Commission of Inquiry, *Maintenance of Vegetation cover in New Zealand with Special Reference to Land Erosion*, Department of Scientific and Industrial Research Bulletin No. 77, Government Printer, Wellington, 1939.

20 Frederick Furkert, 'The Control of Rivers', *New Zealand Journal of Science and Technology*, vol. 10, 1928, pp. 434–47.

21 A. R. Acheson, *River Control and Drainage in New Zealand*, Ministry of Works, Wellington, 1968, p. 22.

22 P. Temm, *The Waitangi Tribunal: The Conscience of the Nation*, Random Century, Auckland, 1990.

13 On the edge: making urban places

1 Anon, *Auckland, The Gateway to New Zealand*, Auckland, 1931, p. 1; Cilla McQueen quoted in David Eggleton, 'Introduction', *Here on Earth: The Landscape in New Zealand Literature*, Craig Potton Publishing, Nelson, 1999, p. 14. The census definition of 'urban' in New Zealand includes all places with more than 1000 people, compared with 2500 in the United States. Many 'urban-dwellers' therefore lived in very small places.

2 The rural focus is clearly reflected in sources such as the collection edited by C. Merchant, *Major Problems in American Environmental History, Documents and Essays*, D. C. Heath & Co., Lexington, 1993. Also William Cronon, 'Modes of Prophecy and Production. Placing History in Nature', *Journal of American History*, vol. 76, no. 4, 1990, p. 1131; Stephen Dovers (ed.), *Environmental History and Policy: Still Settling Australia*, Oxford University Press, Melbourne, 2000, p. viii; Jock Phillips, *A Man's Country? The Image of the Pakeha Male: A History*, Penguin Books, Auckland, 1987, p. 39. Among historical geographies of New Zealand, see, for example: A. H. Clark, *The Invasion of New Zealand by People, Plants and Animals, South Island*, Rutgers University Press, New Brunswick, 1949; K. Cumberland, *Landmarks*, Reader's Digest, Surry Hills, 1981.

3 C. M. Rosen & J. A. Tarr, 'The Importance of an Urban Perspective in Environmental History', *Journal of Urban History*, vol. 20. no. 3, 1994, pp. 299–310; M.V. Melosi, 'The Place of the City in Environmental History', *Environmental History Review*, vol. 17, no. 1, 1993, pp. 1–23; Maureen A. Flanagan, 'Environmental Justice in the City: A Theme for Urban Environmental History', *Environmental History*, vol. 5, no. 2, 2000, pp. 159–64.

4 G. Davison, 'Cities and Ceremonies: Nationalism and Civic Ritual in Three New Lands', *New Zealand Journal of History*, vol. 24, no. 2, 1990, pp. 97–117.

5 J. E. Vance, *The Merchant's World: The Geography of Wholesaling*, Prentice-Hall, Englewood Cliffs, 1970; J. Gottmann, *Megalopolis: The Urbanized Northeastern Seaboard of the United States*, Twentieth Century Fund, New York, 1961; N. C. Quigley, Patterns and Processes in the Development of Frontier Canterbury, 1850-1890, MA thesis, University of Canterbury, 1980; E. Pawson & N. C. Quigley, 'The Circulation of Information and Frontier Development: Canterbury 1850–1890', *New Zealand Geographer*, vol. 38, no. 2, 1982, pp. 65–76; W. Cronon, *Nature's Metropolis: Chicago and the Great West*, W. W. Norton, New York, 1991.

6 A. Siegfried, *Democracy in New Zealand*, repr. Victoria University Press/Price Milburn, Wellington, 1982 (first published 1914), pp. 252–3.

7 James Belich, *The New Zealand Wars and the Victorian Interpretation of Racial Conflict*, Auckland University Press, Auckland, 1986; *Making Peoples: A History of the New Zealanders from Polynesian Settlement to the End of the Nineteenth Century*, Penguin Books, Auckland, 1996.

8 A. Hurley, 'Common Fields: An Introduction', in A. Hurley (ed.), *Common Fields: An Environmental History of St Louis*, Missouri Historical Society Press, St Louis, 1997, p. 10.

9 J. Cowan, *New Zealand Cities*, Auckland, Whitcombe & Tombs, Auckland, 1917, pp. 10–11; J. Barr, *The City of Auckland New Zealand, 1840–1920*, Whitcombe & Tombs, Auckland, 1922, p. 199.

10 Anon, *Auckland, The Gateway*, p. 4.

11 Robert McGregor, *The Art Deco City: Napier, New Zealand*, Art Deco Trust, Napier, 1998; Patrick van Daele & Roy Lumby, *A Spirit of Progress: Art Deco Architecture in Australia*, Craftsman House, North Ryde, 1997.

12 Anon, *Auckland City and Province, Gateway to New Zealand*, Auckland, c. 1950.

13 J. Cowan, *Official Record of the New Zealand International Exhibition of Arts and Industries, Held at Christchurch 1906–7. A Descriptive and Historical Account*, Government Printer, Wellington, 1910, pp. 12, 21.

14 G. Anderson, 'Wakefield Towns', in The Friends of the Turnbull Library, *Edward Gibbon Wakefield and the Colonial Dream: A Reconsideration*, GP Publications, Wellington, 1997, pp. 143–58; D. Hamer, 'Wellington on the Urban Frontier', in D. Hamer & R. Nicholls (eds), *The Making of Wellington 1800–1914*, Victoria University Press, Wellington, 1990, pp. 227–54.

15 *Taranaki: The Garden of New Zealand*, 1906; *New Plymouth: Health, Sunshine, Happiness*, New Plymouth Tourist and Expansion League, 1922; *Guide and Map of Gisborne and the Picturesque East Coast*, Gisborne Publishing Co., 1942; *Come to Sunny Gisborne on Sea: The California of New Zealand*, Gisborne 30,000 Club, 1946; see also D. Alessio, Colonial Views: Images of the New Zealand City and Town, 1880–1930, PhD thesis, Victoria University of Wellington, 1992.

16 *The Future's in Rotorua: A Complimentary Brochure*, City of Rotorua Publications Office, 1962; Wellington Early Settlers' and Historical Association Inc., *Pioneers Progress*, Wellington, 1960, p. 19.

17 F. Whitford, 'The City in Painting', in E. Timms & D. Kelley (eds), *Unreal City: Urban Experience in Modern European Literature and Art*, Manchester University Press, Manchester, 1985, p. 57.

18 N. J. Ericksen, *Creating Flood Disasters? New Zealand's Need for a New Approach to Urban Flood Hazard*, Water and Soil Miscellaneous Publication No. 77, National Water and Soil Conservation Authority, Wellington, 1986; M. Davis, *Ecology of Fear: Los Angeles and the Imagination of Disaster*, Metropolitan Books, New York, 1998; see also K. Hewitt, *Regions of Risk: A Geographical Introduction to Disasters*, Addison Wesley Longman, Harlow, 1997.

19 Rodney Grapes, *Magnitude Eight Plus: New Zealand's Biggest Earthquake*, Victoria University Press, Wellington, 2000.

20 Ericksen, *Creating Flood Disasters?*, p. 46.

21 Report on the Waimakariri River by James M. Balfour, Marine Engineer, 9 April 1866, National Archives, Christchurch, MS, CP 631a/1.

22 G. Nelson, *Report on the Waimakariri River (New Zealand)*, Cook, Hammond & Kell, London, 1928, p. iv.

23 F. W. Maclean, J. M. Willis & J. G. Alexander, *Water of Leith and Lindsay's Creek*, 'The Engineers' Commission', 1931, Hocken Library, Hoc Bliss and RUS MacL; W. J. Watt, *Dunedin's Historical Background*, Dunedin City Council, Dunedin, 1972.

24 W. Pratt, *Canterbury and Incidentally New Zealand, AD 1900*, Christchurch Press, Christchurch, 1900, pp. 93–4.

25 E. Pawson, 'Confronting Nature', in J. Cookson & G. Dunstall (eds), *Southern Capital: Christchurch, Towards a City Biography*, Canterbury University Press, Christchurch, 2000, pp. 60–84.

26 Report of the Commission of Inquiry into Certain Alleged Nuisances in Districts Within or Contiguous to the Southern Auckland Metropolitan Area (Fumes Inquiry) August 1955, *Appendices to the Journals of the House of Representatives*, H31A, 1955; C. J. Sparrow, 'Some Geographic Aspects of Air Pollution in Auckland', in *Auckland Air Pollution Symposium*, Royal Society of Health, Auckland, 1968; G. Bush, *Moving Against the Tide: The Brown's Island Drainage Controversy*, Dunmore Press, Palmerston North, 1980; *Finding of the Waitangi Tribunal on the Manukau Claim*, (Wai 8), Government Printer, Wellington, 1985.

27 Pawson, 'Confronting Nature'.

28 D. Hamer, 'Centralization and Nationalism (1891–1912)', in K. Sinclair (ed.), *The Oxford Illustrated History of New Zealand,* Oxford University Press, Auckland, 1990, pp. 125–52; M. Fairburn, 'The Rural Myth and the New Urban Frontier. An Approach to New Zealand Social History, 1870–1940', *New Zealand Journal of History*, vol. 9, no. 1, 1975, pp. 3–21.

29 Siegfried, *Democracy*, p. 247; Cowan, *New Zealand Cities*, p. 42; Eggleton, 'Introduction', p. 21.

30 The advertisements referred to in this section are from the archives of H. G. Livingstone Ltd, Christchurch, and the Hocken Library, Dunedin. See also Caroline Miller, 'Images and Reality: Selling Suburbia', *Proceedings of the Twentieth New Zealand Geography Conference*, New Zealand Geographical Society, Hamilton, 1999, pp. 223–6.

31 D. C. Thorns, 'Owner Occupation, the State and Class Relations', in C. Wilkes & I. Shirley (eds), *In the Public Interest: Health, Work and Housing in New Zealand Society*, Benton Ross, Auckland, 1984, pp. 213–30; E. Pawson, 'The Social Production of Urban Space', *New Zealand Geographer*, vol. 43, no. 3, 1987, pp. 123–9; Fairburn, 'The Rural Myth', p. 16.

32 Anon, *Auckland. The Gateway*, p. 10; S. P. Hays, *Beauty, Health and Permanence: Environmental Politics in the United States 1955–1985*, Cambridge University Press, Cambridge, 1987.

33 Penrose Industrial Progress Association Inc., *Penrose Progress: The Growth of a Great Industrial Centre*, Penrose, 1946, p. 5.

34 Ministry of Works, *The New Zealand Environment. National Report to the United Nations Preparatory Committee for the 1972 Conference on the Human Environment*, Town and Country Planning Division, Wellington, 1972, p. 7.

35 Ericksen, *Creating Flood Disasters?*, pp. 64–9.

36 'Sunny Timaru Welcomes You', *Shopping Week*, September 27 to October 2, Timaru Post Co., Timaru, 1926, p. 7.

37 R. Shields, *Places on the Margin: Alternative Geographies of Modernity*, Routledge, London, 1991. Shields uses Brighton in Sussex as the focus of his argument.

38 'Sunny Timaru Welcomes You', p. 35.

39 *Timaru Herald*, 18 December 1922.

40 I am grateful to Tom Brooking, Richard Le Heron, and Peter Holland for their comments and encouragement, and to the late David McDonald, of the Hocken Library in Dunedin, for his enthusiasm and help with finding original materials.

14 Exotic natives and contrived wild gardens: The twentieth-century home garden

1 W. Shepherd & W. Cook 1988, *The Botanic Garden Wellington: A New Zealand History 1840–1987*, Millwood Press, Wellington, 1988; A. Hale, *The Pioneer Nurserymen of New Zealand*, Reed, Wellington, 1955; S. Challenger, 'Early Nursery Catalogues: An Historical Resource', *N.Z. Libraries*, vol. 41, no. 4, 1978, pp. 107–8.

2 For example, B. Douglas, *Pictures in a New Zealand Garden*, Alexander McCubbin, Melbourne, c. 1917; E. K. Morton, *Gardening's Such Fun!*, Oswald-Sealy (NZ) Ltd, Auckland, 1944; N. Woodhouse, *Flowers*

for Four Seasons, A. H. & A. W. Reed, Wellington, 1968; J. Lawrence, *Gardens Full of Wings*, Millwood Press, Wellington, 1976; F. Preston, *From Rocks to Roses*, Craig Printing, Invercargill, 1978; K. Carman, *Portrait of a Garden*, Reed, Wellington, 1983; D. Anthony, *Seven Summers at Valley Homestead*, Godwit Press, Auckland, 1994.

3 *Yates' New Zealand Garden Guide*, 20th New Zealand edn, Arthur Yates & Co., Auckland, 1934, cover. Before this, editions published from 1895 to the 1920s were written primarily with Australian (NSW) conditions in mind, despite the inclusion of 'New Zealand' in the title.

4 For example, the following handbooks: M. Murphy, *Gardening in New Zealand*, 4th edn, Whitcombe & Tombs, Christchurch, 1907; D. Tannock, *Manual of Gardening in New Zealand*, Whitcombe & Tombs, Christchurch, c. 1914; J. A. McPherson, *Whitcombe's Complete New Zealand Gardener*, Whitcombe & Tombs, Christchurch, 1943; J. W. Matthews, *Matthews on Gardening: A Practical Approach to the Growing of Fruits, Flowers and Vegetables*, A. H. & A. W. Reed, Wellington, 1960.

5 T. Strongman, *The Gardens of Canterbury: A History*, Reed, Wellington, 1984; cf. R. Tipples, *Colonial Landscape Gardener: Alfred Buxton of Christchurch, New Zealand 1872–1950*, Department of Horticulture and Landscape, Lincoln College, Canterbury, 1989.

6 Murphy, *Gardening*, p. 5; Tannock, *Manual*, p. 65.

7 For example, Tannock, *Manual*, pp. 30–1; J. Young & D. A. Hay, *Flower Gardening in New Zealand*, 2nd edn, Whitcombe & Tombs, Christchurch, c. 1925, pp. 57–66; cf. B. Elliott, *Victorian Gardens*, Batsford, London, 1990, pp. 90–1, 130–1, 137, 203, 209–11.

8 Murphy, *Gardening*, p. 228; Tannock, *Manual*, p. 139; McPherson, *Whitcombe's Complete N.Z. Gardener*, pp. 154–6; Tipples, *Colonial Landscape Gardener*, pp. 101–4, 106; H. M. Leach, 'Analysing Change in the New Zealand Home Garden—by Style or Element?', *New Zealand Garden Journal (Journal of the Royal New Zealand Institute of Horticulture)*, vol. 1, no. 2, 1996, p. 15.

9 J. W. Chapman-Taylor, 'A Simple Cottage', *Progress*, vol. 6, no. 1, 1910, p. 451; Tannock, *Manual*, pp. 48–52, 160; Murphy, *Gardening*, frontispiece; Young & Hay, *Flower Gardening*, p. 86.

10 Murphy, *Gardening*, p. 27; Elliott, *Victorian Gardens*, pp. 40–1; Tannock, *Manual*, pp. 29, 52; Douglas, *Pictures*, p. 10; Leach, 'Analysing Change', p. 14; W. Robinson, *The Wild Garden or the Naturalization and Natural Grouping of Hardy Exotic Plants with a Chapter on the Garden of British Wild Flowers*, John Murray, London, 1870; H. Leach, *Cultivating Myths: Fiction, Fact and Fashion in Garden History*, Godwit Press, Auckland, 2000, pp. 77–96.

11 Tannock, *Manual*, pp. 65, 68, 138; Murphy, *Gardening*, p. 222.

12 Murphy, *Gardening*, pp. 226–7; Tannock, *Manual*, p. 159; cf. H. M. Leach, 'Native Plants and National Identity in New Zealand Gardening: An Historical Review', *Horticulture in New Zealand (Journal of the Royal New Zealand Institute of Horticulture)*, vol. 5, no. 1, 1994, pp. 28–33.

13 Murphy, *Gardening*, p. 237.

14 Murphy, *Gardening*, pp. 80, 242; Tannock, *Manual*, p. 143.

15 W. C. Hyde, 'The Homestead Beautiful', *The Journal of Agriculture*, vol. 7, 1913, pp. 127–8; J. A. Campbell, 'Landscape Gardening: Laying Down and Maintaining Lawns', *Journal of Agriculture*, vol. 7, 1913, p. 260.

16 Tannock, *Manual*, pp. 23, 24.

17 *Yates' Garden Guide for Australia and New Zealand*, 15th edn, Arthur Yates & Co., Auckland, 1922, pp. 44–6; D. Tannock, *Practical Gardening in New Zealand*, Whitcombe & Tombs, Christchurch, 1934, p. 3.

18 H. Orsman (ed.), *The Dictionary of New Zealand English*, Oxford University Press, Auckland, 1997, p. 113; *Yates'*, 1922, pp. 89, 93–4, 97.

19 *Yates' Garden Guide for Australia and New Zealand*, 19th edn, Arthur Yates & Co., Sydney and Auckland, 1931, pp. 40, 84; *Yates'*, 1934, pp. 42, 80; D. Tannock, *Rock Gardening in New Zealand*, Whitcombe & Tombs, Christchurch, 1924, p. 32; McPherson, *Whitcombe's Complete N.Z. Gardener*, p. 181; *Brett's Gardening Guide for New Zealand Gardeners*, revised edn, New Zealand Newspapers Ltd., Auckland, 1945, pp. 203–5; J. Young, *Rose Growing in New Zealand*, Whitcombe & Tombs, Christchurch, c.1922, pp. 52–3; H. M. Leach, 'The European House and Garden in New Zealand—a Case for Parallel Development', in B. Brookes (ed.), *At Home in New Zealand: Houses History People*, Bridget Williams Books,

Wellington, 2000, pp. 73–88; D. Elliott, 'Planning the Small Town Garden for Use, Convenience and Enjoyment', *New Zealand Gardener*, vol. 3, no. 10, 1947, p. 540.

20 Strongman, *Gardens of Canterbury*, pp. 74, 100; G. Jekyll, *Wood and Garden*, introduced and revised by G. S. Thomas, The Ayer Co., Salem, New Hampshire, 1983.

21 *Yates'*, 1922, p. 12; M. Halligan, 'A Sufficiently Exciting Occupation', in P. Timms (ed.), *The Nature of Gardens*, Sue Hines/Allen & Unwin, St Leonards, NSW, 1999, pp. 7–8; *Yates'*, 1931, pp. 7, 12; *Yates'*, 1934, p. 9.

22 Tannock, *Practical Gardening*, p. 131; L. Cockayne, *The Cultivation of New Zealand Plants*, Whitcombe & Tombs, Christchurch, 1923, pp. 8, 12.

23 Tannock, *Practical Gardening*, pp. 132–8; McPherson, *Whitcombe's Complete N.Z. Gardener*, pp. 178, 180; 'M', 'Some Colourful New Zealanders. Shrubs Noted for Gay Flowers and Foliage', *New Zealand Gardener*, vol. 2, no. 8, 1946, p. 339.

24 Anon, 'The New Flowers have Arrived: Seed You Can Sow this Year', *The New Zealand Gardener*, vol. 2, no. 10, 1946, pp. 439–40; N. M. Taylor, *The Home Front: Official History of New Zealand in the Second World War 1939–45*, Government Printer, Wellington, 1986, p. 814; *Yates' New Zealand Garden Guide*, 28th New Zealand edn, Arthur Yates & Co., Auckland, 1943, p. 127; *Yates' Garden Guide*, 1st edn [n.s.], Arthur Yates & Co., Auckland, 1950; cf. *Brett's Gardening Guide for New Zealand Gardeners*, revised edn, New Zealand Newspapers Ltd, Auckland, 1951, pp. 39–41; *Yates' Garden Guide for New Zealand Home Gardeners*, 39th edn, Arthur Yates & Co., Auckland, 1957, p. 10.

25 C. Firth, *State Housing in New Zealand*, Ministry of Works, Wellington, 1949, p. 13.

26 Elliott, 'Planning the Small Town Garden', p. 539; *Yates'*, 1957, p. 4, chapter 3; *Yates' Garden Guide for New Zealand Home Gardeners*, 41st edn, Arthur Yates & Co., Auckland, 1961; *Yates' Garden Guide*, 61st edn, Yates New Zealand Ltd, Auckland, 1987.

27 Tannock, *Practical Gardening*, p. 37; *Yates'*, 1957, pp. 215, 275–6; J. A. McPherson, *Whitcombe's Complete New Zealand Gardener*, 5th edn, Whitcombe & Tombs, Christchurch, 1964, pp. 12–13.

28 *Yates'*, 1957, p. 275; B. McDonald, *Home Landscaping in New Zealand: A Design Guide*, Collins, Auckland, 1980, p. 33; J. Say & N. Weal, *Developing a New Garden in New Zealand*, A. H. & A. W. Reed, Wellington, 1981, pp. 3, 8.

29 *Yates' Garden Guide*, 3rd edn [n.s.], Arthur Yates & Co., Auckland, 1953, pp. 222–3; *Yates' Garden Guide for New Zealand Home Gardeners*, 46th edn, Arthur Yates & Co., Auckland, 1970, p. 17; J. P. Salinger, *The New Zealander's Guide to Pebble Gardens*, Collins, Auckland, 1971, p. 9.

30 *Yates'*, 1953, pp. 222–3; *Yates' Garden Guide for New Zealand Home Gardeners*, 40th edn, Arthur Yates & Co., Auckland, 1958, facing p. 1; *Brett's Gardening Guide for New Zealand Gardeners*, revised edn, New Zealand Newspapers Ltd., Christchurch, 1963; J. P. Salinger, J. S. Say, & K. H. Marcussen, *Flower Gardening with The Journal of Agriculture*, Whitcombe & Tombs, Christchurch, 1962, pp. 93, 96; Salinger, *The New Zealander's Guide to Pebble Gardens*, pp. 37–8; M. E. Fisher, E. Satchell, & J. M. Watkins, *Gardening with New Zealand Plants Shrubs and Trees*, Collins, Auckland, 1970; L. J. Metcalf, *The Cultivation of New Zealand Trees and Shrubs*, A. H. & A. W. Reed, Wellington, 1972; Leach, 'Native Plants', pp. 32–3.

31 This conclusion has been reached for Australia as well, where George Seddon applies the term 'exclosure' to contrast with 'enclosure'—see G. Seddon, 'Mission Statements', in Peter Timms (ed.), *The Nature of Gardens*, Sue Hines/Allen & Unwin, St Leonards, NSW, 1999, pp. 159–60.

32 Tannock, *Manual*, p. 137; Tannock, *Practical Gardening*, p. 137; J. W. Matthews, *Garden Treasures: Choice Flowering Shrubs for Australia and New Zealand*, A. H. & A. W. Reed, Wellington, 1947, p. 56.

33 Tannock, *Rock Gardening*, facing p. 3, pp. 16–17; *Yates'*, 1934, p. 43; McPherson, *Whitcombe's Complete N.Z. Gardener*, 5th edn, p. 116; Matthews, *Matthews on Gardening*, p. 196; Young & Hay, *Flower Gardening*, p. 101.

34 Murphy, *Gardening*, p. 226; Cockayne, *Cultivation of N. Z. Plants*, pp. 13, 103; McPherson, *Whitcombe's Complete N.Z. Gardener*, p. 189; D. Elliott, *Planning Your Garden*, A. H. & A. W. Reed, Wellington, 1950, p. 52.

35 'Maecanas', 'Planning a Garden: Fundamentals of Landscape Architecture', *New Zealand Gardener*, vol. 2, no. 12, 1946, p. 562.

36 J. C. Loudon, *The Suburban Gardener, and Villa Companion*, Longman, Orme, Green & Longmans, London, 1838, pp. 138–40, 429; Robinson, *The Wild Garden*.

37 Young & Hay, *Flower Gardening*, p. 97, 102; Elliott, *Planning*, p. 37; Tannock, *Rock Gardening*, p. 8; Tannock, *Practical Gardening*, p. 142; McPherson, *Whitcombe's Complete N. Z. Gardener*, p. 156; Matthews, *Matthews on Gardening*, p. 200.

38 G. Dutton, *Some Branch Against the Sky: The Practice and Principles of Marginal Gardening*, David & Charles, Newton Abbot, 1997, pp. 15, 167; M. Pollan, *Second Nature: A Gardener's Education*, Bloomsbury, London, 1996, pp. 266–7; Leach, *Cultivating Myths*.

15 Companions, stowaways, imperialists, invaders: Pests and weeds in New Zealand

1 Personal interview with A. France, Holbrook station, 17 November 1991.

2 H. Guthrie-Smith, *Tutira: The Story of a New Zealand Sheep Station*, University of Washington Press, Seattle/Godwit Press, Auckland, reprint 1999, pp. 361–5.

3 G. M. Thomson, *The Naturalisation of Animals and Plants in New Zealand*, Cambridge University Press, Cambridge, 1922, p. 2.

4 A. H. Clark, *The Invasion of New Zealand by People, Plants and Animals: The South Island*, Greenwood Press, Westport, reprint, 1970.

5 A. W. Crosby, *Ecological Imperialism: The Biological Expansion of Europe, 900–1900*, Cambridge University Press, Cambridge, 1986, pp. 7, 270.

6 Discussion of red deer, except as otherwise noted, based on K. A. Wodzicki, *Introduced Mammals of New Zealand: An Ecological and Economic Survey*, DSIR Bulletin No. 98, Department of Scientific and Industrial Research, Wellington, 1950, pp. 176–202; Clark, *Invasion of New Zealand*, pp. 274–8; G. Caughley, *The Deer Wars: The Story of Deer in New Zealand*, Heinemann, Wellington, 1983, pp. 1–117; R. Nelson, *Deer and Resulting Devastation in New Zealand: A Review of the Concern and Evidence Presented over the Last 100 Years*, Royal Forest and Bird Protection Society of New Zealand, Wellington, 1979, pp. 1–28. On the Wildlife Service, see R. Galbreath, *Working for Wildlife: A History of the New Zealand Wildlife Service*, Bridget Williams Books/Historical Branch, Department of Internal Affairs, Wellington, 1993.

7 Quoted in Nelson, *Deer and Resulting Devastation*, p. 4.

8 B. Crump, *A Good Keen Man*, A. H. & A. W. Reed, Wellington, 1960.

9 D. Yerex, *Deer Farming in New Zealand*, Agricultural Promotion Associates, Wellington, 1979, pp. 7–10; personal interview with M. & P. Garden, Avenel station, Millers Flat, 9 November 1991; exhibits at Deerworld Museum, Taupo.

10 Major sources on possums are Wodzicki, *Introduced Mammals*, pp. 21–43; Parliamentary Commissioner for the Environment, *Possum Management in New Zealand*, Wellington, 1994; *Possum Management in New Zealand: Critical Issues in 1998*, Parliamentary Commissioner for the Environment Progress Report No. 1, Wellington, 1998. See also the 'Possum Bibliography', compiled by Stephen Sarre, <http://possum.massey.ac.nz>.

11 'Kiwis for Kiwis', press release, New Zealand Forest and Bird Society, 11 September 1998, <http://www.nxwwa.com/education/conservation/forest-bird/page3.htm>.

12 Quote from summary of *Possum Management* at <http://www.pce.govt.nz/reports/possum.htm>.

13 Quote from summary of *Critical Issues* at <http://www.pce.govt.nz/reports/possumreview.htm>.

14 Northland Regional Council, 'Animal and Plant Pests',_<http://www.northland.ac.nz/nrc/pests.htm>.

15 Parliamentary Commissioner for the Environment, *The Rabbit Calicivirus Disease (RCD) Saga: A Biosecurity/Bio-control Fiasco*, 1999, quote from summary posted at <http://www.pce.govt.nz/reports/rcd.htm>.

16 Major early sources on rabbits include Wodzicki, *Introduced Mammals*, pp. 107–20; Thomson, *Naturalisation of Animals and Plants*, pp. 85–91; *New Zealand Parliamentary Debates*, vol. 21, 1876, pp. 626–8; vol. 68, 1890, pp. 91–9; Rachel E. Egerton, Unconquerable Enemy or Bountiful Resource? A New Perspective on the Rabbit in Central Otago, BA Honours thesis, University of Otago, 1993. See also *Appendices to the Journals of the House of Representatives* (hereafter *AJHR*), annual reports of the New

Zealand Department of Agriculture (1894–1915), and the *New Zealand Journal of Agriculture* (hereafter *NZJA*) for the period under review. Archival material providing details of rabbit policy and controls during this period is in the National Archives of New Zealand, AG Series 1 and 40, from which the author examined numerous files.

17 *Environmental Impact Report on a Proposal to Introduce Myxomatosis as Another Means of Rabbit Control in New Zealand*, John Bamford Associates, Nelson, 1985, updated 1987; Parliamentary Commissioner for the Environment, *Investigation of the Proposal to Introduce Myxomatosis for Rabbit Control*, 3 vols, Wellington, 1987; *Report of the Rabbit and Land Management Task Force (Amended Impression)*, 1988; P. Jarvis, J. Kelly & B. Beckingsale, *Rabbit and Land Management Programme Final Report: Financial/Economic Monitoring Report*, Ministry of Agriculture and Fisheries, Christchurch, 1995.

18 Personal interview with J. M. Williams, Director, Rabbit and Land Management Programme, 21 February 1996; R. Wilkinson & G. Fitzgerald, 'Public Perceptions of Biological Control of Rabbits in New Zealand: Some Ethical and Practical Issues', *Agriculture and Human Values*, vol. 14, 1997, pp. 273–82.

19 P. W. Smallfield, *The Grasslands Revolution in New Zealand*, Hodder & Stoughton, Auckland, 1970. Of the many classic publications by Leonard Cockayne, the author points particularly to 'An Economic Investigation of the Montane Tussock-Grassland of New Zealand', serial in *NZJA*, vol. 18, no. 1, 1919 through to vol. 25, no. 3, 1922. The pop-ecology view that pests and weeds must be the result of land abuse permeates the Parliamentary Commissioner for the Environment's report, *Sustainable Land Use for the Dry Tussock Grasslands in the South Island*, Wellington, 1991.

20 Parliamentary Commissioner for the Environment, *Sustainable Land Use*, pp. 1–21; G. G. Hunter et al. (eds), *Vegetation Change in Tussock Grasslands, with Emphasis on Hawkweeds*, New Zealand Ecological Society Publication No. 2, 1992; personal interview with F. McRae, Policy Development Manager, Otago Regional Council, 12 November 1991; T. P. Grundy, *An Economic Evaluation of Biological Control of Hieracium*, Research Report No. 202, Lincoln College Agribusiness and Economics Research Unit, 1989.

21 *New Zealand Farmer*, February 1888, p. 55, September 1889, p. 362; A. H. Cockayne, 'Californian Thistle: A Suggestive Field for Investigation', *NZJA*, vol. 4, no. 5, 1912, p. 346.

22 *New Zealand Farmer*, September 1893, p. 339, October 1893, p. 355; F. S. Pope to Minister of Agriculture, 10 June 1911, Pope to Director of Fields Division, 14 August 1916, Records of the Noxious Weeds Act, AG, Series 1, File 3171, National Archives; A. H. Cockayne, 'Noxious Weeds in New Zealand: Notes on a Recent Inquiry', *NZJA*, vol. 14, no. 5, pp. 339–44.

23 J. S. N., 'The Story of Gorse', *New Zealand's Nature Heritage*, vol. 6, 1974, pp. 2238–42; Clark, *Invasion of New Zealand*, p. 362; R. P. Hargreaves, 'Farm Fences in Pioneer New Zealand', *New Zealand Geographer*, vol. 21, no. 2, 1965, pp. 144–55.

24 Komata, 'Hints on Making Ditches', *New Zealand Farmer*, June 1888, p. 192.

25 *New Zealand Farmer*, June 1888, p. 218, August 1888, p. 276; J. Forrest, 'Mechanical Cutting of Gorse Hedges', *NZJA*, vol. 78, no. 1, 1949, pp. 45–6; station diaries for Clayton station, 1877–84, and Rakaia station, 1867–96, Manuscripts Department, Alexander Turnbull Library, Wellington; *Ashburton Guardian*, 26 August 1880, 28 August 1880; personal interviews with Sid Lister, Temuka, 22 November 1991, and with Alister & Warwick Wooding, Geraldine, 23 November 1991.

26 *New Zealand Farmer*, December 1888, p. 471.

27 *New Zealand Farmer*, August 1900, p. 320; T. W. Lonsdale, 'Eradication of Gorse and the Utilization of Gorse-Infested Lands', *NZJA*, vol. 50, no. 4, 1935, pp. 235–7; J. E. Bell, 'Destruction of Gorse and Blackberry: Methods of Eradication and Control', *NZJA*, vol. 58, no. 2, 1939, pp. 111–16; R. P. Hill, 'Clearing Gorse Land with Tractor and Giant Discs', *NZJA*, vol. 75, no. 2, 1947, p. 151; A. A. Duncan, 'Gorse Control on Hill Country', *NZJA*, vol. 88, no. 4, 1954, pp. 359–67; L. J. Mathews & P. B. Lynch, 'Aerial Application of Weedkillers to Gorse', *NZJA*, vol. 92, no. 2, 1956, pp. 121–5; W. F. Leonard, 'Thorough Planning Essential in Control of Gorse', *NZJA*, vol. 103, no. 6, 1961, p. 564.

28 D. Miller, 'Control of Gorse by Seed Weevil', *NZJA*, vol. 75, no. 4, 1947, pp. 341–4; R. Hill, *The Biological Control of Gorse (*Ulex europaeus L.*) in New Zealand: An Environmental Impact Assessment*, Entomology Division, Department of Scientific and Industrial Research, Christchurch, 1987, pp. 12–13, 32; R. Hill, *Biological Control of Gorse: Implications for the Natural Environment and for Primary*

Production, Entomology Division, Department of Scientific and Industrial Research, Christchurch, 1986; L. W. Price, 'Hedges and Shelterbelts on the Canterbury Plains, New Zealand: Transformation of an Antipodean Landscape', *Annals of the Association of American Geographers*, vol. 83, no. 1, 1993, pp. 119–40.

29 New Zealand Forest and Bird Society, press release, 14 August 1998, <http://www.nzwwa.com/education/conservation/forest-bird/page3.htm>.

30 W. T. L. Travers, 'On the Changes Effected in the Natural Features of a New Country by the Introduction of Civilized Races', *Transactions New Zealand Institute*, vol. 2, 1869, p. 312.

31 R. Hengeveld, *Dynamics of Biological Invasions*, Chapman & Hall, London, 1989; C. S. Elton, *The Ecology of Invasions by Animals and Plants*, Methuen, London, 1958.

32 C. Lever, *Naturalized Animals: The Ecology of Successfully Introduced Species,* T. & A. D. Poyser, London, 1994; Parliamentary Commissioner for the Environment, *Sustainable Land Use*.

33 Department of Conservation and Ministry for the Environment, 'Draft Biodiversity Strategy', <http://www.biodiv.govt.nz/>.

34 Crosby, *Ecological Imperialism*, p. 307.

35 K. F. O'Connor, 'Alien Animals in New Zealand Grasslands', unpublished lecture, copy courtesy of the author.

36 The author expresses thanks to the New Zealand Fulbright Foundation for funding his research in New Zealand in 1991 and 1996, and to the editors and fellow authors of this book for their helpful comments on this chapter in manuscript.

16 Bound to the land: Māori retention and assertion of land and identity

1 I. H. Kawharu, *Maori Land Tenure: Studies of a Changing Institution*, Clarendon Press, Oxford, 1977; David Williams, *Te Kooti Tango Whenua: The Native Land Court 1864–1909*, Huia Publishers, Wellington, 1999.

2 Joe Pere, '*Hitori Maori*', in Colin Davis & Peter Lineham (eds), *The Future of the Past: Themes in New Zealand History*, Department of History, Massey University, Palmerston North, 1991, p. 30. See also Te Ahukaramu Charles Royal, *Te Haurapa: An Introduction to Researching Tribal Histories and Traditions*, Bridget Williams Books/Historical Branch, Department of Internal Affairs, Wellington, 1992, p. 13; Monty Soutar, Towards An Acceptable Record: An Analysis of Tribal History, BA Hons essay, Massey University, 1991.

3 Dispatch from his Excellency Governor Gore Browne, C.B., to the Right Hon. Sir E. B. Lytton, 29 March 1859, *Appendices to the Journals of the House of Representatives* (hereafter *AJHR*), E2, 1860, p. 2.

4 Eddie Durie, 'The Law and the Land', in J. Phillips (ed.), *Te Whenua Te Iwi*, Allen & Unwin/Port Nicholson Press, Wellington, 1987, p. 78.

5 Petition No. 19/1925 (1925), Le 1/1925/12, National Archives, Wellington.

6 Ngā Ruahine, for example, itself comprised hapū and did not therefore necessarily operate under the mana of Ngāti Ruanui, the tribe to which it was long thought affiliated as hapū; Tom Ngati, Ngā Ruahine, personal communication, November 1992.

7 Lou MacDonald, Ngāti Mutunga, personal communication, October 1992.

8 Kawharu, *Maori Land Tenure*, p. 47.

9 Tipene O'Regan, 'Old Myths and New Politics: Some Contemporary Uses of Traditional History', *New Zealand Journal of History*, vol. 26, no. 1, 1992, p. 25.

10 E. T. Durie, *Custom Law*, Research Paper, Waitangi Tribunal, Wellington, 1994, p. 96.

11 MacDonald, personal communication, October 1992.

12 I. L. G. Sutherland, 'Maori and European', *Journal of the Polynesian Society*, vol. 61, no. 1, 1952, p. 139.

13 'Evidence relating to the origin of the Native insurrection, 1860'; *AJHR,* E4, 1861, p. 1.

14 MacDonald, personal communication, October 1991.

15 'Thomas Gore Browne, The Governor's Despatch', *AJHR*, E1, 1861, p. 8.

16 Angela Ballara, Origins of Ngati Kahungunu, PhD thesis, Victoria University of Wellington, 1993.

17 Petition No. 87/1925 (1925), MA 85/5, National Archives, Wellington.

18 MacDonald and Ngatai, personal communications, October–November 1992.

19 Petition No. 291/1880 (1880), Le 1/1880/6, National Archives, Wellington.

20 Kawharu, *Maori Land Tenure*, p. 37.

21 Exhibits and miscellaneous papers, Sim Commission (1927); MA 85/6, National Archives, Wellington.

22 MacDonald, personal communication, October 1992.

23 ibid.

24 ibid.

25 Tapa Te Waero to Native Affairs Committee (1867); Le 1/1876/7, National Archives, Wellington.

26 Minutes of Evidence, Sim Commission (1927); MA 85/1, National Archives, Wellington.

27 ibid.

28 Report for Commissioners, Sim Commission (1927); MA 85/5, National Archives, Wellington.

29 Hamilton, Cambridge, Mercer, and Urenui were established as town centres for such military settlers.

30 New Zealand Settlements Amendment Act 1863.

31 New Zealand Settlements and Continuance Act 1865.

32 Papers Relating to the Sitting of the Compensation Court at New Plymouth, *AJHR*, A13, 1866, p. 3.

33 Keith Sinclair, *Kinds of Peace. Maori People After the Wars 1870–85*, Auckland University Press, Auckland, 1994, p. 7.

34 E. Durie, personal communication, May 1994.

35 To some Taranaki Māori, 'kūpapa' means to crawl on all fours, or to even crawl on one's belly—in other words, tantamount to a traitor. But more broadly speaking, 'kūpapa' is a highly contested term. Various tribal districts see 'kūpapa' in quite different terms. One needs to understand the complexities of local tribal involvements in warfare, for or against the Crown and settlers, or among each other, before one can confidently assert who was 'kūpapa' and who was not—or even what the term means, for individual tribal districts. We should also acknowledge the view held by Māori that 'kūpapa' should not necessarily carry a negative connotation.

36 Petition No. 284/1878 (1878), Le 1/1878/6, National Archives, Wellington.

37 ibid.

38 Hon. Sir W. Fox to Hon. Native Minister, 25 February 1882; *AJHR*, G5, 1882, p. 16.

39 Petition No. 75/1940 (1940), Le 1/1940/8, National Archives, Wellington.

40 ibid.

41 Alistair Morrison, 'Tribunal Motunui Recommendation Defines The Treaty' in *Tu Tangata. Maori News Magazine,* Issue 13 June–July 1983, p. 2.

42 Morrison, *Tu Tangata*, p. 2; *Report, Findings and Recommendations of the Waitangi Tribunal on an Application by Aila Taylor for and on Behalf of Te Atiawa Tribe in Relation to Fishing Grounds in the Waitara District*, Claim Wai 6, Waitangi Tribunal, Wellington, 1983.

43 *The Taranaki Report, Kaupapa Tuatahi*, Claim Wai 143, Waitangi Tribunal, GP Publications, Wellington, 1996.

44 *Indigenous Flora and Fauna of Aotearoa*, Claim Wai 262, Waitangi Tribunal, 9 October 1991.

17 A history of New Zealand environmental law

1 'Environmental law includes judicial decisions, legislation, and administrative regulation directly concerning the use, management, and protection of the physical and biological elements of the biosphere and the effects of human and natural interactions within and between these physical and biological elements.' (D. A. R. Williams, *Environmental and Resource Management Law*, 2nd edn, Butterworths, Wellington, 1997, p. 7, which is the text relied on generally in this chapter.)

2 See *Wi Parata* v. *Bishop of Wellington* (1877) 3 New Zealand Jurist Reports (New Series) Supreme Court, p. 77, per C. J. Prendergast, and the discussion in E. T. Durie, 'F. W. Guest Memorial Lecture 1996: Will the Settlers Settle? Cultural Conciliation and Law', *Otago Law Review*, vol. 8, 1996, pp. 449–65. For a description of Māori environmental law, see T. S. Ruru, The Resource Management Act 1991 and Ngā Iwi Māori, LLM thesis, University of Otago, 1997.

3 Even before the abolition of the provinces in 1875, local government had entered a period of 'variegated fragmentism' (G.W.A. Bush, *Local Government and Politics in New Zealand*, George Allen & Unwin, Auckland, 1980, p. 20), which persisted until the Local Government Act 1974 was enacted. The 'tinkering' approach is invited by the outdated view of nature as a 'perfectly intelligible clockwork ... [whose] moving parts were automata or mechanisms in miniature': J. B. Callicott, 'La Nature est Morte, Vive la Nature!', *Hastings Centre Report*, vol. 22, 1992, pp. 17–18.

4 T. Bührs & R.V. Bartlett, *Environmental Policy in New Zealand: The Politics of Clean and Green?*, Oxford University Press, Auckland, 1993, p. 92.

5 The presumption of protection has obvious merits, but also 'has the strange effect of not specifying by name [the wildlife which is] protected. For instance, nowhere in the statutes of New Zealand will one find a provision which specifically protects the kiwi ...' N. Wells, 'Protection of Wildlife in the Environment', *Auckland University Law Review*, vol. 4, 1980–83, p. 392. The kiwi is New Zealand's national bird.

6 N. Peat, *Manapouri Saved! New Zealand's First Great Conservation Success Story*, Longacre Press, Dunedin, 1993, p. 1.

7 Peat, *Manapouri Saved!*, p. 33.

8 A. F. Mark, 'Foreword' in Peat, *Manapouri Saved!*

9 *Royal Forest and Bird Protection Society of New Zealand Inc.* v. *Bay of Plenty Regional Water Board* (1978) 6 New Zealand Town Planning Appeals, pp. 361–70. The New Zealand waterfowl affected were the grey and blue ducks and the black and brown teal. The association of all four in one habitat was described as nationally unique (p. 365).

10 T. Black, 'Defending the Environment', *New Zealand Law Journal*, 1978, p. 153.

11 R. Wilson, *From Manapouri to Aramoana: The Battle for New Zealand's Environment*, Earthworks Press, Auckland, 1982, p. 20.

12 Town and Country Planning Act Review Committee, *Report to Government*, September 1973.

13 Wilson, *From Manapouri to Aramoana*, p. 63. For a detailed and critical description of events leading to the damming of the Clutha River, see P. Powell, *Who Killed the Clutha?*, J. McIndoe, Dunedin, 1978.

14 See F. M. Brookfield, 'High Courts, High Dam, High Policy: The Clutha River and the Constitution', *Recent Law*, vol. 9, 1983, pp. 62–72.

15 See, for example, *CREEDNZ Inc.* v. *Governor-General* [1981] 1 New Zealand Law Reports, pp. 172–215; *Environmental Defence Society* v. *South Pacific Aluminium* [1981] 1 New Zealand Law Reports, pp. 146–52, *(No. 2)* [1981] 1 New Zealand Law Reports, pp. 153–71, *(No. 3)* [1981] 1 New Zealand Law Reports, pp. 216–21; *Re An Application by NZ Synthetic Fuels Corporation Ltd* [1981] 8 New Zealand Town Planning Appeals, pp. 138–65.

16 T. Bührs, 'Environmental Policy', in R. Miller (ed.), *New Zealand Politics in Transition*, Oxford University Press, Auckland, 1997, p. 289.

17 J. Kelsey, *Rolling Back the State: Privatisation of Power in Aotearoa/New Zealand*, Bridget Williams Books, Wellington, 1993.

18 Bührs & Bartlett, *Environmental Policy in New Zealand*, p. 94. On Labour's programs of reform of environmental administration and local government, see S. Britton, R. Le Heron & E. Pawson (eds), *Changing Places in New Zealand: A Geography of Restructuring*, New Zealand Geographical Society, Christchurch, 1992.

19 Hon. P. Woollaston, 'The Creation of the Position of PCE: the Importance of the Role', in G. Hawke (ed.), *Guardians for the Environment*, Institute of Policy Studies, Victoria University of Wellington, Wellington, 1997, p. 7.

20 Ministry for the Environment, *Introducing the Resource Management Bill*, Wellington, 1989, p. 1. For a description and assessment of the making of the Resource Management Act, see Rt Hon. Sir G. Palmer, 'Sustainability—New Zealand's Resource Management Legislation', in M. Ross & J. O. Saunders (eds), *Growing Demands on a Shrinking Heritage: Managing Resource-Use Conflicts, Essays from the Fifth Institute Conference on Natural Resources Law*, 1992, pp. 408–28. For a history of New Zealand water law, culminating in the Resource Management Act, see N. R. Wheen, 'A Natural Flow—A History of Water Law in New Zealand', *Otago Law Review*, vol. 9, 1997, pp. 71–110.

21 *Greenpeace New Zealand Inc.* v. *Minister of Fisheries*, unreported, High Court, Wellington, 27 November 1995, CP 492/93, per J. Gallen; in these respects confirmed by the Fisheries Act 1996 and *New Zealand Fishing Industry Assn (Inc.)* v. *Minister of Fisheries*, unreported, 22 July 1997, CA 82/97 (Court of Appeal).

22 The flaws are explained in: A. Gillespie, *Burning Issues: The Failure of the New Zealand Response to Climate Change*, Dunmore Press, Palmerston North, 1997; A. Gillespie, 'Burning Follies: The Creation and Failure of the New Zealand Response to Climate Change', *New Zealand Journal of Environmental Law*, vol. 1, 1997, pp. 43–66; K. Bosselmann, 'Power, Plants and Power Plants: New Zealand's Implementation of the Climate Change Convention', *Environmental & Planning Law Journal*, vol. 12, 1995, pp. 423–9.

23 S. Tromans, 'High Talk and Low Cunning: Putting Environmental Principles into Legal Practice', *Journal of Planning & Environmental Law*, vol. 2, 1995, p. 791.

24 *New Zealand Rail Ltd* v. *Marlborough District Council* [1994] New Zealand Resource Management Appeals, p. 86.

25 *North Shore City Council* v. *Auckland Regional Council* [1997] New Zealand Resource Management Appeals, p. 94.

26 G. Palmer, *Environment—The International Challenge*, Victoria University Press, Wellington, 1995, pp. 172–3.

27 See note 10 above and accompanying text.

28 Environmental Law Reports of New Zealand, vol. 2, p. 407; [1997] New Zealand Resource Management Appeals, p. 35. For a critical review on uncertainty and the Resource Management Act, see N. R. Wheen, 'The Resource Management Act 1991: A Greener Law for Water?', *New Zealand Journal of Environmental Law*, vol. 1, 1997, pp. 165–98; I. H. Williams, 'The Resource Management Act 1991—Well Meant but Hardly Done', *Otago Law Review*, vol. 9, 2000, pp. 673–95.

29 *Marlborough District Council* v. *NZ Rail Ltd.* [1995] New Zealand Resource Management Appeals, p. 381.

30 B. Pardy, 'Fast Ferries: New Equilibrium versus Ecological Sustainability', *New Zealand Law Journal*, 1995, p. 204.

31 D. F. Dugdale, 'Framing Statutes in an Age of Judicial Supremacism', *Otago Law Review*, vol. 9, 2000, p. 604.

32 Tromans, 'High Talk and Low Cunning', p. 780.

33 B. Pardy, 'Abstraction, Precedent, and Articulate Consistency: Making Environmental Decisions', *California Western Law Review*, vol. 34, 1998, p. 429.

34 The author wishes to thank Royden Somerville, QC, Associate Professor Ken Palmer, and Dr Benjamin Richardson for their contributions to early research for this chapter.

18 Losing ground? Environmental problems and prospects at the beginning of the twenty-first century

1 Tim Porteous, *The Banks Peninsula Landscape*, Queen Elizabeth II National Trust, Wellington, 1987, p. 13.

2 Klaus Neumann, Nicholas Thomas & Hilary Eriksen (eds), *Quicksands: Foundational Histories in Australia and Aotearoa New Zealand*, UNSW Press, Sydney, 1999.

3 Julian Thomas, 'A History of Beginnings', in Neumann et al., *Quicksands*, pp. 115–31.

4 Stephen Turner, 'Settlement as Forgetting', in Neumann et al., *Quicksands*, pp. 20–38.

5 Alfred W. Crosby, *Ecological Imperialism: The Biological Expansion of Europe 900–1900*, Cambridge University Press, Cambridge, 1986.

6 Tim Flannery, *The Future Eaters: An Ecological History of the Australasian Lands and People*, Reed Books, Port Melbourne, 1995.

7 W. P. Reeves, 'The Passing of the Forest', in P. Temple (ed.), *Lake Mountain Tree: An Anthology of Writing on New Zealand Nature and Landscape*, Godwit Publishing, Auckland, 1998, pp. 84–6.

8 The Ministry of Agriculture and Forestry does not keep natural resource accounts that track gains and losses in 'natural capital', i.e. water, soil, native forests, or the costs of remedying damage caused to natural capital by industrial agriculture, such as water pollution and soil erosion. In 1996 MAF prepared a paper on agri-environmental programmes in New Zealand (available at <www.maf.govt.nz/MAFnet/articles-man/agenv/httoc.htm>), which includes a summary of expenditure on agri-environmental programmes.

This provides an estimate (for 1994/95) of total agri-environmental expenditure of $186,730,000. This includes disaster relief, pesticide registration, funding for native vegetation protection on private land, and $102,700,000 for research, as well as pest management. The pest component, including expenditure on rabbit and land management programs, pest policy, pest surveillance, pest response capability, and quarantine/border control came to $17,660,000. Quite a lot of the research funding would have also gone to pests and bio-remediation.

9 Malcolm McKinnon, 'Opening to the World? External Relations, 1961–1991', *New Zealand Historical Atlas*, plate 100, David Bateman, Auckland, with Department of Internal Affairs, Wellington, 1997.

10 Media release from the Minister of Biosecurity, 'Luxton launches new Biosecurity Authority', 29 July 1999; media release from the Parliamentary Commissioner from the Environment, 'New Zealand Under Siege. A Review of the Management of Biosecurity Risks to the Environment', 14 December 2000.

11 Details of the pests, and control measures, can be found on the Ministry of Agriculture and Forestry website—<www.maf.govt.nz>—under recent media releases and in the media release archive. In 2000, snakes, spiders, and other pests were entering the country frequently, and uncleared seed contaminated with exotic weeds was planted, despite MAF claims that its biosecurity control standards and practices were among the highest in the world.

12 The RHD story can be tracked in the RHD media archive on the MAF website—<www.maf.govt.nz/mafnet/search/index.htm>.

13 New Zealand Press Association, 'Gene Technology to Take Big Bite of Research Funds', Wellington, 2 November 2000.

14 The *New Scientist* magazine on-line has a 'Living in a GM World' section that contains references to research into the environmental effects of genetically engineered plants and animals (<www.newscientist.com/gm/>). Recent examples include 'Modified Crops could Corrupt Weedy Cousins' (evidence of GE canola cross-pollinating with wild brassicas), 'Pockets of Resistance' (GE cotton plants provide refuges for the boll weevil), 'Resistance is Useless' (weeds found to be resistant to three kinds of herbicide) and 'Toxic Leak' (GE toxins in maize plants found to contaminate the soil). See also S. O. Duke, *Herbicide Resistant Crops: Agricultural, Environmental, Regulatory and Technical Aspects*, Lewis Publishers, Boca Raton, 1996.

15 Karl Polanyi, *The Great Transformation*, Octagon Books, New York, 1980.

16 See W. J. Gardner, 'A Colonial Economy', in W. H. Oliver (ed.), *The Oxford History of New Zealand*, Oxford University Press, Wellington, 1981, pp. 57–86, for information on the interplay between primary production, natural resource exploitation, and colonial capitalism in nineteenth-century New Zealand. C. Simkin, *The Instability of a Dependent Economy. Economic Fluctuations in New Zealand 1840–1914*, Oxford University Press, London, 1951, and J. B. Condliffe, *New Zealand in the Making*, Allen & Unwin, London, 1959, provide more on the economy/primary industry relationship. Donald Denoon, *Settler Capitalism*, Clarendon Press, Oxford, 1983, locates the New Zealand experience within a general analysis of capitalism and settlement in the settler colonies.

17 The first history of New Zealand farming remarked on the modernity of nineteenth-century farmers, praising them for 'anticipating by many years the mass-production methods achieved, with some self-congratulation, in the factory' (G. T. Alley & D. O. W. Hall, *The Farmer in New Zealand*, Department of Lands and Survey, Wellington, 1941, pp. 83–4). Similarly, J. B. Condliffe's economic history of New Zealand noted that 'All the essential features of mass production, usually credited only to the newer factories in America, are to be observed in a well-organised shearing shed, and most of them anticipated and were independent of American industrial experience' (Condliffe, *New Zealand in the Making*, p. 147).

18 J. R. McNeill, *Something New Under the Sun: An Environmental History of the Twentieth Century World*, W. W. Norton, New York, 2000, pp. 216–19.

19 S. Challenger, 'Changes in the Canterbury Landscape', *Garden History*, vol. 3, no. 1, 1974, pp. 57–76; Agricultural Landscape Research Project, *Problems of the New Zealand Agricultural Landscape*, Queen Elizabeth II Trust, Wellington, 1984; Shelley Egoz, 'Clean and Green but Messy: The Contested Landscape of New Zealand's Organic Farms', *Oral History*, vol. 28, no. 1, 2000, pp. 63–74.

20 See M. M. Roche, *Land and Water: Water and Soil Conservation and Central Government in New Zealand 1941–1988*, Historical Branch, Department of Internal Affairs, Wellington, 1994.

21 J. T. Salmon, *Heritage Destroyed: The Crisis in Scenery Preservation in New Zealand*, A. H. & A. W. Reed, Wellington, 1960.

22 Ministry for the Environment, *The State of New Zealand's Environment*, Ministry for the Environment/GP Publications, Wellington, 1997, chapter 7.37–39, 67–73.

23 ibid., 8.65–68.

24 ibid., 8.68.

25 ibid., 7.7.

26 Jules Pretty et al., 'An Assessment of the Total External Costs of UK Agriculture', *Agricultural Systems*, vol. 65, no. 2, 2000.

27 Ministry of Agriculture, Fisheries and Food (UK), 'Organic Farming: A Boom Year', MAFF UK website, 1.1.00.

28 David Goodman, Bernardo Sorj & John Wilkinson, *From Farming to Biotechnology: A Theory of Agro-Industrial Development*, Basil Blackwell, Oxford, 1987.

29 Raymond F. Dasmann, 'National Parks, Nature Conservation, and "Future Primitive" ', in *Proceedings of the South Pacific Conference on National Parks and Reserves*, Department of Lands and Survey, Wellington, 1975, pp. 89–96A.

30 A. P. Sturman & N. Tapper, *The Weather and Climate of Australia and New Zealand*, Oxford University Press, Melbourne, 1996.

31 Details on the Fossil of the Day website—<www.fossil-of-the-day.org/15-11-00.html>.

32 Vandana Shiva, *The Violence of the Green Revolution: Third World Agriculture, Ecology and Politics*, Zed Books, London, 1991; Joke Schrijvers, *The Violence of 'Development': A Choice for Intellectuals*, International Books, Utrecht and Kali for Women, New Delhi, 1993; Vandana Shiva, *Monocultures of the Mind: Perspectives on Biodiversity and Technology*, Zed Books, London, 1995; Gilbert Rist, *The History of Development: From Western Origins to Global Faith*, Zed Books, London, 1997.

33 McNeill, *Something New*. p. 6.

34 McNeill, *Something New*, p. 335.

35 The foundational connections between economic ideology and biological science in the nineteenth century are discussed by Donald Worster, *Nature's Economy: The Roots of Ecology*, Anchor Books, Garden City, New York, 1979; and Robert Young, *Darwin's Metaphor: Nature's Place in Victorian Culture*, Cambridge University Press, Cambridge, 1985.

36 Mae-Wan Ho, *Genetic Engineering: Dream or Nightmare*?, Gateway, Dublin, 1999; David Suzuki & Holly Dressel, *Naked Ape to Superspecies*, Allen & Unwin, St Leonards, 1999; Peter Wills, Testimony to the Royal Commission on Genetic Modification, 8 November 2000.

37 Peter Wills, Testimony to the Royal Commission.

38 Christine Dann, 'The Environmental Movement', in R. Miller (ed.), *New Zealand Politics: A Reader*, Oxford University Press, Auckland, 2001, pp. 342–51.

39 Details on the Soil and Health Association and its activities can be found in its bi-monthly magazine, *Soil and Health*, now in its fifty-ninth year of publication. Information on the economic side of the New Zealand organics movement can be found at <www.organicsnewzealand.org.nz>.

40 Phil Twyford-Jones & Robert Doolan, 'The International Market for Organic Food', Department of Primary Industry, Rural Industry Business Services, Queensland, 1998; Reuters Business Report, 'Strategies in Organics', *Reuters Business Insight*, 1999; Commission for Sustainable Development, Department of Economic and Social Affairs, *Changing Production and Consumption Patterns: Organic Agriculture*. Background Paper No. 4, Commission on Sustainable Development, New York, 2000; Hugo Ehrenreich & Siddika Moosa, 'Organic Profits: New Opportunities in Food and Drinks', *Reuters Business Insight*, 2000; Margaret Ritchie, Hugh Campbell & Leda Sivak, 'Investigating the Market for Organic Food: Dunedin, New Zealand and the World', A paper presented to Organics 2020: New Zealand National Conference on Organics, Unitec, Auckland, 19–20 May 2000; Ray Moynihan, 'Organics a go-go', *Australian Financial Review*, 1 November 2000.

41 Michael Roche, 'Case Study 3.4 Wattie and Heinz', in R. Le Heron & E. Pawson (eds), *Changing Places: New Zealand in the Nineties*, Longman Paul, Auckland, 1996, pp. 71–3.

42 New Zealand Press Association, 'Gene Technology to Take Big Bite of Research Funds'.

43 Ministry of Agriculture and Forestry, 'Huge Response to Sustainable Farming Fund', media release, 1 November 2000, <www.maf.govt.nz/MAFnet/press/011100fnd.htm>.

44 Andrew J. Cook. John R. Fairweather & Hugh R. Campbell, 'New Zealand Farmer and Grower Intentions to Use Genetic Engineering Technology and Organic Production Methods', Agribusiness and Economics Research Unit, Lincoln University.

45 For information on how the GE market has fallen and is being artificially propped up, plus details on lobbying expenditure by the biotech industry, see Christine Dann, 'The Inedible Becomes Unprofitable', *Soil and Health*, September–October 2000, pp. 17–18.

46 J. Gamble, S. Mugglestone, D. Hedderley, T. Parminter & N. Richardson-Harman, *Genetic Engineering: The Public's Point of View. Report to Stakeholders*, Mt Albert Research Centre, Horticulture and Food Research Institute of New Zealand, Auckland, 2000; Ritchie, Campbell & Sivak, 'Investigating the Market for Organic Food'.

47 The salient features of the way in which the Australian and New Zealand labour parties and the European social democrat parties made this change are discussed in Chapter 3, 'The Rise and Fall of Social Democracy', in Christine Dann, From Earth's Last Islands the Global Origins of Green Politics, PhD thesis, Lincoln University, 1999.

48 Jane Kelsey, *Reclaiming the Future: New Zealand and the Global Economy*, Bridget Williams Books, Wellington, 1999.

49 Christine Dann, 'Taking the (Engineered) ANZAC Biscuit. A Study of How the Australia New Zealand Food Authority Makes Food Policy Fit the New Trade Rules', A paper to the Agri-Food VII Conference, Sydney University, 15–16 July 1999; Peter Wills, Testimony to the Royal Commission.

50 By 2000 New Zealand's external debt had risen to 8 per cent of GDP, despite significant increases in exports in the previous twenty years. Its economic growth rate was consistently below the OECD average for the same period.

51 For examples of this in the Philippines, see 'The Silent War', in John Pilger, *Distant Voices*, Vintage, London, 1992.

52 Anita Roddick, 'Sleepless in Seattle', *New Internationalist*, April 2000, pp. 20–2.

53 Green Party of Aotearoa New Zealand, *Thinking Beyond Tomorrow*, Green Party, Wellington, 1999.

54 Larry Lohmann, 'Resisting Green Globalism', in W. Sachs, *Global Ecology*, Zed Books, London, pp. 157–67.

55 An editorial ('Common and Secure Ground') in the *Marlborough Express* of 20 November 2000 speaks approvingly of co-operation between Greens and National Party representatives 'to forge common goals: for economic growth to be environmentally and socially sustainable, for Marlborough to recognise the world-wide move to organic farming'.

56 Fair and sustainable trade in global primary commodities is regularly discussed in the *New Internationalist* magazine. Issue 322, April 2000, focuses on fair trade.

57 Wren Green et al., *New Zealand After Nuclear War*, New Zealand Planning Council, Wellington, 1987; B. A. Pittock, *Beyond Darkness: Nuclear Winter in Australia and New Zealand*, Sun Books, South Melbourne, 1987.

Index

Page numbers in *italics* indicate figures and tables.
Species are indexed under their common name.

1080 (poison) 236, 237, 239
2,4,5-T 171, 181, 243, 290
2,4-D 180, 224

acclimatisation societies 233, 234, 277
aerial topdressing 170, *194*, 195, 198
agricultural industry:
  'best use' of land 185
  conservation initiatives 181–2
  deforestation for 109–11, *110*, 112, 114, 116, 185
  land reclamation 61, 63–4
  mass-production in 279, 333*n*17
  migration from 178
  mining conflicting with 92–5, 98, 306*n*24
  pastoralism 63–4, 72–3, *73*, 83, 240
  urbanisation of land 211
  'urine and dung showers' 171
  'war' against nature 11, 178, *178*, 179
agricultural science 78, 171, 172, 174, 177
agri-environmental programmes 332*n*8
agrostology 171, 176–7, 290
alpine regions *see* mountains
aluminium production 263, 267–8, *268*, 269
animals *see* avifauna; fauna
Antarctica *282*, 283
archaeological data, reliability of 27–8
archival repositories 15–16
Arnold, Rollo 7

Auckland 200, 202–3, *204*, 208–9, *208*, 210, 211
Auckland Islands 24, 130
Australia:
  British colonisation of 54, 66
  colonial trade with *37*, 41, 42, 43, 45, 56–7
  resource management 184, 277
avifauna:
  aiding plant naturalisations 76
  albatross colony 267
  conservation of 121–3, 125
  deforestation and 32
  endangered waterfowl 28, 265, 330*n*9
  extinctions 20, 28
  introduced species 54, 78, 82, 233, 234, 245
  pre-colonisation species 27
  wetlands dependency 162, 163–4
  see also kiwi; moa

Ballara, Angela 252
Banks, Joseph 53, 54, 57, 101, 151, 152–3, 154
Banks Peninsula 275
Baughan, Blanche 119, 134, 135, 140, 143
beech, southern (*Nothofagus* sp.) 103–4, 187, 266, 308*n*7
bee-keeping 243, 278
Beker, Karen 14
Binney, Judith 39
biodiversity policy 244–5
biodynamics 179, 181
biofeedstocks 281
biogeography 244
biological control 81, 237, 239–40, 243, 278, 293

biosecurity 13, 237, 277–8, 332*n*11
'biosphere people' 282–3
birds *see* avifauna
Blomfield, Charles 134–5, *134*
Blue Spur goldmine *94*
botanic gardens *see* gardens, public
bovine tuberculosis 236, 237
Bragge, James 2, *2*
Brunner, Thomas 63, 139
Brunner coalfield 307*n*39
Buller, James 42
burning:
  attitudes to 3, 30
  deforestation due to 19–20, 23–4, 30–1
  of forests 104, 110–11, 112, 113
  land degradation due to 71, 193
  for land reclamation 61, 110–11, 112
  tussock grasslands 78–80
Burnt Bush (Baughan) 119
bushfires 111; *see also* burning
Byrnes, Giselle 5

C^{14} dating *see* radiocarbon dating
calicivirus *see* RHD (rabbit haemorrhagic disease)
California 84, 87–8, 95
Campbell, Douglas 169, 170, 171–2, *194*, 195
Campbell, J.A. 220
Campbell Island 130
Campbell Walker, Inches 113, 114, 116
Canterbury Plains 63, 64, *65*
capitalism:
  and environment 184
  expansionist policies 1, 4, 7, 8, 52, 66
  Māori integration 53
  moral economy of 58–9, 63, 66
Carstensen, Vernon 4
catchment boards 195
cattle:
  breeds *76*
  dietary preferences 77, 180
  stock numbers 61, 62, 72, 73, *76*
cattle industry 77, 172, 181
Caughley, Graeme 32
census, Hokianga 43, 45
Chatham Islands 24, 45, 128, *279*, 297*n*2
chemical usage *see individual applications*
Chevalier, Nicholas 139
Christchurch 203, 205–7, *206*, 209, 219
Church Missionary Society (CMS) 38, 39–40, 41, 251
cities *see* urban environments
Clark, Andrew Hill 4, 233, 234
Clifford, Charles 62, 64, 72
climate:
  distribution 25–7
  unpredictability of 74, *75*
  vegetation reflecting 30
  windward–leeward clines *26*, 27, 32–3
climatic change 19–20, 114, 283, 287
clines, windward–leeward *26*, 27, 32–3
Clutha River 88, 92, 197, 266–9, *267*
coal mining 9, 95–7, *96*, 307*n*39–40
coastal environments 211–13, *257*, 258–9, 262, 273–4
Cockayne, A.H. 75, 169, 173, 186, 241
Cockayne, Leonard:
  conservation initiatives 127, 128–30, *129*, 131, 132, 191, 235
  environmental awareness 240, 245
  gardening manual 222
  grasslands management 77, 78, 79–80
  on mountains 143, 147
colonisation:
  Banks' influence 153
  chronology of 22–5, 34, 101
  contemporary issues 13
  environmental change and 276–8
  European colonists' perceptions 1–7
  by Europeans 5, 12, 59–66, 201
  by Māori 24–5, 28
  pre-Māori population 297*n*2
  resource utilisation and 115–16
  Vogel's view 114
Compensation Court 246, 252, 254–6
compost 179, 180, 182, 223–4
Condliffe, J.B. 333*n*17
conflicts *see* wars
conservation:
  aesthetic motives 123–7, 148
  economic factors overriding 125, 127, 262, 265, 266–9, *266*, 283
  economic motives 121, 123
  of ecosystems 125, 128–30
  island reserves 121–2
  nationhood and 131–2, 133
  nineteenth-century legacies 185
  post-1914 management 130–1, 183–4, 187–99
  preservation motives 127–30, *129*, 133–4
  promotion via media *192*, *194*, 195, 196, *196*
  state responsibility for 262–3, 269–74
  of swamps 163–4
Cook, Mount 123, 141, *142*, 144, 146

cosmogony, Māori 1, 35, 253, 258
Cowan, James 132, 202, 203, 209
Cronon, William 4, 6, 200, 201
Crosby, Alfred W. 4–5, 151, 234, 277
Crowder, Bob 181, 182
Crump, Barry 235
cultural relations, Māori–Pākehā 44–5, *44*
Cumberland, Kenneth 4, 19–20, 105, 169, 171, 175, 177
cyanide 90, 91, *238*

Darwin, Charles 115–16, 169, 242, 243–4
Dasmann, Raymond 281–2
DDT 180, 224, 291
deer 131, 234, 235, 237
deforestation:
  consequences of 30–2, 116, 121, 185
  historical studies of 19
  by Māori 19–20, 23–4, 30, 32
  Vogel's view 114–15
  see also forests
'depletion', defined 78
Depression *see* Great Depression
desertification 114, 239
'deterioration', defined 78
Dieffenbach, Ernst 43, 60, 61, 138
'disaster amnesia' 205
disease 46, 165, 236, 237
  see also biological control
DNA analysis 24
dogs 26, 28
Dominy, Michele 14
Donne, Thomas 127, 131
Dovers, Stephen 13, 200
Down to the Sea in Slips (SCRCC) 195
drainage canals *152*, *155*, 157
Du Faur, (Emmeline) Freda 146, 313*n*28
Dugdale, D.F. 274
Duke of Gloucester *see* Henry, Duke of Gloucester
Dunlap, Thomas 4
Durie, Eddie 250
Dutton, Geoffrey 229

Earncleugh station 239
earthquake hazard 205, 207
ecology, as 'science of Empire' 177, 179
economic growth 283, 285, 335*n*50
'ecosystem people' 282
Ell, Harry 123, 127, 132
Elliott, Douglas 222, 225, 228
Ellis, Leon McIntosh 187–8, 191
employment 84, 107, 319–20*n*8
Entrican, Alex 188–90, *189*, 191
'environmental appropriation' 133–4
environmental awareness:
  concern for forests 111–12, 114–15
  future perspective 13–16, 284–7
  by Guthrie-Smith 116
  historical perspective 1–5, 71, 83, 276–80
  modernisation and 5–13, 281–4
  increase in 121–35, *280*
  post-1970 initiatives 181–2
environmental-impact assessments 264, 265
environmental institutions 265
environmental law:
  indigenous 261
  Labour government reforms 269–74
  overview of impact 12–13
  resource management and 261–9
  scope of 329*n*1
  see also conservation, state responsibility for
environmental lobbying 264, 266, 268
environmentalism, approaches to 244
erosion:
  burning increasing 79–80
  conservation mitigating 128
  deforestation causing 32, 107, 114, 116
  growing awareness of 114, *192*
  gumdiggers causing 108
  Guthrie-Smith on 180
  recognition of causes 177–8, 318*n*21
  of soil 4, 172, 193
exotic species *see* forests, of exotic species; pests, introduced; weeds, introduced
exploration, by Europeans 54, 61, 62, 63, 64–6, 139
export market 84, 106, 121, 277, 278–9, 285
extinctions 28, 29

farming *see* agricultural industry
fatalities, alpine 146, *147*
fauna:
  deforestation affecting 32
  environmental law and 262–6
  extinctions 27–30
  glossary of names 288–93
  habitat destruction 265
  native bird protection 121–3, 125, 265
  native herbivores 71
  pre-colonisation distribution 27
  see also avifauna; pests, introduced
Federated Mountain Clubs (FMC) 146–7
fens, England 152–3, 154, 156, 157, 159

Fenton, Francis 253
fernland 69, *104*
ferrets 80, *81*
ferries 273–4
fertilizers:
  availability 171
  home gardens 222, 224
  productivity increased by 170–1, 172, *173*
  usage 172, 174, 180, 279, 280
Field, W.H. 144–5, 146
fire *see* burning
firearms 42, 45, 59, 165
fisheries:
  cyanide disposal affecting 90, 91
  management of 121, 262, 271
  Māori trade 38
  mining debris affecting 90
  swamps and 160, 161
  trout 265
Flannery, Tim 1, 277
flax (*Phormium tenax*):
  Banks on potential of 53
  firearms traded for 165
  processing of 36
  trade commodity 41–2, 55, 57
  trading stations *37*, 38
flooding:
  conservation mitigating 128, 148
  Esk Valley 193, 194
  factors increasing 86, 116
  non-recognition of causes 177–8
  urban vulnerability to 205–7, *206*, 211
  Waihou–Ohinemuri rivers 89, 90
  see also water conservation
flora:
  burning and species succession 30–1
  conservation of resources for 123
  distribution 27, 31
  environmental law and 262–3
  glossary of names 288–93
  see also flax; grasses; weeds, introduced
food plants 25, 26, 27, 32, 38, 53, 58–9
food resources, Te Āti Awa tribe *257*, 258–9
forbs 74
Forest and Bird Protection Society 191, *192*, 236, 243
forests:
  defined 303*n*1
  deforestation for agriculture 109–11, *110*, 116
  deforestation for timber 100, 105–9, *107*, *108*
  depletion debate 111–12, 114–16
  distribution 71, 103–5, *104*, *109*, 119, *186*
  of exotic species 183, 186, *186*, 188–90, 197–8, 319–20*n*8
  management of 112–14, 187–91, 197–8, 266, 271
  perception of 101–2, 105, 120–1, 190–1, *192*
  pre-colonisation species 27
  species of 27, 102–4, *102*, *103*
  state conservation of 184–5, 266
  see also deforestation; kauri
forts (pā) *26*, 32, 133
Fox, William *6*, 62, 63, 123, 139
Fox Glacier 149
Framework Convention on Climate Change 272
France, Ruth 158

Galbreath, Ross 124, 133
gardening publications 215, 216, 218, 221–2, *221*, 226
gardens:
  1920s–30s 220–3, *221*
  1950s–80s 223–6, *223*, *224*
  early twentieth-century 210, 216–20, *219*
  histories of 214–16, 228–9
  organic practices 223–4
  overview 227–9
  possums ravaging 236
  post-1990 226–7
  principle of exclusion 220, 225, 227–8, 229, 325*n*31
  public 214, 216, *218*
  wild 217, 228, 229
genetic engineering 13, 278, 281, 283–4, 285
gold 9, 46, 84–5, 93
gold mining:
  debris disposal 86–7, 88–92, 98
  degradation due to *94*
  land settlement and 92–5, 98, 306*n*24
  laws 85–6
  production data 84, *85*, 92
Gore Browne, Thomas 251
gorse (*Ulex europaeus*) 6, 78, 182, 241–2, *242*, 245
grasses 71, 75, 182
grasslands:
  1840s distribution 70–2, *104*
  burning of 78–80
  defined 303*n*1
  ecology of 240
  exotic species 74, 75, 77, 240–1
  management of 8–9, 77, 82–3
'grasslands revolution' 10–11, 169–78, 181–2

Great Depression 170, 188, 191, 234, 235, 238, 319–20*n*8
Green, W.S. 140, 144
Green Party 284, 286
greenhouse gas emissions 272, 283
Grey, Alan 4
Grey, George 62, 72
Grey River 307*n*39
Grossman, Joseph 192
Guardians for the Lakes 264–5, 267
Gully, John 140, 150
gumdiggers 108, 111
Guthrie-Smith, Herbert 4, 83, 116, 180, 192, 233

Hadfield, Octavius 251
Hall, John 78
Hamer, Paul 133
Hauraki Plains *152*, 153, 154, 155, 156–7, *157*, 160
hawkweed (*Hieracium spp.*) 233, 240–1, 292
Hays, Samuel 184, 209
hazards, natural 205–7, *206*, 211
Heaphy, Charles 60, 63, 138, 139, 158
heather 131
hedges, gorse 242–3
Hengeveld, Rob 244
Henry, Duke of Gloucester 14, *15*
herbicides 171, 172, 174, *178*, 180, 181, 243
herbivores, native 71
Heremia, Kaho 256
Heritage Destroyed (Salmon) 279, *280*
Hermitage, The 123, 141, *142*, 144, *145*, 146
Hickson, Thomas 113–14
Hokianga 43, 45
Holdaway, Richard 22, 28
Holloway, John 19
Holmes, Ian *224*
Holyoake, Keith 182
home-ownership 209–10, *224*
Hongi Hika 39, 40, 44
Hong-key Yoon 138
Horomaka/Banks Peninsula 275
House in Nelson (painting) *6*
Howard, Albert 179
Howard, Mabel 207
hunting 122, 131, 235
Hursthouse, Charles 74, 77, 151, 152, 153, 154, 165
Hyde, W.C. 219
hydroelectric development 13, 149, 263–9, *263*, *267*, 313*n*36

identity, concept of 9–10, 12, 36, 132, 248–9, 260
ideology 283
Indigenous Flora and Fauna claim 259–60
industrialisation, environmental change and 13, 278–81, 333*n*17

Jackson, Moana 251
Janzen, Daniel 162
Journal of Agriculture 175, *175*, *176*, 180, 181, 219–20

Kaharoa ash deposits 24
Kaingaroa Forest 188–9
Kapiti 122, 128, 130, 131
kauri:
  conservation of 111, 127
  distribution of *37*, 103, *109*
  forest management 187
  logging of 42–3, 59, 107–8, *108*
  Puhipuhi forest fire 111
  Waipoua forests 14, *15*, 128, 130
kauri gum 108
Kawharu, Hugh 49, 247
Kehu 139
Kemp, Henry 64
Kennedys Bush *126*
Kermadec Islands 24
King, Philip Gidley 36–7, 55, 56
Kingitanga confederation 48
Kirk, Norman 264, 267
Kirk, Thomas 106, 113, 114, 122, 130
kiwi (*Apteryx* spp.) 122, 236, 330*n*5
'Kiwi' identity 132
Kokianga tidal swamp *161*
Korokoro 39
kūpapa 254, 256, 329*n*35
Kyoto protocol 283

Labour Party environmental policy 264, 267, 269–74
lacustrine environments *104*, 263–5, *263*, *264*
land instability *see* erosion
land tenure:
  compulsory acquisitions 156, 163
  doctrine of property 300*n*3
  Māori assertions 246–60
  Māori system of 35–6
  mining rights and 85–6, 93–5
  Native Land Court policy 48–51, *50*
  Pākehā expropriation 66

pre-New Zealand Wars 72
types of 93
Waste Lands Doctrine 60, 61–2
land utilisation, rational system of 195, *196*, 197
landcare 181, 319*n*32
language, Māori 22, 254, 256, 257, 329*n*35
law *see* environmental law; legislation
legislation:
Certificate of land title 254
English land law 159, 160, 162, 300*n*3
institutional convention breached 268
Māori law 35–6
mining law 85–8, 93–4, 95, 96–9
Rivers Commissions 88, 92
town-planning 211
waterways and swamps 163
see also conservation, state responsibility for; environmental law
Lever, Christopher 244
Levy, Bruce 169, 171, 172, 175, 177, 182, 193
Lewis, T.W. 50–1
Lincolnshire Fens *see* fens, England
'Living Here' (McQueen) 200
longshore drift 211–13

MacDonald, Lou 251, 253
Mackenzie Country 233, 239
male mythology 200
mammals, absence of indigenous 25
mana, Māori assertion of 248–9, 260
mana whenua *see* land tenure
Manapouri controversy 263–5, *263*, *264*, 266
Mantell, Walter 19, 22, 138
Māori:
conservation and 133
founding population 24–5
glossary of terms 288–90
impact of European colonisation 36–8, *37*, 246–50, 252–60
importance of land 250
language 22, 254, 256, 257, 329*n*35
'loyalty' to Crown 255–7
pre-European impact of 7–8, 19–22, 25–34
resource management 6, 261
settlement patterns 161
social structure 36, 38, 250, 252, 328*n*6
socio-economic development 32–3, *33*
'speaking from own paepae' 247
marine environments 12, 266
marine resources *see* fisheries; seals; whales
Mark, Alan 265
Marsden, Samuel 38–9, 41, 58
Marsh, George Perkins 71, 115, 121, 128
Matenga, Hemi 256
Mathias, Frank 78–9
McCahon, Colin 276
McCaskill, Lance 4, 169, 171–2, 175, 193–4
McGlone, Matt 24
McLean, Donald 62, 63, 253
McNeill, John 5, 283
McQueen, Cilla 200
Meinig, Donald 14
Melanesia 22
middens 27
Milford Track 140–1, 145
mining industry:
aluminium 263, 267–8, *268*, 269
coal 84, 95–7, 307*n*39–40
gold 84–95, *85*
overview 9, 98–9
quarrying 84, 87, 97–8, 307*n*42, 307–8*n*46
missionaries 38–9, *39*, 43, 46, 251
moas (Dinornithiformes):
biomass hypothesis 29
distribution of 27
dominant herbivore 71
extinction of 19, 20, 28–9
hunting of 20, 25, *26*, 32, 297*n*2
reproductive strategies 30
modernisation, environmental change and 13, 281–7
motor traffic 143, *143*; *see also* roads
'motto maxims' 138
Motunui claim 258–9
mountaineering 123, 141, 144, 145–6, *145*
mountains:
artists' depictions 138, 139–40, 150
cultural meanings 137–9, 150
fatalities 146, *147*
location map *104*
Māori hunting sites 138
national parks in 147–50
nationalism and 136, 143, 144, 150
sport and 10, 123, 141, 144–7, *145*
tourism 139–43, 144, 148–9
Muir, James 133
Muriwhenua Land Report 35
Muriwhenua Tribunal 46
Murphy, Michael 216, 218
Murray, Haana 259
musket wars 249
myxomatosis 237

names, ownership conferred by 3, 25
'Nation of Waitaha' 20
National Forest Inventory 187
national parks:
  Cockayne's surveys 128–30, *129*
  forests in 119, 191
  inception of 123–7, 133, 185, 262
  landscape representation in 150
  locations of *120*, *148*
  management of 126, 130–1
  mountains in 147–50
nationalism 131, 132, 143, 144, 150; *see also* identity, concept of
Native Bird Protection Society 130, 131, 235
Native Land Court 48–51, 246, 247, 249, 252, 255
native title, extinguishment of 46–8, *47*, *50*; *see also* land tenure
'natural capital' 332*n*8
nature, perception of 2–7, 330*n*3
Nauru Island 170, 172, 223
New Plymouth *62*, 203, 247, *248*, *255*
New Zealand Company 47, 59–60, 61–2, 66, 69, 139, 158
New Zealand Forest Service (NZFS) 190
Ngā Puhi confederation 45
Ngahuruhuru 36
Ngāti Tamaterā 91
Ngāti Te Whiti (hapū) 247, 248
Nicolls, J.W. 179
Nightcaps–Ohai coalfield 307*n*40
Norfolk Island 24, 36, 55
North Island, 1840s landscapes 70
nurserymen 214–15, 222, 223, 225

O'Connor, Kevin 172, 182, 245
Ohai coalfield 307*n*40
Ohinemuri goldfield 9, 88–92, *89*
open-country environments *see* grasslands
organic farming 172, 179–82, 280, 284–5, 335*n*55
Ostler farm *110*
Otago Daily Times 144, *264*, *268*
ownership, names instilling 3, 25
ozone layer *282*, 283

pā (forts) *26*, 32, 133
Paekawa, Tunga 252
paepae 247, 260
Pai Mārire 48
palynology 24
Pardy, Bruce 274
Pascoe, John 146, 149
pastures:
  improvement of 72–5, 176–7
  management of 70, 78–80, 82–3
  soil fertility and 170–1
  suitability for stock 70–1
  see also agricultural industry
patriotism 132
Pere, Joe 248
pesticides 172, 180, 182, 224, 236, *238*, 280
pests, introduced:
  biodiversity policy 243–5
  historical perspective 233–4
  insects 278, 332*n*11
  mammals 131, 234–40, *236*, 244–5
  remediation costs 332*n*8, 332*n*11
  small birds 233, 234, 245
Petchey, Fiona 29
Phillips, Jock 200
Phillips Turner, E. 126
photographic records 2–3, 5, 14, 15–16
pigs 37–8, 54, 56, 61, 234
pine forests *see* radiata pine (*Pinus radiata*)
plants *see* flora; food plants
Point station, The *73*, *81*
poison usage 236, 237, 238, *238*, 239
Polanyi, Karl 278
political parties 264, 267, 268, 269–74, 284, 286
Pollan, Michael 229
pollution *see* waste disposal
Polynesia, colonisation of 22, 24–5
possums 235–7, *236*, 245
potatoes 38, 54, 58, 61
Potts, Thomas 83, 111, 122, 128
Pouakani Report, The (report) 51
Powell, Joe 2, 184
preservation societies 124, 125, 126, 130, 131, 133; *see also* conservation
Pretty, Jules 280
private property rights, defined 86
progress leagues 204
property rights 86, 93, 246–60, 262, 300*n*3, 306*n*24; *see also* land tenure
pulp-and-paper industry 188–9, 198
Pyne, Stephen 4

quarrying 9, 87, 97–8, 307*n*42, 307–8*n*46
Quin, Bert 181

rabbits, European gray:
  biological control 237, 240, 278
  control of 80–1, *81*, 122, 237–40, *238*, *239*, 245

introduction of 80, 237
land degradation due to 76, 233
radiata pine (*Pinus radiata*) 186, 188, 198, 219, 243
radiocarbon dating 22–3, *23*, 24, 71, 292
railways 106–7, 111, 141
Rangitaiki River 156, 265
Rankin, Hone Heke 164
rats (*Rattus* spp.) 22, 28, 54, 138
real estate industry 209
Reeves, William Pember 158, 159
reserves, nature:
avifauna breeding sites 125
forests 113
historic places 126
inception of 133, 185, 262
islands 121–2, 126
land acquisitions for 126–7
management of 126, 130–1
mountains 150
recreational 123–4
scenic 119, *120*, 124–7, *126*
Resolution Island 121–2, 126, 133
resource management:
environmental law and 261–9
by Māori 8, 33, 261
Pākehā development of 9
pre-European Māori lack of 20, 21
state responsibility for 11, 269–74, 285
'tinkering' approach 261–2, 330*n*3
wise use in 184, 197, 198, 199
Resource Management Act 1991 13, 261, 270, 272, 273
revegetation, mining sites 97, 98
RHD (rabbit haemorrhagic disease) 237, 239–40, 278
riparian rights 86–7, 88, 293
roads 141–2, *143*
Roberts, Ben 180
Robin, Libby 177
Rotorua 123, 204
Royal Navy 42, 59, 111
Rua Taranaki 253
Ruatara 38–9, 58
Runte, Alfred 143
'ruralism' 175, *176*

Salmon, John 279, *280*
Sanitary Movement 153, 314*n*11
Sargeson, Frank 100, 101, 116
Savage, John 38
Scales, Sid *264*, *268*
scenery preservation societies 124–7, 133
scrub, defined 303*n*1
seals 27, 29–30, 56–7, 121, 266
Seddon, George 325*n*31
Sefton, Mount 146
Sewell, Henry 3
Shaw, George Bernard *204*
sheep:
breeds *76*, 77
dietary preferences 77–8, 79
introduction of 54, 61
overgrazing by 172
stock numbers 61, 62, 72, 73, *76*, 82, 170
sheep industry 63–4, 69, 77, 173, 181, *279*, 333*n*17
sheep scab 80
shelter belts 243
shrubland 69, *104*, 303*n*1
Siegried, André 201, 208
silver, Crown ownership of 46, 93
Sinclair, Keith 5, 256
skiing 143, 146
Smallfield, P.W. 169, 171, 174, 175, 240
social structure, Māori 44–6, *44*, 49–51
soil:
conservation of 184, 192–7, *194*, 198
erosion of 4, 172, 193
productivity and fertility of 170
Soil Conservation and Rivers Control Council (SCRCC) *194*, 195, 197
South Island, 1840s landscapes 70
Southern Oscillation 74, *75*
sports, mountain 10, 123, 141, 144–7, *147*
Stapledon, Reginald George 176
State Forest Service (SFS) 187, 188, 190, 191, 235, 236
state forests 113, 114, 119, 185, 262
Stewart Island 128
stoats 122
subsidies, agricultural 170, 174, 195, 196, 197
suburbs *see* urban environments
superphosphate *see* fertilizers
sustainability 271–2, 273–4, 284–7
Sutherland, I.L.G. 250
swamps:
1840 distribution *104*
defining of 160–1
drainage of 152–60, *152*, *155*, *157*, 162–3, 164–5, 280
ecosystem of 161–2, *161*
European perceptions of 10, 151–5, 157–60
habitat conservation 163–4

Māori perception of 154, 158, 159, 160, 161, 162

Tannock, David 216, 217, 219, 220, *221*, 222–3
Tapsell, Philip 45, 59
Taranaki 12, 203, 247–60, *248*, *255*, *257*, 272
Tararua Tramping Club (TTC) 144–5, 146, 149
Tasman Pulp and Paper Ltd 188–9, *189*
Taupo eruption 30, 160
Taurua 256
Tawhiao (Potatau II) 48
Taylor, Aila 258
Taylor, Norman 193
'Taylorisation' of labour 279
Te Anau controversy 263–5, *263*, 266
Te Āti Awa 12, *257*
Te Heuheu Tukino IV, Horonuku 124, 133
Te Hiku o Te Ika (North Auckland):
  cultural relationships 44–6, *44*
  Pākehā land claims 38–40, *39*
  pre–1840 resource exploitation *40*, 41–3
Te Ika a Māui 25
Te Kooti Arikirangi Te Turuki 48
Te Kupenga Kaha, Wimeru 250
Te Ruaparaha, Riwha 59
Te Ua Haumene 48
Te Waero, Tapa 253–4
Te Wharekorari 138
Te Wherowhero, Potatau 48
technology, Polynesian 25
Thames (NZ) 90, 91, 159
thermal springs 123, 262
thistle, Californian (*Cirsium arvense*) 82, 241, 245
Thomas, Julian 276
Thomas, Keith 4
Thomson, George M. 122, 130, 132, 233
Timaru 211–13, *212*
timber industry:
  Banks on potential of 53
  colonial reliance on 9, 59, 105–6
  monoculture vulnerability 189
  pre–1840 trade 42–3
  pulp-and-paper 188–9, 198
  resource depletion 14, 104, 112, 114, 127–8, 185
  resources for 185, 319*n*5
  sawmilling 106–8, *107*, 121
  ship spars 42, 56, 59, 111
  species utilisation 106, *108*
  state regulation of 113, 187–90, *189*, 198, 271
  see also kauri
Titokowaru, Riwha 48

Tongariro National Park 124, 128–9, *129*, 130, 131, 133
tourism 123–4, 127, 128, 131, 139–43, 144, 148–9
town-planning 61, *62*, 203, 210, 211, 266
towns *see* urban environments
trade, colonial 54–66, *55*
tramping 130, 144–5, 146
Travers, W.T.L. 71, 83, 243–4
Treaty of Waitangi:
  contraventions 62, 90, 162
  Crown 'loyalty' and 257
  Māori resources 161, 271
  native title under 46–8
  signing of 38, 46
  state adherence to 270
  Waitangi Tribunal and 247, 257
Tregear, Edward 109–10
Tuki Tahua 36–7
Turner, Stephen 275, 276
tussock 69, 70–1, *70*, 77–8, 79
tussock grasslands *see* grasslands
Tutira (Guthrie-Smith) 4, 14, 180, 192, 234
Tutira station 116

Union Steam Ship Company 140
urban environments:
  cultural significance 11, 201–2, 211
  defined 320*n*1
  Dieffenbach's view 60
  historians' neglect of 200–1
  migration to 178
  progressive towns 202–5, *204*
  proximity to mountains *137*, 150
  suburban towns 208–11
  Timaru case study 211–13
  vulnerable towns 205–8, *206*
  Wakefieldian ideals 200
use rights, Māori 162–3
user rights, defined 86

varroa bee mite 278
Victoria (Australia) 84, 85, 87, 95
Vogel, Julius 113, 114, 121, 128
volcanic activity 30, 71, 104
volcanic cones, quarrying of 98, 307–8*n*46

Wade, Nugent 76, 78, 82
Wai 262 claim 259–60, 277
Waihou–Ohinemuri goldfield 9, 88–92, *89*
Waihou River *89*
Waikato swamplands 160

Waimakariri River 205–7, *206*
Waipoua 14, 128, 130, 191
Wairau Plains 72
Waitakere Ranges 149
Waitangi Tribunal:
  destruction of traditional resources 162
  Indigenous Flora and Fauna claim 259–60
  land claim reviews 46, 48
  Māori response to 249
  Muriwhenua Land Report 35
  naming of mountains 139
  pollution investigations 207
  Pouakani Report 51
  role of 20, 247, 257
  Taranaki hearings 247, 248, 249
  Te Āti Awa claim 12, *257*, 258–9
  Wai 262 claim 277
  water management contraventions 197
Wakefield, Edward Gibbon 3, 4, 59–60, 154
Wakefield, William 60, 61, 63, 158
Wallace, Alfred Russel 244
Wallace's Realms 244
Wanaka, Lake 266–7
Warming, Eugene 128
wars:
  'against nature' 11, 178, *178*, 179
  Korean War 175
  Māori internecine 45, 251, 252
  Māori–Pākehā 43, 48, 54, 72, 249
  musket wars 249
  New Zealand Wars 72
  see also World War II
waste disposal:
  agricultural industry 181, 272, 279
  air pollution 207, 266
  gold mining 86–7, 88–92, 98
  marine reefs affected by *257*, 258–9
  Motunui *257*, 258–9
  regulation of 98–9, 121, 262
  sewage 207, 211
  urban 207
Waste Lands Doctrine 60, 61–2
water conservation 192–8, 262, 265–6
weasels 122
weeds, introduced:
  biodiversity policy 243–5
  historical perspective 233–4
  impact of 240–4
  in national parks 131
  naturalisation by 74, 76, 78, 82, 234, 240–3, 292
  remediation costs 332*n*8, 332*n*11
  see also gorse
Weld, Frederick 64, 72
Wellington 203, 204, 205, 210
wetlands *see* swamps
whales, protection of 266
whaling industry 57, 64, 121
whaling stations 37, 38, 41, 43, 60, 65, 121
Wheao River 265
White, Ben 162
White, Richard 4
Whitford, Frank 204–5
Wihongi, Del 259
wilderness areas 149, 201
Williams, David 49–50, 247
Williams, Michael 184
Wills, Peter 283
Wilmshurst, Janet 24
Wiremu Kingi 254
Wooding, Alister 242
Wooding, Warwick 242
Woollaston, Phillip 269
World War II 170, 171, 191, 223, 238; *see also* wars
Worster, Donald 14, 184, 198
Worthy, Trevor 28

Yates, Arthur 215
Yates' Garden Guide 215, *215*, 221, 223, 225, 226, 323*n*3
Yerex, G.F. 235